I. Asimov

I. Asimov

A MEMOIR

Isaac Asimov

DOUBLEDAY
New York London Toronto Sydney Auckland

PUBLISHED BY DOUBLEDAY
a division of Bantam Doubleday Dell
Publishing Group, Inc.
1540 Broadway, New York, New York 10036

DOUBLEDAY and the portrayal of an anchor with a
dolphin are trademarks of Doubleday, a division of
Bantam Doubleday Dell Publishing Group, Inc.

Library of Congress Cataloging-in-Publication Data

Asimov, Isaac, 1920–1992
    I. Asimov : a memoir/Isaac Asimov.—1st ed.
    p. cm.
    Includes bibliographical references.
    1. Asimov, Isaac, 1920–1992.—Biography. 2. Authors, American—20th century—
Biography. 3. Scientists—United States—Biography. 4. Science fiction—Authorship.
I. Title.
    PS3551.S5Z468   1994
    813'.54—dc20
    [B]   93-8644
    CIP

ISBN 0-385-41701-2
Copyright © 1994 by the Estate of Isaac Asimov
Jacket Photograph © by Jill Krementz
All Rights Reserved
Printed in the United States of America
April 1994
First Edition

10 9 8 7 6 5 4 3 2 1

Dedicated to

My dear wife, Janet,
My partner in life and thought

Contents

Introduction

In 1977, I wrote my autobiography. Since I was dealing with my favorite subject, I wrote at length and I ended with 640,000 words. Since Doubleday is always overwhelmingly kind to me, they published it all—but in two volumes. The first was *In Memory Yet Green* (1979), the second *In Joy Still Felt* (1980). Together, they described the first fifty-seven years of my life in considerable detail.

It had been a quiet life and there was no great excitement in it, so even though I made up for that by what I considered a charming literary style (I never bother with false modesty, as you will quickly discover), the publication was not a world-shaking event. However, some thousands of people found pleasure in reading it, and I am periodically asked if I will continue the tale.

My answer always is: "I have to live it first."

It was my notion that I ought to wait till the symbolic year of 2000 (always so important to science fiction writers and futurists) and write it then. However, I will be eighty years old in 2000 and it may just be possible that I may not make it till then.

When, just before my seventieth birthday, I was stricken with a rather serious illness, my dear wife, Janet, said to me severely, "Start that third volume *now.*"

I protested feebly and said that the last twelve years had seen my life turn quieter than ever. What could I possibly have to say? She pointed out that the first two volumes of my autobiography were strictly chronological. I recounted events in precise order according to the calendar (thanks to a diary I've kept since I turned eighteen, to say nothing of an excellent memory) and I had said almost nothing about my inner being. She said she wanted something else for the third volume. She wanted a retrospective in which the events were secondary to my thoughts, my reactions, my philosophy of life, and so on.

I said, even more feebly, "Who would be interested?"

And she said firmly, for she is even less falsely modest on my behalf than I am on my own, "Everybody!"

I don't think she's right, but she might be, so I intend to try. I don't intend to start where the second volume left off. In fact, it would be dangerous to do so. The first two volumes are out of print and many people who might pick up this volume and find it interesting (stranger things have happened) would be unable to find the first two volumes in either the hard- or soft-cover incarnation and grow seriously annoyed with me.

So what I intend to do is describe my *whole* life as a way of presenting my thoughts and make it an independent autobiography standing on its own feet. I won't go into the kind of detail I went into in the first two volumes. What I intend to do is to break the book into numerous sections, each dealing with some different phase of my life or some different person who affected me, and follow it as far as necessary—to the very present, if need be.

I trust and hope that, in this way, you will get to know me really well, and, who knows, you may even get to like me. I would like *that*.

I. Asimov

1
Infant Prodigy?

I was born in Russia on January 1, 1920, but my parents emigrated to the United States, arriving on February 23, 1923. That means I have been an American by surroundings (and, five years later, in September 1928, by citizenship) since I was three years old.

I remember virtually nothing of my early years in Russia; I cannot speak Russian; I am not familiar (beyond what any intelligent American would be) with Russian culture. I am completely and entirely American by upbringing and feeling.

But if I now try to discuss myself at the age of three and the years immediately beyond, which I *do* remember, I am going to have to make statements of the type that have always led some people to accuse me of being "egotistical," or "vain," or "conceited." Or, if they are more dramatic, they say I have "an ego the size of the Empire State Building."

What can I do? The statements I make certainly seem to make it clear that I think highly of myself, but only for qualities that, in my opinion, deserve admiration. I also have many shortcomings and faults and I admit them freely, but no one seems to notice that.

In any case, when I say something that sounds "vain," I assure you it is *true* and I refuse to accept the accusation of vanity until somebody can prove that something I say that sounds vain is *not* true.

So I will take a deep breath and say that I was an infant prodigy.

I don't know that there is a good definition of an infant prodigy. The Oxford English Dictionary describes it as "a child of precocious genius." But how precocious? How much genius?

You hear of children who can read at two, who learn Latin at four, who enter Harvard at the age of twelve. I suppose those are undoubted infant prodigies, and, in that case, I was *not* one.

I suppose that if I had had a father who was an American intellectual, well off and lost in his study of the classics or of science, and if that father had discovered in me a likely candidate for prodigiousness, he might have driven me onward and gotten something like that out of me. I can only thank whatever chance has guided my life that this was not so.

A force-fed child, driven relentlessly to the very top of his bent, might break under the strain. My father, however, was a small storekeeper, with no knowledge of American culture, with no time to guide me in any way, and no ability to do so even if he had the time. All he could do was to urge me to get good marks in school, and that was something I had every intention of doing anyhow.

In other words, circumstances conspired to allow me to find my own happy level, which turned out to be sufficiently prodigious for all purposes and yet kept the pressure at a sufficiently reasonable value to allow me to chug along rapidly with no feeling of strain whatever. It meant that I kept my "prodigiousness" for all my life, in one way or another.

In fact, when asked if I was an infant prodigy (and I *am* asked this with disconcerting frequency), I have taken to answering, "Yes, indeed, and I still am."

I learned to read before I went to school. Spurred on by my realization that my parents could not yet read English, I took to asking the older children on the block to teach me the alphabet and how each letter sounded. I then began to sound out all the words I could find on signs and elsewhere and in that way I learned to read with a minimum of outside help.

When my father discovered that his preschool youngster could read and, moreover, when he found on questioning that the learning was on my own initiative, he was astounded. That may have been the first time he began to suspect that I was unusual. (He kept that feeling all his life, though he never hesitated to criticize me for my many failings.) The fact that he thought I was unusual, and made it clear that he did, gave *me* the first inkling that I was unusual.

I imagine there must be many children who learned to read before going to school. I taught my younger sister to read before she went to school, for instance, but I *taught* her. No one taught me.

When I finally entered the first grade in September of 1925, I was astonished at the trouble the other children were having with their reading. I was even more astonished at the fact that after something had been explained to them, they would forget and would have to have it explained *again* and *again*.

That, I think, was what I noticed very early in the game; that in my case it was only necessary that I be told once. I did not realize that my memory was remarkable until I noticed that my classmates didn't have memories like it. I must instantly deny that I have a "photographic memory." I have been accused of that by those who admire me beyond my deserts but I always say, "I only have a near-photographic memory."

Actually, my memory for things that are of no particular interest to me is not much better than normal, if that, and I can be guilty of appalling lapses, when my self-absorption gets the better of me. (I can be remarkably self-absorbed.) I once stared at my beautiful daughter, Robyn, without recognizing her, because I did not expect to see her at the time and was only aware of a vaguely familiar face. Nor was Robyn in the least hurt, or even surprised. She turned to the friend at her side and said, "See, I told you that if I just stood here and didn't say anything, he wouldn't know me."

For things that do interest me, and they are many, I have virtually instant recall. Once when I was out of town, my first wife, Gertrude, and her brother, John, were having some small argument, and little Robyn, about ten at the time, was sent up to my office to get down the appropriate volume of the Encyclopaedia Britannica to settle the matter.

Robyn went rebelliously, saying, "I wish Daddy were home. Then you could just ask him."

There are, however, difficulties and disadvantages to everything. I may have been gifted with a delightful memory and a quick understanding at a very early stage, but I was not gifted with great experience and a deep understanding of human nature. I did not realize that other children would not appreciate the fact that I knew more than they did and could learn more quickly than they did.

(Why is it, I wonder, that anyone who displays superior athletic ability is an object of admiration to his classmates, while one who displays superior mental ability is an object of hatred? Is there some hidden understanding that it is brains, not muscles, that define the human being and that children who are not good at athletics are simply not good, while those that are not smart feel themselves to be subhuman? I don't know.)

The problem was that I did not try to hide my superior mentality. I demonstrated it every day in the classroom, and I never, never, never thought of being "modest" about the matter. I cheerfully made it clear, at all times, that I was very bright, and you can guess the result.

The results were all the more inevitable in that I was small for my age, weak for my age, and younger than anyone else in the class (eventually two and a half years younger due to my being shoved ahead periodically, yet still the "smart kid").

I was scapegoated. Of course I was.

Eventually, it became plain to me why I was scapegoated, but I spent many years accepting this because I could not bear to hide my brilliance from the eyes of others. In fact, I was scapegoated, with diminishing intensity, right into my early twenties. (Let me, however, not make it seem worse than it was. I was never physically assaulted. I was merely sneered at, derided, and excluded from the society of my peers—all of which I could bear with reasonable equanimity.)

In the end, though, I did learn. There is still no way of hiding the fact that I am unusual, considering the vast number of books I have written and published, and the vast number of subjects I have covered in those books, but I have learned, in ordinary life, to refrain from being on display. I have learned how to "turn it off" and meet people on their own terms.

The result is that I have many friends who treat me with the greatest of affection and for whom I feel the greatest of affection in return.

If only an infant prodigy could be prodigious in grasping human nature and not in memory and quickness of intellect alone. But then, not everything is inborn. The truly important parts of life develop slowly with experience, and that person is lucky who can learn them more quickly and with greater ease than I did.

2
My Father

My father, Judah Asimov, was born in Petrovichi, Russia, on December 21, 1896. He was a bright young man who received a complete education within the limits of Orthodox Judaism. He studied the "holy books" assiduously and was fluent in Hebrew as pronounced in his particular Litvak (Lithuanian) dialect. In later life, in our conversations he would delight in quoting from the Bible or the Talmud, in Hebrew, then translating it into Yiddish or English for my benefit and expounding on the matter.

He also gained secular knowledge and could speak, read, and write Russian with great fluency and was well read in Russian literature. He knew Sholem Aleichem's Yiddish stories virtually by heart. I remember him once reciting one to me, in Yiddish, a language I understand.

He knew enough mathematics to serve his father as bookkeeper in the family business. He survived the dark days of World War I without, for some reason, serving in the Russian army. This last was a good thing, for, had he served, the chances were excellent that he would have been killed and I would never have been born. He also survived the disorders that followed the war, marrying my mother sometime in 1918.

Until 1922, despite the dislocations of war, revolution, and civil turmoil, he was doing fairly well in Russia, though, of course, if he had remained there who knows what would have happened to him and to me in the even darker days of Stalin's tyranny, World War II, and the Nazi occupation of our native region?

Fortunately, we need not speculate on that, because in 1922 my mother's half brother, Joseph Berman, who had gone to the United States some years before, invited us to come to that land and join him, and my parents, after some agonizing introspection, decided to do so. It was not an easy decision. It meant leaving a small town in which they had lived all their lives, in which all their friends and relatives were to be found, and heading out into an unknown land.

But my parents decided to risk it, and they got in just under the wire, for in 1924 stricter immigration quotas were imposed and we would not have been allowed to enter.

My father came to the United States in the hope of a better life for his children, and this he certainly achieved. He lived to see one son a successful writer, another son a successful journalist, and a daughter happily married. However, this was all at a great cost to himself.

In Russia, he was part of a reasonably prosperous merchant family. In the United States, he found himself penniless. In Russia, he had been an educated man, looked up to by those about him for his learning. In the United States, he found himself virtually illiterate, for he could not read or even speak English. What's more, he had no education that would be counted as such by secular Americans. He found himself looked down upon as an ignorant immigrant.

All this he suffered without complaint, for he concentrated entirely on me. I was to make up for everything, and I did. I have always been very grateful to my father for this sacrifice of his, once I was old enough to understand what it was he had had to do.

Once in the United States, he turned his hand to any job he could get, selling sponges door to door, demonstrating vacuum cleaners, working for a wallpaper concern and later in a sweater factory. After three years, he had saved enough money for a down payment on a small mom-and-pop candy store and our future was assured—and shaped.

My father never pushed me toward prodigiousness, as I have already explained. He also never punished me physically; he left that to my mother, who was very good at it. He contented himself with long, improving lectures whenever I misbehaved. I think I preferred my mother's blows, but I always knew my father loved me, even if it was difficult for him to put it into words.

3
My Mother

My mother was born Anna Rachel Berman. Her father was Isaac Berman. He died when she was young, and it was for him that I was named.

My mother, who looked like a typical Russian peasant woman and was only about four feet ten inches tall, was literate and could read and write both Russian and Yiddish. —And here I have a complaint against both my parents. They spoke Russian to each other when they wanted to discuss something privately that my big ears were not to hear. Had they sacrificed this trivial urge for privacy and spoken to *me* in Russian, I would have picked it up like a sponge and had a second world language.

This, however, was not to be. I presume my father's defense was that he wanted me to learn English and make it my first language, untroubled by the complexities of another, so that I could become a complete American. Well, I did that, and since I consider English the most glorious language in the world, perhaps all is for the best.

Aside from literacy and the knowledge of enough arithmetic so that she was able to serve as cashier in her mother's store, my mother was not educated. In orthodox Judaism women simply weren't educated. She knew no Hebrew and had no secular knowledge.

Nevertheless, I have heard her sneer at my learned father's Russian handwriting, and I think she was probably justified. It is my experience that women's handwriting is, for some reason, more attractive and more legible than men's handwriting. My sister's writing, for instance, makes mine look crabbed and semi-literate. It would not be surprising to me, then, if my mother's Russian was more elegantly written than my father's.

My mother's role in life could be explained in one word—"work." In Russia, she had been the oldest of numerous siblings and had to take care of them in addition to working in her mother's store. In the United States, she had to raise three children and work endless hours in the candy store.

She was all too aware of the limitations of her life, of the lack of the kind of freedom others had. She was often lost in self-pity, and while I cannot blame her for that, I was the most frequent recipient of her self-pitying tirades. And since she made it clear that I was part of the cross she had to bear, and not the lightest part either, I was filled with guilt.

Her hard life made her short-tempered as well, and her rage found its outlet chiefly on me. I won't deny I gave her cause, but she hit me frequently, and with no light hand either. This didn't mean she didn't love me to distraction, because she did. I wish she had had some other way of showing it, though.

My mother never had a fair chance as a cook. She had to prepare meals quickly and on the run because of the candy store, so that all during my youth (till I got married, in fact) I ate fried foods of all kinds with occasional boiled beef or boiled chicken with boiled potatoes. We were not strong on vegetables, but we were very strong on bread. —I'm not complaining, though. I loved it all.

However, I think that my mother's cooking started me on a way of life that led to troubles with my coronary arteries in late middle age. On the more positive side, her cooking inured my alimentary canal to difficult tasks, so that I developed an iron digestion.

My mother did have some specialties, though—grated radish with onions and hard-boiled eggs that were heaven going down but repeated on you for a week and forced people to grant you privacy.

She also prepared jellied calf's feet with onions and hard-boiled eggs, and who knows what else. It was called *pchah,* and I would rather have had that than Elysium. Even after I was married, I would occasionally be given a vast container of *pchah* to take home. It is an acquired taste, of course, and it was a sad day for me when my wife, Gertrude, acquired the taste. It instantly cut the supply in half. I remember sadly the last bit of *pchah* my mother made for me.

My present wife, Janet, the dearest woman in the world, has carefully looked up recipes and occasionally makes *pchah* for me even now. A pleasure, but not quite like mother's, I'm afraid.

4
Marcia

My younger days were spent in the company of my younger sister, Marcia, who was born on June 17, 1922, in Russia and came to the United States with us when she was eight months old. She has frequently complained that I rarely speak of her in my writings, and that is true. In 1974, however, I published a book in which I *did* mention her and said she was born in Russia.

I phoned her to read the passage to her as proof that I *did* speak of her sometimes and she immediately broke into loud, hysterical wails. I said, in consternation, "What's the matter?"

She said, between sobs, "Now everyone will know how old I am." (She was fifty-two at the time.)

"So what?" I said. "Is this going to disqualify you for the Miss America contest?"

It didn't help. I could not placate her, and now you know the sort of relationship my sister and I have had too often.

Marcia is not her original name. She had a very nice Russian name which I am not allowed to use. She chose Marcia for herself in later life and that's what I must call her.

We did not get along well when we were children. That's not surprising. Why should we have? Our personalities were completely different and had we been independent individuals we would never have chosen each other for friends. Yet here we were, bound together and in constant irritation with each other.

Almost anything one of us did aroused umbrage in the other. There would be an argument that quickly escalated to a shouting match and then to a ferocious howling. Things might have been better if we had had parents who could pull us apart, listen patiently to each one of us as we detailed the high crimes and misdemeanors of the other, and then adjudicate the matter fairly. Unfortunately, our parents had no time for that.

My mother would come running upstairs from the store and hurl her ukase at us: "Stop fighting." She would then launch into an angry oration, the burden of which was that we were the only children in the neighborhood, nay, in the whole world, who fought in this disgraceful manner, and that all other children were nothing but sweetness and light. She would also say that customers and neighbors at a distance of two blocks would hear us and come running to the store to find out what was happening and that, as a result, she was embarrassed beyond description by all this. If we hadn't heard that speech a hundred times, we hadn't heard it once. Nor did it have any effect on us, especially since I *knew* that other siblings did not get along any better than we did.

Now here's a funny thing. Marcia remembers that I taught her to like Gilbert and Sullivan and that I had friends in the science fiction world who were interesting and witty, but she doesn't remember that we ever fought. She pictures an idyllic existence between us and I have found this to be true of other people who have shared memories with me. They wipe out whole continents of fact and construct some fairy tale that never existed and insist that that's the way it was. Maybe it is more comfortable to create your own past, but I can't do it. I remember things too well—although I don't say that my own past is entirely immune to reconstruction. When I wrote my autobiography and consulted my diary, I was astonished at the things I had forgotten, as well as the things I remembered that weren't so. They were all matters of trivial detail, however.

Marcia was a bright child. I taught her to read (somewhat against her will) before she went to school, and she raced ahead, just as I did, graduating from high school, again as I did, at the age of fifteen. Then the male chauvinism of Judaism raised its head to Marcia's great disadvantage. My father was poor, but he managed, somehow, to send both his sons to college. There was no thought, however, of sending poor Marcia to college. Girls, after all, were simply meant for marriage.

Marcia, therefore, at fifteen had to find work. She was too young for marriage and, as a matter of fact, she was also too young to work, at least too young to work legally. I think she must have lied about her age. In any case, she got a secretarial position and did quite well at it.

She did not marry until she was thirty-three. With a brother's inability to see the virtues of a sister, I was not surprised. I remember that when I was getting ready for marriage thirteen years earlier, some woman (obviously of the old school) expressed surprise.

"Brothers," she said, "shouldn't marry till after the sister is married."

That may have been a viable custom in Eastern Europe in the days when marriages were arranged and any girl could be (and usually was) married off as a teenager as long as the dowry was right. But here? In America?

I said, "If I wait for my sister to marry, I'll die a bachelor."

I was wrong, though. A man of thirty-seven, Nicholas Repanes, who was passive, quiet, and gentle, was smitten by her. They married, had two handsome sons, and were happy together for thirty-four years till Nicholas died on February 16, 1989, at the age of seventy-one. Janet and I drove out to the wilds of Queens to see him lying in state (wearing his glasses). I owed him that much for making Marcia so good a husband.

Marcia, by the way, is just five feet tall, has a ready smile, and is a really generous person. I'm sorry we couldn't get along better.

5

Religion

My father, for all his education as an Orthodox Jew, was not Orthodox in his heart. For some reason, we never discussed this—perhaps because I felt it to be a very private thing with him and I did not wish to intrude upon it. I think that while he was in Russia he went through the motions only in order to please his father. —This sort of thing is, I believe, very common.

It may be that since my father was brought up under the Tsarist tyranny, under which Jews were frequently brutalized, he turned revolutionary in his heart. He did not, to my knowledge, engage in any actual revolutionary activity; he was far too cautious a man for that.

One of the ways a Jew could be a revolutionary, could work for a new world of social equality, of civil liberty, and of democracy, would be to shake off the dead hand of Orthodoxy. Orthodox Judaism dictates one's every action at every moment of the day and it enforces differences between Jew and Gentile that virtually make certain the persecution of the weaker group.

It followed, then, that my father, when he came to the United States and was freed of the overwhelming presence of his father, could turn to a secular life. Not entirely, of course. Dietary laws are hard to break, when you've been taught that the flesh of swine is the broth of hell. You can't entirely ignore the local synagogue; you are still interested in biblical lore.

However, he didn't recite the myriad prayers prescribed for every action, and he never made any attempt to teach them to me. He didn't even bother to have me bar mitzvahed at the age of thirteen— the rite whereby a young boy becomes a Jew with all the responsibilities of obeying the Jewish law. I remained without religion simply because no one made any effort to teach me religion—any religion.

To be sure, at one period in 1928, my father, feeling the need for a little extra money, undertook to serve as secretary for the local synagogue. To do so, he had to show up at the synagogue services and, on occasion, took me with him. (I didn't like it.) He also, as a gesture, entered me in Hebrew school, where I began to learn a little Hebrew. Since that meant learning the Hebrew alphabet and its pronunciation, and since Yiddish makes use of the Hebrew alphabet, I found I could read Yiddish.

I showed my father I could, in rather halting fashion, and I was astonished when I found that he was thunderstruck and asked how I did it. By this time, I thought, he should be past being surprised at anything I did.

My father didn't stay secretary long; he couldn't swing both it and the candy store. After some months, therefore, I was taken out of Hebrew school, to my great relief, for I didn't like it either. I didn't like the rote learning, and I didn't see the value of learning Hebrew.

I may have been mistaken in this. Learning *anything* is valuable, but I was only eight years old and hadn't quite got that into my head. One thing, though, remained from this early period and from my father's lectures on this and that which he would illustrate with biblical quotations. I gained an interest in the Bible. As I grew older, I read the Bible several times—the Old Testament, that is. Eventually, and with a certain circumspection and hesitation, I read the New Testament also.

By the time I was reading the Bible, however, science fiction and science books had taught me their version of the universe and I was not ready to accept the Creation tale of Genesis or the various miracles described throughout the book. My experience with the Greek myths (and, later, the grimmer Norse myths) made it quite obvious to me that I was reading Hebrew myths.

In my father's old age, when he had retired to Florida and found himself at a loss for something to do, he felt he had no choice but to join with other elderly Jews whose life centered in the synagogue and in the discussion of the minutiae of Orthodoxy. There my father was in his element, for he loved arguing over trifles and was always convinced he was right. (I have inherited some of that tendency.) In fact, I sometimes say sardonically that my father never backed down from any opinion he had, except when that opinion happened, by accident, to be correct.

In any case, in the last few months of his life, he became happily Orthodox again. Not in his heart, I think, but in his outer actions.

I am sometimes suspected of being nonreligious as an act of rebellion against Orthodox parents. That may have been true of my father, but it was not true of me. I have rebelled against nothing. I have been left free and I have loved the freedom. The same is true of my brother and sister and our children.

Nor, I must add, is it simply that I find Judaism empty and that I must search for something else to fill the spiritual void in my life. I have never, in all my life, not for one moment, been tempted toward religion of any kind. The fact is that I feel no spiritual void. I have my philosophy of life, which does not include any aspect of the supernatural and which I find totally satisfying. I am, in short, a rationalist and believe only that which reason tells me is so.

Mind you, this isn't easy. We are so surrounded by tales of the supernatural, by the easy acceptance of the supernatural, by the thunders of the powers that be who attempt with all their might to convince us of the existence of the supernatural, that the strongest among us may feel himself swaying.

Something like that happened to me recently. In January 1990, I was lying in a hospital bed one afternoon (never mind why—we'll discuss that at the proper time) and my dear wife, Janet, was not with me, but had gone home for a few hours to take care of some necessary chores. I was sleeping, and a finger jabbed at me. I woke, of course, and looked blearily about to see who had awakened me and for what purpose.

My room, however, had a lock, and the lock was firmly closed and there was a chain across the door too. Sunlight filled the room and it was clearly empty. So were the closet and the bathroom. Rationalist though I am, there was no way in which I could refrain from thinking that some supernatural influence had interfered to tell me that something had happened to Janet (naturally, my ultimate fear). I hesitated for a moment, trying to fight it off, and for anyone but Janet I would have. So I phoned her at home. She answered immediately and said she was perfectly well.

Relieved, I hung up the phone and settled down to consider the problem of who or what had poked me. Was it simply a dream, a sensory hallucination? Perhaps, but it had seemed absolutely real. I considered.

When I sleep alone, I often wrap myself up in my own arms. I also know that when I am sleeping lightly, my muscles twitch. I assumed my sleeping position and imagined my muscles twitching. It was clear that my own finger had poked into my shoulder and that was it.

Now suppose that at the precise moment I had poked myself, Janet, through some utterly meaningless coincidence, had tripped and skinned her knee. And suppose I had called and she had groaned and said, "I just hurt myself."

Would I have been able to resist the thought of supernatural interference? I hope so. However, I can't be sure. It's the world we live in. It would corrupt the strongest, and I don't imagine I'm the strongest.

6
My Name

My first name, Isaac, is, of all first names, with the possible exception of Moses, the most clearly Jewish. I am quite aware that there are Isaacs among old New Englanders, and among Mormons, and here and there elsewhere, but nine times out of ten, I believe, it signifies a Jew.

I knew nothing about that as a youngster. I just liked the name. I was Isaac Asimov, and I would never dream of being anything else. That was so even when I was quite young and perhaps it had something to do with my feeling that I was remarkable. Since my name was part of me, it had to be remarkable also.

The trouble was that not everyone was enamored of my name. When my mother was in her first years of immigrancy, the neighbors felt it incumbent upon themselves to warn her that she was loading me down with undesirable baggage. The name Isaac was advertising my Jewishness, and establishing a stigma, and it made no sense to worsen the disadvantages I would inevitably be laboring under. Why rub it in other people's noses. —So went the arguments.

My mother was nonplussed. "What do I call him, then?" she asked.

The answer was simple. You keep the initial letter so that my mother's father, for whom I was named, would still be honored, but you adopt some old and honorable Anglo-Saxon family name. In this case, it should be Irving, pronounced, in Brooklyn, as "Oiving."

(Actually, such changes of name do little good. If enough Isaacs and Israels become Isidores and Irvings, the old aristocratic names come to wear a Jewish effluvium and you're right back where you started.)

However, it never came to that. I must have been five years old at

the time, and I listened to the exchange, and when I heard the suggestion that I be called Irving, such a wail went up from me as my mother
had never heard before.* I made it quite plain that under no circumstances would I consent to be called Irving, that I would not answer
to the name Irving, that I would yell and scream anytime I heard the
name Irving. My name was *Isaac* and that it would stay.

And it did, and to this day, I've never been sorry. Stigma or not,
Isaac Asimov is I, and I am Isaac Asimov.

Of course, I had to endure being called, in taunting manner, Izzy
and Ikey and I bore it stolidly because I had no choice. When I
reached the point where I could better control my environment, I
insisted on my name in full. I am Isaac, no nicknames allowed (except
for old friends who are so used to calling me Ike that I don't think
they can change).

I remember meeting someone once who commended me on keeping the name Isaac, telling me it was a rare act of courage. He then
referred to me as "Zack" and I had to correct him with considerable
irritation.

But then, in my late teens, when I was beginning to try to write, the
problem of my name arose again. I couldn't help but notice that the
writers of popular fiction all seemed to have simple names of Northwestern European extraction—especially Anglo-Saxon. Possibly those
were the writers' real names, and possibly they were pseudonyms.

Pseudonyms were common among writers of popular fiction. Some
wrote in a variety of different genres and used a different name for
each. Some were not particularly interested in having it known that
they wrote popular fiction. And some felt that a simple American
name might lead to greater reader acceptance.

Who knows? In any case, the names were largely Anglo-Saxon.

This is not to say that there weren't Jewish writers. Some even used
their own names. Two of the best science fiction writers of the 1930s
were Stanley G. Weinbaum and Nat Schachner, both Jewish. (Weinbaum published for only a year and a half, during which he immediately established himself as the most popular science fiction writer in
America, before dying tragically of cancer while still in his thirties.)

Note, though, that the last names were German, and that was semi-
acceptable. Despite World War I, Germany was still Northwestern

---

* I told this story in my earlier autobiography. You must forgive me, but it is sometimes
essential that I repeat stories in order to have a proper retrospective. Remember, too, that a
number of readers of this book will not have read the earlier one.

European. The first names were certainly acceptable. Stanley was another one of those old English family names. (My brother was named Stanley at my mother's insistence, over the votes of me and my father, who wanted Solomon.) As for Nathan, if it is shortened to Nat, it sounds all right.

What I had, though, was a blatantly Jewish first name and a (good heavens!) Slavic last name. I was warned that editors would probably want to call me John Jones. At this suggestion, I rebelled. I would not allow any story of mine to appear except under the name of Isaac Asimov.

It might seem eccentric of me to be willing to sacrifice a career as a writer rather than not use my odd and peculiar name, but so it would have been. I identified myself so strongly with my name that to have the story appear without my real name would have been no satisfaction to me. Rather the reverse.

It never came to that, however. My name was, in the end, used, and without objection. Over a period of more than half a century, it has appeared on books, in magazines, in newspapers, wherever any of my prolific output was to be found. And as time went on, Isaac Asimov appeared in bigger and bigger letters too.

I don't want to claim more than is mine by right, but I think I helped break down the convention of imposing salt-free, low-fat names on writers. In particular, I made it a little more possible for writers to be openly Jewish in the world of popular fiction.

And yet—and yet—

Somehow that doesn't seem to be enough. A friend in Atlanta sent me an article that appeared in the *Atlanta Jewish Times* on November 10, 1989. It quotes the thoughts of someone named Charles Jaret, who is described as "a Georgia State University sociologist, [who] has made a study of Jews and Jewish themes in science fiction."

Here is another quote from the article: "Probably the best known Jew in science fiction is writer Isaac Asimov. But Asimov's connection with Judaism is tenuous at best. 'You'll find more themes in his work that derive from Christianity than Judaism,' Jaret says."

This is unfair. I have explained that I have not been brought up in the Jewish tradition. I know very little about the minutiae of Judaism. Surely this is not something to be held against me. I am a free American and it is not required that because my grandparents were Orthodox I must write on Jewish themes.

The fact that I am, by the usual definition, Jewish does not bind me hand and foot. Isaac Bashevis Singer writes on Jewish themes because he wants to. I don't write on them because I don't want to. I have the same rights he does.

I am tired of being told, periodically, by Jews, that I am not Jewish enough.

Let me give you an example. I once agreed to give a talk on a day that happened to be the Jewish New Year. I didn't know it was the Jewish New Year, but if I had it would have made no difference. I don't celebrate holidays, not the Jewish New Year, not Christmas, not Independence Day. Every day is a workday to me, and holidays are particularly useful because there is no mail and no telephone calls to distract me.

But I received a call from a Jewish gentleman soon afterward. He had noted in the paper that I had spoken on the holy day and he berated me for it rather harshly. I kept my temper and explained that I didn't observe holidays, that if I hadn't given the talk I certainly would not have attended synagogue services.

"That doesn't matter," he said. "You should serve as a role model to Jewish youth. Instead, you are simply trying to hide the fact that you are Jewish."

This was too much for me. I said, "Pardon me, sir, you have an advantage over me. You know my name, but I don't know yours."

I was taking a chance, of course, but I won. I won't use his real name, but it was completely equivalent to the following. "My name," he said, "is Jefferson Scanlon."

"I see," I said. "Well, if I were trying to conceal the fact that I was Jewish, the first thing I would do, the very *first* thing, would be to change my name from Isaac Asimov to Jefferson Scanlon." He hung up the phone with a bang and I never heard from him again.

Another time I was given the back of the hand for not being Jewish enough by someone whose first names were Leslie Aaron but who used only the Leslie portion.

Why do all these people hound me? They sit around with their simon-pure first names of Charles and Jefferson and Leslie and they scold me for hiding my Jewishness when I have plastered the name Isaac all over my writings, and have discussed my Jewishness in print, freely and openly, whenever it was appropriate to do so.

7
Anti-Semitism

This leads me to a more general discussion of anti-Semitism.

My father told me rather proudly that there was never any pogrom in his little town, that Jews and Gentiles got along. In fact, he told me that he was good friends with a Gentile boy, whom he helped with his schoolwork. After the Revolution, that boy turned up as a local functionary of the Communist Party and helped my father with the paperwork required for emigration to the United States.

This is important. I have frequently had hotheaded romantics assume that our family fled Russia to escape persecution. They seem to think that the only way we got out was by jumping from ice floe to ice floe across the Dnieper River, with bloodhounds and the entire Red Army in hot pursuit.

No such thing. We were not persecuted and we left in a quite legal manner with no more trouble than one would expect from any bureaucracy, including our own. If that's disappointing, so be it.

Nor do I have horror tales to tell about my life here in the United States. I was never made to suffer for my Jewishness in the crass sense of being beaten up or physically harmed. I was taunted often enough, sometimes openly by young yahoos and more often subtly by the more educated. It was something I accepted as an inevitable part of the Universe that I could not change.

I also knew that vast areas of American society were closed to me because I was Jewish, but that was true in every Christian society in the world for two thousand years, and I accepted that too as a fact of life.

What was *really* difficult to endure was the feeling of insecurity, and even terror, because of what was happening in the world. I am talking about the 1930s now, when Hitler was becoming more and more dominant and his anti-Semitic madness was becoming ever more vicious and murderous.

No American Jew could fail to be aware that the Jews, first in Germany, then in Austria, were being endlessly humiliated, mistreated, imprisoned, tortured, and killed, merely for being Jewish. We could not fail to realize that Nazi-like parties were arising in other parts of Europe, which also made anti-Semitism their central watchword. Even France and Great Britain were not immune; both had their Fascist-type parties and both had long histories of anti-Semitism.

We were not safe even in the United States. The undercurrent of genteel anti-Semitism was always there. The occasional violence of the more ignorant street gangs always existed. But there was also the pull of Nazism. We can discount the German-American Bund, which was an open arm of the Nazis. However, people such as the Catholic priest Father Charles Coughlin and the aviation hero Charles Lindbergh openly expressed anti-Semitic views. There were also homegrown Fascist movements that rallied round the anti-Semitic banner.

How could American Jews live under this strain? Why did they not break down? I suppose that most simply practiced "denial." They tried hard not to think of it and went about their normal way of life as best they could. To a large extent, I did this too. One simply had to. (The Jews in Germany did the same thing till the storm broke.)

I also had a more positive attitude. I had enough faith in the United States of America to believe that it would never follow the German example.

And, as a matter of fact, Hitler's excesses, not only in his racism but in his nationalistic saber rattling, his increasingly obvious paranoia, were rousing disgust and anger among important sections of the American population. Even if the United States was, on the whole, rather cool to the plight of Europe's Jews, it was becoming increasingly anti-Hitler. Or so I felt, and I found comfort in that.

I also tried to avoid becoming uncomfortably hooked on anti-Semitism as the main problem in the world. Many Jews I knew divided the world into Jews and anti-Semites, nothing else. Many Jews I knew recognized no problem anywhere, at any time, but that of anti-Semitism.

It struck me, however, that prejudice was universal and that all groups who were not dominant, who were not actually at the top of the status chain, were potential victims. In Europe, in the 1930s, it was the Jews who were being spectacularly victimized, but in the United States it was not the Jews who were worst treated. Here, as anyone could see who did not deliberately keep his eyes shut, it was the African-Americans.

For two centuries they had actually been enslaved. Since that slavery had come to a formal end, the African-Americans remained in a position of near-slavery in most segments of American society. They were deprived of ordinary rights, treated with contempt, and kept out of any chance of participation in what is called the American dream.

I, though Jewish, and poor besides, eventually received a first-class American education at a top American university, and I wondered how many African-Americans would have the chance. It constantly bothered me to have to denounce anti-Semitism unless I denounced the cruelty of man to man in general.

Such is the blindness of people that I have known Jews who, having deplored anti-Semitism in unmeasured tones, would, with scarcely a breath in between, get on the subject of African-Americans and promptly begin to sound like a group of petty Hitlers. And when I pointed this out and objected to it strenuously, they turned on me in anger. They simply could not see what they were doing.

I once listened to a woman grow eloquent over the terrible way in which Gentiles did nothing to save the Jews of Europe. "You can't trust Gentiles," she said. I let some time elapse and then asked suddenly, "What are you doing to help the blacks in their fight for civil rights?" "Listen," she said, "I have my own troubles." And I said, "So did the Gentiles." But she only stared at me blankly. She didn't get the point at all.

What can be done about it? The whole world seems to live under the banner: "Freedom is wonderful—but only for me."

I broke out, under difficult conditions, once in May of 1977. On that occasion I shared a platform with others, among them Elie Wiesel, who survived the Holocaust (the slaying of six million European Jews) and now will talk of nothing else. Wiesel irritated me when he said that he did not trust scientists and engineers because scientists and engineers had been involved in conducting the Holocaust.

What a generalization! It was precisely the sort of thing an anti-Semite says. "I don't trust Jews because once certain Jews crucified my Saviour."

I brooded about that on the platform and finally, unable to keep quiet, I said, "Mr. Wiesel, it is a mistake to think that because a group has suffered extreme persecution that is a sign that they are virtuous and innocent. They might be, of course, but the persecution process is no proof of that. The persecution merely shows that the persecuted group is weak. Had they been strong, then, for all we know, they might have been the persecutors."

Whereupon Wiesel, very excited, said, "Give me one example of the Jews ever persecuting anyone."

Of course, I was ready for him. I said, "Under the Maccabean kingdom in the second century B.C., John Hyrcanus of Judea conquered Edom and gave the Edomites a choice—conversion to Judaism or the sword. The Edomites, being sensible, converted, but, thereafter, they were in any case treated as an inferior group, for though they were Jews, they were also Edomites."

And Wiesel, even more excited, said, "That was the only time."

I said, "That was the only time the Jews had the power. One out of one isn't bad."

That ended the discussion, but I might add that the audience was heart and soul with Wiesel.

I might have gone further. I might have referred to the treatment of the Canaanites by the Israelites under David and Solomon. And if I could have foreseen the future, I would have mentioned what is going on in Israel today. American Jews might appreciate the situation more clearly if they imagined a reversal of roles, of Palestinians ruling the land and of Jews despairingly throwing rocks.

I once had a similar argument with Avram Davidson, a brilliant science fiction writer, who is (of course) Jewish and was, for a time at least, ostentatiously Orthodox. I had written an essay on the Book of Ruth, treating it as a plea for tolerance as against the cruelty of the scribe Ezra, who forced the Jews to "put away" their foreign wives. Ruth was a Moabite, a people hated by the Jews, yet she was pictured as a model woman, and she was the ancestress of David.

Avram Davidson took umbrage at my implication that the Jews were intolerant and he wrote me a letter in which he waxed sarcastic indeed. He too asked when the Jews had ever persecuted anyone.

In my answer, I said, "Avram, you and I are Jews who live in a country that is ninety-five percent non-Jewish and we are doing very well. I wonder how we would make out, Avram, if we were Gentiles and lived in a country that was ninety-five percent Orthodox Jewish."

He never answered.

Right now there is an influx of Soviet Jews into Israel. They are fleeing because they expect religious persecution. Yet at the instant their feet touched Israeli soil, they became extreme Israeli nationalists with no pity for the Palestinians. From persecuted to persecutors in the blinking of an eye.

The Jews are not remarkable for this. It's just that because I'm a Jew I am sensitive to this particular situation—but it is a general phenomenon. When pagan Rome persecuted the early Christians, the Christians pleaded for tolerance. When Christianity took over, was there tolerance? Not on your life. The persecution began at once in the other direction.

The Bulgarians demanded freedom for themselves from an oppressive regime and made use of that freedom by attacking the ethnic Turks in their midst. The Azerbaijani demanded freedom from the centralized control of the Soviet Union, but they seemed to want to make use of that freedom to kill all the Armenians in their midst.

The Bible says that those who have experienced persecution should *not* in their turn persecute: "Thou shalt neither vex a stranger, nor oppress him; for ye were strangers in the land of Egypt" (Exodus 22:21). Yet who follows that text? When I try to preach it, I merely make myself seem odd and become unpopular.

8

Library

Once I could read, and as my ability to read improved rapidly, there turned out to be a serious problem. I had nothing to read. My schoolbooks lasted me just a few days. I finished every one of them in the course of the first week of the term and thereafter was educated for that half year. The teacher had very little to tell me.

My father bought a candy store when I was six and the store was filled with reading material, but my father wouldn't let me touch it.

He felt it to be trash. I pointed out that the other kids read it, and my father said, "So they get trashy brains and their fathers don't care. I care."

And I chafed.

What to do? My father got me a library card and, periodically, my mother would take me to the library. The very first time I was ever allowed to go somewhere by myself was to the library after my mother grew tired of taking me.

Here again, happy circumstance took care of me.

Had my father had the time, and had he been of American culture, he would surely have guided me in greater detail than that of merely protecting me from the ephemera he sold in the candy store. He might have directed me to what he considered good literature and, without meaning it, have narrowed my intellectual horizons.

However, he couldn't. I was on my own. My father assumed that any book that was in a public library was suitable reading and so he made no attempt to supervise the books I took out. And I, without guidance, sampled everything.

By the purest of circumstances, I found books dealing with the Greek myths. I mispronounced all the Greek names and much of it was a mystery to me, but I found myself fascinated. In fact, when I was a few years older, I read the *Iliad* over and over and over, taking it out of the library every chance I could, and starting all over again with the first verse as soon as I had completed the last. The volume I read happened to be a translation by William Cullen Bryant, which (looking back on it) I think was a poor one. Nevertheless, I knew the *Iliad* word by word. You could recite any verse at random and I could tell you where it would be found. I also read the *Odyssey*, but with lesser pleasure, for it wasn't as bloody.

Now here's the thing that puzzles me. I don't remember the very first time I read a book on Greek mythology, but I must have been very young. Could I, or could I not, tell that they were made-up stories and not the truth? The same could be asked of fairy tales (and I read every volume of fairy tales in the library). How does one know these are just "fairy tales"?

I presume that in ordinary families children's books are read to children and the child is somehow made to understand that bunny rabbits don't really talk. I don't know. Oddly enough, I don't remember how it worked with my kids. I didn't read to them very much (being so self-absorbed) and I don't recall specifically saying, "This is just a made-up story."

Of course, some youngsters are frightened of witches and monsters and tigers under the bed and all the dreadful things they read about, so they must accept them as true to begin with (and, if sufficiently unsophisticated, into adult life as well). I never was frightened of such things, so I must have known right from the start when tales were simply fiction—but I don't know *how* I knew.

Of course, I might have questioned someone on the matter, but whom? My father was entirely too busy in the candy store to be bothered, and my mother (past the ability to read, write, and calculate) was completely uneducated. I had the uneasy feeling that I mustn't ask them questions. And I certainly didn't ask my peers. It would never occur to me to consult them on intellectual matters. The result was that I was left to myself and ended upright—except that I don't remember how that came about.

In fact, despite my excellent memory, there are innumerable things that are of the greatest importance to me that I do not remember and that no amount of scrambling through my childhood can make me remember.

For instance, when I was quite young I got hold of a volume containing the complete works of William Shakespeare. It can't have been from the library, for I have a memory of keeping it for a long time. Perhaps someone gave it to me.

I remember, with perfect clarity, working my way through *The Tempest,* which was the first play in the book, even though it was the last Shakespeare wrote (and the only one in which he made up his own plot). I remember, as an example, how puzzling the word "yare" was. Shakespeare used it to give an impression of sailor lingo, but I never saw it before or (I think) afterward.

I remember enjoying *A Comedy of Errors* and *Much Ado About Nothing.* I even seem to recall enjoying the Falstaff scenes in *Henry IV, Part One.* In short, I liked the comic scenes as one might expect. I also remember disliking *Romeo and Juliet* because it was too mushy.

But now comes the part that drives me crazy. Did I, or did I not, try to read *Hamlet* or *King Lear*? I have absolutely no recollection of it. In fact, I cannot remember when I read *Hamlet* for the first time. Surely, there must have been a moment when I read it, or at least began to try to read it, for the first time. Surely I must have had some reaction. —But no, nothing. A blank.

It raises a whole series of problems, when you stop to think of it. When did I first learn that the Earth travels about the Sun? When did I first hear of dinosaurs? Presumably, I read about this and other matters in books on popular science for youngsters which I obtained in the library, but why don't I remember saying, "Oh, my goodness, this whole Earth is speeding about the Sun. How amazing!"

Does everyone else remember when they first heard of such things? Am I an idiot for not remembering?

On the other hand, is it possible that once you firmly accept something as a youngster, you wipe out your earlier state of "not knowing" or "wrong knowing"? Does the memory function of the brain simply clear the earlier stuff? There would be usefulness to that, since it would surely be harmful to live under the childish impression that bunny rabbits talked once you found out they didn't. I'll accept that, and decide I'm not an idiot.

I therefore assume that I eventually read and appreciated *Hamlet* so much that the memory function of my brain simply settled down to the easy belief that I had known it through all eternity. And I suppose I learned things from my books that I adopted not only at that moment but retrospectively too.

One thing leads to another, even accidents. Once, when I was ill and couldn't go to the library, I persuaded my poor mother to go for me, promising I would read any book she brought me. What she brought back was a fictionalized life of Thomas Edison. That disappointed me, but I had promised, so I read it and that *might* have been my introduction to the world of science and technology.

Then, too, as I grew older, fiction drew me to nonfiction. It was impossible to read Alexandre Dumas's *The Three Musketeers* without becoming curious about French history.

My introduction to ancient Greek history (as opposed to mythology) came about, I believe, because I read *The Jealous Gods* by Gertrude Atherton (thinking it was mythology, I imagine). I found myself reading about Athens and Sparta, and about Alcibiades, in particular. The picture I have of Alcibiades, as drawn by Atherton, has never left me.

Again, *The Glory of the Purple* by William Stearns Davis introduced me to the Byzantine Empire and to Leo III (the Isaurian), to say nothing of Greek fire. Another one of his books, the title of which I can't recall at the moment, introduced me to the Persian War and to Aristides.

All this led me to history itself. I read Hendrik van Loon's book on history, then decided I needed stronger stuff, so I remember reading a history of the world written by a nineteenth-century French historian named Victor Duruy. I read it several times.

This was all miscellaneous reading and I can't even begin to tell you how far it stretched and how silly it must have seemed to others. At one library I attended (I used to go to every one within reach) I found bound volumes of *St. Nicholas,* a children's magazine that flourished a century ago. I took out one volume after another—big, bound volumes each including a year's worth of monthly issues in microscopic print, and read as much as I could of them.

In those volumes, I came across the serialization of *Davy and the Goblin,* which I rather frowned on because I thought it an imitation of *Alice's Adventures in Wonderland,* but not as good. (There! When did I first read *Alice?* I can't remember, but I'm absolutely sure that whenever I read it, I loved it.)

There were also doggerel poems in each issue about a band of innocent goblins who were always having troublesome adventures. The illustration for each was particularly delightful, especially since one of the goblins was always dressed as a stage Englishman (top hat, tails, and monocle) and was having more trouble than all the rest put together.

I skipped a lot, of course, but I read a lot too.

When I grew a little older, I discovered Charles Dickens (I have read *Pickwick Papers* twenty-six times by actual count and *Nicholas Nickleby* some ten times). I even worked my way through such unlikely books as Eugène Sue's *The Wandering Jew* (attracted by "Jew") and *The Mysteries of Paris* (attracted by "mysteries"). I found myself appalled. I couldn't stop reading, but I was horrified from beginning to end by the picture Sue drew of the poor and criminal. Even now, I shudder when I think of it. Dickens's pictures of poverty and misery always had the leaven of humor, which made it more tolerable. Sue hammered away.

I also read a justly forgotten book, *Ten Thousand a Year* by Samuel Warren, which had an excellent villain by the name of Oily Gammon. I think that was the first time I realized that a villain, not a "hero," might be the true protagonist of a book.

About the only thing that was almost totally left out of my reading was twentieth-century fiction. (Not twentieth-century nonfiction, which I read voluminously.) Why modern fiction was left out I don't

know. Perhaps I was attracted to the dustier books. Perhaps the libraries I went to were themselves poor in modern fiction.

That childish bent has remained. I still only very rarely read a piece
of modern fiction (other than mysteries).

All this incredibly miscellaneous reading, the result of lack of guidance, left its indelible mark. My interest was aroused in twenty different directions and all those interests remained. I have written books
on mythology, on the Bible, on Shakespeare, on history, on science,
and so on.

Even my lack of reading modern fiction has left its mark, for I am
perfectly aware that there is a certain old-fashioned quality about my
writing. However, I like it, and there are enough readers who also
seem to like it to keep me from impoverishment.

I received the fundamentals of my education in school, but that was
not enough. My *real* education, the superstructure, the details, the
true architecture, I got out of the public library. For an impoverished
child whose family could not afford to buy books, the library was the
open door to wonder and achievement, and I can never be sufficiently
grateful that I had the wit to charge through that door and make the
most of it.

Now, when I read constantly about the way in which library funds
are being cut and cut, I can only think that the door is closing and
that American society has found one more way to destroy itself.

9

Bookworm

Everything conspired to force me into an abnormal way of life as a
youngster—"abnormal," of course, only if compared to the average
way of life of the average youngsters by whom I was surrounded. To

me, it was not abnormal. It was desirable. I sat by myself with my books and felt sorry for the other kids.

Mind you, I was not completely isolated. I was not a misanthropic or super-shy "loner." I am as a matter of fact (I am told this by others) highly extroverted. I am loud, I am noisy, I chatter, and I laugh a lot. (I use the present tense, because I am apparently still like that.) It meant that I could talk to my schoolmates and to the neighbor kids, and even on occasion play with them. However, only on occasion, and this for a variety of reasons.

1. Once I was pressed into labor in the family candy store, my hours of leisure were cut down to almost nothing. There was no time for play.

2. Even if, under unusual circumstances, playing could take place, I refused to engage in any play that had any chance of violence, even friendly violence. I was small, I was weak, and in any roughhousing I was the one who got roughhoused.

3. Many games, whether with checkers, tops, marbles, or other objects, were played "for keeps." The winner got the loser's objects. Very early, I learned that I wasn't made to play for keeps. If I lost my preciously hoarded objects, there was no chance of getting them replaced. My father wasn't going to stake me to indefinite amounts of these gewgaws, and I knew that well. I would only play "for fun"— that is, games in which the glory of winning was all, but everyone kept his own objects. To most people, playing for fun just wasn't any fun, and I got few chances to play my way.

Looking back at this, it seems rather shabby of me never to want to bet any trivial possession on my skill, but it had its uses. It kept me, throughout my life, from any temptation to gamble. Only once, only *once* did I fall from this state of rigid nongambling purity. In my early twenties, I succumbed to the temptation to be "one of the boys" and I joined in a poker game when I was assured the stakes would be very low.

Later, riddled with guilt, I confessed to my father and told him I had played poker for money.

"How did you do?" asked my father calmly.

"I lost fifteen cents," I said.

"Thank God," he said. "Think if you had *won* fifteen cents." He was well aware of the addictive qualities of the vice.

This bias against gambling goes even further. It is more than simply not playing poker or betting on the horses. In every step of my life, I have tried to estimate the chance I would have of succeeding. If, in my opinion, the chances of success were far less than the risk I would have to take, I did not take the risk. This works, if you're capable of making good judgments, and I apparently have been capable of this. At least, the things I've attempted have almost always worked out well, even when, *to others,* they would seem long shots. If, *to me,* they did *not* seem long shots, I went after them wholeheartedly, and almost always with success.

Thus, I have written books no one but an idiot, perhaps, might have thought would sell, and yet they managed. On the other hand, I have always estimated that any but the most trivial connection with Hollywood, however profitable it might *seem* at the moment, would end in disaster, and I have stayed away from the place. I have never regretted it either.

As you can see from all this, I did not form part of the neighborhood gang, and, as I grew older, I formed less and less of it. Extrovert or not, cheery prattler or not, I was essentially an outsider, and I might easily have broken my heart over it, and poisoned the rest of my life. (I have friends who have led more or less poisoned adult lives because they were outsiders when young.)

But outsideness simply didn't bother me. I don't recall ever mourning being left out. I don't recall ever watching the other kids running about madly and wishing I could join them. Rather, I thought of the possibility with distaste.

You see, I had my books. I would rather read.

I remember the hot summer afternoons when business was slow and my father, with or without my mother, could handle the candy store without me. I would sit outside the store (always available for emergencies) with my chair tipped back against the wall, and read.

I remember that after my brother, Stanley, was born, and I was given the task of tending him, I would wheel him around the block some twenty or thirty times, with a book propped against the handle of the baby carriage, reading.

I remember coming back from the library with three books, one tucked under either arm and reading the third. (This was reported to my mother as "peculiar behavior" and my mother would scold me, for both she and my father had this horror of offending customers. You may be sure that I paid no attention.)

I was, in other words, a classic "bookworm." To those who are not bookworms, it must be a curious thought that someone would read and read, letting life with all its glory pass by unnoticed, wasting the carefree days of youth, missing the wonderful interplay of muscle and sinew. There must seem something sad and even tragic about it, and one might wonder what impels a youngster to do it.

But life is glorious when it is happy; days are carefree when they are happy; the interplay of thought and imagination is far superior to that of muscle and sinew. Let me tell you, if you don't know it from your own experience, that reading a good book, losing yourself in the interest of words and thoughts, is for some people (me, for instance) an incredible intensity of happiness.

If I want to recall peace, serenity, pleasure, I think of myself on those lazy summer afternoons, with my chair tipped back against the wall, the book on my lap, and the pages softly turning. There may have been, at certain times in my life, higher pitches of ecstasy, vast moments of relief and triumph, but for quiet, peaceful happiness, there has never been anything to compare with it.

10
School

I liked school. There was nothing in what they tried to teach me, in grammar school and in junior high school at least, that I found formidable. It was all easy and I shone—and I loved to shine.

I had problems, of course. There are always problems. Even leaving out of account the fact that I was not popular with my classmates, I was not popular with most of my teachers either. Despite the fact that I was inevitably the brightest kid in the class (and the youngest), I was also among the worst-behaved. When I say that, you must understand that the standards of "worst-behaved" were incredibly different sixty years ago than they are today.

We live in a society today in which schoolchildren are involved with drugs, in which they carry weapons to school with them, in which they beat up and, sometimes, rape teachers.

Such behavior could not have been imagined in the schools of my time. I was worst-behaved because I whispered in class. I always had a lot to say about what was going on, and wild horses couldn't prevent me from making those comments in a whisper to whoever sat next to me.

My victim was likely to titter and that would attract the attention of the teacher. Since the one tittering was always sitting next to me, the deduction was obvious and a sharp eye was kept on me. I never managed to evade it.

Why did I do it? Why didn't I learn better? I don't know. Perhaps it was a matter of reacting before thinking. I've been doing it all my life, although with diminishing frequency. Sometimes, even now, something funny but extremely inappropriate occurs to me and I say it before my teeth can bite it back.

Thus, one day, during intermission in the lobby of a theater showing one of the Gilbert and Sullivan plays (a passion of mine), a woman came up to me to ask for an autograph. I obliged (I have never refused an autograph) and she said, "You're only the second person I ever asked for an autograph."

Idly, I asked, "Who was the other?"

"Laurence Olivier," she said.

And, with horror, I heard myself say, "How honored Olivier would feel if he knew."

It was meant as a joke, of course—humor by reversal—but she staggered away and I'm sure that she has told everyone she knows what a monster of vanity and arrogance I am.

And it's not just saying things, it's doing things. On that very same occasion, an elderly woman said to me (by this time, you understand, I was an elderly man), "I went to grammar school with you."

"Did you?" I asked, no memory stirring, of course.

"In PS 202."

I grew more interested. I did, indeed, attend PS 202 between 1928 and 1930.

She said, "The reason I remember you is that once the teacher said something—I forget what—and you told her she was wrong. She insisted she was right and at lunchtime you ran home, came back with a big book, and proved that she was wrong. Do you remember that?"

"No," I said, "but that was Isaac Asimov all right. There's not another schoolchild ever invented who would go to all that trouble to humiliate a teacher and make himself hated just to prove he was right over some trivial point."

Yes, I had trouble with teachers all through school, well into my doctoral studies. Beyond that, I had trouble with any people who were above me in any hierarchy. I never found true peace till I turned my whole working life into self-employment. I was not made to be an employee.

For that matter, I strongly suspect I was not made to be an employer either. At least I have never had the urge to have a secretary or a helper of any kind. My instinct tells me that there would surely be interactions that would slow me down. Better to be a one-man operation, which I eventually became and remained.

I am sometimes asked if there was any particular teacher at school who was an inspiration to me, and if I would give details. In fact, I remember virtually none of my teachers, not because they were particularly unmemorable, but because I am particularly self-centered. There are, however, three who stand out in my mind.

There was a teacher I had for a month in the first grade who was stout and warm and loving (and black—the only black teacher I ever had). She had me pushed ahead, and when I was forced to leave the class I cried and said I wanted *her,* and she patted me and told me I had to go. When I tried to sneak back into her class the next day, she took me by the hand and led me out again.

There was a Miss Martin in the fifth grade, who (unlike most teachers) liked me despite my faults and was kind to me. What a relief that was to me.

There was a Miss Growney in the sixth grade who had the reputation of being "strict" and threw students into terror. She scolded and shouted at them and, on occasion, at me too. I, at least, was used to that and endured it stolidly. I think she liked me too, perhaps because I was clearly unafraid of her. (I discovered quite early that the "smartest kid in class" could sometimes get away with murder.)

11
Growing Up

I presume every child wants to grow up and become an adult, with all the rights and privileges of an adult. It stands to reason that a child is aware of the circumscribed life he leads, with his parents always telling him what to do and what not to do, without a chance to make his own decisions, and so on. He therefore sees adulthood as a time of incredible freedom. (Later, he is likely to learn that it is merely a passport to a far more onerous slavery . . . but never mind.)

When I was young there were certain physical concomitants to growing up. Children wore "shorties"—that is, breeches that buckled just under the knees rather like the trousers of aristocrats of the eighteenth century. You had to wear long stockings, of course, that reached to the knee. As one grew older, a smoldering hatred for the shorties burgeoned, for they were a mark of childhood. Children waited for the time they could put on "longies" for the first time—ordinary trousers that come down to the ankles and require no buckles.

I remember the time when I first put on longies. I was so proud I couldn't stand it. I walked out in the street and paraded around hoping that everyone would see me and notice that a new adult had come into the world. Actually, I was only thirteen at the time, and I quickly found out that longies did not make me an adult.

Nevertheless, I was stricken when, not long after that, shorties disappeared from the scene. Kids don't wear them anymore. They don't have that stigma and I don't think that's fair. Why was I forced to carry that badge of shame when nowadays no one does?

I lived to see other changes in dress. When I was young, all youngsters wore caps. These were cloth hats with a visor. You could snap them on, snap them off, crush them out of shape, do anything you wanted to them, and they always remained serviceable. They were the most convenient headwear I've ever worn; some of them even came with earflaps for the cold weather.

Now they're gone, all gone. The story I've heard was that caps were always worn by the bad guys in the early gangster movies, and the American public, never notable for thinking for themselves, therefore rejected them.

It didn't matter. I graduated to a fedora, which was the "adult" hat. Eventually I got to hate it, even though it was universal. In the movies everyone wore a fedora outdoors. Even when they got into a fistfight, which was often in the cheaper movies, the fedora stayed on no matter what.

It was a relief to me when fedoras disappeared also and everyone went hatless. Of course, as I got older, I found it was useful to wear a hat for warmth, but I now wear a Russian-style fur hat which, like the caps of my childhood, can be stuffed into a pocket. Full circle.

I have seen other changes in men's clothing. Suits used to come with two pairs of pants. No more. Vests largely disappeared. Trousers lost their cuffs (very useful for collecting lint and pebbles). The watch-fob pocket disappeared.

Buttons on trouser flies were replaced by zippers. This was a dispensation from heaven, for when I was a kid a favorite game was to walk up to some unexpecting victim and rip open his fly to the sound of taunting laughter. I don't know that anything of note was ever exposed in this way, but the embarrassment was extreme, especially if there were girls about. Apparently, if the perpetrator managed to rip off a button or two, he was even more triumphant, and someone's poor mother would have to sew them on again.

12
Long Hours

The overriding factor in my life between the ages of six and twenty-two was my father's candy store.

It had its numerous good points. My father worked for himself and could not be fired. This was all-important once the Great Depression began with the stock market crash of 1929. With millions unemployed, with no unemployment insurance, no welfare, no feeling that society had to do anything at all about the unfortunate except to toss them an occasional dime for a cup of coffee ("Buddy, can you spare a dime?"), one could only stand on corners in ragged coats selling apples, or scrounge in garbage cans, or starve.

No one can possibly have lived through the Great Depression without being scarred by it. In the United States at least, its devastation was greater than that of World War II (if you ignore the military casualties, which is, of course, hard to do). No "Depression baby" can ever be a yuppie. No amount of experience since the Depression can convince someone who has lived through it that the world is safe economically. One constantly waits for banks to close, for factories to shut down, for the pink slip of discharge.

Well, the Asimov family escaped. Not by much. We were *poor*, but we always had enough to put food on the table and to pay the rent. Never were we threatened by hunger and eviction. And why? The candy store. It brought in enough to support us. Only minimally, to be sure, but in the Great Depression, even minimally was heaven.

There was a price, of course. Everything has its price. Making the candy store work required the total time of my mother and father (though my mother managed to find just a bit of time to keep the house in approximate order and to prepare meals).

This meant that, from the age of six, I lost the chance of having traditional parents—a mother who stays about the house, who spends hours in the kitchen, who is available, on demand, for this and that; and a father who shows up when work is done and who does things with you over the weekend.

On the other hand, I always knew where they were. They were in the store and I could be sure of finding them there. That, I suppose, was a measure of security.

When I was nine, and my mother was pregnant again, I was pressed into labor. My father had no choice. And, once in the store, I never emerged until I left home and was replaced by my brother, who was, after all, the occasion of my enslavement. (Not that I considered it enslavement, as I shall shortly explain.)

What was really remarkable about the candy store was the long hours. My father opened the store at 6 A.M., rain, shine, or blizzard. He closed it at 1 A.M. He had four to five hours of sleep at night. He made up for it by taking a two-hour nap every afternoon. That was *every* day, Saturdays, Sundays, and holidays included.

When we happened to own a store (we owned about five, one after the other) in a Jewish neighborhood, we closed for the most important of the Jewish holidays, to spare the feelings of our neighbors, but most of the time we were in Gentile neighborhoods and then we did not. As a matter of fact, on the rare occasions when the store was closed, I remember feeling distinctly uneasy about it, as though it were a weird phenomenon out of nature. I was relieved when the store reopened and the even tenor of our life resumed.

How did the long hours affect me?

On the adverse side of the ledger, they cut down my free time to virtually nothing. They wiped out any hopes of a social life even during my teenage years, and in the time when I might have discovered women, I could only do so from afar.

At school, I could not engage in "extracurricular activities," join any of the after-hours clubs or teams, because I had to go home and get into the store. This hurt my record. I never qualified for the honor society in high school because I did not engage in extracurricular activities, but I never tried to advance my home situation as an excuse. It would have sounded as though I were complaining about my parents, and I did not wish to do that.

Yet I didn't resent it.

Of course, I would have had to be a lot less intelligent than I was not to understand that the candy store stood between us and destruction. I also would have had to be a lot less decent a human being than I hope I am if I were able to watch my father and mother work as hard as they did and not pitch in.

It's more than that, even. There's a positive side to the ledger. I must have liked the long hours, for in later life I never took the attitude of "I've worked hard all my childhood and youth and now I'm going to take it easy and sleep till noon."

Quite the contrary. I have kept the candy-store hours all my life. I wake at five in the morning. I get to work as early as I can. I work as long as I can. I do this every day in the week, including holidays. I don't take vacations voluntarily and I try to do my work even when I'm on vacation. (And even when I'm in the hospital.)

In other words, I am still and forever in the candy store. Of course, I'm not waiting on customers; I'm not taking money and making change; I'm not forced to be polite to everyone who comes in (in actual fact, I was never very good at that). I am, instead, doing things I very much want to do—but the schedule is there; the schedule that was ground into me; the schedule you would think I would have rebelled against once I had the chance.

I can only say that there were certain advantages offered by the candy store that had nothing to do with mere survival, but, rather, with overflowing happiness, and that this was so associated with the long hours as to make them sweet to me and to fix them upon me for all my life. I will now explain what I mean.

13
Pulp Fiction

In the 1920s and 1930s, there was no television. There were virtually no comic books. (There was radio, to be sure, and such programs as *Amos 'n' Andy* became national fixations for a time.) On the whole, though, the environmental niche devoted to trash food for the mind consisted of the "pulp magazines."

These were so called because they were made of cheap pulp paper that didn't last long but quickly tended to turn yellow and grow fragile. They were rough-edged and rough-surfaced. This was in contradistinction to the "slick magazines," which had smooth surfaces, better paper, and which, in my opinion, were a rather classier trash food for the mind.

The pulp magazines were issued once a month, in some cases twice a month, and in a few cases even every week. To begin with, they were eclectic jobs offering melodramatic action fiction of a variety of types (examples were *Argosy* and *Blue Book)* but it eventually turned out that specialization was what was desired.

People wanted to read detective stories, or love stories, or Western stories, or war stories, or sports stories, or horror stories, or jungle stories, or any of a number of other classifications, often to the exclusion of anything else. They would therefore buy magazines devoted to their particularly desired specialty.

Perhaps the most successful of all the pulp fiction magazines were those devoted to the superheroes. There was, of course, the greatest of all, the Shadow, who, twice a month, foiled evildoers with his weird laugh and his ability to move like a ghost. There was Doc Savage, the "Man of Bronze," and his five, sometimes comic, assistants. There was the Spider and Secret Agent X and Operator 5. There was G-8 and his Battle Aces, who single-handedly defeated the Kaiser's Germany by foiling the evil scientific machinations of the German scientist Herr Doktor Krueger, and doing it month after month.

It was from this pulp fiction that my father tried to save me by getting me a library card and, on the whole, he was right, because he had no way of knowing the use to which I would put this (no, I won't call it trash again, for I owe it too much) rather low-class scribbling.

Once I began to work in the store, however, it became harder and harder to keep me from the pulps, and I became more and more strident in my demands for permission to read them. I pointed out that my father read the Shadow magazines constantly. My father replied that he was trying to learn English and I already knew English and had better things to do. He was right, but I continued with my demands and my father finally gave in, so I added the pulp magazines to my library reading.

It was those pulps that the candy store gave me that I valued far above anything else; that reconciled me to the work, to the long hours, and to everything else that might seem wearisome; that pinned me to a way of life even after the candy store had disappeared. If I weren't in the candy store, I couldn't possibly have afforded the magazines. As it was, I read them all, very carefully, and returned them, seemingly untouched, to the stands for sale.

By the time I reached my mid-teens and was ready for a writing career of my own, I had read with equal voracity the "good books" in the library and the "low-class material" in pulp fiction. What was it that influenced me in my writing, then?

I'm sorry. It was the pulp fiction.

In the first place, I wanted to write for the pulp magazines, or for a particular variety of the pulp magazines anyway (I'll get to that), and so I wanted to write the way the stories in the pulp magazines were written. I thought, in my innocence, that that was the way to write.

The result, of course, was that my early writing was extremely pulpish. It was heavy on adjectives and adverbs. People "snarled" rather than "said." There was lots of action, the dialogue was stilted, the characterization was nonexistent. (I don't believe I knew what characterization meant.)

The amazing thing was that my early stories, or at least some of them, were published at all. I attribute this to two things. First, the pulp magazines devoured material at so huge a rate that standards had to be low or they couldn't publish. The standards were low enough to include me.

Second, the particular branch of pulp fiction that interested me as a *writer* was the smallest and the neediest and the one, therefore, I was most likely to break into. As it happens, the vicissitudes of time have greatly increased the literary standards of my particular medium and I am very well aware (as I frequently say) that if I were starting *today* as a teenager, with only the evident talent that I actually had as a teen-ager, I could not possibly break into the field.

It is so important to be in the right place at the right time.

To be sure, I didn't stay pulpish. My writing rapidly improved with time and the pulp faded, but perhaps never entirely. I suspect that a keen eye reading my stuff even today can detect the pulp ancestry, and for that I'm sorry—but I do the best I can.

Let me make a few points about pulp fiction while I'm at it. It flourished in pre-World War II days, and in those days racism and racial stereotypes were an ingrained part of the American scene. It was not till World War II and the fight against Adolf Hitler's racism that it became unfashionable for Americans to express racist views.

I don't mean by that that racism disappeared after World War II, but merely that Hitler's example killed its respectability except among the troglodytes we always have with us. People still may feel racist in many respects, but they are cautious about expressing it, and if they are decent (and most people are), they try to fight it in themselves.

Pre-World War II pulp fiction was racist outright and everyone accepted the fact. Even the people who were victimized by it accepted it. There was very little militancy among the minorities, very little self-assertion.

So the heroes of pulp fiction were invariably solid Americans of Northwestern European extraction.

As for everyone else, well— If they were mentioned at all, Italians were greasy organ-grinder types, Russians were dreaming mystics, Greeks were olive-skinned and untrustworthy, Jews were comic characters when they were money-mad, African-Americans were comic characters who were either cowardly or murderous, according to the needs of the plot. Chinese were subtle and cruel (it was a time when Dr. Fu Manchu was a perfectly acceptable villain). Everyone but the Northwestern Europeans spoke with thick accents unheard in real life. (For that matter, motion pictures of the period were no better, and many of them would be extremely embarrassing to enlightened viewers if they were seen now.)

And even I accepted it all.

When it came time for me to write, however, no matter how pulpish my writing was, I avoided stereotypes. That much I did owe myself. But all my characters had names like Gregory Powell and Mike Donovan and so on. It wasn't till further on that I began to indulge in ethnic names.

There was another characteristic of pulp fiction that was quite curious. Though women were routinely threatened by the villains, the nature of the threat was never explicitly stated. It was a period of strong sexual repression, and sexual acts and threats could only be referred to in "family magazines" in the most distant way. Of course, no one minded if there was a continuous display of violence and sadism—that was all right for the family—but no sex.

This reduced women to little mannikin figures who never contributed actively to the plot. They were there to be (namelessly) threatened, to be captured, to be tied up and imprisoned—and, of course, to be rescued unharmed.

The women were there solely to make the villains more villainous, the heroes more heroic. And in being rescued, they played a purely passive role, their part consisting mostly of screaming. I can't recall (though I'm sure there must have been rare cases) any woman trying to join the fight and help the hero; any woman picking up a stick or rock and trying to lambaste the villain. No, they were like does, idly cropping the grass while they waited for the stags to stop fighting so that they would know which harem they would belong to.

Under the circumstances, any red-blooded male reading pulp fiction (like me) grew very impatient with the introduction of females. Knowing in advance they would merely be stumbling blocks, I wanted them out. I remember writing letters to magazines complaining about women characters—their very existence.

This was one of the reasons (not the only one) that in my own early stories I omitted women. In most cases, I left them out altogether. It was a flaw, of course, and another sign of my pulpish origins.

14

Science Fiction

One of the branches of pulp fiction was "science fiction"—the smallest and least regarded branch. It came into being in the pulp world in the form of *Amazing Stories,* whose first issue appeared in April 1926. Its editor and, therefore, the founding father of magazine science fiction, Hugo Gernsback, called it "scientifiction," an ugly portmanteau word.

He was forced out as editor in 1929, and went on to found two competing magazines that summer, *Science Wonder Stories* and *Air Wonder Stories,* which were soon combined into *Wonder Stories.* In connection with these magazines, he first made use of the term "science fiction."

The presence of the word "science" in the new magazine was a gift from heaven for me. I managed to con my naive father into thinking that a magazine entitled *Science Wonder Stories* was all about science. The science fiction magazines were, therefore, the first pulp magazines I was allowed to read. That may have been part of the reason that, when the time came for me to be a writer, it was science fiction that I chose as my medium.

Another reason was science fiction's more extended grasp on the young imagination. It was science fiction that introduced me to the Universe, in particular to the Solar system and the planets. Even if I had already come across them in my reading of science books, it was science fiction that fixed them in my mind, dramatically and forever.

There was, for instance, a three-part serial entitled *The Universe Wreckers* by Edmond Hamilton, which appeared in the May, June, and July 1930 issues of *Amazing.* In it, Earth was threatened with destruction by aliens from beyond the Solar system, but they were foiled by the derring-do of the heroes, who traveled out to Neptune in order to save the world. (How much more exciting and suspenseful that was than merely catching a criminal!)

It was in that tale that I first heard of Triton, the larger of Neptune's two satellites. Alpha Centauri also played a minor role and that may be the first time I heard of it and realized that it was the nearest star.

The first time I ever heard of the uncertainty principle, one of the basic foundations of modern physics, was through my reading of a two-part serial entitled *Uncertainty* by John W. Campbell, Jr., in the October and November 1936 issues of *Amazing*.

Mind you, I am not saying that science fiction was necessarily a good source of true scientific knowledge. In fact, rather the reverse when I was a youngster. In those early days, many of the science fiction writers were pulp writers who tried their hand at this field as well as at the others, and did so with only the barest rudiments of science. There were also eager teenage youngsters whose knowledge of science was almost as poor.

Still, among the garbage there were bound to be pearls and it was up to the discerning reader to find them. For instance, beginning with the September 1932 issue of *Amazing*, a writer named J. W. Skidmore wrote a series of stories about two entities he called "Posi" and "Nega," which stood for "positive" and "negative" of course, and I suspect that it was in the 1932 story that I first got the notion of protons and electrons kicked into my mind.

How fortunate I was, then, that my father had a candy store and not some other kind of store. Except that one mustn't blame fortune. It was inevitable. Because my father was an immigrant without any skills beyond the ability to handle bookkeeping accounts, he had no choice. He did not have the specialized skills to be a butcher or a baker and he might not even have been able to handle a grocery store. A candy store, which sold only packaged items (aside from the preparation of soda-fountain specialties, which is easy to learn), was the least specialized form of store and required the least knowledge. It was rock bottom.

One difficulty in my magazine-rack reading, by the way, was that I had to do it quickly to minimize the chance that the magazine would be needed for a customer. If a customer came in and asked for a Doc Savage when I was reading the only copy, it would be snatched out of my hands faster than a cobra strike. Fortunately, the demand for science fiction was not great. I don't recall a single instance when I had to give up a copy before I was done. Of course, if we received several copies of a particular magazine, which was frequently the case, I was home almost free.

Often, one or more of the magazines on my desirable list remained unsold at the end of their publication period. You might think I could then keep a copy as a permanent possession, but when the new issue of a magazine came out, any old issue left unsold was returnable at the wholesale price, and my father returned them. Never once was I allowed to keep one—but I knew that we existed on the knife edge, so I didn't complain.

After all, I did get other things for free. I could have a chocolate soda periodically, although I always had to ask. Ignorant people call them "egg creams," though they have neither egg nor cream. What they have is thick chocolate syrup and carbonated water. And don't try to get the equivalent today. I don't know what kind of synthetic garbage they use for syrup nowadays but it totally lacks the gooey, chocolaty riches of the stuff in my father's candy store. And often my mother would make me a chocolate malted milk under the impression that it was good for a growing boy. And it *was* for *this* growing boy. It was milk and malt and a generous dollop of that good chocolate syrup whipped into a froth that filled one and a half large glasses and left you with a mustache you hated to wipe off.

But I digress—

You might wonder what all this pulp fiction reading did to me and to my intellectual development. My father called it "trash," and though I hate to admit it, the old man was about 99 percent right. This, however, is what I think.

However trashy pulp fiction might be, it had to be *read*. Youngsters avid for the corny, lightning-jagged, cliché-ridden, clumsy stories had to read words and sentences to satisfy their craving. It trained everyone who read it in literacy, and a small percentage of them may then have passed on to better things.

Now consider what has happened since. In the late 1930s, comic books began to flood the market, and the pulp magazines weakened under the competition. World War II introduced paper shortages and there was a further weakening. With the coming of television, what was left of the pulp magazines died (all except, for a wonder, science fiction).

In general, the trend over the last half century or so has been away from the word to the picture. The comic magazines increased the level of looking, decreased the level of reading. The television set has carried this to an extreme. Even the slick magazines found themselves dying because of competition with the picture magazines of the 1940s and the girlie magazines that followed.

In short, the age of the pulp magazine was the last in which youngsters, to get their primitive material, were forced to be literate. Now that is gone, and the youngsters have their glazed eyes fixed on the television tube. The result is clear. True literacy is becoming an arcane art, and the nation is steadily "dumbing down."

It breaks my heart, and I look back on the days of the pulp magazines with a sigh not only for myself but for society.

15

Beginning to Write

I began to write in 1931, at the age of eleven. I did not try to write science fiction, but tackled something much more primitive.

Before the period of pulp fiction, there was the era of "dime novels." I witnessed the very end of that era. When my father first bought a candy store, he had for sale some old, dusty, browning paperback books involving Nick Carter, Frank Merriwell, and Dick Merriwell.

There were dozens and dozens of books about each of these characters and, I suppose, about others. Nick Carter was a detective who was a master of disguise. Frank and Dick Merriwell were all-American boys who were forever winning baseball games under difficulties for dear old Yale. I never read any of these books. My father was adamantly opposed, and by the time he got around to allowing me to read trash, those dime novels were gone.

"Series books" were hardcover books about some central character concerning whom new volumes were constantly churned out. Some were for very young children, such as those featuring Bunny Brown and his sister Sue (I actually read one or two of these when I was quite young), and, at a very slightly older level, the Bobbsey Twins, the Darewell Chums, Roy Blakely, Poppy Ott, and so on. (Such books existed for decades afterward, notably the Hardy Boys and Nancy Drew.)

The most popular of the series books in my younger days featured the Rover Boys. One of them, *The Rover Boys on the Great Lakes,* contained a young lady named Dora who was so primitive an example of "love interest" that I never noticed. She had an amiable but weak mother who was a continuing victim of an oily con man named Mr. Crabtree. There was also a more vicious pair of villains, father and son (although the father eventually reformed).

When I started to write, I wrote in direct—even slavish—imitation of this book. I called it *The Greenville Chums in College.*

Now the question is: Why did I start to write?

I have frequently written about my writing beginnings, and the story I usually tell is that I felt bad about not having any *permanent* reading material, only books that had to be returned to the library or magazines that had to be returned to the racks. It occurred to me I might copy a book and keep the copy. I chose a book on Greek mythology for the purpose and, in five minutes, realized this was an impractical procedure. Then, finally, I got the further idea of writing my own books and allowing them to be my permanent library.

Undoubtedly this was a factor, but it can't be the entire motive. I must simply have had the terrible urge to make up a story.

Why not? Surely many people have the urge to make up a story. It has to be a common human desire—a restless mind, a mysterious world, a feeling of emulation when someone else tells a story. Isn't storytelling what one does when one sits around a campfire? Aren't many social gatherings devoted to reminiscences and doesn't everyone like to tell a story of something that really happened? And aren't such stories inevitably embroidered and improved until the resemblance to reality becomes distant?

One can imagine early man sitting about campfires telling stories of great hunting feats that exaggerate the truth ridiculously but which are not questioned because every other person present intends to tell similar lies. A particularly good story would be repeated over and over and attributed to some ancestor or some legendary hunter.

And some people would, inevitably, be especially skilled at telling a story, and their talents would be in demand when there was some leisure time. They might even be rewarded with a haunch of meat if the story was really interesting. This would make them labor to invent bigger, better, and more exciting tales, naturally.

I don't see how there can be any doubt about it. The storytelling impulse is innate in most people, and if it happens to be combined with enough talent and enough drive, it cannot be suppressed. That was so in my case.

I just *had* to write.

I never finished *The Greenville Chums in College,* of course. I wrote eight chapters and ran down. Then I tried writing something else, and when that ran down, I tried writing something else, and so on, over a period of seven years.

Writing was exciting because I never planned ahead. I made up my stories as I went along and it was a great deal like reading a book I *hadn't* written. What would happen to the characters? How would they get out of the particular scrape they were in? The excitement was all I wrote for in those early years. In my wildest dreams it never occurred to me that anything I wrote would ever be published. I didn't write out of ambition.

As a matter of fact, I still write my fiction in that manner—making it up as I go along—with one all-important improvement. I have learned that there's no use in making things up as you go along if you have no clearly defined resolution to your story. Not having one was why my early stories all ran down.

What I do now is think up a problem *and a resolution to that problem.* I then begin the story, making it up as I go along, having all the excitement of finding out what will happen to the characters and how they will get out of their scrapes, but working steadily toward the known resolution, so that I don't get lost en route.

When asked for advice by beginners, I always stress that. Know your ending, I say, or the river of your story may finally sink into the desert sands and never reach the sea.

16
Humiliation

I have explained that I have always thought of myself as a remarkable fellow, even from childhood, and I have never wavered in that opinion. Need I say that the feeling was not universal?

I am not talking about people who recognized the existence of my faults, of my talkativeness, my self-assertiveness, my self-absorption, my social gaucheries. I recognized those faults too and labored (with indifferent success) to correct them. I'm talking about people who didn't think that I was remarkable intellectually or that I had unusual talents (or any at all).

I had sailed through the first six years of my schooling with remarkable ease and with the comfortable knowledge that no one in any of my classes could touch me. That ended, however, when I entered high school in 1932 and joined the tenth grade.

One trouble was that I didn't go to the neighborhood high school, Thomas Jefferson High School. I wanted to go to Boys High School, which was a considerable distance away, though it was still in Brooklyn, of course, the borough in which I spent my entire youth. Boys High School was, in those days, an elite school, and my father and I thought it would make it easier for me to get into a good college if I graduated from Boys High.

But that meant that Boys High collected the "smartest kids" from all over the borough and some were smarter than I was, at least as far as getting high grades was concerned. I suspected this at once when I tried to join the math club (Boys High invariably won the math competitions) under the impression that I was a hotshot mathematician. I quickly found out that the other students knew math I had never heard of, and I dropped out in confusion.

I also discovered after a while that there were a number of students who got better grades in this particular subject or that than I did. This did not ruffle me. I remember that in junior high school one boy won the biology prize but was terrible in math, and another boy won the mathematics prize but was terrible in biology—and I was runner-up in *both*.

Unfortunately, I also discovered that some students ended up with better overall averages than I did. Their averages were not only higher but stayed higher. These averages were posted, and I had the annoyance of seeing my name down in tenth or twelfth place. (It was no disgrace but I was no longer the "smartest kid.")

Such was the impression this made on me that I actually remember, after more than half a century, the names of three of the students who did better than I. This is remarkable for someone like me who is so self-centered that he does not consider the names of other people worth remembering. Obviously, *these* students hit me hard.

None of this shook my own belief in my remarkability, but I did seek an explanation in my own head. I always seek explanations in my own head, and in this case I had no choice. There was no way I could go to anyone, certainly not to any teacher, and say, "Why are these students getting better grades than I am?"

The obvious answer would have been: "Because they're smarter than you, Asimov, you rotten kid, and I'm glad they are." This was not an answer I wanted to hear, or proposed to believe.

Instead, I reasoned out that these extraordinary kids came from settled and well-to-do families, that they had been raised in an intellectual atmosphere, that they had plenty of time to study, and they *were* bright after a fashion.

As for me, I still had the candy store to work in, so that my time for studying was limited. Besides, I made no real effort to find time for study. My stubborn notion was that I simply didn't have to study. I read the schoolbooks and I listened to the teacher and that was it.

Well, saying so doesn't make it so, and if I had truly wanted to compete, truly felt that I had to get higher marks, I would have swotted away—but I refused. I decided I didn't have to because I needed no record marks to prove to myself that I was remarkable. My enjoyment in being me wasn't affected. After all, I wasn't just a student; I was a writer.

But even there I was doomed to suffer humiliation in high school. I suffered, indeed, the hardest blow my ego has ever received. In 1934, one of the English teachers, Max Newfield, who was the faculty adviser of the school's semiannual literary magazine, decided to give a special writing class, hoping he could get more material for the magazine in this way. I quickly joined up. I was only fourteen and everyone else was sixteen or seventeen, but I was a *writer*.

It was a huge mistake. We were all asked to write an essay and I wrote one that was absolutely and terminally rotten. When Newfield asked for volunteers to read their essays, my hand shot up. I had read only about a quarter of it when Newfield stopped me and used an opprobrious barnyard term to describe my writing. (I had never heard a teacher use a "dirty word" before and I was shocked.) The class wasn't, however. They laughed at me very uproariously and I took my seat in bitter shame and humiliation.

I remained in the class, however. I knew the mistake I had made. I had tried to be "literary" when I didn't know how to be. I would never make *that* mistake again. (And I never have either. Other mistakes, perhaps, but not that one.) I was determined to do better.

Finally, we were asked to write something particularly for the literary semiannual, and I grimly tried again. I wrote an essay called "Little Brothers" about a new little baby entering our house five years before. I tried to be funny about it. Newfield actually accepted it and eventually it was printed, the very first significant piece of my writing ever to be printed.

I tried to thank Newfield, hoping he would tell me how much I had improved, but no such thing. Apparently, this being in the depth of the Great Depression, every student in the class, badly scarred by it, had written tragic Dostoyevskian pieces. Only I, rescued by the candy store, wrote a lighthearted piece. Newfield needed a lighthearted piece and mine was the only one. He had the bad grace and needless cruelty to tell me that that was the only reason he had taken it. He even added an editorial note in the semiannual, virtually apologizing for including it.

Now how did I survive that?

I must tell you that I was shaken to the core, and I cannot remember what arguments I used to convince myself that I was, indeed, a good writer, and would succeed. I suppose that I simply held on, stubbornly, to my own good opinion of myself and found refuge in hating Newfield. (I hate very few people, but I hate *him*.)

To all those who "make good," there must be some feeling such as "If only so-and-so knew about this, he'd be sorry he said such and such." Or "She'd be sorry she turned me down." The whole world might know you and acclaim you, but someone in the past, forever unreachable, forever unknowing, spoils it all. That remains a blot, a splotch of darkness, a never to be assuaged pain.

In my case, it's Newfield. I suppose he died before I became a truly famous writer, so that he never knew what he had done. Every once in a while, though, I wish I had a time machine and could go back to 1934 with some of my books and some of the articles that have been written about me and say to him, "How do you like that, you rotten louse? You didn't know whom you had in your class. If you had treated me right, I could have recorded you as my discoverer, instead of branding you a rotten louse."

As a matter of fact, I have been so rubbed raw over the more than half a century of suffering I have endured that I have recently written a story entitled "Time Traveler," in which a character who suffered exactly as I had *did* go back in time. Unfortunately, being a writer I was forced to end the story dramatically and appropriately, and not in such a way as to truly satisfy me. (No, I won't tell you how it worked out.)

The one satisfaction I have is this: There must be a few copies of that literary semiannual with "Little Brothers" in it. I own a copy, for instance. I assure you that, except for mine, there is no name in the table of contents that is well known. A number of poems are included by Alfred A. Duckett, a talented young African-American who went on to do considerable writing, but, overwhelmingly, the one familiar name is my own. There are collectors who, if faced with that copy, might well be willing to pay a sizable sum for it, if for no other reason than that it contains my first published piece of writing, the one Newfield apologized for.

When the graduation yearbook came out, there was a listing of the best all-round scholar, the best writer, the best this and the best that. Needless to say, I was not named the best anything, and needless to say, none of the best this and the best that have (as far as I know) made names for themselves. In fact, the only place in the entire yearbook where I was mentioned was immediately under my photograph and there it said, "When he looks at a clock, it not only stops, it goes backward." Schoolboy wit.

No, my high school career was not a success in any worldly sense, though I did end up with a very high overall grade average. And this despite the fact that I discovered, to my considerable horror, that there were subjects I could not handle at all.

I was used to taking up any academic subject, from grammar to advanced algebra and from German to history with equal ease. At Boys High, however, I had a semester of economics and found, to my utter amazement, that I didn't understand it. Listening to the teacher did me no good, and reading up on it did me no good either. For the first time in my life, I ran up against a mental barrier—a subject that simply could not make its way into my brain.

All this I had to survive. I had to bear up under the humiliation of the writing class, of the fact that I was not even in the first half dozen of grade averages, of the fact that I was totally ignored in the yearbook, and of the fact that there were subjects I could not understand.

I managed. At least, I don't recall being downcast. I was still a remarkable person, and I intended to show the world I was. I finished high school in 1935, only fifteen years old.

17
Failure

My intention was to enter Columbia College, the elite undergraduate school of Columbia University. My father couldn't really afford the tuition, but he proposed to worry about that afterward. The first thing was to be allowed to enter. I went to be interviewed by the appropriate official at Columbia, the campus of which I entered for the first time on April 10, 1935.

The interviewer would not take me. I know why. Columbia College's quota for Jews for the coming year was already filled. It was my first serious experience with the hampering effect of anti-Semitism. He was kind, though, and attributed the rejection to the fact that I was under age. I had to be sixteen to become a Columbia College freshman. He suggested I agree to enter Seth Low Junior College, another undergraduate college of the university. (It also set the minimum age at sixteen, I noticed, but it didn't seem to matter in a non-elite school.) It was located in Brooklyn, it would give me two years of college education, and then I could take the final two years with the students of Columbia College.

I agreed. I could scarcely do anything else.

My father, however, did not agree. He was willing to go to considerable trouble, even borrow money, to send me to Columbia College but not to Seth Low. So I bit the bullet and went to City College, to which I had also applied and which had accepted me. It did not charge tuition, but it was a kind of ghetto school, strongly Jewish, and graduates had little chance of finding cushy jobs.

I spent three miserable days there, and the only thing I remember was the physical examination. Everyone else got their cards stamped WD, but mine was stamped PD. I inquired. WD, I was told, meant "well developed." PD meant "poorly developed." The fact that I was up to three years younger than all the others being examined was not taken into account. I felt bitterly insulted.

But then a letter came from Seth Low. Where was I? My father, having opened the letter, phoned them to explain that I couldn't afford the tuition. They offered him a hundred-dollar scholarship and he couldn't resist that. I switched to Seth Low. Later I got a letter from City College. They had looked at the results of an intelligence test they had had the students take, and they were very anxious to have me come in and discuss my college career. I wrote back rather coldly and told them it was too late. I was going to Columbia. ("Poorly developed" indeed.)

(The incident, by the way, led to a serious argument with my father. In Russia, receiving a letter was such a rare phenomenon that any member of the family who got his hands on it first opened it. I explained rather bitterly that we didn't do things that way in the United States. A letter addressed to me could only be opened by me. My father was puzzled at this strange exclusivity, but from then on my mail was private.)

Seth Low turned out to be a ghetto school, about half Jewish and half Italian-American. It apparently got the overflow of bright students who could not be squeezed into Columbia College's quota.

Seth Low was not a successful school. After my freshman year, it was closed down, and we were transferred en masse to the campus at

Morningside Heights. For the remainder of my college career, I sat in with the Columbia College class, listening to their lectures, taking their tests, and being marked by their standards.

Did that make me a member of the class? It did not. I was classified as a university undergraduate. When the time came to graduate, every member of the Columbia College class got a B.A., or Bachelor of Arts, the gentleman's degree. I got a B.S., or Bachelor of Science, a less prestigious degree. I thought I got it because I majored in a scientific subject, but no, it was a gesture of second-class citizenship, I eventually found out, and it was one more source of annoyance to me.

What's more, the university eventually established the School of General Studies to succeed University Extension. It dealt primarily with those students who took night courses because they had to work during the day. Under that heading, they swept in a variety of miscellaneous categories, including university undergraduates. This means I am listed as an alumnus of the School of General Studies, and any careless biographer is going to conclude from that that I went to night school. *I did not.*

Of course, eventually, Columbia University was sufficiently proud of me to grant me an honorary doctorate and make much of me and have me come in to address this function or that. And when Columbia College itself invited me to speak to *them,* I had enough clout to insist on doing so only if I were made a member of the class of 1939. I was, and in 1979 I attended the fortieth class reunion. This was not because I wanted to (I don't attend reunions in general because I don't value wallowing in nostalgia that much), but I did on this occasion in order to establish the franchise, so to speak. I didn't know any of the others who attended the reunion, and while they all knew of me, I don't think any of them remembered me as a classmate.

In many ways, then, my college career was a failure, perhaps worse than my high school career. It saw a further slippage of my academic expertise too. In grammar school and junior high school, I was *the* smart kid. In high school, I was one of the smarter kids. In college, I was simply a smart kid of no particular distinction.

The largest failure came toward the end of my college career.

You see, there was a danger to the end of college. As long as I went to grammar school, junior high school, high school, and college, I was a schoolboy, content to live at home, work with the family, and live an accustomed and even-tenored life.

As the years crept on, though, college graduation and a bachelor's degree loomed, and I would have to find a job. The year of my graduation would be 1939. I would be nineteen, and jobs were still hard to get.

What's more, some jobs were barred to me, no matter what. There was no chance of my gaining the kind of job from which Jews were automatically barred—the kind that placed one on the stairway of advancement to the most prestigious and profitable positions, of course. But I won't plead anti-Semitism. Even if I were *not* Jewish, but were still myself, I would not qualify. I did not make a good appearance, I was gangly, acne-ridden, had an easily provoked grin that, I think, lent a foolish expression to my face, and, to top it off, I was incredibly gauche socially. I couldn't imagine anyone wanting me.

The only solution was to stay in school and, if possible, to be trained for a job in which I would be self-employed. By an odd turn of circumstance, I had already achieved that goal without knowing it. In my junior and senior years at college, I sold my first two or three stories and had become a professional writer.

There was, however, no way in which I could imagine that I could do anything more with my stories than make an occasional few dollars for pin money. The thought of writing as a *career,* and as a well-paying one to boot, would have occurred only to a megalomaniac, and, for all my self-assurance, I was not that.

The self-employed jobs open to Jews that carried the promise of social prestige and a good living were the professions: doctor, dentist, lawyer, accountant, and so on. Of course, it was best to be a doctor. A great many New York doctors were Jews, and it was a sure way for a Jew to succeed in a society that was moderately anti-Semitic.

As it happened, my father had assumed this for a long time. Once I got out of college, he reasoned, I would naturally get into medical school and become a doctor. Since it never occurred to me to disagree with my father in such matters, I naturally assumed it too.

As time went on, however, certain doubts began to gather within my mind. First of all, where on earth was the money to come from? There was no way I could afford tuition, books, and equipment. I made it through college by the narrowest of chances, with the aid of summer jobs, a couple of story sales, a couple of very small scholarships, and the scraping together of all the available family money. There was never anything to spare. Medical school would be much more expensive. There was no chance at all that I could make it.

To make matters worse, my father developed angina pectoris in

1938 and there was serious question whether he could continue to work in the candy store, and whether I would not have to take over altogether and give up all hopes of becoming anything but a store-keeper myself.

Fortunately, my father, who weighed 220 at the time, lost weight with all deliberate speed, coming down to 160, and remaining there for the rest of his life. He stayed on medication and continued to work in the candy store, but that still left a medical school career more questionable.

On a more personal note, there was the matter of my having to leave home. What if I were accepted by a medical school in Ohio or Nevada?

The fact is that I had lived at home all my life and had only on the rarest of occasions, and for the briefest of intervals, left New York City. Again, as in the case of long hours, I might have rebelled against this, and when the occasion arrived and I was no longer compelled to stay at home, I might with the greatest of joy have undertaken to see the world. My brother, Stanley, has reacted in just this way. He and his wife travel the world over and love it.

Unfortunately (or, perhaps, fortunately—who can tell in these matters?) the urge to travel withered in me. I didn't want to leave home. In fact, I was terribly frightened of leaving home. I couldn't sleep when I thought that I might have to go to another state and be entirely on my own and have to take care of myself. I didn't know *how* to do that.

To be sure, as life went on, I was eventually forced to leave home, and to live on my own, and to take on the responsibilities of a wife and children of my own. However, whenever I established myself to the point of calling somewhere home, I instantly fixed myself firmly there and didn't want to leave.

This has continued all my life long, and my aversion to travel, my desire to remain at home in my own comfortable and familiar environment, has strengthened. At the present moment, I live in Manhattan, and have lived here for twenty years. I do my level best never to leave Manhattan if I can possibly help it. To be utterly frank, I am not very excited about leaving my apartment. I am jealous of the fictional detective Nero Wolfe, who virtually never left his house on West Thirty-fifth Street.

The third reason was the simplest of all. The more I thought of it, the more I realized I didn't want to be a doctor, any kind of doctor. I can't stand the sight of blood, I am queasy at any mention of wounds, I am unhappy at any description of illness. I realized that one grows hardened. I grew hardened to dissection when I took zoology in college, but I didn't want to have to go through that painful process again.

Fortunately, the problem of medical school was decided for me by the medical schools themselves and the decision was the proper one. I applied only to the five medical schools in the New York area (since I was determined not to leave home). Two of them, including Columbia University's College of Physicians and Surgeons, rejected me out of hand, probably because their quota for Jews was filled. The other three interviewed me and, as usual, I made an unfavorable impression on the interviewers. This was not done on purpose, mind you; I did my best to be charming and lovable, but that sort of thing simply wasn't in me; at least, not at that time of my life.

I was rejected by all five while still in my junior year at college and when, the next year, I applied again, I was rejected even more rapidly.

It was a great disappointment to my father. It was the first time his remarkable son had tackled something he felt to be of great moment and had been defeated. I believe he felt the fault was, to some extent, mine (which it certainly was), and relations between us were cool for a while. As for me, I felt a certain hurt pride; I would not have been human if I hadn't. My best friend in college, with lower grades but with far greater social presence, *was* admitted to medical school, and briefly I was smitten by a painful emotion I almost never feel—envy.

I recovered, however, and the passing of the years has only confirmed my notion that I would never have made it in medical school. I would have suffered the far greater humiliation of having to drop out, even if I had had all the money that was required, simply because I lacked the necessary ability and, even more, the suitable temperament.

What a blow *that* would have been. From that, I might not have recovered. I never think of that dangerous period in my life without feeling enormously grateful to the perspicacity and intelligence of the various people in charge of entrance requirements who carefully barred me from entrance into medical school.

18

The Futurians

I had become a science fiction "fan" (the word is short for "fanatic" —I'm not joking) by the mid-1930s. By that I mean that I did not confine myself merely to the reading of science fiction. I tried to participate in the machinery. The simplest way was to write letters to the editor.

The science fiction magazines all had letters columns, and readers were encouraged to write. The magazine that now most attracted me was *Astounding Stories*. This began its life in 1930 under the management of Clayton Publications. It, and Clayton, were forced out of business by the Depression after the March 1933 issue, but the title was picked up by Street & Smith Publications, the largest of the pulp fiction publishers.

Half a year after its death, then, *Astounding* was resurrected with the October 1933 issue. Under the imaginative direction of its editor, F. Orlin Tremaine, it quickly became the most successful of the science fiction magazines, and the best. It still exists today, although it has changed its name to *Analog Science Fact–Science Fiction*. In January 1990 the magazine celebrated its sixtieth anniversary (but illness, to my utter disappointment, prevented me from attending).

It was to *Astounding* that I wrote my first letter in 1935, and it was printed. In the usual fan fashion, I listed the stories I liked and disliked, said why, and asked for smooth edges, rather than the typical messy rough edges of the pulps that shredded and left paper lint everywhere. (The magazine did provide smooth edges, eventually. Nor were they holding back out of callousness. Smoothing the edges cost money.)

By 1938, I was writing letters to *Astounding* every month, and they were usually printed. This turned out to be more significant than I could have imagined.

There were other ways of being a fan too. Individual fans might get to know each other (perhaps from the letters column, since names and addresses were given). If they were within reach of each other, they could get together, discuss the stories, swap magazines, and so on. This developed into "fan clubs." In 1934, one of the magazines invented the Science Fiction League of America and fans who joined could make friends over still wider areas.

Stuck in the candy store as I was, I knew nothing about the fan clubs and it never occurred to me to join the League. However, a young man who had gone to Boys High with me noted my name on the letters in *Astounding* and sent me a card in 1938 inviting me to attend meetings of the Queens Science Fiction Club.

The chance to do so excited me extremely and I began negotiations with my parents at once. First I had to make sure that for the time of the meeting I could be spared from the candy store. After that I had to persuade them to give me the necessary carfare plus a few extra dimes in case we would eat something at the club and I had to make a purchase.

I might say at this point that I never got an allowance of any sort. I worked at the store for food, board, clothing, and an education and my parents felt that that was enough, and so did I. I had heard of allowances for children in movies, in comic strips, and so on, but I always had the vague feeling that that was a romantic departure from reality.

Of course, if I needed money for some legitimate purpose (carfare to school, lunch, or even something frivolous like the movies) it was never denied, but I had to ask. It was only after I started receiving checks for my stories that I was able to start a bank account of my own and then under the completely understood condition that the money was to go for tuition and other unavoidable school expenses and for nothing else.

It struck me as strange, later in life, that despite keeping me penniless, my father had no hesitation in allowing me access to the cash register. Of course, the register recorded all sales and if I had abstracted an occasional quarter it would show, but it was perfectly possible for me to have made some small sale of candy or cigarettes and then "forgotten" to put the money in the register and pocketed it myself. However, I was carefully brought up and it never once occurred to me to do such a thing, nor, apparently, did it ever occur to my father that I might.

In any case, I received permission to attend the fan-club meeting and was given the necessary funds for the purpose, and on September 18, 1938, I met, for the first time, other science fiction fans. However, between the first invitation and a second card giving me instructions on how to get to the meeting place, there had been a split in the Queens club, and a small splinter group formed a new fan organization. (Eventually, I came to understand that science fiction fans were a quarrelsome and contentious bunch and that clubs were forever splitting up into hostile factions.)

My high school friend belonged to the small splinter group and, in all ignorance that I was not going to the Queens club, I joined them. The splinter group had broken off because they were activists who felt that science fiction fans ought to take a stronger anti-Fascist stand, while the main group held that science fiction was above politics. Had I known about the split I would have resolutely sided with the splinter group, so that by ending up there I came to the right place.

The new group gave themselves a rather long and grandiloquent name but they are popularly known as the Futurians and they were certainly the most astonishing fan club that was ever founded. They consisted of a group of brilliant teenagers who, as nearly as I could tell, all came from broken homes and had led miserable or, at the very least, insecure childhoods.

Once again, I was an outsider, for I had a tightly knit family and a happy childhood, but in other respects I was charmed by all of them and felt that I had found a spiritual home.

To tell you how my life changed, I must explain my views on friendship—

One often hears in books, and movies, of childhood friendships that last throughout life; of onetime schoolmates who associate with each other through the years; of army buddies who are constantly getting drunk and reliving the joys of barracks life; of college chums helping each other through life for the sake of the old school tie.

It may happen, but I am always skeptical. It seemed to me that people who went to school together or were in the army together were living in a state of forced intimacy that they had not chosen for themselves. A kind of friendship-by-custom-and-propinquity might exist among those who happened to like each other independently or who were thrown into social togetherness outside of the artificial environments of school or army, but not otherwise.

In my own case, I had not one school friendship that survived school and not one army friendship that survived the army. Partly this was because there was no opportunity for social interaction outside either school or army and partly it was because of my own self-absorption.

However, once I met the Futurians, everything changed. Here, although there was little chance for social interaction most of the time, although I sometimes remained out of touch with this one or that one for a long period of time, I made close friendships which lasted in some cases for half a century, right down to the present.

Why?

At last I met people who burned with the same fire I did; who loved science fiction as I did; who wanted to write science fiction as I did; who had the same kind of erratic brilliance that I had. I did not have to recognize a soul mate consciously. I felt it at once without the necessity of intellectualizing it. In fact, in some cases, both within the Futurians and without, I felt soul-matehood and eternal friendship even with people whom I didn't really like.

In any case, I intend to devote small essays in this book to the individuals who strongly influenced my career or whose lives intertwined with mine in certain ways, and I cannot do better than begin with some of the more prominent Futurians.

19

Frederik Pohl

Frederik Pohl was born in 1919 and is just a few weeks older than I am. When we met as fellow Futurians in September 1938, we were each of us edging toward his nineteenth birthday. Despite the equality of our chronological age, he has always been more worldly-wise and possessed of more common sense than I. I recognized this and I would turn to him for advice without any hesitation.

Fred is taller than I, very soft-spoken. He has a pronounced over-bite and an often quizzical expression on his face that makes him look a bit rabbity but, in my eyes, cute, because I am very fond of him. He has light hair that was already thinning when I met him.

Fred is a very unusual fellow. He does not flash from time to time as I do, and as several of the other Futurians did. Instead, he burns with a clear, steady light. He is one of the most intelligent men I have ever met, and he frequently writes letters or columns for the fan magazines or professional magazines, expressing his views on scientific or social issues. I read them avidly, for he writes with clarity and charm, and I have never in fifty years had occasion to disagree with a word he has said. On a very few occasions when he expressed a point of view differing from one I had expressed, I would see at once that I had been wrong, he right. I think he is the only person with whose views I have never disagreed.

I always felt closer to him than to any other Futurian, even though our personalities and circumstances were so different. He had had an unsettled childhood, though he never spoke of it in detail, and the Great Depression had forced him out of high school. He makes the best of it by treating the matter humorously and referring to himself as a "high school dropout." Don't let him kid you, though. He con-tinued his program of self-education to the point where he knows a great deal more about a great many more things than does many a person with my own intensive education.

His social life has been more hectic than mine. For one thing, he has been married five times, but his present marriage, his fifth, to Bette, seems stable and happy.

At the time we met, he and the other Futurians were writing science fiction at a mad pace, alone and in collaboration, under a variety of pseudonyms. I did not join them in this, insisting on writing my sto-ries on my own and using my own name. As it happened, I was the first Futurian to begin to sell consistently, but they tumbled into the field on my heels.

He began to use his own name on his stories in 1952, when he, in collaboration with another Futurian, Cyril Kornbluth, published a three-part serial in *Galaxy* entitled "Gravy Planet." It appeared in novel form as *The Space Merchants* in 1953 and made the reputation of both Fred and Cyril. Each was a major science fiction writer thereafter.

His connection with me?

In 1939, he looked over my rejected short stories, called them "the best rejections I have ever seen" (which was very heartening), and gave me solid hints on how to improve my writing. Then, in 1940, when he was still only twenty years old, he became the editor (and a very good editor too) of two new science fiction magazines, *Astonishing Stories* and *Super Science Stories*. For those magazines he bought several of my early stories. This kept me going till I got the range of the best magazine in the field, *Astounding*. Fred and I even collaborated on two stories, though not very good ones, I'm afraid.

In 1942, when I was stuck and could not proceed with a novelette I was writing that *had* to be submitted in a week or so, he told me how to get out of the spot I had written myself into. I remember that we were standing on the Brooklyn Bridge at the time, but what my difficulty was and what his solution was, I don't remember. (We were standing on the Brooklyn Bridge, I found out many years later, because Fred's first wife, Doris, thought I was a "creep" and wouldn't have me in the apartment. I was struck in a heap when I found this in Fred's autobiography because I had liked her and had never dreamed of her distaste. Nor could I make it up with her, for she had died young.)

In 1950, Pohl was instrumental in the highest degree in getting my first novel published. In short, Fred, more than anyone else but John W. Campbell, Jr. (about whom I shall have more to say soon), made my career possible.

20
Cyril M. Kornbluth

Cyril M. Kornbluth was the youngest of the Futurians and, in some ways, the most erratically brilliant. He was born in 1923 and was only fifteen when I met him. He was short and pudgy, with curly brown hair, and there was a cutting edge to his speech, so that he was not a really pleasant person.

He was brighter than I was and, I think, showed much more promise, but, as in the case of Fred Pohl, his schooling had been aborted for some reason I never found out. I might have envied him his brightness, but it was clear that he was an unhappy person. What he was unhappy about, I don't know, but I suspect it was at finding himself in a world populated by people so much less intelligent than he who appreciated him so little.

On the other hand, he couldn't have lumped me together with the "less intelligent" and yet it was my impression he didn't like me, and that's a mild way of putting it. I have no direct evidence on this. He never told me in so many words that he disliked me, but he did avoid my presence, never spoke to me, and, on occasion, sneered at me. On the other hand, he tended to be morose and sneering at all times, and it may have been overly sensitive of me to feel that he was picking on me. Perhaps he found my consistent loud cheerfulness hard on his nerves, but I didn't do it to irritate him. I was as helplessly cheerful as he was helplessly morose.

Once when I sang the tenor song "A Maiden Fair to See" from *H.M.S. Pinafore,* I sang the high note in the last line with ease, and Cyril muttered, "Nuts! He hit it!" as though he had been waiting for my voice to crack so that he could savor my discomfiture.

And once, when I was giving a talk at a science fiction gathering,

Cyril interrupted me so frequently, and in so unfriendly a manner, that I stopped dead for a few moments in order to build suspense and ensure attention, and then said loudly and clearly, "Cyril Kornbluth— the poor man's George O. Smith."

George O. Smith was another science fiction writer, and an unrelenting bore. In any gathering, he drove everyone to distraction, speaker and audience alike, with his inane non-sequiturish remarks. The comparison of Cyril, unfavorably, with George seemed to stop him dead. There were no further interruptions.

But Cyril turned out to be a brilliantly smooth writer and displayed in his writing a wit and a sense of humor that he *never* displayed in real life. He was at his best in short stories, and his most famous one is "The Marching Morons" (April 1951 *Galaxy*). In it he depicts a world consisting largely of subintelligent morons who have outbred the few bright people who alone keep the world going. I'm sure that Cyril felt a personal application here.

He collaborated with Fred Pohl on "Gravy Planet" and wrote several novels on his own. I'm convinced that he was on his way out of the science fiction field, and would soon be writing mainstream novels and making an enormous name for himself, when it all came to an end.

He had a bad heart, and on March 21, 1958, he shoveled snow after a surprise vernal-equinox storm. He then ran for his train, had a heart attack at the station, and died. He was only thirty-five years old.

21

Donald Allen Wollheim

Donald Allen Wollheim was the oldest of the Futurians, having been born in 1914. He was the most dynamic member and dominated the society, but, then, he was probably the most active science fiction fan in the country, with the possible exception of Forrest J. Ackerman of Los Angeles.

He was not a handsome man, for he had a rather bulbous nose, and when I first met him, he also had (as I did) a bad case of acne. There was undeniable force to him, however, even though he was as dour as Cyril Kornbluth. In 1941, he became the editor of two science fiction magazines, *Stirring Science Fiction* and *Cosmic Stories*. These were put out on a frayed shoestring. In fact, he didn't have the money to pay for the stories and had to depend on fellow Futurians to supply him with material that they could not otherwise sell. He even asked me for a story, and I gave him one called "The Secret Sense," which appeared in the March 1941 issue of *Cosmic*. I had not been able to sell it, because it was a real stinker, even in my own eyes, so I was willing to contribute it, without pay, for friendship's sake.

But F. Orlin Tremaine, who had edited *Astounding* till 1938, had also started a new magazine, *Comet Stories*, and he paid the top rate of a penny a word. He told me that writers who gave stories to magazines that didn't pay helped such magazines take readers away from magazines that *did* pay. Such writers were harming their fellow writers and science fiction in general, and should be blacklisted.

That scared me. I promptly called Wollheim and asked him for ten dollars for my story (a fifth of a cent a word) just so that I could say I had received money for it. Wollheim paid, but along with the check he sent a very nasty letter.

He went on to do great things. He wrote a number of short stories, the first being "The Man from Ariel" (January 1934 *Wonder Stories)*, which came out five years before my first story. The one that struck me the hardest was "Mimic" (September 1950 *Fantastic Novels)*. He also wrote a number of science fiction novels, mostly for youngsters.

However, it was clear that he, like the legendary John Campbell of *Astounding,* would rather edit than write. He edited the first anthology of magazine science fiction, *The Pocket Book of Science Fiction,* in 1943. He was an editor at Ace Books for a long time, doing creditable and innovative work. He then founded DAW Books, the first paperback publishing house to deal exclusively with science fiction and, in the process, has developed a number of the contemporary luminaries of the field.

A book of his entitled *The Universe-Makers* was published in 1971. It was a history of science fiction in which he attempted to debunk some of the wilder aspects of the Campbell legend. He also spoke favorably of stories of mine belonging to the Foundation series (which I will discuss myself in due course) and argued they had established modern science fiction. I didn't go along with him completely on either argument, but I accepted his praise gratefully and finally forgave him the "Secret Sense" incident. (Yes, I am susceptible to praise. Just about everyone finds this out very soon, especially my editors.)

Don suffered a stroke in 1989, which largely immobilized his body, but not his mind. DAW Books continues without a hitch under the guidance of his wife, Elsie (his *only* wife, a situation I sometimes think is very unusual among science fiction writers), and his daughter, Betsy.

22
Early Sales

It was not till I was seventeen that it occurred to me that I ought to think up a story with a defined ending instead of simply making things up randomly. I began such a story in May 1937, called it "Cosmic Corkscrew," and worked on it by fits and starts, sometimes allowing it to remain in my desk drawer untouched for months at a time.

In early 1938, however, *Astounding* changed its schedule without warning, and it did not arrive on the expected day. Fearing that it had ceased publication, I called Street & Smith and discovered it would come out on another day. The momentary panic that had resulted when I thought the magazine would be gone forever caused me to fish out "Cosmic Corkscrew" and finish it. I wanted to submit the story while there was still something to submit it to. I finished it in June 1938.

Why the sudden urge to submit? It seems to me that by 1938 I had tired of all the pulp fiction magazines *except* science fiction. I was reading science fiction exclusively and its writers were beginning to seem like demigods to me. I wanted to be a demigod also.

Then, too, I might earn a little money if I sold any of my stories and I was desperate to be able to pay off some of the college tuition without turning to my father. I had had a summer job for a few weeks in the summer of 1935, but I had disliked it intensely, and I would much prefer to make my money at the typewriter.

But now that I had written my story, how did I submit it? My father, no more worldly-wise than I was, suggested I take it to the editor in person and hand the manuscript to him. I said I would be too frightened to do such a thing. (I envisaged being kicked out of the office with loud, contumelious phrases.) My father said, "What's to be afraid of?" (Sure, *he* wasn't going.)

Obeying my father was a long-ingrained habit, so I traveled to Street & Smith by subway and asked to see Mr. Campbell. I couldn't believe it when the receptionist called him and then told me the editor would see me. What made that possible was that I was not an unknown quantity to him. He had been receiving and printing my letters, so he knew I was a serious science fiction fan. Besides, as I found out, he was a nonstop talker who needed an audience, and at the moment he felt I would provide him with one.

John Campbell treated me with the greatest respect, took my manuscript, promised a quick reading, and kept his promise. I received it back by virtually return mail, but his rejection letter was so kind that I instantly began writing another story, called "The Callistan Menace." This took me only one month to write.

After that, I wrote a story a month and brought it in to Campbell, who would read it and return it with helpful comments.

It was not till October 21, 1938, exactly four months after my first visit to Campbell, that I managed to sell my third story, "Marooned off Vesta," but not to Campbell, who had rejected it. I sold it to *Amazing Stories,* which had just come under a new publisher, Ziff-Davis, who decided to publish pulpish action stories, and who, in driving down the quality, raised the circulation.

It was then under the editorship of Raymond A. Palmer, a four-foot-tall hunchback with a most lively and unorthodox mind. In later years, he created, virtually single-handed, the flying saucer craze and he took to publishing magazines on pseudoscience. He died in 1977 at the age of sixty-seven. I never met him in person, but he was the first editor to buy one of my stories, and the time came when he would mention that fact proudly.

I received $64 for the story, and it appeared in the March 1939 issue of *Amazing.* This issue reached the stands on January 9, 1939, a week after my nineteenth birthday. My father sent vain, ornate letters to all his friends (I didn't know he had any) and seemed prepared to do so with each succeeding story I sold. I had a very difficult time putting a stop to this.

Later, I sold my second story, "Callistan Menace," to Fred Pohl, and it appeared in the April 1940 *Astonishing.* I never sold my first story, "Cosmic Corkscrew," or some seven other early stories of mine. None of these exist any longer. I suspect that when I left town in 1942 (for reasons I'll get to), my mother, unaware of what she had, threw them out. Literarily, they were no loss; indeed, the world gained by their disappearance. Historically, however, it was a shame. There's always a certain interest in juvenilia.

The first story I sold to John Campbell was called "Trends," and it appeared in the July 1939 *Astounding*. By then, *Amazing* had published another story of mine, a very poor one called "The Weapon Too Dreadful to Use" (May 1939 *Amazing)*, so that my first *Astounding* story was my third published story.

I have never quite liked that. I have always dismissed those first two stories because I didn't approve of the Ziff-Davis *Amazing* and felt embarrassed at having my stories in such low company. It was in *Astounding* I wanted to appear, and in my heart I try to consider "Trends" my first published story.

I am wrong to do so, however, for those two stories in *Amazing* may have saved me from a fate worse than death. John Campbell was a great believer in nice simple names for his writers, and I am sure that he would ordinarily have asked me to use a pseudonym on the order of John Smith, and I would have absolutely refused to do so, and perhaps aborted my writing career.

However, those two early stories in *Amazing* appeared under my real name—Isaac Asimov. Palmer didn't care about that, bless him, and perhaps because the deed was done and my name, such as it was, had graced the contents page of a science fiction magazine, Campbell uttered not a murmur and my name appeared in *Astounding*'s august pages in its proper form.

All told, in my senior year at Columbia I had earned $197. This was not much, though it meant considerably more in 1939 than it would now, but it marked a beginning. It was not only the beginning of the time when I could pay off my own tuition expenses, but the beginning of my freedom from bondage, the beginning of my ability to support myself.

It meant much more than that too, for there was something I wanted even more than money. What I wanted—what I dreamed of— what I lusted for—was the sight of my name on the contents page and, in even larger letters, on the first page of the story itself.

And that I had, and it warmed my heart.

23

John Wood Campbell, Jr.

John Wood Campbell, Jr., born in 1910, was only nine and a half years older than I was, although when I first met him I thought of him as ageless. He was a tall, large man with light hair, a beaky nose, a wide face with thin lips, and with a cigarette in a holder forever clamped between his teeth.

He was talkative, opinionated, quicksilver-minded, overbearing. Talking to him meant listening to a monologue. Some writers could not endure it and avoided him, but he reminded me of my father, so I was perfectly willing to listen to him indefinitely.

Like so many brilliant science fiction personalities, he had had an unhappy childhood. I never learned the details, because he never volunteered any, and if someone doesn't volunteer, I don't ask. For one thing, I lack an instinct for nosiness; and for another, I'd rather talk about myself than about someone else anyway.

He went to MIT for his undergraduate work and never finished. My understanding is that he couldn't manage German. He switched to Duke University in North Carolina, best known in my youth for the work of Joseph B. Rhine on extrasensory perception, and that may have influenced Campbell's later views on the subject.

His first published story was "When the Atoms Failed," in the January 1930 *Amazing*. It was a time when the most famous writer in science fiction was Edward Elmer ("Doc") Smith, who wrote "super-science stories." Smith was the first writer to feature interstellar travel in his *Skylark of Space* (August, September, and October 1928 *Amaz-*

ing), and Campbell wished to imitate him with tales of superhuman heroes tossing stars and planets about. With "Piracy Preferred" (June 1930 *Amazing)* he began his famous "Wade, Arcot and Morey" series, which put him nearly into Smith's class.

Smith, however, continued to write his superscience till he died in 1965 at the age of seventy-five. He was one of the most beloved science fiction writers there was, but he remained in one place. His earliest stories were ten years ahead of their time, and his latest ten years behind their time, though Campbell continued to publish them faithfully in *Astounding.*

Campbell, on the other hand, grew tired of superscience and moved in other directions. In 1936 and 1937, he wrote an eighteen-part series for *Astounding* on the latest developments in solar system science. This was one of the first ventures of a science fiction writer into the realm of straightforward science.

Even more important was a change in the style of his stories. Instead of superscience, he began to write mood pieces. So drastically different were these new stories from his old that he had to use a pseudonym to avoid disappointment among readers who would read the stories thinking they would be superscience. His pseudonym was Don A. Stuart, a simple variation of his first wife's maiden name, Dona Stuart. The first story under this pseudonym was "Twilight" (November 1934 *Astounding),* an all-time classic.

He abandoned his Campbell stories and continued with his Stuart line until he published "Who Goes There?" (August 1938 *Astounding).* This may possibly be the greatest science fiction story ever written.

By that time, though, he had found his true métier. In 1938, he took over the editorship of *Astounding* and kept it for the rest of his life. He promptly changed the title of *Astounding Stories* to *Astounding Science Fiction* (usually referred to as *ASF.)*

He was the most powerful force in science fiction ever, and for the first ten years of his editorship he dominated the field completely. In 1939, he started *Unknown,* a magazine devoted to adult fantasy which was one of a kind, and marvelous—but it was killed by the paper shortages of World War II.

He discovered and developed a dozen top-ranking science fiction writers in those wonderful ten years of his, including me.

It would have seemed impossible for this giant to go into a twilight of decline, but he did. His very success, lending science fiction a new respectability as a purveyor of tales of scientists and engineers rather than of adventurers and superheroes, created competition. In 1949, *The Magazine of Fantasy and Science Fiction (F&SF)* was inaugurated under the editorship of Anthony Boucher and J. Francis McComas and proved successful. In 1950, *Galaxy Science Fiction,* edited by Horace L. Gold, appeared on the scene and was also successful. Campbell, in the shadow of both, declined.

Campbell's decline was accelerated by his own quirks of character. He enjoyed dabbling with the fringes of science, slipping over the edge into pseudoscience. He seemed to take seriously such things as flying saucers, psionic talents such as extrasensory perception (the influence of Rhine), and even more foolish items called the "Dean drive" and the "Hieronymus machine." Most of all, he championed "dianetics," a kind of offbeat mental treatment invented by the science fiction writer L. Ron Hubbard. Its tenets were first published in an article entitled "Dianetics" (May 1950 *ASF).*

All these things influenced the kind of stories Campbell bought and, in my opinion, greatly weakened the magazine. A number of writers wrote pseudoscientific stuff to ensure sales to Campbell, but the best writers retreated, I among them. I did not stop writing for him, nor did I break off my friendship with him, but there was just a bit of coolness, for I would not accept his odd views and said so.

I wrote a story called "Belief" (October 1953 *ASF),* which dealt with psionic talents *my* way. After long arguments, I agreed to change the ending for him, and I never quite forgave him that.

Campbell continued to edit *ASF,* whose name was changed to *Analog* in the early 1960s, till his death on July 11, 1971, at the age of sixty-one. However, in the last twenty years of his life, he was only a diminishing shadow of what he had once been.

24
Robert Anson Heinlein

In my first couple of years with John Campbell, I met a number of people who were eventually to become science fiction stars of the first magnitude. The friendships formed in this way, as always when they were within the science fiction community, proved lifelong.

The reason for this, I think, is that we all felt part of a tiny group, derided and maligned by the vast majority who totally failed to understand us. We clung together, therefore, for warmth and security and formed a brotherhood that never failed. Nor did competition for sales make enemies out of us. There was so little money involved in science fiction in those days that there was nothing to compete for. We were writing for love, actually.

(Nowadays, I suspect it is different. There are ten times as many science fiction writers as there were in 1939, and the money involved, in advances, movie sales, and so on, is sometimes huge. It seems to me that the old sense of brotherhood cannot exist under such conditions.)

In some ways, my most important friendship was with Robert Anson Heinlein. He was a very handsome man, with a neatly trimmed mustache, a gentle smile, and a courtly way about him that always made me feel particularly gauche when I was with him. I played the peasant to his aristocrat.

He had been in the U.S. Navy, but was invalided out in 1934 for tuberculosis. In 1939, when he was thirty-two years old (late for a science fiction writer), he turned his hand to the writing of science

fiction, and his first story, "Lifeline" (August 1939 *ASF),* appeared
one month after my story "Trends." From the moment his first story
appeared, an awed science fiction world accepted him as the best science fiction writer in existence, and he held that post throughout his
life. Certainly, I was impressed. I was among the very first to write
letters of praise for him to the magazines.

He became the mainstay of *ASF* at once, and he and Campbell
became close friends, although Heinlein made it a condition of the
friendship, apparently, that Campbell never reject one of his stories.

Heinlein never got over his navy discharge. At the news of Pearl
Harbor, he tried to enlist but was rejected. He therefore came East
looking for a way to serve in a civilian capacity.

He managed to locate a position at the Naval Air Experimental
Station and he looked about for other bright scientist/engineer types
who might join him. He recruited Sprague de Camp (about whom I
will soon have more to say) and offered me a job as well. In the end,
after much travail, which I will describe later, I accepted.

My friendship with Heinlein, by the way, did not follow the smooth
and even course that marked all my other science fiction friendships.
That this would be so appeared almost at once when we worked together at the NAES. I never openly quarreled with him (I try never to
quarrel openly with anyone) and I never turned my back on him. We
greeted each other warmly when we met right down to the end of
Heinlein's life.

There had to be a certain circumspection in the friendship, however. Heinlein was not the easygoing fellow that other science fiction
personalities I knew and loved were. He did not believe in doing his
own thing and letting you do your thing. He had a definite feeling
that he knew better and to lecture you into agreeing with him. Campbell did this too, but Campbell always remained serenely indifferent if
you ended up disagreeing with him, whereas Heinlein would, under
those circumstances, grow hostile.

I do not take well to people who are convinced they know better
than I do, and who badger me for that reason, so I began to avoid
him.

Furthermore, although a flaming liberal during the war, Heinlein
became a rock-ribbed far-right conservative immediately afterward.
This happened at just the time he changed wives from a liberal
woman, Leslyn, to a rock-ribbed far-right conservative woman, Virginia.

Ronald Reagan did the same when he switched wives from the liberal Jane Wyman to the ultraconservative Nancy, but Ronald Reagan I have always viewed as a brainless fellow who echoes the opinions of anyone who gets close to him.

I can't explain Heinlein in that way at all, for I cannot believe he would follow his wives' opinions blindly. I used to brood about it in puzzlement (of course, I never would have dreamed of asking Heinlein—I'm sure he would have refused to answer, and would have done so with the utmost hostility), and I did come to one conclusion. I would never marry anyone who did not generally agree with my political, social, and philosophical view of life.

To marry someone at complete odds with myself in those basics would be to ask for a life of argument and controversy, or (in some ways, worse) one that comes to the tacit understanding that these things were never to be discussed. Nor could I see any chance of coming to agreement. I would certainly not change my own views just for the sake of peace in the household, and I would not want a woman so feeble in her opinions that she would do so. No, I would want one compatible with my views to begin with and I must say that this was true of both my wives.

Another point about Heinlein is that he was not among those writers who, having achieved a particular style, cling to it during their lives, despite changing fashions. I have already mentioned that E. E. Smith was such a clinger and so, I must admit, am I. The novels I have been writing lately are the kind I wrote in the 1950s. (I have been criticized for this by some critics, but the day I pay attention to critics is the day the sky will fall.)

Heinlein, on the other hand, tried to keep up with the times, so that his later novels were "with it" as far as post-1960s literary fashions were concerned. I say "tried" because I think he failed. I am no judge of other people's writings (or even of my own) and I don't wish to make subjective statements about them, but I am forced to admit that I always wished that he had kept to the style he achieved in such stories as "Solution Unsatisfactory" (October 1941 *ASF)*, which he wrote under the pseudonym of Anson MacDonald, and such novels as *Double Star,* published in 1956, which I think is the best thing he ever wrote.

He made a mark outside the limited magazine world of science fiction too. He was the first of our group to break into the "slicks," publishing "The Green Hills of Earth" in *The Saturday Evening Post.*

I was quite envious of this for a while till I reasoned out that he was advancing the cause of science fiction generally and making it easier for the rest of us to follow in that direction. Heinlein was also involved with an early motion picture that tried to be both sensible and science-fictional—*Destination Moon*. When the Science Fiction Writers of America began to hand out their Grand Master Awards in 1975, Heinlein received the first by general acclamation.

He died on May 8, 1988, at the age of eighty to an outpouring of sentiment from even the non-science-fiction world. He had kept his position as greatest science fiction writer unshaken to the end.

In 1989, his book *Grumbles from the Grave* was published posthumously. It consists of letters he wrote to editors and, chiefly, to his agent. I read it and shook my head and wished it hadn't appeared, for Heinlein (it seemed to me) revealed, in these letters, a meanness of spirit that I had seen in him even in the NAES days but that I feel should not have been revealed to the world generally.

25

Lyon Sprague de Camp

Lyon Sprague de Camp was born in 1907, the same year that saw the birth of Robert Heinlein. He is tall and handsome, holds himself erect, and has a beautiful baritone speaking voice (though he cannot sing a note). When I first met him, he had a neat mustache and in later years he added a neat close-cut beard. There is something very British about his appearance.

Of all the people I know he is the most unchanging in his looks. I met him when he was thirty-two. Now, fifty years later, he is quickly and certainly recognizable—a little thinner in the hair, a little grayer in the beard, but still L. S. de Camp. Others have changed and if placed near a picture of their younger selves would seem to be some other person, but not he.

He seems formidable and aloof, but that is a delusion. What he is (quite unbelievably) is *shy*. I think that is why he and I get along so well, for in my presence no one can be shy; I don't allow it. He can relax with me. In any case, my feeling for him is one of the deepest affection. From the start, when we met in Campbell's office in 1939, when I was a callow youth of nineteen and he was already a seasoned writer, he treated me with grave respect and won my heart. And in all the years since, we have remained in touch by phone and letter whenever we were in different cities.

I was always too affected by awe and reverence to call Campbell by his first name, and I was always just unfriendly enough with Heinlein to avoid using his first name. De Camp, however, is "Sprague" to me, always has been, always will be.

He has now been married to his wife, Catherine, for over fifty years (when I met him they were newlyweds). She was born the same year he was and she has kept her looks every bit as well as he has. Seemingly ageless, they keep up a busy life of writing and travel.

Sprague had trouble making a living during the Depression (didn't we all?) and in 1937 turned to the writing of science fiction. His first story, "The Isolinguals," appeared in the September 1937 *ASF*. This was in the pre-Campbell days, and when Campbell took over he introduced such changes in the field that many authors who were renowned before Campbell's time couldn't make the transition and fell by the wayside. (It was like the carnage among the silent-film stars once talking pictures arrived.) Sprague, however, weathered the change easily.

He is one of those science fiction writers who can manage fiction and nonfiction with equal ease. He has written many books on fringe aspects of science and has always maintained the strictest rationality in doing so. He has also written wonderful fantasy and excellent historical novels.

Heinlein, Sprague, and I were at the Naval Air Experimental Station together during World War II. We were all civilians when we started. Heinlein wasn't allowed to achieve officer status and I strongly did not want to. Sprague, however, bucked for it and soon became a lieutenant in the navy. Before the war's end, he had been promoted to lieutenant commander, though his duties kept him behind a desk at NAES.

I will now repeat a story that I told in my earlier autobiography—

For security reasons, we all had to wear identifying badges when we entered the grounds of NAES. If we forgot our badges, we were put through a period of humiliation, given a temporary badge and docked an hour's pay.

In our early days there, Sprague and I often went to work together, and one time when Sprague and I reached the gate he clasped his hand to his jacket lapel and said, "I've forgotten my badge!" To him this was serious, for he imagined that such an incident, entered on his record, might hamper his attempt to attain officerhood.

So I unpinned my own badge and said, "Here, Sprague, take this and wear it. No one will look at it and you'll get through. You can give it back to me after work."

He said, "But what will you do?"

"So I'll be jerked about a bit. I'm used to it."

Sprague's voice became husky as he muttered, "Kind hearts are more than coronets."

Ever since, Sprague has never ceased to sing my praises, by word and by print, though he claims he doesn't remember the incident. I like to think my action was motivated out of my sincere love for Sprague, but if I were a true cynic with the gift of foresight, I would have considered it a sound business investment.

After World War II, Sprague stayed in Philadelphia while I returned to New York. I attended the celebration of his eightieth birthday on November 27, 1987. In 1989, Sprague and Catherine moved to Texas to take advantage of a warmer climate and to be near their two sons, Lyman and Gerard. It doesn't matter. We spoke on the phone yesterday evening.

26

Clifford Donald Simak

Clifford Donald Simak was born in 1904 and was a journalist by profession, working in Minneapolis. My first contact with him was when I read a story, "The World of the Red Sun," in the December 1931 *Wonder Stories.* I loved it to such an extent that during lunchtime at my junior high school, I sat on the street curb and told it in detail to a crowd of attentive kids.

I paid no attention to the fact that the author of the story was Cliff Simak. I didn't even realize this till over forty years later when I was putting together an anthology of my favorite stories of the 1930s, which was published as *Before the Golden Age* (Doubleday, 1974). By that time, Cliff was an old and valued friend and I was thunderstruck to find the story I had loved was his.

Actually, "The World of the Red Sun" was Cliff's very first story. He wrote a few more and then quit because he didn't like the science fiction being published. When Campbell took over *ASF*, however, Cliff was galvanized into renewed action and quickly became one of Campbell's mainstays.

I must here tell the story of how we became friends, though I have told it often before.

Cliff Simak wrote "Rule 18" (July 1938 *ASF),* and in the monthly letter that I was then writing to the magazine, I said that I hadn't liked that story and gave it a very low rating indeed.

Promptly, there came a polite letter to me from Cliff, asking me for the details of what was wrong so that he could improve. His courtesy and his sweetness took my breath away and, frankly, I cannot conceive of myself showing the same courtesy and sweetness to any brash young whippersnapper who had the temerity to criticize one of *my* stories.

This, however, was typical of Cliff, who was surely one of the least controversial figures in science fiction. I never heard a bad word about him but only universal approval and approbation.

In any case, I promptly reread "Rule 18" (I had now reached the point where I was *keeping* my science fiction magazines) and I found, to my intense embarrassment, that it was a very good story and that I liked it.

What had thrown me was that Cliff had slipped from scene to scene without any interlarding material and on my first reading, since I wasn't used to the technique, I got confused. On the second reading, I understood and realized what he had done and why. It had immensely speeded the story.

I wrote a very humble letter and explained my error. A correspondence and friendship thus began even before I had sold my first story, and it lasted till Simak's death.

More than that, the incident caused me to read his stories carefully and to imitate his easy and uncluttered style. I think I have succeeded to an extent and that it has immeasurably improved my writing. He is the third of the three people, then, who formed my writing career. John Campbell and Fred Pohl did it by precept, and Cliff Simak by example.

I have told this story so often that Simak, a most unassuming fellow, asked me in some embarrassment if I were ever going to stop praising him.

My answer was in one word. "Never!"

Cliff was one of those who received the Grand Master Award from the Science Fiction Writers of America, and well deserved it was.

He died on April 25, 1988, at the age of eighty-four. Heinlein, however, died less than two weeks later, so that Simak's death was relegated to second place in the minds of most science fiction readers. I felt bad about this, for although Heinlein was the more successful writer, I could not help but feel that Cliff was the better man.

27
Jack Williamson

Jack Williamson is the kind of Anglo-Saxon name that just fits the pulp magazines, but he comes by it honestly. His actual name is John Stewart Williamson, and Jack is the natural nickname.

He was born in 1908 and he is the unquestioned dean of science fiction writers at this time, for his first story, "The Metal Man," appeared in the December 1928 *Amazing,* and he is still writing actively now, a record unmatched in the field by any major writer, as far as I know. He is another beloved figure, above all controversy and criticism, second only to Cliff Simak. His writings in the 1930s were among the stories I most loved.

He was one of the few who made the transition from pre-Campbell to Campbell without trouble, and he was the second person (after Heinlein) to get the Grand Master Award from the Science Fiction Writers of America.

My first experience with Jack's goodness came in 1939, when after my first story, "Marooned off Vesta," appeared, I received a postcard from him saying, "Welcome to the ranks." It was the first event that made me *feel* like a science fiction writer and I have never stopped being grateful to him for this thoughtful and generous gesture.

Williams had an impoverished background in the Southwest and had only a limited education at the time he started writing. In the fullness of time, however, he went back to school and eventually obtained a professorial position. A most amazing gentleman.

As in the case of Cliff Simak, I have only seen Jack on those rare occasions when we are both attending the same science fiction convention.

28
Lester del Rey

Lester del Rey (the simple form of a sonorous Spanish name) was born in 1915. He is a short, slight fellow with a big voice and a pugnacious personality. He has a triangular face, narrowing to his chin, and wears thick-lensed glasses since he was operated on for cataracts. He was clean-shaven when I met him in 1939, but he has since grown a sparse beard. I always have the irresistible feeling that he is what Gandalf in Tolkien's *Lord of the Rings* looks like.

Horace Gold (a science fiction writer and editor, of whom I will have more to say later) liked to say that Lester "had the body of a poet and the soul of a truck driver" and that sounds right to me. Unfortunately, Horace tried to complete the epigram by saying, "And Isaac has the body of a truck driver and the soul of a poet." There I think he was wrong on both counts.

Lester is one of those people whom good luck has thrown my way. He is completely honest, a man of his word, and absolutely trustworthy. After all, one meets so many phonies in the world, so many sleazeballs, so many people who lie and twist and whose word cannot be trusted, that one sometimes gets the sick feeling that life is a garbage pit in which people are the rotting banana peels. Yet *one* honest man refreshes the air fouled by a thousand devious rascals. For that reason I value Lester and the other honest men I have met in and out of science fiction.

There is a story in Jewish moralistic literature that God refrains from destroying this wicked, sinful world only for the sake of the few just men who can be found in it in every generation. Were I religious, I would believe this devoutly, and I can never be sufficiently grateful that so many just men have come my way, and that I have so rarely fallen into the hands of the wicked.

Lester has had four wives altogether. I don't know if there is something about writers that encourages divorce. Perhaps writers are so self-absorbed as a necessary part of their profession, so consumed by their writing, that they have little or no time for their families. It's a rare spouse who can endure this for long, I imagine. This may be especially true because writers so seldom become affluent and a mate cannot even mutter to herself (or himself), "Well, at least he (or she) is a good provider."

I knew Lester's third wife, Evelyn, quite well. She was thin-faced, attractive, and intelligent. I believe she was not fond of me at first. (I don't know why; I never know why.) However, as she got to know me better, she got to like me better. I liked her all the time. She helped me get back into science fiction after I had been out of it for a while (something I will explain in due course). She said to me in March of 1967, "Why don't you write science fiction anymore, Isaac?"

I said, sadly, "You know very well that the field has moved beyond me. I'm a back number."

And she said, "You're crazy, Isaac. When you write, *you* are the field."

I hugged that to my bosom and it *did* help me get back into science fiction in time.

Evelyn died tragically in an automobile accident on January 28, 1970. She was only forty-four years old at the time.

There was a period during Lester's earlier days when it seemed to me that he drank too much. I may have exaggerated this because of my antipathy to alcohol, and in any case, if he had a problem, he defeated it decades ago.

It does raise the question, though, as to whether alcoholism is an occupational hazard for writers. I have heard this seriously suggested and I think I can understand why it might be. Writing is a lonely job. Even if a writer socializes regularly, when he gets down to the real business of his life, it is he and his typewriter or word processor. No one else is or can be involved in the matter.

What's more, a writer is notoriously insecure. Is he turning out pure junk? Even if he is a popular writer who is sure of publishing whatever he writes, he might still worry about quality. It seems to me that the combination of loneliness and insecurity (plus, in some cases, the inexorable pull of the deadline) makes it all too easy to seek the solace of liquor. And, certainly, I know many science fiction writers who are heavy drinkers.

How did I escape? For one thing, I was brought up as a nondrinker by a strict father. For another, the causes that drive writers to drink don't exist in my case. I *like* being alone, though I can be very convivial if I find myself in a group and if I am allowed to do all the talking. Nor do I ever think that my writing might be junk. I am totally uncritical and I like everything I write.

What surprises me is that Harlan Ellison (whom I will write about later), who is a more talented writer than I, but has had a far more difficult literary life, also doesn't drink at all. We and Hal Clement (whom I will also write about later) are, I think, the three most prominent teetotalers in science fiction.

But I digress—

Lester's life changed completely when he married his fourth wife, Judy-Lynn. That was a most dramatic event that I will deal with later.

Lester's first story, "The Faithful" (April 1938 *Astounding)*, was written under circumstances that are often met with in fiction but not in real life. Having read a science fiction story he didn't like, he threw the magazine against the wall and said, "I could write a better story than that."

Whereupon his girlfriend, to whom he had made the remark, said, "I dare you to." He promptly sat down to write the story and the rest is history.

My favorite del Rey story is "The Day Is Done" (May 1939 *ASF)*, which I read in the subway and cried over. I incautiously told him that once and he has held it over my head ever since.

29

Theodore Sturgeon

Theodore Sturgeon, born in 1918, had originally been named Edward Hamilton Waldo, but he adopted his stepfather's name. Like Fred Pohl, Jack Williamson, Lester del Rey, and others, Ted had a difficult childhood and a limited education. (Does a limited education turn people to writing because of the lack of a more obvious profession?)

Ted rattled from job to job until he finally turned to writing science fiction. His first story was "Ether Breathers" in the September 1939 *ASF*. That was one month after Heinlein's first and two months after my first. Campbell was discovering major writers on a monthly basis in those happy days.

Ted was, like Ray Bradbury, a particularly poetic writer. (Bradbury was the one major writer of the 1940s who had not been discovered by Campbell and who virtually never sold to Campbell. The two just didn't fit each other, but it didn't bother Bradbury, who went on to fame and fortune anyway.)

The trouble with writing poetically is that if you hit the target, the result is beautiful; if you miss, it is rotten. Poetic writers are usually uneven. A prosaic writer like me, who consistently misses the heights, also avoids the depths. In any case, Ted's stories were usually on the button.

Sturgeon was a fey individual. (I'm not sure what that adjective means, but whatever it means, it fits Ted.) He was soft-spoken, sweet, and seemed shy and he was just the type of person that young women loved to mother—even after he grew older. The result was that he had an elaborate sexual life and a complicated marital one that I never tried to get straight. This was reflected in his fiction too, which dealt increasingly with love and sex in its different varieties.

He wrote quite prolifically in the 1940s and 1950s, but then writer's block became an increasing problem, and the later portion of his life saw him reduced to a considerable state of insecurity. At times, he would write to me for small sums to keep from having to undergo embarrassing contretemps and I would send them to him.

I'm a "soft mark" in that sense and dozens of writers have put the bite on me for small amounts, now and then. The thing is that my wants are few and I have little occasion to spend my money wildly. Even in the army, other soldiers would line up for small sums from me to be paid back on payday. If you don't smoke or drink, the money stays in the pocket. My own feeling is that every time I lend money it is a way of expressing my deep gratitude that I am lending it rather than borrowing it.

Nor do I expect to get it back. By considering each loan a virtual gift, I am, in the first place, accepting the matter realistically. People who are forced to borrow from friends are often not in a position to repay, and, of course, I *never* dun them. In the second place, by not expecting it back, I avoid disappointment. I must say, however, that in many cases, though not all, the money does come back.

A Gentile friend once came to me for a small sum and, without saying a word, I pulled out my checkbook and made out the check. He promised he would pay me back in six weeks, and so he did. He then said, "I asked all my Gentile friends first and they all turned me down. I came to you last because you were Jewish, and you lent me the money."

I said, with what I hope was only gentle irony, "Gee, and I didn't charge interest either. I must have forgotten I was Jewish."

But back to Sturgeon. Ted was among those who *always* repaid, in one case so long after the loan that I had forgotten I had made it.

It worked both ways, of course. Once Ted had arranged for a number of science fiction writers to participate in some sort of radio project. Unfortunately, the impresario who was in charge of the project couldn't make it go and abandoned it while owing the writers money —not large amounts, but still it was money. Ted worked for months to get the impresario to disgorge. He finally did, and checks were sent to each writer concerned, including me.

A few weeks later, I got a rather plaintive letter from Ted. He detailed all the work he had had to do to get the money and then he said, "And of all the writers to whom I had checks sent, you were the only one to write and thank me."

It always seems to me that it's not hard to be nice to people in small ways, and surely that must make them more willing to be nice in small ways in return.

30

Graduate School

But despite how full 1939 was with science fiction writing and with meeting science fiction people, a major problem remained. I couldn't live on $197 a year, so I had to view writing as merely a delightful avocation and nothing more.

My failure to get into medical school left me with the problem of what to do as my college career came to a close. It still seemed useless to me to simply walk off with my bachelor's degree. I would find no job—so I had to stay in school.

If an M.D. was out, I would have to work toward a Doctor of Philosophy degree (Ph.D.). Whether a Ph.D. would help me get a job, I couldn't be sure, but the crucial point was that it would keep me in school anywhere from two to four years and the passage of time might solve the problem.

But if I went for my Ph.D., in what subject should I do so? When I was in college, I continued to be fascinated by history, just as I had been in my early library reading. I had long since graduated to the reading of Herodotus and Edward Gibbon.

I had thought, and I remember this distinctly, that perhaps I ought to become a professional historian. My heart longed for it, but I thought further that as a professional historian, I could only find a place on a college faculty, probably a small one. I might have to go far from home, and I might never make much money.

So I decided I would have to become a scientist of some sort, for then I would have the opportunity of working in industry or in some important research institution. I might make a great deal of money, gain a great deal of fame, win (who knows) a Nobel Prize, and so on.

But a fat lot of good careful reasoning can do sometimes. I *did* become a scientist and what was the result? I found a place on a college faculty, a rather small one and far from home, and I never made much money. (Fortunately, events nullified all that, as I shall explain later.)

Yet you know, I never quite let go of my desire to be a historian. My brother Stan's son, Eric, after he had completed his college education, went to Texas to work toward a doctorate in history, and I felt a distinct twinge of envy and wondered how my life might have been changed if I had done this. (However, Eric had a change of heart, returned to New York, and became a journalist like his father.)

If I decided on getting my Ph.D. in science, which science would that be? Fortunately, that question answered itself. I had selected a major when I entered college, and because I was under the impression I was aiming for medical school and that I would therefore take a premed course, I majored in zoology. It was one of my more incredible mistakes. I could not endure zoology. Oh, I would have done well enough if it were a mere matter of book learning, but it wasn't. There was a laboratory and we dissected earthworms, frogs, dogfish, and cats. I disliked it intensely but I grew inured to it.

The trouble was that we had to find a stray cat and kill it by dumping it in an ashcan which we filled with chloroform. Like a fool, I did it. After all, I was only following the orders of my superior, like any Nazi functionary in the death camps. But I never recovered. That killed cat lives with me, and to this day, over half a century later, when I think of it, I double up in misery.

I dropped zoology at the completion of the year.

This, incidentally, is an example of the division between intellectual and emotional understanding. Intellectually, I understand the necessity for animal experimentation if medicine is to be advanced (provided the experimentation is absolutely necessary and is carried through with a minimum of suffering). I can argue the point eloquently.

However, I will never, under any circumstances, participate in such experimentation or even observe it. When the animals are brought in, I always leave.

With zoology eliminated, I had to choose either chemistry or physics. Physics was quickly eliminated, for it was far too mathematical. After years and years of finding mathematics easy, I finally reached integral calculus and came up against a barrier. I realized that that was as far as I could go, and to this day I have never successfully gone beyond it in any but the most superficial way.

That left me with chemistry, which was not too mathematical. What it amounted to was that chemistry won by default, scarcely a good basis for a profession, but there was nothing else to do.

Unfortunately, because I had not aimed for a Ph.D. but for an M.D., I found that applying to graduate school was a problem. I did not have enough in the way of undergraduate chemistry courses. For medical school, yes; for graduate school, no. In addition, the head of the chemistry department did not like me. I gathered, in fact, that he very much didn't like me.

This did not disturb me greatly in itself. I had a long history of teachers and professors who did not like me, undoubtedly for good and sufficient reason. However, the head of the department could keep me out of graduate school and it seemed to be his intention to do so.

There began a duel between us. He kept ordering me out of the office; I kept returning with rule books that showed I could qualify for graduate school if I was put on probation until I had passed the undergraduate course I had missed—physical chemistry.

Sheer dogged persistence won the day for me. I was gaining the sympathy of the other members of the department and the head gave in, but didn't make it easy for me. I could take physical chemistry, provided I took a full program of other courses (for all of which physical chemistry was the prerequisite). What's more, I would have to achieve at least a B average or I would get no credit at all for any of the courses, and all the money I would have spent on a year of tuition would be thrown away. These were draconian terms, but I agreed. What choice did I have?

I managed. In the physical chemistry course given by Louis P. Hammett, I was one of only three students in a large class who obtained an A. That shifted me from probation to a regular graduate student after only half a year.

I was twenty at the time and that happened to be my last scholastic triumph.

As a matter of fact, my academic career had gone steadily downhill from my remarkable beginnings. In college, I had still been a smart student. By the time I reached graduate school, I was simply no better than mediocre. The other students, in general, seemed to understand the material better and more easily than I did, and I was simply hopeless in the laboratory. Experiments rarely worked for me, and when they did, I showed less deftness and expertise than anyone else in the class.

In a way, this was not surprising. The other students had made chemistry their life's work. They were seriously heading for positions in academe or industry. I was merely marking time, working on chemistry on an everything-else-is-worse basis, merely in order to stave off the evil day when I would have to look for a job and (I gloomily felt) not find one.

But what happened to my view (held so firmly in childhood) that I was a remarkable person? Now that I was no longer a monument of glittering smartness, but merely a quite ordinary B-level student (*still* disliked by my professors), would I have to draw in my horns, lose at least some of my self-assurance, take a back seat, and prepare for obscurity and for regrets over a life so well begun and so poorly maintained?

Oddly enough, none of this happened. I was entirely unshaken and my opinion of myself remained firm. You see, I had become wiser. I began to realize that scholastic achievement was more than grades and test marks, because they were only more or less arbitrary and trivial criteria designed to judge youngsters' progress in their schooling. The true value of what I had done in school (and in the library) was to lay a groundwork of knowledge and understanding in a wide variety of fields.

It did not matter that the graduate chemistry students about me were all better in chemistry than I was. Most of them were virtually illiterate in each of a dozen areas of knowledge in which I felt quite at home.

I was beginning to see that I was not a specialist; that in *any* field of knowledge there would be many who would know far more than I, who could make a living and attain fame, perhaps, working in that field, whereas I could not. I was a *generalist,* who knew a considerable amount about almost everything. There were many specialists of a hundred or a thousand different kinds, but, I told myself, there was going to be only one Isaac Asimov. This feeling was only dim to begin with, but grew rapidly stronger with time.

Megalomania? No! I had a firm understanding of my own abilities and talents and I intended to show them to the world.

As my success in chemistry continued to fade (and, alas, it did) my success in writing continued to grow, and my sense of being remarkable was more firmly (and, perhaps, more logically) fixed than ever.

31

Women

As luck would have it, I never felt any confusion or doubt over sex. Even in kindergarten, I found that little girls were a great deal more pleasant to look at than little boys were. I never asked myself, at that time, why that should be. I just accepted it as a fact.

As time went on, I did, of course, learn about the nature of sex. This was not from my parents, you understand. My father and mother would not have dreamed of discussing sex with me (or, I suspect, though I may be wronging them, even with each other). And I, for my part, would not have dreamed of approaching them with questions on the subject.

Nor did I learn about sex from any reasoned source of instruction. I learned about it from the distorted and imperfect knowledge of other boys. This is the usual fate enforced upon youngsters by a society that is too prim and too hypocritical to have sex taught like any other branch of knowledge.

Considering how important sex is, how great a source of joy, how enormous a source of misery and disease, how it permeates the workings of courtship and marriage, isn't it strange that we go to great lengths to teach our children to play football and make no effort whatever to teach them to play sex?

Any attempt to introduce sex education classes into the school curriculum is always met with fierce opposition. The feeling among those who oppose it (after you strip off the hypocrisies of "morality") is that learning about sex will encourage youngsters to experiment with it and lead to unwanted pregnancies and disease.

To me, this seems ridiculous. Nothing on earth can stop youngsters from experimenting with sex, unless they are kept so brutally in ignorance and captivity that their lives are distorted and ruined. By stripping away the mysteries of sex and treating it openly, the act is robbed of its illegality, of its attraction as "forbidden fruit." In my opinion, good knowledge of all aspects of sex, including proper methods of contraception and hygiene, will actually reduce unwanted pregnancies and disease.

I might, of course, have gone on to learn a bit more about sex than the boys told me and to put my dim and imperfect knowledge to the test. It would surely have been easy to experiment with willing young women. I might, best of all, have met a young woman with sexual experience who would have been pleased to teach me.

The fact is that I did not. It was not for lack of desire on my part. I looked at young women longingly and learned how to flirt in a rather heavy-handed way, but nothing ever came of it.

The chief reason is that I had no time. There was my swotting away in college and my pegging away in the candy store. To put the cherry on it, my father decided to get the early night-before edition of the *Daily News,* which was not delivered directly to the newsstands. Therefore, each night of my late teenage years, without exception and whatever the weather, I had to walk about half a mile to a distribution center, wait for the truck to come, collect the papers, pay for them, and then carry them back to the store. That effectively occupied my evenings, and made it impossible for me to have even an innocent social relationship with a young woman.

In fact, I didn't have a date with a girl until I was twenty years old.

The situation was exacerbated by the fact that between the ages of twelve and nineteen I attended Boys High School, Seth Low Junior College, and Columbia College, from all of whose classes girls were excluded. It meant that at school I remained in monastic solitude.

This may not have been all bad. The absence of the opposite sex meant I could concentrate on my studies without the distraction that their presence would have ensured. Besides, because of my having been pushed ahead, all the young women in my classes would have been two years older than I and they would have looked down upon me as a child and rejected, with contempt, any advances I dared make.

It was not all good either. The absence of women contributed to the distortion of my social development. It also meant that I started my wedding night (at the age of twenty-two) as a virgin, with a new wife who was also a virgin. To moralists that may sound like a wonderful thing, but I think it turned out to be disastrous.

32
Heartbreak

Finally, on entering graduate school at the age of nineteen, I found myself in classes that included young women. As luck would have it, the young woman at the adjoining desk in my synthetic organic chemistry course was blond, attractive, only a year older than I, and a much better chemist than I.

(When I was one of three who got an A in physical chemistry, she was another of them, and she did it much more easily than I did.)

Under the circumstances, I don't consider it surprising that I promptly fell in love. It was stupid to do so with such celerity but, I think, very natural.

It did not bother me in the least that she was a much better chemist than I was. That is to me, as I look back on it, the strongest evidence that, by that time, I had rearranged my priorities. In earlier life, when grades were all-important to me, I had never really been fond of the students who did better than I or who even threatened to do better than I (though I never wasted my time in strenuous hate or envy). If I had still had that view of "smartness," her being better than I at chemistry would have turned me off.

The young woman was a sweet and kind girl who went out of her way to make sure that she never hurt my feelings even though she was not in the least interested in me romantically. We went out together a few times (my first dates) and she bore up under my incredible gaucheries. For instance, she taught me that self-service cafeterias were not the only places where one could eat, and led me to a small restaurant after warning me, very gently, that I would have to leave a tip.

In fact, the happiest day of my life, up to that point, came on May 26, 1940, when I took her to the World's Fair, spent the whole day with her, and even managed to give her a few small pecks I thought of as "kisses."

That was the end, though. She had obtained her master's degree by then and that was enough for her. She got a job in industry in Wilmington, Delaware, and on May 30 she said goodbye and left me behind feeling quite woebegone.

I saw her twice after that. Once I actually went down to Wilmington to visit her and we went to the movies together. And a quarter century later, I was giving a talk in Atlantic City to the American Chemical Society and a woman who was quietly waiting to speak to me after the lecture was over said, "Do you remember me, Isaac?"

It was she and I did recognize her, but there was no emotion involved. I had dinner on the boardwalk with her and her husband. By that time, she had had five children.

What followed after our parting seems to me now *(now,* after half a century) to be the most interesting part of the whole event. I suffered heartbreak, for the first and only time of my life.

Heartbreak, as I judge from my limited experience, is the pain one feels at the loss of a love object, in the case where the love object, not returning the love, breaks off (whether kindly or cruelly) and disappears. The person you love is gone, but still exists, and is simply not available. This is a rather benign situation as compared with the irrevocable loss through death of someone you love, but it is, nevertheless, painful.

For a long time, I wandered about unsmiling and unhappy. For me, the clouds hovered close and sunshine was meaningless. I somehow couldn't think of anything but the young woman, and when I did think of her there was a constriction of the chest and I found it difficult to breathe. I decided there was no meaning to life and I was quite, quite, *quite* certain that I would never get over it. In fact, I wasn't sure it might not be a good thing simply to lie down and die of heartbreak.

The odd thing is that I did get over it and I don't remember exactly how. Was it in stages? Did the load lighten slowly day by day? Or did I just wake up one morning whistling? I'm not even sure how long it took to recover.

And when it was over, it left not a scar behind. That's why I say it's benign. I presume that the younger you are when you experience heartbreak, the milder the attack and the cleaner the recovery. (I wonder if anyone has ever investigated such matters?) Assuming that this speculation of mine is true, I'm glad I experienced it no later than twenty.

I would like to make the further guess that heartbreak confers a certain amount of immunity, if a person is not incredibly emotional. At least, after my experience with heartbreak, I was very careful not to allow my emotions to run away with me. I held my feelings for young women in check, and let them grow only if justified by the response I seemed to sense. The result was that I never suffered heartbreak again.

I did marry twice, eventually, each time for love, but I did so, I like to think, sensibly; and more sensibly the second time than the first.

33

"Nightfall"

By the spring of 1941, I had published fifteen stories, four of them in *ASF*. I had also written ten stories or so that had not been sold. Most of my published stories had been poor indeed. By then, though, I had begun to write a series of stories about "positronic robots" that were to achieve a certain renown. I had published three of them. They were "Strange Playfellow," for which I later used the title "Robbie" (September 1940 *Super Science*), "Reason" (April 1941 *ASF*), and "Liar!" (May 1941 *ASF*). They were fairly good.

However, I had as yet, in almost three years of selling, failed to do anything outstanding.

On March 17, 1941, however, when I visited Campbell's office, he read me the following quotation from an early essay entitled "Nature" by Ralph Waldo Emerson:

"If the stars should appear one night in a thousand years, how would men believe and adore, and preserve for many generations the remembrance of the city of God."

Campbell said, "I think Emerson is wrong. I think that if the stars would appear one night in a thousand years, people would go crazy. I want you to write a story about that and call it 'Nightfall.' "

Alexei Panshin, an important historian of science fiction, is convinced that Campbell had decided that I, specifically, was the one he wanted to write the story. I don't believe that. I think that Campbell was just waiting for any one of his reliables to walk in, and I happened to be the one. If so, how fortunate for me. It might have been Lester del Rey or Ted Sturgeon and I would have lost the opportunity of a lifetime.

I worked away at "Nightfall" just as I would any other story and sold it to Campbell in April. It appeared in the September 1941 issue of *ASF.*

To me, it was just another story, but Campbell, a much better judge of such things, treated it as something unusual. He paid me a bonus for the first time, sending me a check for one and a quarter cents a word rather than the usual penny. (Nor did he tell me he was doing this, so that I had to brood a bit and then, in accordance with the strict code of ethics inculcated in me by my father, I phoned to tell him he had paid me too much. Campbell was very amused. He was used to complaints that he paid too little; this was the first time he received a complaint that he had paid too much. He explained, of course.)

He also gave me the cover—the first time I ever had an *ASF* cover—and it was the lead story in the magazine.

The story, "Nightfall," has since come to be considered a classic. A great many people think it was the best story I ever wrote, and some even think it was the best magazine science fiction story anyone ever wrote. Frankly, I think this is ridiculous and have always thought so.

First, the story still shows ample signs of pulpishness in the writing. By my reckoning, I didn't get rid of my pulp magazine heritage till 1946.

While I grant the story has an interesting and mind-expanding plot (about a world in perpetual light that experienced darkness only once in a long, long time), I have since written stories—quite a number of them—that I like much better than "Nightfall."

In later years, Campbell established something he called an "Analytical Laboratory," which reported on readers' votes as to the relative popularity of the stories in a particular issue. If this had existed in 1941, I am quite convinced that the story "Adam and No Eve" by Alfred Bester, which appeared in the same issue with "Nightfall," would have been voted the top story. It should have, for Bester was a better writer than I was (then and afterward) and his story was extremely good.

In later years, increasingly prestigious awards were given out by science fiction organizations for the best stories of the year in different length categories. The two most important of these are the Hugo, given out at the World Science Fiction Convention, and the Nebula, given out by the Science Fiction Writers of America. If these had existed in 1941, I am convinced that "Nightfall" would not have received an award in the novelette category. In that year, Robert A. Heinlein and A. E. van Vogt were far and away the most popular writers in science fiction and the absolute mainstay of *ASF*. They would surely have swept all the awards.

And yet "Nightfall" retains its retrospective position. In a number of readers' polls since as to all-time favorite stories, it has regularly finished in first place. Even nowadays, I get word with fair regularity that when "Nightfall" is included among the stories studied in science fiction classes, it is invariably the top favorite.

I'll never understand it.

Still, it was a turning point, even if I can't figure out the reason. After "Nightfall" was published, the rejections stopped. I simply wrote and sold, and within a year or two, I had reached the Heinlein/van Vogt level, or almost.

When, forty years after the story was published, I got around to establishing a corporation, I had no choice. I called that corporation Nightfall, Inc.

34

As World War II Begins

At almost precisely the time I began my graduate studies, World War II broke out in Europe.

I hesitate to look for external reasons for my decline in academic scholarship, but the war took my attention away from my studies. It had to. No bright Jewish youngster who had been following the situation in Europe with painful attention for years could possibly dismiss the war as something that didn't concern him just because his own nation was not part of it and maintained its neutrality. Every Jew in the world was at risk if Hitler's Germany won the war.

I desperately wanted Hitler defeated. Desperately!

The school year during which I had my feckless little love affair began with the destruction of Poland and ended with the destruction of France. I spent hours *(hours)* each day listening to the radio and reading the newspapers in a vain search for good news, for anything to lift my spirits. During the summer of 1940, the time of my heartbreak was made heavier by something very akin to it over the plight of Europe.

I'm sure my schoolwork had to suffer. It was hard to concentrate on it, or to think of it as important. It is amazing to me that I continued writing. I can only explain it by my experience in later life. When I have felt depressed and unhappy, the only anodyne I had (since I have never smoked, drunk, or drugged) was to write. It was only writing that dulled my anxiety. Once, when Robyn had broken her ankle and I was in despair, thinking it might interfere with the growth of that leg and leave her with a permanent limp, my only escape was to sit down and write three long essays one after the other.

But even writing in that wretched time was scarcely enough. Only a few months after I sold "Nightfall," German forces invaded the Soviet Union on an enormous scale and with enormous strength. By the time "Nightfall" appeared in print, the Soviet Union seemed on the point of destruction.

Still the United States maintained its neutrality. To be sure, every victory by Hitler weakened the isolationist forces within the United States. Every victory frightened more and more people into wanting the United States to do something actively to aid those who were fighting Hitler. In particular, Great Britain's remarkable stand against Hitler in the fall of 1940, its victory in the Battle of Britain, galvanized American sympathies to the point where we were at everything but a shooting war with Germany. Even those (quite many) who feared the Soviet Union more than Germany were shouted down by the great many who shared the increasingly universal execration of Hitler.

35

Master of Arts

Eventually, one had to take tests in order to see (a) if one deserved to be granted a Master of Arts degree (M.A.) and (b) if one deserved, further, to be allowed to move on beyond that for a degree of Doctor of Philosophy (Ph.D.).

The young woman with whom I had been in love had had no trouble at the end of one year of studies in passing her tests and getting her M.A. and could have gone on for her Ph.D. if she had wanted to. It is a sign of the degree to which my academic quality had fallen that when I took the tests, I got my M.A. but it was strictly a consolation prize in my own eyes, for my test grades were not sufficient to allow me to go on for a Ph.D.

That put me in a quandary—the same quandary I had been in for some years. If I accepted my M.A. and left it at that, I would have to leave school and find a job. On the other hand, I might continue to take courses, for I would be allowed to take the tests a second time.

Of course, the job situation had changed considerably. The United States was now gearing up for war if that should be necessary or, failing that, at least for serving as what Franklin Roosevelt called the "arsenal of democracy."

Feelers were therefore out for bright students in the sciences who could take on war work. I would have been glad to take such a job and feel that I was contributing to the fight against Hitler.

Unfortunately, I had two things going against me. I was no longer a bright student, at least not in chemistry. Second, there was the old, old trouble—the professors thought little of me, and it was they who had to be relied on to recommend this student or that.

I had encountered another professor who enjoyed hectoring his students. I refused to submit to that and I assume he felt I was disrespectful to him, so he was therefore not likely to recommend me for anything, and he had a powerful voice. So there I was, in graduate school and still unable to establish a decent working relationship with my teacher.

Then I got into trouble with Professor Arthur W. Thomas, a curmudgeon of the worst kind, and in sheer desperation I asked for an interview, at which I could try to present my version of the problem. (He was receiving complaints that I was singing in the chem lab and distracting the other students—very like my early problems about whispering in class.) I labored hard to make myself look good and to win him over and, for a wonder, I succeeded.

To my astonishment, he became pro-Asimov, and shortly after that became acting head of the chemistry department. I suspect that one reason for his switch in attitude was that he had given instructions to the lab assistants (they told me a year later) to give me difficult analytical problems and get rid of me through failure. I stubbornly worked my way through them, however, and did so without complaint because I was too stupid to suspect conspiracy.

I have often thought of my talk with Thomas and wondered what course my life would have taken if I had consistently turned on the charm when I thought that would be useful instead of taking the attitude that "I'm right—you're wrong—and I don't intend to compromise." But I never did. Until the time came when I was fully self-employed, I continued to be in serious trouble with anyone who could be considered my hierarchical superior.

When I took my tests a second time, I finally received permission on February 13, 1942, to go on for my Ph.D., perhaps through the intercession of the now kindly Professor Thomas. But that did not end my troubles either. I had to find a professor who was willing to take me on and give me a problem to work on and supervise that work in a competent and friendly manner. Unfortunately, the professors I knew in the department would not have me under any circumstances, and Thomas himself was immersed in administrative work and was not doing research.

A fellow student, however, told me that his own professor, Charles Reginald Dawson, was a kindhearted fellow who took on all the "lame dogs" others didn't want. I was not offended by the appellation, for I recognized aptness.

I rushed to Dawson and he took me on. He was a man of medium height, soft-spoken, and of a quiet temperament. He never lost his temper, he was never angry. (This may have been at a price, for he suffered badly from duodenal ulcers.) He was endlessly patient and he was amused by me. I was pleased by that. I don't mind being considered a queer duck, if the alternative is to consider me a problem student.

Dawson was an inspiration to me and a gentleman of impeccable kindness. Despite my hopeless lack of ability in laboratory work, Dawson supervised me carefully and tirelessly, and saw to it that I managed. I believe that he somehow had the notion that I was an enthusiastic inventor of ideas and that I was a remarkable person. (At least, on one or two occasions when I overheard him talking about me to another professor, I had difficulty in recognizing myself from his description.)

The result? Well, he lived to see me become what I am, has had books of mine dedicated to him, and I have praised him in print on a number of occasions. (I may have many sins, but I have never practiced the sin of ingratitude.)

In fact, he told me—with what I am sure was affectionate exaggeration—that his greatest claim to fame, it eventually turned out, was that I had been a student of his. I cannot believe that, but how I wish it were true, because I can't think of any better return I could make for all he did for me.

36

Pearl Harbor

Two months before I qualified to go on for my Ph.D., the Japanese bombed Pearl Harbor, so that on December 7, 1941, we were in the war.

I suppose it would be wonderful if I could say that I instantly dropped everything and volunteered to join the armed forces, and then fought through the war, winning medals and wounds.

If the world were ideal and I were perfect, I would have, but it isn't and I'm not, and I didn't. I've always admitted that there is nothing physically heroic about me.

If I had been drafted, I would have gone, of course, even though I would have been frightened to death every step of the way. I can't imagine what kind of soldier I would have made, and it paralyzes me to think that under enemy fire I might have turned coward and fled screaming, or done something else equally terrible. I console myself with the thought that human beings rise to the occasion, that even cowards will find some reservoir of strength when it is demanded.

Well, perhaps—but I thought I could surely use my brains in my country's service to better effect than I could use my shrinking body.

Yes, of course, I'm ashamed that I didn't rush to volunteer, but I'd be a lot more ashamed if I tried to pretend to a bravery I do not possess. In any case, I wasn't drafted, at least not for quite a while, and I just kept on writing, and began work toward my Ph.D.

37

Marriage
and Problems

I had joined the Brooklyn Authors Club in 1941. We would get together, read manuscripts and criticize them. It was rather a fun thing to do. Another young man at the club, Joseph Goldberger, liked one of my stories and suggested that he and I go out on a double date. I explained that I had no girlfriend, and he said he would supply one. Very nervously, I agreed.

As I found out eventually, Goldberger's girlfriend, Lee, was trying to decide whether to marry him or not and she wanted to introduce him to her best friend in order to get an independent opinion. She therefore suggested to that best friend, whose name was Gertrude Blugerman, that she go on this blind date, if only to survey Goldberger. Reluctantly, Gertrude obliged. I was described to her as a mustachioed Russian and heaven only knows what kind of exotic personality she imagined. The date was set for February 14, 1942. The fact that it was Valentine's Day did not enter into any of our consciousnesses, I'm sure; certainly not into mine.

I *had* been wearing a mustache for a year now, but it was a very ugly one, and a classmate had bet me a dollar against my mustache that I would qualify for a Ph.D. When I did on February 13, I shaved off my mustache, and met Gertrude bare-faced.

She took one horrified look at me and (I think) tried to back out of the date with a sudden splitting headache, but Lee wouldn't let her. It's only for a few hours, she said, and I want you to help me decide about Joe.

It was quite otherwise with me. I had seen *Captain Blood,* which introduced Errol Flynn and Olivia de Havilland, and although I'm not one of those who fall in love with movie stars, I do admire some more than others. Olivia de Havilland struck me, at that time, as the epitome of feminine beauty. Gertrude, to my dazzled eyes, was the complete image of Olivia de Havilland. She was actually an extraordinarily beautiful girl.

My reaction was inevitable, but I was now three years older than I was when I fell in love in the chem lab. I had no intention of ever going through heartbreak again. I therefore reacted cautiously, working it through by stages.

But I was determined. Such was my address and firmness, such my insistence on further dates, such my calm certainty that we would be married, that she gave in. She certainly did not find me an object of romantic adulation (who on earth would?), but I managed to talk her into such a daze that she agreed to take a chance on me. (Of course, she admired my cleverness. That helped.) On July 26, 1942, less than half a year after we had met, we were married.

It was not an easy marriage. After all, she was not in love with me, I'm pretty sure. We were both virginal (even though she was two years older than I was) and sex didn't work out too well, with neither of us possessing experience. There were other incompatibilities too that developed and that would be hard to describe. I don't even intend to try.

There was one incompatibility, however, that I ignored during my courtship (for the simple reason that I had not the slightest idea it was vital) and that served in the end to raise enormous difficulties in the marriage.

Gertrude smoked!

Let me go back now and discuss tobacco. One of the large components of the candy store's sales was tobacco. We carried cigarettes by the pack and by the carton, cigars by the single and by the box, and pipe tobacco of various kinds. I don't remember whether we, at any time, had pipes for sale, but I do remember a vertical dispenser of round containers of Copenhagen snuff. I don't think we ever sold chewing tobacco.

Pipes and cigars were rather exotic, but the smoking of cigarettes was almost universal. Individual packs of twenty cigarettes of the leading brands were thirteen cents each, and some lesser brands were ten cents each. What's more, we kept one pack of each of the leading brands open so that people could buy single cigarettes for a penny. Many of the teenagers who patronized the store and who were my contemporaries would buy single cigarettes in this fashion, light up, and go off puffing.

The cigarettes were obviously available to me. I had but to take one from an open pack. However, my father had laid down strict rules. The goods in the store were to *sell,* not to *consume.*

This was a hardship on me where the candy was concerned. We had boxes and boxes of candies, all open and on display in the counter, and youngsters came in with their pennies and nickels and selected what they wanted and I gave it to them. I was *never* allowed to take a piece of candy for myself, however.

No, I was not starved for them. I could always ask my father or (much better) my mother, "Mama, may I have a Hershey bar?" Sometimes, but by no means always, the answer was yes, and I would be happy. What went for all the delightful succulences in the store also went for cigarettes. I would have to say, "Pappa, may I have a cigarette?"

I never did. Not once. I knew the answer would be no. The result is that I have never smoked. You can see, then, that I am a nonsmoker by circumstance. A small change in my father's attitude and I might well have become a heavy smoker.

My sister and brother have never smoked either, and my mother never did. Stanley tells me that for a period of time (but only for a period) my father smoked heavily and I hear this with the utmost astonishment. My brother swears to it, and I cannot doubt him, for he is an upright man, but try as I might I cannot recall my father with a cigarette in his hand.

It may be that such is my retrospective detestation of smoking that I have simply blocked out all memories of my father doing so.

In 1942, however, although I did not smoke myself, I had no objection to smoking. People smoked in the candy store and that suited us, for tobacco sales made up a large part of our small revenue. So I was accustomed to the effluvium and thought nothing of it. The fact that Gertrude smoked, therefore, did not strike me as an item I ought to weigh in my developing plan to marry her, and that was a disaster.

If I had felt then as I feel now, or as I felt a few years after I had married her, nothing could possibly have persuaded me to marry a woman who smoked. Dates, yes. Sexual adventure, yes. But to pin myself permanently inside closed quarters with a smoker? Never.

Never. Never. Beauty wouldn't count, sweetness wouldn't count, suitability in every other respect wouldn't count.

But I didn't know. I had never actually lived in a house or apartment that was always filled with smoke and with the reek of dead ashtray contents. When I found that living with Gertrude meant that and that there was no escape, our relationship withered.

I must say that Gertrude was, in many, many respects, a very good wife. Aside from remaining beautiful, she was a careful housekeeper, a good cook, absolutely loyal to me, and strict with the household accounts.

These are big things and yet little things can ruin it. There is the story of the man who was planning a divorce from a wife whom all his friends considered ideal. They argued with him, praising her qualities and virtues, and he listened as long as he could. Then he pulled off his shoe, held it out to the others, and said, "Can any one of you tell me where this shoe pinches my foot?"

And remember, it was not merely the reek of tobacco. I began to be aware of the health problems involved in tobacco. There was early talk of respiratory problems and lung cancer, and I failed to see the difference in inhaling the smoke into the lungs freshly or only after it had emerged from someone else's lungs.

I therefore began a campaign to get Gertrude to stop smoking, or failing that, to cut down, or failing that, never to smoke in the bedroom or in the automobile or when we were eating. Unfortunately, none of this succeeded. As the years passed, the issue was like a sore that rubbed and chafed itself into blisters that grew more and more painful.

I endured it longer than I might have for three reasons. First, I knew she smoked when I married her and it seemed unfair to penalize her for something I had accepted at the start.

Second, I was always aware that I had talked her into marrying me and that she had been most unwilling to do so. It seemed I ought to endure the situation, therefore.

Third, by the time I was secretly considering divorce, I had two small children. I could divorce Gertrude, given what seemed adequate reasons, but there was no way in which I could abandon my children. I had to wait till they grew up.

It may seem odd to let a simple thing like smoking break up a long-term marriage that was suitable in so many ways, but, of course, it was more than a simple thing. Besides, there were other irreconcilabilities less easy to talk about. For one thing, I don't think that Gertrude ever liked me much and that hurt my self-esteem. After about twelve years, I grew tired of being in love all by myself and fell out of love, though the marriage continued for many more years through simple inertia.

I'll give Gertrude credit, however. She may not have liked me much but she never denigrated my intelligence. (That would *really* have been too much to bear.)

In the army, for instance, I took a sort of intelligence test, called the AGCT, which stood for something I have forgotten. I scored 160, which none of the army people running the test had ever seen before. It must have been very nearly the maximum possible. I phoned Gertrude to tell her this.

At my next furlough, she told me indignantly that she had told a friend I had scored 160. "You must mean 116," said the friend. "No," said Gertrude, "160."

Her friend said, "How do you know?"

She said, "Isaac told me."

Her friend laughed and said, "He lied," and sent Gertrude into a paroxysm of fury.

I said to Gertrude, curiously, "How do you know I didn't lie?"

I wanted her to tell me the simple fact that I never lied, but she didn't. Instead, she said, "For you 160 is just normal. Why should you have to lie?"

Then, too, about twenty years later, Lee, the girl who had arranged the original double date, came to visit. (I think by that time she had married and divorced Joe Goldberger.) She said to Gertrude, "Did you ever dream when you first met Isaac that he would become what he is today?"

"Certainly," said Gertrude, "I expected it."

"Why should you have expected it?"

"Well, he *told* me at the start that it would happen."

There is a similar story I have to tell about Fred Pohl. When we were both out of the army, he said to me, "My AGCT score was 156. What was yours?"

I hesitated, then said, reluctantly, "I'm sorry, Fred. It was 160."

He said, "Oh ———."

But he didn't question my word. He knew that I was incapable of lying just to score him off, and I loved him all the more for that.

38
In-Laws

Getting married meant I had another family, the Blugermans. I was to see more of them than my own folks during my marriage. We returned to New York periodically after I had moved out of town and we always stayed at the Blugermans', for that's where Gertrude wanted to stay. Nor did I blame her. My family, with its candy store, could offer far less in the way of hospitality.

Gertrude's father, Henry Blugerman, was a very quiet, very sweet, very gentle person, beloved by all, even by his son-in-law. To me, he resembled Edward G. Robinson in looks. (Considering that Gertrude's father and mother were quite plain, I marveled that they could give birth to someone as beautiful as Gertrude, or as handsome as their son.)

Henry was the traditional passive Jewish father. My joke, never spoken in Gertrude's hearing, was that at the age of fourteen she asked her mother, "Who is that man who always eats with us?"

In later years, I heard the story of a would-be actor who came home excitedly saying that he had finally landed a part. "What kind of a part?" asked a friend. Said the actor, "I'm playing a Jewish father." To which the friend replied, "What's the matter? Couldn't you get a speaking part?"

That was Henry.

It was Gertrude's mother, Mary, who utterly dominated the family. She was just about five feet tall and, to my eyes, just about five feet wide. She was obese. She was also the center about which the little family revolved. She ran everything with a loud voice, corrected everything, insisted on her own way in everything, and, in my opinion, broke the spirit of her children and managed to make them utterly dependent on her and incapable of forming true bonds outside the family.

I think it was Gertrude's attachment to her mother (not, in my opinion, a healthy one) that made it impossible for her to commit herself to me entirely. It is significant, I think, that after the marriage, as we were leaving for our honeymoon, her mother called out in a loud voice, right there in the street, "Remember, Gittel, if it doesn't work out, you can always come home to me." You can imagine the self-confidence with which that filled me.

Mary was forty-seven when I met her and was in bad health. At least she said she was in bad health and this helped keep the rest of the family in line. At crucial moments, she would manage to deteriorate rapidly, to the vast alarm of her family.

Gertrude was convinced that her mother (I repeat—forty-seven years old) was an old, old woman, incapable of taking care of herself. In fact, on a number of occasions in the first year of our marriage, she wished to go back to New York to take care of her poor superannuated parent. "She's an old woman," she would say indignantly when I suggested her place was with me. However, Gertrude never actually carried out her threat to go to New York to serve as her mother's round-the-clock nurse.

Many years later, when Gertrude had passed her fiftieth birthday, I asked if she remembered how she had wanted to go home to her old, old mother and take care of her. Incautiously, Gertrude remembered, and I said (with a touch of malice, I'm ashamed to say), "Well, she was four years younger then than you are now."

Gertrude had a brother, John, who was nineteen at the time of my marriage. I never understood him. He was a little taller than I, had a good body, and was extremely handsome. To my eyes, he looked as much like Cary Grant as his sister looked like Olivia de Havilland.

John was quite intelligent and apparently took pleasure in puncturing the boyfriends that Gertrude would occasionally bring home. It was apparently one of my few good points in Gertrude's eyes that John could not succeed in puncturing me. (I wasn't even aware he was trying to.)

The peculiar thing about John was that he was a deeply depressed person with no reason that I could see for the depression. It was obvious to me that, despite his looks and his intelligence, he suffered from a feeling of lack of self-worth. So, in fact, did Gertrude.

I have theories concerning this. I believe that John was pushed by his wildly adoring mother to a point where he was past his level of competence. He felt himself quite unable to gain the goals expected of him, or to reconcile himself to alternate and lesser goals. He failed to get into medical school and went to dental school, so that eventually he became, in his mother's words, a "doctor of dental surgery." However, he never opened an office of his own.

He grew interested in Jungian psychiatry and went to Switzerland to become a lay analyst, but he returned after a lengthy period without completing the course. And he never got married.

Gertrude was six years older than John (she was born on May 16, 1917) and was made much of by her mother till John was born. John was a *boy*. Gertrude dropped to second-class citizenship at once and the shock to the little girl was severe. Furthermore, Gertrude told me that her mother consistently told her she was *not* beautiful to keep her from getting swell-headed. No wonder poor Gertrude suffered from a lack of self-worth.

Once, I remember, during an argument between me and Gertrude when I complained of her needlessly depressed attitude toward life, she said, "Anyone married to you would be depressed."

Whereupon I said, "But your brother, John, is even more depressed than you are and he's not married to me. Is there anything that you two share in common?"

Gertrude saw my point. She must have, for she grew furious.

My mother-in-law and I did not get along. She could not dominate me. I wouldn't allow it for a moment. I suppose my clear antagonism to her counted as a black mark against me.

It also bothered her that my gathering success seemed to cast a shadow on her beloved son, whom she always referred to as "Sonny" in what seemed to me a deliberate attempt to keep him infantilized. Once she said to me, quite loftily, "My Sonny is an *artist*, not a businessman like you."

To which I replied, "I'm a college professor and a novelist. Isn't that artistic enough for you?" (It was; chalk up another black mark.)

Mary's business advice to Henry, who passively followed that advice, was disastrous. He quit his job after World War II, at her insistence, and opened an ill-fated business of his own, which soon failed. Nevertheless, Mary always insisted on avoiding all responsibility and placed the blame squarely on the head of poor, innocent Henry.

I was the only member of the family who objected and tried to put the responsibility for disaster where it belonged, and that was still another black mark against me.

But let me give the devil her due. I don't know that there was ever a better cook than Mary Blugerman. When I ate her roast stuffed chicken, or her noodle pudding with bits of liver, or her strudel, I was ready to forgive her anything. It also meant that Gertrude, having learned from her mother, was also a good cook, though not *quite* as good.

39
NAES

Robert Heinlein, in the spring of 1942, tried to recruit me to work at the Naval Air Experimental Station in Philadelphia, along with him and Sprague de Camp. It put me into a real quandary, for there were strong arguments in my mind for both taking and rejecting the offer.

Against going to Philadelphia was the fact that I didn't want to go anywhere. I wanted to stay at home. Although I was now twenty-two years old, I still feared the task of taking care of myself.

Second, I wanted to continue toward my Ph.D. I didn't want to interrupt it for an indefinite period, perhaps forever.

The arguments *for* going to Philadelphia were, however, much stronger. I wasn't sure that I would be allowed to complete my Ph.D. work in any case. The first few months after Pearl Harbor had not been good for the United States and, although in Europe the Soviet Union had rallied and was holding the German army, that might be the last Soviet stand.

The draft was going to bite deep into young American manhood, and I could scarcely argue that my Ph.D. was more important than the war effort. If I worked for the NAES, my labors might serve as directly useful for that war effort, and I knew I could do more as a reasonably capable chemist than as a panicky infantryman, and perhaps the government would think so too.

Another argument for Philadelphia was simply that it was a job. I wanted to marry Gertrude but how was I going to support a wife? I had accumulated $400 in the bank and that struck me as a good starting sum, but I needed a job to supply me with a secure and continuing income. The job that Heinlein offered would bring me $2,600 a year. That should be enough.

My desire to get married carried the day. I moved to Philadelphia on May 13, 1942, and managed to live there for some ten weeks by myself (with weekend visits to New York to see Gertrude). After I married I had a week's honeymoon in Allaben Acres in the Catskills.

There I managed to demonstrate my intelligence to Gertrude when I volunteered to take part in a quiz contest and assured her I would win. She sat in the balcony all by herself to avoid having everyone see her embarrassment when I failed, but, of *course*, I won. I gained the hostility of many of the people at the resort because when I stood up to answer questions—very anxious lest I humiliate Gertrude—the anxiety on my face was interpreted as stupidity and everyone laughed. (They didn't laugh at anyone else.) When I won they seemed to take the attitude that I had no right to look stupid and mislead them.

After the honeymoon, I took my bride to Philadelphia and we found an apartment (and then a better one) for a rent of a little over forty dollars a month. I found that I didn't mind being away from home after all, for with Gertrude I *felt* at home. Unfortunately, Gertrude did not feel the same way. The apartment was small, it did not have air conditioning (in those days almost no one did), or even cross-ventilation, and we had a hot, muggy Philadelphia summer. Gertrude had to sit home alone in the heat while I worked in an air-conditioned laboratory. She resented it bitterly, all the more so because she missed her mother and her old home.

Every week, we would leave for New York on Friday evening. I would return on Sunday evening and she would stay on till Wednesday, with her mother doing everything she could to make her supercomfortable at home so that she would be all the more miserable in Philadelphia. And every week, I would think that she would not come back—but she always did. Just the same, there was simply no chance of my making her happy, and that sometimes reduced me to despair.

I remained at the NAES for three and a third years from 1942 to

1945. I hope that what I worked on was useful to the war effort; they told me that it was.

The job did keep me out of the draft during the war and I couldn't help but note that there were a great many young men my age (and in better physical condition) who also worked there and who apparently didn't seem to mind in the least that they weren't being drafted. I, always conscious of my lack of bravery, was forever caught between the desire to stay out of the army and shame at staying out of it. In the end, needless to say, the desire overcame the shame, especially since I was desperately in love with Gertrude and couldn't bear the thought of leaving her.

The stay at the NAES was not really a happy one for me. On the whole, I was a drastic failure. I'm convinced that if it hadn't been wartime and that if I hadn't been in the civil service and therefore subject to the incredible inertia with which it is plagued in all societies, I would have been fired. As it was, I received one promotion rather early in the game that raised my salary from $2,600 to $3,200 per year and that was it. It was made quite plain to me, without its actually being said, that I should look for nothing else.

Why? The usual thing. I'm sure you're tired of hearing it. (The wonder is that I wasn't tired to death of *living* it.) I didn't get along with my superiors. Of course, in later years, those superiors who survived treated me with great affection, and I was very friendly in return (why not?), but surely we are all cynical enough to know how little that means. When they were dealing with me during the war, I was the "problem" in the laboratory.

It really puzzles me as I look back on it that I didn't make a greater effort to placate the powers that be. After all, for the first time, I had more than myself to please. I might shrug off a failure to get further salary increases on the grounds that it was a temporary job, and that I would have a far greater career stretching out ahead of me. But I had to face Gertrude with that evidence of failure, and she was disturbed, as it was, at the fact that other people made more money than I did. I would say, "Stick with me, kid, and in ten years you'll be wearing diamonds." Though she said afterward that she had believed me, it didn't seem that she was much impressed at the time.

And what about my writing?

The pressures of a six-day-a-week job, and my desire to spend what spare time I had with Gertrude, sharply cut into my writing. In fact, during my first year at the NAES, I didn't write at all. Still, even jobs and marriage couldn't hold off the urge forever and in 1943 I began to write again.

I had written a story called "Foundation," which appeared in the May 1942 *ASF*. I also wrote a sequel called "Bridle and Saddle," which appeared in the next issue. It was "Bridle and Saddle" in which I found myself stuck and from which Fred Pohl had unstuck me on the Brooklyn Bridge. "Bridle and Saddle" appeared on the stands the very month in which I began work at the NAES.

These two stories were the first of my Foundation series, and when I returned to my writing while I was at the NAES, I wrote and published four more sequels that appeared in *ASF* during the war years. They were "The Big and the Little," "The Wedge," "The Dead Hand," and "The Mule."

Now let me explain the significance of this.

I have described my early interest in history, my urge to major in that field, and even to go for my Ph.D. in it. I cast all that aside because I didn't think it would work out well. I went for chemistry instead, but my interest in history remained.

I love historical novels (if they contain neither too much violence nor too much sleazy sex) and I still read them today whenever I get a chance. Naturally, just as loving science fiction led me to the desire to write science fiction, the love of historical novels led me to the desire to write historical novels.

To write a historical novel was, however, impractical for me. It would require an enormous amount of reading and research and I just couldn't spend all that time at it. I wanted to *write*.

Early on, then, it occurred to me that I could write a historical novel if I made up my own history. In other words, I might write a historical novel of the future, a science fiction story that *read* like a historical novel.

Now, I won't pretend that I made up the idea of writing histories of the future. It had been done numerous times, most effectively and startlingly by the British writer Olaf Stapledon, who wrote *First and Last Men* and *The Star Makers*. These books, however, read like histories and I wanted to write a historical *novel*, a story with conversation and action just like any other science fiction story except that it would deal not only with technology but with political and sociological problems.

I tried to do this as early as 1939, when I wrote a story called "Pilgrimage." It was terrible and Campbell would have nothing to do with it. I finally sold it to *Planet Stories*, under the title (editor's choice, not mine) of "Black Friar of the Flame" and it appeared in the Spring 1942 issue of that magazine. It is very likely the worst story I have had published and the one with the worst title. (It was revised seven times before I sold it, each revision making it worse. Since then, I do not revise substantially, except under very extraordinary circumstances.)

That rather daunted me, but the urge to write a historical novel of the future still had me by the throat. I had just finished reading Edward Gibbon's *History of the Decline and Fall of the Roman Empire* for the second time and it occurred to me that I could write a story about the decline and fall of the Galactic Empire.

On August 1, 1941, I came to Campbell with the idea and he caught fire. He wanted not a single story, but a long open-ended saga, of the fall of the Galactic Empire, the Dark Ages that followed, and the eventual rise of a Second Galactic Empire, all mediated by the invented science of "psychohistory," which enabled skilled psychohistorians to predict the mass currents of future history.

As it happens, the Foundation series proved to be the most popular and successful of all my writings, and my continuation of these stories in the 1980s after a long hiatus proved even more popular and successful. These stories contributed more than any others to making me more nearly rich and famous than I could have imagined. Most of the Foundation series was being written even while I was a complete failure at the NAES.

Of course, I had no way of knowing what was to come while I was working as a chemist during World War II, but looking back upon it, I note that chemistry, my profession, continued to fail and to do so more drastically with time. Not only didn't I get along with my superiors but I was not a particularly good chemist and never would be.

But *history*, which I had discarded, made its appearance in the most unlikely form, as a series of science fiction historical novels of the future, and lifted me to the heights.

I knew I would succeed, but I could not possibly have predicted the precise manner in which success was to show itself.

40
Life at War's End

On September 2, 1945, the war was over and the United States celebrated V-J Day with wild jubilation. On September 7, 1945, I received my draft notice.

What an excellent chance for self-pity! Everyone was celebrating, and I was staring at a letter that began: "Greetings." I was only six weeks short of my twenty-sixth birthday and, after V-E day, twenty-six had been fixed as the top age for being drafted. Had they waited only six weeks I would have been safe.

Self-pity is a horrible feeling and I did my level best to argue myself out of it. After all, the draft had held off through all the long years of bloody fighting, and when the finger finally tapped my shoulder, there was peace. The guns were stilled. I should rather be grateful that my cowardice would never be asked to rise to the needs of heroism.

What's more, I knew why I had to go just as I was getting ready to return to my research. I was to go into the army to allow a soldier who had borne the heat of the battle to go home. I was taking his place in safety. I should look upon it as an odd and interesting experience.

All that was logic and reason speaking. It went for naught. I was terribly sorry for myself anyway.

I entered the army on November 1, 1945. At the end of my first full day in the army, the evening of November 2, I looked about at the desolation of the base and thought, "Two years! Two years!" I was looking into the abyss of eternity.

Actually, I was not mistreated in the army in any way. I had to undergo the rigors and tedium of basic training, and I didn't get along with most of the other soldiers (surprised?), but I was never punished for anything. My 160 on the AGCT score established me in the eyes of the officers as someone who was far too stupid to be a soldier and they studiously ignored me—which suited me right down to my toenails.

By February 1946, I had grown more or less accustomed to army routine. Camp Lee, in Virginia, where I had gone through basic training, had been close enough to home for me to have occasional furloughs when I could see Gertrude. I hoped fervently that I would be placed somewhere still closer to New York.

Not a chance. The atomic bomb was to be tested at the atoll of Bikini in the South Pacific, and a number of soldiers were assigned to participate in that task, and I was among them. I would be some ten thousand miles from home for an indefinite period and at that moment I think I would have welcomed death.

A kindly librarian asked me why I looked so awful and I poured out my sad tale to her in piteous accents. She listened, then said, coldly, "Listen, there's not a person here, not a person in the world, who doesn't have troubles. What makes you think yours are so special?"

You know, it put me face to face with my foolishness and resigned me to my fate.

I won't go into the details of my army experiences, which were dull and tedious. Just as I had finished dead first in my AGCT score, I finished dead last in the physical contests—and by a healthy margin in both cases. I had to do an occasional KP but mostly I escaped because I was a rapid typist and typists were (a) in great demand in administration and (b) immune to KP.

I developed, of course, an absolute detestation of the army, of its routine, of its mindlessness, of its callousness, of its meaninglessness, but, looking back on it, this hurt me far more than it hurt the army.

My refusal to accept the situation rationally prevented me from observing a curious subculture that I might have used in my essays and stories, and kept me from enjoying what there was to enjoy. En route to Bikini, for instance, I spent ten weeks in Hawaii with no duties. I would have been perfectly able to spend all my time enjoying that beautiful place—but I never allowed myself to do so. I persisted in considering it all a hateful exile. (I did manage to pick up a mild case of athlete's foot in Hawaii, something I have never entirely shaken.)

While I was in Hawaii, incidentally, something took place that in itself could not possibly have seemed to be of much importance, but that, looking back upon, I have always considered a turning point in my social life—the greatest turning point, perhaps.

The group of soldiers who were sent to Bikini by way of Hawaii included six "critically needed specialists" (that is, soldiers with some scientific training, and I was one of them) amid a large number of high school graduates and less. ("Farm boys," I thought of them, rather unkindly—but they thought even less kindly of me and sometimes showed it. I was the oldest person in the barracks and sometimes they called me "Pop," which hurt my feelings, for inside me I was still an infant prodigy.)

We "critically needed specialists" clung together, of course, and, indeed, palling around with them on the train and ship that carried us from Camp Lee to Hawaii was the nearest I came to having a good time in the army. We played innumerable games of bridge. I was terrible at it, but it didn't matter, because we played for fun.

In any case, I was in the Honolulu barracks once, at a time when the other five specialists were off somewhere, so that I was the only one present. Unable to socialize with the farm boys, I lay in my bunk reading.

There were three of the farm boys further down the barracks and they were preoccupied (as we all were, considering the nature of our mission) with the atomic bomb.

One of the three took it upon himself to explain to the other two how the atomic bomb worked, and needless to say, he got it all wrong.

Wearily, I put down my book and began to get to my feet so that I could join them, assume "the smart man's burden," and educate them. Halfway to my feet, however, I thought, "Who appointed you to be their educator? Is it going to hurt them to be wrong about the atomic bomb?" And I returned to my book.

This is the first occasion I can remember in which I deliberately resisted the impulse to put my remarkability on display.

It doesn't mean that my character changed suddenly and completely, but it was a step, a tiny first step, in the forging of what I can only describe as a new me. I was still obnoxious to many, I still failed to get along with my superiors, but I began to change. I began to be able to "turn it off," to not be forever putting my cleverness on display.

I answer questions if asked, I explain if an explanation is requested,

I write educational articles for those who *wish* to read them, but I have learned not to volunteer my knowledge, unsolicited.

It's amazing the change that produced. It would seem that, very slowly, I mellowed. I did, in the process, seem to change the most important item in my makeup, the I-know-it-all syndrome that led to my unpopularity with others. In fact, if I may trust what others have told me with increasing vehemence over the years, I seem to have become a much-beloved elderly person. Remembering how things were nearly two-thirds of a lifetime ago, I always feel astonished, especially when beautiful young women treat me as though I were a cuddly teddy bear. Fortunately, I have learned to bask in the adulation.

And I trace it all, I swear I do, to that moment in the Honolulu barracks.

Why did it happen just then? Perhaps my unaccustomed role as oldest in the place, as "Pop," formed within me an age-induced gravity. Perhaps my decline in academic prowess, which had not escaped my attention, you may be sure, kept me from feeling so terribly all-fired "smart" in the scholastic sense.

Everything we do, obviously, is the result of various changes in the conditions about us over which we rarely have control. I did not begin the conversion from obnoxious kid to beloved patriarch because I had made a conscious decision to do so, but because life, in several ways, simply shaped me as a more or less unconscious object.

I can only be glad it shaped me in the right direction—but I deserve no personal credit for it.

What's more, I lost nothing by it. The delights of explaining and educating were not lost. The time was to come when I was to write thousands of essays, all designed to educate and enlighten my readers; when I was to give hundreds of talks, all designed to educate and enlighten my audience; when even my science fiction had its educational aspects.

But, and this is the crucial point, no one is forced to read what I write, and, indeed, the vast majority of Earth's population does *not* read what I write. My educational efforts are only for those who, voluntarily, wish to subject themselves to it.

This is utterly and entirely different from forcing my impulse to educate on unwilling victims, and it is only that that I have chosen to give up—and it has made all the difference.

Another unusual event in the course of my army stay was that I did manage to write one story while I was in the army. During basic training, I persuaded the librarian to lock me in the library when it closed for lunch and to allow me to use the typewriter. After a few sessions, I had completed a robot story, which I mailed to Campbell. It was called "Evidence" and it appeared in the September 1946 *ASF*.

The interesting thing about the story is that when I reread it recently because it was appearing in a collection and I had to check it for typographical errors, I realized that it was the first story I wrote that sounded as though I might have written it forty years later.

The worst of the pulpishness was suddenly gone and from "Evidence" onward I wrote much more rationally (at least so it seems to me). Why my writing should have suddenly matured while I was in the army, I don't know. I have brooded about it, but have no answer.

As it happened, I did not stay in the army for two years. Through a clerical error, Gertrude received a notice that her allotment as an army wife was being stopped because I had been discharged. I went at once to my captain with the letter. He considered the matter and said he wouldn't concern himself with it but would send me back to Camp Lee to straighten the matter out. (He was probably glad to get rid of me.)

As a result, I left for Camp Lee the day before the ship left Hawaii for Bikini. This meant that I never saw a nuclear bomb explosion close up. It also meant that, perhaps, I did not die of leukemia at a comparatively early age.

Once back in Camp Lee, I began to pull the strings for a "research discharge" since I was now not doing anything in the army and since I would go back to scientific research if I was discharged. So they discharged me (and again might have been glad to get rid of me). I was out of the army on July 26, 1946, which was, as it happened, my fourth wedding anniversary. I had served eight months and twenty-six days.

41

Games

I mentioned in the previous section that I had played innumerable games of bridge with the "critically needed specialists" and that I was no good at it. I am simply no good at games generally.

I am not talking about the rough-and-tumble of street play, or the calisthenics of gym classes, or the organized efforts of sports requiring a quick eye and good reflexes, such as tennis and golf.

My ignorance of all these things is pathetic.

In 1989, I gave a talk at a high-powered country club and found myself among a group of the elite who had come there for their conference in order to have an opportunity to play tennis and golf in the off-hours. They had some objects on display that the competing players could win for excellence in their scores, and one object was utterly strange to me. I studied it carefully and finally said to a young man who looked as though he might answer a polite question, "Pardon me, what is this?"

He stared at me a moment, and said, "A golf bag."

"Oh, is it?" I said, as naively as though I were only seven, instead of old enough to be the young man's grandfather. "I've never seen one before."

I'm sure that that story spread and everyone must have wondered, in great alarm, why they had invited me to speak to them. However, I proved to them that you might not know what a golf bag was and still give a very good talk.

Failure at physical sports has never bothered me. I even consoled myself in my younger and more foolish days with the thought that it was just a by-product of being "smart," but as I grew older, I found that I was no good at competitive activities that involved the mind either. I was not only no good at bridge, I was no good at any card games, which has its advantages too, for it kept me from the folly of gambling.

What bothered me, though, was my failure at chess. When I was quite young and had a checkerboard, but no chess pieces, I read books on the game and learned the various moves. I then cut out cardboard squares on which I drew the symbols for the various pieces, and tried to play games with myself. Eventually I managed to persuade my father to get me real chessmen. Then I taught my sister the moves and played the game with her. Both of us played very clumsily indeed.

My brother, Stanley, who watched us play, learned the moves and, eventually, asked if he might play. Ever the indulgent older brother, I said, "Sure," and prepared to beat the pants off him. The trouble was that in the first game he ever played *he* beat *me*.

In the years that followed, I discovered that *everyone* beat me, regardless of race, color, or religion. I was simply the most appallingly bad chess player who ever lived, and, as time went on, I just stopped playing chess.

My failure at chess was really distressing. It seemed completely at odds with my "smartness," but I now know (or at least have been told) that great chess players achieve their results by years and years of studying chess games, by the memorization of large numbers of complex "combinations." They don't see chess as a succession of moves but as a pattern. I know what that means, for I see an essay or a story as a pattern.

But these talents are different. Kasparov sees a chess game as a pattern but an essay as a mere collection of words. I see an essay as a pattern and a chess game as a mere collection of moves. So he can play chess and I can write essays and not vice versa.

That's not enough, however. I never thought of comparing myself to grand masters of chess. What bothered me was my inability to beat anyone! The conclusion that I finally came to (right or wrong) was that I was unwilling to study the chessboard and weigh the consequences of each possible move I might make. Even people who couldn't see complex patterns might at least penetrate two or three moves ahead, but not I. I moved entirely on impulse, if not at random, and could not make myself do anything else. That meant I would almost certainly lose.

And again—why? To me, it seems obvious. I was spoiled by my ability to understand instantly, my ability to recall instantly. I expected to see things at once and I refused to accept a situation in which that was not possible. (Just as I refused to swot away and study in high school and college.)

It is my good fortune that in both my writing and my speaking engagements I see patterns effortlessly and at once. If I had to think things through, I imagine I would have failed at both. (And I wouldn't be at all surprised if my unwillingness to take time to think things through contributed to my failure as a scientist.)

42

Acrophobia

I do not take airplanes because of my acrophobia, and that is a legitimate excuse, as I shall soon explain. Nevertheless, I did fly in a plane once while I was at the NAES and once while I was in the army. I must explain the circumstances.

At the NAES, I was working on "dye markers," which pilots who were ditched in the ocean could use to color the water about them and make themselves more easily visible to searching planes above. (I loved working on that because it clearly contributed to the welfare of our fighting men and excused my not being among them—at least, a little.)

The usual way of testing various dye markers was to go up in an airplane and study their comparative visibilities. I, however, had worked out a test that, I thought, would do the job without the expense of a plane flight. In order to make sure that my test was suitable, however, I would have to compare its results with those given by air surveillance. If both gave the same results, well—

Such was my enthusiasm over this (and I believe it was the last spark of true enthusiasm I felt for actual scientific research) that I actually asked to go up in an airplane to observe the dye markers. I went up in a small two-engine NAES plane, piloted by one of the NAES officers. In my interest in watching for the tiny green smears on the water, I forgot my acrophobia and did *not* go into panic. I was even planning to go up again, but my superiors wanted to know if I could *guarantee* results.

I said, "Of course not. If I could, I wouldn't have to go up in the plane."

So, with incredible stupidity, they canceled my flights.

My second time in a plane was on my return from Hawaii. I had asked for the first available sea transportation to San Francisco, which meant six days on the ocean. I preferred that to a plane flight.

In the army, however, "sea transportation" means a plane. I protested vehemently, but the sergeant in charge of me simply ordered me onto the plane, and I had no choice but to board it. It took off instantly and propelled me through the night for twelve hours till we reached San Francisco. It all happened so quickly, and left me in such a state of uncertainty and confusion, that I had no time to panic.

Neither trip sold me on airplanes. To be sure, they had little chance to do so. The first was a small plane not in the least meant for civilian transportation, and the second was an eviscerated DC-3 in which all the passengers had to sleep, or try to sleep, on the curved wooden floor.

What if I took a modern plane, with comfortable seats, stewardesses bringing food, movies to watch, and so on? What, indeed? I'll never know, for there is no chance I'll ever talk myself into trying a flight (unless Janet or Robyn were far away and needed me desperately and quickly). What's more, there is always the extraordinary publicity and macabre detail with which every airplane crash is greeted, and with each grisly incident, my firm intention never to fly is strengthened.

But do I really have acrophobia, or is that just an excuse to avoid airplanes? As Lester del Rey once implied, am I a coward rather than an acrophobe?

Believe me, I'm an acrophobe. I first became truly aware of it the very first time I put it to a true test. When I visited the New York World's Fair in 1939, with my chem-lab ladylove, it occurred to me to ride on a roller coaster. From what I had seen of it in movies, it seemed to me that my date would scream and would cling to me, something which, I thought, would be delightful.

The instant the roller coaster topped the first and highest rise and began to swoop downward, I reacted like an acrophobe. I screamed in terror and I hung on desperately to my date, who sat there stolid and unmoved. I got out of the roller coaster half dead, and if I had been older and had had a less youthful heart, I am certain it would have killed me.

I don't think that that experience *caused* the acrophobia. I think I was an acrophobe all along but till then I had had no occasion to be high up and in a position to fear falling. I wonder if I was actually born with the phobia, if it is part of my genetic makeup. I wonder if such things have even been studied.

After I came to know I was an acrophobe, I studiously avoided anything that might activate the sensation. Only once was I cajoled into violating this sensible precaution.

In December 1982, a large menorah, thirty feet high, was set up at Chanukah time in Columbus Circle, within walking distance of my apartment. A rabbi phoned me to ask me to light some of the lamps with a blowtorch on a certain day, give a short speech, and repeat a short prayer after him. I had no desire at all to do this but I am reluctant to behave in such a manner as to seem to have no Jewish feelings at all.

"How do I get up there?" I asked.

"With a cherry picker," he said, referring to those buckets in which men are lifted to work on trees.

"I can't do that," I said. "I'm an acrophobe. I have a morbid fear of heights."

"Nonsense," he said. "I'll be going up in a cherry picker too, and remember, the higher up you go, the closer you are to God."

That was nonsense, if you like. Even if God existed, he would not exist in some region "up there." He would be immanent in all creation. But I let myself be talked into it. Looking back on it, I can't believe I was so incredibly stupid—but I was.

On the evening in question I walked to Columbus Circle, along with Janet and her niece, Patti. Janet was furious with me for agreeing, partly because it meant participating in a religious rite and partly out of her fear of my acrophobia. As for myself, I thought, "It's mind over matter. I shall simply ignore the fact that I'll be moving up in the air."

However, once I got into the cherry picker and felt myself move upward, it was at once apparent that the phobia would not be conquered by mind alone. I collapsed to the bottom of the cherry picker, and my clutching fingers, white with pressure and clinging to the lip of the picker, was all anyone could see. I was suffering from bouts of angina pectoris at the time and, usually, it manifested itself only when I was walking. For the first time it hit me when I wasn't moving, clamping down hard on my chest.

All I could think of was the possibility of a fatal heart attack and I thought, "If I die now, Janet will *kill* me."

But I got up to the menorah, still alive, and managed with the greatest of difficulty to light the necessary number of lights with the blowtorch. (I had never before held a blowtorch in my hands and learning how to control its flame while I was in the grip of my phobia was difficult indeed.)

I gave a speech that lasted a few minutes, though I haven't the foggiest notion of what I said, and then, pretty much in agony, I repeated the Hebrew syllables the rabbi intoned. (He was not phobic.)

Finally, *finally,* we began to descend and I thought thankfully that with every foot downward I was getting farther from God and nearer the blessed ground.

My troubles were not over. When we were back at ground level, I found I was suffering from nervous paralysis. I could not move my legs and had to be lifted out of the cherry picker. I stood upright, and with Janet supporting me on one side and Patti on the other, I managed to shuffle. As they walked me home, my leg muscles slowly returned to normal.

I winced over what Janet would say to me, for she maintained an ominous silence while we walked home (as my mother used to do when she was contemplating the spanking I was going to get once I was safely in the apartment). To avert that, I said, pathetically, "I was afraid if I had a heart attack and died that you would kill me, Janet."

And she said, "No, but I would have killed that rabbi."

Once I had a chance to observe a non-acrophobe in action and I still can't believe it. There was a weak spot in the wall of our apartment house, and during gusty storms, the wind would blow water right through the wall into the apartment. On December 17, 1986, a man was on a scaffolding suspended from the roof to gouge out the bricks and look for the weak spot. The scaffolding seemed a frail structure and it was thirty-three stories above the ground.

I wondered at his nonchalance, and with my stomach twisting, I asked him if he minded being up in the air like that. He looked down, then up at me, and said, "No."

He found a piece of metal in the wall that obviously represented the weak spot, and as he tried to wrench it away, it came with a sudden yielding. As the workman staggered back, I reacted like an acrophobe, emitting an unearthly scream. He was stopped by the back of the scaffolding, looked a little perturbed for a moment, and then went back to putting new bricks into the portion of the wall he had excavated.

That's what it's like, *not* being an acrophobe.

43

Claustrophilia

While I'm at my phobic peculiarities, I might as well mention a very mild condition that I also suffer from. It is claustrophilia, or a liking for enclosed places.

Let me tell you how I became consciously aware of the condition. Every once in a while I would go to a department store with Gertrude. (I hate shopping and can't be trusted to buy my own clothes in a sensible manner, so that Gertrude had to come with me to supervise, and once she was there, she would shop for herself too.)

As we wandered through the store, I would look at the displays about me and find myself particularly interested in the furniture displays. The stores would set up sample bedrooms or living rooms and show the furniture properly placed within it. I found those rooms extraordinarily attractive, warm, and friendly. I seemed to prefer them to the ordinary rooms that existed in my apartment or in those of my friends.

But why? The rooms I lived in were adequately furnished and not essentially different from the model rooms in the department store. I puzzled over the matter and, one day, studying one of the model rooms with my usual desire to live in it, I finally saw the difference.

The model room had *no windows*. It existed only under warm, artificial light. There was no intrusion of harsh sunlight.

Suddenly, I understood a few things about myself I had earlier simply taken for granted. In one of the candy stores we owned, we had an apartment on the floor above. There was also a little room in the back of the store equipped with a stove and other kitchen utilities, for when we bought the store, it had also served as a primitive luncheonette. My parents put an end to that, but I frequently had lunch in that little room.

I much preferred this little room to the kitchen upstairs. Once I learned about my claustrophilia, I remembered that the little room had had no window and that I had sat there eating lunch, even in the blaze of noon, by the light of an electric bulb.

The subways in those days had newsstands which sold newspapers and magazines and candies. At night, the wooden sides were folded in and locked, and the whole thing resembled a closed box till it was opened for business before the morning rush hour.

I used to have a yearning to own such a newsstand, and I fantasized that when it was closed, I would remain inside with an electric light going. I would then have a chance to read, in strict isolation and enclosure, the magazines I liked, while hearing the occasional rumble of a subway train. (Such mundane problems as how I would manage to visit the bathroom in the middle of the night never occurred to me.)

My claustrophilia is not extreme. While I prefer enclosed places, I can get along very well in sunlit rooms and in the open. I don't have any touch of agoraphobia (the morbid fear of open places), though I would rather walk the canyons of Manhattan with tall buildings hemming me in than in Central Park, which is open.

My claustrophilia does show up in my office, where I keep the window blinds down at all times and work only under artificial light no matter how bright and sunlit the day. What's more, my typewriter is always so arranged that when I am using it, I face a blank, windowless wall.

At present, however, my word processor is located in our living room, which is open to sunlight, for the window blinds here are never drawn. Nevertheless, however bright the room, I turn the overhead electric lamp on.

Once my claustrophilia stood me in good stead.

As one gets older and more rickety, and as medical technology advances, doctors love to play with their toys, using you as their victim. At one time they ran a magnetic resonance test on me, a noninvasive, nondangerous way of probing your interior. (I'll tell you right now they didn't find anything disturbing.)

To do this they put my entire body inside a cylinder and left me there for an hour and a half, while strange banging noises took place. The crucial fact was that the cylinder was a tight fit, most coffinlike, and you were supposed to lie still, most corpselike.

It was boring and I was prey to the fear that the doctors had forgotten about me and gone home, but the close quarters of the embracing cylinder did not bother me. I don't know how they could test claustrophobes (those with a morbid fear of enclosed places). I suspect they can't.

It might even be argued that my whole way of life is an expression of my claustrophilia. My total absorption in writing creates a warm artificial enclosing world about me (one without windows) that shuts out the harsh outside world with its glaring sun. And it is no accident, perhaps, that in my book *The Caves of Steel* (Doubleday, 1954) I pictured underground cities on Earth, the ultimate in windowless enclosure.

Heinlein, in connection with my story "Dreaming Is a Private Thing" (December 1955 *F&SF*), accused me, good-naturedly, of coining money out of my neuroses. Actually, *The Caves of Steel* is a much better example of that. —And I'm not ashamed. Every writer, I am convinced, makes use of his own neuroses to the fullest possible extent in his writing.

44

Ph.D. and Public Speaking

It is easy to suppose, when one interrupts one's Ph.D. work for a period of years, that one will never return to it. I must admit that I had that woebegone feeling myself and that it was another small factor that argued against my accepting the job in Philadelphia. In fact, one of my schoolmates was convinced I would never come back, not so much because of the job as because of my planned marriage. He felt that my family responsibilities would force my life into other, more mundane channels.

By the time that the war and my NAES job came to an end and by the time my army stint was over, four and a half years had passed. Fortunately, my marriage had not yet developed the complication of children and I was determined that my Ph.D. work was *not* to be abandoned. In September 1946, therefore, I presented myself at Columbia, ready to go back to work. Professor Dawson was still there, remembered me well, and was delighted to see me.

However, you can't go home again. It wasn't the same. I was four years older, four years more disillusioned with science, four years more convinced that I was inadequate in scientific research. Worse yet, while I had been gone, there had been a revolution in chemistry with the application of quantum mechanics to it, something brought on largely by the work of the great Linus Pauling.

I had not kept up with that change and was appalled to find that chemistry had turned into Greek for me. Fortunately, I had taken all my course work before leaving for Philadelphia and there was no need for me to do anything but research. This was incredibly fortunate, for there was now scarcely a course that I could reasonably have needed to take that I would have had any perceptible chance of passing.

It was another step in my decline. I was not just a mediocre student; I was a sure-fail student.

Nevertheless, one good thing happened during my doctoral research, something in which coming events cast their shadow.

As part of my duties as a doctoral candidate, I was expected to give a seminar on the work I was doing. (It was research into the kinetics—that is, the speed of working—of some obscure enzyme.)

I had attended such seminars and they were usually resounding failures. The person giving the seminar (however good a chemist he might be) usually had no particular talent at spoken exposition. Moreover, his subject was arcane and was not easy to understand, without considerable careful explanation, by anyone but himself. As for the audience, knowing from experience they would not understand anything after the first five words, they were prepared only for suffering and attended only because they were expected to.

I approached the task with enthusiasm, however. For one thing, it was something I could do that did not involve my hands. I would not have to worry about breaking equipment or having experiments go mysteriously wrong.

But it was more than that. I looked forward to speaking, and really I don't know why. I had no experience at all in public speaking, and it is usually looked on as the ultimate test of self-assurance, as a way of ruining the bravest. There are people who would sooner face a charging rhinoceros than a peacefully somnolent audience. One feels so exposed on a public platform. There is the possibility of making such a public ass of one's self. Why on earth I should not have shared this extremely common feeling I don't know.

I walked into the room well before the seminar was due to begin and covered the ample blackboard with mathematical and chemical equations so that I would not have to interrupt the even tenor of my talk by writing them down. (What gave me the notion that this was the right thing to do? I can only assume the answer was some kind of instinct. Just as I had an almost inborn grip on the essentials of writing so that I could begin doing so at the age of eleven, I seemed to have an almost inborn grip on the essentials of public speaking.)

Of course, when the audience arrived and saw the equations, there was a palpable shock and a buzz of anxious uncertainty. I'm sure that no one felt he was going to be able to make head or tail of the talk. But I raised my arms and, with complete self-confidence, said, "Just listen to everything I say and all will be as clear as a mountain pool."

How did I know? Surely this was a piece of arrogant self-confidence that was more fitting for my grammar school years than for the years of grim disillusion with my own abilities that I had experienced in college and beyond.

But this was something I had never done before, you see. I had not had occasion to be disillusioned with speaking, and I was pawing the ground in my eagerness to try.

And it worked! There were no terrors, no butterflies in my stomach. I spoke easily and smoothly, starting at the very beginning (seminar speakers rarely did that, but nervously plunged into their own intricacies at the start—perhaps to demonstrate their erudition). I progressed along the line of equations, explaining each clearly as I came to it, then going on.

In the end the audience seemed enthusiastic and Professor Dawson told someone (who promptly passed it on to me) that it was the clearest presentation he had ever heard.

This was the first time I had ever presented a formal hour-long talk to an audience. I had no occasion to present another for several years, nor did I have any plans or thoughts about any others. Nevertheless, from that point on I knew forevermore that I could speak in public without trouble.

This whole thing raises an interesting point. I obviously had a talent for public speaking that must have been lying latent within me for quite a while. There had just been no occasion that would serve to exercise it. When the first occasion arose, at the age of twenty-seven, I spoke with sufficient mastery to do well.

Suppose the occasion had arisen earlier. At what age could I have delivered a good talk without trouble? Obviously, I don't know. Or suppose the occasion had not arisen till considerably later—or not at all. Is it conceivable that I might have lived and died without knowing that I was an excellent public speaker?

Perhaps so.

It makes me wonder. Do I have any other talents, the exercise of which would have been amusing and useful to me, that I have just never had occasion to tap? I don't know.

For that matter, the same applies to everyone. Who knows what talents lie unrealized among the vast population of humanity, and how much we all lose because those talents are never brought into play?

—Another unexpected development that arose during my doctoral research came about in the following manner:

I was sitting at my desk, preparing the materials for the day's experiments, and brooding over the approaching necessity of writing a doctoral dissertation. A doctoral dissertation is a highly stylized document, and ironclad rules necessitate that it be written in a stiff and abnormal (even stupid) way. I did not want to write in a stiff, abnormal, and stupid way.

It struck me, therefore, in a Puckish moment, to write a spoof of a doctoral dissertation that would relieve my soul and enable me to approach the real thing with more spirit.

As it happened, I was working with tiny feathery crystals of a compound called catechol, which was extremely soluble in water. As I dumped some of it into the water, it dissolved the moment it hit the surface. I said to myself, "What if it dissolves just a split second *before* it hits the surface. What then?"

The result was that I wrote a pseudo-dissertation written as stodgily as I could manage about a compound which dissolved 1.12 seconds before you added the water. I called it *The Endochronic Properties of Resublimated Thiotimoline.*

I submitted it to Campbell, who enjoyed it and who had no objection to running an occasional spoof article. I realized that it would appear in the magazine at just about the time I would be taking my make-or-break doctor's orals, and I was cautious enough to instruct Campbell to run it under a pseudonym.

It appeared in the March 1948 *ASF* and Campbell forgot about the pseudonym. There it was, Isaac Asimov plastered all over it, and, of course, the entire Columbia University chemical faculty got wind of it and passed it from hand to hand.

I turned really sick. I knew what would happen. Whatever I did at the doctor's orals, they were going to turn me down on the grounds of personality deficiency. All those years, all those years, and I was going to lose out for the old, old crime of irreverence to my superiors.

But it didn't work out that way. After the professors had put me through the hell of a doctor's orals, Professor Ralph Halford asked the last question: "Mr. Asimov, can you tell us something about the thermodynamic properties of resublimated thiotimoline?"

I burst into hysterical laughter, because I knew they wouldn't play games with me if they intended to flunk me, and they didn't. I passed, and one by one they emerged from the testing room, shook my hand, and said, "Congratulations, Dr. Asimov."

That was May 20, 1948. I was twenty-eight years old and I mourned over the loss of four years because of World War II. I might have got my doctorate at twenty-four and retained a bit more of my prodigious infancy—which was ridiculously stupid of me, considering the uncounted millions of people who lost a lot more than four years during the war.

The graduation ceremonies were on June 2, but I refused to attend formally, since I disapproved of the medieval claptrap involved. However, I did sit in the audience with my father, who was most unhappy that I wasn't up there on the platform in academic robes. But at least he was there witnessing my becoming a doctor after all, even if it was the wrong kind.

45

Postdoctorate

I had started worrying about getting a job in 1938, in my junior year at college, when I first applied to medical school. Since then, my life had been one long delaying action. There was graduate school, the NAES, the army, and graduate school again. Ten years had passed and it was now 1948 and I was about to get my Ph.D. and there was still that same old problem. What did I do about a job?

I must admit that Professor Dawson, however wonderful a research director he was, was not among the most powerful members of the faculty when it came to getting jobs for his students. Nor was my work sufficiently worthwhile to attract much attention. As a result, I did not find a job.

What saved me was the offer of a job as a postdoctorate student for a year. This meant I could continue to do research and be *paid* $5,000 for the year. I was to work on antimalarial drugs, trying to find a better synthetic substitute for quinine than those that already existed.

I did not particularly want to work on the problem, I was disenchanted by chemistry, and I was well aware of my insufficiencies as a researcher. In fact, I remember almost nothing of the work I did that year, a sure sign of its total lack of interest for me.

As the year 1949 progressed, however, I found the hope of a real job going glimmering. No job! Not even a distant nibble. I became so desperate that I had about made up my mind to throw myself into the antimalarial project in the hope that I would be kept on for year after year.

That was perhaps the low point of my chemical career, for I was considering condemning myself to a job I didn't like just for the money. I was twenty-nine years old and a complete and utter failure, despite all my boastings and certainties that I was going to be the kind of success that would amaze the world.

And then I learned one of the uncomfortable facts of postwar academic life. Increasingly, academic research was supported by government grants. Those grants usually lasted for one year. Each year, if continued support was desired, the professor who was running the research had to apply for renewal and present justification for it.

The results of this, I have always thought, were pernicious. First, the professor who wished a government grant had to choose a subject that would sound as though it was worth spending government money on. Scientists therefore crowded into the money fields, to coin a phrase, and left the less dramatic areas of science untended. This meant that the money fields were overfinanced, so that much money was wasted, while the neglected parts of science might have produced an important breakthrough if they had not been neglected.

Further, the harsh competition for government money exacerbated the chances of fraud as scientists (being human) tried to improve or even invent experiments that would drag in the dough.

Still another result of the grant system is that the second half of each year is spent, increasingly, on the preparation of documents dealing with renewal of the grant rather than with research.

Finally, the lower echelons of the research groups, whose salaries are paid out of the grant instead of out of university funds, are in a continual state of insecurity. They never know when a failure of renewal will send them flying out the door. I found this out when toward the end of the year my grant was not renewed.

Only one good thing happened in the postdoctorate period. A neighbor of ours asked, curiously, what the nature of my work might be. I told him I was working on antimalarials, and he asked, in all innocence, "What's that?"

I therefore painstakingly explained what I was doing, complete with chemical formulas, and when I finished, he said, with obvious sincerity, "You make it very clear and simple. Thank you."

The result was that, for the very first time, it occurred to me that I might write a *nonfiction* book on science. Nothing came of it right then, but it stayed in my mind and eventually resulted in copious fruit.

46

Job Hunting

The low point of my job hunting came about as follows. An acquaintance of mine who was employed at Charles Pfizer, a pharmaceutical firm based in Brooklyn, said he had obtained an interview for me with a high official of the firm. The appointment was for 10 A.M. on February 4, 1949, and you can be sure I was there on time. The official I was to see was not. He did not show up until 2 P.M. It was foolish of me beyond words to sit there for four hours, through lunch, but it was one of those occasions when I was governed by stubborn rage rather than by good sense. I wasn't going to be driven away in so cavalier a fashion.

The official came at last, probably because he was told I showed every sign of refusing to leave until he did come. I was treated with clear indifference and not too much time was wasted on me.

I saw enough of Charles Pfizer to know I didn't want to work there, and would have refused a job if one was offered, but that made no difference. I was in a rage over my treatment, and it is one case in which that rage has never died down. It is as fresh in my heart as though it happened yesterday. I'm not proud of holding a grudge and I probably would not have done so, except for one crowning incident.

Despite everything, I had given the official a copy of my carefully produced, carefully bound Ph.D. thesis. I did not expect to impress him, but I had planned to do it, so I did. A few days later the copy was returned to me in the mail with a brief, cold covering note stating that he was returning my "pamphlet." That, to my mind, was an insult. I could not believe that this miserable being did not know a Ph.D. thesis when he saw it, especially since it said plainly on the cover that it was a Ph.D. thesis. To call it a "pamphlet" was like calling a writer a "scribbler" and I have never forgiven him.

One closing item about Charles Pfizer. Many years later they asked me to speak to a group of their executives. They offered me $5,000 and I don't generally haggle over fees. At that time, $5,000 was enough for a talk to be given in Manhattan. However, for Pfizer I made an exception. I demanded $6,000 and wouldn't budge. They finally agreed.

That extra thousand was to assuage my hurt feelings of so many years before, and what's more, after I had completed my speech to considerable applause and pocketed my check, I told them exactly why they had had to pay an additional thousand.

It made me feel better. It was small and mean of me, but I'm only human. I had not sought revenge, but it had been handed to me and I could not refuse.

Although the Pfizer incident was the very worst ever in my job hunting, nothing else was much better. I simply couldn't get a job.

47

The Big Three

But while my job hunting remained a fiasco, what about my writing?

There, I was not a failure but an increasing success. I continued both my robot stories and my Foundation stories, even though I slowed up a bit while I was actually engaged in my research. I sold all the stories I wrote to *ASF* to the drumbeat of increasing popularity.

There was no question that by 1949 I was widely recognized as a major science fiction writer. Some felt I had joined Robert Heinlein and A. E. van Vogt as the three-legged stool on which science fiction now rested.

As it happened, A. E. van Vogt virtually ceased writing in 1950, perhaps because he grew increasingly interested in Hubbard's dianetics. In 1946, however, a British writer, Arthur C. Clarke, began to write for *ASF,* and he, like Heinlein and van Vogt (but unlike me), was an instant hit.

By 1949, the first whisper of Heinlein, Clarke, and Asimov as "the Big Three" began to be heard. This kept up for some forty years, for we all stayed alive for decades and all remained in the science fiction field. In the end, we all three commanded large advances and found our books on the best-seller lists. (Who would have thought it in the 1940s?)

Now that Heinlein has died and Clarke and I are increasingly decrepit, one is bound to ask, "Who will be the next Big Three?" The answer, I'm afraid, is that no one will ever be. In the early days, when the Big Three were chosen by general consent, the number of science fiction writers was small and it was easy to choose the outstanding examples.

Nowadays, however, the number of science fiction writers, and even of *good* science fiction writers, is so great that it is simply impossible to pick three writers whom everyone will agree on.

But perhaps that is no great tragedy. I have always thought that the constant harping on the Big Three was in a way a self-fulfilling phenomenon. We were the Big Three because we were successful, but how much of our continuing success arose from the fact that we were referred to, day in and day out, as the Big Three? Even though I benefited from it, I have always been uneasily aware that it might have been cheating the rest of the field.

But in that case, if my writing was doing so well, why was I so worried about a job? The problem, as perhaps you might guess, was money.

By 1949, I had sold sixty stories and was universally considered a leading light of science fiction. Yet in all the eleven years I had been writing and selling science fiction, I made a total of $7,700—that's for *all* eleven years. An average earning of $700 a year was clearly not going to support a married couple, and so I needed something else.

48

Arthur Charles Clarke

Arthur Charles Clarke was born toward the end of 1917 in Great Britain. He is another science fiction writer who has been thoroughly educated in science and he did extremely well in physics and mathematics.

He and I are now widely known as the Big Two of science fiction. Until early 1988, as I've said, people spoke of the Big Three, but then Arthur fashioned a little human figurine of wax and with a long pin—

At least, he has told me this. Perhaps he's trying to warn me. I have made it quite plain to him, however, that if he were to find himself the Big One, he would be very lonely. At the thought of that, he was affected to the point of tears, so I think I'm safe.

I'm very fond of Arthur, and have been for forty years. We came to an agreement many years ago in a taxi which, at the time, was moving south on Park Avenue, so it is called the Treaty of Park Avenue. By it, I have agreed to maintain, on questioning, that Arthur is the best science fiction writer in the world, though I am also allowed to say, if questioned assiduously, that I am breathing down his neck as we run. In return, Arthur has agreed to insist, forever, that I am the best science writer in the world. He *must* say it, whether he believes it or not.

I don't know if he gets credited for my stuff, but I am frequently blamed for his. People have a tendency to confuse us because we both write cerebral stories in which scientific ideas are more important than action.

Many a young woman has said to me, "Oh, Dr. Asimov, I don't think your 'Childhood's End' was up to your usual standard." I always answer, "Well, dear, that's why I wrote it under a pseudonym."

Childhood's End, by the way, was the first science fiction book my dear wife, Janet, read. *I Robot* by her future husband, was only second. But neither of us wins top place in her literary affections. Her favorite science fiction writer is Cliff Simak, and I think that shows good taste.

Arthur and I share similar views on science fiction, on science, on social questions, and on politics. I have never had occasion to disagree with him on any of these things, which is a credit to his clear-thinking intelligence.

There are, of course, some differences between us. He is bald, is over two years older than I, and is not nearly as good-looking. But he's pretty darned good for second-best.

From the start Arthur was interested in science fiction and in the more imaginative aspects of science. He was an early devotee of rocketry and, in 1944, was the first to suggest, in a serious scientific paper, the use of communications satellites.

He turned to the writing of science fiction, and his first published story in an American magazine was *Loophole* in the April 1946 *ASF.* He was instantly successful.

Arthur cheerfully admits that when he was a schoolboy he was called "Ego" by his mates. However, he is an incredibly bright person who writes fiction and nonfiction with equal ease. Despite his ego, he is an extremely lovable person and I've never heard a bad word seriously advanced against him, although I have said lots of bad words against him unseriously—and vice versa. He and I have the same mock-insult relationship that I have with Lester del Rey and with Harlan Ellison. I find that women are often perturbed by our banter. They don't seem to understand male bonding in which the remark "Howdy, you ornery ole hoss thief" translates into "How are you, my dear and charming friend?"

Well, Arthur and I do the same, but, of course, in formal English to which we endeavor to introduce a soupçon of wit. Thus, when a plane crashed and roughly half the passengers survived, it turned out that one of the survivors had kept calm during the perilous attempts to land by reading an Arthur C. Clarke novel and this was reported in a news article.

Arthur, as is his wont, promptly xeroxed five million copies of the article and sent one to everyone he knew or ever heard of. I got one of them, and at the bottom of the copy he sent to me, he wrote in his handwriting, "What a pity he didn't read one of your novels. He would have slept through the whole wretched ordeal."

It was the work of a moment to send Arthur a letter which said, "On the contrary, the reason he was reading your novel was that if the plane did crash, death would come as a blessed release."

I suspect that Arthur is one of the wealthiest of the magazine science fiction writers, for he has written a number of best-sellers and been involved with several motion pictures, including the first of the big science fiction movie spectaculars, *2001: A Space Odyssey*.

He was once briefly married, but ever since he has lived a comfortable bachelor life. At one time, he was an ardent scuba diver and, indeed, almost got killed on one of his dives.

49

More Family

Back to the postwar world: when my job misadventures had brought me to the ranks of the unemployed, and my literary endeavors were brilliant but moneyless, there was a certain coolness between my parents and me. For a while, Gertrude and I lived on the first floor of the same two-story house in which my parents lived. It was not a comfortable arrangement, and I hated to be within reach of the candy store. Consequently, when Gertrude and I were told, in 1948, that an apartment was available for us in a new and modern development called Stuyvesant Town, we moved to Manhattan. My parents took it hard, however, and were quite angry with me. Naturally, it didn't last.

Even if my father had known and if he had dismissed me, with a heavy heart, as a failure, after all the promise I had shown, he had a second string to his bow, my younger brother, Stanley. (In adult life, he preferred to shorten his name to Stan, and I'll follow him in this.)

Stan was born on July 25, 1929, the first member of our family to be born in the United States. My mother's pregnancy and the need to care for the new infant were what made it necessary for me to take up my duties in the candy store. In addition, I had to spend part of my time taking care of Stan, feeding him his bottle and wheeling him about in the carriage. As a result of all this, Stan seemed to me to be *my* baby rather than my mother's and to this day I confuse Stan and my real son, David, tending to call each by the other's name.

Stan was a good kid. He never talked back to our parents and always did as he was told. He was a great relief to our parents after me (with my sharp tongue) and Marcia (with her self-willed attitude). It has always been a mystery to me that between Stan and me, I, who gave my mother infinite trouble, was always her favorite, when Stan gave her no trouble at all.

Of course, women, according to tradition in romances, always go for the charming rascal and ignore the poor fellow of solid worth, but I don't think that was the answer in this case. I was the older son, the first child, and when I was two years old, I nearly died of pneumonia in an epidemic that swept through the children of our village and of which I was the only survivor, my mother says. What's more, I survived only because of my mother's frantic and assiduous nursing, day and night, she going without sleep and almost without food, and this (she believed) had saved me. Of course, I was doubly and triply precious to her after that. Still, in all fairness, Stan should have been her favorite—or anyone's.

When I left home for Philadelphia, Stan took over my duties in the store. He was not quite thirteen at the time, but I had no qualms about that. I was only nine when I started, and Stan was stronger than I had been (being better nourished as a child, I suppose, in the United States than I was in Russia) and more deft. He could ride a bicycle, for instance, from the moment he got on one, while I have never mastered the trick to this day.

Stan did well in school. He went to Brooklyn Technical High School, then to New York University, and finally to the Columbia School of Journalism.

In 1949, the year when things were looking blackest for me, Stan was in college. I visited my father, who confided in me that he was having trouble raising the tuition. Well, things might not be going well for me, but I wasn't penniless and I didn't want my father scrabbling for dough and I didn't want Stan's schooling to be interfered with.

So I said, "That's all right, Pappa. I'll pay the tuition."

Whereupon my father stiffened and said, "God forbid the day should ever come when I would have to go to my children for money."

And he clung to that and paid the tuition himself.

A couple of weeks ago, when I was thinking of this section of this book, I dredged up that memory and told it to Janet and grew indignant.

"My father made it sound," I said, "as though I were the kind of wicked son who would begrudge him the money, or would make him feel that he had to come to me hat in hand. On the contrary. I would willingly have paid and considered it totally inadequate compensation for all he did for me. Why couldn't he understand that?"

And Janet said, "But, Isaac, you're just the same yourself. Would you take money from your children?"

I frowned and said, "That's *different*. I have my pride."

Whereupon she went into gales of laughter and ordered me to put the story into the book. I said, "Why?"

She said, "Your readers will know why."

When Stan was in school, he had engaged in extracurricular activities. (Either the candy-store duties had grown lighter or Stan was more adventurous than I was.) He got involved in the school newspapers, and by the time he was finishing college, he was co-editor of the college paper. He had found his vocation and was going to be a journalist. Eventually, he joined the staff of *Newsday*, a newspaper based in Long Island, and worked his way up through the ranks to become the much-loved vice president in charge of editorial administration.

Stan is a good man in the old-fashioned sense of the word—honest, ethical, kind, reliable. Stan once said of me that I was industrious, efficient, puritanical, and absorbed in my work, so that I had all the unlovable virtues. Well, Stan has all the lovable virtues and, in point of fact, everyone loves him. Even his brother does (and the love is reciprocated). I used to say, jokingly, that I might be the brilliant brother, but he's the good brother—and this may not be entirely a joke.

Here's what is to me the key example of his goodness. Considering his last name, he is in constant danger of losing his identity. People without number will say to him when he is introduced, "Are you a relative of Isaac Asimov?" He stays good-natured under the onslaught and says, patiently, "Yes, he's my brother." He does not allow it to poison our relationship, for which I am infinitely grateful to him. If the situation were the other way around, I would hate it, and it would be a source of trouble between us. But that's the point. *He's* the good brother.

In the 1950s, he met a sweetly gorgeous divorcée, Ruth, whom he at once decided to marry (even though her first question to him when they were introduced was whether he was related to me). They did marry and have lived in perfect accord ever since.

They have a son, Eric, and a daughter, Nanette, both of whom have followed their father's example and become journalists. (Ruth also has a son, Daniel, by her previous marriage, and Stan has adopted him, so that he is Daniel Asimov. He is a mathematician.)

It is, perhaps, a measure of Stan's success as a father that his children were willing to follow in his footsteps. I sigh sometimes when I think that my own children have not followed in my footsteps, but that's silly of me. Why should they?

My daughter, Robyn, when she was twelve years old, wrote a small story all on her own initiative and brought it to me to read. I was astonished. It seemed to me that it was a better piece of work than I would have managed at that age.

I said, "Robyn, if you feel like writing, please go on and do so. I'll help you if I can and, when the time comes, I'll try to open doors for you."

Robyn said, "Oh, no. I don't want to live like you."

"What do you mean?" I asked.

"Work. Work. Work. I won't do it."

I said, "Writers don't have to work, work, work. That's just the way I do it. You could write only when you wanted to."

"No," she said. "I won't take the chance." And she never did.

Well, maybe it's for the best. Years later when she was trying to write a memo at her job, she scratched out and revised and scratched out and revised, just as everyone always does. And finally, she threw down her pen and exclaimed to the world in general, "Would you believe I'm my father's daughter?"

50
First Novel

Yet the same year, 1949, which saw me at my nadir also witnessed the turnaround, though it was not terribly obvious and I did not see myself as passing through the bottom and beginning the climb. It involved a science fiction *novel* rather than a magazine story.

Actually, science fiction first became prominent through novels. Science fiction in the modern sense began, in my opinion, with the French writer Jules Verne. Writing in the second half of the nineteenth century, he was the first writer whose major output was recognizable science fiction and who made a good living out of it. His books, particularly *From the Earth to the Moon* (1865), *Twenty Thousand Leagues Under the Sea* (1870), and *Around the World in Eighty Days* (1873), were enormously popular all over the world. Verne was the one science fiction writer my father had read—in Russian translation, of course.

Other science fiction writers, less well-known, followed, and in the 1890s the British writer Herbert George Wells became popular with his *The Time Machine* (1895) and *The War of the Worlds* (1898).

Still other science fiction books followed, for the most part by British writers, such as Aldous Huxley's *Brave New World* (1932), Olaf Stapledon's *Odd John* (1935), and George Orwell's *1984* (1948). On a somewhat lower level, the American writer Edgar Rice Burroughs wrote a popular series of books set on Mars, the first being *A Princess of Mars* (1917).

The coming of the science fiction magazines, presenting science fiction of an admitted low grade, tended to swamp the science fiction novel, however. After all, the novels were relatively few and far between and the magazines poured off the presses every month.

In general, science fiction readers of the 1930s and 1940s tended to consider *only* the magazines and to ignore totally the occasional literary novels. There would have been excitement if some of the magazine stories had appeared in book form or if original novels by recognized magazine science fiction writers had appeared. This, however, did not happen. Some very small-scale amateur publishers, run by science fiction fans, did put out magazine science fiction in book form, but the productions were poor, the printings were small, and the distribution virtually nonexistent.

In the days after World War II, things changed. Science fiction suddenly became more respectable. First there was the nuclear bomb; then there were the German rockets, which raised hopes for the possibility of space flight, then the electronic computer. All these things were staples of science fiction and all these things had become reality in the immediate postwar period.

Doubleday & Company, a major publishing firm, therefore decided, in 1949, to put out a line of science fiction novels, and for this they had to have manuscripts.

As it happened, I had written a 40,000-word novella in 1947 that I could not sell anywhere—my worst literary failure up to that time. I had put it in a drawer and tried to forget about it. I, of course, did not know that Doubleday was planning to put out a line of science fiction novels, but Fred Pohl did, and he urged me to submit the novella to them. "If they like it," he said, "you can rewrite it to suit their needs."

I let him have the manuscript and that initiated a three-year period during which he acted as my agent.

Walter I. Bradbury, the editor at Doubleday who was to be in charge of the new line, did see possibilities in the story and he asked me to expand it to 70,000 words. Later, he also gave me a check for $750, the first time in my life I had been paid for a piece of writing I had not yet done—with the promise of more when it was completed.

I got to work with lightning speed, and on May 29, 1949, Bradbury phoned to tell me that Doubleday would accept and publish the novel, which, later on, I called *Pebble in the Sky*.

I had sold my first novel, which marked an enormous advance in my literary career (though I did not quite realize it at the time). The only trouble was that I was suddenly faced with an *embarras de richesse*. Not only had I made a literary leap but I also had a job.

Let me explain how that came about.

51
New Job at Last

I suppose that any writer, even one who has written very little, must get an occasional letter from a reader.

I rather suspect that science fiction writers are particularly bombarded by such letters. For one thing, I think science fiction readers are more articulate and opinionated than are other types of readers. For another, the letters column in the science fiction magazines encouraged such letter writing.

I loved the fan letters and tried to answer them all, and continued to do so for many years. As the number of letters increased, along with the number of my commitments, the time came when I had to grow selective, something that has never ceased to bother me. I cannot help but feel that anyone who takes the trouble to write to me deserves an answer, but time and strength are limited, unfortunately.

Nor were the letters all merely from enthusiastic youngsters. Some of the letters came from weighty members of society. Thus, during my doctoral and postdoctoral years I was getting a number of letters from William C. Boyd, a professor of immunochemistry at the Boston University School of Medicine. He had been very impressed by my story "Nightfall" and had been a fan of mine ever since.

I was very impressed by *him*. The correspondence between us flourished, and when he came to New York every once in a while, he would find occasion to spend time with me.

Naturally, in the course of our friendship, I told him of my job troubles and he wrote to tell me that there was an opening in the biochemistry department at his school in Boston and that he was willing to recommend me for the job.

I desperately did not want to leave New York a second time, but I even more desperately needed a job. I had already been following leads out of town, even traveling to Baltimore with a fellow-student job seeker, looking for a position that would involve working on plant chemicals. My fellow student got the job (he knew something about botany) and I (knowing nothing about botany) did not.

I felt I had to investigate the new opportunity, and, with sinking heart, I took the train to Boston and walked into the office of Burnham S. Walker, head of the biochemistry department. I wasn't impressed with the Boston University School of Medicine. It was small and seemed ramshackle. It was located in a slum area too.

However, Walker seemed pleasant and the offer was that of an instructorship that would make me a member of an academic faculty. The salary attached would be $5,500 a year.

What bothered me, however, was that I wouldn't be working directly for the school. I would be working for Henry M. Lemon, a completely humorless individual, whom I was introduced to, and with whom I felt instantly uneasy. What's more, I would be paid out of a grant, which meant I would have to live from year to year.

I went home in a sad quandary, and as unhappy as I had been when I faced induction into the army. —But what was the use? I needed a job and no other was being offered to me. I therefore accepted the post at BUSM.

And then, just a few weeks after I accepted the position, I sold that first novel to Doubleday. Instantly, I was tempted to seize upon that as an excuse to stay in New York. With the sale of the novel, I could count on some money and be able to stretch out additional time to find a job in the New York area. In fact, if the novel did well, I might not need a job at all.

It was a temptation. I have heard often of young writers who sell a book, or sometimes just a magazine story, and at once give up their jobs to devote themselves to writing. And usually the tale goes on to tell of how they do not succeed in selling another item and must then try to get their jobs back or find others.

I was sure of selling other things, of course, but I knew that I would not get enough money to support myself and a wife. Nor could I be sure that the novel would do anything for me. All I had gotten out of it, in total, was a $750 advance, and if it didn't sell I might never see another penny. (If I had sold it to *ASF* I would have gotten $1,400 for it.)

Furthermore, I had accepted the position in Boston, and if I now decided not to go there, I would, in a sense, be breaking my word, and I have a peculiar horror of doing that. So, much against my will, I went to Boston at the end of May, sorrowing, and took an equally unhappy Gertrude with me. We had been married almost seven years and there was no sign yet of the diamonds she was going to wear.

This is one of the places where we can play the jolly but useless game of "what if?"

What if I had not been offered the job in Boston? What if I had sold the book a few weeks earlier, *before* I had committed myself to Boston. In either case, I might well have remained in New York, gambling that the $750 and the prestige of a book would give me time to find a job closer to home.

How can anyone tell what would have happened? My tendency is to look on the matter constructively and optimistically. In the end, I remained in active service at BUSM for nine years. In those nine years, I taught and lectured and branched out literarily in ways I might not have done otherwise. What's more, I gained the cachet of the professorial title which established my bona fides as a science writer.

Painful as the move was, then, it broadened my horizons and I am convinced it made me a better and more successful writer than I would otherwise have been, so it was important I go to Boston.

And besides, doing so meant that I kept my word.

52

Doubleday

Pebble in the Sky was published on January 19, 1950, less than three weeks after my thirtieth birthday. I have remained with Doubleday ever since in perfect happiness. They have, as of this moment of writing, published 111 of my books, and on January 16, 1990 they seized the opportunity of celebrating both my seventieth birthday and the fortieth anniversary of the publication of *Pebble in the Sky*. A large cocktail party was planned for the restaurant Tavern on the Green and hundreds of people were invited.

Came the day and I was hospitalized. But I could not disappoint all those people, so that afternoon I quietly sneaked out of the hospital. Janet pushed me in a wheelchair and my faithful internist, Dr. Paul R. Esserman, came along. The party went off very well, although I had to receive everyone in my wheelchair and make a speech from it as well. Then I sneaked back into the hospital, in the fond hope that no one had noticed my disappearance.

Fat chance! It was an amused item in The New York *Times* the next morning and *everyone* knew. The nurses lectured me. Lester del Rey phoned me and called me names because he said I had risked my life. When I called Los Angeles on business, the first words of the young woman who answered me were: "Oh, you naughty boy—"

Three days later there was the sixtieth anniversary of *ASF* and I had been slated to give a talk, and that time I did not dare try to get out, so I had to miss it. That was one of the times I was very sorry for myself. I felt as though I had betrayed John Campbell.

People have often asked me why I stayed with Doubleday all these decades. The general feeling seems to be that once a writer becomes famous and a "hot property," he should shop about among publishers, letting himself be bid for, and taking the highest offer. In this way, he becomes richer and richer—but I can't do that. Doubleday has been good to me and there is no way in which I can return evil for good. I have made a fetish of gratitude and loyalty all my life and I've never regretted the possible loss of money because of it. I would rather lose money than feel like an ingrate.

I am told, "Well, of course, they treat you well, Isaac. Why shouldn't they when you make so much money for them?"

People who say that miss the whole point. I have to explain that when I submitted my first story and no one at Doubleday could possibly have known whether it would do well or not, or whether I would ever write another, they were very good to me *then*.

The agent for goodness was my first Doubleday editor, Walter I. Bradbury (whom everyone called "Brad"). He was of middle height, just a shade plump, and looked very much (in my eyes) like the British actor Leo Genn. He was kind and gentle and he had a paternal, non-condescending air toward me that made me comfortable at a time when I was most uncertain of myself. He advised me gently on my writing, helped me read my first set of galleys, was always willing to talk to me on the phone, even once when I called him at home in agitation over something or other and his child was ailing. He still spoke to me kindly and without haste. He was the third man, after Campbell and Dawson, to help me in my career for no other reason, apparently, than out of goodness of heart.

But I'll have to repeat a story in order to give you the full flavor of the man. Another publisher offered me a $2,000 advance for paperback rights to one of my early novels, *The Currents of Space* (Doubleday, 1952). I was delighted, for the sum was a monstrously large one to me at the time. I said that Doubleday controlled the rights but that they would do what I said.

I then phoned Bradbury to give him the news, and when there was a silence at the other end, my heart sank. I said, "Did I do something wrong?"

Brad said, "Well, Bantam has just offered $3,000."

I was silent and Brad said, kindly, "Did you commit yourself, Isaac?"

I said, "Well, I said Doubleday controlled the rights but yes, I did commit myself."

"In that case, we'll take the $2,000."

I said, "Doubleday needn't lose by it, Brad. Your half of $3,000 would have been $1,500. You can take that $1,500 out of the $2,000. I'll be satisfied with the remaining $500."

"Don't be silly," said Brad. "We'll split half and half."

In other words, Brad (and Doubleday) were willing to give up $500 merely to save my word of honor. It may not have been a large sum to them but that didn't matter. My word means everything to me and to have Doubleday respect that meant that thereafter wild horses couldn't have made me break faith with them, and I never did. (Of course, I also never again tried negotiating on a publisher's behalf.)

Money has, for a long time, ceased being an issue with me. I have enough. There are other things I want more and the chief of these is the gift of being able to write what I want to write in the way I want to write it, and do it with the comfortable certainty that it would be published. This Doubleday made possible for me quite early on.

Thus when I brought in an enormous manuscript for *Asimov's Annotated Gilbert & Sullivan* (Doubleday, 1988) without even warning them I was doing it, they published it without a murmur. They couldn't possibly have anticipated doing better than breaking even on it, but they insisted on giving me a larger advance than I felt the book would be able to support. I said so strenuously, but they wouldn't listen. They always give me larger advances than is safe, but somehow they always manage to make it back. (I don't mean to be unfair to my other publishers. Quite a few are now ready to oblige me in any reasonable way, but Doubleday did it first and on the largest scale.)

I am a friendly person and I make friends of all my editors and publishers, simply because I can't help it. Unless I am ill, or in a rage, or consumed by worry (all of which hardly ever happens), I am all smiles and jocularity and friendliness. And because I am, and because I never make trouble or get "prima-donnish," my editors and publishers seem to like me, treating me as a friend. That also makes it difficult for me to walk away from Doubleday—how would I explain it to all my friends there?

To tell you the truth. I like it. I like friendship and informality in my business relationships. (It may be bad business, but that's the way I do it.)

Thus, I once had lunch with about a dozen members of the Doubleday editorial staff, and the conversation turned on the iniquity of writers. (Had the lunchers been a group of writers, the conversation would have turned on the iniquity of editors and publishers, I'm sure —but I have never allowed myself this type of confrontational attitude.) In any case, at this luncheon, one editor said, passionately, "The only good writer is a dead writer," and I laughed. No one at the table seemed aware of my presence. I was so firmly a member of the Doubleday family that they simply did not think of me as a writer.

My attitude toward editors was, of course, strongly influenced by my early dealings with John Campbell. He was totally atypical of the breed, though I did not know that at the time. In the first place, he was a fixture. He remained editor of *ASF* for thirty-three years and there was never any question of replacing him. Only death removed him.

Naturally, I thought that all editors were godlike, dominating fixtures, and it came as quite a shock to me when I found that editors frequently jumped from company to company.

Thus, I lost Brad when he moved on to another company, and I was devastated. (He eventually returned to Doubleday.) Naturally, I was assigned another editor, and when he vanished, I received still another, and so on. Altogether I have had about nine editors at Doubleday, every last one of them a delight.

Thus, Timothy Seldes succeeded Brad as my editor. He was tall, thin, and had a craggy face that was quite attractive and that seemed always to wear a half smile. He always affected gruffness and would address me as "Asimov" with a growl, but that didn't fool me at all. In fact, he was so friendly I would bait him. Having carefully gotten him to admit that Gilbert Seldes, the writer, was his father, George Seldes, the writer, was his uncle, and Marian Seldes, the actress, was his sister, I said, with wide-eyed innocence, "How does it feel, Tim, to be the only member of the family without talent?"

I was just getting even with him for introducing me to one distressing fact. He and I were having lunch, and when I came to the heavy door of the restaurant, I forced it open and held it for him to pass through. (I knew my place.) Timothy seized the door, however, and motioned me through.

I protested, "You're the editor, Tim. You go first."

"Not on your life," said Tim. "My mother taught me I must always be respectful to my elders."

And it was borne in on me that I was indeed older than he was. The infant prodigy was now older than his editor. (At the present moment, he is older than the Pope and the President of the United States and he is two and a half times older than his present Doubleday editor.)

My friendship with editors and my joy at dealing with them made it difficult for me to get an agent. When I started writing, of course, I had never even heard of agents. I dealt directly with Campbell because I couldn't imagine any intermediary. Then, when I *did* hear of agents, it seemed to me it was unreasonable for me to give them 10 percent of my earnings when I was selling every story I was writing without them. (I had never heard of dickering for better terms, of subsidiary sales, and so on, which an agent could handle and I could not.)

Of course, after Fred Pohl helped me sell my first novel I had no choice but to accept him as my agent. He ran the Dirk Wylie Literary Agency, named for another Futurian, who had, like Cyril Kornbluth, died young, and for three years he handled my novels. Fred was a very good agent, just as he was very good at whatever he turned his hand to, but the Dirk Wylie Literary Agency did not do well for some reason and in 1953 he gave it up. This created a problem for me and, for a time, relations between us were cool, but that blew over and we were eventually more friendly toward each other than ever.

Since then, in any case, I have had no literary agent, except for a couple of individual projects in which I couldn't avoid one. I prefer it that way. I like to make my own sales, and have the publisher take care of the subsidiary sales. It saves me trouble.

As a matter of fact, I have no help of any kind, no secretary, no typist, no manager. I am a one-man operation, working alone in my office, answering my own phone and my own mail.

This surprises people too, but it is not really puzzling. My workload has increased so gradually that at no time was there the sudden jump that would have made me look for help. The situation is something like that described in the ancient Greek legend of Milo of Crotona, a celebrated weight lifter. He is supposed to have lifted a newborn calf and then continued to lift it each day as it grew until he was lifting a full-grown bull.

I have rationalized the situation to my own satisfaction. If I had employees, I would have to have an office and I like working out of my apartment. Then too, if I had employees, I would have to give them instructions, keep an eye on them, go over what they did, point out their errors, grow exasperated, and so on. It would all slow me down and make me miserable.

I prefer my life as it is.

53

Gnome Press

Doubleday did not publish *everything* I wrote in those early years. This became evident after it occurred to me that it was not absolutely necessary for me to write a new novel each year. Why could I not take advantage of work I already had done?

For instance, in 1950, I had given up the Foundation series. I had worked on it for eight years and written eight stories, totaling some 200,000 words altogether, and I had grown tired of them and wanted to pass on to other things. However, the stories still existed and it seemed to me they might be worth republishing.

So I took the carbons of the stories (which were not in the best of shape, since I had never thought them worth anything) and showed them to Brad. He studied them and then turned them down, explaining that he wanted new novels, not old ones. (This was a huge mistake on Doubleday's part, and even though it was eventually corrected, it meant a loss of eleven years of earnings both for them and for me.)

Once I had moved to Boston, I took the manuscripts to the Boston publishing firm of Little, Brown, and they turned it down also.

There was, however, another publishing firm in the field. I mentioned earlier that there were semipro publishing firms run by science fiction fans. One of these, perhaps the last and best, was Gnome Press, run by a young man named Martin Greenberg. (In later life, I worked with a wonderful man named Martin Harry Greenberg. It is important to remember that these are two different people.)

Martin Greenberg of Gnome Press was a glib young man with a mustache, quite charming, as glib young men often are, but, as I found out in the end, not entirely trustworthy.

However, he seemed willing to publish collections of my old stories and that rather glorified him in my eyes. I put together nine of my robot stories—eight that had appeared in *ASF* and the first one, which I now restored to its original title of "Robbie." He published it toward the end of 1950 under the name of *I, Robot,* a name that Martin himself had suggested. I pointed out that there was a well-known short story of that name by Eando Binder, but Martin shrugged that off.

He then published the Foundation series in three volumes, which came out in successive years—*Foundation* (1951), *Foundation and Empire* (1952), and *Second Foundation* (1953). I wrote a special introductory section to the first book in order to introduce the saga in more specific terms, so that the very first part of the very first book was actually the last portion written.

Gnome Press also published books by Robert Heinlein, Hal Clement, Clifford Simak, L. Sprague de Camp, Robert Howard, and others. Virtually all the books Martin published, including mine, have since been recognized as great classics of science fiction, and it boggles the mind that Martin had them all.

However, he could not exploit them properly. He had no capital, could not advertise, had no distribution facilities, no contacts with bookstores, and the result was that he didn't sell many copies.

In addition, Martin had a peculiarity. He had an unalterable aversion to paying out royalties and, in point of fact, never did. At least, he never paid me. The royalties could never have been very high, but, however small they were, he wouldn't pay.

He always had excuses, enormous excuses. His partner was sick. His accountant was dying. He had been caught in a tornado. I suggested that I was willing to wait for the money but couldn't I at least get a statement of sales and earnings so I could keep track of what he owed me? But no, that too seemed to be against his religion.

Yet he had the unmitigated gall to complain when I gave him no further books. He had received four books that Doubleday foolishly didn't want, but I certainly wasn't going to give him any that Doubleday *did* want, and Doubleday by now wanted all of them.

So when Martin complained, I simply said, "Where are my royalties, Martin?" and that shut him up.

In 1961, Tim Seldes handed me a letter from a Portuguese publisher who imagined that Doubleday was the publisher of the Foundation books. He offered to do a Portuguese edition of them. I looked at the letter, shrugged my shoulders, and said, "It's no use. Gnome Press doesn't pay royalties."

"What?" said Tim indignantly. "In that case, let's get the books away from him." He sent the corporation lawyers after Martin.

Martin had the nerve to set conditions too profitable to himself, and Tim wanted to fight, but I said, in alarm, "No, Tim, give him whatever he wants and take it out of my royalties. We've just got to have those books."

That was good advice, and Tim did as I asked, but never took the money out of my royalties.

Other authors also wormed their stories out of Martin's grip, and he was forced out of business. What happened to him afterward, I do not know.

Now, *if* Martin had kept reasonable books and paid the miserable royalties we had earned, none of the writers would have been able to withdraw their books. As each writer's *other* books became increasingly famous and popular, the demand for the Gnome Press books would have increased and Greenberg might have become prosperous and made Gnome Press an important science fiction publishing house. He chose a different path, however.

Once Doubleday had *I, Robot* and the Foundation books, they began to earn money at a surprising rate and Martin never got a penny of it.

Yet though I resented the situation at the time and had hard feelings against Martin, time has shown me that, as in so many other cases, though a person didn't mean to do me good, he succeeded in doing so.

After all, whether Martin paid me or not, he produced those four books when Doubleday would not. They *existed* and remained alive until it was time for Doubleday to take the Gnome Press caterpillar and turn it into a butterfly.

54

Boston University School of Medicine

Moving to Boston meant making a new set of friends and acquaintances.

Burnham Walker, head of the department, was forty-nine years old when I arrived. He was a quiet, noncommunicative New Englander, who was extremely bright and who, in his quiet way, did not seem to mind my boisterousness. I liked him and I must admit that he made my life at the medical school tolerable for me.

William Boyd, forty-seven years old when I arrived, had been instrumental in getting me the job. He was a shambling bear of a man, who struck me as one who labored under a deep disappointment. He had gone to Harvard University, where J. Robert Oppenheimer had been one of his classmates. Bill could not keep up with him, of course (nor would I have been able to), and that, I think, upset him.

He was kindness itself to me, as was his wife, Lyle. I was frequently at their house, and met their friends. That did more than anything else to make me feel at home in the new city. When he accepted a job in Alexandria, Egypt, where he was going to join the civil service at a much higher salary than he commanded in Boston, he offered to take me along. I shuddered and refused. Not only would I not go to Africa, but I warned him about the civil service and told him what it would be like. (Of course, I was influenced by the fact that I very much didn't want him to go. He was my most effective friend in Boston and his departure would leave me alone in a strange world.)

Boyd went off on September 1, 1950, three months after I had come to Boston, but soon returned to Boston and to his old job. He confided to me that everything I had warned him about the civil service was precisely accurate and that he wished he had listened to me.

Henry M. Lemon, the person I worked for, seemed to take an instant dislike to me, and perhaps he was not entirely unjustified in this. On the occasion of our first meeting on the top floor of the hospital, he pointed out the window and talked of the beauties of the "Boston skyline," which was not something to make a point of when talking to a Manhattan resident.

I was not happy to be in Boston in the first place, and I looked out at an endless sea of two-story brick houses, and thought achingly of my home canyons, and said grumpily, "Who's interested in the Boston skyline?"

It was a stupid thing to say and our relationship went downhill from there. He was dedicated to his work on the relationship of cancer to nucleic acids (actually a very fruitful line of investigation, which, unfortunately, neither he nor I had the capacity to exploit properly) and I was not. I was increasingly dedicated to my writing. He wanted me to attend all sorts of scientific conferences, and I did attend some, but what I wanted to do was to go to New York periodically and see my publishers. Increasingly the relationship became one of mutual hatred.

One good friend appeared outside the school. At Bill Boyd's house, I met Fred L. Whipple, an astronomer at Harvard University. He was forty-three when I met him, a courtly, good-natured person who won his way into my heart almost instantaneously. This is one non-science-fiction friendship that has endured. Like Sprague de Camp, Fred does not change in appearance. He's now in his eighties, still slim, lithe, active, and rides his bicycle to work. He is the very model of agelessness. We call each other without fail on our respective birthdays.

But, of course, I was not at the medical school to cultivate friendships. I was expected to work. In addition to doing research for Lemon, I had to lecture on biochemistry to the freshman class in the medical school. It was rather a thankless task. Medical students want to get their hands on stethoscopes and patients at once, and to have to spend their time listening to lectures as though they were still in college must have been exasperating.

I found ways of avoiding the research. There were lab assistants and graduate students and as far as possible I let them do the research, while I supervised the results. (They were better than I was at handling equipment anyway.) What I wanted to do was to escape from research altogether. In my heart I was through with it; I had made the wrong turning.

However, the job was not all bad. I enjoyed being a professor (I was promoted to professorial rank as an assistant professor of biochemistry in 1951), and lecturing was simply made for me. The various members of the department divided up the lectures, each taking the subjects he felt most comfortable with. I (with a trace of my old arrogance) said that I would wait till everybody had made his choice and then I would take whatever was left. The result was that I ended up with the more chemical lectures, eleven of them.

These, given in the spring of 1950, were the first significant lectures I gave since the seminar in graduate school three years earlier. Like the seminar, they were given to a captive audience—students who had no choice but to attend and listen. This, you can well imagine, is not the recipe for an enthusiastic audience.

In addition, these lectures, like the seminar lecture, had to be carefully prepared. I never went to the length of writing them out, let alone memorizing them, but I had to have a pretty good notion what I was going to say and there had to be a lot of formula writing on the blackboard that I couldn't afford to get confused over.

As my research continued to decline, my lectures continued to improve. By the time my active period at the medical school was drawing to its end, I was generally recognized as the best lecturer in the school. The account reached me, in fact, of two faculty members talking in one of the corridors. The distant sound of laughter and applause reached them, and one said, "What's that?"

The other replied, "It's probably Asimov lecturing."

My utter failure at research didn't bother me in the least, considering my excellence at lecturing. I reasoned it out this way. The prime function of a medical school is to teach medical students to be doctors and one important way of doing this is through lectures. Not only was I capable of informing and educating the class with my lectures but I roused their enthusiasm as well.

The proof of that was their reaction to my lectures. It was customary to applaud each professor at the conclusion of his final lecture of the course. It was, of course, applause that was halfhearted and perfunctory, the product of custom rather than of conviction. I alone would get applause in mid-course lectures, and real applause too. And while that took place, I felt invulnerable.

How wrong I was! I had left one factor out of my calculations. Lecturing helps only the students. Research, on the other hand, means government grants, and a portion of the grants is invariably marked for "overhead," which goes to the school. What it amounts to is that the school chooses research over lecturing every time—money for itself over education for its students. That meant I was not invulnerable at all, but rather a sitting duck once my research vanished altogether, which it did.

You might argue that the school was correct in choosing itself over the students, since if the school were forced to curtail its facilities through lack of funds, the students would suffer. On the other hand, surely one could strike a balance. A superior teacher might be forgiven failure at research. That, however, as I shall explain later, was not to be.

55
Scientific Papers

An important, even the most important, function of a researcher was to write papers on the work he was doing and get them published in some appropriate learned journal. Each such paper was a "publication," and a scientist's hopes for promotion and prestige rested on the quality and number of his publications.

Unfortunately, the quality of a publication is a hard thing to estimate, while the number is very easy to determine. The tendency arose, then, to judge by number alone, and this provoked scientists into writing a great many publications with somewhat less regard for quality than is quite becoming.

Publications appeared that had just barely enough additional data to qualify as a new item. Some publications were broken into fragments, each fragment published separately. Some publications were signed by everyone who had had anything to do with the work, in however tangential a manner, since it would then count as a publication for each named author. Some senior scientists insisted on putting their names on every paper produced by their department, even if they had had nothing to do with the work at all.

I never got into this game, nor did I plan to. In the first place, I hardly ever produced any data that was worth publishing. In the second, I didn't like the writing style required for such papers and didn't want to expose myself to it. And in the third place, I had no hope whatever of achieving any renown in research, and I had no intention of engaging in a useless struggle for it.

I was not totally lacking in papers. My Ph.D. thesis counted as one and a condensed version of it was published in *The Journal of the American Chemical Society*. In the course of my years of research, I also added my name as senior scientist to perhaps a half dozen papers written by various assistants and students in the department. (In those cases, however, I at least supervised the research, read the papers, and did a little polishing.)

That was everything, and it was absolutely pitiful in both number and significance. As far as I know, not a single research paper to which my name was attached ever proved of the slightest importance, was ever cited by anyone else, or ever led to anything of any great moment.

An idea, however, occurred to me. *The Journal of Chemical Education* was a good and useful journal that published articles that would be of interest to chemistry students at the college level. It seemed to me that it would be interesting to write such essays and have them published. They would be fun to do and they would count as publications. I did about half a dozen of these in the early 1950s and they were all published.

One of these turned out to be important, actually, for I pointed out the particular danger of the isotope carbon 14 as a generator of deleterious mutations in the human body. The reason this was important was that Linus Pauling later made the same point in a very detailed and convincing manner (and may conceivably have been spurred on by my own strictly speculative suggestion). The testing of nuclear bombs aboveground added carbon 14 to the atmosphere, and that meant a disproportionate increase in birth defects and in cancer. This was a factor in leading to the outlawing of such atmospheric tests, and it pleases me to think that my paper might have contributed its microscopic bit to this desirable event.

The addition of these short papers to my list, however, turned out to be totally nonsignificant. They did not, after all, involve research. They did, on the other hand, as I shall explain in due course, lead to something much more important than merely supplying me with numbers.

But the scientific papers I produced did not represent the only learned writing to engage me during my teaching years.

In 1951, Bill Boyd determined to write a textbook on biochemistry for medical students. It occurred to him further that he could use my writing expertise and so he suggested it to me as a joint project.

As usual, when I am presented with a new project like that, my mind goes into a whirlwind of pros and cons. Against the idea was the fact that I didn't feel I knew enough about biochemistry to write a text and (although I may be wronging the man) I didn't feel that Boyd did either. For it, however, was the fact that it was a challenge. Far beyond that was this: working on the textbook would give me a chance to drop research on the grounds that another important scholarly task preoccupied me.

The pros had it and I agreed to join Boyd, provided that Professor Walker, the department head, gave his permission and agreed to protect me against the entirely just wrath of Dr. Lemon.

We got rather more than we bargained for, for Walker insisted on joining the project. This was good on three counts. It would reduce my share of the work from one-half to one-third; Walker could supply the biochemistry expertise that Boyd and I lacked; and, finally, if he himself were part of the project, he would *have to* protect me.

Actually, doing the text was not as much fun as I had expected it to be. The writing styles of the three authors were so different that we were forever arguing over what we each wrote. I almost never got my way, so that the book was the usual stilted and turgid text. It finally came out as *Biochemistry and Human Metabolism* (Williams & Wilkins, 1952). A second (revised) edition appeared in 1954, and a third in 1957. Although the work was enormous, the financial return was nonexistent. All three editions were complete and utter flops since other, far better texts appeared in the 1950s. After the third edition, therefore, I let the book die a much-deserved death.

I would consider the book to have been an incredible waste of time and effort, but everything has its uses. It gave me a great deal of practice in writing nonfiction and, more important still, it taught me that writing nonfiction (when I was not being interfered with by co-authors) was easier and, in some ways, more interesting than writing fiction. This strongly influenced the later course of my writing career.

One final point must be made about *Biochemistry*. It was only my eighth book (and my first nonfiction book, which is a point in its favor where I am concerned) and it had not yet occurred to me that the actual number of my books was a matter of concern or interest.

Consequently, the second and third editions, although each required more work than the average fiction book, were not added to my list as separate books. Later in my career I always considered a substantially revised book to be a new book on the basis of the work it required. This failure to count the two later editions means that if I should feel myself to be unable to work further and if I knew it meant that I would end with, say, 498 books, I would be annoyed at having not counted those two editions and having in that way deprived myself of the full count of 500.

However, this is an incredibly trivial point which can seem important to me, but, I'm sure, can only amuse others.

56

Novels

Despite all this bother about research, scientific papers, and textbooks, the chief labors that involved me during my teaching years remained the writing of science fiction. Even before *Pebble in the Sky* was published, Walter Bradbury asked me to do another novel. I did and sent in two sample chapters. The trouble was that now that I was a published writer, I tried to be literary, as I had in that never-to-be-forgotten writing class in high school. Not nearly as badly, of course, but badly enough. Brad gently sent those two chapters back and put me on the right track.

"Do you know," he said, "how Hemingway would say, 'The sun rose the next morning'?"

"No," I said, anxiously (I had never read Hemingway). "How would he say it, Brad?"

Brad said, "He would say, 'The sun rose the next morning.' "

That was enough. It was the best literary lesson I ever had and it took just ten seconds. I did my second novel, which was *The Stars, Like Dust—*, writing it plainly, and Brad took it. This is the list of my Doubleday novels in the 1950s:

> *Pebble in the Sky,* 1950
> *The Stars, Like Dust—,* 1951
> *The Currents of Space,* 1952
> *The Caves of Steel,* 1954

The End of Eternity, 1955
The Naked Sun, 1957

Of these six novels, the first three made up what were eventually to be lumped together as "the Empire novels." *The Caves of Steel* and *The Naked Sun* were the first two of my "robot novels," which introduced the detective team of Elijah Baley and R. Daneel Olivaw. (Daneel was a humaniform robot and possibly the most popular character in all my writings.) As for *The End of Eternity*, that was an independent novel with no connections.

In addition to this, Brad asked me in 1951 to write a short science fiction novel for youngsters, one that could be adapted to the television scene. It was to be about a Space Ranger and was to be for television what the Lone Ranger had been for radio. No one quite understood the new medium, and it was taken for granted that programs on TV would be as long-lived as those on radio had been. It seemed that, if it worked out, a Space Ranger character would serve as a long-term annuity for both Doubleday and me. (Of course, we didn't know how few programs would run for even one season, let alone for twenty, but we also didn't know about reruns.)

I was less than enthusiastic. I feared that television would ruin any stories of mine they used and that my literary reputation would suffer. Brad had the answer. "Use a pseudonym."

At the time I was a great Cornell Woolrich fan, and I knew he had adopted William Irish as a pseudonym. I thought I would use a nationality too, and so I used the name of Paul French. It was a terrible mistake. Of course, nothing happened as far as television adaptation was concerned. Another program, *Rocky Jones, Space Ranger*, beat us to it and was just as terrible as I feared television would make such things. And besides this, people took to saying that "Isaac Asimov writes science fiction under the name of Paul French," as though I were trying to protect my respectable persona as a scientist by hiding the fact that I was also writing cheap thrillers. You have no idea how that bothered me.

In any case, I was relieved that television left us alone, and since my first juvenile did fairly well simply as a book, I did five others before stopping. I began by calling my hero David Starr. Something more glamorous was asked for, so I substituted his nickname and made him Lucky Starr. I began by having him a semi-mystical Space Ranger with a mask of radiation, but I dropped that quickly and instead made use of elements associated with my stories—such as positronic robots. I wanted to make no secret of my authorship and in later editions I insisted on having my name on it to bury the hated Paul French forever.

Here are my six Lucky Starr books:

> *David Starr: Space Ranger,* 1952
> *Lucky Starr and the Pirates of the Asteroids,* 1953
> *Lucky Starr and the Oceans of Venus,* 1954
> *Lucky Starr and the Big Sun of Mercury,* 1956
> *Lucky Starr and the Moons of Jupiter,* 1957
> *Lucky Starr and the Rings of Saturn,* 1958

Writing the novels, whether adult or juvenile, did not keep me from writing shorter pieces for the magazines. My own favorite among all my magazine stories, "The Last Question," appeared in 1956, and my third favorite, "The Ugly Little Boy," appeared (under the horrible title of "Last-Born") in 1958. (My second favorite was not written till the 1970s and I'll get to it later on.)

By this time, Doubleday no longer objected to collections of my shorter pieces, and in the 1950s they published three such collections:

> *The Martian Way and Other Stories,* 1955
> *Earth Is Room Enough,* 1957
> *Nine Tomorrows,* 1959

Add to these the four Gnome Press books, *I, Robot* and the three Foundation novels, which Doubleday was soon to take over, and it turns out that during the 1950s I wrote 32 books, of which 19, all science fiction, were Doubleday's. The remaining books were not.

What startled me most from almost the very start of the 1950s was the effect of these books on my income. For the eleven years in which I had been writing exclusively for the magazines, I was accustomed to single payments and then nothing (except for tiny sums for anthologization—something I'll come to later).

Books, however, earned royalties and *continued* to earn royalties. Not only did the books continue to sell for a few years but there was a constant drizzle of subsidiary rights—second serial, paperback, foreign. By the time *The Stars, Like Dust*— was published and began earning royalties, I was still getting some money for *Pebble in the Sky*. By the time my third novel began earning royalties, there was still money coming in from the first two, and so on. As a matter of fact, since *Pebble* was published I have received eighty semiannual statements from Doubleday, and *Pebble* has earned a respectable amount of money on every one without exception.

The result was that my royalty statements from Doubleday tended to climb steadily (as they did from other publishing houses too, but less steeply). In no time at all, I realized that I *could* make a living writing. In fact, by 1958 (a crucial year at the school), I was making three times as much money from my writing as I did from the school. You can well imagine that that increased my feeling of independence.

It also gave me something to think about. Had I gambled on the first book, broken my word to the medical school, and stayed in New York, I now realized, I would indeed have been able to support myself by writing alone. I had had no need of a job. (In fact, I never again had the need of a job.)

By the middle 1950s, I was wondering if I ought not to quit my job and return to New York. Prudence still won the day. What if Doubleday for some reason abandoned its science fiction line? What if I suddenly got writer's block? I felt the psychological need, if not the financial need, of a secure base, of a salary, even a small one, that was not subject to the insecure fluctuations of writing. (Besides, I still didn't want to give up my lecturing or my professorial title.)

However, I felt strong enough to threaten to resign if I was not taken out of Lemon's clutches and put on a salary paid out by the school. I had my way, and that meant that I could put an end altogether to my research, and that my school income was independent of the vicissitudes of grants.

57

Nonfiction

All the time I was at the medical school, I wrote my science fiction evenings, weekends, and holidays. I *never* wrote science fiction during school hours, however pressing my deadlines, for that would have been unethical. I wasn't being paid for writing science fiction.

I was, however, paid for scholarly activities, and it struck me that when I wasn't teaching, I could do either research or scientific writing. Either would redound to the benefit of the school. That was the reasoning that made it possible for me to work on the two textbooks on school time without any pangs of conscience.

But what could I do when I was neither teaching nor working on the texts? I didn't *want* to do research. I wanted to *write* and that meant nonfiction. I felt free to do so once I had gotten out from under Lemon (who had been livid, and with some justification, over my work on the textbook).

The question was: *What* could I write?

The idea that occurred to me was to write the type of article I wrote for *The Journal of Chemical Education,* but to make it longer, more informal, more *jovial,* if I may use the term, and yet keep it strictly scientific. Thus, I had written a brief article for *The Journal of Chemical Education* on the number of different ways a protein molecule could be built out of hundreds of different amino acids of twenty different types. (The number of ways is more than astronomical. It is inconceivable.)

I proceeded to write another article on the subject, much longer and more informal, and called it "Hemoglobin and the Universe." My intention was to sell it to *ASF,* which printed science articles that were imaginative enough to appeal to science fiction readers. Campbell took it and it appeared in the February 1955 issue of the magazine.

"Hemoglobin and the Universe" was the first science essay I wrote and published for which I received payment. I discovered, to my surprise, that writing such an article took less time, was easier, and was much more fun to boot than writing a science fiction piece of equal length. (And I didn't have to plot anything. The material was factual.) It opened the floodgates, for from then on, I was eager to write essays on science or, occasionally, on nonscientific topics, and, indeed, by the present time I have written, quite literally, thousands of such pieces.

A peculiar advantage to writing nonfiction was this: When I was working on fiction, I could deal with only one story or novel at a time. To try to write two of them simultaneously would surely lead to a confusion of characters and events. Nonfiction pieces, however, were sharply different. If I were writing on vitamins in one essay and on stellar evolution in the other, there was no chance of confusing the two. I discovered I could work on many nonfiction pieces at once, switching from one to the other as it suited my convenience.

Nor were essays the only form of nonfiction that I could write.

Boyd, who had stumbled me into the textbook disaster, now made up for it. A small publisher wanted him to write a book for teenagers on biochemistry. Boyd didn't feel up to it, and suggested that I do it instead. I accepted eagerly. I *wanted* to write for youngsters and had actually made stabs at this sort of thing, but had aimed too high and had not been able to persuade Little, Brown to publish such a book.

Now I *had* a publisher and I realized that I was going to write it at the level of the bright junior high school youngster. I produced a book called *The Chemicals of Life*, published by Abelard-Schuman in 1954.

It was the first nonfiction book I published for the general public and it too opened the floodgates, for I wrote many more books of this type thereafter. Although my novels take me seven to nine months to write, *The Chemicals of Life* took me only six weeks. I could only ask myself, "Hey, how long has this been going on."

During the 1950s, I wrote eight such books for Abelard-Schuman. They were:

> *The Chemicals of Life*, 1954 (biochemistry)
> *Races and People*, 1955 (genetics)

Inside the Atom, 1956 (nuclear physics)
Building Blocks of the Universe, 1957 (chemistry)
Only a Trillion, 1957 (science essays)
The World of Carbon, 1958 (organic chemistry)
The World of Nitrogen, 1958 (organic chemistry)
The Clock We Live On, 1959 (astronomy)

As you see, I was beginning to exercise my range.

58

Children

Despite the fact that the 1950s seemed filled with medical school affairs, textbooks, popular science books, and enormous quantities of science fiction, I still had a private life, a marriage, and even (to my astonishment) children.

I might as well be frank and explain that I don't like children. When I was quite young, my mother got the idea into her head somehow that I loved babies and children. Perhaps she thought she was subtly training me to supply her with grandchildren someday. In any case, whenever a customer brought a child under five into the candy store, my mother would ululate, "Oh, Isaac loves children," and I would be pushed forward in order to be visibly gratified.

It was a terrible ordeal for me. One glance gives me all I want to know about a baby. Additional glances are unprofitable. If the children are old enough to be freely mobile, I am anxious to keep my distance. Such children are overactive, overnoisy, and invariably undercontrolled. They are also likely to have sticky fingers and unsettled stomachs. I want to have nothing to do with them.

It is not surprising, then, that when I married I had no specific plans for having children. Nor did Gertrude. We might very well have settled down to a childless existence, and why not? The greatest single problem facing humanity today is the multiplicity of people. No environmental problem can possibly be solved till the population is stabilized and brought under control. Under these circumstances, it would seem that any young couple who were indifferent to children and showed no disposition to add to Earth's burden ought to be encouraged and made much of.

The truth, however, is quite the contrary. The world would not let us be childless. People who met us invariably asked if we had children, and when we said we didn't, they would look at us with disapproval or with sorrow. Our fellow young marrieds, one by one, had children and then would talk of nothing else but the joys of parenthood. (In my more cynical moments, I wondered if they were so appalled by the expense, the work, and the responsibility of parenthood that they were infuriated at our having escaped it, and therefore did their best to inveigle us into the trap.)

Since we were only human, we were not proof against the propaganda and the pressure, and we began to try for children. For some years, we failed, and, apparently, with good cause. Gertrude's periods were radically irregular, and when I visited the doctor, it turned out I had a low sperm count. We could still have children, but the chances for doing so were less than normal.

As a result, we resigned ourselves (without too much difficulty) to continuing to lead child-free lives. I bought a primitive recording device so that I could dictate my stories, with the thought that Gertrude would then type them up and we could, in this way, have a collaborative career.

I often wonder what would have happened if that had indeed come to pass. Would we have grown closer? Would the marriage have been a happier one? There's no way of telling, for we had no chance to try it out. I had dictated three stories, which she typed up (all of them sold; all of them were successful), and then, as you can probably guess, she became pregnant, and the possibility of a child-free, collaborative career vanished.

It took a doctor's test to convince us that Gertrude was pregnant and even after that we went about in a kind of daze of disbelief until Gertrude began to display obvious physical signs of the condition.

And, in the due course of time, I found myself the amazed and not entirely gratified father of a son, David.

59
David

David was born on August 20, 1951. It was a difficult delivery and he weighed less than six pounds. (I think it is a well-established fact that the children of smoking mothers, especially if they smoke during pregnancy, which Gertrude certainly did, tend to be underweight at birth.)

It early became apparent that David could not play with other children on a give-and-take basis and could not make friends. As he grew older, we found that school was an unhappy period for him because he tended to be scapegoated. Still later in life, it appeared he could not keep a job because he could not get along with his fellow employees.

All this I accepted with a certain resignation, for I recognized the condition. I had been exactly like that. In fact, even at the time David was a child and I was teaching at the medical school, I couldn't get along with people, so that my job was constantly at risk.

What David didn't have, however, was my quick intelligence. He was perfectly normal in mental capacity, you understand, and not retarded in any way. (We didn't take chances. We had him tested neurologically and consulted psychiatrists.) But normality is not enough when one is socially inept. I got away with my ineptness only through my display of brilliance and even so I barely made it.

Mind you, he is a good and loving person, ordinarily gentle and understanding. He does have a tendency to become mulish when crossed (so do I) and does not display good judgment at such times.

When he was still in his teens, it was apparent to me that he was not going to be able to support himself in mature life and so I took measures to take care of him by setting up a trust fund for him, so that he is free of economic worries.

David's great hobby is to tape the television shows he likes and to build up an enormous library of such things. It seems to me to be rather a lonely life, but, like me, he seems to enjoy being alone and being thrust on his own resources. He doesn't smoke, drink, take drugs, or present me with any problem other than that of supporting him, which is no trouble, and (if not exactly a pleasure) is my duty.

People sometimes assume that since I have a son and since I am so remarkable a person myself, my son must be remarkable as well. They ask me what he does, expecting me to say he is a nuclear physicist at the very least. My answer is invariably that he is a "gentleman of leisure." If they inquire further, I tell them frankly that I support him and that he lives a quiet and blameless life.

If they act as though they seem to think I should be disappointed, I tell them (sometimes masking a little irritation) that my son lives his own life and doesn't have to labor to cast glory on me. I can manufacture my own glory. My only wish for my son is that he be happy and I labor to make that possible. When I speak to him on the telephone, he always sounds happy, and I would rather have a happy gentleman of leisure as a son than a possibly unhappy nuclear physicist.

60

Robyn

I must admit that although I don't like children, I find little girls far more tolerable than little boys. When Gertrude had David, I took it almost for granted that he would be my only child. After all, we had had so much trouble producing one child, it seemed unlikely that we would find it within ourselves to produce another, especially since by David's birth Gertrude was thirty-four years old.

I had therefore hoped earnestly for a girl but I didn't neglect David because he was a boy (I wouldn't have dreamed of that). In fact, I remember that he was a bottle-fed baby, and since Gertrude was a sound sleeper and I was not, it was I who wakened each night at the slightest infant cry, and it was I who routinely warmed the bottle and fed him his formula in the small hours.

And, in 1954, to another bout of amazement, Gertrude was pregnant again and on February 19, 1955, had a girl we named Robyn Joan. The "y" in Robyn was at my insistence, for I didn't want people to think she was a boy, and Joan was added as a very plain alternative in case when she grew up she decided she disliked Robyn. Fortunately, she did not. She took to Robyn as I had taken to Isaac, and any other name for her is inconceivable.

Robyn didn't cry much; she was good-natured; she toilet-trained quickly; and in all ways she was satisfactory, except that she did have the habit of (once in a while) drinking her formula and then quietly giving it back to me all over my shirt.

Most of all, she grew into a beautiful, blond-haired, blue-eyed child. At seven, she looked precisely like the John Tenniel illustrations of Alice in *Alice in Wonderland*. This was so marked that when she walked into a new class at school, the teacher took one look at her and asked her to play Alice in the class play.

I was delighted and could never hug and kiss her enough and tell her how beautiful she was. Gertrude objected (thinking perhaps of her own childhood) and said I shouldn't do that. "What if she grows up to be a plain woman?" she said.

I said stoutly, "She won't. And even if she does, she'll be beautiful in my eyes, and I want her always to know that."

And, as it happened, she grew up to be extraordinarily beautiful in anyone's eyes. She is five feet two inches tall, her mother's height, and still has blond hair, though her eyes have darkened. More important than beautiful, she is a sweet girl, softhearted and loving, who returns her father's affection in full.

On the negative side, she does have a sharp tongue (I can't imagine where she gets it from) and I have to be careful with her, for she is perfectly capable of slashing me with a phrase. For instance, I liked to wear loud bow ties in the 1960s and Robyn had grown to be very conservative with respect to my clothing (not her own) and objected. One time, I rebelled and put on a tie with bright orange stripes and walked into the kitchen, where she was sitting, making every attempt to be brave about it.

She took one look at me, and said, "Very effective, Dad. Now if you'll only paint your nose red—"

Also, it took her some years to adapt herself to my sense of humor. (She succeeded eventually and we enjoy ourselves enormously because we understand each other. "I've spent my whole life laughing," she once said to a friend.)

The difference in Robyn's appearance from that of either parent is so great (though blondness exists in my family) that more than one person has asked me if it was possible that there had been a mix-up in the hospital. To which my response is always to seize Robyn, squeeze the breath out of her, and say, "If so, it's too late. I'm keeping this one."

Robyn was born to have friends and get along with people. I used to say that if she curled up like a bowling ball and if I rolled her through a crowd of strangers, she would come through at the other end with five friends stuck to her. This social instinct has made her life relatively easy. Robyn has had two long-term relationships with young men I would refer to, dryly, as my "sins-in-law," but as of this writing she is still single.

I have made it plain to her that she can have children if she wishes but she doesn't need to feel impelled to have a child she doesn't want just to give me a grandchild.

I have frequently expressed my absolute horror at the growing overpopulation of the earth, and Robyn shares my feelings. Neither of us feels that it will do humanity much good to bring additional children into the world merely because it is the thing to do. Therefore, Robyn feels no compulsion to have children, or I to have grandchildren.

Robyn attended Boston College, where she majored in psychology, then went on to get her master's degree in social work at Boston University.

Robyn enjoys her last name, by the way. It pleases her to have people ask if she is related to me and she apparently takes pride in announcing that I am her father. It warms the cockles of my heart.

However, once when I mentioned the warm affection she had for me, the woman I was speaking to said (perhaps a little cynically), "Look, if you have a well-off father who dotes on you, what's not to love?"

That bothered me a bit, but I am close enough to Robyn to be able to ask her difficult questions and rely on a truthful answer. I said to her, therefore, "Robyn, would you love me if I were poor?"

She answered without hesitation. "Of course. You'd still be crazy, wouldn't you?"

And that satisfied me. It was clear that she valued spending her life laughing and considered that more important than any money I might have.

61
Off the Cuff

By the summer of 1950, I had given a number of successful talks, but always to a professional audience and always well prepared. But then I was asked to speak at a science fiction convention on the subject of robots. I agreed but balked at spending the time required to prepare the talk. It seemed to me that the subject was so familiar to me as to require no preparation.

Gertrude, who knew I hadn't prepared any talk, sat in the last row for fear that I would mess things up. She wanted to be in a position to escape quietly if I did.

I began to talk, and found that even without preparation, each sentence led naturally to another. A little to my surprise and a great deal to my pleasure, I discovered that the audience invariably laughed when I wanted them to laugh. Even more to my pleasure, I found that Gertrude had suddenly gained confidence and changed her seat to one in the front row.

This talk was another turning point, for I found I could speak easily and, as it eventually turned out, on any subject, and do so off the cuff and without preparation. From then on, except for my school lectures, I never prepared a talk. Never!

In one case, I wrote out a talk that was scheduled to be published, but in that case I delivered it without once looking at the written page. Generally, if it is important for a talk of mine to be published, they must tape it and then type it up from the tape.

Another turning point came not long afterward when I gave a talk to a PTA group in a southern suburb of Boston at the request of a fellow faculty member. To my surprise, I was paid $10 for it. I tried not to take it, feeling I couldn't accept money just for talking, but they insisted.

I grew more willing to charge for my labors as time went on and my speaking fees have steadily risen. Once I spoke at MIT for $100 and over dinner found out that they had paid Wernher von Braun $1,400 for a talk some weeks previously.

I asked, with a frown, "Was he fourteen times better than I was?"

"Oh, no," they answered artlessly. "You were much better."

That was the last time I offered to speak for as little as $100, you can well imagine. Eventually, I received as much as $20,000 for an hour's talk. This may seem exorbitant (it does to me), but the money is delivered with smiles and expressions of gratitude, and that goes far to soothe my overtender conscience.

Why? One reason is precisely that my talks are off the cuff. A speech that is carefully written in literary English, and is then read, is not delivered in *spoken* English (spoken English and written English are two different languages, believe it or not) and sounds unnatural. Besides, in reading it, the turning of the pages and the occasional stumbling over words adds an artificial note. Memorizing a speech may remove some of the artificiality, but it is hard work, and the result is still in unnatural written English.

If you speak off the cuff, however, you can speak colloquially, and you can easily shift moods and emotions to suit the reaction of the audience.

Continued success at anything tends to breed arrogance, if you are not careful, and every once in a while I am tripped into arrogance over my ability to give talks. Thus, I am frequently on a platform with two or three other speakers and, in such a case, I always suggest that I speak last. If anyone asks why, I answer truthfully (but with the sound of arrogance), "Because I am an impossible act to follow."

Usually, I go on to prove that, but every once in a while, a fellow who speaks before me is *so* good that I have to stretch myself to the limit to surpass him, and, every once in a long while, I wonder uneasily if I have been successful.

On one occasion, for instance, the speaker before me lectured on Kissinger and the doctrine of the balance of power. It was an important topic and was delivered with such smoothness and aplomb that my heart sank into the cellar. I would never surpass that. I *tried*, of course, but I felt that I had fallen short.

At the reception afterward, someone said to me, "I greatly enjoyed your excellent talk, Dr. Asimov."

Glumly, I answered, "I'm afraid that the talk on Kissinger was much better."

"Oh, no," said the other. "I heard him speak on Kissinger before and this was the same speech, word for word. I've heard you speak before too, but your talks are always different."

That's another point. If you go to all the trouble of memorizing a long and complicated speech, you can't waste it by using it on only one occasion. You must use it over and over again, and heaven help those who find themselves sitting through it a second time.

Off the cuff, on the other hand, allows infinite impromptu variations, and although I have undoubtedly given a couple of thousand talks in my lifetime, no two of them have ever been exactly alike.

Incidentally, such is the fame of my talks (thanks to word of mouth from gratified listeners) that I am forever being invited to give talks in every state of the Union, to say nothing of other countries (even as far away as Iran and Japan). My aversion to travel, however, allows me to talk only fairly close to home. If that were not so, I could make a good living out of talks alone, and see the world in addition.

But I'm not sorry. My vocation is writing, not talking.

There are any number of funny stories that involve my talks and I can't resist telling a few. Many involve the introductions I receive.

When someone gives a talk, it is incumbent on someone else to introduce him. There is a risk in this, for unless the introduction is short and matter-of-fact, there can be trouble. A long, dull introduction cools the audience. A witty introduction, long or short, casts the speaker into the shade.

On the whole, I would prefer no introduction at all. I would like to walk out onto an empty stage at the time my talk is slated to start, advance to the podium, and say, "Ladies and gentlemen, I am Isaac Asimov"—and then begin the talk. That is all the introduction I want and need but it has never yet happened. There is always someone who wants his moment in the sun.

In 1971, I spoke at Penn State University, where my science fiction friend Phil Klass was teaching. He was tabbed to introduce me and my heart sank. I remembered Phil's speeches at science fiction gatherings. He was a funny, funny man, so I hoped his introduction would be short and matter-of-fact.

It wasn't. Phil spoke brilliantly for fifteen long minutes, giving a ridiculously exaggerated description of my character and ability that had the audience convulsed. I sank lower and lower in my seat. He was speaking for nothing, and I was speaking for $1,000. He was delighting the audience and I would be a sorry anticlimax.

Finally, when I had begun to contemplate sure disaster, Phil came to his concluding sentence. "But don't let me give you the idea that Asimov can do anything. For instance, he never sang in *Rigoletto* at the Metropolitan Opera."

There was a loud burst of laughter and I leaned over toward Janet and muttered grimly (as Thomas Henry Huxley had once said regarding Samuel Wilberforce at the great evolution debate), "The Lord has delivered him into my hands."

I walked out on the stage to the podium, faced the audience, waited for the applause to die down, and then stood there for about fifteen seconds of silence. I stared solemnly at the audience and let them wonder what was going on.

And at the precise moment when puzzlement had mounted to the requisite pitch, I burst out, without warning, and in as ringing a tenor as I could manage: "Bella figlia dell'amore"—the opening bars of the famous Quartet from *Rigoletto,* and the very epitome of all operatic pieces.

The audience collapsed in delight and I had them in the palm of my hand. (A speaker has to know how to do these things.)

Another bit of snatching victory from the jaws of defeat came on March 21, 1958, when I spoke at Swarthmore College near Philadelphia. I arrived the night before and the president of the school warned me I would be speaking at the convocation at eight o'clock the next morning. Student attendance was compulsory at this one function and many students resented that.

"It may be," said the president, "that a number of students will ostentatiously read newspapers during your talk. This will not be to show any displeasure toward you personally, but only to register their disapproval of the convocation as an institution."

"Never fear," I said, with a wave of my hand, "no one will read a newspaper while *I* am speaking."

However, that night Philadelphia experienced the worst slush storm it had had in a hundred years. (This was the storm, by the way, that killed Cyril Kornbluth.) The slush stood two feet deep—wet, clinging, heavy slush that destroyed many gardens and damaged many trees.

I watched the students walking toward the convocation hall the next morning, struggling through the deep slush in boots, and thought in alarm that if they resisted convocation under ordinary conditions, how they were going to resent *this* one! I was going to have an ice-cold audience, figuratively as well as literally.

What to do? I seized upon the date and began my talk with "Gentlemen, I come to you on the day of the vernal equinox, when the storms and shocks of our winter of discontent have departed the scene, and the buds of spring tremble on the brink of appearance; when the harsh winds moderate into gentle sweetness—"

I kept at it, growing wilder and wilder in my encomiums, while keeping a look of holy rapture on my face, and the audience began to chuckle and then to guffaw. When I felt I had warmed them up sufficiently, I launched into my talk and no one read a newspaper.

Once I averted a much more serious catastrophe by sheer luck. I was speaking in Ohio in the 1960s for no more than $250 in order that I might get a plaque from some organization interested in communications. I was going to give them what I called my "Mendel talk," various versions of which I had given here and there with great success. It was about Gregor Mendel, who had discovered the laws of heredity, but, through a failure of communication, these laws remained unknown to science for thirty-three years.

Here I got another long and witty introduction, and I sat in the huge dining room waiting, with increasing depression, for the introducer to sit down, and aware of how I would have to stretch myself to avoid anticlimax. The fellow at my right whispered to me during the introduction, "We're all waiting eagerly for your speech, Dr. Asimov."

I felt depressed enough to reply, "How do you know I'll be any good?"

"Because I've heard you before at the Gordon Research Conference. You gave a talk on Mendel."

I sat bolt upright. "On Mendel? Was anyone else in this place present at the conference?"

"Almost all of us," he said.

I had five minutes to organize a different talk. I managed, but every time I think of how close I came to giving a talk to an audience that had already heard it in essence, I break into a cold sweat.

Another time the person introducing me asked permission to read from the correspondence that had preceded our agreement on terms. I didn't remember what I had said in those letters, but I knew I never wrote anything that was actionable, so I said, "Sure! Go ahead!"

He went on to read the letters, and it turned out that I had been adamant in demanding three times the fee he had offered on the ground that I was three times as good as anyone else. That meant I had to get up before an audience badly cooled down by the fact that I had gouged their organization out of lots of money, and prove to them that I was three times as good as anyone else. It was a hard job, but I succeeded.

The worst introduction I ever received was in Pittsburgh. It's the only one I look back on with anger rather than with amusement. I was on the platform waiting for the proceedings to begin and the self-important woman running the show stood in front of the podium, directing people to seats in a shrill, monotonous voice.

Finally, it was time to begin and she introduced me. I stepped to the podium, the applause started up—and may I die if she didn't step in front of me and wave the audience to silence in order that she might direct a few last-minute stragglers to their seats. I had a strong impulse to shove her off the platform, but I resisted.

I had to start the lecture to a cold audience and was too enraged to devise any tricks to warm them up again. The talk wasn't a flop, but it was far from a success. What a stupid woman!

One cannot speak often without developing a special clock inside oneself. When I lectured to the medical students, I routinely completed the last sentence as the closing bell rang. Of course, there was a big clock in the room that was in plain view, so I could pace myself. Even so, it was good practice and helped set the internal clock.

Routinely, before I speak, I say to the person in charge, "How long do you want me to speak?" If they give me a specific time of duration, that's what they get, plus a question-and-answer session. If they say, "As long as you please," they get forty-five minutes.

On May 18, 1977 (a date I remember for a reason I will explain later), I gave a commencement address at Ardmore College in suburban Philadelphia. Just before I got up, the president of the college leaned toward me and whispered, "Talk for about fifteen minutes."

"Sure," I said, got up, and cheerfully announced that I had been asked to talk for only fifteen minutes, so I wouldn't keep them long. (That put the audience in a good humor at once. They hadn't come to hear me. They had come to get their diplomas or to watch their young hopeful get one.)

After the talk, one of the graduates came to me and said that he had just happened to have a stopwatch in his pocket. He had clicked it on as soon as I mentioned the fifteen-minute limit.

"It took you fourteen minutes and thirty-six seconds," he said, "and I never saw you looking at your wristwatch. How did you do it?"

"Long practice, my boy," I said.

My brother, Stan, set me an even worse task later on, and left me in ignorance of it too. *Newsday* was inaugurating a weekly science section and, as a favor to Stan, I came down on September 13, 1984, to address an audience of potential advertisers on the importance of science.

"Speak for sixty minutes," said Stan.

So I did—for *exactly* sixty minutes.

Stan was jubilant. "I told them," he said, "that if I told you to speak for sixty minutes, you wouldn't speak for fifty-nine or sixty-one."

I was horrified. "Why didn't you warn me?"

"I had faith in you," said Stan.

I was quite annoyed. I'm good, but I'm not *that* good.

Incidentally, *Newsday* had offered me $4,000 for the talk months earlier, when it had all been arranged. For some reason, perhaps because I was doing it for Stan, I didn't record the matter and, as it happened, by the time I gave the talk I had altogether forgotten about the promised fee.

Weeks after the talk, *Newsday* called me and wanted my social security number.

"Why?" said I, suspiciously.

"So we can send you a check."

"For what?" I asked, and they had to explain.

"Oh," I said, unable to keep my mouth shut. "I thought I was doing it for nothing."

That evening I called Stan. "Stan," I said, "the paper wants to pay me for the talk and I forgot all about that. If they come to you and ask if they really have to pay me since I told them I was under the impression I was speaking without a fee, please say they must pay."

There was a short pause and then Stan said peevishly, "Why do you call me on Friday night to tell me this?"

I was surprised. "What does it matter when I tell you?"

"Because now," said Stan, "I have to wait till Monday morning before I can tell my latest stupid-brother-Isaac story."

But I digress—

Only twice, that I can remember, did I speak for substantially longer than sixty minutes. Once it was my fault and once it was the fault of the audience.

It was my fault on May 30, 1967, when I talked in downtown Boston. Gertrude was immobilized with rheumatoid arthritis, Robyn had a cast on her left leg because of a hairline fracture at her ankle, and David had just developed a fever—and I had to give a talk, the seventh of the month. I was so distraught I took a taxi downtown because I didn't think I could trust myself behind the wheel of my car. Once there, I actually accepted a drink instead of turning it down as I invariably do. I thought it might deaden the anxiety, but it didn't. I might as well have had a drink of ginger ale.

I then launched into my talk and *that* was my anodyne. All my troubles vanished, but I knew they would return when I was done. I was therefore reluctant to stop. The talk lasted an hour and a half before I could bring myself to a halt (and, of course, the anxiety immediately returned).

To explain the other case, I must tell you that I like the light on in the auditorium when I speak. I want to be aware of the audience. To talk into darkness makes me uneasy. Of course, being aware of my audience doesn't mean I have to look at them. That could be distracting, especially when a young woman in a miniskirt sits in the front row and crosses her legs. (This is so distracting that I dare not look at her, and I wonder if some of them don't do it just to be distracting.)

What I do, then, is *listen* to the audience. I hear the coughings, the stirring about, the sighing. It all tells me the state of those listening to me. It tells me when I ought to be funny, when I ought to be serious, when I ought to change the subject, and so on.

I can't tell you exactly which sounds go with which changes. I don't really know in any conscious way, but something inside me knows. I do know, though, what I listen for with particular relish. It is the sound of *silence*.

When all the rustling stops, and my voice rings out as the only sound in the room, then I know I've *got* them and must continue on the route I am taking. I have to tell you, though, that I achieve this ultimate only rarely.

Once I was speaking to a bunch of IBM people at King of Prussia, Pennsylvania, and I received the silence. Exultantly, I continued, waiting for the renewal of sound which might indicate I had better approach the end of the talk. (What I call my internal clock may be, at least in part, my unconscious reaction to audience sound.) But the silence continued and when I could bear it no longer, I looked at my watch and an hour and a half had passed. I stopped suddenly and said, rather helplessly, "I've been talking for an hour and a half."

"Keep going!" came the shout from the audience, and I did, but I gave them only five minutes more.

What every speaker wants is loud and prolonged applause, of course, and I received that almost every time. Better still is a "standing ovation." Applause by itself can be pretty automatic, but standing up takes an effort, and is something beyond applause. I *love* a standing ovation.

Once I discovered something even better than a standing ovation. I gave a talk at Carnegie Tech in Pittsburgh and it went so well and received such audience response that I considered a standing ovation a sure thing. However, when I finished, all I got was prolonged applause. Not one person stood up.

I tried to mask my disappointment, smiled, bowed, waved, and retreated into the wings to brood. The applause continued, however, and finally my introducer came to me and said, "They won't stop. Go out there."

I went out, grinning my face in two, and *took a second bow*. It was the only time that ever happened to me, but it is a treasured memory.

62

Horace Leonard Gold

In the 1940s, virtually all my stories were sold to *ASF*. That made me a little uneasy. It is rather risky to be a one-magazine, one-editor writer. What if Campbell decided to retire as editor, or died; what if the magazine failed? My writing career might then come to a sudden end. Who could tell whether I could sell to another editor or find another magazine outlet?

My fears were alleviated when I sold *Pebble in the Sky* to Doubleday. There, at least, was another, and very prestige-filled, market. Even more important in a way was the founding of two new magazines.

The Magazine of Fantasy and Science Fiction (*F&SF*) was not truly a market for me. It featured fantasy and literary writing and I was not very strong in either direction. The other magazine, *Galaxy*, was, however, strictly science fiction and with its very first issue it demonstrated that it was a serious contender for "best science fiction magazine." Campbell's absolute rule was shaken and was never to be restored to what it had been.

Galaxy asked me for a story and I wrote one called "Darwinian Poolroom." It appeared in the October 1950 issue, its very first. It was a very weak effort, but the magazine wanted more stories. In the second issue, a stronger story appeared, which I called "Green Patches," but the title was changed by the editor to "Misbegotten Missionary," which I disliked.

Then *Galaxy* serialized my novel *The Stars, Like Dust—*, which the editor retitled *Tyrann*, something I disliked even more. What's more, the editor made me insert a subplot that I disapproved of, and when I wanted to take it out prior to book publication, Brad decided he liked it and insisted that it stay. Because of this I have never liked the novel as much as I might have.

All this could not have happened at a better time, for in 1950 Campbell began to push the pseudoscience of "dianetics." I disapproved of that so strongly that I wished to distance myself from Campbell. I did not stop selling to him, but I welcomed the chance to sell to others.

The editor of *Galaxy,* the one who changed titles and insisted on lousy subplots, was Horace Leonard Gold (better known as H. L. Gold). He was almost as colorful a character as Campbell himself. He was as talkative and as opinionated as Campbell, and much more likely to be bad-tempered than the invariably sunny Campbell. Gold was not a bad-looking man even though he was almost as bald as a bowling ball.

Between 1934 and 1937, he had written a number of stories under the pseudonym of Clyde Crane Campbell (a case of masking a Jewish name). Once John Campbell became editor of *ASF,* the Campbell pseudonym was not tenable and Horace began writing under his own name.

He served in World War II, and while I don't know the details of what he suffered, it left him with a profound agoraphobia and xenophobia (a morbid fear of open spaces and of strange people). When I met him, he literally could not leave his apartment.

The first time I met him, we spoke in the living room of his apartment. I had no knowledge of his affliction, and he shocked me by suddenly rising and leaving the room. I thought I must have offended him somehow and I was utterly confused when his wife, Evelyn, assuring me I had not offended Horace, nevertheless asked me to leave.

I was just going out the door when the telephone rang and Evelyn, answering, said to me, "It's for you."

"Who knows I'm here?" I asked blankly.

But it was Horace. He couldn't stand the company of a stranger. So he went into the bedroom, made use of a second phone, and called me. We had a long conversation, he in the bedroom, I in the living room.

The fact that he had trouble speaking to people in person made him a terror on the telephone. Once on, never off, as I soon learned.

Speaking to Horace on the telephone was an exercise in making excuses to get off: "I'm sorry, Horace, but I must go. My house is on fire."

As nearly as I could make out, his one relaxation was a weekly poker game with his cronies. Since I don't play poker (or any other game of chance), I never attended.

Horace was, at least potentially, an extremely good editor, but he had a fatal flaw. He was bad-tempered, and as time passed, he seemed to grow steadily more irascible. He changed titles and made unnecessary editorial alterations in the story and grew nasty when writers objected. He also grew angry when one tried to get off the telephone after an hour or two.

Worst of all was his pernicious habit of writing insulting rejection letters. To some writers, like me, any rejection at all was unsettling even when the editor (mindful of writers' fragile egos) was careful to be polite about it. When one got a savage and destructive commentary on a story, the insult was extreme.

Thus, I had offered him a story called "Profession," the first story I wrote on an electric typewriter. He rejected it with vile references to my laziness and my "mental bloat" and implied that I thought I could sell any piece of junk just because my name was on it. (He then asked to see other stories that I would write to better effect.) The rejection rocked me. "Profession" might not be the best story in the world, but it was certainly not the terrible hunk of tripe Horace thought it was.

I took the story to Campbell, who accepted it at once. It ran in the July 1957 *ASF* and was very well received by the readers.

I had occasion some time afterward to write a comic poem entitled "Rejection Slips," with one verse for each of the three most important editors in science fiction. The second verse was meant for Horace. It goes:

> Dear Ike, I was prepared
> (And, boy, I really cared)
> To swallow almost anything you wrote.
> But, Ike, you're just plain shot,
> Your writing's gone to pot,
> There's nothing left but hack and mental bloat.
> Take back this piece of junk;
> It smelled; it reeked; it stunk;
> Just glancing through it once was deadly rough.

But, Ike, boy, by and by,
Just try another try.
I need some yarns and, kid, I love your stuff.

I was not the only one to suffer such indignities. Horace treated all his writers like that, and many, refusing to subject themselves to abuse, refused to send him any further stories. I myself was one of the "strikers," though I thought I was doing it all on my own.

Horace was reduced to such straits that he was forced to publish a letter in a fan magazine which he knew was read by many writers, asking for submissions, and promising to reject politely, if rejection was necessary.

I must, however, give the devil his due. I wrote a story about a Neanderthal boy who had been brought into the present and showed it to Gold. His criticisms (carefully couched in the politest of tones) struck me as so valid that I tore up the story and wrote a completely different one (the only time I ever did that). The result was "The Ugly Little Boy," which, as I said before, is number three on my list of my favorite stories.

Some time after this, Horace lost his job as editor and was replaced by Fred Pohl, who carried on in his usual capable manner.

63

Country Living

I'm a city boy, but occasionally the world forces me into the country. When I was quite little, my mother would go off for two weeks to the Catskills and take Marcia and me with her. This happened, I believe, in 1927, 1928, and 1931. This meant my father was left in the store and how he managed I don't know.

In 1941, for some reason, it fell into my head to go on my own to the same small place in the Catskills where my mother used to take me. I stayed a week—six days, actually, for I left a day early when Germany invaded the Soviet Union and I thought this might be the beginning of total Nazi victory.

In each case, I hated it and longed to get back to the city streets.

When I married Gertrude, we spent our week's honeymoon in the country, and thereafter we went off most summers, for one week or sometimes two, to someplace or other. I didn't hate this quite as much as when I was a child, but I didn't love it.

If we met some interesting people, it wouldn't be too bad, but you couldn't count on that. Failing that, I simply had nothing to do, except engage in the silly activities that were de rigueur. I particularly remember being expected to play volleyball.

Once I tried to spend my time writing a story, and turned out one called "Lennie," which eventually appeared in the January 1958 *Infinity*. However, Gertrude objected to my sitting indoors to write, so I took it outdoors and held the pages down with rocks.

Naturally, people asked what I was doing, and when I said that I was a writer and that I was writing a story, they grew extremely hostile. Apparently, one is not supposed to be happily at work on a vacation, one is supposed to suffer at volleyball.

Only once in my years with Gertrude did we go for a vacation in the country that I *really* enjoyed. This was in 1950, when we went to a place called Annisquam.

For a while I thought it was just another volleyball purgatory, but then I learned that the Annisquam staff was trying to prepare a comic musical as a presentation to the guests. For the purpose they were using the music of Cole Porter's *Kiss Me, Kate* and were trying to write appropriate funny words to fit the music.

However, none of them, I quickly discovered, had any notion of scansion, or rhyme, or how to fit words to existing notes.

I said to them, "Each note has to have a separate syllable. You have to make sure that the meter and the rhyming are exactly similar to Cole Porter's. You can't improve on it."

They stared at me blankly, and I said, "You're working on the song 'Wunderbar,' aren't you? Well, let me show you." (That was me, educating the ignorant without being asked—but I couldn't bear to listen to them mangling the songs.)

I thought a while, then asked for a piece of paper and wrote:

> Annisquam, Annisquam
> We've taken ocean trips
> But when the sea ain't calm
> Take the train to Annisquam.

They stared at the words in bemusement and I said, impatiently, "Well, sing it."

They did and were overwhelmed. The words fit the music exactly. "Do more," they said.

"You bet," I said, and for days and days and days I sat in the recreation hall with them and worked on the lyrics of song after song, and showed them how to sing them, and rehearsed them over and over, and, in the end, sang the lead role myself.

Gertrude was, predictably, furious. Apparently, we were spending a lot of money to be at the camp for a couple of weeks and I spent it indoors, *working* for the camp.

I tried to explain that it was money well spent considering that I was in seventh heaven working on the musical and that the alternative was a stint in purgatory playing volleyball. It was no use. She didn't understand.

Actually, the man who ran the camp gave me twenty dollars when I was leaving as payment for my help, but I didn't do it for money. I gave it to the staff and told them to divide it among themselves.

64
Automobile

As long as I lived in New York City, there was absolutely no need for an automobile. Thanks to the candy store, the family rarely went anywhere. Of course, I had to get to school, but the city was rich in public transportation facilities and you could get anywhere for a nickel (and then another nickel to return). And, of course, if you only had to go a mile or so, you walked.

In Philadelphia, public transportation facilities were also satisfactory. Besides, it was wartime and gasoline use was carefully restricted, so I was a passenger in a car pool.

Once I got to Boston, I found myself in a city in which rapid transit was less satisfactory, especially if you wanted to live in one of the suburbs. In 1950, I came to the conclusion that I would need a car. Aware of my lack of deftness, I despaired of ever learning to drive a car safely. My plan was to have Gertrude learn to drive and then have her chauffeur me.

I was, however, sport enough to be willing to take lessons, and as soon as I felt the car moving with myself at the controls, I found, to my utter astonishment, that I loved to drive. Having learned to drive, I bought a Plymouth.

The best advice I ever got in driving was from Sprague de Camp. I told him about driving to New York and boasted about the speed with which I drove and my utter confidence.

He said, "Goodbye, Isaac."

I said, in surprise, "Where are you going, Sprague?"

"I'm not going anywhere," he said, "but if you drive a car at speeds like that, you haven't got long to live, and so I'm saying, 'Goodbye.' "

I'm a quick learner, and I slowed down.

65

Fired!

My history, well into middle age, was marked by my inability to get along with my fellows and my superiors. Even as a professor at a medical school, I demonstrated this unlovely aspect of my personality for one last time.

Perhaps it was not all my fault. I suspect I was not popular with much of the faculty and perhaps couldn't be no matter how sweet I might try to be. Being the best lecturer in the place might please me and please the students, but it would not necessarily win me medals from the other lecturers.

Furthermore, it was impossible for me to hide the fact that I had an outside career and that I made money out of it. That was another reason for struggling faculty members not to love me. Nor was the range of my writing something to be approved of. I wrote *The Human Body* (Houghton Mifflin, 1963), a very good book (if I do say so myself) on anatomy. I asked one of the professors of anatomy to go over it to see if I had made some egregious errors. She found a few, the most important of which was that I had placed the spleen on the wrong side of the body, something she found very amusing.

As I left, I heard one of the anatomists say, "How would he like it if I wrote a book on biochemistry?"

Finally, I had completely abandoned any pretense of doing research and spent all my spare school time on the writing of nonfiction, which could not help but displease the administration.

I tried to make up for my outside income by never asking for a raise. (It would be ridiculous for me to scramble after a few more school dollars when my writing earnings were steadily increasing.) The result was that in 1958 I was earning only $6,500 a year, an additional thousand dollars having been given me over the course of nine years without my having asked for it. It was the lowest professorial salary in the medical school, and perhaps in all the university. This, which I considered, in my innocence, to be ethical behavior on my part, proved to be another point against me. To be paid so little was interpreted as meaning that that was all I deserved.

Worse than any of this, of course, was the offense I had given Henry Lemon in abandoning his research. He dedicated himself to the task of getting rid of me. I was reasonably safe, however, as long as James Faulkner was dean and Burnham Walker was department head. Both seemed to like me despite my peculiarities.

But then Dean Faulkner announced he would resign at the end of the 1954–55 school year. This was a terrible blow, for not only was the loss of a highly placed ally disastrous but he was likely to be replaced by Chester Keefer, perhaps the medical school's most renowned faculty member. Keefer was a close friend of Lemon's and I was sure that he would fire me.

Walker must have thought that too, for in May 1955, just a month before Faulkner left, Walker obtained a promotion to associate professor for me as of July 1, 1955. That automatically gave me tenure, so that I could not be fired without cause. I imagine he did that before Faulkner left because he knew there would be no chance thereafter. And to be sure, Keefer did succeed as dean of the medical school.

Keefer had a handle on me. In 1956, I had received a small government grant in order that I might write a book on the bloodstream. (It had been offered to me; I had in no way asked for it.) I wrote the book, and it was eventually published as *The Living River* (Abelard-Schuman, 1960). Keefer waited.

And then Walker resigned (for family reasons) as of November 1, 1956, and Bill Boyd became acting department head. Bill, I suppose, was hoping to be made the permanent head, but in the summer of 1957 Keefer brought in an outsider, F. Marrott Sinex, to be head of the department. Sinex was a short man with a perpetual nervous smile, a loud voice, a still louder laugh, and, as it turned out, was a rather difficult lecturer to follow. The word reached me that Sinex had gotten the job only after he agreed he would do nothing to keep me from being fired.

Keefer could now act. It had come time to collect the money that was assigned to me in the grant for the book on blood and Keefer refused to let me have it. He said the money had been given to the school. I pointed out that the school had received an overhead, but that a certain sum had been specifically allocated to me. He went on to sneer that any faculty member could write a book if paid to do so. I retorted angrily that I didn't need to be paid to write a book, that I had already done over twenty, and that if he didn't let me have my money, he could expect me to raise hell with Washington. He let me have it, and got ready for the more important task of firing me.

On December 18, 1957, I was called into Keefer's office for the final showdown. Sinex was there, but he did no talking. His role was merely to ratify. Keefer was quiet and simply said that he did not want me to write on school time. I had to do research. As he fully expected I would do, I refused, and pointed out that my duty was to teach medical students and that I was, by common consent, the best lecturer in the school. He insisted that the sole point was research and I finally grew angry enough to say:

"Dr. Keefer, as a science writer, I am extraordinary. I plan to be the best science writer in the world and I will shed luster on the medical school. As a researcher I am merely mediocre and, Dr. Keefer, if there's one thing this school does *not* need, it is one more merely mediocre researcher."

Keefer, I am sure, interpreted that as an insulting sneer at the medical school, and he was right to do so, because that was how I meant it. It put an end to everything. He said, "This school cannot afford to pay a science writer. Your appointment will come to an end as of June 30, 1958."

I was ready for that too. I said, "Very well, Dr. Keefer. You may refuse to pay me a salary." (With heroic self-control I refrained from telling him where he could put my salary.) "In return, I will do no teaching for the school. However, there is no way you can take away my title. I have tenure."

He claimed I didn't and I insisted I did and there followed a desultory two-year fight over the matter. Even though my stint at the medical school did come to an end on June 30, 1958, and even though after nine years I had been fired, I continued to come to school fairly regularly to pick up my mail and run other odd jobs, but mainly to maintain the franchise, to show that I was a member of the faculty and was not to be run off.

The rest of the faculty avoided me for fear that too close an association with the school leper might get them into trouble too. One of them, however, approached me cautiously once and, making sure we were not under observation, he told me that he was proud of me and of my bravery in continuing to fight for academic freedom.

I shrugged. "There's no bravery about it. I *have* academic freedom and I can give it to you in two words."

"What's that?" he asked.

"Outside income," I said.

It's true. The average faculty member is under an enormous disadvantage in a fight with the administration. He need not even be fired, he need merely be harassed, and he *must* start looking for a new position. They are not easy to find and generally, if he waits too long, he might find he *is* fired and, without a salary, he can be in deep financial trouble.

In my case, though, what did I care what the administration did? I was in no financial trouble at all.

After two years, it finally came to a vote by the faculty senate (or whatever the group was that had to approve the decision). They voted *against* Keefer, and I kept my title. I have it to this day. In fact, on October 18, 1979, I was promoted to full professor.

Looking back on it, I wonder: Why did I bother?

There were two reasons. First, I didn't want to give up my professorial title. I had struggled too long to get it, under sometimes adverse circumstances, and I wasn't going to give it up lightly.

Second, it was a mere matter of mulish pride. They were determined to kick me out, and I wasn't going to let them do it.

At the time, I was furious with Lemon and Keefer, but they unwittingly did me the greatest favor I ever received since the various medical schools turned me down twenty years earlier. Had they left me alone, my native caution would have kept me at the school and forced me to waste large parts of my time on matters of no importance. By getting me out, they compelled me to turn to full-time writing and that was an important turning point for me.

I'm sure that Lemon and Keefer had not the slightest intention of doing me good, but I can dismiss the intention for the sake of the result. I have therefore long since forgiven them.

In 1961, when one of my science books received particular acclaim, I was at a party at school. Keefer was also present and he held out his hand and congratulated me. I thought that was a classy thing to do, so I took his hand and thanked him in all sincerity. Lemon also congratulated me and I nodded and smiled, but that was the last time I ever saw him. Later that year, he left the school and joined the faculty of the University of Nebraska Medical School.

One postscript— In the spring of 1989, I traveled to Boston in order to participate in the sesquicentennial celebration of Boston University. I gave one of my talks on the future to a large audience of BU students, speaking with my customary élan, and in the question-and-answer period, one of the students said, "We've been hearing some very good speeches, Dr. Asimov, and since you are on the BU faculty, why aren't you lecturing to us regularly?"

And I said, "Forty years ago I was placed on the faculty and I gave lectures for nine years, about a hundred of them altogether, and they were the best lectures the students ever had, but"—a short pause of about two seconds to make sure they were listening—"I was fired."

There was a kind of collective gasp from the audience and I was gratified. During my fight with Keefer, I said to the assistant dean, Lamar Soutter (who was on my side), that if the school fired me, then people in the future would find that unbelievable. It had sounded like braggadocio, I suspect, but I knew it wasn't, and I was glad to get confirmation of it, even at that late date.

66
Prolificity

I must admit that I was a little nervous on July 1, 1958. There I was, thirty-eight years old (definitely middle-aged), with an unhappy wife, two children aged seven and three, and no job.

Things weren't all bad. We had bought a house in 1956 and paid off the mortgage almost at once, so that we owned it free and clear. I had a decent sum of money in the bank and now that we had been married for nearly sixteen years I could fulfill my promise and buy some diamonds (rather small ones, I must admit) for my first wife, Gertrude—but she didn't want them. And, of course, there was my writing, which was now bringing in, all by itself, somewhat in excess of $15,000 a year.

The trouble was psychological. From 1942 to 1945 and again from 1949 to 1958, I had had a job and a fixed salary. The salary wasn't high but it was something to fall back on and gave me the illusion of security. Now the question was: Could I write full-time without the security of a basic salary as fallback? Could I write full-time without my mind quickly wearing itself out and running dry? Would the basic problems of a writer's insecurity quickly overwhelm me?

Gertrude was quite sure it wouldn't work. She took to her bed for three days, leaving me to take care of the children. That did nothing to reassure me and alleviate my doubts.

In fact, I was sufficiently nervous to make a halfhearted attempt to find another academic post. I went to Brandeis University, which was quite close to home, and investigated the possibility of a place in the biology department. The head of the biology department was not interested in me, however, and I beat a quick retreat. This was the last time in my life I ever looked for a job.

The only thing I could do, then, was to throw myself into my writing chores with a real frenzy in order to get as much as I could out of my mind while it lasted.

As it turned out, I needn't have worried. In the years since I turned to writing full-time, I have averaged thirteen books a year (I'm my own book-of-the-month club). I am the most prolific American author on record apparently. Furthermore, whereas most really prolific writers tend to write almost entirely in one genre (mysteries or Westerns or romances), my books range over every division of the Dewey decimal system (according to one enthusiastic librarian). No one in history has written more books on more different subjects than I have. Please understand that I am so modest, it is embarrassing for me to say such a thing, but—I cannot tell a lie.

The question is: How does one become a really prolific writer?

It is a matter to which I have given much thought and it seems to me that the very first requirement is that a person have a passion for the process of writing. I don't mean that he must enjoy imagining he is writing a book or enjoy dreaming up plots. I don't mean that he must enjoy holding a finished book in his hands and waving it triumphantly at people. I mean he must have a passion for what goes on between the thinking of a book and its completion.

He must love the actual operation of writing, the scratching of a pen across a blank piece of paper, the pounding of typewriter keys, the watching of words appear on the word-processor screen. It doesn't matter what technique is used as long as he loves the process.

Mind you, the passion is not required just to be a writer; not even to be a great writer. There are many great writers who detest writing and who turn out a book once every ten years. The book may be a marvel of technique, and the writer may make himself immortal with it, but he cannot be a *prolific* writer, and I am talking only about prolific writers right now.

I have that passion. I would rather write than do anything else. In fact, some wise guy, knowing of my penchant for gallantry to young women, asked me during a question-and-answer session once, "If you had to choose between writing and women, Dr. Asimov, which would you choose?"

I answered instantly, "Well, I can type for twelve hours without getting tired."

People say to me sometimes, "How disciplined you must be to get to work at the typewriter every day."

I answer, "I'm not disciplined at all. If I were, I could make myself turn away from the typewriter now and then, but I'm such a lazy slob I can never manage it."

It's true. It doesn't take discipline for someone like Bing Crosby or Bob Hope to play golf all day long. It doesn't take discipline for Joe Six-Pack to snooze in his chair while watching television. And it doesn't take discipline for me to write.

And I am unseducible. The fact that it is a perfect day outside makes no impact on me. I have no desire to go out and get some healthful sunshine. In fact, a perfect day fills me with the nameless dread (usually fulfilled) that Robyn will come to me, clapping her little hands in excitement, and say, "Let's take a walk in the park. I want to go to the zoo."

Of course, I go, because I love her, but I tell you I leave my heart behind, stuck in the typewriter keys.

So you will understand when I tell you that my favorite kind of day (provided I don't have an unbreakable appointment that is going to force me out into it) is a cold, dreary, gusty, sleety day, when I can sit at my typewriter or word processor in peace and security.

Then, too, a compulsive writer must be always ready to write. Sprague de Camp once stated that anyone wishing to write must block out four hours of uninterrupted solitude, because it takes a long time to get started, and if you are interrupted, you would have to start all over again from the beginning.

Maybe so, but anyone who can't write unless he can count on four uninterrupted hours is not likely to be prolific. It is important to be able to begin writing at any time. If there are fifteen minutes in which I have nothing to do, that's enough to write a page or so. Nor do I have to sit around and waste long periods of time arranging my thoughts in order to write.

I was once asked by someone what I did in order to start writing.

I said, blankly, "What do you mean?"

"Well, do you do setting-up exercises first, or sharpen all your pencils, or do a crossword puzzle—you know, something to get yourself into the mood."

"Oh," I said, enlightened, "I see what you mean. Yes! Before I can possibly begin writing, it is always necessary for me to turn on my electric typewriter and to get close enough to it so that my fingers can reach the keys."

Why is this? What is the secret of the instant start?

For one thing, I don't write only when I'm writing. Whenever I'm away from my typewriter—eating, falling asleep, performing my ablutions—my mind keeps working. On occasion, I can hear bits of dialogue running through my thoughts, or passages of exposition. Usually, it deals with whatever I am writing or am about to write. Even when I don't hear the actual words, I know that my mind is working on it unconsciously.

That's why I'm always ready to write. Everything is, in a sense, already written. I can just sit down and type it all out, at up to a hundred words a minute, at my mind's dictation. Furthermore, I can be interrupted and it doesn't affect me. After the interruption, I simply return to the business at hand and continue typing under mental dictation.

It means, of course, that what enters your mind must stay in your mind. I always take that for granted, so that I never make notes. When Janet and I were first married, I would sometimes say, during a few wakeful moments at night, "I know what I ought to do in the novel."

She would say, anxiously, "Get up and write it down."

But I would say, "I don't have to," turn over, and let myself drift off to sleep.

And the next morning I would remember it, of course. Janet used to say that it drove her crazy at first but she got used to it.

The ordinary writer is bound to be assailed by insecurities as he writes. Is the sentence he has just created a sensible one? Is it expressed as well as it might be? Would it sound better if it were written differently? The ordinary writer is therefore always revising, always chopping and changing, always trying on different ways of expressing himself, and, for all I know, never being entirely satisfied. That is certainly no way to be prolific.

A prolific writer, therefore, has to have self-assurance. He can't sit around doubting the quality of his writing. Rather, he has to *love* his own writing.

I do. I can pick up any one of my books, start reading it anywhere, and immediately be lost in it and keep on reading until I am shaken out of the spell by some external event. Janet finds this amusing, but I think it's natural. If I didn't enjoy my writing so much, how on earth could I stand all the writing I do?

The result is that I rarely, if ever, worry about the sentences that reel out of my mind. If I have written them, I assume the chances are about twenty to one that they are perfectly all right.

"There you are. Asimov's literary output expressed as a function of the expanding universe."

I am not completely certain, of course. Robert Heinlein used to tell me that he "got it right the first time" and sent off the first draft. That is also supposed to be true of the mystery writer Rex Stout. I'm not quite *that* good. I do edit the first draft and make changes that usually amount to not more than 5 percent of the total, and *then* I send it off.

One reason for my self-assurance, perhaps, is that I see a story or an article or a book as a *pattern* and not just as a succession of words. I know exactly how to fit each item in the piece into the pattern, so that it is never necessary for me to work from an outline. Even the most complicated plot, or the most intricate exposition, comes out properly, with everything in the right order.

I rather imagine that a grand master in chess sees a chess game as a pattern, rather than as a succession of moves. A good baseball manager probably sees the game as a pattern rather than as a succession of plays. Well, I see patterns too in my specialty, but I don't know how I do it. I simply have the knack and had it even as a kid.

Of course, it also helps if you don't try to be too literary in your writing. If you try to turn out a prose poem, that takes time, even for an accomplished prose poet like Ray Bradbury or Theodore Sturgeon.

I have therefore deliberately cultivated a very plain style, even a colloquial one, which can be turned out rapidly and with which very little can go wrong. Of course, some critics, with crania that are more bone than mind, interpret this as my having "no style." If anyone thinks, however, that it is easy to write with absolute clarity and no frills, I recommend that he try it.

Being a prolific writer has its disadvantages, of course. It complicates the writer's social and family life, for a prolific writer has to be self-absorbed. He *must* be. He has to be either writing or thinking about writing virtually all the time, and has no time for anything else.

This is hard on one's wife. Janet is tolerance personified, and is very fond of me and of all my quirks and peculiarities, but even she is sometimes goaded into remarking that we don't talk to each other sufficiently.

My daughter, Robyn, is very affectionate, as I've already said, and recently I asked her, "Robyn, what kind of father have I been?"

I wanted her to tell me I was a loving father, a generous father, a warm and protective father (all of which I like to think I was, and am), but she thought about it and finally said, "Well, you were a *busy* father."

I imagine it does weary a family to have a husband and father who never wants to travel, who never wants to go on an outing or to parties or to the theater, who never wants to do anything but sit in his room and write. I daresay that the failure of my first marriage was partly the result of this.

Gertrude once said, bitterly, as I was closing in on my hundredth book, "What good is all this anyway? When you are dying, you will realize all you missed in life, all the good things you could have afforded with the money you make and that you ignored in your mad pursuit of more and more books. What will a hundred books do for you?"

And I said, "When I am dying, lean close over me to get my dying words. They are going to be: 'Too bad! Only a hundred!' "

Having reached 451 books as of now doesn't help the situation. If I were to be dying now, I would be murmuring, "Too bad! Only four hundred fifty-one." (Those would be my next-to-last words. The last ones will be: "I love you, Janet.") [They were. —Janet.]

I was once interviewed by Barbara Walters, by the way, and while we were off-camera, she seemed very interested in my prolificity and wondered whether I didn't sometimes want to do other things, rather than writing.

"No," I said.

She said, "What if the doctor gave you six months to live. What would you do?"

I said, "Type faster."

67

Writer's Problems

All writers have problems. In my case, the most amusing is that of handling people who don't or can't believe I am so prolific. After all, I don't make a point of it. I don't say to anyone, "Fine weather we're having, and by the way I've published umpty-ump books."

But it does come up sometimes. Back in 1979, the first volume of my autobiography had just appeared, and, as it happened, it was my 200th book. I was at a cocktail party or something of the sort and someone who didn't know me and hadn't ever heard of me (there are billions of such people, unfortunately) said to me, "What do you do?"

"I write," I said, this being my standard answer.

I expected him to ask me what I wrote, but he didn't. He said, "Who is your publisher?"

I said, "I have a number of publishers, but Doubleday is the most important of them. They have done three-eighths of my books."

He chose to interpret that remark as a way of aggrandizing myself. Up went his eyebrows, sneer went his lips, and he said, "I suppose that by that remark you mean that you have written eight books and that Doubleday has published three."

"No," I said quietly. "It means I have written two hundred books and Doubleday has published seventy-five."

At which those people around the table who did know me smiled, and my questioner looked suitably silly.

A similar case took place about seven years later when I had just published my 365th book. I was standing holding a copy at the Doubleday elevator when a young man came rushing out. He was a new employee and he wanted to meet me. We shook hands, and he said, "How many books have you published, Dr. Asimov?" (I am frequently asked that.)

I held up my book and said, "This is my three hundred sixty-fifth."

Just then someone came into the hall who didn't know me.

I said to the young man, "I've published a book for every day in the year."

And the stranger, passing me as I said this, smiled paternally, and said, "I'm sure it must seem like that sometimes," and passed on.

But writers have far worse troubles than that. After all, the writer's life is inherently an insecure one. Each project is a new start and may be a failure. The fact that a previous item has been successful is no guard against failure this time.

What's more, as has often been pointed out, writing is a very lonely occupation. You can talk about what you write, and discuss it with family, friends, or editors, but when you sit down at that typewriter, you are alone with it and no one can possibly help. You must extract every word from your own suffering mind.

It's no wonder writers so often turn misanthropic or are driven to drink to dull the agony. I've heard it said that alcoholism is an occupational disease with writers.

One young woman, gathering data for an article she was writing, must have assumed so, for she phoned me and asked me brightly, "Dr. Asimov, what is your favorite bar, and why?"

"Bar?" I said. "You mean a place where you drink?"

"Yes," she said.

"I'm sorry," I said. "I may sometimes pass through a bar to get to a restaurant, but I've never stopped in one. I don't drink."

There was a short pause, then she said, "Are you Isaac Asimov?"

"Yes," I said.

"The writer?"

"Yes," I said.

"And you've written hundreds of books?"

"Yes," I said, "and I've written every one of them cold sober."

She hung up, muttering. I seemed to have disillusioned her.

The question is, of course: Why don't I drink?

And one answer (if you disregard the stern conditioning of my father) is that, as a writer, I am not insecure. With trivial exceptions I have sold everything I have written in fifty years.

The most serious problem a writer can face, however, is "writer's block."

This is a serious disease and when a writer has it he finds himself staring at a blank sheet of paper in the typewriter (or a blank screen on the word processor) and can't do anything to unblank it. The words don't come. Or if they do, they are clearly unsuitable and are quickly torn up or erased. What's more, the disease is progressive, for the longer the inability to write continues, the more certain it is that it will continue to continue.

In this connection I think of a cartoon I once saw. It shows a writer at his typewriter. He needs a shave. Several empty cups of coffee are on his desk. The ashtray is heaped high with butts. The floor about him is littered with torn and crumpled pieces of paper, and a little girl is standing there and speaking. The caption reads: "Daddy, tell me a story." Talk about one's heart bleeding.

In real life, some science fiction writers, and very good ones too, have had serious episodes of writer's block that sometimes extend for years. There are some very good science fiction writers who have written quite prolifically for a period of years and have then stopped cold. Perhaps they were simply written out; perhaps they had said everything they had to say and could think of nothing more; and perhaps that is the reason for writer's block too. A writer can't put anything on paper when there's nothing left (at least temporarily) in his mind.

It may be, therefore, that writer's block is unavoidable and that at best a writer must pause every once in a while, for a shorter or longer interval, to let his mind fill up again.

In that case, how have I avoided writer's block, considering that I never stop? If I were engaged in only one writing project at a time I suppose I wouldn't avoid it. Frequently, when I am at work on a science fiction novel (the hardest to do of all the different things I write) I find myself heartily sick of it and unable to write another word. But I don't let that drive me crazy. I don't stare at blank sheets of paper. I don't spend days and nights cudgeling a head that is empty of ideas.

Instead, I simply leave the novel and go on to any of the dozen other projects that are on tap. I write an editorial, or an essay, or a short story, or work on one of my nonfiction books. By the time I've grown tired of these things, my mind has been able to do its proper work and fill up again. I return to my novel and find myself able to write easily once more.

This periodic difficulty of getting the mind to deliver ideas reminds me of how irritating that perennial question is: "Where do you get your ideas?"

I suppose that all writers of fiction are asked that, but for writers of science fiction, the question is usually phrased: "Where do you get your crazy ideas?"

I don't know what answer they expect, but Harlan Ellison answers, "From Schenectady. They have an idea factory and I subscribe to it, so every month they ship me a new idea."

I wonder how many people believe him.

I was asked the question a few months ago by a top-notch science fiction writer, whose work I admire greatly. I gathered that he was suffering from writer's block, and phoned me as one notoriously immune to it. "Where do you get your ideas?" he wanted to know.

I said, "By thinking and thinking and thinking till I'm ready to kill myself."

He said, with enormous relief, "You too?"

"Of course," I said, "did you ever think it was easy to get a good new idea?"

Most people, when I tell them this, are dreadfully disappointed. They would be far readier to believe that I had to use LSD or something like that so that ideas would come to me in an altered state of consciousness. If all one has to do is *think*, where's the glamour?

To those people, I say, "Try thinking. You'll find it's a lot harder than taking LSD."

68
Critics

When *Pebble in the Sky* appeared, I naively expected that *The New York Times* would review it prominently on the day of publication. They didn't, of course, then or ever, and I quickly learned that "prestige reviews" for writers like me were virtually nonexistent. As an example, not one of my books was ever as much as *mentioned* in *The New Yorker*, though I myself as a human being have been.

I quickly learned something else. When reviews of my books began to appear in minor publications (and were sent me by the publishers or by the clipping service I patronized in the early days), I found that they were not necessarily favorable—and I found that I disliked, nay, hated, an unfavorable review.

Such reviews are another source of insecurity, and a particularly pernicious one, for it arises *after* a book has been safely published. What will the critics say? Might not a terribly bad review kill the book after all the work you've done?

It is a terrible power that a writer imagines critics have, but it's just imagination. Any review (even unfavorable) is useful because it mentions the book and helps bring it to the reader's consciousness. Or as Sam Goldwyn is supposed to have said, "Publicity is good. Good publicity is even better."

But even if a critic doesn't really have the power to kill, he does have the power to hurt a writer's fragile ego. It is not surprising, then, that writers universally detest and execrate critics. One could make quite a long (and, to a noncritic, amusing) essay if one simply quoted all the vituperation hurled at critics' heads by writers.

One writer once said, "A critic is like a eunuch in a harem. He sees what's being done and he can criticize the technique, but he can't do it himself." And I have been known to say, "A critic is not considered professional till he produces satisfactory evidence to the effect that he beats his mother."

But let's put prejudice to one side and point out that good, professional critics perform a useful function. The statement that "they can't do it themselves" is not always true, and even if it were, so what? You don't have to be able to lay eggs to know when one of them is rotten.

Criticism and writing are two different talents. I am a good writer but I have no critical ability. I can't tell whether something I have written is good or bad, or just why it should be either. I can only say, "I like this story," or "It was easy to read," or other such trivial nonjudgmental remarks.

The critic, if he can't write as I do, can nevertheless analyze what I write and point out its flaws and virtues. In this way, he guides the reader and perhaps even helps the writer.

Having said all that, I must remind you that I'm talking about critics of the first caliber. Most critics we encounter, alas, are fly-by-night pipsqueaks without any qualification for the job other than the rudimentary ability to read and write. It is their pleasure sometimes to tear down a book savagely, or to attack the author rather than the book. They use the review, sometimes, as a vehicle for displaying their own erudition or as an opportunity for safe sadism. (Sometimes reviews are not even signed.)

It is these reviews, when I am the victim, that send me into a rage.

Lester del Rey solves the problem by never reading reviews (though he himself once conducted a column of book reviews—and was very good at it too).

"If you must read a review, Isaac," he said, "then at the first unfavorable word, stop reading and throw it away." I have tried to follow this sage advice but have not always managed.

My first really unpleasant experience with a critic came in the early 1950s when someone named Henry Bott attacked my books with ferocity. In his review of *The Caves of Steel,* he made no mention of any part of the plot and his reference to the background of the novel was so ludicrously wrong that it was clear he had not bothered to read the book. I was furious.

I wrote an essay denouncing the idiot and sent it to a small fan magazine, feeling that I would get the bile out of me and that no one of importance would read it. Even that turned out to be disastrous, however. It is never safe to answer a critic, however incompetent and libelous his reviews might be. Everyone who read that fan magazine sent his copy to the editor of the magazine in which Bott's review appeared, and the editor wrote an editorial denouncing me.

He offered to let me answer the editorial, but I decided to cut my losses and let it go, but then I read the next issue of the magazine. The infamous Bott reviewed *Lucky Starr and the Pirates of the Asteroids* and gave it a favorable review because he didn't know that I was Paul French. (It was the only favor a pseudonym ever did me.) I promptly wrote a letter to the magazine, thanking Bott for the review on French's behalf, and didn't mention that I was French till the last line. It effectively demolished the villain.

The editor of the magazine later admitted he was merely attempting to start a feud that would benefit the circulation. My neat ending spoiled that plan and the magazine eventually folded.

I must admit that in the early days of my book production I was asked to review some science fiction books and I acceded. However, I quickly stopped this for two reasons. First, I recognized that I had no talent as a critic and could not tell bad from good. Second, it seemed to me that it was unethical for me to review science fiction books. The writers were mostly friends of mine and there was too much danger of my leaning backward to avoid saying anything nasty. And even if the writer was unknown to me, he was, nevertheless, a competitor, and could I be sure of being fair to him?

Other science fiction writers seem not to be troubled by this ethical dilemma. I have read reviews of unmeasured vituperation written by one science fiction writer about a book written by another, and competing, science fiction writer. I have even been the victim of such reviews myself.

I can't help remembering the names of those who wrote reviews of this sort. I do nothing about it, you understand—I never lift a finger or say a bad word against these wicked malefactors. However (I tell myself), someday one of these miserable worms will come to me for a favor and I'll turn him down.

This has actually happened. A writer who in a review once accused me (wrongfully) of nepotism had the infernal gall some years later to ask a favor of me. —Favor requested; favor denied. That was the extent of my revenge.

69
Humor

One advantage of being prolific is that it reduces the importance of any one book. By the time a particular book is published, the prolific writer hasn't much time to worry about how it will be received or how it will sell. By then he has already sold several others and is working on still others and it is these that concern him. This intensifies the peace and calm of his life.

Then, too, once enough books are published, a kind of "ever-normal granary" is established. Even if one book doesn't do well, all the books, as a whole, are bringing in money, and one fall-short isn't noticeable. Even the publisher can take that attitude.

It also makes it easier to experiment. If an experimental short story goes sour—well, what's one story in hundreds?

An experiment I kept wanting to try was that of writing a funny science fiction story. I don't really know why but I have this strong drive to make people laugh. I'm an excellent raconteur, as it happens, and I've even written a reasonably successful jokebook, containing not only 640 funny stories but endless advice about how to tell them, what to do, and what not to do. The book is *Isaac Asimov's Treasury of Humor* (Houghton Mifflin, 1971).

That book was written because Gertrude and I and another couple were driving to the Concord Hotel in the Catskills. As usual, I desperately didn't want to go, even though it was just for the weekend, and in order to drown my sorrows, I told an endless series of jokes while we were driving. The other woman said, "You're very good, Isaac. Why don't you write a jokebook?"

I started to say, "Who'd publish it?" but choked it off, because I realized any of my publishers would publish it. Consequently, I spent the entire weekend at the Concord with a small notebook I had bought, scribbling jokes in it as fast as I could think of them. I even did it when we attended the nightclub (the largest in the world supposedly) and were afflicted with unbelievable noise. It was all that helped me survive that miserable place.

It was only natural, then, that I should have the desire to write a funny story. At the very beginning of my career, I attempted humor with "Ring Around the Sun" (*Future Fiction,* March 1940), "Robot AL-76 Goes Astray" (*Amazing,* February 1942), and "Christmas on Ganymede" (*Startling,* January 1942). The humor in all three stories was quite infantile and, in quality, they stand very close to the bottom of the list of my stories.

The trouble was that I was trying to imitate the slapsticky humor I found in other science fiction stories and I wasn't good at that. It was not until I realized that my favorite humorist was P. G. Wodehouse and that the proper way for me to be humorous was to imitate him— use my full vocabulary and say silly things with a straight face—that I began to write successful humor.

My first Wodehousian story was "The Up-to-Date Sorcerer" (*F&SF,* July 1958). Thereafter, things were easier for me. In the 1980s, I began to write a whole series of stories about a tiny demon named Azazel, who was constantly being asked to help people and who did as he was told—but always with disastrous results. A number of these stories were collected in *Azazel* (Doubleday, 1988) and they were just as Wodehousian as I could possibly make them.

I'm not ashamed of being "derivative" in this respect and I never try to hide the fact that I am. Sam Moskowitz, who has written many historical accounts of science fiction, says, with some bitterness, that I am the *only* science fiction writer who will admit to being influenced. All the others, he says, imply that their writing is the original production of a mind that owes nothing to anyone.

I have to allow for Sam's exaggeration in this respect. I'm sure that any writer, if pressed, will admit to being influenced by some other writer whom he admires (usually it's Kafka, Joyce, or Proust, although with someone as humble as I am it's Cliff Simak, P. G. Wodehouse, and Agatha Christie). And why not? Why not take someone worthy as a model? And no imitation is truly slavish. I'm sure that no matter how Wodehousian a story I write may be, I can't prevent it from being somewhat Asimovian as well. (As an example, my humor is distinctly more cruel than Wodehouse's is.)

It is, of course, difficult to tell why there should be this strong drive to write humor, not only in myself but in many other writers as well. After all, humor is difficult. Other kinds of stories don't have to hit the bull's-eye. The outer rings have their rewards too. A story can be fairly suspenseful, moderately romantic, somewhat terrifying, and so on.

This is *not* the case with humor. A story is either funny or it is not funny. Nothing in between. The humor target contains only a bull's-eye.

Then, too, humor is entirely subjective. Most people will agree on the suspense content of a story, on the romantic nature, on the mystery or horror of it. But over humor there is bound to be violent disagreement. What is howlingly funny to one person is merely stupid to another, so that even my best humorous stories are often skewered by readers who dismiss them as silly. (Of course, they are dull, humorless clods to whom I pay no attention.)

Having said all that, let me get back to the realm of spoken humor. I have said I am a good raconteur, and in this my fiction writing is of great help. I have a fund of a number of complex stories that are actually mini-short stories that have to be told with skill, because I must make sure that humor exists throughout the narrative. It is possible for me to talk anywhere from five to ten minutes, holding audience interest, before exploding the final punch line.

I love these stories because the people who listen to them can never repeat them with success. If they want to hear one again, they have to come to me. And every once in a long while (for I won't repeat these jokes too often) they prevail on me to tell it again. They know the punch line but they just want to hear the story.

And where do I get such a story from? Why, from someone who told it to me in bald, abbreviated form, which I then elaborate into a short story. I once watched a person listen with delight to a story I was telling, and when I was done, I said to him, "But you told me that joke." And he replied, still laughing, "Not like that."

Sometimes my facility with jokes gets me into trouble. I was on television once with the great humorist Sam Levenson, and he said to me, "Do you know the joke about the Jewish astronaut?" That was my cue to say, "No, Sam, tell me the joke about the Jewish astronaut," so that he could tell it. But, of course, I had forgotten I was on television, and I said, "Yes, I heard it."

Sam threw himself back pettishly and said, "Then you tell it."

I was thunderstruck. I wasn't ready. I wasn't even sure I had the same joke, but I said, "An Israeli said to an American, 'Do you think reaching the Moon was such a big thing? We Jewish astronauts are going to land on the Sun.' The American protested, 'You can't. The heat! The radiation!' 'Don't be silly,' said the Israeli. 'Do you think we're fools? We're going to go at night.' "

That was the joke and I got the laugh, but I perspired a lot.

My tendency to overlook little things like microphones and cameras showed up again about half a year ago during a radio interview at the Hotel Algonquin. Along with me was a musician who was accompanied by his gorgeous wife. One of the questions was whether sex interfered with the creative process. I answered in the negative, of course, and rather disdainfully at that. The musician also answered in the negative but admitted that on the night before a big concert, he usually abstained from sex.

Whereupon, I stage-whispered to the gorgeous wife, "Give me a call on those nights," and then realized I had stage-whispered directly into the microphone. A look of horror crossed my face but, fortunately, the interview was not live and that line could be edited out.

70

Literary Sex and Censorship

Despite my prolificity, one thing I never experimented with was vulgarity and sex.

In the days when I started writing, writers, whether for the printed or the visual media, found it impossible to use vulgar language or even some proper words. It was for this reason that cowboys were always saying, "You gol-darned, dag-nabbed, ding-busted varmint," when undoubtedly no cowboy ever said anything like that. We know what they really said but it was unprintable and unusable.

Words like "virgin," "breast," and "pregnant" were also unprintable and unsayable. It was even impossible, in some quarters, to say, "He died." One had to say, "He passed away," or "He went to his reward," or "He was gathered unto his fathers."

This type of prissiness was a great bother to writers, who found themselves unable to present the world as it was, and there was enormous relief in the 1960s when it became possible to use vulgarisms in writing, and even, to an extent, on television. The prissy were horrified, but they live in some never-never land and I am in no mood to worry about them.

And yet, despite all that, I have not joined the revolution. This is *not* out of prissiness of my own. I have published five books of naughty limericks that I constructed myself and that are quite satisfactorily obscene. What's more, they are not hidden under a pseudonym. They appear under my own name.

Those, however, are limericks. In my other writing, sex and vulgarity are absent. In fact, my early stories usually excluded women altogether. Even as late as 1952, when I wrote "The Martian Way" (*Galaxy*, November 1952) I omitted women. The plot did not require them. Horace Gold stated, in his irascible way, that I had to include a woman or he would not take the story. "Any sort of woman," he said.

So I gave one of my characters a shrewish wife. Horace objected, of course, but I shook my head. "A deal is a deal," I said, so he had to take it. However, he misspelled my name on the cover, giving Asimov a double "s." I wouldn't be surprised if he did it on purpose.

I did introduce women in a few early stories, but my first *successful* female character was Susan Calvin, who appeared in some of my robot stories. Her first appearance was in "Liar" (*ASF*, May 1941). Susan Calvin was a plain spinster, a highly intelligent "robopsychologist" who fought it out in a man's world without fear or favor and who invariably won. These were "women's lib" stories twenty years before their time, and I got very little credit for that. (Susan Calvin was very similar, in some ways, to my dear wife, Janet, whom I didn't meet until nineteen years after I had invented Susan.)

Despite Susan Calvin, my early science fiction stories were sometimes considered sexist because of the absence of women. A few years ago, a feminist wrote to excoriate me for this. I replied gently, explaining my utter inexperience with women at the time I began to write.

"That's no excuse," she replied angrily, and I dropped the matter. Clearly, there is no percentage in arguing with fanatics.

As my writing progressed, I became more successful with women characters. In *The Naked Sun,* I introduced Gladia Delmarre as a romantic interest, and I think I did her well.

She appeared again in *The Robots of Dawn* (Doubleday, 1983), where she was even better, in my opinion. In *The Robots of Dawn* I even made it clear that the hero and heroine had sex (adulterous sex at that, for the hero was a married man), but I gave no clinical details and the episode was absolutely essential to the plot. It was *not* included for titillation.

In fact, in my last few novels, I have made it a practice to exclude not only all vulgarisms but all expletives of any kind. I exclude even "dear me" and "gee whiz." It is difficult to do this, for people use such expressions (and much worse) almost routinely. I do it partly out of deliberate rebellion against the literary freedom of today and partly as an experiment. I was curious to see if any readers would notice. Apparently, they do not. (Do you notice that in this book there are no vulgarisms and no expletives?)

Nevertheless, I have had trouble with censorship. I'm not talking about my books of naughty limericks. I never had any trouble with them because they were never sent to libraries or schools. They never had much of a sale either, because my readers are not the dirty-limerick type. I wrote those books entirely for my own amusement.

My *Isaac Asimov's Treasury of Humor* received some lumps. All through the book, I stressed the desirability of *not* using vulgarisms unnecessarily. They were likely to embarrass some in the audience and did not add to the humor of the story. In fact, I pointed out, the humor was more effective when the ribaldry was merely hinted at. The listener fills in the lacunae in his mind according to his own tastes, and I give several examples of jokes where the wicked details are left out to the improvement of the tale.

The last two jokes in the book, however, were examples of cases where the use of vulgarisms was necessary. The last joke, in fact, illustrated the manner in which overuse of a particular vulgarism deprives it of all meaning.

Somewhere in Tennessee, the *Treasury of Humor* was violently attacked. An attempt was made to indicate that the last two jokes were typical of the book as a whole, and no mention was made of my strictures against the use of vulgarisms.

This is not surprising. Bluenose censors, in their attempt to cut off anything they don't like, do not hesitate to distort, deceive, and lie. In fact, I think they would rather. They failed, however. The *Treasury of Humor* was removed from the junior high school shelf but remained in the town library. I hope the publicity meant that more students read it, though they must have been disappointed if they expected real obscenity.

(What strikes me in this is that the junior high school kids, if they are like all the junior high school kids I've ever known, know and freely use the wicked word found in those last two jokes. So, I suspect, do the censors themselves, for they are undoubtedly steeped in every possible aspect of hypocrisy.)

The Robots of Dawn also took its lumps. Parents in some town in the state of Washington found themselves appalled by the book and demanded it be withdrawn from the school library. Some who made this demand admitted they didn't read the book, because they wouldn't read "trash." It was enough to *call* it trash and burn it.

One school board member actually had the guts to read the book. He said he didn't like it (having to stay on the side of the angels if he wanted to keep his job) but actually had the surprising courage to say that he found nothing in it that was obscene. So it stayed.

At a time when obscene books are published without remark and are openly read by young women on buses, the fact that anyone, anywhere, can waste their time over my harmless volumes amazes me. Sometimes, though, I wish that the people who did this weren't the pitiful and petulant pipsqueaks they are and that they made a real stink over some book of mine. How that would improve sales!

71
Doomsday

Something else I have avoided in my prolific fiction writing has been the "doomsday" scenario (with one small exception I'll get to).

Humanity has been damaging the planet and its ecological balance since it learned how to develop stone weapons and to band together to hunt down the larger herbivores. There is no question in my mind that human hunting bands are responsible for the disappearance of the magnificent mammoths and the other large mammals that roamed the Earth twenty thousand years ago.

Ten thousand years ago, human beings devised the techniques of agriculture and herding and slowly began the process of destroying the environment by overgrazing and by overfarming.

Still, not all that human beings could do in the wildest excesses of war and rapine could seriously damage the planet until 1945. In that year, the first nuclear bomb was exploded, and the Industrial Revolution, fed by cheap oil, went into high gear. We are now perfectly capable of damaging the planet beyond repair in any reasonable time, and are, in fact, in the process of doing so.

Science fiction writers are more aware of this than many others and, immediately after World War II, stories of atomic doom became popular. In fact, such stories were already being written before the news arrived of the nuclear bombing of Hiroshima on August 6, 1945. U.S. intelligence agents even investigated *ASF* because it published Cleve Cartmill's "Deadline" in its March 1944 issue. The story described a nuclear bomb with too much accuracy.

As almost always happens, such atomic doom stories became so popular as to dominate the field and to fall victim to their own success as readers grew tired of the endless repetition. Other types of doomsday stories followed—tales of a poisoned atmosphere, of incredible overpopulation, and so on, and science fiction became tinged with gray and red doom.

This was, in a way, useful. The science fiction writer Ben Bova says that science fiction writers are scouts sent out by humanity to survey the future. They return with recommendations for world improvement and warnings of world destruction. In times like these, when humanity is complacently working its own devastation, it *must* be warned—over and over again.

However, I have never joined the gloom and doom procession. This is not because I don't believe humanity can destroy itself. I believe this heartily and have written numerous essays on different aspects of the problem (particularly on the subject of overpopulation). It is just that I think there are enough science fiction writers shrieking, "The day of judgment is at hand!" and I won't be missed if I am not of their number.

To be sure, in *Pebble in the Sky,* I described an Earth all but destroyed by radioactivity, but humanity is pictured in that book as existing in a great Galactic Empire, so that the fate of one small world means little for humanity as a whole.

My books tend to celebrate the triumph of technology rather than its disaster. This is true of other science fiction writers as well, notably Robert Heinlein and Arthur Clarke. It seems odd, or perhaps significant, that the Big Three are all technological optimists.

72
Style

I have already mentioned that I have deliberately cultivated a simple and even colloquial style, and I would like here to go into that matter in greater depth.

Orson Scott Card, one of the best of contemporary science fiction writers, is very generous in his approval of my writing. He thinks it is uniquely clear and that while other writers have idiosyncrasies that make it possible to imitate them, I have none, and that no one, therefore, can imitate me successfully. (I must stress the fact that it's *he* who says so, not I. Since I have no talent as a critic I have nothing to say in this matter.)

Others are not so kind. They find my novels, particularly, to be too talky and my style to be too flat.

Again, not being a critic, I didn't know how to defend myself. Fortunately, Jay Kay Klein came to my defense.

Jay Kay is a plump fellow, mostly bald, has a ready smile, a quick wit, and is a much-loved presence at all science fiction conventions. He is science fiction's ace photographer and is never without his camera equipment. He has taken many thousands of photographs of science fiction personalities, including me. He once collected a few dozen photos of me kissing different young women. He flashed them on the screen, accompanying them with a commentary that had the audience convulsed, especially me.

Jay Kay defined two kinds of writing and I expanded on his thesis, making it my theory of "the mosaic and the plate glass."

There is writing which resembles the mosaics of glass you see in stained-glass windows. Such windows are beautiful in themselves and let in the light in colored fragments, but you can't expect to see through them. In the same way, there is poetic writing that is beautiful in itself and can easily affect the emotions, but such writing can be dense and can make for hard reading if you are trying to figure out what's happening.

Plate glass, on the other hand, has no beauty of its own. Ideally, you ought not to be able to see it at all, but through it you can see all that is happening outside. That is the equivalent of writing that is plain and unadorned. Ideally, in reading such writing, you are not even aware that you are reading. Ideas and events seem merely to flow from the mind of the writer into that of the reader without any barrier between. I hope that is what is happening when you read this book.

Writing poetically is very hard, but so is writing clearly. In fact, it may be clarity which is harder to get than beauty, if you will let me continue with my metaphor of mosaics and plate glass.

Colored glass of the type used in mosaics has been known since ancient times. Getting the color out of the glass, however, proved so difficult a task that the problem was not solved till the seventeenth century. Plate glass is a comparatively recent invention and was the great triumph of Venetian glassmaking art, kept secret for a long time.

And so it is in writing. In the past, virtually all writing was ornate. Read a Victorian novel, for instance. Read even Dickens, the best of all the Victorians. It is only comparatively recently that writing has, in the hands of some writers, become simple and clear.

Simple, clear writing has its advantages for me. I have received a number of letters from people who tell me that they hated to read until they stumbled across one of my books and, for the first time, found reading to be pleasant. I have even received some letters from dyslexics who found that my books were worth working slowly through and that their reading improved as a result. And I once received a letter from a grateful mother whose son I had lured into reading.

This sort of thing pleases me. I write primarily for personal pleasure and to make a living, but it is delightful to find that, in addition, you are helping others.

But how does one go about writing clearly? I don't know. I presume you have to start with an orderly mind and a knack for marshaling your thoughts so that you know exactly what you want to say. Beyond that, I am helpless.

73

Letters

Since I've just been mentioning some of the letters I receive, perhaps I ought to go into the matter more fully.

Most of the letters I get are, of course, completely pleasurable. They come from people who have read some of my books (sometimes a great many), enjoy them, and are kind enough to write and tell me so.

In the past I have tried to answer all such letters at least with an acknowledging postcard. I must admit, though, that as the years pass and my energy reserve dwindles while my writing commitments seem to increase, it becomes harder and harder to do so. I'm afraid I'm becoming remiss and no longer answer every letter.

A subdivision of such letters consists of those written by youngsters in pencil on ruled paper, stating they had read some of my stories in school and have liked them. The last sentence is usually: "Please write back." It is almost impossible not to do so—because the kids don't understand the "I'm too busy" ploy and are dreadfully disappointed if you don't reply and I couldn't bear that, so additional postcards go out.

I might say, in passing, that the postcard is a noble invention. It saves enormous amounts of time and postage. It sacrifices privacy, but I have never written a postcard I haven't been willing to have the postman read.

Of course, there is the case of the jovial woman editor with whom I carried on a genial mock flirtation. (In my younger days, I flirted almost indiscriminately with every woman in sight and not one of them ever took me seriously—which may not be exactly complimentary, now that I think of it.) In any case, I wrote her a brief card and, out of sheer habit, ended with a double entendre.

Back came a letter: "Dear Isaac. I have been propositioned before— but never on a postcard."

However, I digress—

One version of the little-boy letter that I view with gathering outrage is the kind that begins: "I am so-and-so in the 7th grade of such-and-such school and my teacher has asked me to write some author and ask him questions about his work." There would then follow the tritest questions you can imagine—always the same. When did I start writing? How? Why? Where do I get my ideas? Do I intend to write another story?

When such letters first started arriving, I would answer briefly, but as they continued to flood in, I developed a towering burn.

All over the country, it seems to me, idiot teachers are urging their students to assail busy writers and subject them to demands for what is clearly homework. What right have the teachers to do that? The only commodity I have to work with is time and every single day my total supply of time decreases by one day. Must I expend my diminishing supply answering stupid questions from kids who wouldn't dream of bothering me if they were not egged on by their obtuse teachers who don't want to waste *their* time and limited capacities by thinking up better things for their students to do? Undoubtedly, other writers may have secretaries who send off form letters, but I don't have one.

Occasionally, my anger reaches such a pitch that in particularly egregious cases I write an angry letter to the teacher. In one such case, my letter was sent to a local newspaper (without my permission!), which presented it as an example of an arrogant writer. This was clipped out and sent to me by some friend of the teacher who berated me for refusing to take the "five minutes" required to make a child happy.

She shouldn't have done that. My cup of wrath boiled over. I wrote to her to ask if she were imbecilic enough to think I only received *one* letter like that. I receive hordes of such letters, each one asking for five minutes—an indication of the general low level of compassion and understanding in much of the teaching profession. I'm afraid I let myself go and let her have the rough edge of a very articulate and, when necessary, vituperative tongue. I never got an answer, because I probably scared her to death.

Nowadays, I have no trouble. As soon as I come to the magic words "my teacher has asked me to"—my wastebasket finds itself richer by one letter. It saves a lot of time and a lot of wear and tear on my emotions.

Sometimes I get letters pointing out errors in my nonfiction writing (or, more rarely, in my fiction). Cards of thanks go out routinely in such cases and when the mistakes are real bloopers, I make changes for the book version, or for the next edition if it is already in a book. A bad mistake is embarrassing, but unavoidable now and then when one writes as much and as quickly as I do. The wonder is not that I make mistakes but that I make so few.

I can always count on my readers to backstop me. I have had men as great and as famous as Linus Pauling write to point out errors.

Of course, there is the very occasional letter denouncing my writing and telling me what a monster of arrogance and conceit I am, and describing other character shortcomings from which I suffer. These I don't answer. If they want to dislike me, let them.

A number of letters ask for information, and if the question is specific and can be answered briefly, I try to oblige, especially if it is an interesting question and the answer is not easily available. It is very odd, but I almost never get a letter of thanks in return for answering such questions. I honestly don't know why that is.

Sometimes the request for information clearly shows I am mistaken for a public library. "Please send me all the latest data on the space effort" is a common request—usually from youngsters who, having been told to write an essay on new developments in space, think it would be a good idea to have me write it for them. —Wastebasket.

Sometimes (and surprisingly often) someone from prison asks if I can send them a book or two because they have read all the Asimov books in the prison library and want more. I always feel a pang of pity for prisoners, whatever they may have done, especially if they read my books (which convinces me at once that they may have been wrongfully convicted). In such cases, I arrange to have Doubleday send out a book or two and invariably they refuse to deduct the expense from my royalties—which, of course, prevents me from abusing the privilege.

Sometimes I receive a request for money, but I never send out money to strangers. I may be a soft touch, but I'm not *that* soft.

A still more embarrassing type of request is one in which I'm asked to read a beginner's manuscript and give him a careful critique of it. That's impossible. I lack the time and I lack the critical ability, but no matter how I explain that, I am always left with the uncomfortable feeling that the letter writer considers me a fat cat who is too selfish and meanspirited to help a beginner. Some even take unfair advantage of my frankness in describing my life by saying, "John Campbell helped you when you were a beginner, so why can't you help me?" The answer to that is that helping was Campbell's business and he had the talent for it; it is not my business and I have no talent for it. Nor did Campbell help all beginners indiscriminately. He was careful to pick and choose. He waited for an Isaac Asimov and he knew how to recognize him when he saw him; I don't. But how do I explain all that?

The same goes for the many beginners who think there's some special trick to selling stories, a trick I know and could easily pass on to them. No matter how earnestly I try to tell them that there is no trick, that it is a matter of inborn talent and hard work, I'm sure they think I'm just hugging the secret to my breast out of fear of competition.

Some letters are argumentative, disputing some view I have expressed. On occasion, a particularly well-reasoned letter forces me to modify my views and I usually answer in that case and sometimes find an excuse to write an essay expressing my modified view. More often, such letters are merely unpleasant and argumentative and I ignore them.

A subset of such disagreements involves my openly expressed lack of religious feeling. I receive letters from people who sorrow for me and pray for me and I don't mind. It makes them feel better, I'm sure.

It is a little irritating when I am sent little tracts touting some sectarian belief in the fond hope that this will make me "see the light." I don't know why it never occurs to such people that my views are fixed firmly and are not to be swayed by little tracts.

Sometimes I am irritated into answering. Once, when a religionist denounced me in unmeasured terms, I sent him a card saying, "I am sure you believe that I will go to hell when I die, and that once there I will suffer all the pains and tortures the sadistic ingenuity of your deity can devise and that this torture will continue forever. Isn't that enough for you? Do you have to call me bad names in addition?" I never received an answer, of course.

Then there are the autograph hounds. (What people want with autographs is more than I can figure out.) The letters asking for them (particularly from youngsters who will throw them away once they get them) are like snowflakes in a constantly accelerating blizzard. The flattery of it wore off long ago, and if someone wants an autograph and sends me a card to sign and a stamped self-addressed envelope to put it in, I oblige. Otherwise, I no longer do. (I am particularly suspicious of those who tell me what a great writer I am and how they enjoy my work and yet don't mention a single title of anything they've read. I suspect these of being form letters.)

In recent years, a new wrinkle has been added. An autograph is not enough. A signed photograph is what is wanted; an 8 × 11 glossy is sometimes specified. Well, I have no photographs. I'm not in show business. My face is not my fortune. If someone *sends* me a photograph along with a stamped self-addressed envelope, I'll oblige. Not otherwise.

Some people send me books to sign and return. Usually, they include stamped self-addressed mailers, but even so it is a pain in the neck. The packages are bulky and make my day's mail weigh a ton or so. Then I have to go out and find a mailbox that will take bulk. When asked in advance, I always suggest they send me nameplates, which I will sign and return and which they can then paste into their books.

However, few are thoughtful enough to ask in advance and of those who do, few accept the nameplate notion.

Another foul development of recent years is the "celebrity auction." Someone discovered that a good way to raise funds is to write to a number of celebrities and ask each for something personal—an old sock, a laundry list—which could then be auctioned off to those who valued such junk. Usually, the causes for which the money is being raised sound worthy, so the first few times I received such a request, I sent off signed paperback books.

That put my name on a computerized list that was circulated throughout the country and then came the deluge. Every celebrity auction in the United States sent me a begging letter. I have received as many as four in a single day and there are very few days in which I receive none. What can I do? As soon as I glance over a suspicious letter and see the magic words "celebrity auction," there is a weight increase in my wastebasket.

I also get a small number of crazy letters—from people who are being manipulated by strange rays, who have encountered extraterrestrial aliens, who have uncovered secret conspiracies, or who are simply incoherent. I sigh and dump them.

Then there are the people writing "nonbooks." A nonbook is produced when some person sends each of several hundred celebrities some inane questions, collects answers, and puts them together into a book from which he hopes to draw royalties.

There are numerous celebrity cookbooks, for instance. Why should anyone go about concocting and testing recipes when he can get a number of celebrities to submit "favorite" recipes? I have been asked for my favorite recipes a million times, but the only recipe I have is for boiling water and using it to convert a freeze-dried powder into coffee. That's the extent of my culinary skill.

(Of course, every once in a while, when Janet is busy, she sets up all the necessary utensils, all the necessary ingredients, and a carefully prepared recipe. I then get to work, mixing, adding, adjusting temperatures, and, in general, doing whatever must be done. Invariably, the dish, however complex, turns out excellent because I am meticulous about following the recipe, as Janet almost never is, and because I am not a chemist for nothing. But in such cases, I get so dictatorial about not allowing anyone to enter "my kitchen" and so smug and self-satisfied about the outcome that Janet can rarely bring herself to let me do it.)

I rarely oblige any of the nonbook purveyors, partly because the questions are often so silly.

Thus, one woman wanted me to write an essay on my father and why I admired him, and she sent me a list of other celebrities she was asking to write such essays. Actually, I have frequently written about my father (as in this book) and it is perfectly clear that I *do* admire him. Still, I thought the idea was a silly one because she could scarcely expect to get anything but saccharine essays about fathers. What celebrity was going to admit his father was an alcoholic wife-beater, even if he was?

I was incautious enough to write and tell her this and she returned a virulent letter, accusing me of hating my father. I was sorry I had written, but I never heard of the book being published, so maybe it didn't work out.

One time I was asked to describe the very worst date I had ever had. I answered briefly and truthfully that I had never had a bad date. I had rarely dated anyone but the two women I eventually married and I always made it my business to see that the date would be a pleasant one. They *printed* that letter in among a whole mess of others describing disasters so horrible they nauseated me when I tried to read them. (I've been luckier than I knew.)

I was once asked to say what I wanted for Christmas in the way of computers. I was urged to describe anything I could imagine, whether it was feasible or not. I answered briefly and truthfully that I had an antediluvian electric typewriter and a medieval word processor and printer and both worked properly. They were all I needed, and I didn't want, for Christmas or for any other time, anything beyond what I really needed.

The questioner replied that it was a pleasure to receive my letter among all the letters of unalloyed greed that she had received but her editor wouldn't let her print it because it would make everyone else in the nonbook look bad. (Besides, I thought to myself, not being greedy is probably un-American and subversive.)

In the same letter she asked me to tell her what made traveling pleasurable for me and how did I compare travel for business and travel for pleasure. I had to explain that I didn't travel. (Un-American again.)

There are other things I have written that are apparently un-American and unfit to print. The Chicago *Tribune* asked me to write an essay on Christmas. "Anything you want to say," they assured me. I agreed gladly, and seized the occasion to denounce the crass commercialism of the holiday. You can guess the nature of the remarks when I tell you the title was "And Now, a Word from Scrooge." It was accepted enthusiastically and was paid for, but, as far as I know, it was never printed.

74

Plagiarism

One of the plagues of the prolific writer is the constant concern over the possibility of plagiarism, which is the appropriation of someone else's words with the pretense that they are your own. This is, in my opinion, the greatest crime a writer can commit, and there isn't any chance at all I'll ever do that. The trouble is that I want to avoid even the *appearance* of plagiarism and I write so much that this is sometimes difficult.

For instance, Jack Williamson's 1934 story "Born of the Sun" had a scene in which a bunch of fanatics tried to destroy an astronomical observatory at which a startling new theory had been developed. I read the story and was undoubtedly impressed by the scene, which remained in my unconscious mind.

Seven years later, I published "Nightfall," in which there was a scene in which a band of fanatics tried to destroy an astronomical observatory at which a startling new theory had been developed. It wasn't till thirty years after "Nightfall" had been written, when I reread "Born of the Sun" because I wanted to include it in an anthology of mine which I called *Before the Golden Age* (Doubleday, 1974), that I realized what had happened and was embarrassed by it.

It was not really plagiarism, of course, for ideas and situations are repeated over and over again in different stories—but in different words, in different contexts, and with different consequences. Ideas and situations can even be deliberately borrowed provided they are used sufficiently differently.

I borrowed freely from Edward Gibbon's *History of the Decline and Fall of the Roman Empire* in planning the Foundation series, and I believe that the motion picture *Star Wars* did not hesitate, in turn, to borrow from the Foundation series.

I learned not to consider overlapping of ideas to be a crime when I was writing "Each an Explorer," which appeared in 1956 in the undated *Future Fiction* #30. Halfway through I recognized that the idea was uncomfortably similar to that in Campbell's great story "Who Goes There?" I broke into an immediate perspiration. I phoned Campbell, told him what was happening, and asked his advice.

Campbell laughed and said that duplication of ideas was unavoidable and, in the hands of honest, capable writers, harmless. "I can give the same idea to ten different writers," he said, "and get back ten completely different stories."

Even so, however, I labored to make it as different from "Who Goes There?" as possible.

Again, I wrote a story called "Lest We Remember," which appeared in the February 15, 1982, issue of *Isaac Asimov's Science Fiction Magazine (IASFM)*. As I wrote it, I recognized a similarity in idea to that in Daniel Keyes's classic "Flowers for Algernon" (April 1959 *F&SF)* and labored like a Trojan to make my story as different as possible.

The closest call I ever had was in a short short story I wrote for someone who asked me to portray a computer at the moment of self-awareness. I wrote of one that stopped working for a while, then began to ask the question "Who am I? Who am I?"

It appeared in an amateur computer newsletter, but was later reprinted in a children's magazine. Another writer saw it and sent me a tear sheet of one of his own stories that also ended in a computer asking, "Who am I? Who am I?" (The stories were otherwise completely different.)

The other writer told me where his story had appeared and I realized with a sinking heart that it had been included in an anthology that also contained one of my stories and that I therefore had in my library. I looked for it and there was the other story, published years earlier than mine.

What could I do? I wrote to him admitting that his story had been available to me and that the ending might have clung to my mind. I asked if he would be satisfied if I were never to allow my story to be published again anywhere. He replied that that would be satisfactory and was kind enough to say that he never thought for a moment that I had committed a plagiarism.

But what can I do? The danger is always there. Scraps of this and that cling to my tenacious memory and I might at any time think that one of these scraps is my own creation. Worse yet, I haven't read even a small fraction of all the science fiction stories written, and I might overlap ideas with something I have never read, through sheer coincidence.

Once Theodore Sturgeon and I independently, and almost simultaneously, wrote stories which made use of the word "hostess" in a double meaning, the *same* double meaning. What's more, two of his characters were Derek and Verna and two of mine were Drake and Vera. Both stories were sent to *Galaxy*—pure coincidence. Since Ted's story arrived in Horace's office a few days earlier, it fell to me to make a few cosmetic changes. (Vera was changed to Rose, for instance.) My story appeared as "Hostess" in the May 1951 *Galaxy*. No matter how carefully I try to stay far away from even the hint of plagiarism, there is nothing I can do about being plagiarized myself. All over the country, students are being asked to write essays and stories and a very small percentage of them are cretinous enough to seek the shortcut of copying some existing item.

I say "cretinous" because any kid so uncertain of his own abilities that he is forced to plagiarize must be a rotten writer, even for a kid. If he suddenly hands in a polished professional piece of work, whom can he possibly fool, unless he has an equally cretinous teacher?

One professor from a Rhode Island college once sent me a copy of a long manuscript. One of her students had submitted it as his own work. However, it had robots in it, and was far too good for the student. She knew that I was known for my robot stories and she felt I could tell her whether the student had plagiarized.

Yes, indeed, he had. The dumb jackass had copied my story "Galley Slave" (December 1957 *Galaxy*), and had done so word for word. He lacked the capacity to paraphrase so that he might plead coincidence and he didn't even have the wit to change the names of the characters.

I reported all this to the professor, and I hope the young man was duly punished.

A few years ago, someone came across a high school literary magazine which contained, under some student's name, my story "Nothing for Nothing" (February 1979 *IASFM*). I wrote an indignant letter to the school and so did Doubleday, but there was never any answer. Either the people at the school were too embarrassed to answer or (and I don't consider this impossible) they were annoyed at my objection to one of their very own students finding such a clever way of fulfilling an assignment.

If you doubt that the latter viewpoint could be possible, listen to this (even though it doesn't involve a plagiarism). A young man wrote me once for a recommendation letter. He was trying to get into some school, had read my stories, and thought that my name on a letter saying how great he was would carry much weight. He admitted that I didn't know him, but he felt it wouldn't be very difficult for me to pretend I did, and to speak highly of his intelligence and character, in order to help him. After all (the old bromide) hadn't Campbell helped me?

I boiled over. I wrote back an austere letter pointing out that he was asking me to commit an unethical act and that he insulted me by assuming I was capable of one. His letter, I said, showed neither intelligence nor character.

That, I thought, was that, but to my surprise, I got an answer, not from the young man, but from his mother. She castigated me quite eloquently for making her son feel bad when he had only been joking. What was the matter with me (and my colossal ego, I suppose) that I could not take a joke?

I boiled over again. I replied even more austerely that if she and her son did not change their minds about what was funny and what was not, the young man would someday end in jail. This time I got no answer.

The funniest plagiarism story involving me took place on May 23, 1989. Tor Books had put out a "double." It was a paperback that contained a Ted Sturgeon novella. If you turned the book over, top to bottom, you found yourself facing another cover, with another story reading from that end. The other story was my "The Ugly Little Boy."

After the double had been announced as a forthcoming event and the stories briefly described with teasers, I received a furious letter from a young woman accusing me of plagiarism. Apparently, one and a half years earlier (in 1987 or 1988) she had written a story, submitted it, and had it rejected. She sent me a précis of the story, which had a little boy in it (as did Charles Dickens's *Oliver Twist*). She felt that the editors had been unwilling to print her story under her unknown name, so they gave the idea to me in order to have it appear under my own famous name and sell better. In this way "The Ugly Little Boy" was written. "How else can you explain it?" she demanded.

It had to be answered. No matter how ridiculous, a charge of plagiarism must be nailed to the wall. I was cruel enough to address her as "Dear Crazy Lady."

I then told her that if she had *looked* at the Tor double instead of merely reading an announcement of its forthcoming appearance, she would have seen that "The Ugly Little Boy" was a reprint and that the copyright notice, right there in the book, showed it to have been published in 1958, long before she wrote her story, and, possibly, before she was born. How had it happened, then? Perhaps she had plagiarized me.

She never answered, though the decent thing would have been to apologize rather humbly.

That reminds me that I am frequently asked by beginners whether their stories might be stolen if they submitted them to an editor. The answer is: "Not a chance." If the story were good enough to steal, the editor would want the writer more than the story, for the writer might then write *more* good stories. Why steal one when you can get many legitimately?

75

Science Fiction Conventions

The same push that caused science fiction to gather into local clubs and that had led to the formation of the Futurians, for instance, also acted to force the local clubs into larger associations.

In 1939, it occurred to Sam Moskowitz to set up a World Science Fiction Convention. It was held on July 2, 1939, in a hall in midtown Manhattan with only a few hundred people. Sam, who was a member of the Queens Science Fiction Club, from which the Futurians had broken away, refused to allow any Futurians to participate. I, however, had not yet been firmly associated with them in Sam's mind, and I had already sold three stories, so I was able to get in.

Thereafter, a World Science Fiction Convention has been held every year (except the war years of 1942, 1943, and 1944) in different cities. At each there is some important guest of honor and there are speeches, fancy-dress parties, banquets, and so on. It is always held over the Labor Day weekend, unless it is held outside the United States where Labor Day is not a factor.

Attendance has generally increased with time until it is possible to have as many as six or seven *thousand* people at a convention. Other, smaller conventions were set up and the time came when a really enthusiastic conventioneer such as Jay Kay Klein or Sprague de Camp could, if he wished, attend some convention or other nearly every day of the year.

Since I don't like to travel, I rarely attend a World Science Fiction Convention, but on those occasions when I was present I used to be often asked to serve as master of ceremonies at the banquet. But there was one time when I muffed things badly, giving an award, mistakenly, to a writer who had not won it. My embarrassment was so extreme that I have usually refused to toastmaster at convention banquets since.

There was one exception. In 1989, in Boston, we celebrated the golden anniversary of that first convention in 1939, and I was one of the few people who had attended it (and certainly the most prominent of the survivors). I therefore consented to travel to Boston and serve as toastmaster for the "nostalgia luncheon" that served as the celebration. I was delighted to do it too.

The guest of honor of the World Science Fiction Convention is usually chosen from some section of the country far from the place where the convention is being held. After all, the bulk of the attendees are locals and they don't want to see someone they are likely to see at local meetings. A distant guest of honor not usually seen by local fans drags in the registrations and helps pay the expenses of the convention. Since I only attend conventions close to home, I am usually not suitable as a guest of honor. In 1955, however, the convention was held in Cleveland and they asked me to be the guest of honor. I was not proof against the flattery and I drove to Cleveland so that I could serve.

This is the only time I have ever been the guest of honor at a World Science Fiction Convention (some people have served as such twice or even three times) but that doesn't bother me. I have been the guest of honor at a number of lesser conventions and, in fact, I have a set of plaques and scrolls that line my walls and fill my closets.

My fourteen honorary doctorate degrees, moldering in a trunk, have their inconvenient side, for I am considered an alumnus of each college and therefore fair game for fund-raising letters. (That reminds me of the man who complained that his wife was always after him for money, day and night. A friend said, "What does she do with it?" The man replied, "Nothing. I don't give her any.")

But I digress—

The Cleveland World Science Fiction Convention of 1955 was the thirteenth (for those of you who are superstitious). It was very nearly the smallest of all the conventions. Only three hundred attended. This had its advantages. In later years I was sometimes at a convention with an attendance in the many thousands, which means large hotels, enormous programs, crowded halls and function rooms, and hordes and hordes of unknowns among whom it was impossible to find one's friends and cronies. There was simply too much confusion, chaos, and anarchy.

When I am asked to sign books at one of these large conventions, the line stretches out anaconda-like. This is very flattering, but one gets tired of signing books too after a steady hour and a half of it. As I am a prolific writer, it is not unheard of for some eager reader to come with a suitcase containing two dozen books for me to sign. And even when it is not a formal signing time, fans stop me in the halls to sign programs and scraps of paper too.

It's partly my fault. Arthur Clarke, for instance, is notorious for being willing to sign only hardcover books, but I can't bring myself to refuse anyone who is actually standing there and looking at me with what *might* be devotion.

An attendance of three hundred was just right. There was no confusion. Writers met each other without trouble. Book signing was limited. For years, the 1955 convention was looked back upon as the friendliest one of all.

In the 1953 convention awards had been handed out for the best books of the year in different categories. That was viewed as just a gimmick made use of by that particular convention. In 1954, for instance, it wasn't done.

In 1955, however, the custom was revived and made permanent. From then on, the grand climax of the convention was always the banquet at which a series of awards were handed out very much in the fashion of the movie Oscars. The awards were called Hugos in honor of Hugo Gernsback, who had founded the first all-science-fiction magazine twenty-nine years earlier.

When I was toastmaster, I usually handed out the Hugos and I used the Bob Hope technique of complaining that I didn't get one. After all, "Nightfall," my robot stories, and the Foundation stories were all done before there was such a thing as a Hugo.

Of course, I eventually won Hugos, but I will leave that for later discussion.

76
Anthony Boucher

The Magazine of Fantasy and Science Fiction (F&SF) had begun publication in 1949. I was destined to be closely associated with it over a period of decades, but I had no inkling of this at the start. My early efforts to get a story into it were insufficient and I didn't manage to break in until I wrote a story called "Flies," which appeared in the June 1953 *F&SF*.

The editor of *F&SF* was Anthony Boucher, first with J. Francis McComas and later alone. His real name was William Anthony Parker White. He was born in 1911 and he entered the science fiction scene with his fantasy "Snulbug" in the December 1941 *Unknown*. He also wrote mystery stories. One of these, *Rockets to the Morgue* (1942), was a roman à clef in which a number of science fiction authors, notably Heinlein, appeared in recognizable guises. There was a brief mention of me and my robot stories.

During the early 1950s, there was a Big Three of magazine editors: John Campbell, Horace Gold, and Tony Boucher.

They were distinguished from each other, for one thing, by the nature of their rejection letters to established authors.

Campbell was ponderous and would send off single-spaced letters anywhere from two to seven pages long explaining why a particular story was unacceptable. It was often hard to tell what he was talking about. I once received a letter concerning a science essay I had submitted and that letter sounded like a rejection to me. I tried unsuccessfully to place the piece elsewhere until Campbell asked me impatiently what was holding up the revision. I went back to his letter, puzzled out what he had asked for, made the change, and sold him the piece.

I have already written about Horace Gold and his vicious rejections, but I can add one more little story here. He once, to my face, told me that a story of mine was meretricious. (The word is from a Latin word meaning prostitute and Horace was implying that I was prostituting my talent by writing junk just in order to make money.)

I controlled my annoyance and said innocently, "What was that word you used?"

Horace, proud of his vocabulary and delighted to have (as he thought) caught me out, said haughtily, "Meretricious!"

"And a Happy New Year to you," I responded. It was a silly remark, but it soothed my feelings, especially since it clearly enraged Horace.

Tony Boucher's rejections, on the other hand, were so gentle and so courteous that they could easily be mistaken for acceptances, except that the manuscript was returned. In the same bit of doggerel in which I satirized Horace's rejections I also satirized Tony's in a third verse. This went as follows:

Dear Isaac, friend of mine,
I thought your tale was fine.
Just frightful-
Ly delightful
And with merits all a-shine.
It meant a quite full
Night, full,
Friend, of tension
Then relief
And attended
With full measure
Of the pleasure
Of suspended
Disbelief.
It is triteful,
Almost spiteful
To declare
That some tiny faults are there.
Nothing much,
Perhaps a touch,
And over such
You shouldn't pine.

> So let me say
> Without delay
> My pal, my friend
> Your story's end
> Has left me gay
> And joyfully composed.
> P.S.
> Oh, yes,
> I must confess
> (With some distress)
> Your story is regretfully enclosed.

If Tony had a fault, it was that he sometimes sat on manuscripts for an inordinate length of time. That editors sometimes do so is a common complaint among writers, but the delay is actually understandable. Editors, even of small science fiction magazines, get huge quantities of submissions, mostly from unknowns and beginners (the "slush pile"). Large slick magazines have "readers" whose sole job it is to glance through the manuscripts and quickly weed out the impossibles so that the editor need read only those few manuscripts that offer some distant hope of acceptance.

At science fiction magazines, however, it is frequently the editor himself who must go through the slush pile. You can well imagine how the editorial gorge must rise after reading hundreds of impossible stories. There comes a point when the reading is actually painful and yet must be done on the off chance that somewhere in the slush pile is a budding Heinlein, but the editor is slow about it.

Writers don't always understand the physical and psychological difficulties of dealing with the slush pile. They sometimes don't understand that the many, many rejections that are sent out to unknowns can't, each one, have an accompanying letter that lovingly details the faults of the story. Sometimes, a true rejection would have to say, "You have no visible writing talent," and editors are loath to say such things. So a form rejection slip is enclosed, bland and uninformative.

I get letters in my capacity as figurehead editor of a magazine (I'll get to that later) complaining that Campbell sent me long, helpful letters when I was a beginner. Why can't I do that for other beginning writers?

Well, for one thing, Campbell's great mission in life was to send long letters (not always helpful) and it isn't mine. For another, Campbell sent them only to writers that showed promise. The vast, vast majority got only form rejection slips from Campbell, just as they got them from any other editor.

Beginning writers sometimes don't even understand the necessity of sending a stamped self-addressed envelope in case of rejection. At the magazine, I once got a letter from an outraged beginner who asked if he weren't worth a small amount of postage. I replied that he certainly was worth it but we had to return hundreds of manuscripts each week and the postage would mount up unbearably. It was far easier, I said, for each writer to bear his own cost of rejection than for the magazine to bear all. Of course, I got no answer.

I was very fond of Tony Boucher, as everyone was, but the only time I had a chance to socialize with him considerably was at the 1955 convention, where he was toastmaster. He saddened us all by dying in 1968 when he was only fifty-seven years old. He was succeeded in the editorial post by his managing editor, Robert Park Mills, about whom I will have more to say later.

77

Randall Garrett

I had met Randall Garrett on earlier occasions, but I got to know him really well at the Cleveland convention. During the days we spent there we were boon companions.

He was seven years younger than I was, a bit taller, and (as I was) markedly overweight. He and I were equally convivial, noisy, and extroverted. The difference was that he was quite a heavy drinker and I didn't drink at all, but when we were together and in full shriek, no one could tell the difference. We were so much alike in appearance and behavior that once when the two of us were on the platform at a science fiction convention, the deadly-tongued Harlan Ellison called out, "There they are: Tweedledum and Tweedledee."

And I called back, "Come stand between us, Harlan, and be the hyphen."

I knew Randall as Randy, but late in life he insisted on Randall and I'll adhere to his wishes. Randall was an incredibly prolific writer of short stories in the 1950s, simply pouring them out, under a variety of pseudonyms, though few were of much distinction.

He was quick-witted and fearsomely intelligent. He wrote excellent comic verse, infinitely better than anything I could turn out. He could sing Gilbert and Sullivan songs better than I could. He could turn out virtually lifelike clay figurines of the characters in the "Pogo" comic strip.

He was, of all the people I've met, probably the most perfect example of the supertalented person who simply wasted his talents. Partly, this was because of his drinking, I think, and partly because the talents were in so many directions that he had trouble making up his mind which track to follow.

A woman editor once said to me, "I can't stand Randall. He's loud, raucous, and flirts insistently with women."

I said, in embarrassment, "But that describes me!"

And she said, "Not quite! You can turn it off."

A true puritan does not have to choose a course of action. He remains sober, grave, and disapproving of hilarity at all times. An alcoholic doesn't have to choose either. He is always hilarious, noisy, and foolish. I, however, have to make a choice—hilarious or grave—to fit the occasion.

Randall's inability to "turn it off" was bad for him. It kept him from being taken with the seriousness he deserved.

Eventually, he moved to California and I lost touch with him. However, there was one last contact. In December 1978, I was in California. (It sounds unbelievable, but I will get to this later.) On December 12, I gave a talk in San Jose and Randall was in the audience.

I was speaking to a group of doctors and lawyers on the future of medicine and had much to say about clones. (It's important to realize, though I did not make a point of it in my talk, that a clone of a particular human being is the same sex as that human being. Of course, a male has an X and Y chromosome, while a female has two X chromosomes. If, therefore, the Y chromosome of the male clone could be changed to X, it would become a female.)

After I had been talking about clones for a while, Randall came quietly to the podium and placed a piece of paper before me. I read it while continuing to talk (not as easy as you might think) and could tell at once that it was a piece of comic verse about clones, designed to be sung to the tune of "Home on the Range." I therefore sang it at the close of the talk and it elicited a storm of applause.

I eventually wrote four more stanzas to the song and have sung what I have called "The Clone Song" innumerable times to innumerable gatherings. I have written a number of pieces of comic verse to one tune or another, but none have been as popular as "The Clone Song." This is not surprising, since the conception was Randall's, not mine. Here are the words to "The Clone Song," if you're curious:

(1) Oh, give me a clone
Of my own flesh and bone
With its Y chromosome changed to X
And after it's grown
Then my own little clone
Will be of the opposite sex.

(Chorus) Clone, clone of my own
With its Y chromosome changed to X
And when I'm alone
With my own little clone
We will both think of nothing but sex.

(2) Oh, give me a clone
Is my sorrowful moan,
A clone that is wholly my own.
And if she's X-X
And the feminine sex
Oh, what fun we will have when we're prone.

(3) My heart's not of stone,
As I've frequently shown
When alone with my own little X
And after we've dined,
I am sure we will find
Better incest than Oedipus Rex.

(4) Why should such sex vex
Or disturb or perplex
Or induce a disparaging tone?
After all, don't you see
Since we're both of us me
When we're having sex, I'm alone.

(5) And after I'm done
She will still have her fun
For I'll clone myself twice ere I die.
And this time without fail
They'll be both of them male
And they'll each ravage her by and by.

Some years after this last encounter, Randall was struck down by some form of meningitis that burned out his mind. After lingering in this mindless state for some years he died in December 1987 at the age of sixty.

78

Harlan Ellison

The most colorful character I ever met at science fiction conventions in the 1950s was Harlan Ellison, who was barely out of his teens at the time. He claims he is five feet four inches tall, but it doesn't really matter. In talent, energy, and courage he is eight feet tall.

He was born in 1934 and had a miserable youth. Being always small and being always enormously intelligent, he found that he could easily flay the dimwits by whom he was surrounded. But he could only do so in words, and the dimwits could use their fists. He spent his childhood (as Woody Allen once said of himself) being beaten up by everyone regardless of race, color, or religion.

This embittered him and did *not* teach him to keep his mouth shut. Instead, as he grew older, he made it his business to learn all the different arts of self-defense, and the time came when it was absolutely dangerous for some big hulk to attack him, for Harlan would lay him out without trouble. (I admire this greatly, for when *I* was scapegoated for similar reasons, I only studied the various arts of running and hiding. However, I must admit I was never as orally poisonous as he was, so I was scapegoated in minor fashion compared to his ordeal.)

Harlan uses his gifts for colorful and variegated invective on those who irritate him—intrusive fans, obdurate editors, callous publishers, offensive strangers. Little real harm is done, but it is particularly hard on editors who are young women, who have not been hardened to auctorial peculiarities. He can reduce them to tears in three minutes. The result is that many editorial staffs and many Hollywood people too (for Harlan is not just a science fiction writer—he is a *writer* in the fullest sense of the word) are reluctant to deal with him. What's more, he is so colorful and his personality sticks out so far in all directions that many people take pleasure in saying malicious things about him.

This is too bad, for two reasons. In the first place, he is (in my opinion) one of the best writers in the world, far more skilled at the art than I am. It is simply terrible that he should be constantly embroiled and enmeshed in matters which really have nothing to do with his writing and which slow him down tragically.

Second, Harlan is not the kind of person he seems to be. He takes a perverse pleasure in showing the worst side of himself, but if you ignore that and work your way past his porcupine spines (even though it leaves you bleeding), you will find underneath a warm, loving guy who would give you the blood out of his veins if he thought that would help.

I have a fairly good gift for invective myself and I am the only person I know who could stand up to him on a public platform for more than half a minute without being eradicated. (I think I can last as long as five minutes.)

I enjoy a public set-to with him, as I enjoy it with Lester del Rey and Arthur Clarke. It's a game with us. In private, though, there is never a cross word between Harlan and me, and if I tell you he is warm and loving, pay no mind to anything else you've heard. I know better and I am right.

One last word. Harlan has incredible charm and I have no idea how many tall, beautiful women he has been involved with. He has been married five times altogether. The first four marriages were brief and disastrous, but his fifth, with a sweet young woman named Susan, seems stable and Harlan seems mellowed. I hope so. He deserves far more in the way of happiness than he has had hitherto.

79

Hal Clement

When I moved from New York to Boston, I left behind me (so it seemed to my saddened self) the world of science fiction. This was not so, as it turned out. Boston was a lively center of science fiction fandom, and MIT, in particular, was littered with enthusiasts. That school has one of the great collections of old science fiction magazines, for instance, and every year they would set up a picnic in the hills south of Boston. I always attended and sometimes was even persuaded to accompany the students on a hike to the top of the hill. It was easier to persuade me to eat my fill of all the comestibles they brought along—such a mix of poisonous fast foods as would warm the cockles of any heart.

There was also a Boston science fiction club, which eventually set up semiannual conventions called "Boskones." This was a word out of E. E. Smith's famous story "Galactic Patrol," a four-part serial which began in the September 1937 *ASF* and which, when I first read it, I thought was the best thing ever written (though it didn't stand up when I reread it as an adult). It was also a form of "Boscon," standing for "Boston Convention." Eventually, the Boskones, in size and elaboration, were second only to the World Science Fiction Convention.

At the Boston science fiction club, I met Hal Clement, whose real name is Harry Clement Stubbs. Born in 1922, he has spent his adult life teaching science at Milton Academy, and since he wished to keep his writing career separate, he dropped his last name and used a familiar form of his first. He has not been a prolific writer, but his stories are always characterized by a rigid adherence to scientific fact and legitimate scientific speculation.

Hal Clement has a blunt-featured face and is quiet and soft-spoken. He is a gentle man. On occasion, he has pointed out errors in my science essays, but does so with such kindness and even diffidence that it would be impossible to be annoyed over it, even if I were the sort of person who got annoyed at being corrected. And any time he corrected me, I took it seriously, for he was always right.

At the 1956 World Convention in New York, Hal and I shared a room. (Sprague de Camp used our room as a kind of safety-deposit vault for his liquor supply, in order to keep it from being guzzled by science fiction's more notorious alcoholics. He knew, of course, that in our room it would not be touched.)

Hal was the ideal roommate, for he did not snore. (I was once forced to room with a thunderous snorer and I wouldn't repeat that experience for quite a lot of money. Janet says I snore but that she doesn't mind it because then she knows I'm alive. When I sleep quietly, as I often do, she gets nervous and makes sure I'm breathing.)

Hal attends almost every science fiction convention of any size, and is beloved by the fans. It is one of my regrets that since I have left Boston I rarely see him.

80

Ben Bova

The other prominent science fiction writer I met in Boston was Benjamin William Bova, who is universally known as Ben Bova. He was born in 1932, wore a crew cut when I first met him, but has a normal head of hair now. He has a keen sense of humor and we love swapping jokes. He is the source of some of my good ones.

He didn't start publishing till 1959, but he has been producing steadily ever since. He is another one of those science fiction writers who are quite at home in the writing of nonfiction.

Ben's big chance came in 1971, when, after Campbell's death, he was hired as editor of *ASF*. Filling Campbell's shoes was an enormous task, but Ben did it most creditably for seven years. He then became editor at *Omni*, a new slick magazine. Still later, he was involved with societies that were interested in space exploration and, indeed, Ben has written excellent books on the subject.

After his first marriage broke up Ben (who is of Italian descent) confessed to me that he thought he was in love with "a nice Jewish girl." In mock alarm, I offered to stake him to some money so that he could quickly leave town, but he really was in love. He married Barbara, a vivacious and attractive brunette, for whom it was also a second marriage, and they have been happy ever since.

Ben has always been a very good friend of mine. When I was incapacitated for a time in 1977 I asked him to substitute for me in certain talks that I was unable to give. I had no qualms about that because I had heard him speak and I knew him to be very good. He obliged me and, in doing so, asked that the payment for the talks be sent to me. I was horrified and you can bet that I told him quite flatly that any checks made out to me would be instantly torn up. But that's the kind of fellow he is.

I have many other close friends, and I shall never cease marveling over my good fortune in meeting so many wonderful people in the course of my life.

81
Over My Head

I don't want to give the impression that my writing is of uniform quality. We all have our bad days and our good days. I have turned out science fiction stories, even late in the game, that I refer to, in an embarrassed way, as "minor Asimov." I like to think, though, that (except for some of my very early stories) even minor Asimov is not very bad.

On the other hand, I occasionally write better than I ordinarily do. I call it "writing over my head," and when I reread one of these stories or passages, I find it hard to believe that I wrote it, and I wish ardently that I could write like that all the time.

Others might call it "being on a roll." Everything seems to break right, as with a baseball player who one day hits four home runs in a single game and may never again hit even two in one game.

When I was handing out Hugos in Pittsburgh in 1960, one of the winners was "Flowers for Algernon" by Daniel Keyes, which I had loved. It was surely one of the best science fiction stories ever written, and as I announced the winner, I grew very eloquent over its excellence. "How did Dan do it?" I demanded of the world. "How did Dan do it?"

At which I felt a tug on my jacket and there was Daniel Keyes waiting for his Hugo. "Listen, Isaac," he said, "if you find out how I did it, let me know. I want to do it again."

I suppose I was writing over my head when I wrote "Nightfall." It couldn't get all the praise it did if it weren't better than my usual, though frankly I don't see it. I reread it once, years ago, just to see if I could tell what all the fuss was about. Perhaps it was because the structure of the story was unusual. Every scene (if I remember correctly, for I don't intend to go back to the story to check on this) was interrupted. Before it could come to a natural conclusion, I'd be off in another direction, which was again interrupted. This lent a breakneck and breathless pace to the story. I stated at the start of the story that there would be a catastrophe in four hours. The four hours passed in a wild toboggan slide, and there was indeed a catastrophe.

It may be, then, that the story was written in such a way as to raise the suspense to a steadily higher pitch until it exploded. If so, I swear to you that I had no conscious plan for doing that. It was not deliberate. I did not know enough back in 1940 to do such a thing deliberately. I was just writing over my head.

In my favorite of the stories I've written, "The Last Question," it is not the writing that is over my head. It is the idea and the manner in which I constructed the climax. For years, people have phoned me to ask about a story they had read, whose name they had forgotten, and concerning whose authorship they were uncertain, though it *might* have been me. They could identify the story by the last sentence, however, and they wanted to know where they could find it for re-reading. The story in question was always "The Last Question."

My second favorite is "The Bicentennial Man," which appeared in an anthology of original stories in 1976. Here at last, it is the writing. I reread it recently and marveled at how much better it was than the general run of my writing.

My third favorite, "The Ugly Little Boy," is unusual in the same way. My stories tend to be cerebral and unemotional. How is it possible, then, that I could make up a story that builds up emotion to the point where, at the end, the reader can't help but cry? I cry every time I reread it, but, of course, I weep easily. However, I once *told* the plot of the story to an audience that fell absolutely silent as I talked because tears trickling down cheeks make no noise.

When Robyn was twelve or thirteen, I gave her the story to read and she came out of her room periodically to assure me she was greatly enjoying the story. Then, for a long while, I did not hear from her. Finally she came out, her face red and swollen and her bloodshot eyes staring at me accusingly. "You didn't *tell* me it was a sad story," she said.

Now *that* was writing over my head.

I'm not going to try to tell you that every story I wrote was great. I would be hard put to find another one to compare with "The Bicentennial Man" and "The Ugly Little Boy." However, the biggest and most effective over-my-head writing I ever produced was not in a short story but in a section of a novel.

The novel in question was *The Gods Themselves* (Doubleday, 1972). It was in three parts, and the second part dealt with aliens in another universe. I'll risk being accused of a "colossal ego" again by giving you my opinion that they were the best aliens ever described in science fiction, and also the best writing I ever did, or am likely to do. I received plenty of confirmation of this from my readers.

One more word on the subject—

It is much harder to write over your head in nonfiction than in fiction. The closest I ever came to such a thing, in my opinion, was in an essay entitled "A Sacred Poet" in the September 1987 *F&SF*. Ordinarily, in such essays, I discuss some scientific subject, but I was moved in another direction this time. I had had a set-to with someone I considered a narrow-minded scholar and, as a result, I decided to write an essay on poetry.

I wasn't such a fool as to think I could write anything about the literary quality of poetry. I just wanted to write about poems that *moved* people and affected their actions. I began with Oliver Wendell Holmes, for instance, and his poem "Old Ironsides," which elicited a howl of public protest against scrapping the ship, one that has kept it in existence right down to this very day.

I was afraid I would get cold letters that would say, in effect, "Stick to science, Asimov. You're an ignoramus in the humanities." Not so! I got an outpouring of letters, more than for any other essay I had ever written, and every last one approved of the essay. There was not even one dissenting vote.

82

Farewell to Science Fiction

I have been spending a long time on the 1950s, the decade of my greatest science fictional triumphs. It is strange, therefore, that as the 1950s ended, I should also end most of my involvement with the field.

After "The Ugly Little Boy," I seem to have simply dried up, at least partially. I have said that science fiction writers were sometimes written out. It usually takes ten years, in my opinion. In my case, it took twenty. But why? I have wondered about that frequently.

In the first place, I had moved away from Campbell and his peculiar ideas. I also moved away from Horace Gold, and *F&SF* was not a reliable market for me. I had even grown tired of writing novels. In 1958, I started a third robot novel and bogged down quite early and couldn't make myself continue. It took me years to persuade Doubleday to take back the $2,000 advance they had given me.

In the second place, even as I was writing "The Ugly Little Boy," the Soviet Union sent up the first artificial satellite and the United States went into a panic, feeling it would be left behind in the technology race. It seemed to me that it was necessary for me to write science books for the general public and help educate Americans.

So you must understand I did not suffer from writer's block. I merely switched the main focus of my endeavors. I worked as hard as ever, kept the same long hours I always did, but for some twenty years I wrote nonfiction rather than fiction.

I did this not without some worry. Aware that my chief source of income was my fiction, I anticipated a sharp decrease in annual income just when I no longer had a base salary from the school to fall back on. I tried to tell myself that writing nonfiction was the patriotic thing to do and one must be willing to suffer in a patriotic cause, but, in all honesty, that did not make me feel much better.

However, things did not work out as I expected. In the first place, writing nonfiction was much easier and much more fun than writing fiction, so it was precisely the thing I ought to have done in switching from part-time to full-time writing. If I had tried to write *fiction* full-time, I would undoubtedly have broken down.

Then, too, just as I began to think I ought to write on science for the general public, the publishers began to think they ought to publish such books. The result was that they took everything I could write even when I wrote at my fastest. My income did not go down, but rose rapidly.

Was I astonished? Yes, indeed.

But life was not all roses. The same thing happened to science fiction after I had left it that had happened to chemistry while I was spending years at the NAES and in the army. A revolution took place.

Science fiction, after all, has its fashions as everything else does. In the first dozen years of magazine science fiction, it was extremely action-oriented. Many science fiction stories were essentially Westerns set on Mars, so to speak, and were written by authors who knew little or nothing about science.

Beginning in 1938, Campbell changed everything. He insisted on having characters who were real scientists and engineers and who talked as such people naturally would. Stories became idea-oriented and puzzle-oriented and I was particularly good at that.

Even more than Heinlein (who was a law unto himself) I think that I epitomized what it was that Campbell wanted. The robot stories and, even more so, the Foundation stories were his babies, and during the 1940s and 1950s science fiction writers, whether consciously or unconsciously, tried to follow my lead.

But then came the 1960s, and again there was a radical change. A new breed of science fiction writers came into being. Television had killed the general magazines that had been heavy with fiction. The new writers had lost their natural market and turned to science fiction because it had survived television. They brought to science fiction something called "the New Wave." Stories rich in emotion and stylistic experimentation began to appear, as did mood pieces and stories that were downright surrealistic and obscure.

In a word, science fiction became completely "non-Asimovian" and I was glad that instinct had caused me to leave the field. Far better to leave voluntarily than to be cast out as obsolescent.

I also thought, ruefully, that if I should wish to return to the field, I couldn't. It had passed beyond me, just as chemistry had passed beyond me with the advent of resonance and quantum mechanics.

83

The Magazine of Fantasy and Science Fiction

An odd thing transpired, however. Even though I was not writing science fiction in the 1960s, I remained one of the Big Three, partly because my novels continued to sell and partly because I appeared in anthologies. The most important reason, however, involved a decision I made that I hoped would achieve a certain purpose and that, for a wonder, did indeed achieve it. (My gunnery is not usually so accurate.)

It came about through the help of Robert Park Mills, who was first managing editor of *F&SF* and then, beginning in September 1968, editor, succeeding Tony Boucher. Bob Mills was tall and gangly with prominent angles to his jaw that stuck out on either side just under his ears. He was another of these slow-speaking, soft-voiced fellows. He was born in 1920 and, like Fred Pohl, was within a couple of weeks of my age.

In 1957, a sister magazine of *F&SF* came into being. It was called *Venture Science Fiction* and Bob Mills was made its editor. Anxious to try something new, he asked if I would be willing to write a regular science column for *Venture*.

I had been continuing to write occasional nonfiction pieces for *ASF*, but these were not entirely satisfactory. I did not really have a free hand with Campbell, who had definite notions of the kind of article he wanted and would now and then turn down my suggestions.

What *Venture* offered was not only a regular column but a free hand. As long as I met the deadline, I could write on any subject I wished in any way I wanted. That was exactly the sort of thing I was after and, since I had no fears of failing to meet the deadline, I accepted with a whoop of delight.

I promptly wrote an essay for the January 1958 *Venture*, its seventh issue. Three more essays appeared in the eighth, ninth, and tenth issues of the magazine, but with the tenth issue the magazine ceased publication. My days as a science columnist had ended so quickly (and just as I was getting into the swing of it) that I was chagrined.

On August 12, 1958, however, I had lunch with Bob Mills. He had just succeeded to the editorship of *F&SF* and he suggested that I continue my science column for that magazine—obviously a much more stable outlet than *Venture* had been.

I was overjoyed. I had just come to the decision that I was not going to be writing science fiction, but I didn't want to leave the field. By writing a science column for *F&SF* I would be appearing every month in one of the major science fiction magazines and my name would be kept before the science fiction public.

Of course, I agreed, for the terms were the same. As long as I met the deadline, I would have a completely free hand.

The magazine and I both held to the agreement. My first column appeared in the November 1958 issue of *F&SF* and, from that time to the present moment, almost thirty-two years later, I have never failed to meet the deadline, and have never failed to have an essay in every single issue, whatever the vicissitudes of life held for me. And Bob Mills and the succeeding editors kept to the agreement also. They never suggested a topic, never rejected an essay, and carefully sent me galleys of each so I could make sure that everything was exactly as I wanted it to be.

My *F&SF* essays have never palled on me and they have remained my favorite of all the writing I do (despite the fact that they also represent the lowest word-rate payment). Though I have now written 375 of these essays of 4,000 words or so apiece (1,500,000 words), I never run out of ideas or enthusiasm.

What's more, these essays have done exactly what I wanted them to do. They have kept my name before the science fiction public and assured, more than anything else, that I would remain one of the Big Three. (It's also true that the twenty-year gap was not *entirely* devoid of science fiction, as I shall explain in due course.)

Bob Mills and I always maintained a pleasant relationship. In my essays I referred to him frequently as the "Kindly Editor." In fact, he became known by that sobriquet to the fans generally. When he retired as editor in 1962 and was replaced by Avram Davidson, almost the first thing Avram did was to let me know that he didn't wish to be called the "Kindly Editor."

There was no danger of that. Avram was a class-A writer, but he was a cantankerous individual I would never think of as "kindly."

Bob became an agent for some twenty years, and then, in the mid-1980s, he retired and went to California. He died, rather unexpectedly, in 1986 at the age of sixty-six.

84

Janet

All through the 1950s, filled as the decade was with science fiction triumphs and medical school disasters, I was also leading a private life. The children were growing up, and Gertrude and I were growing older—and unhappier with each other.

I don't suppose marriages turn sour in a moment. You don't fall off a precipice. It's just that annoyances multiply, frictions come slowly to seem irreconcilable, forgiveness comes more reluctantly and with worse grace. And then, one day, you're shaking your head with the knowledge that the marriage isn't working.

I don't know when that happened to me—probably about 1956 after I had been married for fourteen years. Gertrude had talked about divorce earlier, but it was about then that I began to consider it. It did not seem possible, for there was no tradition of divorce in my family. My mother and father remained married for fifty years. It was a stormy marriage at times but there was no whisper of divorce. Such a thing would have been incredibly unthinkable.

The thought of divorce would have horrified me even if only Gertrude were involved, but it was worse than that. There were also David and Robyn. Even if I could bring myself to divorce Gertrude, I could not possibly leave two little children in the lurch no matter what my personal unhappiness. So I sighed, and made up my mind to stay married till the children grew up—and, who knows, by then things might even have improved.

My unhappiness did leave me in a vulnerable emotional condition and laid the groundwork for my fortuitous meeting with Janet Opal Jeppson.

The first meeting took place in 1956, and I didn't even know it. Janet has a younger brother, John, who had gone to Boston University Medical School and who had been in the last biochemistry class I had helped teach. He was a science fiction fan and he had converted his sister, Janet, to the true faith. He also told her about me and what a terrific lecturer and eccentric fellow I was. It roused her curiosity.

In 1956, the World Convention was held in New York, and Janet (who had been born on August 6, 1926, and had just turned thirty at the time) attended some of the sessions, meaning among other things to meet me and get my signature on one of my books. Unfortunately I was suffering a kidney-stone attack.

My first attack of the sort was in 1948. It didn't last long and I put it down as a sudden bout of indigestion and forgot about it. In 1950, I had a much worse attack and, in fact, I had to be hospitalized and was even given morphine (for the only time in my life). Between 1950 and 1969, I must have had at least two dozen attacks, of which even the smallest was terribly painful. They then disappeared for reasons I will advance later.

But in 1956, I had a bad one. I did my best to do what I was supposed to do and I stood in line signing books, but there was a fearsome frown (actually a look of moderate agony) on my face and I was not my usual winsome and charming self.

Janet approached with her copy of *Second Foundation* and I asked her name so that I could write it in the book.

"Janet Jeppson," she said.

"And what do you do?" I asked as I wrote, just to make conversation.

"I'm a psychiatrist," she said.

"Good," said I, automatically, as I completed the signing. "Let's get on the couch together." I didn't even look at her, and you can bet I had no desire whatever, at that moment and under my kidney-stone condition, for any sort of dalliance.

Janet told me years later that she went off thinking, "Well, he may be a good writer, but he's a *pill.*"

"Pill" was the term Janet always used for someone who was irredeemably difficult.

At the time, I hadn't had the faintest idea of what I had done, that I might well have tossed away my future happiness and ruined the best thing in my life.

Fortunately, my faux pas was correctable and the time came when I found out all about Janet.

She suffered from a lack of a sense of self-worth. This wasn't true at first, for as a little girl she was a doll-like beauty, with flaxen hair and blue eyes, who was idolized by her parents. When she was nine, her brother, John, was born. He was the nearest thing to a child that Janet was ever to have and for a long time her attitude toward him retained a touch of the maternal.

The trouble was that Janet remained small while her age-mates grew taller and larger. She eventually shot up and is now five feet seven inches tall, but like many children of Scandinavian descent she was slow to develop physically. (But not mentally. She was considerably more intelligent than her better-upholstered companions—which did not necessarily make her life easier either.)

Janet, in adult life, is not classically beautiful. She has a small chin that she thinks detracts from her looks. Because she did not consider herself pretty and because she worked hard at her studies, she did not have an active social life. By the time she reached her thirties, she had her B.A. from Stanford University, her M.D. from New York University Medical School, had completed her residency in psychiatry at Bellevue Hospital, and was in the William Alanson White Institute of

Psychoanalysis. She had a career, therefore, that would keep her busy and give her a constructive life, whether she married or not.

Her fugitive meeting with me in 1956 did not prevent her from reading other books of mine and she decided, from what I revealed of myself in my books, that I couldn't be quite the "pill" that I had shown myself to be. She decided she would give me another chance.

In 1959, the Mystery Writers of America was holding its annual banquet in New York, and I, having written a mystery novel that was definitely not a success, thought I'd attend. I was encouraged to do this by one of my Boston friends, Ben Benson, who had written a series of well-received mysteries in which the Massachusetts State Police were featured. I liked the books and I liked Ben, who had come through World War II, ending up with a badly damaged heart. I didn't expect that I would know anyone at a mystery writers convention, but Ben could introduce me to various people.

The day of the banquet was May 1, and on the evening before, while having dinner at the home of an editor, I found out that Ben Benson had had a heart attack and had died on the streets of New York. I was terribly depressed and spent the night wondering if I shouldn't go back to Boston. It seemed to me that I didn't want to go to the banquet without Ben.

The next day I visited Bob Mills, who also planned to attend the banquet, hoping he might cheer me up, but there was no chance of that. Bob was in the dumps too, over some problem involving his job. More than ever I ached to go back to Boston, not knowing that, if I did, the misadventure of 1956 would be confirmed and my life would be ruined.

Fortunately, Judith Merril showed up in Bob's office just as I was leaving. Judy was one of the few important women science fiction authors of that time, her most notable story being "That Only a Mother" in the June 1948 *ASF*. She had been Fred Pohl's third wife.

She rallied me and urged me to go to the banquet, where, she assured me, people were probably expecting me and were anxious to meet me. I let myself be persuaded and for that I shall forever be grateful to Judy.

Meanwhile, Janet's friend the mystery writer Veronica Parker Johns was in charge of the seating arrangements at the banquet. She persuaded Janet to go, because Eleanor Roosevelt was speaking, and Janet could sit next to Isaac Asimov and Hans Santesson.

When I arrived at the banquet, I found that Judy was right. There were a number of people there who knew me and whom I knew and in no time at all I felt exactly as I would have felt at a science fiction convention and found myself having a good time.

It was time to be seated at last and Hans Stefan Santesson came to get me. He was a plump, bottom-heavy fellow with a smooth oval face and a faint Swedish accent. He was editor of *Fantastic Universe Science Fiction,* to which I had sold an occasional story. (He died in 1975 at the age of sixty-one.)

He said, "Come, Isaac, there's someone who wants to meet you." Looking in the direction he was indicating, I saw Janet Jeppson, at the table, smiling widely in greeting.

My lonely heart was looking for something at this time, and it was not beauty. I had had beauty in heaping handfuls and it wasn't working out. I was looking for something else—I wasn't sure what, and I may not even have realized, consciously, that I was looking for anything at all.

What I wanted, perhaps, was warmth—pleasant, undemanding affection—something to which beauty was irrelevant. Whatever I was seeking, I found it at that dinner. Janet was warm, unaffected, cheerful, and artlessly glad to be with me. By the end of the dinner, she looked beautiful to me and I have never wavered in that opinion at any time since. When she walks into a room and I see her face unexpectedly, my heart, to this day, jumps with delight.

Of course, I didn't have a kidney stone on that day of the banquet so that I was in my usual state of sweetness and light. Janet was delighted and decided that I wasn't a pill after all.

When a pneumatic young woman, so artificial that I suspected a tap of a finger would cause her to disintegrate, advanced to take some award, Janet said, "Oh, I wish I looked like that," and I told her in all honesty that she looked a lot better than that.

And when I told her that my mystery novel was probably the worst ever written, she decided I wasn't the monster of arrogance that people said I was.

We remained in touch thereafter, writing letters back and forth. The correspondence saw me through the bleak years. I phoned her now and then. I occasionally saw her on my visits to New York and all these contacts merely strengthened my conviction that she was the kind of person who suited me perfectly.

I'll have more to say about her later on.

85
Mystery Novels

In my childhood, as I explained, I read mysteries as well as science fiction. I continued reading both as I grew older and, in fact, although my interest in reading science fiction waned, my interest in mysteries did not. To this day mysteries are virtually the only light reading in which I indulge.

I do not, however, like modern tough-guy mysteries, too violent suspense novels, or studies of criminal psychopathology. I have always liked what are now called "cozy mysteries," those that involve a limited number of suspects and that are solved by ratiocination rather than by shooting.

Of course, my ideal mysteries are those by Agatha Christie and my ideal detective is Hercule Poirot. I also liked the novels of Dorothy Sayers, Ngaio Marsh, Michael Innes, and any others who wrote in literate fashion without undue stress on either sex or violence. When I was young I was particularly fond of John Dickson Carr/Carter Dickson, but in later years when I reread him I found that his books seemed overemotional and even unnatural.

Just as I wanted to write science fiction, I also wanted to write mysteries, and indeed I did. John Campbell had once said, incautiously, that it was impossible to write a good mystery in the science fiction mode, because the detective could always produce some technologically advanced device that would help him solve the problem.

I privately thought that this was a foolish statement, because it was only necessary to set the background at the start and avoid introducing anything new in the remainder of the book. You would then have a science fiction mystery that was legitimate.

In 1952, Horace Gold suggested I write a robot novel. I demurred, saying I could only handle robots in short stories. He said, "Nonsense, write a novel about an overpopulated world in which robots are taking human jobs."

"No," I said. "Too depressing."

"Make it a mystery," he said, "with a detective and a robot sidekick who will take over if the detective muffs the case."

That was the germ of *The Caves of Steel,* which was a good science fiction novel and, at the same time, a straightforward mystery. It was the first time (in my opinion) that anyone had brought the two genres into quite so perfect a fusion.

Then, to show it was no accident, I wrote another science fiction mystery, *The Naked Sun,* which was a sequel to the first. By the time the latter book appeared, in 1957, I was aching to write a "straight" mystery, one without science fiction trappings.

As it happened, Doubleday's mystery editor asked me to write a straight mystery novel and I jumped at the chance. Since I knew nothing about police procedure and preferred to avoid violence (when my mysteries involve a murder, there is only one, which takes place offstage, usually before the story opens), I decided to place the scene in a chemical laboratory at a university. In this way, though the story might not have a science fictional background, it did have a scientific one.

For the purpose, I used my memories of Columbia University together with the professor and graduate students I had known in order to fix the characters in my mind. The events, naturally, were wholly fictional (and a good thing too, since they included a murder). I showed Doubleday the first two chapters and they approved, but when I submitted the entire novel, I was told, when I phoned to inquire, that it was *rejected.* There was no revision requested, it was *rejected.* It was the only novel I ever submitted to Doubleday that was rejected.

This rejection (how I keep repeating the word) came at a very bad time. My quarrel with Keefer at the medical school was approaching a climax and I only phoned Doubleday in order to be told the book was taken so that I could have some relief from tension. Instead—well, I won't use the word, but it wasn't taken.

That was a low point for me. I closed and locked my laboratory door and sat there for quite a while in misery. Then I decided I must not give way to self-pity and I occupied myself in writing the funniest bit of comic verse I ever wrote. No, I won't quote it here—it's too long. I felt much better when it was done, but was still far from my usual sunny self. I think the shock of the (I won't say it) refusal helped bring me to the decision to switch to nonfiction during the time that followed.

I tried to sell the mystery novel elsewhere and, for a while, had no luck whatever. Finally, Avon took it, without any real interest. I suspect they were hoping the acceptance would lead me on to doing a science fiction book for them. (I'm afraid I didn't.) They published the book in 1958 under the title of *The Death Dealers,* which was not my title, and they made use of a completely misleading cover.

What was even worse, the book simply dropped dead. Avon made no effort to sell copies and the book earned back only a portion of its advance. The embarrassment was extreme, and it is no wonder that when I met Janet at the mystery writers banquet not long afterward I should tell her, ruefully, that I had written the worst mystery novel in existence. It was the only book of mine published in the 1950s, by the way, that was neither science fiction nor science, though, I repeat, it had a science background.

And yet *The Death Dealers* underwent a resurrection. One of my publishers, Walker & Company, came across the book in 1967 in a display of my books that Boston University put on in honor of my eightieth book. Realizing it was out of print, Walker asked me to get it back from Avon. I did, and Walker put out a hardcover edition in 1968, ten years after its first appearance, and used *my* title, *A Whiff of Death.* It went through two hardcover printings and a number of paperback editions, to say nothing of several foreign languages, so that it was a reasonable success after all. That gave me the courage to reread it and I revised my earlier notion. It may not have been the best mystery ever written, but it was far from the worst.

Indeed, there was one curious thing about *A Whiff of Death.* It had a lower-class homicide detective of Irish origin who found himself trying to solve a mystery that involved a large number of intellectuals who could not help but look down upon him. The detective, Doheney, was very humble, very respectful, asked questions almost hesitantly, but, in the end, it suddenly turned out he was ahead of them all and knew exactly what he was doing.

The time was to come (and still exists) when Peter Falk's *Columbo* was my favorite TV show and I always noted the resemblance of Columbo to Doheney. I never for one moment thought that *Columbo* had been taken from *A Whiff of Death,* and if it had, I wouldn't have minded, for they improved the idea so greatly. In fact, the resemblance only increases my enjoyment of the TV show.

The resurrection and success of *A Whiff of Death* gave me the comfortable feeling that Doubleday had made a mistake in 1958 and also gave me the courage to try again, when Larry Ashmead (my Doubleday editor at the time) asked me to attend a meeting of the American Booksellers Association (ABA) in 1975. It was one of their rare meetings in New York, so I *could* attend, and they were celebrating their seventy-fifth anniversary.

Larry didn't want me there just for a good time. He wanted me to collect local color and write a mystery entitled *Murder at the ABA*. He explained that he wanted the book for the next meeting of the Association a year later.

"I'll have the manuscript for you well before that time, Larry," I said.

"Not the manuscript," he said, "the finished book."

I was appalled. That gave me only two months to write the book, so I objected. Larry came back with what I've heard a million times from editors, "You can do it, Isaac."

I attended the ABA meeting and wrote the book in seven weeks, as compared with seven to nine months for a science fiction novel. Why the difference?

To me, the answer seems simple. In writing a science fiction novel, you must invent a futuristic social structure which is complex enough to be interesting in itself apart from the story and which is self-consistent. You must also invent a plot that only works within that social structure. The plot must develop without unduly obscuring the description of the social structure, and the social structure must be described without unduly slowing the plot.

Making a science fiction novel fulfill this double purpose is difficult even for an experienced and talented old hand such as myself. Every other kind of writing is *easier* than science fiction.

Writing a story like *Murder at the ABA* requires no invention of a social structure. The social structure is that of here and now. In fact, the structure was precisely that of the ABA meeting I had attended. All I had to do was write the plot. No wonder writing a mystery took seven weeks instead of seven months.

Doubleday published the book in 1976 and I was very pleased with it. I thought it was written in sprightly fashion and that it was a delightful tour de force. I had a Harlan Ellison-like character named

Darius Just tell it in the first person. (I was careful to get Harlan's written permission, of course, and I dedicated the book to him.) I myself, under my own name, appeared in the book in the third person as comic relief. As an added bit of comedy, Darius and I argued some points in footnotes. Some critics objected to this, but there are idiots in every walk of life.

Naturally, I at once thought of doing a series of mystery novels featuring Darius Just. At seven weeks apiece, it would be a delightful snap. Alas, it never happened. Doubleday wouldn't have it. If I were to write fiction, they wanted science fiction. They had just allowed *Murder at the ABA* as a one-shot aberration.

But that's all right, I managed to write mysteries anyway, but, alas, not novels. I'll explain that in due course.

86

Lawrence P. Ashmead

I have had a great many editors in my life, but, of course, some of them stand out particularly. John Campbell and Walter Bradbury are examples of that, and I've discussed them. Another is Lawrence P. Ashmead.

In 1960, he was working as an assistant to Richard K. Winslow, who succeeded Timothy Seldes as my editor at Doubleday. I was busy writing a book called *Life and Energy*, which was published by Doubleday in 1962. Since I couldn't get Doubleday to take back the $2,000 they had advanced for the third robot novel in 1958 that I never wrote, I persuaded them to transfer it to *Life and Energy*, and got rid of the obligation in that way.

Larry Ashmead, who is a scientist (his degree is in geology), went over the manuscript of *Life and Energy,* and suggested a number of corrections. After he sent back the corrected manuscript for me to deal with, Dick Winslow learned of what he had done and, knowing of writers' peculiarities, was uneasy over my reaction.

However, though I have many peculiarities, they are not the ones other writers usually have. My next time at Doubleday, I handed in the corrected manuscript and asked who had done the corrections. Larry said he had (possibly steeling himself for a writer's tantrum).

I said, "Thank you, Mr. Ashmead. They were very good corrections and I'm glad you made them."

I had no way of knowing that when Dick left Doubleday, Larry would succeed him as my editor and that from the moment I had thanked him he was determinedly pro-Asimov. I just work on the principle that of all the virtues gratitude (next to honesty) is the greatest, and that has helped me on numerous occasions in my life.

After the medical school kicked me out and my time became completely my own I made it a practice to visit New York once a month regularly. I always followed the same regimen. I would come in on Thursday, spend the rest of the day and all of Friday on editorial rounds, relax on Saturday, and return by Sunday noon. And when I came in on Thursday, the first thing I would do after dropping off my baggage in the hotel room and washing up was to chase out to Doubleday and have lunch with Larry at Peacock Alley. (This has always been my favorite restaurant.)

When, in 1970, I returned to New York, I worried a little about my relationship with Doubleday. While I was in Boston, I bothered Doubleday only once a month, which was tolerable. While in New York, might I not be tempted to bother them day in and day out till they kicked me out of the building?

Not at all. The monthly luncheon with Larry continued, and it was made quite clear that I could drop in at any time in between, though you can bet I was careful not to spoil matters by overexploiting the privilege. In recent years I have settled down a regular visit to Doubleday of perhaps half an hour's duration every Tuesday, though under later editors, lunch is rarely involved. Doubleday is used to my weekly appearance and on the rare occasions when I can't come there is the invariable complaint that "it didn't feel like Tuesday."

My favorite luncheon-story-with-Larry is the following:

After the usual fine Peacock Alley meal was finished, the maître d' (who knew us well, of course) brought around the elaborate dessert sampler. I had already helped myself to the excellent cookies that were routinely placed on the table with the coffee, so, mindful of my weight problem, I got a very small and relatively harmless dessert.

Whereupon Larry said, "Come on, Isaac, that's not enough. Take something else in addition. It's on Doubleday." (Larry is short, good-looking, and, at that time at least, slender enough, though not exactly thin.)

"Go ahead, Dr. Asimov," chimed in the maître d'. "Have something else."

I said, feebly, "Janet wouldn't like it if I had two desserts."

And Larry said, "She'll never know."

I am nothing if not weak. I took a second dessert.

When I got home, there was Janet waiting for me at the door with a severe no-nonsense look on her face. "What is this," she demanded, "about two desserts?"

Kindly old Larry had phoned her with the news as soon as I had left him. I forgave him because I loved him and therefore classified his vile deed under the heading of "practical joke."

Larry, by the way, whenever anyone asked him to suggest a writer to do some difficult task, invariably suggested me. And since I hated, as a matter of principle, ever to refuse him, I found myself in some uncomfortable situations at times. I had to write an article on sex in space for *Sexology,* for instance.

That particular piece got me an interview with Dr. Ruth on her popular answer-and-question show involving sex. I had to discuss sex in space with her. I didn't mind, for she was a clever and cute little woman. I watched a taping of the interview and her last remark to me was: "I hope you come to see me again, Dr. Asimov." My reply, as the sound faded, was: "What do you have in mind, Dr. Ruth?"

But editors are all editorially mortal and on October 24, 1975, Larry phoned me to say he was taking a job with Simon & Schuster, presumably at a higher salary. I was the first one he told, for he didn't want me to hear it in any other way. It was an awful moment. I sat in my chair staring at nothing for an hour.

Actually, it wasn't as bad as I thought. Doubleday got me another highly satisfactory editor, Cathleen Jordan, and I did get to see Larry every once in a while, for no publisher is a stranger to me. He is now at Harper's and I have just written a book for Harper's.

87
Overweight

Since, in the previous section, I mentioned my "weight problem," I had better say something about an embarrassing but significant matter.

The Asimovs are prone to overweight. My father, slim as a youth, weighed 220 pounds when he was in his early forties and was quite obese. (My mother also gained weight with age, but to a lesser extent.)

But the Asimovs have another ability. If they lose, they lose. I have known a number of obese people who, by dint of strenuous dieting, lose fifty pounds or more, become slim—then allow all the weight to be regained. To me this is such a tragedy. One must work so hard, so grimly, giving up the pleasure of food, in order to become comparatively thin and better-looking, and then—gain it all back? It doesn't bear thinking of.

When my father developed angina pectoris in 1938 at the age of forty-two and was ordered by the doctors to lose weight, he did. He went down fairly rapidly to 160 and stayed at that weight for the remaining thirty years of his life. He would not have had those thirty years otherwise.

As for myself, I was a skinny boy. I weighed 153 pounds in college and I never gained weight no matter what I ate. That was because I really didn't eat much (I almost never ate breakfast, for instance), but I didn't realize that.

Once I got married to Gertrude and had a chance to eat cooking that was better than my mother's, I ate freely, always assuming that I would not gain, and in a matter of a few months, I had gained thirty pounds. By 1964, when I was forty-four, I weighed 210 pounds. I was just my father's height and only ten pounds under his maximum.

I grew frightened. I was already two years past the point where my father had developed angina. To be sure, I had escaped and seemed in perfect health, but how long could I get away with it? My fear accelerated when the actor Peter Sellers, who was *not* fat, had a well-publicized heart attack.

I began to lose weight by cutting my food intake, and little by little I declined, first to 180, then, some years later, to 160. My weight is now a steady 155, about what it was when I married Gertrude—but the damage had been done.

88

More Conventions

After I met Janet, conventions had more meaning to me. In 1959, I traveled to Detroit by train to attend the World Convention there. It was only a few months after the mystery writers banquet, yet I remember being very dissatisfied with the fact I was there alone. After all, Janet was a science fiction fan in her own right. If she had also attended the convention, we could have had meals together, and attended talks together. She could listen to me give a talk and check out her brother's insistence that I was a great lecturer.

However, she wasn't there.

What I remember most clearly about the Detroit convention was that one time I stayed up virtually all night, laughing and kidding with other writers. (This was the only time I ever did that.) When I finally got to my room, dawn was well advanced and I felt it was useless to go to sleep, so I just washed up and went down to breakfast.

Early breakfast is almost unheard of at the conventions, for the nightly dissipation is such that only a few can shake off their swinish slumber before 10 A.M. and most sleep till noon. So I walked into an empty dining room—or, at least, almost empty, for there were John Campbell and his (second) wife, Peg, at breakfast. They led orderly lives as (almost always) I did.

"Well," said Peg, with approval, "I'm glad that *someone* goes to bed at a decent time and can have early breakfast with us."

And I said, with completely straight-faced and unashamed hypocrisy, "I try to live right, Peg."

The next year, 1960, the convention was in Pittsburgh and again I felt I could go. What's more, this time I persuaded Janet that she ought to go also, so she did. That made Pittsburgh very successful indeed. What I remember particularly about that convention are these events:

Early on, Theodore Cogswell, a science fiction writer who had the faculty of charming the girls, took Janet by the arm and led her away. There was no reason he shouldn't. Janet didn't belong to me and I was a married man anyway. The odd thing is that I felt a pang of jealousy, an emotion to which I had always considered myself immune. Fortunately, Janet came back in a few minutes.

I introduced Janet to John Campbell, who, once he learned that Janet was a psychiatrist, characteristically undertook to lecture her on psychiatry and (also characteristically) got everything wrong.

(In this connection, I once had lunch with George Gaylord Simpson, the great vertebrate paleontologist of Harvard University. He was a science fiction fan and wanted to know what John Campbell was like. "George," I said, "if you ever meet a fellow who, on finding out you are a vertebrate paleontologist, tells you all about vertebrate paleontology, gets it all wrong, and never gives you a chance to get in a word edgewise, you have met John Campbell.")

At one dinner, I of course invited Janet to be my guest, and Judith Merril (an advance women's rights advocate even in those days) asked me if I had paid for Janet's meal. (Of course, I had, but if Judith were a true women's libber, she'd have wanted Janet to pay for herself, wouldn't she?)

In any case, I put on an innocent look and said, "No, Judy, I didn't pay for her. Should I have?"

And she said. "I knew it. You dumb jerk, you invited her, didn't you?"

"Gee," I said, took the necessary money out of my wallet, and walked over toward Janet as though I meant to offer it to her.

Outraged, Judy overtook me and *slapped* me so that my head rang. It's the only time a woman ever slapped me and I was just having my little joke.

89

Guide to Science

In my first two years as a full-time writer, I continued my practice of writing primarily for teenagers. There were several reasons for this.

1. I honestly thought teenagers most needed an introduction in science (and, for that matter, in the humanities). Once they were out of their teens, it might be too late to affect them much.

2. Writing for young people meant I could best indulge in the informal writing that I considered my forte.

3. The writing I had done for adults—those blasted textbooks—had traumatized me in that respect.

But then, on May 13, 1959 (two weeks after I had met Janet), I heard from Leon Svirsky, an editor at Basic Books. He was a little fellow with a prominent nose who wanted me to write a summary of twentieth-century science for adults. I was flattered to be asked to do so, since I supposed (quite rightly) that my reputation as a science writer was beginning to outpace my position as a science fiction writer.

I must admit here to a bit of unnecessary snobbery. I did have some fears that my career as a science writer might be aborted by publishers who would dismiss me as "just a science fiction writer." This was unnecessary because the problem never arose. My reputation as *both* kept rising and one never interfered with the other. My Ph.D. and my professorial position may have helped and I have always been glad I fought to keep the latter title.

The result is that I have never found it necessary to hide my science fiction. When asked by people who don't know me just exactly what it is that I write, I answer, "All sorts of things, but I am best known for my science fiction."

Yet flattered though I might be at Svirsky's proposal, I was a bit frightened. He came to Boston to see me and left a contract to read over and, if I approved, to sign.

For days I was in a state of dire uncertainty. I wanted to sign and yet I was afraid to sign and I wavered painfully. It was all too much for me, but I remembered my new friend, Janet Jeppson, with whom I had already exchanged pleasant letters. I wrote to her, unburdening myself, expressing all my desires, doubts, and fears.

I did not actually ask for advice since I have always had a reluctance to load anyone else with responsibility for my decisions, but in this case I did not have to ask. She replied that of *course* I could do it, and I *must* do it. I could not turn down a challenge like that and expect to rise in my profession.

She was perfectly right, so I signed. That advice was the first of a countless number of examples of kindness and good sense that Janet has shown me.

I tore into the book with a fury and in a period of eight months had written and put into final form half a million words—remarkable even for me. The book was published by Basic Books in 1960 under the title of *The Intelligent Man's Guide to Science.*

I objected to the title on the ground that "man" seemed unduly restrictive. I wanted women to read the book too and would have preferred *The Intelligent Person's Guide to Science.* Svirsky would have none of it. He was intent on imitating the title of George Bernard Shaw's book *The Intelligent Woman's Guide to Socialism and Capitalism.* Naturally, there were protests from women and all I could do was smile wryly and say, "by 'intelligent man' I am referring to the writer, not the reader."

The book did far better than I expected, or, for that matter, than Basic Books expected. It came out in a two-volume boxed set and was snapped up. George Gaylord Simpson gave it the best review of any I have ever received. He called me a "natural wonder and a national resource"—a phrase you won't blame me for remembering.

My first royalty check for the book was for $23,000, the largest check I had ever received up to that time, and my income suddenly doubled. (In a way, that saddened me, for I thought it was a one-time blip that would never repeat and that my 1962 income would reach a peak I would never again attain. —But that proved not to be so. In fact, I never had an annual income as *low* as 1962's thereafter.)

Frankly, I found it unbelievable. Four years after having been kicked out of school, my income had risen to ten times what my school salary had been. It was about this time that one of my friends at the school told me earnestly that he had good reason to think that, if I played my cards properly, I could be reinstated to an active teaching position at the school, and with a salary. I smiled and said, "Too late, I'm afraid. I couldn't afford it."

Even so, I had not broken off all connection with the school. After all, I was still an associate professor. I gave an occasional lecture, usually the very first lecture of the semester. Since biochemistry was a first-semester subject and given in the morning, my lecture was the very first the med students heard. It was a professional-quality lecture they heard, and it was also the last of that sort they were going to hear. I was once incautious enough to say so out loud, and a student, to my infinite embarrassment, promptly repeated that to the new dean, who was on the scene. The dean sighed and said, "He's probably right."

I might mention some side issues raised by *The Intelligent Man's Guide to Science*. At the start, Svirsky had asked me to read over the contract and this was more than I could do. I have had many hundreds of contracts to sign and I have never really read one. I have glanced through them to see if the advance was as promised but that was usually as much as I could manage. The rest was just too dull to endure and I wasn't going to read through many hundreds of them.

This is considered very eccentric of me.

At one time, the president of Doubleday was discussing with me a dispute I was having with some movie people. He asked me what the contract had said with respect to a particular point. I said, "I don't know, Henry. I just signed it. I never read it."

He looked at me with a mixture of amusement and incredulity and said, "Isaac, you need a keeper."

Then he added, "But don't worry, Doubleday will be your keeper."

Actually, my not reading contracts is not as crazy as it sounds.

After all, most contracts are standard, and if the publisher is a reputable one and if the writer is not interested in stipulating special clauses (which I never do, because I ask only that I be permitted to write in peace and that I be rejection-free), there is no danger in signing them unread. I believe, quite firmly, that my editors are not out to cheat me but to make money along with me.

Then, too, I judge matters by results. If the royalties seem adequate and if the publisher is cooperative, then I am satisfied. And if I think that a publisher is playing fast and loose with me, the response is automatic. I would not audit his books. I would not sue. I would simply give him no more books. This happened in a very few cases.

Another point is that though *The Intelligent Man's Guide to Science* was a great financial and critical success, I was not happy with the book. That is not a strong enough statement. I was bitterly *unhappy* with the book.

The trouble was Leon Svirsky himself. He was a nice fellow, but he turned out to be an editorial villain—one of the very few I have encountered. He had worked for years as an editor at *Scientific American* and was used to receiving important scientific essays from scientists reporting upon their research. Unfortunately, the scientists responsible for the essays could rarely write their way out of a paper bag and it was Svirsky's job to cut, prune, and wrench their essays into shape.

Apparently, he had never gotten over the habit, because I found, when I received the galleys, that he had cut, pruned, and wrenched *my* book into what he thought was "shape." I objected strenuously. Since I was still working on the last part of the book when I received the galleys of the first part (that was one reason the book was published so quickly), I threatened to stop work on the book unless he stopped his shenanigans.

He did, to an extent, but even so, when the book came out it was sufficiently different from what I had written to make it impossible for me to look it in the face. Despite its huge financial success, I hated the book and to this day have a feeling of nausea when I see it on my shelf.

A second villainy that Svirsky committed was to get George Beadle to write a foreword. Beadle was a great geneticist and a Nobel laureate, but I didn't want *anyone* to introduce any of my books. In time to come, I introduced a hundred books, at least, for other people, but I feel no need to have anyone introduce one of mine.

Svirsky started the second volume by saying that scientific advance had all but wiped out the distinction between life and nonlife. It was *his* statement, not mine, and of course it was vulnerable to denunciation.

Barry Commoner denounced it, for instance. He attacked the book in a totally overreactive way in a major article in *Science*. I was caught by the headline, glanced over the first few paragraphs, and was almost knocked over when I realized he was denouncing *my* book. His most stupid remark was to ask what would happen to biology as a science if the distinction between life and nonlife was wiped out.

I wrote a brief and reasoned response (which *Science* dutifully printed) in which I pointed out that Copernicus, over four centuries ago, had wiped out the distinction between Earth and the other planets—and what had happened to geology as a result? Nothing.

Years later, I met Commoner, or at least sat at the opposite end of a long table from him. The discussion was on atmospheric pollution (Commoner being an environmentalist of note) and I endured the cigarettes as best I could. But when Commoner pulled out a large cigar and lit it, I was out the door.

I then wrote a letter to the people who had arranged the meeting and expressed my contempt for environmentalists who talked in high-flown terms about a clean atmosphere even as they polluted it with tobacco smoke. I received no answer.

But I digress. The subject is Svirsky. I had agreed to do another book for him even while I was working on the *Guide to Science*. This was to be a short one on the discovery of the various elements. It was called *The Search for the Elements* and was published by Basic Books in 1962. I wrote this second book before I had quite realized Svirsky's lust to rewrite. The result was that he also manhandled the second book and that was that. I steadfastly refused to write any other books for him. He yelled at me on the phone, but that didn't move me.

Petrovichi, Russia, where Isaac Asimov was born in 1920. *Asimov family photo*

An Asimov family photo. Isaac is standing fourth from the left.

Asimov's parents, Anna and Judah Asimov.

Robyn Asimov as a child.

Isaac in 1940 at age twenty, superimposed on a page of Marcia's diary.

Asimov at a science fiction convention with Robert Silverberg and
a young fan. *Photo by Jay Kay Klein*

At Lunacon '71, from left: Unidentified woman, Judy-Lynn del
Rey, Lester del Rey, John W. Campbell, Janet Jeppson, and Isaac.
Photo by Jay Kay Klein

Janet and Isaac Asimov.
Photo by Jay Kay Klein

Isaac with long-time friend and fellow writer, Lester del Rey. *Photo by Janet Asimov*

Isaac and friend Andy Rooney, at Rensselaer Polytechnic Institute.
Photo by Janet Asimov

The three siblings: Marcia, Isaac, and Stanley Asimov. *Photo by Janet Asimov*

In costume as a member of the Gilbert and Sullivan Society. *Photo by Janet Asimov*

Isaac receiving his honorary degree from Columbia University.
Photo by Janet Asimov

In Central Park. *Photo by Janet Asimov*

Isaac and daughter Robyn, 1989. *Photo by Janet Asimov*

With Janet and long-time
collaborator Martin H. Greenberg.
Photo by Rosalind Greenberg

Isaac at home, wearing one of his
favorite bolo ties. *Photo by Bruce
Bennetts*

The Good Doctor. *Photo by Alex
Gotfryd*

90

Indexes

The Intelligent Man's Guide to Science reintroduced me to the difficulty of index preparation.

A nonfiction book that is a systematic study of one topic is useless
without an index, and the first index I ever prepared was that for
Biochemistry and Human Metabolism, our ill-fated textbook. No one
ever taught me how to do indexes, nor did I ever seek instruction. I
did it according to my own system, which is probably close enough to
what people are supposed to do.

I take an incredible number of blank 3 × 5 cards and go through the
page proofs of the book, writing down each topic in the fashion that
people might conceivably look it up, limiting myself to not more than
one subheading, and noting the page on which it appeared. Then I
alphabetize all the cards, consolidating all those with the same item
into one card with all the different pages on it. Then I type up the
whole thing.

In recent years I've been urged to use a computer for the purpose,
but I resist. I *like* fooling around with the cards, alphabetizing and
consolidating them. That kind of nitpicky sort of thing amuses me.
Besides, as I sometimes say, "Happiness is doing it rotten your own
way."

With *The Intelligent Man's Guide to Science,* it was clear the index-
ing would take days. It was not nearly as bad as the later volumes of
the textbook, but there was a difference. The textbook index I did at
school, and the family was unaware of the work. By the time I was
working on the *Guide to Science* there was no school and I worked at
home. The easiest way of doing it was to spread out the page proofs
and the cards in the living room in the evening, while we were watch-

ing television, so that I didn't waste too much writing time. The television only required half a brain, as did the index, so I could do both together comfortably. The only trouble, however, was that I was converting a time of recreation into a time of business and I suspect the family resented that.

One problem with a book that deals with contemporary science is that in a very few years it becomes ludicrously out of date, and the pressure to prepare a new edition starts rising. The actual preparation was not too odious a task, for it didn't catch me completely by surprise, and in the case of the *Guide to Science* I kept notes on scientific advances I would have to include in a new edition.

When it was clear that the second edition could not be delayed, I found out that Svirsky had retired to Florida.

I agreed to do a second edition, adding new data to the book, putting back all the good stuff Svirsky had taken out, and cutting out all the felicities he had put in. What's more, I managed to imply to the new editor that I would not welcome any changes but the merely cosmetic. The second edition was published by Basic Books as *The New Intelligent Man's Guide to Science* in 1965.

Happy ending? Not quite. Even though the bulk of the second edition was more or less identical with the first, the new material had to be indexed, and the page numbers of all the old material had been changed. In short, a new index, even more elaborate than that of the first edition, had to be prepared. The editor talked me into using an index specialist to do the index. It cost me $500, for Basic Books did not pay the indexer themselves but took it out of my royalties, and it was a *rotten* index. It wasn't even successfully alphabetized. The result was that I could never bear the second edition any more than the first. It was not till a third edition was published by Basic Books in 1972 that I finally had one that was both written my way and indexed my way and that I could look at and use pleasurably.

In 1984, I prepared still another index for the fourth edition. I don't know if there will ever be a fifth. I think I've gotten too old for the task. Of course, I don't want the book to die. I want a fifth edition and a sixth and so on indefinitely, but it will have to be done by others, and (pardon my conceit) I doubt they will ever again find a single person to do it. It will take a consortium.

91

Titles

I'm pretty careful about titles. I always believe that a short title is better than a long title and I like (when possible) to have one-word titles such as "Nightfall" or *Foundation*. What's more, I like to have a title that describes the content of the story without giving it away, but which, when the story is finished, is seen by the reader to take on an added significance.

For that reason, I dislike the manner in which editors sometimes change the title to suit *their* personal tastes. For instance, my first robot story was called "Robbie"; that was the name given to the robot nursemaid by the little girl he took care of. Its use emphasized the emotional content of the story. Fred Pohl changed it to "Strange Playfellow," which contributed nothing. The story has appeared dozens of times since in dozens of places and *always* under *my* title of "Robbie."

A more egregious example is that of "The Ugly Little Boy." Horace Gold thought the word "Ugly" was a downer and changed it to "Last-Born," which was ridiculous. "Ugly" is essential. The little hero of the story *is* an ugly little boy because he is a Neanderthal child, yet in the end, he receives the kind of love that means more than life and the reader sympathizes. The story would have no meaning if the boy had been pretty. But go explain subtle points to Horace!

I can live with title changes in stories, because I can almost always change them back when I place them in one of my collections. Sometimes, however, I do accept editors' titles when I consider them an improvement. I wrote a story for Fred Pohl once which I called "The Last Tool." This was a significant title, but Fred changed it to "Founding Father," which was so much better that I was chagrined at not having thought of it myself. It appeared in the October 1965 *Galaxy* and it has kept that title ever since.

Book titles are more important, for they tend to be permanent. Even there I managed to change *The Death Dealers* into *A Whiff of Death*. This is inconvenient, though. I sometimes have to explain the situation to readers who think they are two different books and want a copy of each.

The subject of book titles came up after T. O'Conor Sloane of Doubleday (who was the grandson of the man who succeeded Hugo Gernsback as editor of *Amazing*) suggested I prepare a book of short biographies of about 250 important scientists to fit a series of books they were doing on musicians, artists, philosophers, and other intellectual groupings.

I was willing, but the book grew in my hands (as books often do). I did the biographies, not of 250, but of 1,000 scientists, explorers, and inventors, and the biographies were longer than they should have been. Furthermore, instead of listing them in alphabetical order I listed them in chronological order of birth. After all, science is a cumulative subject, while music, art, and philosophy are not.

It ended as a book much longer than Doubleday had counted on, but they took it without a murmur and did it my way.

It proved to be a book that required a pair of enormous indexes (one of names and one of subjects discussed), but I had numbered the biographies and keyed the indexes to the number of the biography rather than to the number of the page. That meant I could prepare the index from the manuscript while I was hot and hand it in with the manuscript. I did not have to wait months for the page proofs.

I wanted to call the book *A Biographical History of Science,* which was the shortest way of describing the book accurately. Sloane, however, insisted on adding "and technology" to the title, though I thought that was unnecessary. Furthermore, Sloane maintained that "history" was a bad word that would slow sales. He insisted on substituting "encyclopedia," though I objected to it as a misrepresentation. Finally, he appended "Asimov's" to the whole.

The title of the book was therefore *Asimov's Biographical Encyclopedia of Science and Technology* (Doubleday, 1964). Two more editions have been prepared since, each time with a completely new index.

I must admit I swallowed the clumsiness of the title because of the first word. Sloane said that the salesmen insisted it would sell better if my name was in the title and that flattered me past imagining. It turns out that this conception of my name as something magic has become prevalent. There are over sixty of my books that have my name somewhere in the title.

Well, come on, how can I not be pleased? It shows that the publishers expect people to accept me as a name that can be attached to any kind of book—science fiction, mysteries, science books, humanities books, anthologies—as a guarantee of quality.

92

Essay Collections

I continued to gather various short stories into collections. During the 1960s, Doubleday published three of them: *The Rest of the Robots* (1964), *Asimov's Mysteries* (1968), and *Nightfall and Other Stories* (1969).

The New English Library also published a collection of four of my stories, a collection not for sale in the United States. This was *Through a Glass, Clearly* in 1967.

Since then I have continued to publish story collections in rather large numbers and they tend to overlap. I have individual stories that appear, so far, in as many as five different collections. This does not seem to be fair, really. One can imagine readers buying a collection and finding that they have read all, or almost all, the individual stories in it. My conscience did pang a little over the matter, especially when one important science fiction writer (admittedly not one with a sunny disposition) remarked, more or less sarcastically, that I was a master at recirculating my products.

However, there is a rationale behind it.

Books are mortal. A hardcover is likely to go out of print after a couple of years. A paperback can be buried in the crowds of other paperbacks that are continually inundating the stands. It happens, then, that when a reader writes to ask where he can find a particular story of mine that he wants to read (or reread), I am in a quandary. I can't refer him to the original issue of the magazine in which it appeared. Except in a few private collections and in a few specialty back-number shops, such issues are simply unavailable.

If I give him the name of a collection in which the story appeared, that, too, may be unobtainable. Yes, there are secondhand bookstores, but if I may say so without being instantly pilloried as a monster of vanity, my books rarely appear there. People who own my books tend to keep them. A new collection, then, containing some recent stories, plus some of the old reliables for those who can't find them elsewhere, would seem to be in order.

Then, too, they say that among science fiction readers, a generation is three years long. In other words, after three years, there are a large number of new readers who have never read, and may never even have heard of, the old stories. To them a collection of my stories is new even if some of them, to veterans, would seem like old chestnuts.

The most important reason for preparing endless overlapping collections, however, is that they sell. Publishers are willing to do them for that reason and I have no objection to that.

But if my stories can be collected and re-collected to the profit of readers, publishers, and me, what about my nonfiction essays, which I was producing in quantities even greater than my fiction?

I had actually produced such an essay collection rather early on. This was *Only a Trillion* (Abelard-Schuman, 1957). This contained a number of the science essays I had published in *ASF*, but I was not entirely satisfied with them. My *ASF* essays were tailored for John Campbell and they seemed to me to be rather stiff and formal.

The essays I was writing for *F&SF*, on the other hand, I wrote without any editorial interference at all, and they existed solely to please me. They were informal and, for the most part, lighthearted. I felt that they would be much better examples of what I could do than the *ASF* essays had been. What's more, I wanted a major publisher to do them.

In 1957, I had met Austin Olney, editor of the juvenile division of Houghton Mifflin, Boston's most important publishing house. He was my age, slim, good-looking, with deep-set eyes, and although a true Boston Brahmin, he had absolutely none of the superciliousness and arrogance supposedly associated with them. He was a sweet, amiable person, and we have remained friends ever since.

Many's the time I was to have lunch with him at the fabled Locke-Ober's restaurant in Boston. I love tripe, something few people do, apparently, and I always ordered tripe with mustard sauce. But the time came when I was to leave Boston and after nineteen years I returned with Janet and we were put up in a hotel near Locke-Ober's. Jubilantly, I took her there and ordered my tripe with mustard sauce, and although it was still on the menu, they no longer made it. I could have broken down and cried. I suppose that with me gone, no one ever ordered it.

In any case, Houghton Mifflin was soon publishing several science books of mine, the first being *Realm of Numbers* in 1959, a book which dealt with arithmetic, from addition to transfinite numbers, for junior high school students. Austin was kind enough to send me a proof of the cover and to ask me for my opinion. I phoned him and I said I approved highly, except for one thing.

Austin didn't know me thoroughly as yet and he decided that I must be one of those author's (of whom editors are very wary) who feel like art critics and try to dictate the nature of the cover. Actually, I couldn't care less. My only interest is the inside of a book.

At hearing that I had a point of disapproval, the temperature dropped fifty degrees instantly. Austin said, coldly, "What don't you like about it?"

I said, "Well, I hate to mention it and, undoubtedly, it's a small thing I shouldn't worry about, but you spelled my name wrong."

Of course, they had to redo the cover. Austin was very apologetic.

In any case, in 1961 I came to him with a bunch of *F&SF* essays. Since they were intended for adults, Austin passed them on to the adult division, which rejected them. Austin, embarrassed, offered to publish them as a juvenile book, if I would consent to simplify them. Not in a million years, I said, but no hard feelings, and took them to Doubleday.

Tim Seldes was not exactly enthusiastic, but neither did he want to turn me down, so that my first book of *F&SF* essays was published by Doubleday in 1962 as *Fact and Fancy*.

Tim knew me quite well by this time, so he warned me not to compile another collection of science essays until he had a chance to see how well *Fact and Fancy* sold. I could see the justice in this, so although I was eager to go on, I held back.

However, *Fact and Fancy* earned back its advance with startling speed and a somewhat amazed Tim said, "All right, Asimov, I'll take another." As a matter of fact, before the 1960s were over, Doubleday had published seven of my essay collections, and they've been continuing to do so ever since. *All* my *F&SF* essays eventually find their way into one collection or another, except for seven very early ones, and some find their way into more than one collection. (Yes, I recycle my essays also.) Many of my essays from sources other than *F&SF* have also been collected. All told, I have nearly forty books of science essays.

I don't think I need any excuse for this. The books sell and the readers enjoy them, if I may judge from the letters I receive, and if any further justification is needed, what might that be?

In fact, these collections are a source of great satisfaction to me. In the first place, I think I hold the world record for having published more essay collections than anyone else in history. (Please note that I make no claim whatever as to writing the *best* or even nearly the best, merely the most.)

What's more, I have always heard that collections of essays are "poison at the box office" and publishers are extremely reluctant to publish them except for certain surefire cases like Stephen Jay Gould, Martin Gardner, or Lewis Thomas. I'm sorry if it makes me sound self-satisfied, but I *do* enjoy being surefire.

Not everyone enjoys my essays, of course. Recently, Arthur Clarke, while vegetating at his home in Sri Lanka, came across a rotten review of an essay collection of mine and, fearing that I might not see it, carefully clipped it and sent it to me for my delectation. The first sentence was: "This is a book that should never have been written."

By Lester del Rey's system, that review should at once have been discarded—but I had to glance over it to see if I could tell, without reading much of it, *why* it should never have been written. Apparently, he was appalled at the miscellaneous character of the book and at the way I jumped from subject to subject. I can only conclude that he had never seen or heard of an essay collection. I suppose illiteracy is a requirement for his job.

Actually, the value, in my opinion, of such a collection of essays is precisely the variety it offers. You are not being asked to invest the time required to read an entire treatise. You are reading short items, and if you find one such item dull or disappointing, you have not lost the value of an entire book, but of only a fragment of it. You can pass on to the next fragment, which may delight you. Moreover, short pieces are perfect reading at bedtime or in other small scraps of leisure.

Then, too, the readers of my science essays can (and *do*) play the enchanting game of "Let's catch Isaac in an error." They do this often enough to make the game worthwhile. I have always been grateful for and, actually, touched by the almost invariable gentleness with which such corrections are made and how careful all are to attribute a mistake to my haste and carelessness, rather than to my stupidity.

If I haven't praised my readers before, let me do so now. They may not be as many in number as are the fans of rock stars or of sports figures, but in *quality* my readers are the pick of the lot, the cream, the elite, and I love them all.

93

Histories

Houghton Mifflin was doing a series of American history books for youngsters, and Austin Olney asked if there was some subject I could handle that would fit into the series.

After thinking about it, I said I could do a book on Franklin's investigations of electricity and its influence on the course of the American Revolution. Austin was willing, so I wrote a book entitled *The Kite That Won the Revolution*.

The writer Sterling North was the general editor of the series, and when he saw my manuscript he clearly wanted to rewrite it closer to his heart's desire. At least I received back a hacked-up manuscript that froze my blood. I had just escaped from the clutches of Svirsky and I did not propose to fall into those of North.

I told Austin I would have to withdraw the manuscript and explained why. Austin offered to publish it as I had written it, but explained that it could not then be entered as part of the series and probably wouldn't sell as well, for the series was well established and large sales would be virtually guaranteed. I said I didn't care about sales at all, only about having a book of mine published as I wrote it and not as someone else wrote it. It was published in 1963 and its sales were only moderate, but I was happy.

After agreeing to do *Realm of Numbers,* which Austin had suggested, I argued him into *Words of Science,* a series of 250 one-page essays on derivations and explanations of scientific terms, arranged alphabetically. I remember working on those essays at the medical school with an unabridged Webster's on the desk to one side of me. (After all, I couldn't make up the etymologies of the words. I had to know precisely the forms of the Latin and Greek words from which they came.) Matthew Derow wandered in, looked over my shoulder, stared at Webster's, and said, "All you're doing is copying the dictionary."

"That's right," I said. I closed the dictionary, lifted it with an effort, and handed it to him. "Here's the dictionary, Matthew. I dare you to write the book."

He didn't take the dare.

The book did quite well, but the important thing was that I enjoyed doing it enormously, so I did *Words from the Myths* (1961), *Words on the Map* (1962), *Words in Genesis* (1962), and *Words from the Exodus* (1963), all by Houghton Mifflin.

I hadn't had enough, so I cast about for other places besides mythology, geography, and the Bible that would serve as a source of words. I thought of my old passion, history, and prepared a book entitled *Words from Greek History,* in which I told the history of Greece, stopping every once in a while to discuss words that we used that were derived from that history.

Austin went over the manuscript and said he liked the history far more than he did the word derivations and that was all I had to hear. I discarded the manuscript and set about writing a straight history of Greece for young people. I called it *The Greeks* and it was published by Houghton Mifflin in 1965.

Just as Tim Seldes had asked me not to do a second essay collection until we had a chance to see how the first did, so Austin now asked me not to do any other histories till we saw how *The Greeks* did.

Once it was published, I waited some time, then walked into Austin's office and said, "Is *The Greeks* doing well?"

"Quite well," said Austin. "You can do another history."

"It's already done," I said, and brought out the manuscript of *The Roman Republic*. I eventually wrote fourteen history books for Houghton Mifflin, not only on Greece and Rome but on Egypt, on the Near East, on Israel, on the Dark Ages, on the early history of England and France, to say nothing of four volumes of American history from Native American times to 1918.

The books were pure fun to write, and since I crammed each one with dates, places, and assorted facts, they became important reference works for me in my later writing.

I couldn't help but notice that my books with Houghton Mifflin didn't do nearly as well as my books with Doubleday, even if one compared nonfiction with nonfiction. My histories, for instance, never appeared in paperback editions, while virtually all my Doubleday books, of whatever kind, did appear in this way. Then, after my fourth volume of American history, *The Golden Door*, was published in 1977, Houghton Mifflin told me (gently, to be sure) that they didn't want any more. That bothered me a great deal, because I don't like to be kept from writing what I want to write. The result is that I have written very little for Houghton Mifflin since 1977.

94

Reference Library

I mentioned in the previous section that I use my histories as reference works for my later writings, and that reminds me that I am frequently asked whether I have a reference library.

Of course I have one. Once I reached the stage of affluence where I could buy books, I began accumulating one. I now have some 2,000 books divided into sections: mathematics, history of science, chemistry, physics, astronomy, geology, biology, literature, and history. I have an Encyclopaedia Britannica, an Encyclopedia Americana, a

McGraw-Hill Encyclopedia of Science and Technology, a complete Oxford English Dictionary, books of quotations, and so on.

An interviewer who inspected my library on June 21, 1978, wrote afterward, in a contemptuous way, that it was quite small, but he didn't know what he was talking about. I *deliberately* keep it small by getting rid of old books as I get new ones. I have no use for books that are out of date or that, for one reason or another, I have had no occasion to use. What I have is a *working* library, and not one for show.

Of course, my most important reference is my mind and memory. My memory is excellent and very useful, but some of my friends view it with exaggerated, even superstitious awe. I am, every once in a while, called by one friend or another who has failed to locate some piece of information and has, in desperation, said to himself, "I'll call Isaac. *He'll* know."

Sometimes I do. Lin Carter, a fellow member of my club, the Trap Door Spiders, once called me and said, "Isaac, I need to know who said, 'Liberty! What crimes are committed in thy name!' " I answered at once, "Madame Roland, as she passed a statue to Liberty on her way to the guillotine in 1794." Carter dined out on that incident for months, I think, and it just encouraged others to use me as a handy and portable encyclopedia.

Sometimes I don't come through. Some months ago, Sprague de Camp called me from his new home in Texas to ask me about the wavelengths of the supersonic squeaks of bats. That piece of information could not be dredged out of my memory, so I said with chagrin (for I *like* being able to answer arcane questions offhand) that I'd have to call him back.

I then ransacked my library and finally came across an excellent article on sound in my Encyclopedia Americana which contained precisely the information Sprague needed. I phoned him, read off the information, received his thanks, and then, after I had hung up, I found that the encyclopedia article was one that I had myself written!

As I said, my own books are extremely good sources of information for me. In order to make use of them, though, I have to remember in which book I included a particular piece of information and where it might be. Prolificity has its terrors too.

When I first began to write, I naturally saved the issues of those magazines in which I appeared, but I had no idea of the sheer volume of material I was destined to publish. Soon I realized there would be no room in the small apartment in which I lived to keep all those magazines, so I did something I knew Sprague had done. I carefully detached my stories from the magazines, together with the table of contents (and the cover if my name appeared there), and had the stories bound into a single hardcover volume. I continued to form new volumes of such "tear sheets" as time went on. I also bound paperback editions of my novels.

What with one thing and another I now have nearly 350 such bound volumes, and though I live in a much larger apartment than I once did, I have run out of room for them. I am forced to send the less significant volumes of bound material to Boston University, which collects my papers.

Originally I kept a copy of each of my books, every edition, whether English or foreign, but they soon began to encroach on everything, so I sent all the foreign editions to Boston University. I now save *only* the English-language editions and I'm having trouble with that.

I keep my books in chronological order, but even that doesn't ensure that I can find a particular book easily out of a total group that now includes 451 different titles, many of them in multiple English-language editions. What I have done, then, is to Scotch-tape a number (in chronological order) on each different title. Otto Penzler, a book-dealer and bibliophile, warned me that that would ruin the monetary value of the collection, but I told him I didn't keep those books as a financial investment but for needed reference.

Of course, the numbers mean nothing unless I have the books catalogued by them. I do keep a card catalogue for all my books, listing their number and all their editions (even the editions I don't save). I use other cards to record the writing and publishing history of each book, and still other cards for short stories and essays.

My catalogue system is primitive in the extreme and I can use it only because I know it so well, but when I started, I had no idea that I would ever have to deal with more than a couple of hundred cards for everything I wrote. Who could imagine that I would have to deal with somewhere close to 5,000 cards? The problem grew acute so slowly that at no time did it occur to me to get a professional to set up a filing system for me, or, better yet, to computerize the whole thing.

However, considering that I'm a science fiction writer and a professional connoisseur of change, I'm really a clod. I like to keep things the way they have always been. After all, I can still make my system work, limpingly, and my professional career is undoubtedly approaching its end, so let it go—let it go.

My very good friend Martin Harry Greenberg *(not* to be confused with the Martin Greenberg of Gnome Press) has a desire to do a complete bibliography of all I have written. I hate to refuse Marty anything, because he's such an unbelievably good soul, but I didn't want that. It would be bound to involve me, and I could see myself throat-deep in a project that would require a book of a 1,000 pages of small print, which no one would want, or could afford if he did want it.

I said, "Gee, Marty, wait till I'm dead, then you'll know you'll have the entire corpus and you won't have to watch the bibliography grow instantly out of date."

"Nothing will stop when you're dead," said Marty. "There'll be new editions of all kinds of a great many of your books, and they'll keep coming out for years and years."

"Really?" I said with astonishment, but after a moment of reflection I realized he was right and I suddenly saw an advantage to dying. I wouldn't have to be involved with all that stuff.

95

Boston University Collection

I mentioned, in the previous section, that Boston University collected my papers. It came about in this fashion.

In 1964, Howard Gotlieb, the curator of Boston University's Special Collection, told me he wanted to collect my papers. The university was specializing in twentieth-century writers and it seemed ridiculous to neglect a prolific writer who was on the BU faculty.

It took him quite a while to convince me that he wasn't kidding. After all, I considered my "papers" (old manuscripts, second sheets, galleys, and so on) to be trash, which is exactly what it was, and is, no matter what Gotlieb says. Every once in a while I would gather a ton or so of this office-choking material and burn it in the barbecue pit in the backyard of our West Newton home. We used the barbecue pit for nothing else (never for barbecues, you can bet), but I always felt it to be an enormously useful adjunct to the house just for its use as a way of disposing of unwanted material.

Gotlieb was very upset when he found out I burned my papers, but I gave him whatever I had, and since then I've given him a copy of every book in every edition, English and foreign, every magazine containing a story or essay of mine, all my correspondence and manuscripts, and so on. When I lived in Boston, I'd bring the stuff in periodically and have lunch with him. Once I moved to New York, I brought it in to Doubleday, which has always been kind enough to mail the material to Gotlieb as an accommodation to me. Periodically, I tell them to take the postage out of my royalties, and invariably they make derogatory comments on my intelligence and refuse to do it.

But I *still* think most of my papers are junk, and I'm beginning to rebel. Gotlieb is convinced that students of twentieth-century literature will study my papers and that innumerable doctorates in literature will result. I think he's crazy—cherubic and amiable, and I love him dearly—but crazy.

The special vault in which my junk is stored has already come in handy. The general public is allowed to pore over the contents of the vault to their heart's content, and one ardent young fan managed to find the manuscript of a story I had recorded as "lost." It wasn't, and it had even been published under a pseudonym, something I had never listed, for some reason, and had utterly forgotten. I saw to it that it was published in the next appropriate book.

Then, too, Charles Waugh of Maine (with whom I have collaborated on various books), found older versions of two of my novels and one novelette in the vault. One of the finds was the original version of the story that became *Pebble in the Sky*. I had those early versions published as *The Alternate Asimovs* in 1986 just for the historical interest (and to make up for the shock, in 1947, of having had the proto-*Pebble* rejected). It even sold a few copies.

On the whole, though, my vault at Boston University must be the largest and the most varied collection of junk in the world. I have a nightmarish feeling that someday it will be packed too tightly and it will explode. I can see the headlines in the Boston *Globe* now: "Asimov Vault Explodes. Commonwealth Avenue Devastated. Nineteen dead."

96

Anthologies

When I was at the NAES in the early 1940s, the first science fiction anthologies began to appear.

An anthology is a collection of stories—not by a single author, but by many. It performs the same function as a collection does, bringing to the reader stories he may be glad to have a chance to read again or stories he may have missed altogether. New readers are able to read the more notable stories of the past.

Publishers pay for the privilege of using stories in anthologies. One early anthology, published by Crown in 1946, was *The Best of Science Fiction,* edited by Groff Conklin (eventually to become a good friend of mine). It contained a rather minor story of mine, "Blind Alley" (March 1945 *ASF).* Street & Smith Publications had bought all rights, so the money ought to have gone to them, but Campbell insisted that in such cases it go to the authors. (It was a kindly deed, and typical of Campbell.)

I received $42.50 for the anthologized "Blind Alley." It wasn't much, but it was the very first time I ever received additional payment for something I had already written and sold and been paid for in the past. Within a year, another anthology, *Adventures in Time and Space,* edited by Raymond J. Healy and J. Francis McComas, contained "Nightfall," and I got $66.50 for that. I would get many more anthology payments in the future, but I never suspected in the 1940s that such a thing could possibly happen.

In time, science fiction anthologies appeared by the hundreds and a great many of them included stories of mine. Some individual stories of mine have been anthologized forty times or more, but I imagine that some of Arthur Clarke's and Harlan Ellison's do even better.

Of course, I suspect that many anthologists, particularly those people who prepare "readers" for schools, do not go back to original sources in their search for material, but to other anthologies. This means that once a story has been anthologized a few times, it keeps on appearing in still others out of sheer inertia.

Then, too, as writers become better known, and as their stories come into greater demand, the tendency is to demand larger fees for their use. My principle has been the reverse. I never ask for much, in the hope that this will encourage the use of my stories in anthologies. I want my stories and my name broadcast widely, believing that, in the end, this would be more profitable than gouging would be.

Although many anthologies appeared, some being edited by my science-fiction-writing friends, and although I knew that the editor usually got half the royalties (the other half being divided among the authors), I was never tempted to edit one myself. It would mean reading back numbers, deciding on which to include, writing to different authors for permissions, and so on. Too much work. I wanted to spend my time writing rather than fiddling with anthologies.

In 1961, however, Avram Davidson had an idea. He had published a short story, "Or All the Seas with Oysters" (May 1958 *Galaxy),* and it had won a Hugo. Avram always needed money and knew he could make some if that story were anthologized. It would be sure to be anthologized if someone could be persuaded to edit an anthology of Hugo Award winners.

Avram's agent, Bob Mills, thought of getting someone as editor who (1) was a well-known science fiction writer and (2) had never won a Hugo. He thought of me at once. I was reluctant, but since I didn't have to select the stories and Bob Mills would get the permissions, the job seemed easy and I agreed.

The Hugo Winners, the first anthology I edited, was published by Doubleday in 1962, and it did very well. However, I found that I had miscalculated in one respect. Every six months, royalties for *The Hugo Winners* would arrive. I would have to send 10 percent to Bob Mills, divide what was left in half, keep one half, and divide the other half among nine authors in pro rata shares according to the length of their stories, and mail checks to them or to their agents.

I might have endured this for one or two royalty periods, but the anthology kept selling, one way or another, for twenty years. I grew deathly tired of the task and determined never to do another anthology unless I could persuade someone to do *all* the paperwork.

I held to that resolution. By 1977 I had edited eight anthologies, and others did the paperwork, in every case. The anthologies I did in this period included two more volumes of Hugo winners, a volume of Nebula winners, an anthology of science fiction short short stories with Groff Conklin, a book of science fiction stories selected by Doubleday, and one called *Before the Golden Age,* which was entirely my idea.

On April 3, 1973, I dreamed that I had prepared an anthology of the great stories I had read and enjoyed in the 1930s (including Cliff Simak's "World of the Red Sun," Jack Williamson's "Born of the Sun," Charles Tanner's "Tumithak of the Corridors," and so on). I told the dream to Janet and she said, "Why don't you do it?"

Why not? I called Larry Ashmead, stressing the historical importance of such an anthology, and he gave me the go-ahead. I called Sam Moskowitz, the unofficial historian of science fiction. Sam said he had always hoped to do such an anthology himself, but no publisher was willing to have him do it, whereas he could see they would be willing to have me do it. He then loyally got me tear sheets for all the stories I needed in record time, and I paid him for it, of course.

The book was published by Doubleday on April 3, 1974, the anniversary of my dream. It sold only moderately well, but it was a book that gave me enormous satisfaction. I wished with all my heart that I could go back in time to that junior high school boy I once was and tell him what I had done to preserve the stories he loved so.

And that sated me where anthologies were concerned. I didn't anticipate doing any more of them, except, perhaps, additional Hugo Winners volumes, and I wasn't even sure I wanted to do those.

In 1977, however, I met Martin Harry Greenberg and that changed everything, as I shall explain in due course.

97

Headnotes

The Hugo Winners presented me with a problem. Should I or should I not count it as one of my books?

By the time it appeared, I was forty-two years old and had published forty-six books. I was beginning to realize that the most important thing about me, literarily, was the number of books I was publishing. No one ever acclaimed me as a great literary light. I was never a threat to the reign of the Bellows and Updikes and I never could be. Yet we all want recognition, we all want to be known for *something*, and I was beginning to see that there would be a good chance that if for nothing else, I would be known for the vast number of books I would publish and for the range of subjects I wrote about. It would be nice if the good quality of the books were also appreciated, but I had the feeling that no one would notice this; they would notice only the number.

Consequently, I was anxious to count *The Hugo Winners* and make it Book #47, adding by that little bit to my chances for fame. After all, my name was on the cover. There it was: "edited by Isaac Asimov."

Unfortunately, my sense of ethics and all those paternal admonitions about honesty that filled my childhood stood in the way. The fact was that I had *not* edited the book. The nine stories were selected by the science fiction fans. The order in which they were inserted was strictly chronological. I had spent no significant time on the book, and anyone could have done it as easily as I did.

Then I had a brilliant idea. Why did I not introduce myself into the book? I could write a lengthy and highly personal introduction and, in addition, write a lengthy and highly personal headnote for each story.

In that way, I would make the book mine and be able, quite legitimately, to add it to my list.

I did exactly that. I made the introduction a humorous one in which I praised myself fulsomely and objected to the vileness with which I had been deprived of a Hugo (the old Bob Hope attitude toward Oscars). I started reading the introduction to Tim Seldes in his office, and by the time I had finished the first paragraph, there was general shock. Tim's beautiful secretary, Wendy Weil, looked over my shoulder and said, "He really did write that, Tim."

Tim snatched the introduction from my hand and read through it. He said, "Well, I suppose it will go over with science fiction fans, but how about the people in Dubuque?"

"The people in Dubuque," I said, with a show of confidence I didn't really feel, "will love it. They will feel themselves to be inside the world of science fiction."

Tim hesitated, then decided to take the chance. The book was published with my introduction and headnotes exactly as I had written them and it went down in my list as Book #47.

And, as it happened, it was quickly apparent that I had done the right thing. *The Hugo Winners* sold remarkably well for an anthology and the letters flooded in to the effect that the introduction and headnotes were the best part of the book.

I don't need an anvil dropped on my head to get me to see a point. Until then, my collections of stories and essays had been bare. I had just put them together and let them lie there without a single editorial word from me.

Never again! From the time of *The Hugo Winners,* every collection of my stories had extensive wordage from me in the form of forewords or afterwords (sometimes both) for each story. The material I added was highly personal and usually told how I had come to write the story. What's more, the material was cheerful and openly self-appreciative. If I thought a story was good, I said so; if it had achieved some fame, I said so; if I thought it was underappreciated, I said so, and, moreover, I grumbled about it.

The result was, on the whole, a very good one. Readers *did* get the feeling that I was talking to them freely and openly, and, generally, a sensation of warmth and friendliness was generated. I was no longer only a peculiar name, I became a person. I began getting letters that started off: "Dear Isaac, please forgive my use of your first name but I have read so much of what you have written that I feel we are friends."

I even got a letter from a young woman in British Columbia that began as follows: "Today I am eighteen. I am sitting at the window, looking out at the rain, and thinking how much I love you."

She meant, of course, how much she loved my stories, but my headnotes had made me inseparable from them.

I responded with a thank-you letter, but I couldn't resist adding: "I must raise the following question, however. When I was a lonely twenty-one-year-old, where were all you loving eighteen-year-old girls then?"

All this warmth and affection that I generated was infinitely pleasing to me. After all, who doesn't like to be liked? And I was just practical enough to realize that it helped sales too.

Even my science essay collections received my editorial help. In fact, I took to prefacing each one of my *F&SF* essays with a personal, usually humorous anecdote that was, to begin with, quite true, and, secondly, that fit (or could be made to fit) the subject of the essay. It served the function of a headnote and such an initial bit of fun helped slide the reader into a sometimes arcane subject and may even have helped him get all the way through the essay in one piece.

Of course, some people did not like my headnotes. They took them to represent an unhealthy, hypertrophied ego on my part. It's not true, of course. I just like myself, that's all, and I don't think there's anything wrong with that. One critic wrote something I'm willing to agree with. He said, "The man is very immodest, but he has much to be immodest about."

98

My Own Hugos

For a while I made a big deal of the Hugo tirades I had begun in *The Hugo Winners*. It didn't really bother me that I hadn't won a Hugo, since most of my major stories had appeared before Hugos had existed (though I did feel that "The Ugly Little Boy" might have won one). However, it was a good handle for humor, and I made the most of it.

In 1963, the World Convention was held in Washington and was to be run by George Scithers, a fan with whom I had made friends when we left Detroit together, by train, after the World Convention of 1959. George phoned me and asked me if I would be coming to Washington and mentioned that Theodore Sturgeon would be master of ceremonies.

A distant hope awoke. Why should they try to make sure I would come if someone else was to give out the Hugos? Was it possible I might get one for something? —I said I would come and tried to conceal my satisfaction.

But then, some time later, I got another phone call. Ted was having serious family problems and couldn't come to Washington. Would I be master of ceremonies in his place? Well, that obviously meant I was getting no award, but I had already promised to go and I couldn't back out. So I put the best face on it and agreed.

I handed out the Hugos with particular emphasis on the Bob Hope angle, my wit sharpened by my disappointment. When the last envelope was to be opened, I had become too obsessed to note that there was no category written upon it. I waved it in the air for a goodish while as I inveighed against the committee. I had been making even wilder accusations against them to milk all the humor out of the situation that I could and now I actually accused them of ignoring me out of mean and vicious anti-Semitism.

Then I opened the envelope and, of course, it was a special award to me for my science essays in *F&SF*. I stared at the audience helplessly as I found myself unable to complete the pronunciation of my name and they all collapsed in hysteria. (I have a feeling they all knew what was coming except me.)

Afterward I said to George Scithers, "How could you ask me to hand out the Hugos when I was going to get one?"

He said, "We weren't going to till Ted Sturgeon got into trouble and then we decided that you were the only author in science fiction who could hand himself an award without embarrassment."

In 1966, the World Convention was held in Cleveland, where, eleven years before, I had been guest of honor. I decided to go because the convention committee was going to award a Hugo to the best novel series containing three or more novels. As an example, they pointed to Tolkien's Lord of the Rings series of three books (or four, if you count *The Hobbit*). This was a clear indication they expected Tolkien to win, and such was the popularity of his books (I have read through them five times) that I considered him a shoo-in, whatever the competition.

However, other series were nominated just to make it look legitimate: Heinlein's Future History series, Edgar Rice Burroughs's Mars series, E. E. Smith's Lensman series, and my own Foundation series. Obviously, I had to go to Cleveland. Generally, Hugos are valued the more the longer the story, so that the most valuable Hugos are those given for the best novel of the year. But here for the first time (and, so far, the last time too) there was an award for a series of novels, and it was labeled "all-time" too and was by no means merely the best of the year. It was therefore the most valuable Hugo ever offered up to that time (or since). I was pretty sure that Foundation would end in last place, but just being nominated was a great honor, so I went.

This time I took Gertrude and the children with me, which, for a while, I thought might turn out to be a disastrous mistake. The drive by automobile was a tedious one and when we got to Cleveland the hotel proved to be an old one and our room to be a rotten one with virtually no closet space. Gertrude took it all very hard and I anticipated an absolutely awful weekend.

Fortunately, and quite fortuitously, as we went to the registration desk in a blue funk, we bumped into Harlan Ellison and I had a chance to observe his effect on women at close range. In no time at all, he had both Gertrude and Robyn eating out of his hand. Gertrude and I stayed with him virtually all night and Gertrude enjoyed the convention after all. And if she did, of course, so did I.

At the banquet, the Hugos were given out in reverse order of importance, so that the novel series award came last. When that came up, Harlan replaced the master of ceremonies (apparently, he had insisted on this, and no one liked to cross Harlan) and read off the list of nominees, leaving out the Foundation series. I shouted at him in annoyance, but he paid no attention, and read off the winner. *I* was the winner over Tolkien, Heinlein, Smith, and Burroughs. That was why he insisted on making that announcement—to watch my face.

I thought this was Harlan's idea of a joke, and I sat there, frowning and annoyed, until I got it through my skull that I had really won, then I made the kind of faces Harlan was looking for. That was my second Hugo, and the most valuable ever handed out. I was to get three more Hugos, but I'll mention them at the appropriate place.

Incidentally, I pointed out to Doubleday after I had gotten my first Hugo that that really disqualified me from doing further Hugo winner anthologies. (I was hoping that load would be lifted from my shoulders.) That sort of thing never works for me, however. I got the usual answer: "Don't be silly, Isaac."

99

Walker & Company

Editors move from one publishing house to another. Sometimes they carry me along like a virus.

Thus, Edward Burlingame worked for the paperback house New American Library (NAL), under Truman Talley, in the early 1960s. I did some science books for them. One was *The Wellsprings of Life,* which was published in hardcover by Abelard-Schuman in 1960. Two others were *The Human Body* and *The Human Brain* (excellent books, if I do say so myself), which were published in hardcover by Houghton Mifflin in 1963 and 1964, respectively.

But then there was a shake-up at NAL, and Ed left for a position with a small firm, Walker & Company. I had, at the time, written a three-volume book on physics for an adult audience, called *Understanding Physics,* which NAL was to publish in paperback form. Once Ed was ensconced at Walker & Company, he offered to do the hardcover version, and so he did, in 1966. He also persuaded me to do a book on astronomy, *The Universe,* which was also published in 1966. In this way, Walker & Company became a regular publisher of mine.

Walker & Company is a small pop-and-mom publishing house, a breed that is now almost nonexistent. Pop is Samuel Walker, a tall and urbane gentleman with a ready smile. Mom is his wife, Beth Walker, a tall and very attractive woman with a keen sense of humor. She is a joy and pleasure to banter with.

A couple of years ago, for instance, when I had lost a few pounds in weight, Beth patted my abdomen with approval and said, "Keep it down, Isaac, keep it down."

Whereupon I said, "If you do that and I were younger, I wouldn't be able to."

After she finished laughing (she laughs heartily and infectiously), she said, as I have heard so many women say, "Why do I feed you lines like that?" (The answer is simple. The only way to avoid feeding me useful lines is to say nothing at all.)

Walker & Company became my outlet for frivolous books. It was a time, for instance, when *The Sensuous Woman* by J and *The Sensuous Man* by M were selling in runaway lots, though, in my opinion, they were rotten books even on their own terms (judging by what little I could read of them without gagging).

Beth said to me, "Why don't you write a dirty book, Isaac?"

I said, "What about? Being a dirty old man?"

"Great," said Beth, so I wrote *The Sensuous Dirty Old Man,* which Walker & Company published in 1971. I completed it in a weekend and filled it puns and with misquotations and made it sound as though it were forever on the point of becoming "dirty" without ever actually managing to do it. I wrote it in Janet's office, which was not in use weekends (we were not yet married), and hid it nervously when she walked in. I thought she wouldn't approve, but little did I know her. She enjoys ribaldry as much as I do.

The book didn't do at all well. It was too frivolous for my regular readers and not pornographic enough (or at all) for the trashy readers. In connection with this book, I did one of the few things I'm really ashamed of. The cover of the book showed a picture of me with my eyes masked by a brassiere. The author was presented as "Dr. A" to match the initials appended as authors to the other "Sensuous" books. Actually, my true identity was revealed as soon as the book was published.

Nevertheless, Walker arranged to have me interviewed on Dick Cavett's show and to maintain my supposed anonymity by actually wearing a brassiere over my eye. Why I agreed, I cannot tell. Of course, I took it off early in the interview, but not before I had made a colossal fool of myself before a large audience.

Then, early in 1975, I began writing limericks in quantity. I had, earlier in life, occasionally made up a limerick, but now it caught me in a vise, like an addiction. I'm not sure why.

Possibly it was because it was a verse form that had stringent requirements of scanning and rhyme. I resented much modern poetry, because I couldn't understand it (and, worse yet, there was nothing about it that gave me the urge to try to understand it) and because I despised its freewheeling notions of what a poem should look like. (Robert Frost said that free verse was like playing tennis without a net, and I agreed with him.) Therefore, I *wanted* to be constrained by rules, since a successful limerick would then be more of a challenge and more of an achievement.

I chose another constraint voluntarily. The limericks would have to be ribald and I would abandon my resolve not to use vulgarisms in order to have good limericks. However, I remained staunchly determined that no limerick was going to be merely "dirty." They had to be clever and, what's more, cleverer than they were dirty. This made them even harder to write.

For a long time, these limericks filled the wakeful hours of the night. If I couldn't sleep, I constructed a limerick. If I were successful, I would laugh out loud (or even if I managed to stifle it, my body would shake, and shake the bed). Janet would wake up and I would explain I'd just composed a limerick.

"Write it down," she would urge me.

But I scorned that. I would remember, I assured her, and went to sleep. In the morning, of course I did remember.

By the time I had a hundred limericks, I gave them (with notes, of course) to Walker & Company and they were published as *Lecherous Limericks* in 1975. By the end of the 1970s, I had written four more books of lecherous limericks (two in combination with the poet John Ciardi). I also wrote two books of clean limericks.

Altogether, I published nearly 700 limericks that I had made up myself, and then the mania passed and I wrote no more—except for an occasional one on request from people, usually women.

The books scarcely sold. Books of limericks are not usually big sellers anyway, and in my case, once again I fell between two stools. My readers are not big for ribald limericks, and those who are quickly found my limericks not ribald enough. It doesn't matter. It was great fun while it lasted.

I won't succumb to the urge to quote you dozens of my favorite limericks, but I will quote you one, which I wrote about John Ciardi and myself (with exaggeration, of course.)

> There is something about satyriasis
> ']That arouses psychiatrists' biases.
> But we're both of us pleased
> We're in this way diseased,
> As the damsel who's waiting to try us is.

Meanwhile, a new editor at Walker & Company, Millicent Selsam (herself a well-known writer on biological subjects for young people), suggested I write a book to be entitled *How Did We Find Out the Earth Is Round?* It was to be 7,500 words long and to be aimed at bright ten- to twelve-year-olds.

I thought that was a great idea. I dashed it off and it was published in 1973. It did well and Millicent suggested I do an open-ended series of such books. They turned out to be a series of little histories of science on subjects from volcanoes to black holes and from atoms to superconductivity. I have done some thirty-five of them now and the series, as a whole, has proved quite successful.

At this time, I have published sixty-six books with Walker & Company. It stands second to Doubleday both in number of books and in royalty payments.

I like to remember nice things said about me by publishers. Once, when royalties came due in February 1978, in the midst of a heavy snowstorm, I called Sam Walker to say, "I'll pick them up when the weather improves. No hurry."

Sam, however, would have none of that. He delivered the statements and the check *on skis.*

Beth once said to me, "It's odd but you're our best author, and also our nicest."

I know why she thought that was odd. Any creative artist, once he achieves "star" quality, tends to become captious, demanding, and generally disagreeable. I swore to myself at the beginning of my career that if ever I achieved renown I would not fall prey to that. Except for a very few slips, when I was in one of my rages, I have adhered to this resolve.

Once, Patricia Van Doren of Basic Books took me out to lunch and, in the restaurant, we met Robert Banker of Doubleday.

Robert said, "Take good care of him, Mrs. Van Doren. He's Doubleday's favorite author."

And Pat replied haughtily, "Don't worry, Mr. Banker, he's Basic Books' favorite author too."

I can't help loving remarks like that and I can't help repeating them either.

One last word. Walker & Company served me in another unusual way but I'll get to that later on.

100
Failures

Not all my projects in the 1960s were successes.

In 1961, World Book Encyclopedia asked me to join a team that would do writing for their Yearbook. There were seven of us and each would take care of one facet or another of the year's advances. Thus James ("Scotty") Reston would do national affairs; Lester Pearson of

Canada, international affairs; Red Smith, sports; Sylvia Porter, economics; Alistair Cooke, culture; and Lawrence Cremin, education.

I was to do science. Work was light, one 2,000-word essay each year. Pay was good, $2,000. I had not yet reached the stage where I could routinely charge a dollar a word and $2,000 seemed very munificent.

I made only one condition. I was not to be expected to travel.

They agreed, but the agreement was phony. They persuaded me to go to Chicago, then they persuaded me to go to West Virginia. Finally, they tried to get me to go to Bermuda in 1964, and I flatly refused.

They asked me if I wanted more money. I said, "No, you give me more money than it's worth now. I just refuse to travel."

So they fired me.

An even worse situation arose in 1966 when Ginn and Company wanted to put out a series of science books for grade school youngsters. They were assembling a team and they wanted me to join it and write some of the materials for the fourth, fifth, sixth, seventh, and eighth grades.

I was most reluctant to do so, because I had never gotten over my experiences writing textbooks a dozen or so years earlier, especially writing them in committee. However, I was corrupted into it.

By 1966, you see, I was quite certain that my marriage with Gertrude was not going to last many more years, and I was deeply concerned over the matter. I was experiencing Jewish guilt to beat the band. When Ginn and Company assured me that the series of textbooks would be a multimillion-dollar success I got the brilliant idea of arranging to have half the royalties turned over to Gertrude. That, I thought, would take care of her.

So I drew a deep breath, bent my back to the task, and got to work. The team met occasionally as a large group to discuss the book, and I spent the time telling the latest jokes, very much in the way I told jokes on the way to the Concord some years later. I have to do *something* to make the unbearable bearable.

I hated the whole job, and it was all I could do to carry on by thinking of the millions of dollars. Unfortunately, the books were a flop, making not millions but thousands. Gertrude got half the royalties, but that half was so small that she was enraged rather than assuaged.

It was not my fault. Well, in a way it was, come to think of it. One of the reasons the series didn't do so well was that they mentioned evolution and the troglodytes of Texas and other states would therefore not use it. They wanted to teach science à la Genesis.

Publishers, with their usual bravery, dumbed down their books in order to make money at the expense of leaving American children undereducated or, worse, miseducated. Ginn and Company prepared to join the parade to destroy young minds by removing the evolution sections and substituting something vague about "development." However, it was I who wrote the evolution sections (and therefore was responsible, in a dim way, for the poor showing of the books) and I refused to make any changes.

I said to them, haughtily, "It isn't written in the stars that I must make a million dollars, but it *is* written in the stars that I must be true to my principles."

So they fired me. They had someone else do the changes, and on June 26, 1978, I made them remove my name from the books. The project was a fiasco from beginning to end.

What does one do in a case like this? One is helpless in the face of cowardly publishers, pliant school boards, and fanatical ignoramuses. All I can do is write essays denouncing creationism with its belief in Adam, Eve, a talking serpent, and a worldwide Flood, all in a six- to ten-thousand-year-old universe, and in a supernatural creation of all the species of life so that they were different from the start.

Some of my essays appeared in as august an organ as *The New York Times Magazine* and that roused the anger of many Fundamentalists —an anger I am happy and proud to inspire.

101

Teenagers

Earlier in the book, I mentioned my lack of any real feeling of affection for infants and children. I am not exactly sold on teenagers either. I am highly suspicious of any young man under twenty-one and any young woman under eighteen. This was brought to my attention most forcefully after we bought our house in West Newton in 1956.

It was only a block and a half from a junior high school and, in my innocence, I thought of that only as a convenience for my two youngsters as they grew up. I did not think of the other youngsters.

Every school morning a crowd of youngsters, aged twelve to fifteen, walked along the street toward the junior high school. Every school afternoon, the flow ebbed in the other direction. In the morning, it was almost bearable, for they had to be at school at a given time and they rarely woke up early enough not to have to make a brisk walk of it. In the afternoon, however, walking home, many felt no great need to be restored to their loving families at any given time. The walk home therefore meandered and was caught in shallows and stagnation, often right in front of our house.

They were loud, raucous, rude, and, in fact, obscene. It clearly made them feel very adult and hip to be using vile language.

At one time I was writing material on the excretory system for that ever-to-be-deplored Ginn and Company series and I had occasion (very naturally) to use the word "urine" repeatedly.

At one of our frequent get-togethers, the editor-in-chief of the series objected to "urine."

I was confused. "What am I supposed to say?" I asked.

"Say 'liquid excretions.'"

I was still confused. *"Why?"* I demanded.

"Because the students will titter if they hear the word 'urine.' "

Whereupon I reared up in outrage and said, "Listen, I live on a block infested by junior high school students and the only reason they would titter is because 'urine' is a fancy word to them. They're used to calling it 'piss.' I'll change 'urine' to 'piss,' if you wish, but I won't change it to 'liquid secretions.' "

It stayed "urine."

Frankly, the youngsters frightened us. It seemed to Gertrude and me that they were an elemental force. We could not drive them away or, at least, if we did, it was like punching pillows. They always returned and harsh talk from us merely roused a spirit of defiance and rebellion in them and the crowd before the house grew larger and louder.

They were respectable middle-class kids, to be sure, and never was there any violence or vandalism, but it was the volume of noise that bothered me. We learned to recognize the first distant whisper that heralded the forthcoming flood and would shiver in apprehension. It really helped poison our lives. A small thing—but small things can be effective poisoners. Think what the buzzing sound of one tiny mosquito will do to make quiet sleep impossible.

I finally solved the problem, but entirely through accident, as I shall explain.

102

Al Capp

Al Capp is, of course, the famous comic strip artist who devised the world of "Li'l Abner," a world I adored. I met him first in 1954, through the agency of a Boston University professor who knew us both. Al was a man of medium height, with a wooden leg and a strong-featured face, a ready chuckle, and a gift for conversation. I enjoyed being with him.

Our friendship ran a level course, though it was never close. We would occasionally speak on the phone, I visited him at his house once, we went to see Arthur Miller's *The Crucible* together, and so on. The closest we came was at the 1956 World Convention in New York, where he was a featured speaker, and from which he drove Hal Clement and me back with him.

The friendship reached a dreadful climax in 1968, but to explain that I will have to make a detour. Forgive me.

—I have been a liberal all my life. I have had to be. Early in life, I noted that conservatives, who are more or less satisfied with things as they are and even more satisfied with things as they were fifty years ago, are "self-loving."

That is, conservatives tend to like people who resemble themselves and distrust others. In my youth, in the United States the backbone of social, economic, and political power rested with an establishment consisting almost entirely of people of Northwestern European extraction, and the conservatives making up that establishment were contemptuous of others. Among others, they were contemptuous of Jews and in the Hitler years they were not very troubled by the Nazis, whom they considered a bulwark against Communism.

As a Jew, I had to be liberal, first out of self-protection and second because I learned to lean that way as I grew older. I wanted to see the United States changed and made more civilized, more humane, truer to its own proclaimed traditions. I wanted to see all Americans judged as individuals and not as stereotypes. I wanted to see all with reasonable opportunities. I wanted society to feel a reasonable concern for the welfare of the poor, the unemployed, the sick, the aged, the hopeless.

I was only thirteen when Franklin Delano Roosevelt became President and introduced the "New Deal," but I was not too young to get an idea of what he was trying to do. The older I got, the more firmly liberal I became. I disapproved of Roosevelt only when he wasn't liberal enough, as when, for political reasons, he ignored the plight of the African-Americans in the South or the Loyalists in Spain.

Liberalism began to fade after World War II. Times became prosperous and many blue-collar people, having jobs and perhaps feeling themselves secure, turned conservative. They had theirs and they were not willing to discommode themselves for those who were still down at the bottom. And many of those who were worst off and might have fought for a share of the pie retreated into apathy and drugs as the decades passed.

And eventually we came to the Reagan era, when it became de rigueur not to tax but to borrow; to spend money not on social services but on armaments. The national debt more than doubled in eight years and interest payments on the loans soared to over $150 billion a year. This did not immediately affect people. Rich Americans grew richer in an atmosphere of deregulation and greed, and poor Americans— But who worries about poor Americans except people branded with the L-word that no one dared mention anymore?

It makes me think of Oliver Goldsmith's lines:

> Ill fares the land, to hastening ills a prey,
> Where wealth accumulates, and men decay.

As a loyal American, I grow heartsick.

I've watched individuals turn from liberal to conservative as they grew older, fatter, and "more respectable." Those who were conservative from babyhood, like John Campbell, never really bothered me. I argued politics and sociology with him for decades and was never able to budge him, but, then, he was never able to budge me either.

Robert Heinlein, however, who was a burning liberal during the war, became a burning conservative afterward, the change coming at about the time he swapped wives from the liberal Leslyn to the conservative Virginia. I doubt that Heinlein would call himself a conservative, of course. He always pictured himself a libertarian, which to my way of thinking means: "I want the liberty to grow rich and you can have the liberty to starve." It's easy to believe that no one should depend on society for help when you yourself happen not to need such help.

The case I watched at closest range, however, was Al Capp (I've now gotten back to him). What happened to him, I don't really know. Until the middle 1960s, he was a liberal, as one could easily tell from his "Li'l Abner" comic strip. I remember that even as late as 1964, at a get-together, we were both denouncing Barry Goldwater's attempt at gaining the presidency. (Looking back on it, though, I realize that Goldwater was an honest man, and much superior in integrity to Lyndon Johnson, for whom I voted, as well as to Richard Nixon and Ronald Reagan, for whom I did *not* vote.)

And then, overnight, he turned conservative. What impelled this, I don't know. I admit that the "New Liberals" of the 1960s were sometimes hard to take; that they laid themselves open to derision as long-haired, unkempt kooks; and apparently they bothered Al beyond reason, and he turned hard right.

I remember a post-1964 gathering at which Al Capp held the floor and was absolutely acid in his comments on the African-American writer James Baldwin, for instance, on other prominent African-Americans, and on the civil rights and anti-Vietnam War movements generally.

I listened with horror and raised objections, of course, but Al swept them away.

After that, my friendship with Capp was over. I was polite and even friendly on the rare occasions when we met (I've never done anything as rude as to cut or snub anyone, whatever my private opinions might be), but I no longer sought him out.

What bothered me most was that his new attitude made itself strongly felt in "Li'l Abner." His characterization of "Joaney Phoney" as a stereotype of liberal folksingers was vicious. Worse yet, he began a long series of strips that contained what seemed to me to be very thinly veiled attacks on African-Americans.

I grew angrier and angrier at this perversion (in my opinion anyway) of a comic strip I had loved. I was finally sufficiently irritated to write a one-sentence protest to the Boston *Globe*, which ran the strip. It went: "Am I the only one who's grown tired of Al Capp's anti-black propaganda in his comic strip 'Li'l Abner'?"

On September 9, 1968, the *Globe* ran the letter inside a ruled rectangle that made it very prominent indeed. I was fatuously pleased, not thinking what the consequences might be.

The next day, at 3 P.M., Al Capp called. He had seen the *Globe* and he said, "Hello, Isaac, what makes you think I'm anti-black?"

I replied, in surprise, "Why, Al, I've heard you talk on the subject. I *know* you are."

He said, "But can you prove it in court?"

My voice quivered. "You mean you're going to sue me?"

"Darn right—for libel. Unless you call off the Black Panthers."

"I have nothing to do with the Black Panthers, Al."

"Then write a letter of apology to the *Globe* denying I'm anti-black."

I have rarely been put into such a fever of cowardice. I like to believe myself staunch in upholding my principles, but I had never been in court, I had no experience with that kind of nastiness, and I simply quailed.

I went into my office to type the letter of apology and to grovel and I discovered an amazing thing. I might be a coward, but my fingers were brave as lions. They would not type the letter. No matter how I ordered them to, they wouldn't. I stared at the blank sheet of paper and finally I gave up. No letter of apology. Let Al Capp do his worst. I called my lawyer.

He laughed and said Al couldn't sue me without the paper being sued as well for publishing the letter. I said, "But I sent it there precisely in order to have it published."

And he said, "But no one forced the paper to publish it. You call them."

I called the paper, and they laughed. They said that Al Capp was a public figure and what he did was a fair target for comment. He couldn't sue. The same thing, they said, was true of me. (I thought of all the libelous things critics had said of my writing, and I relaxed.) Besides, they said, they would explain to Al that a trial would only publicize his anti-black feelings and he wouldn't want that.

Sure enough, the paper called me the next day. Just twenty-four hours after Al had made his threat, he backed down, and I never apologized.

I met him once afterward at some large function. I greeted him amiably and there was no reference on either side to the late unpleasantness.

Poor Al! His ending was not happy. The popularity of "Li'l Abner" was declining rapidly, perhaps as a result of what I considered his misuse of it. After all, he lost his liberal constituency and conservatives don't read anything but the stock reports.

Then, too, he was overshadowed by the young Charles Schulz and his "Peanuts," which brought a new sophistication to the comic strip that outmoded Al's slapstick (and Al was openly resentful of this). Finally, a campus scandal involving a girl undergraduate put an end to Capp's lecture career. After his death in 1970, no one continued the strip.

How I wish that whatever had happened in the mid-1960s to change Al's views and personality had not happened.

The Al Capp imbroglio had a peculiar result. He had called me with his threat, as I said, at 3 P.M., just at the time the junior high school youngsters were boiling out of school. I was too preoccupied to hear them. The next afternoon, the newspaper call telling me that all was well also came at 3 P.M. I looked for Gertrude to tell her the good news and found her outside lecturing the kids.

I dashed out, full of joviality and human kindness, sent Gertrude inside, gathered the kids around me, put my arms about the two closest, and asked if any of them had ever read one of my stories. A few had and admitted they liked them. I asked if any of them had ever tried to write a story. One lonely hand went up and he admitted it was hard to do.

I said, "Well, I'm trying to write, and if you guys pass the house quietly, it makes it easier for me. How about it?"

One kid said, "Your wife yells at us."

I looked back at the house to make sure Gertrude was out of ear-shot because I was sure she wouldn't understand my next ploy. I stage-whispered, "I have to live with her. How do you suppose I feel?"

There was a loud laugh and instant male bonding. After that, there was no trouble. I made it my business to be outside every once in a while at the time of passing. I'd wave at them with a grin and they would shout back, "How are the stories coming?" It was a real love feast.

Looking back on it, I feel nothing but shame. How could I have allowed my unreasoning dislike for youngsters to grow into feeling that being nasty would achieve more results than being friendly? Why did I have to wait for pure circumstances to teach me something that I already knew at the very core of my being?

I have tried ever since to avoid this mistake, and sometimes it isn't easy. One evening, after dark, I was heading for a meeting with some friends in a large rambling building. I had to climb a flight of stairs to reach the doorway, but on the steps there stood a group of young men who regarded me solemnly as I approached.

The cowardice within me clamored, "They're muggers!" (I have never been mugged so far.) My first impulse was to veer away, but I wasn't going to let myself be swayed by unreasoning fear and I continued on resolutely. I raised my hand in a general greeting as they stared at me at close quarters in the dim light from the building at the head of the stairs.

"Hi, fellows," I said.

As though the sound of my voice was what they were waiting for, one of the young men said, "Say, aren't you Isaac Asimov?"

I stopped dead, in surprise. "Yes, I am."

"I liked the Foundation books," said the fine young man, while the others smiled in friendly fashion.

I thanked them, we shook hands all around, and I went my way, rejoicing.

103

Oases

It is perfectly possible to write a book that is a critical and financial success and yet to hate it. That was true, as I explained, of the first two editions of *The Intelligent Man's Guide to Science*.

A similar situation, on a much smaller scale, existed in connection with "Nightfall." Before its appearance, Campbell added one paragraph toward the very end. It was very poetic but it was not written in my style, and, in my eyes, it was a sheer lump of "non-Asimov." Moreover, in the paragraph, Campbell mentioned Earth, which I was careful *not* to mention in the story, because I didn't want the reader to think of the planet Lagash as alien. Campbell's one paragraph spoiled the story for me and helped cause my reaction of firm denial whenever people praise it in my hearing as my "best story."

The situation was rubbed in hard a few years ago, when the science fiction writer Harry Harrison defended me as someone who could write poetically when he chose. To prove it, he quoted Campbell's paragraph in "Nightfall." That all but sent me into a decline.

Which brings me to the fact that although in the 1960s and 1970s I turned to the writing of nonfiction, that did not mean I wrote no science fiction whatever. There were oases in the nonfiction desert. I wrote a number of science fiction stories in that interval. They included some fairly good ones too. There was "Feminine Intuition," for instance, appearing in the October 1969 *F&SF*. Then there was "Light Verse," a short short I wrote for *The Saturday Evening Post* at their request. It appeared in the September–October 1983 issue, and I liked it very much.

I had previously published stories in *The Saturday Evening Post* (after its revival as a much-diminished shadow of what had once been), but they had all been reprints. The *Post* asked for an original story, and in order to stress that that was what "Light Verse" was, I told them in a covering letter that it was fresh from the typewriter and had been written that very day.

They replied in wonder that I could have written the story in just one day. I said nothing to that. I felt it wouldn't do any good to tell them I had written the story in just one *hour*. People don't understand what it means to be prolific.

I even wrote science fiction novels in the interval and the first of these was *Fantastic Voyage,* concerning which there hangs a tale, for it wasn't really my novel. At least not in my own heart.

A motion picture had been made, entitled *Fantastic Voyage,* in which a miniaturized submarine with a miniaturized crew wanders through a dying man's bloodstream in order to cure him from within. A movie script existed and the plan was to have it novelized. Bantam Books, then under Marc Jaffe, owned the paperback rights and they wanted me to write it.

I hesitated. I had never done anything like that before, and I didn't think I would enjoy writing a novel that, in a sense, was already written. They persuaded me to read the script, however, and I was intrigued. It was an exciting story, and Marc kept buttering me up to the effect that I was the only writer they could trust with it, and so on. As usual, flattery had its effect on me, and I agreed.

It didn't take me long to write the story, even though I had to spend time correcting a few of the elementary mistakes in the script. (The authors of the movie script assumed that matter was continuous and didn't understand that when the human beings were miniaturized to bacterial size, the molecules of unminiaturized air would be too large to breathe. Also, at the end they left the submarine in the body because, they said, it had been eaten by a white cell. I had to point out that, eaten or not, it was composed of miniaturized atoms that would expand and disintegrate the man in whom it had been left.)

Despite losing time over the errors, I finished the novelization in only six weeks.

That was the easy part. Much harder was the implementation of my plans for the book. Paperback novelizations of movies are intended as mere throwaways designed to publicize the picture during the course of its run. They are then never heard of again. I was determined that this was not to happen to one of *my* books. A book of mine might fail and vanish like *The Death Dealers,* but never on purpose. I therefore made it a condition of writing the book that there be a hardcover edition.

Bantam was willing but they controlled only the paperback rights. I had to find a hardcover publisher on my own. Doubleday wouldn't do a hardcover book with the paperback rights already gone. (This was still another mistake for them, especially since the day would come, twenty years later, when Doubleday and Bantam would be part of the same corporate entity.)

I therefore persuaded Houghton Mifflin to do it. Austin was dubious as to whether the hardcover would sell at all since the paperback would come out virtually simultaneously. I assured him that in my case hardcover sales were not affected by the presence of paperbacks. I didn't really know that, but I took a chance, and I was right. The hardcover is still selling now, a quarter of a century later—not in great numbers, I admit, but it's still selling.

I worked so fast and the movies worked so slowly that the hardcover *Fantastic Voyage* was published in early 1966, six months before the picture was released. The result was that everyone was convinced the movie was made from the book. This was terribly annoying because I had to follow the screenplay and I was convinced I could have written a better book on my own. I therefore announced in print and in speech that the book came from the movie and not vice versa. I don't think that helped much.

It was not a bad movie, by the way. For one thing, Raquel Welch was in it, in her first starring role, and she effectively distracted attention from any minor flaws in the film.

The paperback came out at the time the movie was showing in theaters, and to the amazement of Bantam (and of me), it proved not to be a throwaway. It continued to sell long after the film vanished, and, in fact, it continues to sell today after dozens and dozens of reprints. It has sold several million copies. To this day, it sells better than any of my books except the Foundation series.

That doesn't help make me rich, of course. Since it was not an original work but followed the screenplay very closely, I was offered a flat sum of $5,000. Eventually, when Marc Jaffe admitted it had done far better than expected, I got an additional $2,500.

I had insisted on a royalty arrangement for the hardcover, one-quarter of the usual royalties going to me, three-quarters to Hollywood. What's more, I insisted on receiving my share directly and not through Hollywood. That was intelligent of me, for I have every reason to think that if Hollywood had received all the royalties, I would never in this world have seen a penny of it.

I do not like *Fantastic Voyage* and it is one of the few books with my name on it that I wouldn't dream of rereading. This is not because I got so little money for something that proved a runaway, long-time best-seller. Since the book was not original with me, I don't feel I deserve more than I got. The point about the book is that it is *not mine*.

Six years later came *The Gods Themselves*. It was the greatest oasis in the desert of the 1960s and 1970s, since it was the only science fiction novel I published in that double-decade. It was published by Doubleday in 1972, and as I explained earlier, the second part of that novel contained some of the best writing I've ever done—I was writing over my head.

It was nominated for the Hugo, and in 1973 I went to Toronto for the World Convention, just in case. It was a worthwhile trip, for it won as the best novel of 1972! It was my third Hugo and the first for a current fiction story. For me it was a wonderful moment.

By then, the Science Fiction Writers of America were handing out an annual award called the Nebula, and *The Gods Themselves* won that also.

Then, in 1975, a young woman talked me into writing a science fiction short story. The bicentennial of American independence was coming the next year, and she was proposing an anthology of original stories all entitled "The Bicentennial Man." I asked her what the significance of the title was, and she answered, "Nothing. Make whatever you wish of it."

So, intrigued by the notion, I wrote a story about a robot who wanted to be a man and who worked at it for two hundred years before being accepted as one. It intrigued me to the point where I made it twice as long as I had planned to make it.

Again, I was writing over my head. As it happened, the anthology never came to pass. The young woman who proposed it had financial and social problems, and I was the only person who produced a publishable story.

I got the story back from her, therefore, and returned her advance, because (a) she needed the money and (b) I had another outlet for it, obtained in a way which I will shortly describe. It was published in 1976 in *Stellar 2,* another anthology of original stories, and in the end it won both the Hugo and the Nebula as the best novelette of the year. It was my fourth Hugo and my second Nebula.

On this Nebula, by the way, both my names were misspelled. I came out as "Issac Asmimov." Now, I don't expect the ignorant engraver who handled the incision to know how to spell my name, or even to have ever heard of me, but I do think the Science Fiction Writers of America ought to have checked the initial design and noted the misspelling. The SFWA was very embarrassed and offered to redo the Nebula, but I wasn't going to wait the five years or so it would take those jokers to do the job. I simply told them, haughtily, that I would keep it as it was so that it might serve as evidence of the brainpower of the organization.

And, of course, it was at about this time that I wrote my successful mystery novel *Murder at the ABA.*

You would think that with all these successes, I would see my way clear to returning to the mass production of fiction. Actually, I did not. The joys of nonfiction still held me in thrall.

104

Judy-Lynn del Rey

Judy-Lynn Benjamin (to use her maiden name) was born on January 26, 1943, the daughter of a doctor. Most of her life was marked out for her at the instant of conception, for she was born with a genetic deficiency and was an achondroplastic dwarf. This involved a congenital inability to form cartilage normally, so that her arms and legs were always short and, even in adulthood, she was only about four feet tall.

I met her first at a local science fiction convention in New York on April 20, 1968. When I first saw her, I winced and turned away. (I'm sorry about that, but I do tend to turn away from an unpleasant sight, to hold my hands over my ears when people begin talking about an unpleasant subject, and to leave the room when things get too bad. I might try to explain that is because I've got such a sensitive nature, but I suspect it is because I simply want everything to be "nice" so that I don't have to be made to feel bad or unhappy. It is not one of my more endearing characteristics.)

However, Judy-Lynn was working at the time as an associate editor at *Galaxy* and it was her business to get to know science fiction writers, so she struck up a conversation with me, one in which I was obliged to participate, no matter how reluctantly.

And then, the strangest thing happened. I was not talking to Judy-Lynn long before I forgot she was a dwarf. Her luminous intelligence (I can think of no more appropriate adjective) totally obscured her physical appearance. It was only a matter of minutes before I was thoroughly enjoying myself.

No matter how others reacted to her appearance, Judy-Lynn never acted as though she were handicapped. (Lester del Rey said to me one time, "I don't think she knows she's a dwarf.") She had a sense of humor, she was lighthearted, found life a source of merriment, and, in short, became a cherished friend of mine and my companion of choice when we attended conventions together.

I once entered an elevator with her, and behind her walked a woman with a five-year-old child. The child, in all innocence, stared at something he had never seen before and said, "Mama, look, a little woman!"

Judy-Lynn, of course, neither blinked an eye nor turned a hair, but what astonished me (afterward, when I had time to think about it) was that I was so unaware of Judy-Lynn's deficiency that I looked about me, searching for the little woman the child claimed he saw.

She had lived a successful intellectual life. She attended Hunter College, where she majored in English, specialized in the study of James Joyce, and won various honors. She took a job with *Galaxy* in 1965, was associate editor in 1966, and full editor in 1969.

Of course, Judy-Lynn's sense of humor was not always benign. She was intelligent enough to sense in me a certain gullibility, a certain eagerness to believe people, and a nature sufficiently easygoing to be willing to accept being made the butt of a practical joke if it did no physical harm. For two years or more, she therefore made a career of setting up elaborate charades at my expense. Helping her was Lester del Rey, who was also working at *Galaxy* at the time.

Thus, Judy-Lynn once sent me proofs of the cover of an issue of *Galaxy* which was to contain a story of mine, and my name was on that cover, misspelled. Of course, I was on the phone in half a second in a fever of concern, and she insisted my name was *not* misspelled.

Once I wrote the script for a television special and Judy-Lynn used the facilities of the office to prepare a review of the special that looked as though it had appeared in a newspaper. Lester wrote the review, designing it to push every last button that would be sure to send me into a rage. Again I called in a fury, demanding to know the name of the newspaper so I could write them a stiff letter.

Worse than these little pranks was the time I got a letter telling me that Judy-Lynn had been fired. The letter was written by her replacement, one Fritzi Vogelgesang.

I replied with a most indignant letter, demanding to know how the magazine could possibly have let go a woman such as Judy-Lynn. Miss Vogelgesang answered so soothingly and with such innocent flirtatiousness that my anger seemed to disappear, and in no time at all, I was writing pleasant letters back. By the time I had decided that this Fritzi was every bit as nice as Judy-Lynn, she suddenly disappeared forever. I got a waspish letter from Judy-Lynn:

"So, Asimov! How quickly you forget all about me and take up with my replacement."

She had never been fired, and *she* was Fritzi Vogelgesang.

The most elaborate joke consisted of getting the news to me, one morning, that Judy-Lynn and Larry Ashmead had run off to get married. I found myself in a quandary. The news was given to me so seriously that it seemed to me I had to believe it. Yet, knowing each of the two individuals involved, I thought a marriage between them utterly unlikely.

I wasted hours calling everyone who might know anything about the matter, and there was only endless frustration. Either the person I tried to reach was out or if they came to the phone they said only that the marriage was taking place and that they knew no details.

It never occurred to me that Judy-Lynn had bulldozed all of Doubleday (and possibly the entire New York publishing industry) into going along with the joke. Nor did I stop to think that the day was April 1, 1970—April Fools' day.

Which is what it was, an April fool joke, and it was I who played the role of fool. Everyone else enjoyed themselves immensely as my phone calls grew more and more frantic.

Fifteen years later, on April 15, 1985, Janet and I, along with Judy-Lynn, Lester del Rey, and Larry Ashmead, had dinner at a very posh restaurant and celebrated the "anniversary" of that nonmarriage.

But life wasn't just "Let's get Asimov" with her. She made arrangements with Austin Olney to invite me and my family to an intimate dinner celebrating my fiftieth birthday on January 2, 1970, and then, through a complicated fiction, had me led off somewhere to a large surprise party she had arranged—attended by an astonishing number of friends from all over.

But in the same month, Lester's wife, Evelyn, died in an automobile accident. She was only forty-four and the accident all but prostrated me, for Evelyn was one of my favorite people. Lester himself managed to keep hold of himself, but I honestly think he would have fallen apart if Judy-Lynn, a dear friend of both, had not rallied round and offered her strength and warmth in support. Lester appreciated that and, before long, decided he didn't want to do without it. In March 1971, Judy-Lynn Benjamin became Judy-Lynn del Rey. I was at the wedding, grinning.

(Judy-Lynn told me afterward that she had been strongly tempted to interrupt the ceremony and say, "It's just another practical joke, Asimov," because she wanted to see me faint dead away—since I had been pushing the wedding as strongly as I knew how. She had refrained, she said, only because she knew her mother would have been upset if she had said that.)

I was a little bit afraid that Lester might be too much for her, but I needn't have feared. In no time at all, Judy-Lynn had flicked all the rough edges off Lester and he was as tame and devoted a husband as I have ever seen. The next fifteen years were the happiest and most successful of Judy-Lynn's life, and of Lester's life too. Lester always gladly admitted that Judy-Lynn had induced a sea change in all things about him, large and small.

In 1973, Judy-Lynn left *Galaxy* to join Ballantine Books, which had become part of the Random House conglomerate. At once she showed a new facet of her abilities, for she had the knack of recognizing a successful book and of wooing successful writers.

In 1975, Lester joined her, becoming editor of fantasy books, while Judy-Lynn worked on science fiction. Together, they formed a remarkable team, and in 1977, Random House recognized the value of the team by establishing a new imprint, "Del Rey Books." With that, the del Reys reached new heights, for they had books on the bestseller lists, in both hardcover and paperback, almost continuously.

Judy-Lynn was undoubtedly the most successful and dominating force in science fiction since John Campbell was at his height, thirty-five years earlier. And when she dominated, it was with no light hand. I once brought in a set of page proofs of one of my books which I had proofread and which I wanted to give to Judy-Lynn. She was out, so I gave the material to a secretary.

"And don't lose it," I admonished the secretary. "You know Judy-Lynn."

"Don't worry," said the secretary. "I know Judy-Lynn." And I swear she trembled.

Judy-Lynn had a direct effect on some of my science fiction. She once asked me why I didn't write a story about a female robot. I thought that was an interesting idea, and when Ed Ferman (who had succeeded Avram Davidson as editor of *F&SF*) wanted a story for an anniversary issue of the magazine, I wrote "Feminine Intuition" for him. While it was still in press, Judy-Lynn said, "Did you ever write the story about the female robot?"

I said, "Yes, Judy-Lynn. It will appear in *F&SF*."

"In *F&SF!*" she shrieked. "I wanted it for *Galaxy*."

I turned pale. "Did you?" I asked, in all innocence.

She let me have it. Her invective is not in Harlan's style, but she had more different ways of calling me an idiot than you could possibly imagine.

Another time she said, "Why don't you write about a robot who goes to work so he can save money with which to buy his freedom."

I laughed, and said, "Maybe," and forgot about it.

Then came the time when I wrote "The Bicentennial Man," and some time afterward, while it was still in press with the ill-fated anthology that was never to be, Judy-Lynn asked me if I had thought further about a story about a robot buying his freedom.

This time I froze in horror. That was the germ that had given rise to "The Bicentennial Man" and I forgot that it was she who had given me the idea. I tried to explain with more bumbles than you could believe possible, and she came at me with every intent (so it seemed to me) of killing me, screaming, *"Again* you gave my idea to someone else." I ducked behind the furniture.

She seized hold of herself with difficulty. "You give me the carbon, Asimov, and you get that story back from that woman."

"How can I get it back, Judy-Lynn? Be reasonable. I've sold it already."

"That anthology," said Judy-Lynn, "will never appear. You get that story back."

I gave her the carbon copy and the next morning she called me. "Asimov, I did my best not to like it, but I loved it. You get that story back."

Well, I got the story back and it was Judy-Lynn who published it in an anthology she edited and it won the Hugo and the Nebula.

One reviewer said the following, "I read 'The Bicentennial Man' and for an hour I was back in the Golden Age." Why can't all reviewers see as clearly as this one did?

It became customary for Janet and me to celebrate our birthday by taking Lester and Judy-Lynn out to dinner. We never missed, even in 1984, when I was only two days out of the hospital.

She and Lester attended the big bash I threw on January 2, 1985, to celebrate my sixty-fifth "nonretirement" party. On September 18, 1985, she attended the publication party for my novel *Robots and Empire,* and on October 4, Judy-Lynn and Lester and Janet and I had our last meal together, with no thought of time's winged chariot hurrying near.

Judy-Lynn's body betrayed her at last. On October 16, 1985, while she was at work, she suffered a massive brain hemorrhage. Despite speedy work at the hospital, she never emerged from her coma and she died on February 20, 1986, at the age of forty-three. She was a most remarkable woman, really she was. And quite often, Janet will fall into a reverie and say suddenly, "I miss Judy-Lynn." So do I.

105

The Bible

I have always been interested in the Bible, though I can't recall ever having had any religious feelings even as a youngster. There's a swing to biblical language that impresses the ear and the mind. I assume that the Bible is great literature in the original Hebrew or, in the case of the New Testament, Greek, but there is no question that the Authorized Version (that is, the King James Bible) is, along with the plays of William Shakespeare, the supreme achievement of English literature.

I also take a kind of perverse pleasure in the thought that the most important and influential book ever written is the product of Jewish thought. (No, I don't think it was written down at God's dictation any more than the *Iliad* was.) I call it "perverse" because it is an instance of national pride which I don't want to feel and which I fight against constantly. I refuse to consider myself to be anything more sharply defined than "human being," and I feel that aside from overpopulation the most intractable problem we face in trying to avoid the destruction of civilization and humanity is the diabolical habit of people dividing themselves into tiny groups, with each group extolling itself and denouncing its neighbors.

I remember once a fellow Jew remarking with satisfaction on the high percentage of Nobel Prize winners who were Jewish.

I said, "Does that make you feel superior?"

"Of course," he said.

"What if I told you that sixty percent of the pornographers and eighty percent of the crooked Wall Street manipulators were Jewish?"

He was startled. "Is that true?"

"I don't know. I made up the figures. But what if it were true? Would it make you feel inferior?"

He had to think about that. It's much easier to find reasons to consider oneself superior than inferior. But one is just the mirror image of the other. The same line of argument that takes individual credit for the real or imaginary achievement of an artificially defined group can be used to justify the subjection and humiliation of individuals for the real or imagined delinquencies of the same group.

But let's get back to my interest in the Bible. I had already written two small books for Houghton Mifflin that testified to this. They were *Words in Genesis* (1962) and *Words from the Exodus* (1963). In these books, I quoted passages from the Bible (from Genesis in the first book and from Exodus through Deuteronomy in the second) and pointed out how biblical references entered the English language. It was my intention to work through the entire Bible in this fashion, but the books didn't do well—so I turned to other things.

However, the hankering to write on the Bible remained and I had a chance to express this to Doubleday. T. O'Conor Sloane, the editor of *Asimov's Biographical Encyclopedia of Science and Technology*, was astonished at how well it did (and so was I). He said to me, in 1965, "Isaac, are there any other big books you can write?"

I said, "How about a book on the Bible?"

Sloane, a good Catholic, distrusted my religious views or lack of them and he asked, suspiciously, "What kind of a book?"

"Nothing about religion or theology," I said. "What do I know about that? I was thinking of a book that would explain the terms and allusions in the Bible to a modern audience."

He was unenthusiastic, but I went home and began work at once. When I had done a number of pages, I gave a copy to Sloane. A few days later, I had lunch with him and Larry Ashmead. Sloane continued to be unenthusiastic. I was downcast, but after lunch good old loyal Larry told me that if Sloane turned down the book, he (Larry) would be glad to edit it. I cheered up and went back to work.

In the end, Sloane did refuse to do it and Larry did take it over.

We had title trouble over the book. My own working title was *It's Mentioned in the Bible*. Doubleday felt that to be too bland, so I suggested *The Intelligent Man's Guide to the Bible*, to make it match my *Guide to Science*. However, that was felt to be confusing since the two books were in two different publishing houses. I then suggested *Everyman's Guide to the Bible*, but that was turned down also. The salesmen, aware of the success of the *Biographical Encyclopedia*, attributed that to the use of my name and insisted the book be called *Asimov's Guide to the Bible* and so it was.

It was such a long book that Doubleday decided to publish it in two volumes, since it lent itself easily to division. The first volume, dealing with the Old Testament, came out in 1968, the second, dealing with the New Testament and the Apocrypha, came out in 1969.

My father received the first volume in Florida. (I always gave him a copy of every book I wrote, and he would show it to everyone he knew but would not allow them to touch the books. They had to look at it while he held it. He must have made himself, and me, so unpopular.)

He telephoned me to tell me he had read only seven pages and had then closed the book because it didn't reflect the Orthodox viewpoint. This was the period, remember, when he had returned to Orthodoxy so he could have something to do. I felt bad about that, because it was the clearest evidence of his backsliding, and I disapproved.

106

Hundredth Book

As the 1960s approached their end, it was clear that I was closing in on my hundredth book. On September 26, 1968, I had lunch with Austin and he asked me if I had some special plan for the hundredth book. I didn't, so they urged me to think of one and told me I must let Houghton Mifflin do it.

It occurred to me that the best way of memorializing the event would be to prepare a book in which I would present excerpts from the first hundred books. I would divide them into chapters that would take different parts of my range (science fiction, mysteries, straight science in various branches, the Bible, and so on) and I would call the book *Opus 100.*

Houghton Mifflin was enthusiastic, so I prepared the book and it was published in 1969. My smiling face was on the cover, and on either side of it was a pile of my books put together in a deliberately miscellaneous way.

On October 16, 1969, Houghton Mifflin hosted a cocktail party in honor of the publication of the book. One always reads in books and sees in movies how cocktail parties are put on to celebrate book publications and in my younger days I assumed that that was a necessary accompaniment of all publications. However, this was the first cocktail party thrown in honor of one of my books, and I had to write a hundred to get it. I'm not sure what that signifies.

107

Death

a) *Henry Blugerman*— Until 1968, I did not experience death in my immediate family. Death did strike elsewhere. I had an uncle, an aunt, and a cousin of my own age who had all died, but we were never close, so unclose in fact that I do not even know when any of them died or what the circumstances may have been. There were deaths in the science fiction family too, like Cyril Kornbluth and Henry Kuttner.

But then, in 1968, Gertrude's father, Henry, was failing rapidly. He had lung cancer. He had never smoked, but the dust in the paper-box factory in which he worked for many years may have been a factor. In any case, he was hospitalized. While in New York, I had visited Henry in the hospital on February 17 and it was clear that his mind was beginning to wander.

Gertrude was going to go to New York to see him once I got back, but on the evening of the eighteenth we got the news that he had died. He was seventy-three years old.

Gertrude was, of course, desolate, partly because her loved father had died and partly because she had not managed to get in to see him before he died. Naturally, she was going to go to New York for the funeral. And, naturally, the children and I would have to go.

This put me into a quandary. I have a horror of funerals, not only because I dislike anything unpleasant but also because I detect a tang of hypocrisy to the whole thing. As soon as someone dies, he or she becomes transformed into a miracle of angelic behavior and personality which in life was never true, and everyone puts on an attitude of deep sorrow which, in truth, he or she might not feel.

I attended a church ceremony after the death of someone I knew only casually because I felt I ought to, and I watched the widow, all in black, totter down the aisle, face blubbered with tears, while two strong sons supported her on either side. I was astonished, for I knew (and most of the people there may have known) that she and her dead husband were in the midst of messy and hate-filled divorce negotiations when he died.

I suppose that doesn't matter, though. In many cultures, screaming and wailing are de rigueur at a funeral and professional screamers and wailers are hired to add to the din.

To me, however, death is merely death, and a person who was alive is gone, and although sorrow and loneliness may devour you as a result, it should not be put on public display, any more than it must. I realize this is not a popular view and will not prevail.

In any case, I had more than philosophic reasons for not wanting to attend Henry's funeral. I had just returned from New York and I did not feel like making the round trip again. Furthermore, February 19 was Robyn's thirteenth birthday, and I felt attending a funeral was a poor way of celebrating it. However, the necessity of going through the ritual could not be overborne.

I did delay matters a day, though, for Robyn's sake. On the morning of the nineteenth, I drove Gertrude and David to the airport, where they took the plane to New York. Robyn and I then had a birthday dinner at a fancy restaurant and I did my best to make it a pleasant occasion. (Life is for the living.) On the twentieth, she and I drove to New York, and the next day, having attended the funeral, we all drove back.

It was a miserable time for me, not the least because Mary

Blugerman, the widow, was at her self-pitying best. She had wallowed in self-pity all her life, and taught poor Gertrude to do the same, but she had never before had quite as good an excuse.

Other members of the family, of course, showed up. (Even my father and mother came.) Mary seized on Henry's younger sister, Sophie, and favored her with a long, long discourse on the miseries of widowhood and on the misfortunes that now faced her.

I pulled Gertrude to one side, and said to her softly, "Can you stop your mother? Sophie has been a widow for twenty years and it must be hard for her to take your mother's talk of misery and unhappiness."

"What do you mean?" said Gertrude indignantly, for she never allowed any criticism of her mother. "Sophie's husband died when Sophie was still a young woman and could take care of herself."

I stared at Gertrude in disbelief. "Are you trying to tell me that your mother would have been better off if Henry had died twenty years ago, instead of being so selfish as to wait till your mother was old?"

Gertrude said nothing but stalked away. I don't believe she got the point at all. When a true self-pitier is absorbed in that function there seems no way at all of allowing reason to intrude. I remembered then that I had gone through this with Gertrude once before.

Twenty years earlier, when Henry had made his ill-fated business venture after World War II, one of the disasters that struck him was that Jack, his salesman, quit on him.

I asked Gertrude why Jack had quit, and she said, "Because his father-in-law died and left him a lot of money. What a lucky fellow."

I said, "You mean Jack is lucky because his father-in-law died?"

"Of course," she said. "It's so unfair. Why should he get it?"

I said, "Would you prefer it if *my* father-in-law had died and left me money?"

She didn't answer that time either. I suppose that was the hardest thing to take about Gertrude—her insistence on allowing self-pity to take precedence over all else.

I suppose everyone goes through periods of self-pity. I know I do and I have described some of them. It is, however, an unpleasant and undignified emotion, and I do my best to fight it. I always remember the woman who told me, when I was in the army and waiting to go to Bikini, "What makes you think your troubles are so special?"

I have rarely lectured Robyn or tried to impose my views on her, but I did in this one respect, always fearing she would pick up the trick of self-pity from her mother.

I said, "Robyn, in my opinion everybody has a certain share of pity coming to him and no more. If you are sorry for yourself, there is that much less pity available for others to have for you. If you are *very* sorry for yourself, no one else will pity you. If, however, you face your troubles with courage, then you will get all the pity and help you need."

I'm so glad she listened to me, because she has grown up as a merry person who has taken her share of disappointment and misery and has always borne up bravely under them.

b) *Judah Asimov*— My father, as I mentioned earlier, lived for thirty years with anginal pain and on nitroglycerine tablets.

In 1968, the family had a big dinner to celebrate my parents' golden wedding, and it was not long after that that they were to retire to Florida. When we parted, I wondered, with a sad resignation, if I would ever see them again. After all, I was not going to go to Florida and I did not think they would ever come back to New York. My father, at least, I did not, in fact, ever see again.

On August 3, 1969, a feature article about me appeared in the Sunday *New York Times Book Review,* an excellent one which quoted me correctly and said nothing that was silly or wrong. In it, I praised my father most lovingly. I phoned him to make sure he had seen the article and he had. He was a very undemonstrative person but he was clearly touched and pleased. He complained of chest pains, in passing, as he often did, and I expressed my worries and urged him to see a doctor.

He said impatiently, "Why are you worried? If I die, I die."

The next day, August 4, 1969, the pains were worse. My mother had him taken to a hospital and there he died quietly at the age of seventy-two.

My father had had a hard life but it was full of accomplishments. Coming to the United States as a penniless immigrant at the age of twenty-six, he nevertheless managed to educate three children, see his daughter happily married, have a younger son in a high position on a large newspaper and an older son who was a professor and a prolific writer.

My brother, Stan, went to Florida, collected my mother, together with my father's body, and brought them to Long Island. My father did not have a formal funeral (Stan disapproved of them as heartily as I). We merely accompanied the rabbi to the burial site in a Long Island cemetery and watched him buried. I had looked at his face before the coffin was closed, but Stan could not bear to.

c) *Anna Asimov*— My brother placed my mother in a well-heeled nursing home within a few miles of his own home so that he could visit her regularly and frequently. I visited her less frequently, but called her without fail on set days. My father had left enough money to take care of her for the rest of her life, though, of course, my brother and I stood ready to do the job if my father's money failed.

Occasionally, I made it possible for her to bask in my fame. I spoke at a book-and-author luncheon in Long Island that was sponsored by *Newsday,* my brother's newspaper. Stan had my mother brought in by limousine, and she was at a front table during the festivities. I'm afraid that in my talk I made fun of Stan, whereupon my mother stood up and shook her fist at me. (I remember the days when her arm was indeed formidable.) After the talk, when people flocked about, buying my book and those of the other writers present and getting them signed, one brought my book to my mother, who signed it also with the greatest aplomb.

Still later, I gave a talk at the Long Beach library, which was located very near my mother's nursing home, and did it only so that she might attend and play the role of "speaker's mother."

She was, however, declining rapidly. I phoned her on August 5, 1973, it being the regular time for the call. She was quite weepy and spoke about my father, for whom she was always lonely. That night she died and they found her dead in her bed on the morning of the sixth. She had been a widow for exactly four years and two days and she was one month short of her seventy-eighth birthday.

Some relative was needed to identify her officially. They could not reach my brother, and my sister did not have a car, so they got hold of me and I drove out to Long Island with Janet. It was a bad day for it, because it happened to be Janet's birthday, and since she had been in the hospital on her previous birthday, I had wanted this one to be a special one—but not in the way it turned out to be special.

I arrived at the nursing home and identified my mother, who was then covered and taken away, eventually to be put into the prepared plot immediately next to that of my father. I was told that my brother and sister were coming, so we waited, and before long Stan and Ruth were there, and Marcia and Nick.

We looked over my mother's meager possessions to decide what was to go to the Salvation Army and what we wanted to keep ourselves for use or for a memento. I took a ballpoint pen, but nothing else, and I left it to Stan and Marcia to divide what was left.

I did, however, manage to get off one of my gallows-humor specials. Looking about at the family, I said, "If Mama had known we would all be here today, she would have waited." Oddly enough, there was a general laugh and the tension was broken. We all went out for dinner.

I was somewhat concerned at the time that I hadn't felt more grief and sorrow at my parents' death. I seemed to myself to be callous and stonyhearted about it. But there were reasons.

For one thing, as I've already stated, I don't like vast outward shows of sorrow and I don't like to indulge in loud lamentations. Second, both parents had had bad heart conditions in their last years and one would have had to be very foolish not to expect death at any time. We might even view it as a release from growing feebleness. After all, both my parents were in full possession of their minds to the last day of their lives and that is great. I would not have wanted them to live long enough to grow senile.

But I think that the greatest reason for my lack of hair-tearing was that I knew that in life I had gratified them in every way, and on their departure from me I had not one scrap of the guilt I would have experienced if I were conscious of having failed them. And I suspect that a loud and ostentatious sorrow has at its core a feeling of guilt.

To my surprise, my mother left a substantial sum of money behind, and in her will she directed that it be divided equally among the three of us. Naturally, I wouldn't take any of it, feeling that Stan and Marcia (particularly Marcia) needed it a lot more than I did, so I insisted that it be divided into two parts only.

Stan hired a lawyer to supervise this modification to make sure we did nothing illegal, and the lawyer said to me, "You had better get a lawyer of your own."

"Why?" I asked.

"To protect your interests."

I laughed, and said, "It is inconceivable that my brother and I could possibly be at odds with each other over anything as trivial as money. I don't need a lawyer." And I didn't.

d) *Mary Blugerman*— Mary had been in declining health when I first met her and had been failing rapidly ever since. At least that was her estimate of the situation, one that was freely offered to anyone who would listen.

She, however, had been left enough money by Henry to have her old age taken care of and she outlasted the generation. She survived her husband by nineteen years, living in the old apartment in which I had courted Gertrude so many years before until nearly the end, when increasing blindness and debility forced her removal to a nursing home in Brooklyn.

There she died at last on February 12, 1987, at the age of ninety-two. Gertrude was by now approaching her seventieth birthday and was not in good health, so she could not come to New York this time. Nor could John, her brother, who lived in California. Robyn, however, took care of all arrangements and saw Mary buried.

I took the opportunity to call Gertrude, from whom I had been long divorced, and assured her that she was not to worry about the financial end of it. If Mary's own money was not enough to cover matters, I would supply the missing amount. (After all, she was Robyn's grandmother, so I couldn't forsake her, no matter what.) It was one of the few occasions Gertrude said, "Thank you," to me.

108

Life After Death

The coming of death, at last, to my parents, might have given rise in myself to a renewed consideration of the possibility of life after death. How comfortable it would be not only to expect one's own death not to be death but instead to be an opening to (possibly) a more glorious life, and to feel, in addition, that you would also be able to see your parents and other loved ones again, perhaps in the full vigor of their youth.

It is entirely because such thoughts are so comforting and so exhilarating, and so remove us from the otherwise dreadful thought of death, that the afterlife is accepted by the vast majority, even in the absolute absence of any evidence for its existence.

How did it all start? we might wonder. My own feeling, purely speculation, is this—

As far as we know, the human species is the only one that understands that death is inevitable, not only in general but in every individual's case. No matter how we protect ourselves against predation, accident, and infection, each of us will eventually die through the sheer erosion of our body—*and we know it.*

There must have come a time when this knowledge first began to permeate a human community, and it must have been a terrible shock. It amounted to the "discovery of death." All that could make the thought of death bearable was to suppose that it didn't really exist; that it was an illusion. After one *apparently* died, one continued to live in some other fashion and in some other place. This was undoubtedly encouraged by the fact that dead people often appeared in the dreams of their friends and relatives and the dream appearances could be interpreted as representing a shade or ghost of the still-living "dead" person.

So speculations about the afterworld grew more and more elaborate. The Greeks and the Hebrews thought that much of the afterworld (Hades or Sheol) was a mere place of dimness and all but nonexistence. However, there were special places of torment for evildoers (Tartarus) and places of delight for men who were approved of by the gods (Elysian Fields or Paradise.) These extremes were seized on by people who wished to see themselves blessed and their enemies punished, if not in this world, then at least in the next.

Imagination was stretched to conceive of the final resting place of evil people or of anyone, however good, who didn't subscribe to quite the same mumbo jumbo that the imaginer did. This gave us our modern notion of Hell as a place of eternal punishment of the most vicious kind. This is the drooling dream of a sadist grafted onto a God who is proclaimed as all-merciful and all-good.

Imagination has never managed to build up a serviceable Heaven, however. The Islamic Heaven has its houris, ever available and ever virginal, so that it becomes an eternal sex house. The Norse Heaven has its heroes feasting at Valhalla and fighting each other between feasts, so that it becomes an eternal restaurant and battlefield. And our own Heaven is usually pictured as a place where everyone has wings and plunks a harp in order to sing unending hymns of praise to God.

What human being with a modicum of intelligence could stand any of such Heavens, or the others that people have invented, for very long? Where is there a Heaven with an opportunity for reading, for writing, for exploring, for interesting conversation, for scientific investigation? I never heard of one.

If you read John Milton's *Paradise Lost* you will find that his Heaven is described as an eternal sing-along of praise to God. It is no wonder that one-third of the angels rebelled. When they were cast down into Hell, they *then* engaged in intellectual exercises (read the poem if you don't believe me) and I believe that, Hell or not, they were better off. When I read it, I sympathized strongly with Milton's Satan and considered him the hero of the epic, whether Milton intended that or not.

But what is *my* belief? Since I am an atheist and do not believe that either God or Satan, Heaven or Hell, exists, I can only suppose that when I die, there will only be an eternity of nothingness to follow. After all, the Universe existed for 15 billion years before I was born and I (whatever "I" may be) survived it all in nothingness.

People may well ask if this isn't a bleak and hopeless belief. How can I live with the specter of nothingness hanging over my head?

I don't find it a specter. There is nothing frightening about an eternal dreamless sleep. Surely it is better than eternal torment in Hell or eternal boredom in Heaven.

And what if I'm mistaken? The question was asked of Bertrand Russell, the famous mathematician, philosopher, and outspoken atheist. "What if you died," he was asked, "and found yourself face to face with God? What then?"

And the doughty old champion said, "I would say, 'Lord, you should have given us more evidence.'"

A couple of months ago I had a dream, which I remember with the utmost clarity. (I don't usually remember my dreams.)

I dreamed I had died and gone to Heaven. I looked about and knew where I was—green fields, fleecy clouds, perfumed air, and the distant, ravishing sound of the heavenly choir. And there was the recording angel smiling broadly at me in greeting.

I said, in wonder, "Is this Heaven?"

The recording angel said, "It is."

I said (and on waking and remembering, I was proud of my integrity), "But there must be a mistake. I don't belong here. I'm an atheist."

"No mistake," said the recording angel.

"But as an atheist how can I qualify?"

The recording angel said sternly, "*We* decide who qualifies. Not you."

"I see," I said. I looked about, pondered for a moment, then turned to the recording angel and asked, "Is there a typewriter here that I can use?"

The significance of the dream was clear to me. I felt Heaven to be the act of writing, and I have been in Heaven for over half a century and I have always known this.

A second point of significance is the recording angel's remark that Heaven, not human beings, decides who qualifies. I take that to mean that if I were not an atheist, I would believe in a God who would choose to save people on the basis of the totality of their lives and not the pattern of their words. I think he would prefer an honest and righteous atheist to a TV preacher whose every word is God, God, God, and whose every deed is foul, foul, foul.

I would also want a God who would not allow a Hell. Infinite torture can only be a punishment for infinite evil, and I don't believe that infinite evil can be said to exist even in the case of a Hitler. Besides, if most human governments are civilized enough to try to eliminate torture and outlaw cruel and unusual punishments, can we expect anything less of an all-merciful God?

I feel that if there were an afterlife, punishment for evil would be reasonable and of a fixed term. And I feel that the longest and worst punishment should be reserved for those who slandered God by inventing Hell.

But all that is just playing. I am firm in my beliefs. I am an atheist and, in my opinion, death is followed by an eternal and dreamless sleep.

109

Divorce

As the 1960s drew to its close, Gertrude and I found our marriage increasingly intolerable. The situation was made worse by the fact that in 1967 Gertrude developed rheumatoid arthritis, which came and went, but left her very often in pain. It is impossible to be in almost constant pain and to be reasonable.

Then, too, I was increasingly wrapped up in my work and she was left more and more to herself. I can't blame her for resenting it. Furthermore, though our bank account continued to rise, I could see that she felt we got no good out of it. I liked our frugal, stay-at-home life. All I wanted was clean paper and a working typewriter and the money could just stay in the bank.

By 1970, I came to believe that the life we led was driving Gertrude to desperation and, knowing that I could not change, it seemed to me that divorce was the only alternative. I was perfectly willing to give her half of all the money in the bank, plus the house (fully paid off) and all its contents outside my office. I was also willing to make what I thought was a generous alimony settlement.

At the time, David was eighteen and Robyn was fifteen and just entering senior high school. I would have liked to wait till she was eighteen and entering college, but neither Gertrude nor I could have made it.

After we decided I would move out, I put a deposit on a nearby apartment and began the procedures that would lead to a divorce. To my vast astonishment, Gertrude agreed only to a legal separation. Apparently, if I wanted a divorce, I would have to take her to court, where, she made it plain, she would make every effort to strip me dry.

This was horrible. In Massachusetts, the only grounds for divorce were things like insanity, infidelity, cruel and unusual treatment, and so on. Insanity and infidelity were absolutely out of the question, but my lawyer said that if I simply told him tales of my married life, he could work up enough cruel and unusual treatment to satisfy the court. I refused, with considerable anger. I didn't want to accuse Gertrude of such things.

In that case, said the lawyer, I would have to go to a state where no-fault divorces were possible and where I could make out a reasonable case for not taking up residence *just* to get a divorce. The obvious choice was New York, where, after all, I had been brought up and where most of my editors (Doubleday, in particular) were located.

So I made the necessary preparations and on July 3, 1970, I had a moving van come over, load up my writing equipment, my library, my bookcases, and all I needed to make a living—and I left for Manhattan.

That, of course, was not the end. What followed was bitter indeed, for Gertrude hired a lawyer, who did what he could to wear me down. On two different occasions, for example, he set up a court session, and while I was racing to Boston to keep it, he maneuvered a delay, so that on reaching Boston, I simply had to turn around and go back to New York.

I persisted, however, and after three and a third years, the divorce came through. What's more, the judge awarded Gertrude less than I had originally offered. My lawyer was jubilant, but I was not. I said that I wouldn't cheat her and voluntarily raised it to what I had offered.

With that I was free.

I would like to add just one postscript. During those last few deadly and unhappy months before I left, I was busily writing *Isaac Asimov's Treasury of Humor*. I defy anyone to read it and to point out any portion that reflected the state of my despair. The answer is simple. While I was writing, I was not in despair. Writing, as I think I have said before, is the perfect anodyne for me.

110

Second Marriage

I didn't arrive in New York unprepared. I had enlisted the help of Janet Jeppson, with whom I had been corresponding for eleven years. She found me a small apartment on Seventy-second Street only four blocks away from her own apartment. When I moved in I felt exactly as I had the first night at the army camp back in 1945. No, I felt worse. When I entered the army, I had been twenty-five years old and I knew that in two years at the most I would be a civilian again and could take up my old life. Now I was fifty and there was no end possible. I had uprooted myself permanently.

I looked, woefully, about the two rooms I had rented. My library was still in transit, so there was no real work for me to do. It was Independence Day weekend, so there were no publishers to visit.

Janet, who had supplied the kitchen with cutlery and some staples so I could get a start, was with me as I surveyed the scene. She is a remarkably sensitive woman and there is no doubt that she could sense the guilt under which I was laboring over having left my family, and my loneliness. Delicately, she pointed out that she was seeing no patients over the weekend, and I could stay at her apartment during the day. It would be more cheerful.

I was delighted at the chance. Janet's kindness soothed the transition enormously. Remember that we were rather more than friends when I came to New York. That eleven-year correspondence was a romance in itself. Janet wrote long and fascinating letters, and my answers went back by return mail. She addressed her letters to the medical school to avoid raising inconvenient questions at home, and I used to go to the school at least once a week, more for the reason of picking up letters from her than for any other reason. We spoke by phone frequently as well.

It was clear that Janet was as articulate and intelligent as I, and that her views and philosophy were very close to mine. The letters were marvelous. (Janet still has them somewhere and occasionally rereads a few of them.)

Janet, I think, was in love with me all the time. She had no husband, no family, to restrain her. In addition to my letters, she read everything I wrote and had enjoyed my writing before she ever met me. I suspect I loved her too, but, of course I was all tangled up in the feeling that, as a married man, I shouldn't do that.

Let me stress that I was no angel of fidelity. (Gertrude, I'm sure, was. I never dreamed of questioning or investigating the matter, but I'm sure of it anyway.)

I was without sexual experience when I married, and I had no extramarital contacts for eleven years thereafter despite opportunities in the army and at conventions. However, I was not proof against temptation altogether and, eventually, there were occasions when a young woman made her intentions perfectly plain, and when the opportunities were there, and—I succumbed.

It had its importance. With Gertrude, I never felt particularly skilled sexually, but other young women, to my astonished delight, seemed impressed. I realize that sexual prowess is not something an "intellectual" such as myself should place much value on, but biological pride is hard to fight. Frankly, it raised my opinion of myself and made me happier.

I might easily have turned into a Don Juan. I had the impulse to do so—but I lacked the time. Writing still came first, and writing in quantity too, so that the opportunities to have a fling came only rarely. I didn't regret that, for even sex takes second place to writing as far as I am concerned.

What's more, there was no question of "love." Each adventure, in those days of the 1950s, was nothing more than an adventure—on the woman's side as well as mine. After all, there was nothing in common but a fleeting sexual attraction.

Janet was different. Certainly, I found her presence interesting and delightful when we were together at the World Convention in Pittsburgh in 1960 and, again, in Washington in 1963. (In Washington, I remember, we escaped from the convention a while to tour the White House and visit museums.) Then, too, in 1969, when Gertrude and

Robyn were visiting Great Britain with friends, when David was at his special high school in Connecticut, and I was alone at home, Janet came to Boston.

She stayed at a nearby hotel and for a couple of days we drove about in northeastern Massachusetts, visiting such places as Salem and Marblehead. With her, I really forgot about writing, the only time I can think of, offhand, that this happened. In fact, those couple of days may have been the most carefree of my life, for there was nothing hanging over me, not the candy store, not school, not a job, not my family—not even writing. The world, for a little while, was all Janet.

But it was not the delight of her physical presence that was crucial. It was the good fit of our minds and personalities; in fact, it was that good fit that made the physical presence of each so important to the other. The letters would have been enough to make me long for Janet even if I had never seen her, and I know that she reciprocated that feeling.

But once I moved to New York and spent the Independence Day weekend with her, any ambivalence I had in the matter was gone. I was in love with Janet and she was in love with me and we both knew it beyond any possibility of doubt. It was clear in my mind that I would marry her as soon as it became legally possible.

What's more, as divorce proceedings stretched on interminably, there seemed no reason to maintain totally separate establishments. I moved into her apartment and used my own just for daytime work.

Janet was a tower of strength to me during the miserable time of uncertainty that preceded the divorce. She never pushed me; never urged me to agree to anything foolish in order to hasten the divorce; seemed perfectly willing to continue our irregular arrangement for the rest of our lives. If Gertrude was making life harder for me, Janet was making it easier to an even greater extent.

When the divorce finally came through, I insisted (Janet did not) that we get the necessary blood tests and license. We were then married on November 30, 1973. A civil ceremony seemed too bloodless and neither of us wanted a conventional religious ceremony of any kind, so we were married in Janet's living room, by Edward Ericson, a leader at the Ethical Culture Society, which was located four blocks away.

At this time of writing, Janet and I have been married for seventeen years, and it is twenty years since I came to New York. May I say that we have been remarkably happy all this time and are as much in love now as ever. I am still all wrapped up in my work, but Janet is a professional woman with a career of her own. She was a skilled psychiatrist and psychoanalyst, and after she retired, she continued her writing and was, independently of me, successful at it, so she's wrapped up in her work as well.

We both work in our apartment—a larger one that we moved into in 1975, after I gave up the separate office I'd had for five years. We are together constantly, even when we are both working each in our own part of the apartment. In addition, her patience and sensitivity are remarkable and she endures all my faults with unswerving love. I'm sure that I would endure her faults just as lovingly, if she had any.

Not that marriage came easily to Janet at the start. She was forty-seven years old at the time of our wedding and had supported herself all her adult life and been successful in her profession. She wasn't sure how she could adjust to married life and she was in tears the day before the wedding. I asked in alarm what was wrong.

She said, "I can't help it, Isaac. I feel as though I will be losing my identity."

"Nonsense," I said firmly. "You won't be losing your identity; you'll be gaining subservience."

Janet broke into delighted laughter, and all was well.

As to our Darby-and-Joan love affair, consider this—

In 1986, the concierge at our apartment house handed me the New York *Post* and said, "You're on page six."

I went up to the apartment waving the newspaper and said, "Janet, Janet, I made the *Post.*"

"Why?" she said in surprise. (We are not *Post* readers.)

"They caught me kissing a woman."

Janet shook her head (she knows all about my feckless gallantries) and said, "I keep telling you to be careful."

I handed her the paper. We had been at some function at which a science writer's book was being published, and at one point Janet and I kissed each other (which we do frequently, whether we're in public or not). A *Post* reporter saw that and waxed merry over the antics of "sexagenarians," though Janet was actually only fifty-nine at the time.

"See," I said. "There you have our society. If a man kisses his wife in public, it makes the newspapers."

111

Guide
to Shakespeare

My move to New York did not stop my writing. I admit that every time the circumstances of my life changed radically, I would worry about whether I'd be able to continue my writing as before, but the worry has always been groundless. The writing always continued.

After I had handed in *Asimov's Guide to the Bible,* I felt bereft. I had worked on it so long and enjoyed it so much, I resented having to stop. I wondered if there were anything else I could do that would be comparable in pleasure, and what is the only part of English literature to compare with the Bible? Of course—the plays of William Shakespeare.

In 1968, I therefore began to write *Asimov's Guide to Shakespeare,* intending to go over every one of his plays carefully, explaining all the allusions and archaisms, and discussing all his references involving history, geography, mythology, or anything else I thought could use discussion.

I began it even before mentioning my plan to Doubleday, let alone getting a contract. After I finished my analysis of the play *Richard II,* however, I presented that to Larry Ashmead and asked for a contract. Larry obliged and I continued to work on the book furiously.

The most fun I've ever had, writing, was when I wrote my autobiographies. After all, what more interesting subject can I have than myself? Leaving this out of account, however, *Asimov's Guide to Shakespeare* was the most pleasant work I had ever done. I have loved Shakespeare since I was a young boy, and reading him painstakingly, line by line, and then writing at length about everything I read was such a joy.

I was rewarded for this, for soon after I moved to New York, and immediately after the Independence Day weekend was over, when Janet was again with her patients, I received the galleys of the book—a *lot* of galleys, for the book was half a million words long. That gave me something to do, just when I very badly needed something to do to keep my mind off my feeling of guilt and insecurity.

Galleys or "proofs," for those of you who don't know, are long sheets on which the contents of a book are printed, usually two and a half pages or so to each galley sheet. The writer is supposed to read over them carefully, trying to catch all the typos made by the printer and all the infelicities made by himself. Such "proofreading" and corrections are meant to ensure that the final book will be free of errors.

I suspect that most writers find galleys a pain, but I like them. They give me a chance to read my own writing. The problem is that I'm not a good proofreader, because I read too quickly. I read by "gestalt," a phrase at a time. If there is a wrong letter, a displaced letter, a missing letter, an excessive letter, I don't notice it. The small error is lost in the general correctness of the phrase. I have to force myself to look at each word, each letter separately, but if I relax for one moment I start racing ahead again.

The ideal proofreader should be, in my opinion, knowledgeable about every aspect of spelling, punctuation, and grammar, while being slightly dyslexic.

Asimov's Guide to Shakespeare was published in two volumes in 1970, and whenever I use it, or even look at it, I find myself back in those very early days in New York, uncertain of the future and a little frightened.

112

Annotations

On July 16, 1965, I had lunch with Arthur Rosenthal, publisher of Basic Books, which had done *The Intelligent Man's Guide to Science*. Present at the luncheon was Martin Gardner, someone whom I admired extravagantly. I have read (and own) every book of his that I could get hold of. I followed his column "Mathematical Recreations" in *Scientific American* with avidity.

Gardner's most successful book was *The Annotated Alice*. It included the entire books of *Alice in Wonderland* and *Through the Looking Glass* complete with Tenniel's illustrations. In the margin Gardner discussed every aspect of particular lines that he felt required comment. It is a fascinating book that I have gone through several times.

I referred to that at the luncheon, and Gardner (who was kind enough to say he admired my books too—and indeed we have been good friends ever since) told me that if I really wanted to have fun, I should find a book I liked very much and annotate it.

In a way, *Asimov's Guide to the Bible* and *Asimov's Guide to Shakespeare* were annotations, but, of course, I could not include the entire text of either the Bible or Shakespeare's plays. I could only quote selected passages. But still the notion of real annotations remained in the back of my mind.

And why not? My books on the Bible and on Shakespeare had given me courage. Until then, I had confined my nonfiction very largely to science, and even when I ventured outside that realm, as with my histories, I was writing books for young people that were not expected to be terribly deep.

My books on the Bible and on Shakespeare were, however, far outside what one would have thought to be my expertise and they were written for adults. I was quite prepared to meet with a hostile reception along the lines of "Why doesn't Asimov stick to his stupid science fiction and not try to thrust himself into fields he knows nothing about?"

I did get a little of that. I remember a contemptuous short review from a professor of literature at a certain college who made it quite plain that he thought my books on Shakespeare totally unworthy of comment. It was in the Sunday *Times*, and the passage of two decades has not assuaged my anger at it.

In later years, I met a student at the college in question and I asked him if he knew the reviewer (whose name I remember perfectly well but won't mention). Yes, he did.

I said, "How would you describe him?"

"Short," said the student, "and very conceited."

"Good," I said, "that's how I imagined him to be."

The books survived, though, and were generally well received even though they were not the kind of books that would sell lavishly. By the time I had returned to New York, I was quite confident of my ability to write on any subject I pleased without expecting critical obliteration.

In this connection, it happened that in my first week in New York, it occurred to me that I could do anything I wanted to do without let or hindrance. I had no family, and Janet was busy with her patients. Consequently, I went down to lower Fourth Avenue, which in 1970 was still a haunt of secondhand bookstores. There I did something I had always dreamed of doing. I drifted along the musty shelves of such a store, looking at old books.

I came across a copy of Lord Byron's *Don Juan*. There had been a copy in the Blugerman household, and I had tried to read it in the mornings when I woke up before anyone else, and yet was not allowed to do anything lest I wake Gertrude's brother, John, who, his mother would say, "had to have his twelve hours' sleep." As nearly as I could make out, she was serious. However, the type of the edition in the Blugerman bookshelf was microscopic and the surroundings were depressing, so that I could never get into it.

Now, it seemed, I could make a better stab at it. I had never been a good sleeper. I can't manage anything more than five hours a night and in the new apartment I had trouble sleeping at all. Well, if I couldn't sleep, why bother trying? I was alone there. I could put the light on and read all night. Who was to stop me?

That night I got into my very low-quality bed (which came with the apartment and wasn't mine), opened *Don Juan,* and began reading. I had scarcely finished the prologue, in which Byron vilified Robert Southey, William Wordsworth, and Samuel Taylor Coleridge, when I was all on fire. Martin Gardner's words came back to me and I wanted to do an annotation, a real annotation. I wanted to have Doubleday put out an edition of *Don Juan* with comments by me that would explain all the classical allusions and all the topical references for the contemporary American reader.

The next morning I went to Doubleday and sold Larry Ashmead on the idea, and got to work at once. Gardner was right. It was enormous fun. David came to visit me while I was hot on the trail of Byron and it was all I could do to spend any time with him at all. I wanted only to work on the book. It was that which made me a bad father or, in Robyn's gentle phrase, a *busy* father.

I knew it couldn't possibly sell, and so did Doubleday. After all, the public taste was no longer in favor of the romantic poetry of the post-Napoleonic period. For another, the book would have to be priced high—too high for all but a very few readers. However, I wanted to do it and Doubleday wanted to please me.

Doubleday published it in 1972. We couldn't call it *The Annotated Don Juan* because Clarkson Potter (a subsidiary of Crown Publishers), which had published Gardner's *Annotated Alice,* had that form of title copyrighted. It was therefore called *Asimov's Annotated Don Juan.* Doubleday put out a beautiful edition, which won a prize (for its design, not for its contents, I hasten to say), and it actually earned back its advance. (Of course, I had asked for a small advance in the first place, to make sure that it would be earned back.)

As soon as the book was finished, I started working on what was to be *Asimov's Annotated Paradise Lost* because I wanted to get it in to Doubleday before the first was published and, possibly, dropped dead. That was as much fun as its predecessor and it was published in 1974. I also did a smaller book, dealing with a number of well-known poems that had historical meaning, and it came out as *Familiar Poems, Annotated* in 1977.

None of these books made any money to speak of, though none actually lost money, and the pleasure they gave me was worth far more than money to me.

Indeed, I would have liked to do more, but I really felt I couldn't stick Doubleday beyond a certain point. However, in 1979, Jane West of Clarkson Potter asked me to do an annotation for them, leaving me free to choose an appropriate book. Gardner, in that luncheon of ours so many years before, had mentioned Jonathan Swift's *Gulliver's Travels* as an ideal book for me to annotate, and so I suggested that. Jane was enthusiastic and once again I got to work.

This time the book could come out as *The Annotated Gulliver's Travels,* for it was a Clarkson Potter book, and it was published in 1980. It did marginally better than the Doubleday books, but not very much better.

There was one more annotation I was dying to do, and I found my chance in the later 1980s when I was more than ever Doubleday's fair-haired boy, for reasons I will be giving you later. I seized two months of time that I thought I could get away with and worked furiously until I was finished with *The Annotated Gilbert & Sullivan.* I offered it to Doubleday without an advance, so eager was I to get it published. That evoked the famous "Don't be silly, Isaac!" which I was always getting from them, and they proceeded to give me an advance five times higher than I had had for *Don Juan.* It was published in 1988. Although it was a huge book costing $50 and was almost impossible to lift, it actually made back that advance.

But that's all. I can't think of any other annotations I am dying to do. There's Homer, of course, but he's in Greek and you can't go by any of the numerous translations.

113

New In-Laws

I realized that, since I was planning to marry Janet at the first possible opportunity, I was going to have another set of in-laws.

I will confess to a little nervousness there. Whereas Gertrude and her family had been Jewish, Janet was Gentile. I knew that it was a matter of supreme indifference to her that I was Jewish (as it was to me that she was Gentile), but what about her family?

Janet's parents were Mormons, though I gathered they were not active in the church. Janet herself had never been baptized and was emphatically *not* a Mormon. She is, in point of fact, as completely nonreligious as I am.

When the time for marriage was approaching, Janet, anxious to please me in all ways, asked if I would like her to be converted to Judaism.

"Sure," I said, "provided you allow me to be converted to Mormonism." That ended that sort of nonsense forever. (She's a member of the Ethical Culture Society now, but I won't go even that far.)

The Mormons believe in a high birthrate and both Janet's father and Janet's mother had many siblings. The result is that Janet had dozens and dozens of first cousins, uncles, aunts, and assorted other relatives. Fortunately, most of them were in Utah and it would not be necessary for me to meet them all. (Janet was even more relieved at that than I was.)

Janet's father, John Rufus Jeppson, had died in 1958, the year before Janet and I had met at the Mystery Writers banquet. It had been a sudden and unexpected death, for he was only sixty-two, and Janet, who had adored him, was devastated by it.

Her father had had a hard life, working his way up from poverty, working his way through medical school and ending as an ophthalmologist and a respected citizen of New Rochelle. At his side was always his wife, Janet's mother, Rae Evelyn Jeppson (née Knudson). John and Rae had been childhood sweethearts and it was a love match from beginning to end. (This was true of my parents also.)

I met Rae quite early, while Janet and I were living together. My nervousness lay not only in the fact that I was Jewish but in that we were living together though unmarried. I did not fear parental disapproval in itself, but I didn't want to make life difficult for Janet and be the cause of an estrangement between mother and daughter.

Janet assured me that there was nothing to be concerned about, but I remained cautious.

Janet's mother, Rae, was shorter than Janet and with hair still light brown, though she was in her seventies. She strongly resembled Janet in facial appearance and that was enough, in itself, to dispose me in her favor the moment I met her. She was a lady in the old-fashioned sense of the word: genteel, courteous, soft-spoken. (Janet often says that Rae tried to make a lady out of her, but had failed.)

She was honest too. Disregarding the fact that she might embarrass her daughter, she looked me in the eye and said, firmly, "Dr. Asimov, I am sorry for your wife."

But I met her eye and said, just as firmly, "Mrs. Jeppson. Please believe me. So am I."

That was all. The subject never came up again. Rae was satisfied. I think I did myself a great service by resisting the temptation to defend myself. I would surely have come across as a petty whiner if I had, and Rae would not have been pleased.

My future mother-in-law and I got along famously. It was clear that when we remained overnight in her house, she wanted us to have separate bedrooms. I thought we could well endure that, and I pointed out to Janet that it was an innocent way of pleasing her mother. Janet, however, would have none of it. She did not wish, in middle age, to be subject to what she considered her mother's unreasonable wishes, and Rae gave in. I felt guilty about it and I still think there would have been nothing terribly wrong in trying to make Rae feel better about the situation.

The crucial moment of my relationship with Rae came when Janet was in the hospital in 1973, with a sudden subarachnoid hemorrhage. It fell to me to call Rae in order to tell her what was happening, and to explain that it was life-threatening. The situation was worse because Rae's younger sister, Opal (for whom Janet had been named), had died of a subarachnoid hemorrhage at the age of forty-seven and, by coincidence, Janet was forty-seven when it happened to her.

I dreaded telling Rae. Aside from the fact that I was distraught over Janet's condition and could not entirely trust myself to handle the situation with the necessary gentleness and tact, I had to face a possibly equally distraught mother who might, in her sorrow, seek a scapegoat, and blame me. Rae had been brought up with a strict religious training and it was conceivable that she might view what had happened to Janet as God's punishment for her having "lived in sin" with me.

Naturally, I could not accept any such interpretation of events, but neither could I possibly argue the matter with a brokenhearted mother. I steeled myself for an onslaught against which, again, I could make no attempt to defend myself. I got Rae on the phone and told her the news as well as I could. I'm afraid I was weeping as I did so (no, I'm not ashamed of that) and she could not doubt my own misery.

For a while, she said nothing, then, in the softest, warmest possible way, she said, "Whatever happens, Isaac, I want to thank you for making Janet so happy these last few years."

Fortunately, Janet recovered unharmed. Eventually, I told her what her mother had said, and I assure you that after that Rae Jeppson could do no wrong as far as I was concerned. I loved her as another mother of my own, and though Janet, daughterlike, sometimes complained about her, I never did.

After a year of cancer Rae Jeppson died on June 10, 1976, shortly before her eightieth birthday. She remained physically active till almost the end, and mentally alert all the way. It was a quiet death and, unlike the case of my parents, or Gertrude's, she did not die alone or among strangers. She died in her own home, in her own bed, with her daughter at her side, holding her hand.

The last thing Janet said to her was: "I love you, Mother."

Rae whispered, "I love you too, Janet," and drifted softly into death.

And how can one die better than quietly, while receiving and returning love?

Janet's father was the first member of the large Jeppson family to become a physician, but he set the fashion for the family. Not only did Janet become one but so did her younger brother, John Ray Jeppson.

After graduating from Harvard, John went to Boston University School of Medicine and was in the last class I actively taught. He carried the news of me to his sister and also introduced her to science fiction. From this all else followed and I am unspeakably grateful to him.

He married a beautiful young lady named Maureen, while he was still in med school, and eventually he became an anesthesiologist. John now lives in California, and has two children, a girl named Patti and a boy who is a third John.

Janet and I are very fond of Patti, who has chosen historical archaeology as her field. Young John is a dentist, married with a daughter named Sarah. This makes Janet's kid brother a grandfather and herself a great-aunt. (It makes me a great-uncle, of course.)

Janet has a first cousin, Chaucy Bennetts (née Horsley), who is two years older than Janet. They grew up very much as sisters, rather than as cousins, and the sisterly feeling still exists between them.

Chaucy is not her original name. She was christened Shirley, but her father was also named Shirley. Perhaps it was the inevitability of confusion, both in person and in gender, that was part of the inspiration for the name change. However, Chaucy eventually married a very pleasant gentleman named Leslie Bennetts, and when they had a daughter, what was she named? Why, Leslie, of course. I've never understood that.

Chaucy was a highly intelligent and remarkably beautiful young woman who did a little acting, but afterward she turned to editing, becoming an important editor of children's books for many years. Now she's on the copy-editing staff at Doubleday and I frequently stop to see her there when I visit Doubleday. Her husband was considerably older than she was. He was a very lovable, quiet and thoughtful man, who died in 1985 at the age of eighty.

Chaucy's daughter, the younger Leslie, inherited her mother's youthful beauty. I saw the photos taken at her first marriage and in one photograph, where she was shown standing with her mother, she appeared much more beautiful than many a movie star. I looked at the photo with awe and said, "Breathtakingly beautiful. Absolutely breathtaking."

Chaucy beamed at the praise for her daughter, and said, "Yes, isn't she?"

"She?" I said. I looked at the picture again and said, "Oh, yes, Leslie looks pretty good too."

Leslie's marriage was not a success, unfortunately. It lasted only a year, but Leslie then launched herself on a successful journalistic career. She wrote for the Philadelphia *Bulletin,* then the New York *Times,* and is now with *Vanity Fair.* She is a terrific interviewer. (She once described me in an interview, however, and made me two inches shorter than I really am. Since I am only of average height, I couldn't afford the loss and I took it hard. Of course, she is taller than I am, as is Chaucy, and that might have misled her.) She has recently married a second time. Her husband is writer Jeremy Gerard, and they have a daughter named Emily.

Leslie's younger brother, Bruce, is now an actor and photographer. He's also tall, handsome, and intelligent, with an excellent singing voice.

I got along marvelously well with Janet's family and I was introduced to something I had never experienced—the family celebration. My own family never really celebrated, for the candy store was an ever-present anchor that dragged us down. There were occasionally festivities at the Blugerman household, but I was always made to feel an outsider.

Now, though, with the Jeppsons and the Bennettses, I was welcomed into the family wholeheartedly, and made part of the holidays as they came—Easter, Thanksgiving, and Christmas. Chaucy prepared the main dish and she was every bit as good a cook as Mary Blugerman was. Rae would make a special sweet potato and marshmallow dish. Les Bennetts would prepare a liver pâté. There were nuts and candies and fruits and cake, and I just loved the whole thing.

The most remarkable holiday of all was Christmas 1971. I had received the page proofs for the third edition of my *Guide to Science,* and when it was time to go to Rae's house, I looked ruefully at my page proofs, which I wanted to use for the preparation of the index.

Janet said, "Take it with you. You can work there."

So I did. I took the page proofs and several thousand 3 × 5 blank white cards, made sure I had a couple of good pens, and off we went. They gave me Janet's father's old office, with a large comfortable armchair and a perfect desk. They assured me that no one would bother me.

I was about to tell them that I never minded being bothered, but they vanished and for the entire day everyone worked on preparing for a grand feast—except me. I worked on my cards, all alone, with no one daring to disturb the great man at his work. No footstep, no whisper disturbed me. Nothing like that had ever happened to me before and I knew that before long they would discover that I didn't absolutely need isolation and that it would never happen again. But in the meantime I had had hours and hours to myself until I was called in to partake of the great dinner and to open presents. What a pleasant memory.

(Just as a side remark, the third edition of the *Guide to Science* that I was working on that glorious Christmas had title trouble. It couldn't very well be called *The New New Intelligent Man's Guide to Science.* However, my name had grown so much more famous in the last decade that they decided to call it *Asimov's Guide to Science.* When the fourth edition came out it was *Asimov's New Guide to Science.* I don't know what they'll do for the fifth edition, if there ever is one.)

But back to Janet— I introduced her to my family also. She was too late to meet my father, as I was too late to meet hers, but she met my mother in Long Beach. And she met Stan and Ruth. Everyone liked her, of course. (I never met anyone who didn't.) Stan, after he had talked to Janet for a while, pulled me aside and whispered, "She's a pearl, Isaac. How did you find her?"

"I'm talented," I said.

114

Hospitalizations

I had just passed my fiftieth birthday when I returned to New York and I was still essentially intact. I had never had my tonsils, adenoids, or appendix removed. I had thirty-one of my teeth and the only one missing could have been saved if I had had better dental care in the early 1940s. I had never as much as broken a bone.

All this was a matter of smug self-satisfaction with me and I looked forward to going to my grave eventually still intact. However, man proposes and old age disposes—

My certainty concerning my state of health was such that I rarely saw doctors except when it was obviously necessary. In part, that was the result of childhood conditioning too. My parents were poor, and doctors cost money. (Not much, to be sure. In my childish days, doctors paid house calls and charged three dollars to do so, but three dollars was a lot of money to poor people, and the doctor was called only when a child was at least a quarter dead or an adult fully half dead.)

But when I moved in with Janet, I found that things had changed. She was a physician and the daughter of a physician and she was a great believer in perpetual conferences with doctors over every itch and scratch. I was appalled when she began to insist on a general medical once-over.

"I'm perfectly healthy," I protested.

"How do you know?" she said, with a hint of steel in her voice.

(I've discovered that when I hear that hint of steel, the safest thing is to give in gracefully. Janet says I may have discovered it, but I've never yet managed to *do* it.)

In any case, she had picked up from a colleague of hers the name of Paul R. Esserman. He apparently had the reputation of being an internist (which is what we used to call a "general practitioner" or a "GP") of unusual intelligence and medical knowledge. Janet insisted I go to him and I was in his office on December 16, 1971.

Paul, as it turned out, is six feet tall, a trifle overweight, has a soft and soothing voice, and (as I eventually found out) a perfect bedside manner. As usual, I was unable to maintain a business relationship. We became friends and he has been my doctor ever since. I wish earnestly I didn't need his services as a doctor, but, as it turned out, I did.

He carried through the first examination and I asked him how things were with me.

"Perfect," he said.

"I knew it," I said.

"Except for the nodule on your thyroid."

"What nodule?"

He had me bend my head back and sure enough there was a visible bump on the right side of my neck.

"Didn't you ever notice it when you were shaving?" he asked.

"No," I said petulantly. "It was never there before. You put it there."

"Of course," he said agreeably, "and now we'll need a good endocrinologist to tell us what it is and what we ought to do."

The endocrinologist was Dr. Manfred Blum, who subjected me to a test with radioactive iodine. The thyroid nodule was cold; it did *not* take up iodine, and therefore was not performing its function adequately.

"What does that mean, Doc?" I asked.

Blum hesitated.

Whereupon I said, rather coldly, "You're allowed to say 'cancer,' Doctor."

So that's what he said, but he pointed out that the thyroid was so specialized a tissue that a thyroid cancer almost never spread and it could easily be cut out.

So I went to a surgeon, Carl Smith, who cheerfully agreed to take out any affected portion of the thyroid for me and the operation was scheduled for February 15, 1972.

It was the first time that I had ever had to face an operation requiring general anesthesia, and I was not happy about it. I had heard of rare cases where a person was sensitive to a particular anesthetic and died on the operating table. I also knew that I was fifty-two and that my fellow writer William Shakespeare had died at the age of fifty-two, and I thought that the Fates might easily confuse the two of us. In short, I was scared stiff.

So I called Stan, the levelheaded member of the family. A few years earlier he had faced, and survived, a serious operation on his spine. I asked him how he had managed to work himself up to face the grim task.

"I was in dreadful pain," said Stan. "I could hardly walk. I'd have done anything to rid myself of the pain and I didn't fear the operation. I looked forward to it. The trouble with your thyroid condition, Isaac, is that it isn't giving you pain and so you don't really feel the need for an operation."

He was perfectly right and I managed to calm my fears. In fact, before I went in for the operation, they shot me so full of sedatives (over my protests that I was perfectly calm and didn't need them) that, far from being nervous, I was hilarious.

When Carl Smith arrived in his green robe and green mask, I greeted him joyfully, and intoned:

> Doctor, Doctor, in your green coat,
> Doctor, Doctor, cut my throat.
> And when you've cut it, Doctor, then
> Won't you sew it up again.

I don't remember that anyone laughed. I did hear someone say, "Give the anesthetic, will you, and shut him up," or words to that effect. And I passed out of consciousness.

Later, Carl Smith told me exactly how foolish I had been. He explained that he had to cut very carefully to avoid slicing through a nerve, the destruction of which would have left me hoarse for the rest of my life. "Suppose while I was doing that I thought of your little verse," he said severely, "and started to chuckle over it, so that my hand shook."

I'm sure I turned a very pretty green at that point, and I have to repress a shudder every time I think about it, even now.

The operation gave me occasion to prove how delightful it was to be a writer. Carl charged me $1,500 for the operation (well worth it) and I later wrote up a funny article about it (including my little verse) and charged $2,000 for the piece. Ha, ha, and how do you like that, you old medical profession, you? (I was happier than ever I hadn't been accepted by any medical school.)

A side effect of the operation was important.

My last serious remark before my operation was: "Don't touch the parathyroids." It was probably impossible, however, to follow that order. Carl cut out the right half of my thyroid gland and, in the process, two of the four small parathyroid glands normally embedded in the thyroid were undoubtedly cut out also.

The parathyroids control calcium metabolism, and my kidney stones were calcium oxalate dihydrate in structure. Once the diseased half of my thyroid and those two parathyroids were gone, I never formed another painful kidney stone. That alone was worth the operation.

Just the same, I was annoyed about the whole thing. I was no longer intact, and I had the scar across the bottom of my neck to prove it.

Three months after my thyroid operation, Janet's gynecologist found a lump in her left breast. There was, of course, a period of agonizing uncertainty and, finally, it was decided that a bit of exploratory surgery was necessary.

It took place on July 25, 1972, with Carl Smith again officiating. I waited in Janet's hospital room, and as the hours passed my spirits fell. The exploratory surgery had shown the advisability of a mastectomy and Carl Smith performed a radical, taking out the muscle behind the breast also. (Radicals are no longer popular. Janet's may have been one of the last.)

It took Janet two or three days to fully realize what had happened. She had lost one of her two small breasts and she wept bitterly. I managed to worm out of her the real reason for her weeping. She felt "maimed." We were not yet married and she was convinced that, with nothing legal to hold me, I would simply drift off and find someone who was younger, prettier, and had two large breasts.

I was at my wits' end. How was I to convince her that what I loved in her was not something one could see or that a surgeon's knife could reach? Finally, in desperation, I said, "Look, it's not as though you're a showgirl. If you were, and if your left breast was removed, you would fall over to the right. As it is, with your tiny breasts, who cares?

In a year, I'll be squinting my eyes at you and saying, 'Which breast did the surgeon remove?' "

It was a terribly cruel thing to say, but it worked. Janet burst into a laugh and felt much better.

Janet and I both knew how queasy I was, and she feared that at the first sight of her scarred chest I would gasp in agony and leave and never return. And I was afraid that, although I knew I would not leave, I would indeed gasp in agony and make her forever miserable.

So I had Carl Smith tell me in detail just how her chest would look and I practiced pretending I was looking at it. Then a few weeks after the operation, when I thought that she had been carefully concealing the matter long enough, I waited till she was through with her shower and gently drew her towel away from her chest. I did *not* gasp in agony. I maintained a perfect air of indifference and she was infinitely relieved.

To this day, she is occasionally stabbed with regret and embarrassment at the missing breast, and asks if I'm sure I don't mind. And I say, in all truthfulness, "Janet, you know I'm not an observing person. I don't even notice."

And I don't.

I was even able to joke about it to others. Judy-Lynn and Lester del Rey came to visit during the convalescence and carefully talked about everything in the world except missing breasts. Then Judy-Lynn said something or other about "swinging single" bars and said to Janet, "Have you ever been to a swinging single?"

And I interrupted and said, *"Been* to a swinging single? She *has* a swinging single."

Judy-Lynn was infuriated and was about to chastise me in her own eloquent way, but Janet intervened. "Don't listen to him," she said. "He's only boasting. Mine isn't large enough to swing."

A magazine on popular medicine asked me to write on some medical emergency faced bravely by myself or a close relative and I said there was Janet's mastectomy but I didn't want to write about it till after we were married so that the readers would *know* that there was a "happy ending."

After our marriage, I wrote the article. Naturally, I asked Janet's permission, and at first she didn't want to blazon forth her misadventure for all the world to see. But I said, "You know, Janet, it may be the only article ever written on a subject like this in which the writer will *not* carefully give credit to God for giving him the faith and strength to overcome the disaster."

Janet agreed at once, on that basis, and the article was published.

115

Cruises

My animosity toward planes does not extend to ocean liners. Indeed, I love the liners and I suppose it might be a matter of size. When you're on an ocean liner, you don't feel as though you're on a vehicle. You feel as though you are in a hotel that is built horizontally rather than vertically.

My first experiences with ships were involuntary. I traveled by ship from Riga, Latvia, to Brooklyn, New York, in 1923, but I have only the vaguest and most uncertain memories of that. I also traveled by ship from San Francisco to Hawaii in 1946, but I was in the army then, so the trip was not a joyous one for me. The trip to Hawaii was useful, however. I managed to avoid seasickness although the ship pitched and rolled badly, and the sleeping quarters smelled of vomit because others did not have my hardihood. That helped convince me that I had good sea legs. Of course, I would never of my own accord have volunteered to go on a cruise, even though I didn't mind being on ships, because such a cruise was bound to take time and I hated to spend that time away from home.

Once I was living with Janet, however, the pull of the sea grew stronger, because Janet loved it. She had traveled, in her day, much more than ever I had, and this included sea voyages to Scandinavia during the 1960s and earlier to Europe on tramp steamers. She attributed her love to her "Viking ancestry," of which she is proud. (She also feels that she has preserved some Neanderthal genes, because, she says, she has a Neanderthal nose, but I much prefer the theory that she is descended, in some mysterious way, from angels.)

Because of Janet's predilection, I was the readier to listen to a fast-talking young man named Richard Hoagland when he came to tell me of his plans to organize a cruise on the *Queen Elizabeth 2* no less. In December 1972, it was to travel down the coast of Florida to view the launching of Apollo 17, the last of the planned trips to the moon and the only night launching. I had never watched a launching and I knew that Janet would be overwhelmed with delight at a chance of traveling on the *Queen,* so I agreed to go. (Janet was indeed delighted at the prospect.)

As was perhaps usual with plans made by a young man who accepted no limits to his imagination, the reality was not quite the fantasy. We did not go on the *Queen Elizabeth 2* but on the smaller (yet quite adequate) *Statendam.* We did not have a ship filled with eager participants but a ship that was largely empty (which meant we got good service).

A few celebrities did show up. Among the science fiction writers (other than myself) were Robert and Virginia Heinlein, Ted Sturgeon and his current wife, Fred and Carol Pohl, and Ben and Barbara Bova. Also present were Norman Mailer, Hugh Downs (who was the master of ceremonies), and Ken Franklin (an astronomer with the Hayden Planetarium, who had discovered the radio-wave emissions of Jupiter).

A terrible mistake was the inclusion of Katherine Anne Porter. She did nothing particular in the course of the voyage but she had made a hit with her 1962 book *Ship of Fools,* so you can guess what the reporters called us.

Later in the trip, the astronomer Carl Sagan and his second wife, Linda, joined us. I had first met Carl in 1963, when he was only twenty-eight. He was a science fiction fan and we struck up a good and enduring friendship and indeed I signed his wedding certificate as a witness when he married Linda. There is no need to describe him; everyone knows what he looks like. He and Fred Pohl gave the best talks of the voyage.

We did see the launching on the night of December 6–7, 1972. It was beautiful and incredibly impressive even when seen at a distance of seven miles out to sea. We watched Apollo 17 climb into the sky, lighting the night into a copper-colored semi-day, and a full minute after we had watched it do so, the sound waves reached us and the world trembled.

That alone was well worth the trip, even if we hadn't enjoyed ourselves—but we *had*.

In the next year, there was an opportunity for an even more elaborate cruise. This was arranged by Phil and Marcy Sigler; Phil was incredibly retiring and usually talked with his eyes firmly fixed on the floor, while Marcy was incredibly dynamic with her large and beautiful dark eyes transfixing yours. The cruise would be on the Australian liner *Canberra* and was designed to travel to the shores of West Africa in order to observe a total eclipse of the Sun on June 30, 1973. Remembering the pleasure Janet and I had had on the *Statendam*, I agreed at once, even though it entailed my giving four talks on astronomy, each talk to be given twice if they managed to fill the ship.

The cruise was scheduled to leave on June 22, but five days before that Janet had a subarachnoid hemorrhage. What could I do? I knew very well that I was to be the star of the voyage with my talks, but I had to cancel anyway. It was a terrible blow to the Siglers, who begged me to reconsider, but, under the conditions as they existed, I was helpless.

Except that Janet herself changed the conditions. The subarachnoid had temporarily wiped out much of her mind but enough was left for her to be moaning, "I've spoiled everything, I've spoiled the cruise," over and over.

Paul Esserman said to me, "You'll have to go on the cruise, Isaac."

"I *can't* go and leave her in the hospital," I said.

"There's no reason not to. There'll be no operation. We must simply wait for her to recover, but I can't be sure she will if she broods only over the cruise. You *must* go, and I must be able to assure her that you went."

So, immersed in misery, and with enough Jewish guilt to drown all the hosts of Pharaoh, I called the Siglers and uncanceled, to their unbounded joy. I made them agree, however, to arrange it so that I could call the hospital, ship to shore, every day.

I did exactly that, going up every day to the small radiophone room and waiting my turn. I calculated that in the course of the sixteen-day tour I spent about twelve hours in that room. I spoke to her every day but one and received her assurances that she was getting better and that she was happy I was on the cruise. The one day I missed I called Paul Esserman instead to make sure Janet wasn't lying to me. In the end, I saw the eclipse and I was glad I did, for it was the only total eclipse I had ever seen, but all I wanted to do was to get back to Janet (who, by the way, having missed that eclipse, has never seen one to this day).

In order to pass the time and drown my bitter misery while on the trip, I made myself a "tummler." That is a Yiddish word meaning "one who makes a tumult, or noise." They have tummlers at Jewish summer resorts and their function is to tell jokes, organize fun and games, flirt with the plainer and older women, and, in general, create the illusion that there's a hot time in the old town tonight.

I became the tummler for the two thousand people on board ship and, in addition to my eight tálks, I told jokes, sang songs, kissed the ladies, took part in the show organized by the crew, and, in general, made enough noise for fifty. It was all completely successful. For years afterward, people I encountered who were on the *Canberra* told me what a wonderful time they had had.

It reminds me of one of my favorite stories, which, somehow, I never included in *Isaac Asimov's Treasury of Humor*. It goes as follows:

> A gentleman passing through Vienna in the early years of the twentieth century was feeling enormously depressed, even suicidal—so he went to see Sigmund Freud.
>
> Freud listened to him for an hour, then said, "This is a serious and deep-seated condition not to be dealt with in an afternoon. You must seek professional help and prepare yourself for years of treatment. Meanwhile, however, you may find an evening of surcease. The great Grimaldi the Clown is in town and he has his audiences convulsed with laughter. Attend a performance. For two hours, you will surely enjoy yourself and this may have an ameliorative effect that will last for days."
>
> "I'm sorry," said the depressed gentleman, "I can't do that."
>
> "But why not?" asked Freud.
>
> "Because I am Grimaldi the Clown."

This may sound as though I was feeling sorry for myself on the cruise (an emotion I detest, as you know), but I wasn't. I lured myself into thinking I was having a good time simply by acting as though I were. It was only afterward, when I was safe with Janet again, that I could look back on the trip and identify myself as Grimaldi the Clown.

Then, later in the year, soon after we were married, we had a chance to go on a cruise again, this time as a honeymoon couple, and this time it was indeed on the *Queen Elizabeth 2*. It was a "cruise to nowhere." We would simply leave New York, wander over the ocean for a few days without making landfall, and then return to New York —perfect for a person of my tastes.

We got on the ship on December 9, 1973, and I was incredibly happy that this time Janet was with me. In one way the cruise was a failure, for we were watching for the comet Kohoutek, which was touted as a comet that was going to put on a magnificent show. Unfortunately, it was cloudy and rainy every night, and even if it hadn't been, Comet Kohoutek proved a colossal disappointment. It was barely visible to the naked eye. But why should Janet and I care? We were each other's Comet Kohoutek.

Lajos Kohoutek, the discoverer of the comet, was on board ship and was slated to give a talk. Janet and I settled comfortably into our seats and Janet said, "It is so nice to be able to go on a trip with you, Isaac, when you're not the one who has to give a talk."

And at that point, the master of ceremonies told us that Kohoutek was, unfortunately, not feeling well and was confined to his cabin and the talk would have to be canceled. The audience responded with such a pained sigh of disappointment that Janet (ever softhearted) jumped up and said, "My husband, Isaac Asimov, will give a talk."

She claims she didn't do that but that she just gave me the elbow jab all wives use to signify "No back talk" and had then whispered that I must volunteer. I don't see that it makes much difference. Either way, I had to stumble up onto the stage and improvise a talk to an audience waiting to hear someone else.

I managed. In fact, I did so well that the ship's cruise director later invited me to come along on cruises as a speaker and Janet and I made several trips on the *QE2*, all expenses paid.

116

Janet's Books

There was another peculiar side effect of Janet's subarachnoid hemorrhage, but to explain that I will have to backtrack a little.

Janet's early experiences in some ways oddly paralleled mine. Like me, she has wanted to write since she was a child, but, also like me, she realized she could not reasonably expect to make a living this way. She decided on a scientific career. Of course, it was understood she would go to college, for her cultural milieu did not preclude higher education for women, so that she did not suffer the aborted schooling that Gertrude and Marcia had.

Janet wanted to go to Stanford, but World War II was raging and travel to California was impossible. She therefore went to Wellesley in Massachusetts for two years. When the war was over, she did transfer to Stanford for the last two years, and that was the happiest time of her life, she says, before she met me.

She was aiming for medical school, but this was not easy. War veterans had the first choice, and most schools had only a tiny quota for women. (Sexism was quite respectable in 1948.) Accepted by New York University Medical School, she obtained her medical degree in 1952. After an internship at Philadelphia General Hospital, she had a psychiatric residency at Bellevue Hospital. She also graduated from the William Alanson White Institute of Psychoanalysis, and has kept up her connection with the White Institute ever since, becoming Director of Training for eight years. She retired from private practice of psychiatry in 1986, having worked in the field, with considerable distinction, for thirty years.

Through all this time, the urge to write remained with her. She wrote a variety of things, including several mystery novels that she was not able to sell, but they were good practice. (The only real way you can learn to write is to write.) She did sell a mystery short, and a very clever one, to Hans Stefan Santesson, who was then editing *The Saint Mystery Magazine*. It appeared in the May 1966 issue of the magazine.

After her mastectomy, afraid she was going to die, she began to work on a novel. Then, when she was in the hospital the next year with her subarachnoid (and I was on the eclipse cruise), Austin Olney of Houghton Mifflin came, like a good friend, to visit her. Janet enthusiastically began to tell him the plot of her novel. (She says that if she had been in her right mind, she wouldn't have.)

Austin expressed interest. When Janet finally recovered, her close brush with death (which gave her the feeling of mortality) pushed her into finishing the novel and submitting it to Houghton Mifflin. She was asked for extensive revisions and obliged.

Then came November 30, 1973, the day of our wedding. To prevent interruption while Ed Ericson married us, Janet had taken the phone off the hook. When the brief ceremony was over (with our friends Al and Phyllis Balk present as witnesses, so that there were only the five of us—the legal minimum), Janet replaced the phone. Instantly, it rang and it was Austin telling her that Houghton Mifflin would do the novel. It was a day of double happiness.

I always tell people that Janet said, after she had finished talking to Austin, "There! I knew *something* good would happen today." She didn't say it; I made it up; but it always gets a laugh.

Janet's first novel, *The Second Experiment,* was published by Houghton Mifflin in 1974 under her maiden name, Janet O. Jeppson.

She went on to do other books. *The Last Immortal,* a sequel to the first book, was published by Houghton Mifflin in 1980. She also wrote short stories for science fiction magazines, including a series that seemed remarkable to me, for it consisted of gentle satires of psychiatry, featuring the lunchtime conversations of a group of psychiatrists of different persuasions who belonged to a mythical club called Pshrinks Anonymous. These stories appeared in a collection called *The Mysterious Cure and Other Stories,* published by Doubleday in 1984. Meanwhile, she had also worked out a marvelous anthology of humorous science fiction—including verses and cartoons—entitled *Laughing Space,* published by Houghton Mifflin in 1982. My name was on this book in addition to hers because I wrote the introduction and the headnotes, but Janet did 90 percent of the work.

None of these books did well, though they gave Janet and me infinite satisfaction.

Then Walker & Company asked Janet to do a science fiction story for youngsters. For years, she had been revolving in her head a possible story about a conceited, lovable little robot. She now had a chance to write *Norby, the Mixed-up Robot*. My name was wanted on the book (for the betterment of sales, I suppose), so I went over the manuscript and polished it a bit. Again, though, it was Janet who did 90 percent of the work.

The Walkers liked the book very much and wanted more. Janet obliged and, as of this writing, she has published no fewer than nine Norby books, all published by Walker.

A tenth Norby book is being written at this time. These Norby books have done quite well. They have come out in paperback editions by Berkley, and we get fan letters from youngsters concerning them.

Her favorite book, however, is none of those I've mentioned but is one called *How to Enjoy Writing*, published by Walker in 1987. It is a collection of writings about writing (many by me) together with comments by Janet. It is really one of the most charming books I have ever read.

Altogether, Janet has published sixteen books, including two recent science fiction novels, published by Walker, which do not have my name on them. They are *Mind Transfer* and *A Package in Hyperspace*, both published in 1988.

Janet published her first novels, as I said, under her maiden name, and nowhere on the flap matter or in the book was it mentioned that she was my wife. She was anxious not to seem to be riding on my shoulders.

It didn't help. People in science fiction knew, or found out, the relationship and some had a field day as a result. One writer, as I said earlier in this book, accused Janet of having published *The Second Experiment* through nepotism—that the great Isaac Asimov had used his influence to force Houghton Mifflin to publish the book.

Needless to say, this was not true. I never lifted a finger to help Janet publish that book. For one thing, I happen to believe that that would have been an unethical thing to do, and Janet thinks so too. For another, it wouldn't have worked, because not all my so-called influence could persuade a publishing house to do a book they thought was bad. After all, I sometimes had trouble selling items I myself had written. Where was my influence then?

It taught Janet, however, that an attempt to be hyper-ethical in this respect was a waste of time. For that reason, her most recent books, even when I am not involved, have "Janet Asimov" listed as the author.

117

Hollywood

I am frequently asked if any of my books have been made into movies. For a long time, the answer was "No," and that meant I was a happy man.

That seems odd. To most people, Hollywood breathes the aura of romance and, even more than that, of money.

However, to work for Hollywood means, usually, to move to California (as more and more science fiction writers have done in the last decade or two) and I have no intention of doing any such thing ever. I haven't seen much of the world but I cannot believe that any place is more beautiful than New England and the Middle Atlantic States, especially in the fall. I find plains dull, and mountains (real mountains) stark. What I want are hills, and trees, and green vistas, and set in the midst of it all, the glorious skyscrapers of Manhattan.

Then, as I heard stories about Hollywood, I liked it even less. Walter Bradbury of Doubleday would travel to Hollywood once a year on business. When I had lunch with him after such a visit, he would be drawn and strained. He hated the people he had to deal with there, phonies, one and all, he said, and not to be trusted an inch.

After listening to Bradbury, I worked out a theory of my own. I had read a book dealing with publishing in nineteenth-century America and I was astonished to find that publishers were, at that time, sharks, tigers, and crooks. That certainly didn't seem to be so in the case of my own publishing firms in the second half of the twentieth century.

I decided that Hollywood had come along and drawn off the sharks, tigers, and crooks, who, one and all, smelled money, money, money. This left behind, in the publishing houses, those gentle souls who were unfitted for the rat race, even for money.

Well, *I* was unfitted for the rat race too. I knew this all the more when I heard tales of Hollywood from writers such as Harlan Ellison (who likes California and the Californians). I realized, then, that Hollywood was worse than a rat race, it was a *trap*. It lured a person into a lifestyle of sunshine and tans, of barbecues and swimming pools—a life you couldn't afford unless you kept on working in Hollywood. So you kept on working. It was a pact with Mephistopheles that could not be broken.

Consider, too, that as a writer of printed books, I am master. My books may be edited, but that is done lightly, and I have final approval over every changed comma. As a writer for movies or television, it is the producer and director who wield the whip hand and the picture that lords it over the word. The writer is low man on the totem pole in Hollywood, and his work can be tampered with by anyone.

No, thanks, to all the lure of the money and lifestyle, I am immune. I intend to remain in New York at all costs.

All this doesn't mean that Hollywood doesn't come to me now and then. In 1947, Orson Welles bought movie rights to my story "Evidence" for $250. I thought, in my innocence, that, as a result, there would soon be a great motion picture made out of the story. Needless to say, no movie at all was ever made out of it.

After that, it was Doubleday that negotiated movies sales, or, rather, movie *option* sales. That is, someone bought the rights to exclusive use of a particular story or group of stories for a particular length of time in return for a particular sum of money. If by the end of that time the option buyer could raise the necessary money to make the picture, fine! I would then get a lot more money. If he couldn't, he might renew the option for an additional sum of money, or he could give up the option and I, of course, would keep the money paid in up to that point.

Thus, in the late 1960s Hollywood optioned *I, Robot* and the option was renewed year after year for some fifteen years. In the end, however, nothing happened, even though Harlan Ellison wrote a terrific screenplay based on the book. I received other options but nothing ever happened and I developed what I call Asimov's First Law of Hollywood, which goes as follows:

"Whatever happens, nothing happens!"

Still, just a couple of years ago, Doubleday sold an option on my story "Nightfall" to some people. They actually managed to get a picture made. I was not informed of this till friends told me they'd seen an announcement of it in *Variety*. I was never consulted in the making, never saw the script. I was phoned by someone who told me it would open in Tucson, Arizona.

I certainly was not going to Tucson to see it. "When will it open in New York?" I asked.

"New York is pretty expensive," she said.

I realized, then, that the picture had been made on a shoestring and wondered how bad it might be. The picture was advertised, in those few places where it was played, with my name heavily in evidence, and people went to see it on that basis. Then the letters began to arrive and I knew the worst. There was a general agreement that it was the worst motion picture ever made and that it had nothing but the faintest resemblance to my story.

Some blamed me for the picture, as though I had directed it, and at least one demanded his money back. I had to write all around, disowning all responsibility. Fortunately, the picture died a deserved death almost at once and I can only hope that no one who has ever seen it or heard of it remembers it.

And for things like this, do you imagine I want my books to be made into movies?

I acted as "adviser" on several occasions. Gene Roddenberry, of *Star Trek* fame, asked me for some advice in connection with the first *Star Trek* motion picture and I was glad to help out, for he is a friend of mine. I didn't ask for money, but he sent me some and told me I would be listed in the credits. Well, I had never been listed in any movie credits, so I went to see the movie. At the end, everyone started filing out, while an endless series of credits rolled up the screen. Janet and I waited grimly while the house emptied, and finally, the last item, *the very last* was "Science Adviser—Isaac Asimov." Naturally, I applauded loudly, and I distinctly heard a voice in the aisle saying, "There's Asimov, applauding his own name," and another tale of my vanity was born.

I was also adviser, in 1979, for a few episodes of a pleasant science fiction television series, *Salvage 1*, featuring Andy Griffith, an actor I admire enormously. Most important of all, I was roped in as originator and adviser of a television series named *Probe,* a humorous, charming, and quite adult science fiction series. Before the season ended, there had been a two-hour pilot and six episodes, which I liked very much. But then along came a prolonged writers' strike, in the course of which *Probe* died. Too bad!

One odd story should be mentioned in connection with *Probe.* My own contribution to the series was not great, and the head writer, who contributed a great deal to the series, wanted to be listed as co-originator. It made no difference to me. I was not angling for Hollywood influence, status, or prestige, so I said, "Sure!"

I had, however, a contract that described me as sole originator of the series, so Equity (or somebody) phoned me and offered to fight it out on my behalf in the courts.

I said, "I don't want to fight it out in the courts. Let this guy be co-creator. I don't care."

It took me quite a while to convince them that I meant it, and that I had no intention of snarling over every last Hollywood perquisite. It showed me again what Hollywood was like and how fortunate I was to steer as clear of it as possible.

118

Star Trek Conventions

Since I mentioned *Star Trek* in the previous section, let me say a few words about it. This program, conceived and produced by Gene Roddenberry, first aired in 1966 and was an instant hit with science fiction fans. It was the first piece of adult science fiction to appear on television.

At the end of the first year, those who make such decisions decided to cancel the show. This decision was greeted by an instant and massive protest from the fans, which caught the decision makers by surprise. The poor half-wits didn't know just how articulate and impassioned science fiction fans could be. The decision was withdrawn and *Star Trek* continued for two more years before it finally went off the air.

However, it never died. Reruns went on forever, and they still go on. There were five motion pictures made with the old cast up through the late 1980s (by which time they had grown rather geriatric) and a new TV series began in 1988 with a new cast as *Star Trek: The Next Generation*.

Janet is a *Star Trek* enthusiast of the first magnitude. I occasionally write a short piece on some aspect of television for *TV Guide* and back in 1966 they asked me to write something on *Star Trek* and some of the other science fiction shows (much inferior) that were also on the air at the time. I decided to be funny about it and mentioned a few scientific errors, not entirely sparing *Star Trek*. I promptly got a furious letter from Janet and nothing would do but I had to write a separate article praising *Star Trek*'s virtues. That established my friendship with Gene Roddenberry, by the way.

Janet was a wholehearted part of the protest against ending the program after its first year. Ever since, she has watched the reruns assiduously over and over till—I would say jokingly—her lips moved as she recited the lines with the players. She stopped watching the reruns only after she bought all the cassettes, so she could watch without the interruption of advertisements. Of course, she has seen all the movies and she watches the new series avidly. When she is watching a *Star Trek*, old or new, I am not allowed to interrupt her. She won't allow me to call her a Trekkie, however. I don't know what it is that makes her not one.

Others, a great many others, were as enthusiastic as Janet, and one of them was a young lady named Elyse Pines, who had the idea of organizing a *Star Trek* convention at which enthusiasts of the program could gather and talk about it, at which *Star Trek* memorabilia could be sold, and to which, perhaps, some of the actors, could be invited to make a personal appearance. And she wanted me to promise to attend too. Since it was to be held in Manhattan, I agreed.

When Elyse first got the idea for a *Star Trek* convention in 1972, the long-term popularity of the show had not yet been proven, and she expected not more than 400. She got 2,500. Of course, this success meant that Elyse (and others too) organized other conventions throughout the 1970s. I attended virtually all of them that were held in Manhattan, always giving a talk on such occasions. I was present, in fact, at one convention that was incredibly oversuccessful. So many people swarmed into the hotel with the intention of attending the convention that they *crystallized*. The halls and stairways were so full of people that no one *(literally)* could move. Fortunately, I saw that coming just before crystallization was complete and I managed to struggle out somehow into the street.

I am always happy to talk, and signing books (within reason) is flattering and helps public relations. However, I was aware that the focus of attention was on the *Star Trek* people and I was clearly an outsider. The vast majority of the attendees may well not even have known who I was. Disenchantment was complete on one occasion when William Shatner himself (Captain Kirk of the good ship *Enterprise*) held an enormous audience spellbound with a talk that was largely question-and-answer, but eventually, of course, he finished and had to leave.

This created a problem. How could he be gotten out of the hotel without his being mobbed and, probably, suffocated by his adoring groupies. There was a flying wedge of guards designed to protect him, but the crowd, if aroused, would have been overwhelming.

So the organizer of the meeting (not Elyse, who had left the field to others) begged me to hold the crowd while Shatner got away. I had no notice that this would happen, but I got up and began speaking. I was warming up nicely when word came back that Shatner had reached his limousine and had been whisked away. At that point, I was kicked off the stage in mid-sentence.

I appreciate the flattery that led people to believe I was the only one who could pin an audience to their seats, but I did *not* appreciate being so blatantly used. They might have let me complete my talk. After that, I took a leaf from Shatner's book. When I felt like going to a local convention, I arrived just before I was scheduled to speak and disappeared just after.

Of course, I was never in danger from charging groupies.

119

Short Mysteries

But back to my writing career and to a new departure I made in the 1970s.

I have always wanted to write mystery short stories. At the start I was committed to science fiction, of course, and some of my science fiction short stories were very much like mysteries. This was true of several of my robot stories, for instance.

I also wrote a series of five science fiction stories about a character named Wendell Urth, who solved mysteries without ever leaving home. The first of these, "The Singing Bell," appeared in the January 1955 *F&SF*.

The Wendell Urth stories were fun, but they didn't quite satisfy my desires. I wanted to write a "straight" mystery, with no science fiction angle to it. I did write one in 1955, but *Ellery Queen's Mystery Magazine (EQMM)* rejected it. I finally placed it in *The Saint Mystery Magazine,* where it appeared in the January 1956 issue, under the name "Death of a Honey-Blonde." It was set in a chemistry department, however, so that, while it was not science fiction, I had not entirely freed myself from science.

It was not a very good story and I was disheartened. Nevertheless, the urge to write short mysteries persisted. *EQMM* regularly publishes "first stories," usually short-shorts by writers who had never published before. My chagrin finally bubbled over and I thought, "If these amateurs can do it, why can't I?"

So I wrote a short-short on November 12, 1969, and had it in the mail two hours after I had thought of the idea. *EQMM* took it and it ran under the title "A Problem in Numbers" in the May 1970 issue of the magazine.

But that dealt with a chemistry department too, as, for that matter, had *The Death Dealers,* my one straight mystery novel up to that time. It irritated me. I wanted to write nonscience mysteries. Why? Science and science fiction had been so good to me. Why should I abandon a faithful wife (so to speak) to lust after some flirtatious stranger?

Well, I had *done* science fiction. I wanted new worlds to conquer. I had always loved mystery short stories from childhood and I wanted to do mysteries too. Besides, if you want a less idealistic reason, I found mysteries easier to write than science fiction.

Perhaps it was the spirit of emulation that stirred me most. I have noticed that when I watch a good TV show involving lawyers, or musicians, or detectives, or whatever, I at once experience a great longing to be a lawyer, or a musician, or a detective, or whatever myself. I reached the height of the ridiculous once when I watched a good TV show about writers. I turned to Janet and said, "How I wish I were a writer!" (There is one exception. I have never watched a show about physicians that made me in the least want to be one. Rather the reverse.)

Why this spirit of emulation? I suppose it's the desire to do *everything*, to shine in all directions. Even when I confine myself to writing, I sometimes say, in moments of grandiosity, "If I had my way, I would write every book in the world."

Is this mere laudable ambition? Or is it the megalomania that caused Alexander the Great to weep at the fact that there was only one world to conquer? I think rather the former. After all, whatever my impulses, I keep my actual *deeds* firmly under control and do not take on any projects I strongly suspect I can't do. I don't *really* try to be a lawyer, or a musician, or a detective, or whatever. I realize that writing fills my whole life and that to be anything else even just a little bit would force me to cut down on that writing, and that would be impossible.

Nevertheless, I have two abiding sorrows for missed nonwriting opportunities. First, that I never learned Russian, which I could have done with no trouble whatever if my parents had only spoken Russian to me as a child. Second, that there was never any money to give me piano lessons and voice lessons. (I can carry a tune perfectly and have a good natural voice but it is completely untrained.)

Oh, well, I would have to keep using Russian if I weren't to forget it, and I would have to practice music regularly if I played. Writing is rustproof, on the other hand. At least, I find it so. If circumstances keep me from my typewriter for a period of time, I find that I can return to it with my expertise unblunted.

But back to my short mysteries—

My first small sale of a story to *EQMM* did not lead to a flood of mystery writing. After all, I never lacked for other things to do.

In early 1971, however, Eleanor Sullivan, the beautiful blond managing editor of *EQMM,* wrote me a letter *asking* for a story. Eagerly, I agreed, but now I had to think of a plot.

I got one quickly because two stories above our apartment lived David Ford, a corpulent actor with a resonant baritone voice. (Voices, in my opinion, are much more important than faces to an actor, unless he is the vacuous matinee idol type.) He invited us to his apartment once and we found it crammed to the ceiling with what, in Yiddish, are called *chochkes*—that is, miscellaneous objects which strike the fancy of an omnivorous collector. He told us he once had a repairman in his apartment while he was forced to walk his dog. He was sure that the repairman had taken one or two of his *chochkes,* but he was never able to determine what was missing, or, in fact, whether anything was missing at all.

That was all I needed. I wrote the story quickly and it appeared in the January 1972 *EQMM* under the title "The Acquisitive Chuckle."

I thought of it as simply a story, but when it appeared, Fred Dannay's blurb announced it as "the first of a NEW SERIES by Isaac Asimov." (The capitalization was Dannay's.) That was the first I heard of *that,* but I was willing to go along with it.

I wrote more and more stories involving the same characters. When I had written twelve and decided to have them collected in a book, Dannay assumed the series was finished and said so in print. He little knew me. I continued the series stubbornly and I have now written no fewer than sixty-five stories. (What's the good of being a prolific writer if you don't proliferate?)

I call the series the Black Widower stories because each one takes place at one of the monthly banquets of a club of that name. The club is modeled unabashedly on a real club of which I am a member, the Trap Door Spiders, concerning which I will have more to say later.

The stories are entirely conversational. The six club members discuss matters in a quarrelsome, idiosyncratic way. There is a guest, who is asked questions after dinner, and whose answers reveal some sort of mystery, which the Black Widowers cannot solve but which, in the end, are solved by the waiter, Henry.

Eventually, the various Black Widower stories were published, twelve at a time, by Doubleday. The books that have appeared, so far, are:

> *Tales of the Black Widowers* 1974
> *More Tales of the Black Widowers* 1976
> *Casebook of the Black Widowers* 1980
> *Banquets of the Black Widowers* 1984
> *Puzzles of the Black Widowers* 1990

I have written five more stories that will be included in a sixth volume someday when the new total reaches twelve.

A second series of mystery short stories began when Eric Protter, editor of *Gallery,* asked me to do a 2,200-word mystery for his magazine every month. (The Black Widower stories are 5,500 words long, on the average.) *Gallery* is what is called a "girlie magazine," and though it wasn't quite as anatomical as some of the others, it was "girlie" enough to alarm me.

"I don't do erotica, Eric," I said.

He assured me I wouldn't have to. So I set up another background. Four men meet periodically in the library of the Union Club. Three of them engage in a brief conversation which reminds the fourth, Griswold, of a story. Griswold tells it and it always turns out to contain a mystery which Griswold solves. He doesn't tell the solution until the other three demand one indignantly, denying that there can be one. Then he reveals it. I call these the Griswold stories.

I wrote my first Griswold story on March 9, 1980, and *Gallery* published thirty-three Griswolds before it changed publishers in August 1983 and dispensed with my services. I continued to write them occasionally, however, and to place them with *EQMM.*

I have also written some mystery short-shorts for youngsters, many of which have been published in *Boys' Life.* The best of them, in my opinion, was rejected by *Boys' Life* (perhaps because it referred to terrorism) but was snapped up by *EQMM* and appeared in its July 1977 issue under the title "The Thirteenth Day of Christmas."

In the 1970s and 1980s, I wrote something like 120 mystery short stories, far more than the number of science fiction short stories I wrote in that period. I don't think that will change. I enjoy the mysteries more.

Let me explain this. Those 120 mysteries are "old-fashioned." Modern mysteries are more and more exercises in police procedurals, private-eye dramatics, and psychopathology, all of them tending to give us heaping handfuls of sex and violence.

The older mysteries, in which there are a closed series of suspects and a brilliant detective (often amateur) weaving his clever chain of inference and deduction, seem to be, for the most part, gone. They are referred to nowadays, with a vague air of contempt, as "cozy mysteries" and their heyday was Great Britain in the 1930s and 1940s. The great cozy writers were such people as Agatha Christie, Dorothy Sayers, Ngaio Marsh, Margery Allingham, Nicholas Blake, and Michael Innes.

Well, that's what I write. I make no secret of the fact that in my mysteries I use Agatha Christie as my model. In my opinion, her mysteries are the best ever written, far better than the Sherlock Holmes stories, and Hercule Poirot is the best detective fiction has seen. Why should I not use as my model what I consider the best?

What's more, every last one of my mysteries is an "armchair detective" story. The story is revealed in conversation, the clues are presented fairly, and the reader has a reasonable chance to beat the fictional detective to the solution. Sometimes readers do exactly that, and I get triumphant letters to that effect. On rare occasions I even get letters pointing out improved solutions.

Old-fashioned? Certainly! But so what? Other people in writing mystery stories have their purposes, which may be to instill a sense of adventure, or a grisly sense of horror, or whatever. It is my purpose in my mysteries (and, in actual fact, in everything I write, fiction and nonfiction) to make people think. My stories are *puzzle* stories and I see nothing wrong with that. In fact, I find them a challenge, like writing limericks, since the rules for preparing honest puzzle stories are so strict.

This means, incidentally, that the stories do not have to involve pathological acts or violent crime—or, indeed, any crime at all. One of the mysteries that I had most fun in writing recently was "Lost in a Space Warp," which appeared in the March 1990 *EQMM*. It dealt with a man who mislaid his umbrella in his girlfriend's small apartment and couldn't find it. From the information he gave, Henry deduced where it could be found, without stirring from his position at the sideboard.

What's more, I don't intend to alter the format of these stories. They will stay always the same. The guest of the Black Widowers will always have a mystery to tell, the Black Widowers will always be stumped, and Henry will always come up with the solution. Similarly, Griswold will always tell his stories and the other three will never see the solution till it is explained.

Why not? The background is an artificial one designed only to present the puzzle. What I intend is to have the reader greet each new story with the comfortable feeling of encountering old friends, meeting the same characters under the same circumstances, and having a fresh mind stretcher over which to try to outguess me.

120

Trap Door Spiders

During the 1970s, I joined a number of organizations, more through circumstance than through eagerness to do so. Since I mentioned the Trap Door Spiders in the previous section, that would seem a good starting point.

When I first went to Philadelphia, back in 1942, I met John D. Clark, through Sprague de Camp. In their younger days, they had been college classmates. Clark (universally called "Doc" because he had a Ph.D.) had a thin face, a very thin mustache, a keen sense of straight-faced humor, and (unfortunately) was a chain smoker, which kept me away from him.

He was an inorganic chemist who, in the war years, worked on rocket explosives. In the late 1930s, he had written two excellent science fiction stories and then never wrote again. One of them, "Minus Planet" (April 1937 *ASF*), was the first story, I think, to deal with antimatter.

About the time I met him, he was getting ready to marry a large, rather flamboyant would-be opera singer. I didn't particularly like her, but she was Doc's choice, not mine. It turned out, however, that all of Doc's friends didn't like her and it became impossible to engage in social intercourse with him unless his wife was not among those present.

Fletcher Pratt was one of Doc's friends, and had collaborated with Sprague on a number of excellent fantasies in *Unknown*. He was a little man with a thin beard, a bald, retreating forehead, and a formidable intellect. He was an expert on military history and wrote *Ordeal by Fire,* which I consider the best one-volume history of the American Civil War ever written. He invented a war game in which little models of actual warships engaged in naval battles according to a complicated set of rules designed to mimic reality as closely as possible. He also kept marmosets in his apartment, which reeked of animal smell in consequence. He died in 1956 at the age of fifty-nine and, through a quirk of memory, I have a clear picture of the last time I saw him as we separated on the streets of New York, waving at each other.

In 1944, it occurred to Fletcher to establish a club that was to meet for dinner each month and was to be strictly stag. Doc Clark could be made a member and, once a month, he could socialize with his friends without his wife being present. A different member, or pair of members, hosted each meeting (and paid for the meal), and it became customary for each host to invite a guest who, after dinner, could be grilled on his life and work. The club called itself the Trap Door Spiders, the notion being that they had moved into a burrow outfitted with a trap door that would keep out enemies—that is, Doc's wife.

Doc himself apparently couldn't stand his wife eventually, for he divorced her after seven years, but the Trap Door Spiders continued anyway and he remained a member. Also members were my old friends L. Sprague de Camp and Lester del Rey.

I was occasionally invited as a guest when my visits to New York happened to coincide with the meeting day of the club (always a Friday night), but I refused to accept actual membership because I knew I would rarely be in New York on an appropriate day. Once I moved to New York in 1970, however, I was immediately voted in and I have been a member ever since.

It is pleasant to be a Trap Door Spider. The conversation is delightful, and every member is a professional man of some sort. We average some twelve people per meeting. To give you a small notion of the diversity: Roper Shamhart is an Episcopalian minister and is an expert on theology and liturgical music; Richard Harrison is a professional cartographer; Jean Le Corbeiller is a teacher of mathematics; Lionel

Casson is an archaeologist who specializes in the study of Roman life; and so on.

(I was once reading one of Casson's books on Rome while waiting for Robyn—who was visiting me—to return from a date. She was late, which would ordinarily have thrown me into a fever of apprehension, but on this occasion I was so wrapped up in the book, I didn't notice. In fact, when she did come back, *quite* late, I was annoyed because she had interrupted me before I had finished the book. I told Casson this, and he was infinitely pleased.)

I introduced two new members to the club, both of whom were most successful Spiders. One was Martin Gardner and the other was Ken Franklin. The trouble was that both retired (no crime) and then moved out of range (a terrible crime).

As I mentioned in the previous section, my fictional Black Widowers was closely based on the Trap Door Spiders, with the membership cut in half for easier handling. Even the individual members of the Black Widowers are based on individual Spiders.

Thus, Geoffrey Avalon is based on L. Sprague de Camp and Emmanuel Rubin on Lester del Rey. James Drake is a reflection of Doc Clark; Thomas Trumbull of Gilbert Cant; Mario Gonzalo of Lin Carter; and Roger Halsted of Don Bensen. There was no secret about this; I had all their permissions.

Once Ken Franklin's wife, Charlotte, asked about what went on at the Spiders. (I suppose wives can't help wondering about stag meetings—what with vague thoughts of naked women and nameless orgies.) Ken gave her one of my Black Widower books and said, "Like in the book, only not quite as good."

Things don't change in my book, but they do in real life. Three of those who modeled the Black Widowers are now dead: Gilbert Cant, Lin Carter, and Doc Clark himself. Of the remaining three, Sprague has moved to Texas, and Lester is relatively immobile these days and won't come to the meetings.

As for Henry, the all-important waiter, who is always in the background till the end, he is not based on a real person at all. He is entirely my invention, although I must admit that I see a similarity between him and P. G. Wodehouse's immortal Jeeves.

People sometimes ask me if I myself ever appear in the Black Widower stories. I appeared only once, as the guest, Mortimer Stellar, in the story "When No Man Pursueth" (March 1974 *EQMM*). I told

Janet, rather proudly, that I had described myself with great accuracy in that story.

She said, "But that's impossible. The guest is vain, arrogant, self-absorbed, and nasty."

"See!" I said triumphantly. (She was furious. I'm afraid she sees me through rose-colored glasses.)

I am also the narrator, the "I" character in the Griswold stories.

121

Mensa

In 1961, I became acquainted with a young woman named Gloria Saltzberg. She had been a victim of the 1955 epidemic of poliomyelitis, the last one to bedevil the world before the Salk vaccine came into use. She was in a wheelchair, in consequence, but was not embittered. She was a lively woman, full of joy, and I found this admirable. She was also highly intelligent and was a member of Mensa.

Mensa was an organization founded in Great Britain, and it consists of people who are determined, by test, to have "intelligence quotients" ("IQs") that place them (supposedly) among the top 2 percent of humanity in intelligence.

Gloria wanted me to belong but I held back. In the first place, though I have been a lifelong beneficiary of intelligence tests, I don't think much of them. I believe they test only one facet of intelligence —the ability to answer the kind of questions other people with the same facet of intelligence are likely to ask. My IQ rating has always been out of sight, but I am perfectly aware that in many respects I am remarkably stupid. Second, it seemed to me to be beneath my dignity to take an intelligence test. Surely, my life and work were ample testimony to my intelligence (such as it was).

Gloria said, "Can it be that you're nervous about the test?"

I thought about it and I was. I had nothing to gain; everything to lose. If I scored high, that was simply to be expected; but if I scored low, the disgrace would be unbearable. But then, having worked that out, I felt ashamed at doubting myself. So I took the test, scored high, and became a member of Mensa.

It was *not,* on the whole, a happy experience. I met a number of wonderful Mensans, but there were other Mensans who were brain-proud and aggressive about their IQs, who, one got the impression, would like, on being introduced, to be able to say, "I'm Joe Doakes, and my IQ is 172," or, perhaps, have the figure tattooed on their forehead. They were, as I had been in my youth, forcing their intelligence on unwilling victims. In general, too, they felt underappreciated and undersuccessful. As a result, they had soured on the Universe and tended to be disagreeable.

What's more, they were constantly jousting with each other, testing their intelligence on each other, and that sort of thing becomes wearing after a while.

Furthermore, I became uncomfortably aware that Mensans, however high their paper IQ might be, were likely to be as irrational as anyone else. Many of them believed themselves to be part of a "superior" group that ought to rule the world, and despised non-Mensans as inferiors. Naturally, they tended to be right-wing conservatives, and I generally feel terribly out of sympathy with such views.

Worse yet, there were groups among them, as I found out eventually, who accepted astrology and many other pseudoscientific beliefs, and who formed "SIGs" ("special-interest groups") devoted to different varieties of intellectual trash. Where was the credit of being associated with that sort of thing, even tangentially?

Worst of all, I was recognized as a natural target. Every young whippersnapper of a Mensan seemed to think he could win his spurs by taking me on in a battle of wits and winning. I found myself in the position of an old gunfighter who could never hang up his guns because he was constantly being challenged by every fast-draw teenager in the territory.

I didn't want to play that game. I don't mind losing a battle of wits; I've lost a number of them in my life. However, I prefer such things to come to pass naturally. I don't want to be forever on the watch for them. In short, to be metaphorical, I can shoot if I have to but I don't want to spend my life with my hands half an inch from my holsters at all times.

Therefore I stopped attending meetings and I stopped paying my dues. I never formally resigned, but it was just as though I had.

That, however, is not the end of the story. When I arrived in New York, I found Mensans there who considered me one of them. In an unguarded moment, I agreed to attend a gathering to meet Victor Serebriakoff, concerning whom I had a natural curiosity. He was from Great Britain, was the general chairman of Mensa on the international scale, and was its leading spirit.

Serebriakoff was a short man, with an oval, rubicund face and a small grayish beard. He could tell excellent jokes in a variety of accents, including the cockney, and that immediately won me over. Serebriakoff said that he would pay my dues, if I did not, and that would make me a member whether I wanted to be one or not.

Well, I couldn't allow *that,* so I became an active member of Mensa again. And to give the devil his due, there were some good things to be gotten out of it. When Mensa held a national convention in New York, I was usually dragooned into speaking at the banquet or at some other function, and I could speak on abstruse subjects that weren't suitable for the general public. I even dedicated one of my science essay collections, *The Road to Infinity* (Doubleday, 1979), to the Mensa audience.

The old difficulties cropped up, however, and unless I was speaking to a large group of Mensans, I avoided all Mensa functions. It was difficult to resign, for Victor told me that I had been appointed one of the two international vice presidents of Mensa, a post I was to hold for fifteen years. I had not asked for it, I had not wanted it, but I was listed in Mensa literature as filling that office. It was purely honorary, but it made resigning difficult.

There were, of course, many Mensans who were delightful and intelligent, as, for instance, Margot Seitelman, who virtually ran the New York branch of Mensa and who was an indefatigable hostess and an excellent cook. When Victor was in town, Margot and I had dinner with him, usually joined by Marvin Grosswirth, the most congenial of all Mensans. He could tell jokes better than I and could assume an even more authentic Yiddish accent.

I stayed on in Mensa for years, getting more and more tired of it. I couldn't even ignore my membership. Aside from having to pay dues every year, there were always many letters from people who began by announcing themselves as Mensans and therefore, one presumes, my blood brothers and sisters. Almost without exception they wanted me to do something for them that I didn't want to do, write an essay, collaborate on a book, read a manuscript, dig up some information for them, and so on. I felt myself in a ridiculously exposed position.

Eventually, after both Marvin and Margot had died, I did resign.

122

The Dutch Treat Club

Ralph Daigh, who looked a little like Alan Hale—Little John to Errol Flynn's Robin Hood—was editor-in-chief of Fawcett Publications, an important paperback publishing house. He invited me to lunch in April 1971, saying, "We'll go dutch treat."

I met Ralph at the Regency Hotel the following Tuesday. When I pulled out my wallet to pay, Ralph said, "You're my guest."

I said, "But you said we were going dutch treat."

He was horrified. "Do you think I would invite you to lunch and make you pay? This is the Dutch Treat *Club* and you are my guest."

A few weeks later I was invited to join the club as a member.

The Dutch Treat Club was founded in 1905 by a group of newspapermen who met for lunch every Tuesday, each paying for himself (hence Dutch Treat). As time went on, the club expanded to include anyone in the world of the arts. We meet at noon for cocktails and conversation, sit down to lunch at 12:30, and at 1:10 the toastmaster arises. He makes announcements, introduces guests, and then brings on the entertainment, usually a singer, followed by a speaker on some subject of general interest. At 2:00, we adjourn.

It is all very pleasant. At first, my attendance was sporadic, but I enjoyed myself so much when I did go that I began to be one of the regulars. In fact, when I sing "Give My Regards to Broadway" during my morning shower (I am an inveterate shower singer) and come to the lines "Tell them my heart is yearning / To mingle with the old-time throng," it is the Dutch Treaters I think of as the throng.

When I joined the club, the president was William Morris, the well-known lexicographer, jovial, plump, delightful, and with a white tuft of beard that made him look incredibly distinguished. He was forced to resign because his wife was increasingly ill, and he could not be sure of regular attendance. (He lives in Connecticut.) After his wife died, he resumed his regular attendance but not his former office. He is president emeritus.

Succeeding Bill Morris was the famous Lowell Thomas, the most distinguished of the Dutch Treaters during the 1970s. He was in his eighties (though you couldn't tell that from his bearing, his busy life, and his active mind, to say nothing of his young and attractive wife). He insisted that he was only temporary president till the club found someone else, but the club had no intention of finding anyone else. He remained president till he died at the age of eighty-nine.

On May 3, 1981, Janet and I attended one of the festivities in honor of his eighty-ninth birthday. He told me he was tired of all the fuss and feared it would be worse when he turned ninety. He said he would deliberately go on his travels so that no one would get at him on that occasion. —And so he did, though not as he expected, for he died peacefully in his sleep on August 29, 1981, after a day as filled with activity as all his days were, and that's a good end.

Succeeding Lowell was Eric Sloane, the great painter of Americana. One couldn't tell it from his placid exterior, but he had been married seven times. He was a wonderful fellow who occasionally ordered wine for each Dutch Treat table at his own expense. The only trouble was that he spent much of his time in the Southwest and was rarely present to preside at the meetings.

He was aware of the difficulties arising from this and he would speak of having me as president pro tem when he was absent, but I always felt he was joking. I did preside once in a while, though usually it was Walter Frese, the club secretary, who filled in.

Eric was also advanced in years and had a pacemaker. On March 6, 1985, soon after his eightieth birthday, he visited an art gallery on Fifty-seventh Street where they had arranged a display of his paintings for sale. He then walked down Fifth Avenue and his heart must have failed, for he collapsed and died on the pavement. Unbelievably, he had no identification on him, but he did carry a card from the art gallery. The police went there and someone from the gallery made the identification.

At once, Janet decided we had to have an Eric Sloane painting of our own. We went to the gallery and Janet chose three possible paintings and asked me to make the final decision. I did so, choosing the one I liked best, which now hangs on our living-room wall.

At Eric's memorial service, Janet and I were sitting quietly and sadly in our pew when Emery Davis, a Dutch Treater and a well-known bandleader—very bald and very jovial—leaned toward me and said, "You're giving the eulogy."

It was news to me, but I got up and improvised one. It went over well, but I did not foresee the consequences. I had been a member of the board of governors of the club since January 12, 1982, and, as a result of the eulogy, all the other board members at once agreed that I was to be the next president. After some hesitation, I gave in, and assumed the mantle of office on April 16, 1985.

In a way, the Dutch Treat Club changed the routine of my life. Since I was always lunching out on Tuesdays, I made it the day on which I made any visits I had to make to publishers. In particular, I visited Doubleday, and everyone there has grown so used to this that I have been told that on those occasions when I cannot visit, it doesn't feel like Tuesday.

There are many people at the Dutch Treat Club who have become beloved friends of mine (and some of these have died since I joined it). I hesitate to try to list them, for I am sure to leave out a few inadvertently. Let me say instead that the most colorful member of the club is Herb Graff. In his presence, even I tend to wash out.

Herb Graff is a short, balding man, who wore a toupee when I first met him but later abandoned it and grew a scruffy beard instead, which makes him look like a rather screwball variety of rabbi. His field of specialization is the movies of the 1930s.

Herb and I got along famously. For ten years we sat together, gathered kindred spirits, and were the noisiest table in the place. Eric Sloane called it the "Jewish table," though it was Herb, not I, who really deserved Eric's title of "Head Jew." (I once said, in mock complaint during the *Canberra* eclipse cruise, that I always seemed to sit at the noisiest table. Walter Sullivan, the gentlest soul ever invented, who sat at the same table, took me seriously, and said to me in wonder, "But, Isaac, you're the one that makes it noisy.")

Well, I do, but not always. When Herb is at the table, *he* makes the noise. Mind you, I'm a pretty good talker. Only recently, Robyn said casually to a friend, "A conversation with my father means listening to a monologue." When Herb is in the crowd, however, I tend to keep quiet and the conversation becomes a Herb Graff monologue. He knows any number of jokes and amusing stories, and tells them all in skillful nonstop fashion.

Out of a vast number of stories about the Dutch Treat, I'll tell you about the time when one of the regulars had missed a luncheon or two on the petty excuse of his wife's being in the hospital. I said, haughtily and with typical male (false) grandiosity, "The only reason *I* would miss a lunch would be if the gorgeous babe in bed with me simply wouldn't let me leave."

Whereupon Joe Coggins said, sepulchrally, "Which accounts for Isaac's perfect attendance record."

I saw that coming as soon as I made the remark, but it was too late to force it back in my mouth. There was nothing left but to join the group in their laughter.

123

The Baker Street Irregulars

The Baker Street Irregulars (BSI) are a group of Sherlock Holmes enthusiasts. The name comes from the fact that it is what Holmes called a group of street boys who worked for him in some of the early stories.

The organization has an annual banquet on an early Friday in January, the one nearest the sixth of the month, which is, supposedly,

Holmes's birthday. There, after conversation and cocktails, we sit down to a feast. And after that, there are various traditional rituals and "papers."

The game we all play is to suppose that the Sherlock Holmes stories are factually true, and that Dr. John H. Watson actually wrote them, with Arthur Conan Doyle as merely the literary agent.

In actual fact, Conan Doyle was a slapdash and sloppy writer who grew to hate the Sherlock Holmes stories because Sherlock drowned out his other literary works and even forced the author himself to retire into the shadows in comparison. He probably wrote them as quickly as he could to get rid of him. Eventually, he tried to kill Sherlock but reader pressure forced him to resurrect him. He then wrote further stories with even greater resentment.

As a result, the stories are loaded with contradictions among themselves, something Conan Doyle cared nothing about. The BSI, however, assumes the stories to be inerrant and it is the purpose of the "papers" to explain the contradictions in convoluted manner and to propose all sorts of deep and unlikely theories to account for one thing or another in the stories.

In 1973, I was proposed for membership in the BSI by Edgar Lawrence, an elderly member of the Trap Door Spiders (who is now dead). One of the requirements for membership was that the candidates prepare and deliver a paper on the stories. I didn't do this. What's more, I couldn't do it, because I didn't know the Holmes stories well enough and had no intention of doing the necessary research. The requirement was apparently waived in my case.

Fortunately, after a few years, I was asked to contribute to a book of writings about Holmes. When I said that I didn't know enough about the stories, Banesh Hoffman (a physicist who had worked with Einstein and who had an endearingly ugly face and an equally endearingly lovely soul—and who is now dead) suggested I analyze the book *Dynamics of an Asteroid*.

This book is mentioned in one story as having been written by that great mathematician and archcriminal James Moriarty. The story says nothing about what the book contained for the very good reason that Conan Doyle knew nothing about astronomy. I worked out a beautifully reasoned suggestion as to its contents—something that would exactly fit the infinite evil of Moriarty—and wrote the article for the collection. I later expanded it and made it a Black Widower story under the title "The Ultimate Crime." I did not submit it for magazine publication but included it as an "original" in *More Tales of the Black Widowers.*

After that, I felt I was a true Irregular at last.

Still, I must admit (for in this autobiography I tell nothing but the truth) that I am not really a Holmes enthusiast. A couple of years ago, I wrote (by request) a critique of the Sherlock Holmes story "The Five Orange Pips" and pointed out the gaping holes in its logic, which led me to think Conan Doyle had written it while asleep.

One of the banquet rites is to give the six "canonical toasts" to certain definite characters in the stories. One year I was asked to toast Sherlock Holmes himself, and I did so with such flair that, thereafter, I was called on every year to give the closing talk of the occasion. I also took to writing sentimental verses about Sherlock Holmes and singing them to well-known tunes. I sang the first, to the tune of "Believe Me, If All Those Endearing Young Charms," on January 8, 1982.

Not everything was peachy keen at the BSI, however. For one thing, since Sherlock was a heavy smoker, the Irregulars felt it incumbent on themselves to smoke. The air was always heavy with it after the banquet, and it drove me mad. There had been considerable smoking at the Trap Door Spiders and at the Dutch Treat Club, but it had faded off, due in some part to my continual carping, but I could do nothing with the Irregulars.

I pointed out, sarcastically, that Holmes was also a cocaine addict. Should we join the drug culture too, then? That had no effect. I demanded, and got, a smoke-free table, but what good did that do when the effluvium from other tables three feet away filled the air? So I raged—but endured.

One reason I endured was that the fellow running the show was Julian Wolff, a physician and a Dutch Treater. He had retired early from medicine in order to devote himself entirely to Irregular activities. He was short, baby-faced, and exuded an air of love and innocence. We all idolized him. It was he who invited me to speak at the banquet and who urged me to continue with my sentimental verses, and I couldn't bear to resign from the BSI, for that would make him feel bad.

But time passes. In 1986 Julian resigned his post and died in 1990 at the age of eighty-four. Since the new head of festivities did not want me to entertain, I stopped attending the banquets.

124

The Gilbert & Sullivan Society

I have been a Gilbert & Sullivan enthusiast since the fourth grade, when I learned how to sing "When the Foeman Bares His Steel" from *The Pirates of Penzance*. I didn't know it was Gilbert & Sullivan, of course, but I loved the song. I was a boy soprano then (with, I believe, a very sweet voice) and I loved to shrill out the soprano part: "Go, ye heroes, go to glory."

I still have an attraction for soprano songs, by the way, though my soprano days ended nearly sixty years ago, and I am now a baritone (though I can sing tenor if I have to). Some years ago, I joined in a rendition of "God Save the Queen" with a group of other singers, and I couldn't help but notice that the other baritones were not hitting the same notes I was. After it was over, I turned to my good friend Jocelyn Wilkes, a marvelous contralto, who is the best Katisha (in *The Mikado*) ever invented, and said, "I think I was singing the tenor part."

"Not at all," she said, with towering majesty. "You were singing the soprano part."

Well, those were the only notes I knew for the song.

When I was in my teens I heard the Gilbert & Sullivan plays on radio station WNYC, and before I ever saw a Gilbert & Sullivan performance on the stage, I had learned most of the songs and sang them for my own amusement constantly. I also read the plays over and over and was passionate about them.

At science fiction conventions, I used to sing songs from Gilbert &

Sullivan and, sometimes, other songs as well, along with Anne McCaffrey, a Junoesque science fiction writer with white hair who wrote best-selling fantasies. She had a great voice and completely outdid me, especially when it came time to hold a note. Of course, she never bothered to tell me she had had voice training in operatic singing.

At a convention in New York, soon after I returned to that city, I did my Gilbert & Sullivan singing stint, and someone asked me if I was a member of the Gilbert & Sullivan Society. I said I knew nothing about it. He told me where and when to go and I joined up at once.

The Society has always been a great pleasure to me. There is first community singing from one of the plays and then a performance by one of the many amateur G & S groups in the metropolitan area, who do it for nothing as one more rehearsal before a completely sympathetic audience who can join in the choruses.

On rare occasions, I have sung Gilbert & Sullivan before the Society (and once or twice before a larger audience) and I have noticed a peculiar thing. I can step before a crowd of thousands of strangers, without a single note in my hand, and improvise a one-hour talk for which I expect to be paid thousands of dollars, and I do so without a qualm—indeed, without the ghost of a butterfly in my stomach. Get me, however, before fifty friends, who are not paying me anything (and are therefore not risking their money), who are ready to smile indulgently at any mistake I may make, and where I need only sing a song I know perfectly—and I die of apprehension.

Why? My guess is that the song must be perfect to the letter and note, while my talk, being improvised, can go any which way. Even if I goof in the process of talking, I know a hundred ways of covering it up so no one will notice, and I can't do that when I'm singing a Gilbert & Sullivan song.

In short, the song isn't mine and the speech is and that is the difference. It follows, then, that when I sing a comic song of my own creation, I am *not* nervous.

I am also not nervous when I read one of Gilbert's *Bab Ballads*. Of course, I don't memorize it; I read it from the book. There, the trick is to overact. That is, in my opinion, the best part of the plays. In the prose portions between the songs, overacting is the thing to do, at least in my opinion.

Janet has caught the Gilbert & Sullivan fever from me. Together we have now seen every one of the plays, even *The Grand Duke,* which is the last and least of them. The music to the first of them, *Thespis,* has been lost, but we enjoyed a performance even of that, on July 10, 1987, with the company borrowing music from the other plays and fitting it to the songs in *Thespis*.

On November 19, 1989, we watched an Americanized version of *H.M.S. Pinafore* (called for the purpose *U.S.S. Pinafore*). All the songs could be made to fit with minor adaptations except for Sir Joseph Porter's "When I was a lad I served a term." The company turned to me for a completely different set of words, and I obliged.

The revised song was very funny, I thought, and judging by the audience's reaction when it was sung, they thought so too. At the end of the performance, the spotlight was turned on my seat and I rose and took a bow. It was very gratifying.

And then, of course, I had the pleasure of doing *Asimov's Annotated Gilbert & Sullivan*, which I mentioned earlier.

125

Other Clubs

The Trap Door Spiders, the Dutch Treat Club, the Gilbert & Sullivan Society, and even the Baker Street Irregulars were organizations I enjoyed and was glad to belong to, but I was acutely aware that my membership consumed a number of lunches and dinners and kept me away from my typewriter. It was not likely, therefore, that I would ever become a "joiner" and seek out other organizations. Unfortunately, one of the penalties of being a celebrity is that organizations come seeking him.

I found this out when I received a letter from the Explorers Club inviting me to join. I smiled at the thought, and shot back a letter at once telling them they had the wrong man. Not only had I never explored the Himalayas, I told them, but it was only with the utmost difficulty that I could be persuaded to go as far as Hoboken.

That didn't disturb them a bit. They replied that I was a well-known explorer of the galaxy and places beyond, so that I was thoroughly qualified.

I am not proof against flattery, so I joined. However, it was a joining very largely in name only. Many talks on exploration are given at the sumptuous Explorers Club clubhouse, but I have only attended a very few of them. I just cannot afford the time.

I did, of course, attend a special Explorers Club get-together for new members on June 4, 1978, and met Charles Brush, an ardent mountain climber who had just begun to serve a term as president of the club. He drew me to one side and asked if I would emcee the next annual banquet of the Explorers Club. I agreed and for two years was master of ceremonies.

At the banquet the club generally serves unusual hors d'oeuvres (like rattlesnake), but I like to eat exotic things (also commonplace food as well). When "mountain oysters" turned out to be bull testicles, or something like that, I decided that even I had my limits.

There are other organizations too that, one way or another, have laid their traps for me. Many of the members of the Dutch Treat Club are members of the Players Club, and some have urged me to join. I wasn't really enthusiastic. It's way downtown and I didn't see myself as likely to attend its functions very often—and its dues were very high. Nevertheless, I didn't quite have the face to offend my friends by refusing to allow my name to be put in nomination.

You can imagine my relief when the Players Club *blackballed* me. Apparently, one of the votes belonged to a smoker who knew of my extreme antismoking attitude, and he wouldn't have me.

And another friend decided he would get me into the very prestigious Century Club. I wasn't eager since I'm not the Century Club type, really. (I'm just a boy from the slums who views this whole business of being rich and famous with the deepest suspicion.) He insisted, though, and I relied on a blackball. It never came. I'm now a member but almost never take any advantage of my membership.

126

American Way

Now let's get back, once again, to my writing.

I enjoy writing essays, and I particularly enjoy writing a column, for then I know that I can write an essay at regular intervals. My most successful column is, of course, that for *F&SF*, which has been going on, now, for thirty-two years.

It's not the only one. I wrote a column for *Science Digest* till it changed editors. I wrote a fiction column for *Gallery* till it changed publishers. I wrote a series of short science columns for *Sciquest,* a small chemistry magazine intended for high school students, till it ceased publication in 1982, and so on.

One particular column, which I enjoyed very much and which was quite successful during its lifetime, was circulated on airplanes, of all places.

Most airlines have in-flight magazines to be given to airline passengers free of charge as a way of occupying their time, I suppose. American Airlines had an especially glossy magazine called *American Way*. In 1974, the editor of *American Way,* John Minahan, wanted to institute a science column and he asked Larry Ashmead to recommend someone to write it. Well, asking Larry to recommend someone for *anything* gets only one answer: "Isaac Asimov is the man for you."

Actually, I had published an item or two in the magazine, so the editor knew me and approached me at once. It was only a matter of 750 words every month and I jumped at the chance to write a science column for a broadly general audience. Of course, my sense of ethics made it necessary for me to tell him that I never flew in airplanes, but John said that, provided I didn't mention that fact in my column, that would be all right. He also said there were two subjects I could *not* discuss—politics and death.

The essays for *American Way* were easy to do and a great deal of fun, and when the magazine went semimonthly, I did two essays a month and was even asked to make them slightly longer. I was told that the essays were very popular and that the page opposite their invariable position in the magazine commanded a premium price for advertising (so they said). Certainly, it was clear from the letters I received that many people read the column who did not usually read my other writing.

In nearly fourteen years I wrote just over 200 essays for *American Way*, surviving many changes of editor, but then, in October 1987, there was one too many of those changes. The new one decided to do over the entire magazine and I found myself out on my ear.

This would have been dreadful for me but, by the greatest good fortune, the people at the Los Angeles Times Syndicate had, on May 21, 1986, become aware of me and, feeling the need for a science column, asked me to do one for them. I began to do essays for the Syndicate that were similar to those for *American Way*, except that I do one each week, and I am as happy as a lark.

In one way, the Syndicate articles are different. Since, in this case, I am writing for newspapers, it is nice to be topical. I therefore save clippings from newspapers and magazines on such recent scientific advances that I find colorful and interesting. At first, I did have a nervous feeling that I wouldn't find an appropriate topical subject each week, but the situation turned out to be quite the reverse. I have to choose among them.

I stay away from medical advances, though. That is the one branch of science that the newspapers cover thoroughly and there is no use my joining the cacophonous chorus. I would rather write about supernovae, electrons, artificial sweeteners, and endangered species.

I don't allow my various essays to die after their evanescent appearance in a magazine or newspaper. My *American Way* articles have appeared in two collections published by Houghton Mifflin: *Change* (1981) and *The Dangers of Intelligence* (1986). My Syndicate columns have been collected in *Frontiers*, published by Dutton in 1990, with *Frontiers II* due in 1993.

127

Rensselaerville Institute

Left to myself, I would never take a vacation, but I am not left to myself. There are wives, and they *do* want vacations. When I was married to Gertrude, we would go off to some resort in the summer for a week, occasionally for two. Generally, my pleasures in such things were erratic. If there happened to be present some person or persons who were as frenetic as I could be, and whom Gertrude could like, all went well, even hysterically well. Otherwise, it would be rather dull.

Somehow it was different with Janet. If she were with me, I found (to my amazement, at first) that it didn't matter who else was with us or not with us. It was perfectly possible to be uninvolved with anyone else whatever, and simply wander about on our own—just the two of us—and that would be fine.

Janet was so easy to please, she took pleasure in such simple things, such obvious delight just in being with me, even when things went wrong, that I totally lost that old nervousness that came of being with someone who was always on the point of being displeased and turning everything sour. Vacations became delightful, even though I still had to be sparing as to their number and their length, for even under the best of circumstances, the call of my typewriter was supreme.

I found this out in the early summer of 1972, the apprehensive time when we were waiting for Janet's breast biopsy to see whether it would have to come off or not. I received an invitation to go to the Institute of Man and Science for a conference on the future of communications. (That institute, by the way, has since been renamed the Rensselaerville Institute and I now think of it only in that way.)

No money was involved and, ordinarily, I would have turned it down without a second thought. This time, though, I thought carefully. The site was at Rensselaerville, a small village in upstate New York near Schenectady. The Institute was described to me as a very rustic place, and although I am a creature of the city canyons, I knew that Janet loved the country. She was facing an ordeal—even, possibly, the loss of a breast—and I was extremely anxious that she have a few pleasurable days now, in case the worst was to come. I therefore agreed to be there.

We spent the Independence Day weekend there and it was a good thing I did it, for three weeks later Janet's breast *was* removed and I would never have forgiven myself if I had deprived her of that weekend.

The place *was* rustic and beautiful, and Janet was delighted with it. It was set in a large tract of rolling green hills and wooded areas, with a lake drained by a stream that passed down spectacular falls.

The buildings that housed the conference were, however, modern and fitted with pleasant conveniences, including even air conditioning. There was a good restaurant in the area, and there were chipmunks, rabbits, and other creatures to be seen, and this, too, Janet found enchanting. I congratulated myself a thousand times that I had decided to come.

Janet and I asked for separate (but adjoining) rooms in the interest of propriety, for we were not yet married. That, however, proved to be very uncomfortable. Separating at night was simply painful and this was the last time we ever did that. After that, we threw propriety out the window. Why not? Within a year and a half, we were married anyway.

Of course, we had to attend the business end of the conference too, and one talk we particularly enjoyed involved a demonstration of a television cassette that required two large bulky objects to make it work. (This was 1972, remember.) Such cassettes, said the speaker, were the wave of the future, and would replace books, so that people like Isaac Asimov (and he smiled at where I sat in the front row) would starve to death. At this, the audience, faced with the possibility of my famishing, was convulsed with laughter.

As it happened, a major speech was scheduled for the following evening, but the gentleman who was to give it was delayed in Great

Britain and could not arrive to give his speech. I was asked to throw myself into the breach. I protested that I had nothing prepared and was told, "Come, Isaac, it is well known that you don't need preparation."

Since I'm a complete sucker for flattery, I agreed to do it.

In my talk, I took up the subject of TV cassettes and pointed out how bulky and inconvenient the equipment was but insisted (quite correctly) that it would be rapidly simplified. I then speculated on how far it could be simplified—made small and portable, self-contained, with no energy source, and with controls that could start it and stop it or move it back and forth with little more than a mental effort, and so on. And, behold, I pointed out, this was a *book*.

I also pointed out that television yielded so much information that the viewer became a passive receptacle, whereas a book gave so little that the reader had to be an active participant, his imagination supplying all the imagery, sound, and special effects. This participation, I said, gave so much pleasure that television could not serve as a decent substitute.

The talk was such a great success that I was asked to return in 1973 to run a seminar of my own. I wanted Janet to enjoy the surroundings once again, so I agreed. It was just as well. On August 19, 1973, we were at the Rensselaerville Institute again. It gave Janet a chance to rebound from her mastectomy and her subarachnoid hemorrhage, and I, from my mother's death.

In point of fact, we have gone back every year since then. A hard core of "regulars" also returns, and each year there are new attendees too, though there is no way of making room for more than about sixty people.

The group always deals with some science-fictional problem—the coming of some catastrophe, the setting up of a colony in space, and so on. The group is divided into several subgroups, each of which is given a special task, and they go about it with the utmost seriousness, hammering out procedures, solutions, conclusions, arguing with each other fiercely—and all in absolute disregard for the beautiful summer weather outside.

I once delivered a small speech saying that we might be sitting outside sunning ourselves, playing tennis, or swimming in the lake. Instead, I said, we were indoors, arguing and thinking. I then waited a few minutes and said, "How lucky we are!" and everyone broke into applause.

We have, of course, made good friends at Rensselaerville. Preeminent was Isidore Adler, a chemist at the University of Maryland, and his wife, Annie. Izzy was another one of those fellows with a face that is not handsome but is somehow so attractive that young women always flocked about him. He and I swapped jokes endlessly. He was a jock and could beat, at tennis and handball, men young enough to be his grandsons. He would also get up at dawn and jog for several miles down the road and through the town. One extremely attractive young woman, Winnie, felt the need to lose some weight, so she sometimes jogged with him. He was faster, of course, so that townspeople, if they looked out of their windows, could see the unusual sight of a gorgeous girl madly pursuing a plain, old man who seemed intent on escape.

Winnie was a belly dancer, by the way, and extremely spectacular. We always reserved one evening for belly dancing when she was in attendance. And every evening, of course, I was on display, telling my most elaborate jokes. I told some (by popular demand) every year, since no one else could tell them as I could.

Then there was Mary Sayer, who had an artlessness (to say nothing of a figure) that was endlessly attractive. She was a woman with whom flirting was a particular pleasure, because it always threw her into such a delightful confusion. She was a science fiction fan too, and in 1983 I met her at the World Convention in Baltimore. Janet was on an errand, but hadn't returned, so I was getting very restless. Mary, in her gentle way, said there was no use wandering about looking for her in a huge crowd. She urged me to go to my room and wait there, for Janet would surely return. She accompanied me to my room and I sat there in misery, paying Mary no attention, till I heard a key in the door. I was instantly in action.

"Quick, Mary," I said, and dragged her to the door. There I embraced her and managed to plant a kiss on her lips just as Janet walked in.

Janet said, "Hello, Mary." She paid absolutely no attention to the kiss, which she knew was for her benefit. Besides, Mary's transparent goodness made anything else impossible.

During the later years at the Institute, Mark Chartrand (an astronomer) and Mitchell Waldrop (a science writer) began to attend regularly and to take part in the game.

I always gave an introductory hour-long talk on the first evening, a talk that was open to the townspeople too. At Rensselaerville I was lucky enough to become acquainted with the inimitable Andy Rooney, who has a summer house there.

I almost always managed to write a story in longhand while I was at the Institute, usually a Black Widower mystery. I did that on cruises, too. On one cruise, I wrote three stories and later sold them all.

People who catch me writing longhand are always talking to me about laptop computers, but I pay them no mind. I happen to like to write longhand now and then. Why can't they understand that? In fact, most of this book that you are now reading was originally written in longhand, for reasons I will explain later.

But time passes. In 1987, it was found that Izzie Adler was suffering from cancer of the prostate. He continued to attend even though he was in more or less constant pain and in 1989 he attended in a wheelchair. On March 26, 1990, he died at the age of seventy-three.

The news of his death was a source of great sorrow to us, even though it was not unexpected. That, combined with accumulating medical problems of my own, which I will describe later, decided me to make the 1990 session the last. The group will carry on just as well without me—and perhaps better.

128

Mohonk Mountain House

Janet's parents would often spend some time at Mohonk Mountain House, a rambling resort set in many acres of wilderness. Its oldest parts were over a century old, and the whole still breathed a Victorian ambience. It is located in New Paltz, New York, just across the Hudson River from Poughkeepsie.

They went largely because Janet's father was a golfing enthusiast and Mohonk offered good facilities for that. Janet never went with them (she was busy with college and, like most young people, she didn't think a good vacation was one in which you tagged along with your parents). However, they told her much about the beauty of the setting and the pleasantness of Mohonk's aura.

In 1975, when we were barreling down the New York State Thruway from a speaking engagement upstate, Janet said as we came to a sign announcing the New Paltz turnoff up ahead, "There's a place called Mohonk Mountain House in New Paltz. I'd love to see it."

Now, ordinarily, travel—when I must travel—is, for me, only a device for going from A to B as quickly and as directly as possible. I resist the impulse to stop and do a little sightseeing unless Janet presses hard. She wasn't pressing this time, but I must have been in a particularly compliant mood, for I said, "Well, let's turn off and look at it."

We followed a winding mountain road for nine miles and finally reached a large rambling place, with a great variety of architectural motifs madly jumbled together, as picturesque as anything we could imagine. It was surrounded by gardens, hills, wilderness, and a small lake. We had an excellent lunch, followed by a walk to magnificent gardens. Janet was in ecstasies over it, and I am prepared to love anything that will send Janet into ecstasies—and, as a matter of fact, I was impressed by it on my own, so it has become our favorite resort.

Two or three times a year we stay there from one to four days. Arm in arm, we wander through its halls, around its lake, and in its gardens. We once attended five annual sessions of a "murder mystery weekend" in winter, and I later ran two sessions of a "science fiction weekend." We sometimes attend a week devoted to music, and we once went to watch a meteor shower. Sometimes we just go for no reason but to be there. I occasionally give a talk at their request, but of course I accept no money for it, only room and board.

The wildlife at Mohonk, especially the deer, are not frightened of human beings, since no move in anger is ever made against them. One evening, during the kind of gentle walk considered suitable for me, we saw some half a dozen white-tailed deer cropping the grass in the dusk not more than fifty yards from us. We watched enraptured while they ignored us. Finally, Janet said, "Aren't they beautiful?" I answered, "Yes, they look delicious." She groaned, but I notice that she eats venison with delight when it is on the menu.

We once chanced upon a particularly quiet and seemingly un-touched place and sat there in absolute content for half an hour. When we got home, I wrote a Black Widower story, "The Quiet Place," which appeared in the March 1987 *EQMM*.

In 1987, the Washington *Post* asked me to write a piece on some place in my travels that I liked very much. I replied that I didn't travel, unless you counted Mohonk Mountain House, ninety miles from New York. They said that that would be fine and I was then faced with the problem of describing the place—and I'm not a very observant fellow.

I therefore suggested that Janet write it and, after considerable hesi-tation, she did. I then went over it and made a few changes and sent it off. (As is always true in all our collaborations, Janet does 90 percent of the work.) The *Post* loved it, and I insisted that the authors be listed as "Janet and Isaac Asimov." They agreed and it appeared in the *Post*'s Christmas issue under the title "Our Shangri-La."

The piece was apparently sufficiently successful so that they wanted one on the American Museum of Natural History. Since Janet loves that place, I gave her that job also. It appeared in the *Post* in 1988 as "The Tyrannosaurus Prescription" by Janet and Isaac Asimov.

Both of these essays appeared in a collection published by Prome-theus Press in 1989, and the publishers were sufficiently impressed by Janet's essay to name the book "The Tyrannosaurus Prescription."

Janet is a very charming writer of nonfiction. She has sold every one of the few such essays she has written (she sold one of them twice when the first magazine folded and she had to find another) and I keep urging her to write more of them.

129

Travel

Despite all my talk about not traveling, I've been to Evansville, Indiana, and to Raleigh, North Carolina, because it was necessary to attend functions and give talks in such faraway and exotic places. I have been in Mammoth Cave, Kentucky, and seen Indian mounds in Ohio.

Going such unusual distances (for me) requires unusual stimuli. I went to Indiana because Lowell Thomas asked me to do so as a special favor for him. I went to North Carolina at the invitation of the state's governor. With time, even such stimuli became insufficient to budge me, but while I was still in my fifties, I could do it.

The greatest of all stimuli were Janet's desires. She never pushed them or made demands, but I knew, for instance, that she had always wanted to visit the Everglades in Florida. Some people, I imagine, dream of shopping in Paris or of gambling in Las Vegas, but Janet dreams of seeing the flora and fauna of the Everglades, and I wanted desperately to oblige her.

The chance came in 1977, when I received an invitation to lecture to a large group of IBM people in Miami. The offered fee was higher than I was getting at the time, but that would not have influenced me. However, I asked if I could have a conducted tour of the Everglades while there, and they agreed.

So on March 26, 1977, I very nervously undertook the longest trip I had ever taken on my own up to that point. We took the train to Miami.

I don't mind trains very much, although I get nervous when they barrel through the night. I cannot for the life of me convince myself that the engineer can see where he's going, for when I look out the window all is dark. (I know! He has headlights and there are signal lights all along the track, but it's my mind that knows that, not my heart.) It's especially bad when there is a rough stretch of track and the train shakes and rattles. I keep anticipating derailments with who knows what dreadful consequences.

This is not entirely cowardice, though I think I have stressed the fact that I am not physically brave. My fears also reflect a hyperactive imagination. I have trained and used that imagination in my writing for many decades, and I can't turn it off on demand. Dreadful consequences are forever presenting themselves to my eyes in solid and realistic three-dimensional form, and there's nothing I can do about it.

We did our best to be comfortable. We got not one sleeping compartment but two adjoining ones and had them open the door between them. That meant we had two bathrooms, a luxury we greatly appreciated, for when there is only one bathroom there are bound to be conflicts. I am an early riser and am accustomed to retire into the bathroom with a book or a newspaper and to be in no haste to emerge. In our apartment, we have separate bathrooms, so I can luxuriate in the ability to take my time.

Since the sleeping car was the last in the train and the dining car was up near the front, we had to walk through several coaches, which activated my liberalism. There were the proletariat in the coaches sprawled this way and that in their seats trying to get some rest (especially when we passed through early at breakfast time), and there were we with our double room, our separate beds and bathrooms, living the life of luxury. Not only did I feel terribly guilty at having betrayed my class by becoming affluent but I had the uneasy feeling that at any moment all the downtrodden coachers would rise in their wrath, shouting, *"Les aristocrates à la lanterne,"* and hang us, even though, in my heart, I'm one of them.

But we arrived safely, un-derailed and unhanged, and I gave the talks successfully. I was rather amused by IBM's regimentation. The talk was scheduled for very early in the morning and there were no stragglers. (I'm convinced that anyone who came late would have been shot on the spot.) Every one in the audience was in his or her seat, and the men were all in uniform—dark suits, button-down white shirts, narrow ties, and a general air of smooth-shaven wholesomeness.

I was wearing a red jacket, which seemed to blind everyone, but they tolerated it. (A fellow speaker was sent back to his room to get the tie he had neglected to put on.)

My garb made its mark, though. When I returned to New York, I reported to my lecture agent, Harry Walker, who had arranged the trip. While I was there, he happened to get a call from IBM people expressing satisfaction with my talk.

Harry Walker was gratified and he said, "As a matter of fact, he's right here, talking to me." Then a puzzled look crossed his face and he said, "No, he's *not* wearing a red jacket."

We *did* go on the Everglades expedition and it was a complete success, even though the previous winter had been a hard one with the temperature reaching an unprecedented low (for the Everglades) of 19. This killed a good deal of the vegetation, which, after all, was not adapted to cold. There were still distressing patches of plant life that were dead and brown, and Janet mourned over them.

Even so, there was much to see, especially the alligators, who didn't seem at all threatening. We were told we couldn't feed them, but one had a missing leg (presumably chewed off in a fight with a rival) and Janet insisted on feeding *him*. We had a splendid lunch—the weather was perfect—and I stared at the waters of what I was assured was the Gulf of Mexico, something I had never thought to see.

I shuddered at the thought of living in Florida, though, a place where six inches is a high elevation. I like green hills, as I've said before. In Florida, too, there is no real winter, and though winters have their disadvantages, they also have a remarkable beauty of their own. In a winterless climate, such as that of Florida, southern California, and Hawaii, I think I'd go mad with nostalgia for snow.

My good friend Martin H. Greenberg, about whom I will speak in some detail later, was born and brought up in Florida but went to college in Connecticut and saw his first snowfall there. He said it was an unimaginable joy and thrill to see frozen water falling from the sky and to make snowballs. He has now lived many years in Green Bay, Wisconsin, however, and I suspect that he views snowfalls with something less than ecstasy these days.

The next year, 1978, I was faced with an even greater challenge. I was asked to go to Pebble Beach, California, and to San Jose, and to give a talk in each place for a sum that seemed to me to be a great deal at the time.

Never! Never! Never! —But I also knew that Janet had a great longing to visit the San Diego Zoo, and I knew very well that that couldn't be done unless we went to California. The Florida trip had given me confidence, so we left in December 1978.

Janet insisted we leave a day early, something to which I objected strenuously, but she had her way—and a good thing too.

It took us four days and four nights to get to California by train, and then it took us four days and four nights to get back from California—and it seemed longer, both ways. When we had to stop over at Chicago we seized the opportunity to go to the top of the Sears Building, the tallest office building in the world.

I didn't enjoy it as much as I should have, even leaving my acrophobia out of it. The flat midwestern vista struck me as featureless. I want hills, hills.

Worse still, I was offended by the mere existence of the building. My New York patriotism forced me to resent bitterly the fact that any other city had dared to construct a building that outdid all of Manhattan's skyscrapers.

West of Chicago, the train had a coach with a glass dome so that you could watch the scenery more effectively. All was well until Wyoming, where winter had an iron grip on the countryside. We were behind a freight train that was chugging away on a one-track line and, apparently, that slow monster could not be shunted aside because, these days, freight in the trains takes precedence over people.

In the dead of night, something went wrong with the engine in the freight train. It stopped. We stopped, waiting for a new engine to be brought for the freight train so it—and we—could move again. Janet was anxiously awake throughout, but I slept through most of this. When I did wake up, I was enormously indignant at the freight train, the rail network, and the entire philosophy of traveling. To make my point sharper, the train was running out of fuel, losing its power, and all the coaches were becoming winter-cold. Finally, just as the last of our own coach's power was draining away, the freight train was given its new engine and we resumed our trip. We got to Oakland, then took a bus to San Francisco and arrived just twelve hours late, so it was a good thing that Janet had insisted on leaving a day early.

One result of the lost time was that we passed through Utah by day, instead of during the previous night as we ought to have done. Janet pays no attention to her Mormon heritage, but her parents were born in Utah and lived there into their twenties; she has many relatives there; the family homestead was there; and she had visited members of her family in Utah. She was therefore very excited at being able to see the state by daylight, so I decided the delay had been worthwhile.

The stay in California was successful. My two talks went well, though my own views were out of sympathy with the ones that seemed to prevail among the people at Pebble Beach. (I remember defending New York vigorously against the onslaught of non-New Yorkers who thought of the city as a subbasement of Hades.) At the talk at San Jose, I met Randall Garrett for the last time and received the "Clone Song" from him.

Janet was reunited with her brother and sister-in-law for a satisfactory period of time and I rented a car (for the first and, so far, only time in my life) so that we could venture into the redwood forests and see the big trees. I marveled at them and thrilled with anger at recalling one of Ronald Reagan's many, many fatuous remarks to the effect that if you had seen one redwood tree, you had seen them all, and that therefore there was nothing wrong with chopping down those grandest of all the members of the plant kingdom. (Presumably, though, he was only repeating what someone had written down for him on one of his note cards.)

After my talks were done, Janet and I drove the rented car down the coastal highway and I stared at miles of the Pacific Ocean. I can't say I liked the brown countryside. Janet explained that there was a period in spring when it all turned "Kelly green," but I want my countryside either green or with a snow cover—not brown.

We eventually arrived at San Diego, where we had arranged with the managers of the San Diego Zoo for a guided tour the following day, December 17, 1978. Looking at the sky, I asked the hotel doorman if it were going to rain. He laughed heartily. Rain in San Diego, you blighted Easterner? I could hear him saying. Of course not.

The next day it rained buckets all day long.

We couldn't very well miss the San Diego Zoo just because it rained, so we went there anyway, and it all turned out very well. A high official of the zoo turned up in storm gear, looking like the captain of a whaling vessel, and we got our tour. (We were well dressed for the occasion too.)

Whereas ordinarily the zoo would have been crowded with people and we would have had difficulty in moving about and getting a good look at the animals, this time we were in relative isolation, and since we didn't mind the moisture, conditions were ideal.

The next day we drove to Los Angeles, and Janet insisted we stop at Disneyland. I did so with the greatest reluctance, and, to my shame and horror, I enjoyed it tremendously.

They had the exhibit of "It's a Small World After All" that I had enjoyed at the New York World's Fair in 1965. I didn't know that, and as we walked into Disneyland, I said to Janet, "Where's the 'It's a Small World After All' exhibit?" I asked it just to be disagreeable, so that when she said it didn't exist, I could make derogatory remarks about Disneyland, California, and the Universe.

But she said calmly, "Right there, in that building." Naturally, I insisted on seeing it. The seats were full of children aged seven to ten, sitting in moribund silence, plus one child of fifty-eight who couldn't contain his excitement and kept pointing in glee to the various puppets we passed.

In Los Angeles, the rain had temporarily cleared the air, so the Angelenos had their once-a-year chance to see blue skies and cumulus clouds. The weatherman on TV excitedly showed views of the clouds and explained what they were, while in the streets people stared in amazement at the sight of distant mountains, visible in air that was suddenly transparent. (And they knock New York!)

And then we returned the car, took the train, and reached home on December 22. We were away for three weeks altogether, which meant an accumulation of three weeks of mail, three weeks of telephone calls, three weeks of advancing deadlines. When ordinary people go on vacations, their work gets done by an army of assistants, secretaries, helpers, family members, and so on. When I go on vacation, *no one* does my work. It all waits for me and it all has to be done in double time when I return. So what good is a vacation? may I ask. (Incidentally, I have not obliged Janet in all her longings. She also dreams of Vancouver, Canada, and Kyoto, Japan, and I have never taken her there and I suppose I never will.)

After we returned from the trip, Janet wrote an article on the difficulties of crossing the continent with a man who hated traveling and would not fly. She sold it to the New York *Times*'s travel section, to my surprise. The article appeared in the February 25, 1979, issue of the Sunday *Times*, and it attracted a lot of very favorable reader comment.

One person stopped me on the street and asked if I were Isaac

Asimov, and when I admitted it, he said, "Would you tell your wife I really enjoyed her article?"

I stopped at the nearest phone and called her. "Janet," I said, "this nuisance must cease."

130

Foreign Travel

I never expected to leave the borders of the United States after having been brought here in 1923. Even when I went to Hawaii, I hadn't done so, for Hawaii (not yet a state then) was an American territory. That I did so the first time was because Gertrude had been born in Toronto and every once in a while I had to oblige her wish to see it. We drove there on two occasions, and once to Quebec.

We were advised to take our citizenship papers, and sure enough, we had to show them. This bothered me, as a matter of principle. Native-born Americans, on returning from Canada, simply had to state they were native-born. They weren't asked to show their birth certificates, and their word was considered good. But since I was a naturalized citizen, my word wasn't good and I had to present my citizenship papers. This is second-class treatment for someone who is as American as anyone else, and I resented it.

We went to see Niagara Falls, and as I drove up to the town of Niagara Falls, I worried out loud whether we might not get lost and miss the falls somehow. Even as I said it, I turned a corner and *there they were*. That first, totally unexpected sight was magnificent. We stayed on the Canadian side and watched the Horseshoe Falls in silent awe as the very last of the winter's ice pitched over the precipice. The next day, there was no ice, only a blue cascade of water, falling into thunder.

What I remember most clearly, though, is my getting ready for bed in a motel right near the falls, where we could hear it plainly, and my sudden realization that they did not turn off the falls at night. The roar continued throughout the hours of darkness, but it was "white noise" and after a while I got used to it and slept well.

Naturally, we took the children with us, and on our trip to Quebec, David was particularly excited because I had mentioned that the people of Quebec spoke French. David had never heard a foreign language spoken, and he could hardly wait. He spoke of nothing else but the chance of hearing a foreign language spoken.

Once in our hotel room in Quebec, he turned on the television set, of course, and listened to a cascade of French. He seemed completely nonplussed at that.

"That's French," I explained. "That's what you were waiting to hear, David."

And he said, "But I don't understand it."

I had neglected to tell him that a foreign language was not to be understood by those who did not know it. I'm afraid it ruined the trip for him.

In 1973, the World Science Fiction Convention was held in Toronto and my book *The Gods Themselves* was nominated for a Hugo, so I went to Toronto with Janet, even though we were still some three months short of being married. Janet and I have been to Canada three times since then. We visited Quebec as part of a *QE2* cruise and made land trips to Montreal and Ottawa. I gave talks on all three occasions.

On the whole, I am fond of Canada. I found the cities clean and the people friendly. There was a very nice Russian restaurant at which we ate in Montreal and it smote me sadly that I would never eat there a second time, for I felt certain I would never be in Montreal again (there are disadvantages to being a nontraveler too).

In the course of the various cruises we have been on I have occasionally set foot on dry land off the North American continent. In the trips to the Caribbean, Janet and I spent a few hours on each of different islands, including Martinique (where they have a statue to Napoleon's empress, Josephine, who was born there), Tobago, one of the Virgin Islands, and so on. These islands tended to be hot and humid, except for Barbados, which, apparently, had no central mountain peak to catch the rain and where we really had an excellent time.

In the course of one cruise, which docked at a Venezuelan port, everyone went off to look at natural wonders inland, but Janet and I contented ourselves with merely getting off the ship and standing on the pier for a while so that I could say afterward that I had set foot on the South American continent.

I found that on my cruises I liked to be at sea. Docking at a foreign port always bothered me. It meant that I might have to get off the ship. I found that moving from the ship to shore meant "traveling" and I didn't like it. Once I had been on the ship for a few hours it became "home" and I didn't want to leave it. If I had to leave it, I always returned to the ship with the same feeling of relief with which I would return to my own apartment.

I can only suppose that I attach a strong feeling of security to whatever I consider "home." Perhaps it was built up over my first twenty-two years, when, indeed, I virtually never left home (except to go to school) and when my parents were always home too. Any place but home was alien territory, and that may account for my reluctance to travel.

There were times when I refused to get off the ship at all. On the *Canberra* eclipse cruise, I did get off at the largest of the Canary Islands. I carefully insisted on accompanying two young women. After all, I was convinced they could find their way back to the ship when the time came, so that if I never let them out of my sight I would be sure not to find myself lost and stranded. I wandered with them into some retail establishment where they tried to buy something and found themselves stymied since they could not speak Spanish and the storekeeper was innocent of English. I knew no Spanish either, but I managed to conclude the transaction by means of sign language, and gained a great reputation as a linguist in consequence.

However, I refused to get off at Lagos, Nigeria, when the *Canberra* docked there and, as a result, I have never been able to say that I once stood on African soil.

My reluctance to leave reached its apogee when we stopped off at the Dominican Republic, especially since the *QE2* was too large to stop right at the port but had to remain out at sea and take people ashore by tender. I actually agreed to let Janet get off the ship without me. It did me no good. I retained the security of the ship, but I had lost the security of Janet. I was restless all the time she was gone, and about an hour before the tender that was to bring her back was due, I was down at the gangplank anxiously waiting for it.

Our "Astronomy Island" cruises also took us to Bermuda a dozen times, where I gave a lecture to the astronomy fans from the ship plus the Bermuda astronomy group. Beautiful Bermuda soon became familiar enough to me to serve as a kind of home, and I found I could leave the ship without trouble.

When Victor Serebriakoff talked me into rejoining Mensa, he had more in mind than the rejoining. He began a studied campaign to get me to come to Great Britain and talk to Mensa there. I refused, of course, but he kept up the pressure and in time I got to thinking about the matter.

Janet and I are both Anglophiles, since each of us had spent our youth reading through the rich heritage of British literature. British history and geography was almost more familiar to us than the American equivalents. So I agreed to go if someone from British Mensa would consent to drive us about Great Britain, show us the sights, and make all the arrangements for room and board.

They agreed to that, but we still had to get boat tickets and passports (my first) and, on the whole, I grew more and more frightened at the prospect. Janet listened to my outcries of concern and finally said, "Look, Isaac, you always tell me that there may be things I have agreed to do that I don't really want to do, but that, once having agreed to it, I must do it with good grace and a smile. Well, if you can't do that yourself, let's cancel the trip."

It struck me to the heart, for she was dead right. I have indeed lectured to all my nearest and dearest on the necessity of doing what you have agreed to do with good grace and a smile. The trouble is that I am one of that common breed of human being who finds it very easy to strew noble little homilies far and wide but considerably less easy to follow those homilies himself. After Janet had told me this, I must admit I remained just as frightened as before, but I was careful not to let it show.

We embarked on the *France* on May 30, 1974. It was the last cruise for the *France*, for just before landfall, the announcement reached us that the French government was tired of taking a loss and was selling the ship.

We remained in Great Britain for a week and a half and then sailed back on the *Queen Elizabeth 2*. The whole trip took three weeks and, if we except my army career, this was the longest time I ever stayed away from home, though it was equaled four years later by my California trip, which I have already discussed.

I must admit we greatly enjoyed the luxury of the giant ocean liners and, in particular, the food. On the *QE2*, I devoured caviar every chance I had, while Janet loved the chocolate soufflés. We both reveled in beef Wellington, and a lucky thing too, for, as we found out, as one grows older the doctors take you off any kind of food that tastes good, and it's just as well we ate it while we could.

In England, we saw bluebells in the New Forest and a magnificent double rainbow in the Forest of Dean. We visited Stonehenge, Stratford on Avon, and every cathedral we came across. I ate every kind of traditional English food I could find, from shepherd's pie to sausage rolls and from steak and kidney pie to treacle tarts.

In London, I visited Faraday's laboratory and lecture hall (just down the street from Brown's Hotel, where we were staying). When we visited Westminster Abbey, I cried at Newton's grave and saw in its vicinity the graves of four others of the world's greatest scientists.

Quite by accident we saw Queen Elizabeth in a coach with horsemen in red uniform before and after, and discovered something about such equine processions I never saw or heard mentioned. They left the street awash in fresh horse manure.

I signed books in London and in Birmingham and, of course, I gave a talk to Mensans, with Arthur C. Clarke introducing me with genial insults (which, you can bet, I returned in my own speech).

After I began giving lectures on the *QE2*, Janet and I made two more Atlantic crossings. Since I had no interest in remaining in Europe, we planned to stay on the ship, but that could not be done. *All* passengers had to get off the ship in Southampton, even if only to spend one night ashore and then get back on. The ship was officially "dead" while in Southampton, with all power turned off.

So though my second trip across the Atlantic on the *QE2* was delightful, I lived in apprehension over what would take place at Southampton. What if we somehow didn't manage to get back to the ship the next morning and it sailed without us? As usual, these foolish fears of mine turned out to be more foolish even than they sounded. We did *not* miss the ship but returned in time.

I cannot explain, by the way, why I should have this constant fear of being late or getting lost or both. I have almost never been late for anything in my life and I have never been seriously lost. Why I should treat with such anxiety troubles with which I have had no experience?

Might it be because my mother was always so anxious over me that I knew I must never stay away even one minute over my allotted time or she would die a thousand deaths? Very possibly! My own anxiety over the possible lateness of Robyn or Janet has communicated itself to them, so that *they* are never late either, at least under conditions when I am expecting them. It seems a silly and even wicked way of burdening those you love, and since I was always conscious that my mother's fears were an unwelcome pressure on me, I'm amazed that I should, in my turn, have done it to wife and daughter. —But it's no use lecturing me, I couldn't help it.

I even trained Gertrude in the great doctrine of "Never be late." She objected at first, saying it was ridiculous to hurry, but I reminded her that on the most recent occasion we had met a train, we got there with just one minute to spare before the train left and we had to sprint down the station, dragging our baggage. "We get there early," I said, "to *avoid* hurrying," and she saw my point.

But to get back to our trip— We had a great time in Southampton, which to New York eyes seemed extraordinarily clean. We even did a little traveling and looked through Winchester Cathedral and visited Nelson's flagship, *Victory,* in Portsmouth Harbor. One taxi driver, a young woman, said, "You don't want to take a taxi for that trip. It would cost you five pounds."

"That's all right," I said. "I'm a rich American." So she took us where we were going and I tipped her generously for her concern for my wallet against her own best interests.

The third time we made the Atlantic crossing on the *QE2,* Janet petrified me by suggesting that we get off at Cherbourg, France, where the ship docked before it crossed the Channel to Southampton. We could then remain in France for a full day and a half before it would be necessary to board the ship again. What's more, Janet proposed to use the time to go to Paris in the evening of our disembarkation, on September 18, 1979, stay the night, the next day, and another night, and then come back to Cherbourg to catch the return trip.

I did not expect to like Paris, having been told that the French despised anyone who couldn't speak French fluently and that they particularly despised Americans. I was all set, therefore, to get into a rage at the Parisians, but as a matter of fact, I *loved* Paris. A friend had given me two tickets to the Folies-Bergère, but I saw no point to it. Unclad French girls looked no different from unclad American girls. Instead, we walked slowly down the full length of the Champs-Elysées on a perfect night and observed the passing parade. We saw the Arc de

Triomphe and the Eiffel Tower. I wouldn't go up the Eiffel Tower because the structure looked too open and rickety.

We saw the Cathedral of Notre Dame, museums, ate at several excellent restaurants, and, in short, squeezed as much out of thirty-six hours as we could, but I saw no skin shows and Janet did no shopping. And, as I said, we caught the ship.

Before leaving the subject of my travels, I would like to add a few sidelights.

My liking for a place with four seasons was proven to me on one of our Caribbean trips that took place in February. The heat down there at a time when I should have been experiencing cold I found most enervating. As we bore northward through the Atlantic, I exulted as the temperature dropped, though everyone else groaned. I looked forward to setting foot on the New York City docks with the temperature well below freezing. —Not a chance! We happened to come back on a February day when the temperature was 60 F. Words cannot describe my annoyance.

Our last trip on the *QE2*, in July 1981, was the first time the *QE2* had reached Quebec, so there were thousands of people lined up along the river for miles to see us pull in and then, again, pull out. When we pulled out, a fleet of small ships accompanied us quite a distance down the broad St. Lawrence River, like minnows in the wake of a whale, a most unusual sight indeed.

One of the annoyances of ocean travel is, of course, the necessity of having one's baggage pored over by customs inspectors on one's return. Janet and I are not much on foreign purchases. We don't buy liquor, of course, so that the low prices are no inducement to us and that eliminates one great source of customs. Nor do we feel it necessary to shop for bales and bales of clothing and gimcracks that we don't need or can get at home. Usually we show up with a few paperback books and, occasionally, a sweater or a scarf. We invariably fall below the minimum allowed. One inspector, looking at our list, said, "Ah, the last of the big-time spenders."

A last word—

I am frequently asked, when the subject of my travels comes up, whether I have ever visited Israel.

No, I haven't. Getting to Israel without flying would be too complicated a matter. I would have to go by ship and train and I am certain that to try to do so would take up far more time than I could afford and be far more complex than I could endure.

The assumption, however, is that if I don't go, or can't go, then, because I am Jewish, I must be heartbroken, for I must *want* to visit Israel. —But I don't.

I am not, in actual fact, a Zionist. I don't think that Jews have some sort of ancestral right to take over a land because their ancestors lived there 1,900 years ago. (That kind of reasoning would force us to hand over North and South America to the Native Americans and Australia and New Zealand to the Aborigines and Maoris.) Nor do I consider to be legally valid the biblical promises by God that the land of Canaan would belong to the Children of Israel forever. (Especially since the Bible was written by the Children of Israel.)

When Israel was first founded in 1948 and all my Jewish friends were jubilant, I was the skeleton at the feast. I said, "We are building ourselves a ghetto. We will be surrounded by tens of millions of Muslims who will never forgive, never forget, and never go away."

I was right, especially when it soon turned out that the Arabs were sitting on most of the world's oil supply, so that the nations of the world, being pro-oil of necessity, found it politic to become pro-Arab. (Had this matter of oil reserves been known earlier, I'm convinced that Israel would not have been established in the first place.)

But don't the Jews deserve a homeland? Actually, I feel that no human group deserves a "homeland" in the usual sense of the word.

The Earth should not be cut up into hundreds of different sections, each inhabited by a self-defined segment of humanity that considers its own welfare and its own "national security" to be paramount above all other considerations.

I am all for cultural diversity and would be willing to see each recognizable group value its cultural heritage. I am a New York patriot, for instance, and if I lived in Los Angeles, I would love to get together with other New York expatriates and sing "Give My Regards to Broadway."

This sort of thing, however, should remain cultural and benign. I'm against it if it means that each group despises others and lusts to wipe them out. I'm against arming each little self-defined group with weapons with which to enforce its own prides and prejudices.

The Earth faces environmental problems right now that threaten the imminent destruction of civilization and the end of the planet as a livable world. Humanity cannot afford to waste its financial and emotional resources on endless, meaningless quarrels between each group and all others. There must be a sense of globalism in which the world unites to solve the *real* problems that face all groups alike.

Can that be done? The question is equivalent to: Can humanity survive?

I am not a Zionist, then, because I don't believe in nations, and because Zionism merely sets up one more nation to trouble the world. It sets up one more nation to have "rights" and "demands" and "national security" and to feel it must guard itself against its neighbors.

There are no nations! There is only humanity. And if we don't come to understand that right soon, there will be no nations, because there will be no humanity.

131

Martin Harry Greenberg

Sometime in 1972, I received a letter from a Martin Greenberg in Florida. He was doing an anthology and wanted to use two stories of mine. The matter seemed so routine and unimportant to me at the time that I didn't mention it in my diary, and so I don't know on exactly what day the letter was received. That is too bad, for it was the beginning of an extraordinarily close friendship.

I couldn't have foreseen that at the time, of course, not only because I can't look into the future but because I immediately thought of a disturbing possibility. It was Martin Greenberg who had owned Gnome Press and who had, a quarter century earlier, been the first to publish *I, Robot* and the three books of the Foundation series. He had also, as a matter of fact, published several anthologies, and stories of mine had been reprinted in two of them. My relationship with Martin Greenberg had not been a happy one and I was in no mood to reinstate it.

Still, a quarter century had passed, and neither Martin nor Greenberg was an uncommon name. Besides, the letter had been addressed "Dear Dr. Asimov" and surely the previous Martin Greenberg would have begun with a "Dear Isaac."

So in my reply I asked, "Are you the Martin Greenberg who—?"

He wasn't. The gentleman from Florida was Martin Harry Greenberg, and he had been born in 1941, so that he had only been nine years old when *I, Robot* was published. I promptly gave him permission to anthologize my stories and the exchange of letters established friendly relations between us. This is not surprising, since, as I soon found out, Marty (which is how I always refer to him now) is as congenitally friendly a person as I am.

I was not the only one to fuss over Marty's name. It was a stumbling block to his entry into the science fiction world, although he didn't realize it at first. There were, after all, a number of people whose relationship with the first Martin Greenberg had been unsatisfactory.

David Kyle, for instance, had been a partner with the first Martin Greenberg in the management of Gnome Press, and Dave felt he had been ill used. So strongly did he feel this that when he had occasion to visit Marty for the first time, and thinking (as I had) that he might conceivably be the first Greenberg, he arrived with the intention of punching him in the jaw. And to make the punch more authoritative, he carried a roll of quarters in his fist.

Lester del Rey, I understand, warned Marty that he would be well advised to change his name, but I felt that was going unnecessarily far. My advice was that he simply use his middle name, Harry, in connection with his science fiction work, and this he did.

The whole matter became moot with time, however, for Marty has become so famous in science fiction circles that the name Martin Greenberg now applies only to him. The first person of that name is completely obscured and I doubt that any person who lacks my patriarchal age and tenacious memory remembers him.

Even I, who, for some years, addressed all my letters to Marty "Dear Marty, the Other," eventually gave up that habit and "Dear Marty" is now sufficient.

Shortly after I made his epistolary acquaintance, Marty moved to

Green Bay, Wisconsin, which was the hometown of his wife, Sally. There he obtained a position on the faculty of the University of Wisconsin, where he is now a professor of political science and where he teaches science fiction in addition.

He is highly thought of by the college administration, is popular with the student body, and is in all respects an academic success, and yet (as in my case) it was in his avocation that he proceeded to find his real fame. His childhood love of science fiction grew with the years and there are very few people now who can match his knowledge of the field. (He knows much more about it than I do, for instance.)

Marty is a tall fellow and he is large besides. In 1989 (partly as a result of the gentle, but steady nagging of Janet and myself) he undertook a slimming program that shaved sixty pounds off him, but no one would, even now, speak of him as slim.

He is genial, friendly, hardworking, and is utterly to be trusted. I know him well and am absolutely convinced that it is impossible to be more honest and truthful than he is. As I shall explain, there are occasions when he must handle sums of money, part of which is mine, and my part is duly and quickly paid over. For a while, Marty insisted on accompanying each check with a detailed accounting, but I couldn't bear to see him waste his time on such nonsense and I finally persuaded him (with a great deal of trouble) to send me the checks bare, so to speak. I needed no accounting—at least not from him.

It works the other way around too. On rare occasions, I must send him some money. At first, Marty would send me a painstaking account of how the money had to be distributed and to whom, but I managed to persuade him that it was sufficient merely to let me know how large a check I should write out and that I would take the accounting for granted. —And no, in all our relationship, I haven't worried for one second that I was being cheated, either coming or going. I might as well worry that the dawn won't break tomorrow.

Marty's wife, Sally, a schoolteacher, had two daughters by a previous marriage. Marty loved her dearly and raised the two daughters as though they were his own. Sally was a quiet self-contained person who, like me, hated to leave home. It was for her sake that Marty transplanted himself to Green Bay.

He usually traveled without her, at her choice, so, since I don't travel either, I had the chance to meet her on only one occasion. This was in July 1982, when Marty and Sally accompanied us on a Bermuda cruise. They were marvelous company for us.

However, Sally died of kidney cancer on June 10, 1984, at the age of forty-seven, and for a time Marty was inconsolable. At that time, I got into the habit of phoning him frequently to make sure he was getting along and to give him a chance to spend fifteen to thirty minutes at idle chatter that would, at least temporarily, get him out of any blue funk he might find himself in. The habit grew and eventually I was phoning him every night, and I still do, except when physical circumstances make it impossible (which isn't often).

Since Marty travels freely, he comes to New York on fairly numerous occasions, and when he does, we almost always get together and go out for a meal.

On January 2, 1985, I turned sixty-five and celebrated a "nonretirement birthday party," at which I asked everyone not to bring presents but to oblige me by not smoking. We invited over a hundred people to an elaborate Chinese meal (at a good restaurant, for I never entertain at home). We deliberately invited people mainly from the metropolitan area, but Marty came in from Green Bay specially for the occasion.

It was a good thing he did too, for he had known a young woman named Rosalind in very casual fashion, and he seized the occasion of his being in New York to arrange a date with her. One thing led to another, rapidly. I met Rosalind on May 24, 1985, when the four of us had dinner. I approved heartily, and on August 28, 1985, they were married. It seems to me to be a second happy marriage for Marty, and it gives me a warm feeling to know that I was the occasion for it, however indirectly.

Rosalind Greenberg is a very pretty woman, just as genial and friendly as Marty is. She is also tall and large, with a tendency toward overweight. She is an ardent horsewoman and has recently even bought a share of a horse. I view that with extreme concern, for my taste in animals runs exclusively to cats, but Marty is considerably more permissive than I am. Perhaps he may enjoy having a horse-in-law, so to speak.

In July 1986, Marty and Rosalind came to the Rensselaerville Institute and had such a good time, and were so liked by everyone, that I was sure they would become regulars—but something even happier intervened. On July 1, 1987, just before the next Rensselaerville session, Rosalind gave birth to a girl, who they named Madeline, and they have not been able to join us at the seminar since.

Marty was forty-six at this time and it was his first biological child.

It is not hard to tell, even on the telephone, how wildly devoted he is to his daughter. From the photographs he strews about, to say nothing of what I hear of Madeline on the telephone, she is clearly the kind of little girl who is just made to wind herself about her father's heart. (I have a very good knowledge of daughters who have that ability.)

But it's time to get to Marty's professional connection with me. Marty is an anthologist. His encyclopedic knowledge of science fiction, and of other types of genre fiction, too, has enabled him to prepare many anthologies in science fiction, fantasy, horror, mystery, Western, and other fields. Since that first letter of his to me, he has published nearly four hundred anthologies, and there is no question that he is far and away the most prolific and, in addition, the best anthologist the world has ever seen.

He has the knack of thinking up useful "theme" anthologies—that is, collections of stories that cluster about some particular subject. What's more, he has the ability to persuade editors and publishers to do these anthologies. What is still more, he has the industry required to obtain permissions, negotiate contracts, take care of all payments, and disperse them to co-editors and to authors.

In all of this, Marty usually works with co-editors, who are always writers in the field of the anthology, who have names that are valuable on the book covers, but who don't have the time, the energy, or the inclination, or all three, to do the scut work involved.

I'm a natural for this sort of thing, and Marty and I have co-edited over a hundred anthologies.

Marty is under the impression that it is my name that has gained him entrance into publishers' offices and that it is to me that he owes the fact that his income is steadily rising from year to year, but that's just his nonsense. For one thing, he has also co-edited anthologies with Robert Silverberg, Frederik Pohl, and Bill Pronzini, and any one of them could have given him the step-up.

He only needed the help of a companion name at the very start anyway. In a very short time, he became a power of his own. He has been guest of honor at various conventions, has received numerous awards, and finds an instant welcome in the offices of every publisher in the country.

I have told him quite firmly that if I were to retire from the anthology business, he could go right on without a hitch or a hiccup. On the other hand, if he retired, I would be stopped cold. I could not possibly do more than a very occasional anthology without him. Nor would I be likely to work with anyone else, for there is no one else I would trust to display the industry, the reliability, the competence, and the absolute trustworthiness that Marty does.

(Marty has, on some occasions, said that he considers me a surrogate father, especially after his own father died a few years ago at the age of eighty-six. It's not too grotesque a thought. Marty is twenty-one years younger than I am, and I must admit that I feel somewhat as though he is my son.)

Sometimes Marty and I work alone, but usually we add a third party. The third party we work with most frequently is Charles E. Waugh, who is a professor of psychology at a university in Maine. (It is odd that we three co-editors of dozens of science fiction anthologies should all be professors.) Charles is a tall, shy fellow, whom I have met only rarely. He is almost painfully polite and I can't get him to call me Isaac. He has a charming wife who is crazy about teddy bears and they have a daughter of beauty-contest caliber, whom they have never let me meet.

Here's the way things work with us. Charles has a knowledge of science fiction that is as encyclopedic as Marty's. Together they select stories for a particular anthology and prepare xeroxes. All the stories are sent to me and I read them over carefully, since I have veto rights and any story I don't like is instantly eliminated. I must admit, though, that I am chary of making use of that veto. I might not like a story and yet it might be well written, and I must place the writing above my own tastes.

I then write a more or less elaborate introduction to the anthology and, very often, headnotes for each story. Marty takes care of all the financial and legal details, as I've said before.

We split the editors' share into equal halves if Marty and I alone are involved, and into equal thirds if Charles is also involved. I consider it all to be an admirable division of labor.

Though the anthologies do not take as much time as the average book I write myself, they do take *some* time. They take more time, in fact, than many of my smaller children's books. So I add them to my list of books, but I am also honest about it. If it is appropriate to do so, I say, "I have published 451 books, of which 116 are anthologies of other people's stories."

I must stress one point, however. There would appear to be some people who are of the opinion that my sole function in these anthologies is to let my name be used and that I get a free ride. This is *not* so.

Any anthology on my list is one for which I have done significant work.

There are indeed books with my name in the title where I have done no work, where I have selected no stories and exerted no editorial function. Those are *not* listed among my books. If I have written an introduction to a book but have done no editorial work, I do not list it. Any book on the list is a book I have worked on either as a writer or as an editor, or as both.

But why do I do all these anthologies? Of what value are these endless collections of old stories?

Remember that many science fiction short stories (even very good ones) tend to fade into oblivion. The issues of the magazines in which they appeared are in landfills somewhere. Collections in which they may have appeared in book form are often out of print and unavailable. Anthologies bring back these old stories to an audience that has never read them, or perhaps to some who have indeed read them years or even decades before and would like the chance to read them again. Furthermore, writers, many of whom may be past their best years and may not be writing much, will have the benefit of having their early stories brought before the public, something that will brighten their fame and earn them a little extra money too.

I am willing to lend my name, and to do the work necessary to accomplish these things. I am very fortunate to be one of the handful of authors whose books continue to sell and whose stories, however old, continue to be reprinted. It is my pleasure and, even more, my *duty* to do what I can to help other writers not quite as well situated as I am.

And it's Marty who makes it possible for me to do so, and who does his further part in hundreds of anthologies in which I am not involved. As much as Marty is now appreciated by editors, writers, and readers, I cannot help but think that he is still not appreciated enough.

132

Isaac Asimov's Science Fiction Magazine

By the beginning of 1976, I had been writing Black Widower stories for *EQMM* for four years.

The publisher of the magazine is Joel Davis, not very tall, but slim and rather handsome, something that has not changed just because his hair is finally going gray. He always struck me as a rather proper person who was a little confused at my own raucous improprieties but had somehow grown accustomed to them.

One of the executives at Davis Publications had attended a *Star Trek* convention for the sake of his children and was struck by the vast number and the unbounded enthusiasm of the attendees. This, he thought, indicated that a science fiction magazine ought to make a great deal of money for Davis Publications.

In this, he was not necessarily right. What he failed to understand was that the vast majority of the Trekkies were interested in visual science fiction and not in print science fiction. The results, however, were not catastrophic, so we needn't be too concerned about that.

The executive sold Joel on his idea and Joel pondered the matter. He had two fiction magazines, both mystery—*Ellery Queen's Mystery Magazine* and *Alfred Hitchcock's Mystery Magazine*. If he was going to have a science fiction magazine he wanted a name in that too, to preserve the symmetry, and he wanted it, of course, to be a famous name in the field.

Inevitably, he thought of me. I was the one science fiction writer who had obtruded himself on his notice, since I flirted loudly and outrageously with Eleanor Sullivan, the very attractive managing editor of *EQMM*, whenever I visited the magazine.

So on February 26, 1976, he called me into his office and told me he was thinking of starting a new magazine to be called *Isaac Asimov's Science Fiction Magazine (IASFM)*.

I objected on a number of grounds, which I shall list:

1. I had no talent, time, or desire for editing and I simply wouldn't undertake to edit a magazine.

2. The other magazines were edited by friends of mine, in particular Ben Bova, who was then editor of *Analog*, and Edward Ferman, who was editor of *F&SF*. How could I go into competition with my friends?

3. I had a monthly science column in *F&SF*, which I could on no account abandon, not even for the chance of running a similar column in *IASFM*. I didn't try to explain this in detail because I have noticed that there is a certain air of incredulity or amusement in anyone to whom I talk about the importance of loyalty.

4. Authors would refuse to write for a magazine which bore the name of one of their peers. They would feel it beneath them to do so.

Patiently, Joel took up each of my objections. I wouldn't have to edit, he said. We would select an editor who would do the real work and I would confine myself to writing an editorial in each issue and answering the letters in the letters column. In that way, I would give an Asimovian flavor to the magazine, which was all that he wanted.

He agreed that I would continue my science column in *F&SF*, since that was nonfiction, if I would agree to let *IASFM* have first refusal on any of my science fiction.

He stated that since mystery writers were perfectly willing to write for Ellery Queen and for Alfred Hitchcock, science fiction writers would be perfectly willing to write for Isaac Asimov.

That left only the feelings of Ben Bova and Ed Ferman, and so I consulted each separately. Both said the same thing. An additional magazine would strengthen the field by supplying another major market for writers. Since this would encourage science fiction writing, the number of important contributions to all three magazines would increase.

Even so, I hesitated, and it took a great deal of persuasion for Joel to get me to sign the necessary contract. The first issue of the magazine, dated Spring 1977, reached the stands in mid-December 1976.

I mention all this because in 1986 the British science fiction writer Brian Aldiss wrote a history of science fiction, in which he had some harsh things to say about my writing. I didn't mind that. He is certainly welcome to indulge himself in that fashion if it makes him feel better.

However, he also made the insulting statement that I had managed to wheedle my way into having a magazine named for myself. I cannot quote his exact words since I discarded his book after reading that. I did, however, write to him and to his publisher in great indignation, for it was not I who had done the wheedling, but Joel. On January 5, 1987, I received a letter from him, apologizing humbly. That was all I wanted and I dropped the matter thereafter.

The magazine came out at a time when there had been a long interval since a really successful new magazine had been published. The most recent previous success had been *Galaxy*, which had appeared in 1950, and *If*, which had appeared in 1952 and which had eventually become a sister magazine of *Galaxy*. *If*, however, had ceased publication a few years earlier, and *Galaxy* itself was declining toward its demise. *Amazing* was a feeble shadow of what it had once been and was also on the point of dying. Many other magazines had come, existed briefly, and then ceased publication. In 1976, there were only two strong magazines still in the field, the two I had consulted before my own was started: *Analog* and *F&SF*.

What's more, the entire magazine field had weakened to some extent, partly because the ascendancy of television had withdrawn the weaker readers from the magazine audience and partly because the advent of hundreds of paperback novels, collections, and anthologies meant a sharper competition for the readers' money.

There seemed little reason, therefore, to think that *IASFM* would be successful and, since I am no phony, I said so in the editorial I wrote for the first issue. (It was all right for me to say so, of course, but not for others. The editor of one fan magazine predicted that the magazine would last for not more than six issues, whereupon I promptly told Joel to make every effort, even if he were losing money, to publish seven.)

No problem. The magazine is now in its fourteenth year of publication and the latest issue I have at the moment of writing is the 158th.

It began as a quarterly in its first year, advanced to a bimonthly in its second, and a monthly its third. It is now a tetraweekly, with one issue every four weeks and, therefore, thirteen issues a year.

And I have done my part. I have had a 1,500-word editorial in every issue; and I read all the letters to the editor, choose which I suggest be published, and write an answer to each. I show up at the offices every Tuesday morning to pick up letters, deliver editorials (together with stories, which I write for the magazine as often as I can), and discuss problems, when there are any.

Joel was sufficiently satisfied with science fiction to buy *Analog* on February 20, 1980, and sufficiently sensible to keep its excellent editor, Stanley Schmidt. I think he would also buy *F&SF*, if it were up for sale. Joel kept his word to me, by the way. For the full thirteen years-plus of the magazine's existence, I have continued to write my essays for *F&SF*. The situation has, I firmly believe, helped *F&SF* without harming *IASFM*.

I have not missed an issue as far as my editorials are concerned, and I do not ever fear that I will run out of things to say. Readers ask if the real editors want to write editorials sometimes, but they don't. It's a chore they do not wish to undertake, and that's a good thing, because (to tell you the truth) I wouldn't let them. The editorials are *mine* and I love writing them.

Sometimes my editorials discuss some phase of writing, sometimes they deal with science fiction. They are often intensely personal, to the point where some readers begin to grumble about my ego.

Every once in a while, I take up one side of a controversial issue. John Campbell used to do this constantly, to my despair, for he was unrelentingly conservative, and I disliked his biased approach. I, on the other hand, am markedly liberal, and my sort of bias doesn't bother me at all. It bothers some readers, however, but a little controversy is good, I think, and even essential in an open society such as ours, and I have no hesitation about directing the publication of letters that strongly disagree with me or that even include some uncomplimentary remarks about me.

The biggest reaction I got was when I owned up to a hatred of rock-and-roll music. The lovers of that vile noise took out after me with a vengeance. On the other hand, I once made the innocent remark that horses smelled (which they do) and I got letters from indignant horse lovers.

I don't want to leave the impression that I am responsible for the magazine's success, though I hope I have contributed to it somewhat. The credit belongs to the editors.

The first and founding editor was George Scithers, an important science fiction fan and amateur publisher, who had run the Washington convention in 1963, at which I had received my first Hugo. He established the magazine as a viable entity from the start, bringing into prominence such excellent new writers as John Varley, Barry Longyear, and Somtow Sucharitkul. He also strongly favored humorous short-shorts and rather turned away from the obscure and sensational. On September 4, 1978, when only four issues of the magazine had appeared, George won a Hugo as best editor of the year.

Unfortunately, George somehow never quite got along with Joel. The chemistry was wrong. After four years, George decided the magazine was a going venture and needed him no more. He was succeeded by Kathleen Moloney, a relative unknown in the field, who remained only a year before finding a job she liked better. She was succeeded by Shawna McCarthy, who had been managing editor under the first two. Shawna had amazed the dickens out of me when I licked my lips over having an Irish colleen to flirt with, by telling me that despite her name and her appearance, she was Jewish. She turned the magazine in a new direction, emphasizing the experimental and modernistic.

With that, the magazine became a critical success among the aficionados of the field, who had previously criticized it as being too light.

After Shawna left to enter the field of book editing, she was succeeded on May 17, 1985, by the science fiction writer Gardner Dozois, who is still editor and who has continued the Shawna direction. *IASFM* has come to be generally considered to be at the cutting edge of the field. Both Shawna and Gardner have won Hugos, and stories appearing in the magazine receive more nominations for Hugos and Nebulas than do stories in any other magazine.

I might also mention that for some seven years the day-to-day running of the magazine has been in the hands of the managing editor, Sheila Williams, a sweet young woman who sees eye to eye with me on all things connected with the magazine.

I don't say that my own taste in stories is exactly reflected in the magazine, but it is better that it not be. My taste is firmly rooted in the 1950s and I recognize that fact. I have, therefore, never tried to interfere with editorial decisions, or expressed my opinion on any question whatever unless I was asked to.

Once, for instance, in the fall of 1988, *IASFM* had made use of a cover illustration, quite innocently, that was a little too close to one that had earlier appeared in *F&SF,* painted by a different artist. Ed Ferman wanted a reasonable sum of money to be paid to the first artist, but Davis Publications didn't want to seem to admit wrongdoing. So I was asked, "What do we do?"

"Simple," I said, and sent off a *personal* check to the first artist and everything ended satisfactorily.

The stories I write for the magazine are, of course, my kind of 1950-ish stories, but enough readers like them to justify their publication. Besides, *I* like them, and that's all that counts as far as I'm concerned.*

133

Autobiography

Through the 1970s, the people at Doubleday were growing more and more impatient with me. They wanted me to return to the writing of science fiction novels, and, as the years passed, they grew more intense about it. The trouble was that I was afraid to write novels and, as those same years passed, I grew more intense about my fears.

I was quite aware of how the field was changing, of how totally literary the new writers had become, and despite Evelyn del Rey's assurance to me that I *was* the field, I dared not compete. The success of *The Gods Themselves* somehow did not help.

Therefore, I kept trying to think of ways to divert Doubleday's attention. On February 3, 1977, when my editor at the time, Cathleen Jordan, put the pressure on me a bit more firmly, I winced, thought rapidly, and suggested I write an autobiography. As soon as I

* Editor's note: In his next-to-last editorial in *Isaac Asimov's Science Fiction Magazine,* Isaac was pleased to announce to its readers that the magazine had been acquired by Bantam Doubleday Dell Publishing Group.

mentioned the possibility, I caught fire. Such was my sudden enthusiasm that Cathleen didn't see much chance of deflecting me and told me to go ahead.

(Cathleen, a delightful person, had worked for Larry Ashmead and had succeeded him as my editor when he left. Eventually, she left Doubleday too, and began to look for another job. I happened to know that Davis Publications was looking for a new editor for *Alfred Hitchcock's Mystery Magazine* at the time, and I mentioned Cathleen's name. She took the job on August 1, 1981, and has been happily at work there ever since. I've even sold her a couple of stories—editors can't get rid of me just by changing positions.)

The writing of an autobiography was not exactly a new idea to me. I remember that when I turned twenty-nine I felt that my youth was just about over and done with and that I might now legitimately turn to the writing of an autobiography. However, some cool thought on the matter made it plain to me that since not very much had happened to me, there was not much to say about my life—and besides, no publisher would publish it.

As my life progressed and I grew older, I eventually reached the point where I knew that if I did write an autobiography, I could get it published, but it still seemed to me that not very much had happened to me. Mine has been a quiet life (I have never complained about that), and I have been involved with little besides my writing, so there was still nothing to write about.

But an occasional editor would come up with the notion.

Larry Ashmead, for instance, wondered at one time if I had considered writing an autobiography, but I just laughed and said that nothing had ever happened to me that would interest anyone. Larry was so pro-Asimov that I couldn't take him seriously and I doubted that his superiors at Doubleday would support him in this particular project.

Some time after this, Paul Nadan, of Crown Publishers, was trying to get me to do a book for Crown and we got together to discuss the matter over lunch. I would have liked to do a book for Crown and, particularly, for Paul, who was a very pleasant and likable fellow, but my schedule was crowded and I hated to take on something that I then wouldn't do. I therefore tried to deflect him by telling him funny stories about various things that had happened to me.

Suddenly, he said, "Why don't you write an autobiography, Isaac?"

I said, "Because nothing of interest has ever happened to me."

He said, "But all these things you've been telling me are interesting and they would be wonderful in an autobiography. Come, I'll give you a contract for one."

I was tempted, but I resisted. I was terribly afraid I would make a fool of myself, and that I would turn out something that Crown, upon looking it over, would refuse to publish—or, if they published it, that people would refuse to read—or, if they read it, that they would denounce vociferously.

However, when Cathleen began to put the pressure on me for another science fiction novel, I remembered what Nadan had said, and suggested an autobiography. I was still certain it wouldn't work, but my enthusiasm grew over the matter, not because I wanted to do it, but because it would shove any question of a novel to one side for at least a year, maybe two. *Anything* to avoid a novel.

So I had to get to work. I had two things going for me in this connection. I have a remarkably retentive memory and tend to remember things in full detail. This is not always a good thing, of course. Samuel Vaughan, who was then high in the echelons of Doubleday, told me that the art of autobiography was knowing what to leave out, but he was talking to a brick wall and he probably knew it. I didn't intend to leave anything out if I could help it, except for items that might needlessly hurt other people.

Even if my memory failed me, I had a second thing going for me. I had started keeping a diary on January 1, 1938, the day before my eighteenth birthday, and I have been keeping one ever since. (Many young people start diaries, but very few, I believe, keep it going for longer than a few weeks.) To be sure, my diary, after the first year, tended to grow skimpy and to confine itself to a dry accounting of what I was doing with my writing. Some people use a diary to record their feelings and thoughts, but I never did. It was purely a reference book and so dull that even *I* couldn't read it with any interest. I used it only to look up dates and events. The advantage is that I don't have to keep it under lock and key. Anyone can read it who wishes and I defy him, or her, to last more than five pages without brain damage.

The autobiography grew and grew, and I must admit that even I began to have misgivings when I had written 50,000 words and had barely reached the point at which my diary began. If I could write so much out of memory alone, what would I write once I had my diary to help out?

What's more, actually getting down to it and writing the autobiography proved to me that I was right—my life lacked elements of high drama. As you can see from reading this retrospective overview of my existence, the big excitement consists of things like failing to get into medical school and like having a fight with the authorities at Boston University. This is scarcely the material out of which heart-stopping suspense is built.

However, since I realized this, I concentrated on other things. I tried to follow Paul Nadan's suggestion and wrote about everyday things lightheartedly. I depended on my writing ability to mask the unimportance of events generally.

A reader once told me, enthusiastically, after the autobiography was published, that he had read the book with intense interest and that he had been unable to keep from turning the pages and reading on and on and on, laughing all the way.

I said to him, curiously, "Didn't you notice that nothing was happening?"

"I noticed that," he said, "but I didn't care."

(I get that same sort of response when I ask readers if they had noticed that nothing ever happened in the way of whizbang action in my novels. Well, if they don't care, I certainly don't.)

Another thing I did, in my attempt to make the autobiography unusual, was to make it strictly chronological. I could do this, thanks to my diary.

In other words, I tried to describe the story of my life exactly as I had lived it, with different threads all jumbled together and with no foreknowledge indicated as to what was to happen in the future. This, I thought, would lend an air of realism to the account and was something that (to my knowledge) no other autobiographer had ever attempted, at least not with the intensity that I did.

In presenting the matter chronologically, moreover, I tried to make it as factual (and funny) as possible and avoided overmuch subjectivity. I discussed the events that impinged on me externally, but gave comparatively little attention to the thoughts and responses that boiled within me.

By the time I was finished and had carried the tale of my life up through the end of 1977 (which was when I finished the book) I had written 640,000 words, enough to make nine novels the length of *The Caves of Steel*.

I worried about what Cathleen would say when I brought it in. I dreaded the words "We'll have to cut this in half, Isaac," and I prepared myself to say, "No, I can't allow that."

I felt quite certain that I would have to walk away with the manuscript and that I would then have to try to peddle it to Crown or to Houghton Mifflin. Woefully, as I looked at the boxes of manuscript, I felt that I would never sell it anywhere.

Nevertheless, I brought it in to Doubleday with as much confidence as I could manage to pump into my expression and bearing, and said, "Here it is, Cathleen. All of it." (I hadn't told her how long it was getting to be, and since it had only taken me nine months to write it, she had no reason to expect anything more than novel length.)

She took one horrified look at the boxes and consulted Sam Vaughan, who earned my lifelong gratitude by saying, "Well, then, do it in two volumes."

And so it was done. The first volume was published in 1979, and the second in 1980.

There was some discussion over the title. I wanted to call it *As I Remember,* which was accurately descriptive, but the Doubleday people wanted something more dramatic, something that sounded more like the title of a novel. I was at a loss, and said, "Like what?"

Someone (possibly Sam) said, "Find some obscure bit of poetry and use a quotation from it as a title."

So I came up with the following obscure bit:

> In memory yet green, in joy still felt,
> The scenes of life rise sharply into view.
> We triumph; Life's disasters are undealt,
> And while all else is old, the world is new.

I had a vague idea of what it meant, and it seemed suitable to me. So I called the first volume of my autobiography *In Memory Yet Green* and the second volume *In Joy Still Felt.*

I would like to carry on this bit of cribbing by entitling the present retrospective volume, which might be looked upon as a third volume of my autobiography, *The Scenes of Life,* but whether that will survive editorial tampering, I can't say.

As the first volume was being published, I received a plaintive call from Doubleday. They had not been able to locate the source of the verse I had used and they needed to know the author's name. I told them the truth, as is my wont, and said, "I wrote it myself." As a result, they ascribed the verse, in both volumes, to that extraordinarily prolific poet: "Anon."

A satisfactory number of readers, after the appearance of the first volume, bombarded me with queries as to when the second volume would appear. Once the second volume appeared, I began to get questions as to when the third volume would appear. I invariably answered, "I have to *live* the third volume first."

It was my intention to write a third volume in the year 2000 (a nice round figure) as a way of celebrating my eightieth birthday. Circumstances, however, which I will tell you about later, dictated that I do it to celebrate my seventieth birthday instead.

In Memory Yet Green was, by the way, my 200th book. However, I had also written *Opus 200* for Houghton Mifflin, and that was my 200th book. Doubleday was not willing to allow Houghton Mifflin to glory in the 200 mark, and so I said (I always seek a simple solution) that there was no reason I couldn't count *both* books as 200 and let the next book be 202.

Both publishers agreed to that and they even put in a joint advertisement in *The New York Times Book Review* announcing both books. It may have been the only time two publishers had combined their talents in a single advertisement.

134

Heart Attack

My father, as I said earlier in this book, developed angina pectoris at forty-two. One does get superstitious about the possibility of repeating one's father's life, at least as far as physical ailments are concerned. Therefore, I was a little concerned as my forty-second birthday approached.

It came and went, however, and I passed my forty-third and forty-fourth birthdays without any sign of chest pains. Nevertheless, I was nervous enough about the whole thing to start a campaign of weight reduction in 1944 that, as the decades passed, was finally to see me at sixty pounds under my peak at the time of this writing.

I even passed my fifty-seventh birthday with no signs of trouble, but on May 9, 1977, as I was running errands in the neighborhood, I felt a distinct discomfort under my breastbone and a shortage of breath. I stopped walking and the symptoms disappeared. I started walking and they reappeared.

I experienced a chill, for I knew what it was. I had escaped my father's affliction for fifteen years, but now that I was fifty-seven it had finally caught up with me. I was suffering from angina pectoris. A life in which I had, for the most part, eaten too much and too unwisely had succeeded in clogging my coronary arteries to the point where my heart muscle was being placed on short rations as far as oxygen was concerned.

I wasn't sure what to do. I ought to have consulted Paul Esserman at once, but I was in the middle of a heavy speaking schedule and I didn't want that interrupted. After all, my father had lived thirty years with angina, and I might too, and fifty-seven plus thirty equaled eighty-seven, which is a good lifetime. So I decided to let it go for a while till my spate of talks was over and, meanwhile, I intended to be careful how I walked so that Janet wouldn't notice that anything was wrong.

I continued with my schedule, then, and on May 16 we drove to Haverford University, outside Philadelphia, where I was to give a commencement address the next day. (That was the occasion on which I was told to speak for fifteen minutes, and a student timing me found I spoke for fourteen minutes thirty-two seconds, even though I never looked at my watch.)

After the address, we drove to Philadelphia, where I was slated to give two more talks, and at 1:30 A.M. of May 18, 1977, I suddenly sat bolt upright in bed, jolted out of my sleep by a sharp bout of what seemed to be super-indigestion. It was a pain as intense as that of a kidney stone, but it was in the wrong place, the upper abdomen.

Unable to lie, sit, or stand (as in the case of a bad kidney-stone attack), I gasped out to Janet that I wanted no weeping and wailing if I died, that she was to live on cheerfully, and that my will would take care of her and my children for the rest of their lives.

She gave me an antispasmodic and at 3 A.M. the pain began to ebb away, just as it did after a kidney-stone attack. When it was gone, I got back into bed with a feeling of incredible relief over the fact that I was free of pain.

"How do you feel, Isaac?" asked Janet timorously.

"Right now? As if I'd died and gone to heaven," I whispered, and drifted off to sleep.

I still felt rather poorly the next day, but I paid no attention to Janet's demands that I see a doctor. The show must go on, so I gave my two talks. (One of them, as it happened, was to a bunch of cardiologists, and not one of them divined from my expression and bearing what had happened to me two nights before.)

On the evening of the eighteenth, while we were still in Philadelphia, Janet called Paul Esserman and described what had happened. Paul was impressed by my insistence that the abdominal pain was very similar to that of kidney stones, and he speculated that I might have had a gallstone attack because the pain disappeared after the antispasmodic. (I didn't tell him or Janet about my anginal attacks.) Paul urged me to see him as soon as I got home.

Once we got back to New York on the twentieth, Janet wanted me to see Paul at once, but I suspected trouble and I refused. I had a luncheon date with Sam Vaughan and Ken McCormick of Doubleday for May 25, and I didn't want to miss that because I intended to hint that my autobiography might be a long one so that I could get them used to the idea.

From the lunch I walked to Paul's office, about half a mile away, and ran up the stairs, just to see if I could. Paul took an electrocardiogram, and the expression on his face the instant the needle started moving told me all I wanted to know (or didn't want to know, actually). I had not had a gallstone attack; it had been a heart attack.

"How bad?" I asked.

"Not too bad, since you are still alive after running up the stairs," said Paul. "Why did you do that? How would I have felt if you had had a cardiac arrest as you walked through my door?"

"Not as bad as I would have felt," I said. "But as long as it's not too bad, I'll just go about my business."

"No, you don't, Isaac. You'll go into the hospital right now."

"I can't," I said, "I have to give a commencement address at Johns Hopkins day after tomorrow."

"No, you won't."

"Why not? I've lived a week. I can live two days more."

"What if you die on the platform as you give your talk?"

"It will be a professional death," I said firmly.

That seemed to rouse Paul terribly. Physicians seem to think they're the only ones who have professional duties. He ran out into the street, hailed a taxi, and he (with my traitorous wife, Janet) shoved me into it. Within half an hour I was in intensive care.

Just before the deed was done, I called Cathleen Jordan to tell her the news and to assure her that I intended to stay alive despite the worst that the doctors could do. I then left it to Janet to call up Johns Hopkins to explain why I would have to leave them in the lurch, and to cancel some other engagements too.

It was the first time I had ever canceled speaking engagements and the Johns Hopkins cancellation was intensely embarrassing to me. I eventually wrote them a letter of apology in which I said that I owed them one talk without charge. In 1989, the university called in the debt and, though twelve years had passed, I came through. I went to Baltimore and delivered a talk without charge.

In 1977 Ben Bova pitched in and gave some of my talks for me, doing a great job. But then the villain had the nerve to ask those in charge of the speaking engagements to send the checks to *me*. Fortunately, they called me in the hospital to see if they were really supposed to do that, and I was furious. Ben had to keep the checks himself, and serve him right.

I hadn't been in the hospital long before it was clear that I was in no need of intensive care. What I needed was rest and recuperation, and Paul Esserman insisted that I have sixteen days of it. After three hours of it, I was dreadfully bored and said so. —Voluminously.

Paul consulted Janet, who told him I was working on the first draft of my autobiography and that I would stay in the hospital happily if she could bring it in so that I could edit it. The only trouble was that there was only one copy and Janet was afraid of losing it or of having something happen to it in transit or in the hospital.

She therefore brought it to Doubleday, which had it photocopied for the record, so that it could be reproduced if anything happened to it, and she then brought it to the hospital. Day after day, I worked on it, and it was so wonderful to feel that I wasn't wasting time.

Ben Bova visited me and, noticing the manuscript spread out over the bed, asked what I was doing. I explained. "In this autobiography," I said, "I'm including every stupid thing I can remember having said or done."

"Oh?" he said, eyeing the pages. "No wonder it's so long."

Working on my autobiography kept me so cheerful that the residents who came to see me every morning remarked on it wonderingly. The cardiology department was usually filled with depressed people (and having a heart attack is no great cause for elation), so my laughing and joke telling became a topic for awed breakfast conversation.

On only one day—the first Sunday in the hospital—did I break down. I was alone with Janet and a wave of depression swept over me. It had dawned on me that Paul might tell me that I would have to cut down my activities to half of what they had been, so that for the rest of my life I would be forced to work only part-time. That meant, I predicted mournfully, that my 1977 income would represent a peak and that thereafter it would go down steadily and my plans for supporting my wife and children after my death would be placed in peril.

That was bad enough, but something else bothered me too. When I was first placed in the hospital, Paul asked me if I wanted it kept confidential.

"Confidential?" I said. "Why?"

"Some people feel that if the world knows they have had a heart attack they are discriminated against, and don't get jobs or assignments to do work."

I laughed and said, "Nonsense. Tell anyone you please about it. I shall undoubtedly write articles about it." (And so I did.)

But on that Sunday, it suddenly seemed to me that Paul was right and that editors would now avoid me, feeling that giving me assignments was useless if I were likely to drop dead any minute.

Janet consoled me as best she could, and, as a matter of fact, the fears I had were temporary. They vanished before the day was over and never returned. Nor were they justified.

My writing labors have continued at full steam in all the years since the heart attack. As for 1977 representing my peak income, no year since has failed to do far better than that year.

And would editors cease asking me for material?

While I was lying in my hospital bed, I got a call from Merill Panitt, editor-in-chief of *TV Guide*, for whom I had written a number of essays. He asked how I was doing and I said I was coming along well.

He said, "Good. And listen, as long as you're lying in a hospital bed with nothing to do, would you mind watching some daytime television and writing an essay on it?"

I did just that and he accepted it. I could see that if I were given assignments while I was actually in the hospital, I would have no trouble getting them once I was out.

Of course, Paul did insist on my cutting down in one respect.

"Isaac," he said, "two things. First, you must cut down on your speaking engagements. They take a lot out of you. Just give fewer talks and raise your fees so you don't lose income, and don't let personal friends talk you into giving talks for nothing. Do you understand?"

"Yes," I said, "and what's the second thing."

"My group, the New York University Medical School Alumni Association, would like you to give them a talk. Would you?"

I burst out laughing. It was for nothing, of course, but I accepted the talk instantly, for two reasons. First, because Janet was also an alumna, and second, because Paul seemed completely unaware of the mutual exclusivity of his two points.

I eventually gave the talk on May 12, 1979, and I told the story of the two points, imitating Paul's distinctive voice, and that evoked gales of laughter. It seems also that all the alumni wore badges that gave the month and year of their graduation. Paul had graduated during World War II in an accelerated course and he got out in the month of March, which was unusual. I asked him why he alone seemed to have an M on his badge and he explained.

But that's not the way I told it. What I said was this: "I said to Paul, 'Why do you have an M on your badge, Paul?' and he answered, 'It stands for "mediocre." ' " More gales of laughter (especially since he was, in actual fact, an honor student), and I felt I had punished him adequately for having pushed me into the hospital, making me miss the Johns Hopkins commencement.

(Paul forever threatens to sue me for something he calls "patient malpractice.")

Once I got out of the hospital, I lived life normally, except that I took better care of myself. Even so, I would occasionally feel a twinge of angina when I walked too rapidly, and I would stop to let it pass.

When I wrote up the tale of my heart attack in the second volume of my autobiography, one of the reviewers said that I had described it "with characteristic lack of self-pity."

I was glad he had noticed. As I have made plain in this book, I detest self-pity, and when I find myself falling into it, I make every possible effort to fight it off.

And, after all, what reason have I to feel self-pity? What if I had not survived? I had had a reasonably good life, a secure childhood, loving parents, excellent schooling, a happy marriage, a delightful daughter, and a successful career. I had had some disappointments and sadness in my life, but, I honestly think, far less than is true for the average human being, and I have had far more success and gladness than most.

Even had I died at fifty-seven, my life would still have been a full one, especially with regard to Janet and to my writing, and it would have been disgusting of me to have complained. And, as it happened, I continued to live, and continued to have Janet and writing success, and all the various other good things that have so greatly outnumbered the evil things that I have less reason than ever to complain or to feel self-pity.

It seems to me that people who believe in immortality through transmigration of souls have a tendency to think that they were all Julius Caesar or Cleopatra in the past and that they will be equally prominent in the future. Surely, that can't be so. Since some 90 percent of the human race lives (and has always, in time past, lived) in various degrees of poverty and misery, the chances are weighed against any transmigrating personality ending up in happiness. If my personality, on my death, were to transfer into the body of a newborn baby, chosen at random, the chances that I would lead a new life that was far more miserable than the one I had left would be enormous. It's a roulette game that I do not wish to play.

Many people believe that good people are assured a better life at death and wicked people a worse one. If that were true I would strongly suspect that I must have been a very good person in a past life to have deserved the happy life I have led this time, and if I continue to be noble and virtuous, I will have a still happier life the next time. And where will it end? Why, in that happiest state of all—Nirvana; that is, nothingness.

But it is my opinion that we all achieve Nirvana at once, at the moment of the death that ends a single life. Since I have had a good life, I'll accept death as cheerfully as I can when it comes, although I would be glad to have that death painless. I would also be glad to have my survivors—relatives, friends, and readers—refrain from wasting their time and poisoning their lives in useless mourning and unhappiness. They should be happy instead, on my behalf, that my life has been so good.

135
Crown Publishers

I felt rather guilty at doing the autobiography for Doubleday when it had been Paul Nadan of Crown who had first offered me a contract for it, so I let Paul talk me into signing a contract to do a book on the possibility of life and intelligence elsewhere in the Universe. It was to be called *Extraterrestrial Civilizations*. I promised I would do it eventually, although I told him that my schedule was tight and I didn't know when I could start it. He was kind enough not to put a due date into the contract, therefore.

Although Paul was ten years younger than I and was a slim man, he had heart trouble. During the period that this book was lying fallow, so to speak, he was hospitalized with a heart attack.

I visited him in the hospital on this occasion and it was surprising that I did. In general, I do not like to visit hospitalized friends. My normal queasiness and my tendency to turn away from the unpleasant prevent me. Sometimes I manage, though.

To give recent examples, when Herb Graff was in the hospital in Brooklyn, having undergone a triple bypass, Ray Fox (also a member of the Dutch Treat Club) was going to visit him and urged me to come along. I did and, not recognizing the bald man in the bed, thought we were in the wrong room. My obvious shock when I found out it was Herb may have been one of the factors that made him decide to abandon the toupee thereafter. (I think he looks better without one.)

Again, when my brother, Stan, had a prostatectomy, I visited him, going out to the hospital in Long Island at which the operation had taken place.

These were exceptional cases and the fact that I visited Paul Nadan therefore astonishes me. One reason, of course, was that he was such a nice fellow and we had had very good lunches together. Another was my rather intense feeling of guilt. I promised him that I would soon start *Extraterrestrial Civilizations.*

In March 1978, Paul wrote to ask me if I would give him a favorable quote for a book on recombinant DNA by a science writer named John Lear. Now, in 1954, John Lear had referred to my book *The Caves of Steel* in a most insulting fashion, after quoting merely a one-paragraph review of it, and showing no signs of having read the book itself. "What does this author know about science?" he asked.

I promptly wrote Lear a letter telling him flatly that I knew a great deal more science than he did and that, moreover, I was a better science writer than he was, but he never answered. Had he done so, and expressed regret, all would have been forgiven. As it was, I put him on my list of villains. I never did anything about it, of course, but neither was I about to do him favors. Therefore, when Paul Nadan asked for a favorable comment on Lear's book, I returned a flat refusal, and told him why.

He sent me the galleys anyway, along with a covering letter, dated March 21, 1978, in which he said, simply, "To forgive is divine."

That caught me in a quandary. I didn't want to forgive, and yet what he had written made me feel ashamed of my hard-heartedness. And while I struggled with myself over whether I could bring myself to forgive Lear, I received the news that on March 22, the day after he had written to me, Paul had had another heart attack and had died.

I had been caught with my hard and unforgiving heart and now it was too late. All I could do was begin *Extraterrestrial Civilizations* at once. I wished I had not been so dilatory but had begun it when Paul was still alive. But how could I tell it would happen? He was only forty-eight.

I dedicated the book to his memory.

Crown assigned me another editor for the book, Herbert Michelman, whom I met for the first time on November 2, 1978. Once again, I was in luck, for Herbert was another one of those editors I seem to meet with so frequently—gentle, soft-spoken, and delightful. At lunches, we would swap jokes and laugh continually.

Once *Extraterrestrial Civilizations* was done (it was published in 1979), I started a new book for him called *Exploring the Earth and the Cosmos,* dealing with the steady expansion of the human range.

I invited him to have lunch with me at the Dutch Treat Club, and he enjoyed himself enormously on that occasion. As it turned out, Ernest Heyn, one of our older members, knew Herbert Michelman well. He suggested that we invite Herbert Michelman in as a member and I was enthusiastically agreeable. So was Herb. So we voted him in without trouble.

On November 11, 1980, he attended his very first luncheon as a member and said to me, in his gentle way, "May I sit with you, Isaac?"

"Of course," I said. "I wouldn't let you sit anywhere else."

So he sat at the "Jewish table" and joined the fun, but the luncheon entrée was a not very generous wedge of quiche and nothing more. Robert Friedman (the member who had given me my card about critics that I have held on to ever since, and who later resigned in indignation over the fact that the club did not allow women as members) took out his luncheon ticket and tore it in half.

"Here," he said to the waiter, offering one part, "you only deserve half."

I was embarrassed and I hoped against hope that the next week the menu would be a bit more generous and that Herbert would more nearly get his money's worth, but it was not to be. Herbert also had a bad heart, and on that very evening he died at the station of his commuter train line. He was sixty-seven years old and I had known him for only two years.

The next week I came in glumly and was asked where my friend was. I answered, "I'm afraid he died last Tuesday evening, just three hours after he left us."

Bob Friedman couldn't resist saying, "It was that lunch last week. It was the quiche of death."

Such is the nature of humanity that the people at the table all laughed. Even I did.

Exploring the Earth and the Cosmos was published in 1982 and I dedicated it to the memory of Herbert Michelman.

Jane West, who worked for Clarkson Potter, a Crown subsidiary, and who had suggested, in 1979, that I do *The Annotated Gulliver's Travels,* died on September 11, 1981. It was cancer, in her case. In the space of less than three years, then, I lost three good editors in action, all from a single publishing house. It was a most distressing coincidence.

136

Simon & Schuster

Until the late 1970s, I had never done a book for Simon & Schuster. I had the vague idea, somehow, that Simon & Schuster was Doubleday's great competitor and that it would be disloyal to work for them.

In fact, I was once rather shocked when Timothy Seldes introduced me to a visitor in his office who was an editor from Simon & Schuster. Surely, I thought, it would be more appropriate if the employees of the two firms did not talk to each other, but fired when they saw the whites of the enemies' eyes.

I recovered, however, and said to the visitor, "I understand the women at Simon & Schuster are easy."

"What!" said he, scandalized, and Tim did me the honor of letting his mouth fall open too.

"The reason I say that," I said, with as naive an expression on my face as I could manage, "is that recently when I tried to flirt with a young woman here at Doubleday, Tim Seldes said to me, 'Where do you think you are, Asimov? Simon & Schuster?' "

Tim had indeed said that, and he remembered saying it too, and I left him to get out of it as best he could.

As it happened, Larry Ashmead, after he had left Doubleday, moved to Simon & Schuster, and we remained in contact, of course. I don't give up my editorial friendships just because there is a move. Inevitably, Larry asked me if I would do a book for him, suggesting that I deal with all the different ways in which the world might come to an end.

He couldn't have suggested a better book, because I had just written a relatively brief article on the subject for *Popular Mechanics,* which had appeared in the March 1977 issue of the magazine under

the title "Twenty Ways the World Could End." It had been exten-
sively edited and I was unhappy with the result and welcomed the
chance to do an entire book on the subject. I was also anxious to use
my own title, *A Choice of Catastrophes*. I signed the contract gladly
and got to work on it at the first available opportunity.

While I was writing the book, Larry changed jobs again and moved
on to Harper & Row. That didn't bother me, for I assumed that he
would simply take the book with him. This had happened to me
before. When I wrote my book *The Neutrino,* the hardcover was intended for my old editor, Walter Bradbury, who was working with
Henry Holt at the time. While the book was in preparation, Brad
returned to Doubleday and took the book with him. It was published
by Doubleday in 1966. I assumed the same would happen to *A Choice
of Catastrophes.*

It didn't. Simon & Schuster refused to let Larry take the book with
him. He told me this and I was indignant. I went to see the new editor
assigned me by Simon & Schuster and explained that the book had
been Larry's idea and that my whole intention was to do it for him
because of our close friendship.

The new editor shook his head. The contract was with Simon &
Schuster and the top brass intended to keep the book. I reported to
Larry and offered to stop work on the book. Larry said, "No. I don't
want you to lose the book. Just do a different one for me."

So I finished *A Choice of Catastrophes* and it was published by Simon & Schuster in 1979. It did reasonably well, but I was unhappy
over it, because the editor had taken out my section on urban terrorism. He never explained why and I had the uneasy feeling that the
publishers expected that what I said might have unpleasant repercus-
sions. It felt like censorship to me and I brooded over it a bit.

I don't really hold a grudge against Simon & Schuster, but they
have never asked me for another book and *A Choice of Catastrophes*
remains my only book with them.

I kept my word to Larry too. I suggested that I do a book in which
I talked about longer and longer distances, then shorter and shorter
ones; longer and longer periods of time, then shorter and shorter
ones; greater and greater masses, then smaller and smaller ones. In
every case, I would make the increases and decreases very regular and
supply examples from real life—thus giving people some idea of the
scale of everything about us.

It was the kind of book I would love to do, the kind of petty calculations I loved to immerse myself in, and Larry, of course, always let me do whatever I wanted. I produced the book, which I called *The Measure of the Universe,* and it was published by Harper & Row in 1983. It did moderately well too.

Incidentally, in repeating over and over that this book and that book did well, I don't mean to say I haven't had a few real flops. Not many, perhaps, but a few.

There was, for instance, *Our World in Space,* published by New York Graphic in 1974. I contributed essays on the various planets of the solar system as they had been revealed by rockets and probes up to that point, and Robert McCall, a marvelous illustrator of space-age scenes, supplied the paintings. McCall was the senior author, justifiably, and collected 60 percent of the royalties.

My essays weren't bad, but McCall's paintings couldn't be better. It was a large, beautiful book just right for coffee tables and I hoped for great things from it—but it dropped dead and never made back its advance. And in a few years it was out of date.

Then there was the case of Carl Sagan's venture into book publishing. Carl's books were doing better and better until, with his book *The Dragons of Eden,* he won the Pulitzer Prize. (When I read that book in galleys, I predicted to Janet that Carl had a real winner there, and I was delighted at the success of my critical acumen—something I usually feel I lack altogether.)

Carl then made an enormous hit with his television program *Cosmos,* and the book derived from it stayed on the best-seller list almost forever.

It seemed to him (and to me too) that his name was now sufficiently well known so that he could open a publishing firm of his own that would publish books on astronomy and space. He had found, for instance, a book of beautiful illustrations prepared by a Japanese artist named Kazuaki Iwasaki. The captions, however, Carl found insufficient. He asked me to write a more satisfactory set, which I gladly did, and he himself wrote a preface to the book.

Again the artist was the senior author and the title of the book was *Visions of the Universe.* It was published by Cosmos Store (Sagan's firm) in 1981, and I anticipated enormous sales, best-seller listings, and so on. Nothing of the sort. The book never moved and, as a matter of fact, Cosmos Store went out of business.

I'll give you a third example. Harmony Books, a subsidiary of Crown Publishers, asked me, on May 4, 1983, to do a book on robots, their history, their development, their uses in industry and science, and so on. I refused, explaining that although I wrote about robots in science fiction, I knew nothing about them in real life.

They said they had to use my name, and they would get me a co-author who did know about robots. They came up with a young woman named Karen Frenkel, attractive, intelligent, and hardworking. She did the necessary research and much of the writing. I went over it and did some rewriting. Since she did much more than half the work, I arranged to have her get most of the advance. However, I couldn't arrange the credits properly. I wanted her listed as senior author, but the book, entitled simply *Robots,* was published in 1985 with my name coming first and in larger letters. I had protested, but that did no good. It had to be that way, they said, to ensure a better sale.

There was a somewhat grim justice, therefore, in the fact that there was virtually no sale, and the book never made back more than a relatively small portion of its advance (which, fortunately, had gone mostly to Karen).

Some readers may try to draw conclusions from the fact that each of these three flops was a collaboration, but I have published a number of collaborations that have done quite well—the Norby books with Janet, for instance, and various anthologies with Marty.

Several books with only my own name on them may not have been flops, but they didn't really do marvelously well. Such outré ventures as *Asimov's Annotated Paradise Lost,* for instance, while giving me enormous pleasure, did no more than barely earn back its modest advance.

The moral to this, in my opinion, is that my name is not a magic cure-all and putting it on a book does not necessarily ensure success. (Nor should it. A book should be successful on its own terms and not simply because of its author's name.)

137

Marginal Items

I have already spoken of the difficulties I have with my 116 anthologies and my ambivalent feelings about adding them to the list of my books. I have similar feelings with reference to a number of non-anthology items (fortunately not many) that are also marginal.

Some of them are associated in my mind with the publisher S. Arthur ("Red") Dembner, a tall, thin man with a craggy face and gray hair still with a hint of the red that gave him his nickname. He ran a small publishing house and, together with Jerome Agel, a book promoter, proposed that I do a "book of facts" that would contain a great many odd and little-known items, divided into numerous classifications. Many of them, they pointed out, could easily be drawn from my books.

I demurred. I didn't really have the time to engage in the research that would be required.

That was of no consequence, they assured me. They would have a team digging up the facts. I would just have to supply some of my own and go over them all in order to throw out any that I thought were wrong or just dubious.

I considered the possibility. This would be the first book in which I would have a team of researchers doing much of the work. Generally, I did *all* the work myself, no matter how long and complex a book, and I was proud of it. Uneasily, then, I agreed, provided I was not to be described as the author of the book and that every last member of the research team would be named in the front matter. This was agreed to.

So I worked on it, supplied about 20 percent of all the items listed in the book, and looked at all those that I didn't supply and threw out a number of them.

The book was published in 1979 under the imprint of Grosset & Dunlap and, as agreed, I was not listed as the author. However, the title was *Isaac Asimov's Book of Facts*, which implied more credit for me than I deserved. On the reverse of the title page, all the people involved were listed, seventeen of them altogether. I came first as "Editor," but my name was in no larger type than any of the other sixteen.

This satisfied me, and I did enough work on the book to allow me to feel quite comfortable about including it on the numbered list. Less comfortable was the point that, with several thousand items in it, some were bound to turn out to be dubious or even wrong, despite all my efforts to keep that from happening. And when a reader objected to any of them, the objection went to *me*. Almost invariably, the objections were to items that I had *not* supplied, and I had no way of knowing what the source was. I just sent them on to Red.

Then Red came up with another project on June 11, 1981. A Canadian, Ken Fisher, had come up with a quiz book, and Red asked me to look it over. I did so, and ventured the opinion that the quizzes seemed both interesting and competent, so the book might be worth publishing. Red then asked me to select about half of it, correct any mistakes, write an introduction, and allow the book to come out as *Isaac Asimov Presents Superquiz*. In return, I would get a small share of the royalties.

I said at once that this would be unfair to Ken Fisher. Red explained that Fisher would be listed as the author and said that Fisher was eager because the book would have a better sale with my name on it. (Again the superstition of the magic power of my name.)

It is hard for me to say no to nice people and Red certainly fell into the classification of nice people. The book was published by Dembner Books in 1982, with Fisher's name placed prominently on the cover.

Over the next seven years, however, the book was followed by a second volume, a third, and a fourth. In each case, I worked on the book and wrote an introduction. I had to withstand those people who found errors that I had overlooked. The most beautiful case was a question as to the only nation that had the letter combination "ate" in its name. The answer was given as "Guatemala," which is difficult to think of since the "ate" is pronounced with a broad rather than a flat "a." However, it isn't the only nation so distinguished. A reader wrote in to ask why "United States" didn't qualify, and I had no good answer to that at all.

They made a quiz game out of the Superquiz books in an effort to capitalize on the incredible, if predictably short-lived, success of Trivial Pursuit. The Superquiz game did well enough, but it was certainly no Trivial Pursuit. They also derived a question-and-answer syndicated column out of the book, which mentioned only my name and not Fisher's. I complained and, as usual in such cases, my complaint was ignored.

In connection with the Superquiz game, I had a rather miserable experience, the story of which necessitates a detour.

I don't mind arranging to sign books in a bookstore if some halfway effort is made to alert the public I'll be there. With proper promotion, I usually manage to sign a hundred books or more for excited readers. I was once kept busy signing for an hour and a half without a break, even though I had only contracted to do an hour. (It's difficult to look at a long line of hopeful readers and say, "Well, the hour is up. The rest of you are out of luck," so I just kept on going.)

When no promotional effort is made, it can be disastrous, but it's part of the price writers pay. Besides, most writers are willing to travel across the country to promote their books, making an incredible number of one-day stops. I absolutely refuse to do this, aside from making a very occasional venture into the outlying suburbs and once going even as far as Philadelphia. For that reason, I try to make up for it by never refusing a signing in Manhattan and by always agreeing to telephone interviews—and by accepting, with resignation, any misfires.

Some are particularly hard to take, however. On December 16, 1979, for instance, a stack of my books and I were at Bloomingdale's —and the management seated me in the ladies' clothes department, of all places. I sat there for an hour trying to ignore the hostile looks of the passing women, who obviously thought I was a Peeping Tom.

I did sign a few books, however, and one woman rushed up excitedly and congratulated me on my play on Broadway and hoped I would make a million dollars out of it. I told her politely that I hoped I would too, but I felt it would be needlessly embarrassing to her to tell her that I was *not* Isaac Bashevis Singer.

My worst such time, however, came on June 15, 1984, when I had agreed to sit at Macy's for three hours with a pile of Superquiz games which I was offering to sign. In those interminable three hours, there were exactly eight sales. The worst of it was that one of the eight who picked up the box in order to purchase it flatly refused my signature.

There was a second embarrassment in connection with that game that was even more intense. The publishers of the game were anxious to get a little publicity and photo opportunities from the media, and had me attend a demonstration of how the game was played. I was to supply the necessary charisma (which they thought I had).

One elderly gentleman pushed forward his grandson as an incredible genius and demanded that I ask him any question in the Superquiz. The child looked embarrassed, so I hung back, but Grandpa insisted.

I pulled out a couple of questions, chose the easiest, and asked it. The youngster, as I expected, drew a blank. I covered it up as best I could, and managed to find a still easier question. Another blank. So I pulled a card, but ignored its contents, making up, instead, a question that was impossible not to answer. The kid answered it and I made a big hullabaloo over that and sent them away.

If there are any grandfathers reading this book who have genius grandchildren, please give the kids a break and don't embarrass them in public. It's my experience that really bright kids manage to publicize themselves quite obnoxiously and don't need relatives to help them along.

A somewhat similar case of overestimation came when I was invited to attend a bar mitzvah in 1979. A bar mitzvah is held on the thirteenth birthday of a Jewish boy to signify that he has become old enough to be expected to obey all the Jewish ritual laws on his own responsibility. (Neither I nor Stan have been bar mitzvahed, which is a victory for us over hypocrisy, for we would have had no intention of obeying the laws even if we had gone through the rite.)

The few bar mitzvahs I have attended (when I could think of no good excuse to avoid them) I have found utterly boring. However, they were invariably littered with oceans of food that were crammed full of salt, cholesterol, saturated fat, and other life-destroying components and that, in consequence, tasted heavenly. I could always eat.

In this case, however, the proud father was a friend and he told me that his son was extremely interested in Shakespeare, so could I bring in a copy of my *Guide to Shakespeare* for the lad. Well, I wasn't anxious to, for I had but few copies and they were irreplaceable since the book was already out of print, but a bar mitzvah present is, in any case, de rigueur, and a friend is a friend.

I brought with me a copy of the *Guide*, therefore, and presented it with a broad smile to the young bar mitzvah boy. He took it with an unmistakable air of astonishment and disappointment, and from the disheartened way in which he leafed gingerly through the book, I had the distinct impression that, far from being a Shakespeare buff, he had never heard of the bard of Avon. —The book was simply sacrificed to the baseless vanity of a Proud Pappa.

But back to the matter of my marginal books. —For Carolina Biological Supplies I prepared *The History of Biology*, published in 1988, and *The History of Mathematics*, published in 1989. They are long charts, meant for display in schools and libraries, listing a large number of accurate items in the history of those sciences and enlivened by clever cartoons.

I also edited a Dembner book entitled *From Harding to Hiroshima* by Barrington Boardman, subtitled *An Anecdotal History of the United States from 1923–1945*. I *loved* it. I went over it carefully, read and corrected the galleys and page proofs, and it came out as *Isaac Asimov Presents: From Harding to Hiroshima*. Boardman's name was prominently included on the cover as the author.

Then I was sent a collection of a vast number of quotations from scientists and other men on scientific subjects. I was asked to correct or throw out items as I saw fit, to make up little epigrams to head each of the eighty-six classifications into which the quotations were divided, and to write an introduction. I insisted that the editor with whom I was corresponding include his own name as co-editor, and the book came out in 1988, under the Weidenfeld & Nicholson imprint, with the title *Isaac Asimov's Book of Science and Nature Quotations* edited by Isaac Asimov and Jason A. Shulman.

There are a few other items like that scattered among my hundreds of books. Why do I do them? For one thing, they represent work I find interesting, even fascinating. I also always find it difficult to say no to any writing project, especially when it is quite different from anything I do ordinarily.

I should perhaps put up a better fight against blazoning these things as "Isaac Asimov Presents," but the publishers usually insist and, truth to tell, such things do give me a bit of satisfaction. After all, my name may indeed help sell the book to some small extent. It also helps bring my name to the attention of the public and some people may then go out and buy books with my name on it that I have indeed written all of. Everyone is helped and no one is hurt.

138

Nightfall, Inc.

As the 1970s proceeded, my income continued to go up and my business affairs to grow more complicated. Every once in a while my accountant would mutter that I would be better off if I incorporated myself, and each time he said it, I drew off in something very like terror.

Incorporation was another step upward, one more way of submitting to affluence.

Of course, I liked some of the consequences of being relatively affluent. After having spent the first half of my life always conscious of exactly how much money I had in my pocket and carefully weighing every purchase, it was extraordinarily pleasant to walk into any restaurant and order any meal without even looking at the price column. It was a delight to take a taxi anywhere I wanted to go; to make out checks for bills as they came in, without having to worry about the bank balance.

I appreciated all that but I didn't want the side effects that come with affluence. I dreaded the thought that I would be expected to throw fancy parties, that it would be necessary for me to attend social functions in glittering array, that it would be taken for granted that I ought to have my apartment littered with the latest technological advances, that I ought to have a housekeeper, and a fancy office, and a posh automobile, and a boat, and a summer home, and whatever else fancy might suggest.

I didn't want such things. I wanted to live quietly and simply, and every time I indulged in an outward manifestation of being well off, I feared that the world would not allow me my penchant for simplicity.

My accountant, however, grew firmer in his advice, and Janet joined him, and on October 22, 1979, I said, "All right. Go ahead and arrange it." So, as of December 3, 1979, I became president and treasurer of a corporation, while Janet became vice president and secretary.

There was some question about naming the corporation. The accountant firmly vetoed my suggestion that it be simply "Isaac Asimov, Inc." He did not want my name on it. He wanted it to sound much more like an ordinary business firm. "Why don't you name it after something you've written?" he asked.

That brought it down quickly in my mind to two possibilities: Foundation and Nightfall. My accountant chose the latter, perhaps because it sounded more romantic, so that I became "Nightfall, Inc."

I might say that no government agency has ever found anything nontrivial wrong with any of my tax statements, as is not surprising, since I make them out honestly. However, even if they investigate and give me an all clear they have still taken up my accountant's time and he charges me for that, so I wish earnestly they would accept the fact that I am honest and leave me alone.

Once, many years ago, I was interviewed on television and asked, "Suppose you earned a billion dollars. What would you do with it?"

I know the type of answers they expected. Selfish people would buy huge palaces and live like emperors. Idealists would endow universities and support environmental causes. I, however, had a different idea.

I said, "I would walk into the IRS offices and say, 'I have just earned a billion dollars. Here it is, every penny. It's for Uncle Sam. Now please don't ever let me hear from you again for the rest of my life."

The government would undoubtedly make a profit on that deal, for a lifetime of taxes from me comes to far less than a billion dollars; far, far less. However, the dream of not having to keep records, of not having to do any calculations, of not having to deal with accountants and lawyers, would be worth far, far more than money.

139

Hugh Downs

It always comes as a surprise to me when someone I consider a celebrity shows himself to be aware of my existence. I don't have to describe Hugh Downs, because everyone knows him. He has appeared on prime-time television for more hours than anyone else in the United States.

He was on the cruise that took us down to Florida to watch the Apollo 17 launch in 1972, though on that occasion we did not have much in the way of contact. On June 9, 1978, however, I had breakfast with him at his request and we talked astronomy and cosmology.

Hugh is fascinated by science and, despite his TV work, which must take up a great deal of his time, he manages to keep abreast of the latest developments in science (especially cosmology) and he can keep his end up even in discussions with professionals.

Apparently, I passed muster with him. He had the notion of setting up an annual dinner to which about a dozen people interested in science would be invited for an evening of good food and conversation. The first of these was held on May 6, 1980, at the Metropolitan Club, and the dinner was nothing short of lavish.

I have been invited to every succeeding dinner and have missed only one. The cost of the dinners must be high, and each year I offer to pay half the bill. Each year Hugh smiles and tells me it's his pleasure and is well worth it.

Pleasure it certainly is, for the conversation is impressive and I am often the comic relief. I can hold my own in the discussions of the borderlands of science but I can also slip easily into the telling of jokes, for almost everything reminds me of a funny story.

The tale of these annual gatherings got out and I received a phone call once from a reporter, the tenor of whose questions made it plain that she thought that Hugh was an intellectual social climber, that he paid for the banquets in order to be accepted by high-powered egg-heads, who ate his food and snickered at his pretensions.

I put a stop to that very firmly. I told the reporter that Hugh, albeit an amateur, was highly intelligent, was knowledgeable in science, and was liked and respected by everyone there. That probably killed the story and I'm glad of it.

At the gatherings, there are some who, like me, are regulars. Lloyd Motz, an astronomer at Columbia, has never missed a session. Others who sometimes appear and sometimes don't are Walter Sullivan, Robert Jastrow, Jeremy Bernstein, Marvin Minsky, Ben Bova, Mark Chartrand, Gerard O'Neill, Gerald Feinberg, Robert Shapiro, and others. Heinz Pagels appeared at a number of the dinners, but about him I will speak later.

Generally, when I come home, I give Janet a précis of the discussion and of the clever things that different people said (not omitting myself, of course). I do the same after meetings of the Dutch Treat Club and the Trap Door Spiders. She enjoys that, but she sometimes feels resentful over the stag nature of the organizations.

One time, the matter of stagness turned out to be particularly embarrassing. In April 1980, I received an invitation to attend a meeting of physicians who were engaged in research. Lewis Thomas, the great science writer on biology, was going to be the speaker. I accepted quickly and told Janet that, of course, I expected her to come with me because she was very fond of Thomas's essays.

Janet looked at the letter of invitation and then impaled me with an icy glare. She said, "You would have noticed, Isaac, if you really read the letter, instead of absorbing every fifth word, that the organization you have been invited to is *stag*. You can go, but I can't, even though I'm a physician and you're not."

I slunk away and shot off a second letter, explaining that I had incautiously asked my wife to come with me, and that now, in the interest of marital harmony, I was afraid I couldn't come.

Back came a handwritten letter. My wife was invited too. So on April 7, 1980, there we were at a dinner—sixty men and Janet. And don't think Janet didn't love it. She knew some of the people and engaged in lively conversation. It was I, the nonphysician, who was the outsider.

Janet can, of course, as any woman can, attend the Dutch Treat annual banquet and she always goes with me, if only to make sure that I don't let my annoyance at finding myself in a tuxedo lead me into obstreperous trouble. Once she attended a regular meeting under unusual circumstances which I will describe later.

Now, of course, she can occasionally attend the regular meetings as a legal guest on suitable occasions. She came along on April 24, 1990, for instance, when I gave my talk on iambic pentameter and limericks.

140

Best-seller

The two volumes of my autobiography had appeared and had done quite well, and went on to be published as trade paperbacks under the Avon label, but Doubleday wasn't satisfied. They still wanted novels.

Mind you, I hadn't been neglecting Doubleday, with whom I published *The Road to Infinity*, a new collection of science essays, and *Casebook of the Black Widowers*, a third collection of Black Widower tales. In press was still another collection of science essays, *The Sun Shines Bright*, and a collection of essays on science fiction, *Asimov on Science Fiction* and an anthology, *The Thirteen Crimes of Science Fiction*. I was also working madly on another edition of *Asimov's Biographical Encyclopedia of Science and Technology*, so Doubleday couldn't say I was neglecting the firm.

Nor was I neglecting other publishers, by the way, for in 1980 and 1981, I had published twenty-four books. These included *Extraterrestrial Civilizations* for Crown; *A Choice of Catastrophes* for Simon & Schuster; *Isaac Asimov's Book of Facts* for Grosset & Dunlap; *The Annotated Gulliver's Travels* for Clarkson Potter; and four *How Did We Find Out . . . ?* books for Walker & Company.

So I was certainly working full-time, as I always do.

All this meant nothing to Doubleday. It was irrelevant. Their viewpoint was that I should simply not do some of the things I was doing, and write a novel instead. What's more, they were no longer going to ask me; they were going to tell me.

Hugh O'Neill had replaced Cathleen Jordan as my editor after Cathleen had left Doubleday. On January 15, 1981, Hugh called me into his office. He was a young man, new at his job, facing an elderly and distinguished writer. Who could tell how temperamental, or even violent, an elderly and moody writer might get if he were suddenly faced with an ultimatum?

So all he said was that Betty Prashker wanted to see me. Betty was high up in the editorial scale and a very respected editor in the field. I was ushered to her office. This mild middle-aged woman smiled at me and said, "Isaac, we want you to write a novel for us."

I said, "But, Betty—"

She was clearly not going to listen to anything I was going to say, for she ignored my attempted remark and kept right on talking. "We are going to send a contract to you and we are going to give you a large advance."

I said, "But, Betty, I don't know if I can write novels anymore."

Betty said, in the usual refrain, "Don't be silly, Isaac. Just go home and start thinking up a novel."

I was shoved out of the office. That evening, Pat LoBrutto, who was in charge of science fiction at Doubleday, phoned me. "Listen, Isaac," he said, "let me make it clear. When Betty said 'a novel,' she meant 'a science fiction novel'; and when we say 'a science fiction novel,' we mean 'a Foundation novel.' That's what we want."

I heard him, but I couldn't make myself take it seriously. I had written only one science fiction novel in twenty-two years, and I had not written a word of any Foundation story for thirty-two years. I didn't even remember the content of the Foundation stories in any detail.

What's more, I had written the Foundation stories, from beginning to end, between the brash ages of twenty-one and thirty, and had done so under John Campbell's whip. Now I was sixty-one years old, and there was no John Campbell any longer, or any present-day equivalent either.

I had a terrible fear that I would, if I were forced, write a Foundation novel, but that it would be entirely worthless. Doubleday would hesitate to reject it, and would publish it; but it would be lambasted by the critics and the readers; and I would go down in science fiction history as a writer who was great when he was young, but who then tried to ride the coattails of his youth when he was old and incompetent, and proceeded to make an utter jackass of himself.

What's more, my income was high as a result of my vast number of nonfiction books, twenty times as high, in fact, as in the days when I was writing novels. I felt that I might badly damage the state of my private economy if I returned to writing novels.

The only thing I could do was to lie low and hope that Doubleday would forget about it.

They didn't however. On January 19, Hugh told me, with every evidence of satisfaction, that I was going to get a $50,000 advance, which was exactly ten times as much as the usual advance I received for a Doubleday book. I was nonplussed. I worry about large advances. What if I don't earn them back? I know that the proper reaction to that is for a writer to shrug it off and keep the advance, and let the publisher take the loss, but I can't do that. I would have to return the unearned portion of the advance (as I had actually done on one or two occasions in the past). This would give me no pleasure and it would also entail a fight with Doubleday, who would surely refuse to take the return, with their usual and oft-repeated remark of "Don't be silly, Isaac."

So I said to Hugh, "Gee, Hugh, Doubleday will lose its shirt with that kind of advance."

But Hugh already knew the lines. He said, "Don't be silly, Isaac. Have you thought of a plot yet?"

It was clear that Doubleday was dead serious and I must admit that a $50,000 advance was attractive. Even if I turned out a bad book and refused to let Doubleday publish it, or couldn't even finish it, and had to force Doubleday to take back the money, it would be something to be able to say to myself, "I was once promised $50,000 to write a book even before I had turned out a single word or had thought up a single idea."

A week later I was given a check for half the advance (the other half to be handed to me on delivery of the manuscript), and after that there was no longer any chance to fool around. As soon as I could complete projects I was then engaged on, I would have to get started.

And before I got started, I would have to reread *The Foundation Trilogy*. This I approached with a certain horror. After all, I was convinced it would seem rough and crude to me after all these years. It would surely embarrass me to read the kind of tripe I wrote when I was in my twenties.

So, wincing, I opened the book on June 1, 1981, and within a few pages I knew I was wrong. To be sure, I recognized the pulpy bits in the early stories, and I knew that I could have done better after I had taken a few more years to learn my craft, but I was seized by the book. It was a page-turner.

My memory of it was just sufficiently insufficient for me not to be certain how my characters were going to solve their problems and I read it with steady excitement.

I couldn't help noticing, of course, that there was not very much action in it. The problems and resolutions thereof were expressed primarily in dialogue, in competing rational discussions from different points of view, with no clear indication to the reader which view was right and which was wrong. At the start, there were villains, but as I went along, both heroes and villains faded into shades of gray and the real problem was always: What is best for humanity?

For that, the answer was never certain. I always supplied an answer, but the whole tone of the series was that, as in history, no answer was final.

When I finished reading the trilogy on June 9, I experienced exactly what readers had been telling me for decades—a sense of fury that it was over and there was no more.

Now I *wanted* to write a fourth Foundation novel, but that didn't mean I had a plot for it. What I did then was to dig up the beginning of a fourth Foundation novel that I had written some years before. I had written fourteen pages and had then put it aside, largely because there were so many other things I had to do.

Now I went over those fourteen pages and they read well. That gave me the beginning of a novel without an ending. (Always, it's the other way around.) So I sat down to make up an ending, and the next day I forced my quivering fingers to retype those fourteen pages—and then to keep on going.

It was not an easy job. I tried to stick to the style and the atmosphere of the earlier Foundation stories. I had to resurrect all the paraphernalia of psychohistory, and I had to make references to five hundred years of past history. I had to keep the action low and the dialogue high (the critics often complained about that in my novels, but to perdition with them), and I had to present competing rational outlooks and describe several different worlds and societies.

What's more, I was uneasily conscious that the early Foundation stories had been written by someone who knew only the technology of the 1940s. There were no computers, for instance, though I did presume the existence of very advanced mathematics. I didn't try to explain that. I just put very advanced computers in the new Foundation novel and hoped that nobody would notice the inconsistency. Oddly enough, no one did.

There were also no robots in the early Foundation novels, and I didn't introduce them in the new one either.

During the 1940s, you see, I had had two separate series going: the Foundation series and the robot series. I deliberately kept them different, the former set in the far future without robots and the latter in the near future with robots. I wanted the two series to remain as separated as possible so that if I got tired of one of them (or if the readers did), I could continue with the other with a minimum of troubling overlap. And, indeed, I did get tired of the Foundation and I wrote no more after 1950, while I continued to write robot stories (and even two robot novels).

In writing the new Foundation novel in 1981, I felt the absence of robots to be an anomaly, but there was no way I could bring them in suddenly and without warning. Computers I could; they were side issues making only brief appearances. Robots, however, would be bound to be principal characters and I had to continue to leave them out. Nevertheless, the problem remained in my head and I knew that I would have to deal with it someday.

I called the new novel *Lightning Rod*, for what seemed to me to be good and sufficient reasons, but Doubleday vetoed that instantly. A Foundation novel had to have "Foundation" in the title so that the readers would know at once that that was what they were waiting for. In this case, Doubleday was right, and I finally settled on *Foundation's Edge* as the title.

It took me nine months to write the novel and it was a hard time not only for me but for Janet, for my uncertainty concerning the quality of the novel reflected itself in my mood. When I felt that the novel wasn't going well, I brooded in wretched silence, and Janet admitted that she longed for the days when I wrote only nonfiction, when I had no literary problems, and when my mood was generally sunny.

Another reason for my moodiness was, of course, that while I was writing the novel I could not undertake large nonfiction tasks except for the continuing revision of the *Biographical Encyclopedia*. To be sure, during those nine months I co-edited nearly twenty anthologies, did several little science histories for Walker, and turned out a steady stream of short pieces, but I missed my big projects.

I finished the novel, at last, on March 25, 1982, handed it in at once, got the second half of my advance instantly, and received my first copy of *Foundation's Edge* in September.

By that time, Doubleday was reporting large preliminary orders, but I took that calmly and without excitement. Such large orders might well be followed by large returns and actual sales could be small.

I was wrong.

For over thirty years, generation after generation of science fiction readers had been reading the Foundation novels and had been clamoring for more. All of them, thirty years' worth of them, were now ready to jump at the book the instant it appeared.

The result was that in the week of its publication, *Foundation's Edge* appeared in twelfth place on the New York *Times* best-seller list, and I honestly couldn't believe my eyes. I had been a published writer for forty-three years and *Foundation's Edge* was my 262nd book. Having escaped any hint of best-sellerdom for all that time, I scarcely knew what to do with one.

Foundation's Edge reached a high of third place on the first Sunday of December, and remained on the list for twenty-five weeks altogether. I could have hoped for one more, so I could say "half a year," but twenty-five was exactly twenty-five more than I had ever dreamed of in my wildest bits of megalomania, so it would have been ridiculous of me to complain. (And my income, I might add, which I had thought would be damaged by a return to fiction, promptly doubled.)

Incidentally, when Hugh showed me the proof of the cover, I burst into laughter, because it announced *Foundation's Edge* as the fourth book of *The Foundation Trilogy*. When Hugh asked me why I laughed, I pointed out that "trilogy" meant "three books," so that introducing a fourth book was a contradiction in terms.

Hugh was horribly embarrassed and said it would be changed. I said, "No, no, Hugh. Leave it. It will create talk and will be good publicity."

But Doubleday didn't want that kind of publicity. It was changed to a fourth book of the "Foundation Saga." However, I have the original on my living-room wall with the self-contradiction in plain view.

There was, of course, one little flaw in all the excitement of a best-seller. My name on the *Times* best-seller list set off a small tocsin of alarm in my brain and I knew I was doomed. Doubleday would never let me stop writing novels again—and they never did.

141

Out of the Past

As the 1980s opened and I entered my own sixties, I began to experience that phenomenon that comes to all people who approach the end of a normal life span. Their somewhat older contemporaries begin to die—and sometimes their somewhat younger ones also.

Bernard Zitin, who, at the NAES, had been my direct superior, and with whom, of course, I had not gotten along, died in 1979 at the age of sixty.

Gloria Saltzberg, the pleasant girl in the wheelchair who had chivied me into taking the test that had gotten me into Mensa, died on January 25, 1978, at the age of fifty. No doubt the sequelae of infantile paralysis had shortened her life.

John Campbell's widow, Peg Campbell, a plump and pleasant woman who was remarkable for her ability to endure Campbell's peculiarities (much as Janet is able to endure mine), died on August 16, 1979.

Al Capp, who had nearly brought me into court over my letter to the Boston *Globe*, died on November 5, 1979, at the age of seventy.

Sometime late in 1979, Robert Elderfield, who had made life hard for me in graduate school and who had then employed me for a year of postgraduate work, died at the age of seventy-five.

Burnham Walker, who had been head of the biochemistry department when I joined the faculty of Boston University School of Medicine and who had been a good boss to me (one of the few superiors I was always able to get along with—because he left me strictly alone), died on April 3, 1980, at the age of seventy-eight. I had last seen him a year earlier, on May 15, 1979, when I came to the medical school to give a talk and the old faculty of my active days there had assembled to greet me. Walker had difficulty walking and came with an aluminum aid. He had so changed that I did not recognize him at first.

Harold C. Urey, who had almost prevented me from entering graduate school, died on January 6, 1981, at the age of eighty-seven. Ralph Halford, who had asked me about thiotimoline at my doctor's orals, died about that time too, at the age of sixty-four.

There were other markers of passing time. Charles Dawson, my beloved research professor, is still alive at this time of writing, at the age of seventy-nine. However, on February 27, 1978, he retired and I went to Columbia to eulogize him.

Such things can't help but pound into one's head the truth of passing time. The sense of mortality drew closer, and was personally marked by my own heart attack in 1977, and by less important but more immediately noticeable signs such as the graying of my hair, the whitening of my sideburns, and the fact that on March 29, 1978, I had to give in to old age and buy my first pair of bifocals.

An odd bit of the past that had nothing to do with death obtruded itself on my notice at about this time too.

When I was eight years old, I had a brief friendship with a boy my own age named Solomon Frisch. He would make up stories and tell them to me and I listened in fascination. His family moved away from the immediate neighborhood and I lost touch with him, but I never forgot him. It may well be that my experience of listening to him tell stories, and *knowing* that he made them up, was the first thing ever to put the germ of writing into my brain.

I mentioned him in the first volume of my autobiography, and my own fascination with writing was such that I felt certain that Solly, who so eagerly made up stories when he was just a little boy, must have grown up to be a writer, and surely a successful one. It seemed inevitable. And since I knew of no writer named Solomon Frisch, it seemed to me that either he wrote under a pseudonym or he was dead.

Actually, he was alive, and his son, noting the mention of his name in my autobiography, drew it to his attention. He promptly wrote to me and on February 7, 1981, Janet and I had lunch with Solly and his wife, Chicky, a reunion after fifty-three years.

Solly was obviously happily married and he was clearly enjoying life, but, to my astonishment and disappointment, he had never become a writer. He worked for the post office, and as he said to me cheerfully, "I guess I burned myself out at eight as far as literature was concerned."

142
Word Processor

I'm very conservative in my private life. I tend to get into a rut and stay there because it is comfortable to do things as I've always done them. The world of technology advances and leapfrogs all about me and I ignore it until it forces itself on me.

I'm still using an old Selectric III IBM typewriter and dread the day when it breaks down to the point where I must buy a new one. I don't particularly want the new electronic typewriters. They're too fancy for my simple soul. I even use a fabric ribbon (increasingly difficult to get) because a film ribbon that you use only once is consumed too quickly at the speed and constancy with which I work.

And, of course, it never occurred to me to get a word processor.

What! Abandon my faithful typewriter? My curious obsession with the notion of loyalty extends, you see, to inanimate objects. I couldn't bring myself to buy a small calculator because it would mean betraying my slide rule. Then, when I started getting such calculators in the mail from people who wanted to give me one for some reason I couldn't fathom, I tried not to use them. When the convenience of their use forced itself on my stubborn self (especially for addition and subtraction, which slide rules don't handle), I nevertheless kept my two slide rules and I feel very guilty every time I look at them.

I heard many stories about people getting word processors and then never using their typewriters again. I simply wasn't going to do that to my typewriter, so I hardened my heart against the growing clamor all about me to the effect that I *must* get a word processor. My brother, Stan, kept up a steady drumbeat to that effect and used my resistance, I'm sure, for any number of "my stupid brother Isaac" jokes at work.

Finally, in the spring of 1981, a computer magazine (of a kind that had been springing up in uncounted numbers at that time) asked me to do an article on my experiences with my word processor. They naturally assumed I had one, of course, on the same basis that they would naturally assume I was breathing.

I told them I didn't have one and couldn't write the essay. Do you think that saved me? Not at all. The astonished and even outraged editorial staff of the magazine promptly arranged to have a word processor delivered to me. It arrived on May 6, 1981.

I was appalled and did my best to pretend it wasn't there, even though it sat in the middle of my library, well packaged in several boxes. On May 12, 1981, however, two young men arrived from Radio Shack and set it up for me, while I wrung my hands in despair. It was a Radio Shack TRS-80 Model II Micro-Computer with a daisy-wheel printer and a Scripsit program.

In time to come, people would ask me on what basis I had selected this particular word processor, assuming that a person of my over-whelming intelligence would have spent several months weighing the pros and cons of all the varieties that existed and carefully selected the best.

My answer would always be: "Well, this is the one that was given me. Are there other kinds?"

And everyone would then rush off to tell "my stupid friend, Isaac" stories.

The people who set it up showed me how to work it and gave me two volumes of instructions, each one large, heavy, and written in the most opaque possible style. (People who write instruction manuals always assume, it seems to me, that you already know the subject they're trying to explain.)

The instruction didn't take and the manual didn't help. I am hopelessly inept with machinery and nothing I did would make the word processor work. The young men returned on June 4 and gave me a repeat of the instructions and that didn't take either. By June 12, I had had the word processor a full month and I still couldn't make it work the way I wanted it to. By June 14, I decided to ask Radio Shack to remove the device and I sat down to give it one last chance.

—And it worked like a charm. I suppose it sensed my decision and was frightened; it didn't want to be returned. From then on, I've been able to use the word processor and I *do* use it constantly.

However, I use it for only one job and no more—the preparation of manuscripts. I had the Radio Shack people adjust it so that it gave me the margins I wanted, and the double spacing I wanted, and everything else that I wanted. I haven't the faintest idea of how any of these things can be changed. I couldn't make it single space, or adjust the margins, for instance, so I don't use it for anything *but* manuscripts.

I don't know how to repaginate either. That means that when I write something on the word processor, I give each page the minor editing it needs (correcting spelling and punctuation and occasionally adding, subtracting, or shifting a word) and then go on to the next. And once I have gone on to the next, the page before becomes virtually unalterable. Fortunately, since I have never been much of a reviser, this doesn't bother me.

The main thing is that I haven't abandoned my good old typewriter. I use it for correspondence, for my card catalogues, for everything but manuscripts. And even in the case of manuscripts, the typewriter has not fallen completely into disuse. Short pieces of up to 2,000 words or so, I do directly on the word processor, I admit. In the case of anything longer, however, I write the first draft on my typewriter and then transfer it into the word processor, doing the necessary minor editing, page by page.

Good old Stan finds this intolerable. "Why do you do that?" he demands. "You have to type everything twice."

I try to explain to him that with long pieces I want the comfort of a pile of yellow paper, the same pile of first draft I've been accustomed to for decades and decades. If I want to check something I said earlier in a novel, for instance (what color hair did I say my hero had?), I would much rather flip the yellow pages than begin a mad search from floppy disk to floppy disk.

But if I do the first draft of my books on the typewriter, what's the use of a word processor?

In the first place, in the old days, having done a final draft, there was still the necessity of last-minute changes. A word would have to be added or deleted by pen and ink. In addition, there were typos I had to correct. With the word processor, no more pen-and-ink changes.

All changes are introduced electrostatically on the screen. That means I hand in cleaner copy.

Is this important? I think so. Manual corrections make the manuscript look messy. That isn't fatal. My editors will stand a little messiness from me, but with everyone handing in clean copy that has been corrected invisibly on the screen, I'm afraid my messiness would stand out and give editors the subliminal notion that my writing is poor simply because it is messy. My word processor prevents that from happening. I hand in clean copy like everyone else.

Radio Shack had let me have the word processor on approval for the remainder of 1981, with payment by installments afterward. As soon as I got it to work, however, I decided to keep it and I phoned Radio Shack and asked for the total cost of everything so that I could make out the check and get it over with.

They said, "Wait. Don't make out the check. How would you like to be a spokesman for us? If you do it, you can keep the machine, and we'll pay you a monthly stipend."

That sounded good to me and I remained a spokesman for several years. It meant that every once in a while I had to submit to a daylong photo session and the photographs were used in advertisements for Radio Shack products. That made me a little uncomfortable, but my machine worked perfectly, so I felt I was recommending something worthwhile.

Eventually, though, the Radio Shack people decided to do all their advertising work in Texas, where they were based, and, of course, they understood that I wouldn't go to Texas, so they didn't ask me to do anything more and just sent me my monthly stipend. After a while, though, I couldn't endure being paid for nothing, so I told them they would have to either arrange to have me do something or stop the stipend. They stopped the stipend after November 1987.

The first book I turned out by way of the word processor was *Exploring the Earth and the Cosmos*. That was my 252nd book, and I now have 451. If I count the books now in press, this means that in the nine years I have so far had the word processor, I have put just over 200 books through its vitals, and, in addition, I may have written some 200 short pieces that have not yet found their way into one of those books. All told, I may have, as a rough estimate, put 10 to 11 million words through the instrument.

And in all that time, it has given me virtually no trouble. On two occasions, to be sure, my keyboard had to go in for rewiring or oiling, but since I was careful enough to get a second keyboard, I can always use one when the other is being worked on, so I don't lose a moment. On January 13, 1988, an enthusiastic repairman replaced the TV tube, but I doubted that that was actually necessary.

On March 29, 1982, the machine wouldn't start at all. I called in the Radio Shack people and the man who arrived the next day studied the situation, then turned on the wall switch that I had casually turned off and forgotten. I don't think this counts as trouble the machine gave me.

You would think that now that I have a word processor and have caught up with modern times, people would leave me alone, but they don't. As computers go, my nine-year-old Radio Shack word processor is now medieval. In fact, the Radio Shack people don't make it anymore.

Apparently, I am supposed to keep up with the times and buy new machines at every improvement. But I won't give in. I'm not going to switch word processors just so I can keep up with the times. I'm loyal to the one I have. It does everything I want it to do and a new one would just mean going through purgatory learning a new set of reflexes.

So what I tell everyone is this: "When my present word processor breaks down, I'll get a more advanced model."

Fortunately, it doesn't break down.

143

Police

I have never been in serious trouble with the law. In forty years of driving, of course, I've managed to get two tickets for illegal parking and two or three tickets for speeding, but I don't think that's bad.

My worst traffic violation took place on the Massachusetts Turnpike, where I was stopped for speeding and, to my horror, it turned out that my driver's license had expired. The trooper who stopped me pointed this out severely, but he did not (as I had half-expected) drag me off to jail. He simply told me to let Janet drive and that I was not to touch the wheel till I got the license renewed.

What had happened was that in 1975 I had moved from the hotel apartment I had had after I had returned to New York, to the large apartment Janet and I have occupied ever since. The move was only six blocks and our mail continued to arrive through the same post office.

Nevertheless, when the new driver's license came for me, addressed to the old place, the post office, which sends me fifty items a day on the average to the new place, sent it back with an "address unknown" on it. After I got home from my misadventurous trip, I went downtown to get a new license, and later on discussed the matter with the post office.

In 1982, I was returning from a trip feeling rather ill. I got into my apartment elevator and there was a woman puffing at her cigarette, with a "No Smoking" sign staring her in the face. I pointed to the sign and asked her to stop and she puffed smoke in my face.

Whereupon I made as though to flick the cigarette from her fingers and she promptly let out a shriek and attacked me. Janet, knowing that I was ill, pushed in front of me and warded her off. Inside half an hour, there were two policemen and a policewoman at my door because the smoker had reported herself as having been assaulted. I explained the situation and they left.

In February 1983, I was served with a summons and found I was being sued for half a million dollars. It's the only time in my life I was ever sued. More amused than frightened, I called my lawyers, Donald Laventhall and Robert Zicklin, and they got me out of it unharmed.

Although Don and Bob are my lawyers, I give them very little work to do, and since I can't maintain a business relationship with anyone for long, they have become my friends. I brought Bob Zicklin, who lives in the city just a few blocks from me, to the Trap Door Spiders as a guest on two occasions, and he was so effectively entertaining that he was voted in as a member on November 21, 1986. He has become one of our most enthusiastic members too.

Bob taught me the facts of life in connection with this aborted lawsuit. He said, "She had no case and she knew it, and so did her lawyer, but they felt they could get nuisance money out of you. Anyone will do that if they recognize you, so be careful. Avoid any wrangles, because you're a celebrity."

It's hard keeping that in mind, but in our litigious society, I suppose I have no choice.

The oddest contact I had with the police, however, came on October 7, 1989. It was a quiet Saturday evening, and we were both watching television. Janet was watching *Star Trek* in her office, and I was watching a *Kate & Allie* rerun in the living room, when the doorbell rang.

No one from outside can come to our door without being announced, so I assumed it was either some building employee or a neighbor. I went to the door (Janet refuses to be disturbed during *Star Trek*) and called out, "Who is it?"

There was no answer, so I looked through the peephole and, behold, I saw police uniforms. I opened the door hastily and there were four policemen and a policewoman there.

I said blankly, "What's the matter, Officers?"

The one in the lead said, "We have a report of a domestic quarrel here."

"Here?" I said. "You must have the wrong apartment."

"No," he said. "We were given the apartment number and the name." He pointed to where our names were on the door. "Our information is that you're holding a knife to your wife's throat."

Laurence Olivier could not possibly have faked the look of honest surprise on my face. I said, "Me? Her throat?"

Then I realized that Janet was still firmly in her office with the door shut, and I knew I had better produce an unharmed wife or they would think that she was lying a battered corpse behind the closed door.

I yelled, "Janet! Come here!"

It took three shouts (as the police grew increasingly suspicious) before a rebellious Janet could be induced to abandon her show and emerge. She saw the police and was alarmed at once.

I told her what the police had said, and if anyone could act more astonished than I had been, it was Janet.

After the police realized it was a false alarm and left, Janet and I discussed the possibilities. Who had reported such a ridiculous thing? The obvious answer was that a fan of mine, a little the worse for drink perhaps, had thought this would be a funny practical joke, but very few fans would be so well acquainted with my address and apartment number.

Then I remembered that there was someone who had been harassing Janet with phone calls. (Her maiden, and professional, name is in the phone book.)

We called the police. *Which* name had been given them?

Sure enough, it was Janet's.

Within a week, I had written a Black Widower story based on the incident. It was entitled "Police at the Door," and it was published in the June 1990 *EQMM*.

144

Heinz Pagels

I had lunch with Heinz Pagels on April 12, 1982, and got to know him. He was a tall man with a high forehead and a shock of prematurely white hair that contrasted oddly with his youthful face. He looked even younger than his forty-two years. Soon to be head of the New York Academy of Sciences, he was a brilliant physicist. He wrote several books on quantum mechanics, including *The Cosmic Code*, which I read with a great deal of pleasure.

Heinz Pagels was, in my opinion, the brightest of the shining lights who assembled at the Hugh Downs dinners. He also ran the Reality Club, a group of brilliant minds who gathered at roughly monthly intervals at various places in Manhattan to listen to talks on the borderlands of scholarship and to discuss what they heard. I was invited to join, but I have not attended regularly. There were some interesting moments at the few sessions I did attend. For one thing, I gave a talk of my own to the Reality Club on May 7, 1987. I talked about science fiction, of course.

Then, on November 5, 1987, Alan Guth gave a fascinating talk on the subject of the "inflationary Universe," a theory he was the first to advance.

Some time before, I had heard of the inflationary-Universe theory for the first time from Heinz, who explained to me that the Universe might possibly have started as a sub-subatomic particle that represented merely a quantum fluctuation in an infinite sea of "false vacuum."

I was fascinated because years before anyone had suggested such a thing I had written an essay entitled "I'm Looking Over a Four-Leaf Clover" *(F&SF,* September 1966), in which I stated my own belief as to the beginning, and the rule I advanced was "In the beginning there was Nothing," and called it Asimov's First Rule of Cosmology.

It was just an intuitional leap, but I'm fond of my scientific intuition, and this incident pleased me.

I remember some arguments too. One speaker, on February 5, 1987, had spoken of the early Christian church on the basis of some narrow view of his own in which Jesus played the role of magician. Apropos of something he said, I pointed out that the true founder of Christianity was St. Paul, and that without him Christianity might have lived and died as an obscure Jewish sect.

He did not see my point and talked about prosperous Christian communities that St. Paul had never visited. I tried to explain that all those communities were overwhelmed by what the later church considered heresy and, eventually, by Islam, and that it was the regions in which St. Paul was missionary where the mainstream of Christianity survived and flourished.

I tried to quote Horace, who said, "Brave men have lived before Agamemnon, but all are overwhelmed in eternal night . . . because they lack a sacred poet." I tried to explain that St. Paul played Homer to Jesus' Agamemnon, but I could never make my point before he interrupted me to repeat his own view. I wouldn't have minded if he had listened to me and then refuted me, but he never listened, and Heinz had to stop me because he noticed I was growing angrier and he was afraid I might explode and hurt the invited guest's feelings.

On another occasion I was trying to explain that carbon 14 was more dangerous to the body than potassium 40, because carbon 14 was sure to be found even in the very genes, where every breakdown meant, without exception, a mutation, whereas potassium 40 was not present in the genes and therefore did not *necessarily* cause mutations.

The Nobel Laureate Rosalyn Yalow kept objecting that potassium

40 produced more energy in breaking down and was therefore more dangerous. Several times I pointed out that it wasn't the energy but the *location* that constituted the danger and she refused to see it.

Of course, the reader might argue that I was as stubborn in my viewpoint as they were in theirs. Yes, indeed, but I was right and they were wrong and that made the difference.

On another occasion, I remember, I was thinking of fractals. These are a set of curves with fascinating properties. They have fractional dimensions, so that a fractal curve can be neither one-dimensional nor two-dimensional but one-and-a-half-dimensional, which is why they are called fractals. Such curves can be infinite in complexity, so that every small part—no matter how small—is as complex as the whole thing.

The theory of fractals was first developed in detail by a French-American mathematician, Benoit Mandelbrot, whom I met on April 16, 1986, when he was being honored by the Franklin Institute in Philadelphia. On that occasion, I was giving the main speech of the evening, but I had never been informed that it was a black-tie affair. As a result, I was the only male there not in a tuxedo—which didn't bother me a bit.

In any case, Heinz posed the following question one day at a meeting of the Reality Club: "Can science ever explain everything? And can we decide whether it can or not?"

I spoke up at once and said, "I'm sure that science *can't ever* explain everything and I can give you my reasons for that decision."

"Go on, Isaac," said Heinz.

I said, "I believe that scientific knowledge has fractal properties; that no matter how much we learn, whatever is left, however small it may seem, is just as infinitely complex as the whole was to start with. That, I think, is the secret of the Universe."

Heinz looked thoughtful and said, "That's interesting," but no one else present said anything.

On July 25, 1988, during the annual session at the Rensselaerville Institute, Mark Chartrand brought in a half-hour television tape showing a fractal. It started with a dark heart-shaped figure that had small subsidiary figures about it and, little by little, it grew larger on the screen. One subsidiary figure would slowly be centered and grow larger until it filled the screen and it could be seen that it was surrounded by subsidiary figures too, which when enlarged had still other subsidiary figures.

The effect was that of slowly sinking into a complexity that never ceased being complex. It was absolutely hypnotic as I watched the endless unfolding. That, I thought, is what scientific discovery was like, an endless unfolding of deeper and deeper layers of complexity— *forever*.

And I thought of Heinz and looked forward to telling him about the tape, if he didn't already know about it.

But I read no newspapers at Rensselaerville, I listened to no radio, and I watched no television. I didn't know, therefore, that exactly twenty-four hours before I had watched the fractal tape, Heinz Pagels, attending a conference in Colorado, was preparing to come down from a mountain he had climbed. (He was an enthusiastic mountain climber.) He stepped on a loose rock, lost his balance, tumbled down the mountain, and was killed.

I did not find out about it until I returned home and looked over the copies of the New York *Times* that I had missed. I yelled in shock and Janet came running in fright to see what had happened. Heinz was only forty-nine years old when he died.

145
New Robot Novels

Even before *Foundation's Edge* was published, Doubleday was satisfied on the basis of advance sales and on the sale of foreign rights that it was going to be a big moneymaker. I wasn't, simply because I couldn't believe that one of my books could be a best-seller. Having 261 non-best-sellers in a row rather established the pattern, to my way of thinking.

Doubleday, however, was sure enough of their ground to have Hugh O'Neill hand me a contract for another novel on May 18, 1982, a contract that offered me a substantially higher advance than that for *Foundation's Edge*. What's more, as soon as I signed the contract, he gave me a check for the first half of the advance.

I kept calm. I didn't even think of beginning the new novel till *Foundation's Edge* was published and I found out how well it would *really* do.

I found out. When it hit the best-seller list, I realized I had no choice. I began the new novel on September 22, 1982.

Nothing in the contract, or in any verbal communication from Doubleday, however, had said it must be another Foundation novel and I certainly didn't want to do one. Instead, I thought of another series I had never finished.

I had published the book version of *The Caves of Steel* in 1954, and its sequel, *The Naked Sun,* in 1957. In 1958, I had a contract for a third novel about Elijah Baley and R. Daneel Olivaw (the detective and his robot assistant), for my intention was to make another trilogy out of it. I began the third volume in 1958 and bogged down after I had done eight chapters. Nothing more would come and what I had written I felt was unsatisfactory. This was the book for which I tried to return the $2,000 advance Doubleday had paid me. They eventually transferred the advance to my first Doubleday nonfiction book, *Life and Energy.*

Now, in 1982, twenty-four years after I had failed with the third book of the robot trilogy, my thoughts turned to it once more. If I could successfully add a fourth book to the Foundation saga, then surely I could successfully add a third book to the robot saga.

What had stopped me in 1958 had been my intention to have a woman fall in love with a humaniform robot like R. Daneel Olivaw. I had seen no way in 1958 of being able to handle it, and as I wrote the eight chapters I grew more and more frightened of the necessity of describing the situation.

The climate in 1982 had changed, however. Writers were more freely able to discuss sexual situations, and I had become a better writer. I didn't go back to those lost eight chapters (as I had gone back to the fourteen pages of Foundation material). I just didn't want them at all. I decided to start fresh.

I had been asked to make *Foundation's Edge* longer than my early novels, which had been 70,000 words apiece, except for *The Gods Themselves,* which was 90,000 words. For that reason I had made *Foundation's Edge* 140,000 words long. I assumed that my instructions held for later novels and it was my intention to make the third novel 140,000 words long too—that is, as long as the first two robot novels put together. This would give me more room in which to describe the minutiae of the new societies I would deal with, and more leisure to work out complexities of plot.

I called the new novel *The World of the Dawn,* because the chief setting was on a planet named Aurora, who was the Roman goddess of the dawn. However, Doubleday again had the final word. A robot novel would have to have the word "robot" in the title, they said. The novel was therefore named *The Robots of Dawn,* which turned out to be even more suitable.

I enjoyed writing the new novel considerably more than I had enjoyed writing *Foundation's Edge.* Partly this was because, with an actual best-seller under my belt, I had more confidence this time around. Then, too, *The Robots of Dawn,* like the first two robot novels, was essentially a murder mystery and I am particularly comfortable with mysteries.

I finished the novel on March 28, 1983, and by that time *Foundation's Edge* had done so well, and *The Robots of Dawn* was so well liked by the Doubleday editors, that I resigned myself totally to the writing of novels.

As a matter of fact, *The Robots of Dawn* also made the best-seller lists, but for fewer weeks than did *Foundation's Edge,* even though the former was, in my opinion, the better book. There were possibly two reasons for this that had nothing to do with the relative qualities of the two books. For one thing, *Foundation's Edge* had been the beneficiary of the long wait for another Foundation book. The wait for a third robot book had been neither as long nor as intense. Second, a lot depends on the nature of other books being published at the same time. *Foundation's Edge* came out when there was a relative dearth of popular books, while *The Robots of Dawn* faced stronger competition.

Since I had to follow with another novel, my pleasure with *The Robots of Dawn* led me to write a fourth robot novel. In the fourth book, Elijah Baley would be dead, but I had already decided that the robot, Daneel Olivaw, was the real hero of the series, and he would continue to function.

Still, the fact that my robots were becoming increasingly advanced with each robot book, made it seem stranger and stranger that there were no robots in my Foundation series.

Carefully, I worked out a reason for it and, in doing so, I could see that it was going to be necessary to tie my robot novels and my

Foundation novels together into a single series. I intended to begin that process with the upcoming fourth robot novel, and to give a hint of my intention I was going to call it *Robots and Empire.*

I discussed this with Lester and Judy-Lynn del Rey, because Random House had absorbed Fawcett and taken over my paperback fiction. They were, in particular, doing the paperback editions of my new novels of the 1980s and I felt they ought to know. To my surprise and considerable chagrin, the del Reys argued strongly against my plan to fuse the two series into one. They said the readers would prefer to have the two separate and, it seemed to me, they were determined not to publish the paperback versions if I carried through my plan.

I stumbled away very dispirited and explained the situation to Kate Medina. (Hugh O'Neill had taken a position with Times Books, and Kate, whom I had known for years, had now become my editor.)

She said, "What is it you want to do, Isaac?"

I said miserably, "I want to tie the series together."

"You're the writer. Do it."

"You don't understand, Kate. If I do it, the del Reys probably won't buy the paperback rights."

Kate said, "That's not your concern. You write what you want, and it will be Doubleday's job to sell the paperback rights; if not to the del Reys, then to someone else."

(So you see how easy it is to be loyal to Doubleday. After all, they're loyal to me!)

I went ahead and wrote *Robots and Empire* and clearly began the process of fusing the two series. And, in the end, virtue triumphed, for the del Reys *did* buy the paperback rights even so. There was a publication party for the book on September 18, 1985, and Judy-Lynn del Rey attended in fine spirits and never said a word of disapproval for what I had done. (As it happened, it was the last time I was to see her alive—how good it is that we can't see the future.)

Incidentally, though *Foundation's Edge* was published in 1982 and *The Robots of Dawn* in 1983, *Robots and Empire* was not published till 1985. The reason for the year's delay I will explain later.

Robots and Empire did very well and it made the *Publishers Weekly* best-seller list, as did the two earlier novels, but it did *not* make the New York *Times* best-seller list. This was important because the paperback sales allowed bonuses of additional money if the book stayed for a certain length of time on the best-seller list, and only the New York *Times* list counted.

I was very crestfallen as a result; not for the loss of the bonus but for what I thought might be my loss of status in Doubleday's eyes. I went to Kate and told her that perhaps I ought not to write any more novels since I didn't make the *Times* best-seller list.

And Kate said, "Don't worry about that. If the book didn't make the list, that's our fault, not yours. You just write your novels and let us take care of everything else."

So I returned to the Foundation series and wrote *Foundation and Earth*, which was a sequel to *Foundation's Edge*, and the fifth book of the series. It was published in 1986, and it *did* make the best-seller list, not only in *Publishers Weekly* but in the New York *Times* as well.

146

Robyn Again

As I said before, the breakup of my first marriage did not destroy, or in any way weaken, the close affection between Robyn and me.

Robyn graduated from Boston College, having majored in psychology, on May 22, 1978. She then took graduate courses at Boston University, and on May 17, 1981, obtained her master's degree in social work.

I attended both graduation ceremonies. I managed the bachelor's ceremony in such a way that I avoided meeting Gertrude. This was done by the simple expedient of my attending the ceremony itself, while Gertrude attended a reception afterward.

When it came to the master's degree, neither Gertrude nor I were willing to miss the ceremony, and, with much misgiving, Robyn asked each of us to attend and to endure each other. I must admit I was apprehensive, but perhaps because neither of us wished to make Robyn unhappy on a propitious occasion, it worked out. I even invited Gertrude to have lunch with me, just the two of us, and it was reasonably pleasant. She had lost weight and had, I believe, even given up smoking. She had just had her sixty-fourth birthday the day before, but she was still attractive and looked much younger than her age. It was the first time I had seen her since the divorce.

Eventually, Robyn found that she didn't want social work as her full-time career. She was faced so constantly with the unhappiness and misery of the people she was trying to care for, and her warm heart drew her into such empathic misery, that it depressed her. And as the Reagan administration continued to transfer funds from hospitals and other much-needed social institutions into the pockets of arms manu-facturers and politicians, working conditions grew steadily worse.

Robyn decided she wanted to move to Manhattan and find a job there, in the hurly-burly of the most unusual metropolis in the world. I was against it. I love Manhattan and would not live anywhere else, unless I was forced to do so at gunpoint. Nor do I have any fears for myself despite the general impression that New York City is particu-larly prone to street crime. Neither Janet nor I have suffered any violence so far. Still, I must admit that I was uneasy at the thought of Robyn living in Manhattan. Yet, if that was what she wanted, the decision was hers.

I continue to follow my practice of noninterference with Robyn, although she lives in the same city. I don't even demand that she see me very often. I do talk to her on the phone quite frequently, but (deliberately) irregularly. I don't want her to feel tied down and, in fact, one of my great worries is that when it comes time for me to die, she will have trouble reconciling herself to that great and inevitable fact, despite my attempt to limit my intrusiveness into her life.

I would prefer to have her even less firmly tied to me, though that would be at considerable discomfort to myself, if that would lessen her pain when I—most unwillingly—desert her.

I'm also worried about Janet for the same reason, needless to say. Janet and I have been inseparable since I came to New York in 1970. From the way she hovers over me, from her frightened reaction to my every cough and sniff, I can imagine her reaction when I—most un-willingly—desert her.

But what can I do? (I can hear Janet and Robyn say, in chorus, "Live forever! That's what you can do!")

—Well, I'll try, but I must admit that one gradually loses confi-dence in being able to do so as one grows older and sicker.

147

Triple Bypass

Six years had passed since my heart attack, and I had been living a normal life, just as before. My schedule was full of out-of-town lectures, business lunches and dinners, interviews and social engagements. In those six years, I had published about ninety books, including two novels that made the best-seller lists.

Why didn't I take it easier? Surely, a heart attack is a legitimate excuse to slow down.

First, I didn't want to. I dreaded slowing down.

Second, I'm a denier. I had known some hypochondriacs who enjoyed ill health, who insisted on it, who abandoned any doctor who told them nothing was wrong with them, who used the ill health to garner pity and to force others into the position of servants. I was determined not to be like that. I treated any kind of illness as an insult to my masculinity, and so I was a denier—I denied it ever happened. I insist that I am well when I am obviously not well, and if I am forced into illness despite everything I can say or do, I retreat into sullen silence, until I recover—when I promptly deny I was ever sick. As you see, then, my heart attack was a source of serious embarrassment to me and I pretended, as far as I could, that it had never happened and that I could live an uncaring normal life.

Third, I was in a hurry, for despite everything I couldn't rid myself of the feeling that I was mortal; in fact, a lot more mortal than I had felt earlier. When I was young, I looked forward to living till the science fictional year of 2000; in other words, till I was eighty years old. I took it for granted I would make it.

But when both my parents died in their seventies and I had my first operation on a cancerous thyroid, I had to admit that eighty was perhaps unrealistic and that perhaps it was safer to hope I lived to be seventy. Then, with a heart attack at fifty-seven, I couldn't help but wonder if I would have to be satisfied with sixty. There was therefore an urge to speed up rather than slow down, in order that I might get as much work done as possible before I was forced—most unwillingly —to abandon my typewriter.

So put all that together and you can see that my years after the heart attack had to be crammed as tightly with work as I could manage.

But despite all denials, I had one heritage of the heart attack that I could not ignore. That was my angina. It wasn't very bothersome, but if I walked too far, or too quickly, or up an incline, the pain clamped down upon my chest and I was forced to wait in order to let that pain subside. I raged against that evidence of old age and mortality, but there was nothing I could do about it.

For years, however, it remained a minor irritation, since I could avoid it by simply walking at a moderate pace and counting on a natural pause at red lights (so that I could pretend I wasn't forced to stop for internal reasons).

The trouble was that the situation grew slowly worse and finally in 1983 it reached a point where it couldn't be ignored. I could no longer deny very effectively. My coronary arteries were becoming narrower with accumulating plaque and my heart was being more and more starved for oxygen. —And yet I couldn't bring myself to mention the matter in my diary; I couldn't make myself put the truth down in writing.

Over the Labor Day weekend, I went to the World Science Fiction Convention in Baltimore. On September 4, 1983, *Foundation's Edge* won the Hugo by a narrow margin, despite competition from both Heinlein and Clarke. It was my fifth Hugo.

What made the convention most memorable for me, however, was that it was spread over two adjacent hotels, so that we had to travel from one to another constantly over walkways, and I had the greatest difficulty in managing it.

On September 12, I spent some time with George Abell, the astronomer, whom I had met on earlier occasions through Carl Sagan. He was a very intelligent man and very friendly. He was younger than I and seemed absolutely fit, for he kept up a regime of exercise and he lacked any sign of a potbelly.

I thought of my own sedentary and flabby life, and of my increasing martyrdom to angina, and I suppose I would have felt envy if it weren't that I was well aware that my condition was my own fault in that it was the result of a lifetime of dietary and sedentary abuse. I had no right to indulge in envy. Nor need I have done so, for on October 7, poor George died of a heart attack and I lived on. He was only fifty-seven, the age of *my* heart attack.

On September 18, I attended "New York Is Book Country," the annual book-promoting extravaganza along a temporarily closed Fifth Avenue. Robyn showed up with two of her friends and we all went afterward to have dinner. However, I had to beg them all to slow down and creep along, for I could not walk any faster. That was more embarrassment for me, I'm afraid, to say nothing of my concern over the fact that I was clearly frightening Robyn.

By September 24, I actually mentioned my angina in my diary.

Life went on, however, and I even continued to pretend I was well. I kept up my drumfire of lectures, traveling to Connecticut, and to Boston (to give one last talk for the medical school on October 3, 1983), and even as far as Newport News, Virginia.

On September 23, I met Indira Gandhi at a meeting she requested with a number of authors, and we gave her some books. She was a gracious, intelligent woman.

On September 28, I attended a fund-raiser for libraries, and on-stage, as part of the entertainment, Richard Kiley recited Lewis Carroll's "The Walrus and the Carpenter." Toward the end he was stuck for a line, and after a few seconds of agonizing uncertainty on my part as to what I was to do, I shouted the line at him. (I had memorized all eighteen stanzas of the poem in grade school, and I don't forget things.) He continued and I tried to sink into my seat thereafter in order to escape notice, but it was too late. The toastmaster had recognized me and quickly announced who "the prompter" had been.

But on October 17, 1983, on my monthly visit to Paul Esserman, I finally broke down and actually admitted *to a doctor* that I was having anginal problems. I tried to make light of it, but Paul would have nothing of that. Frowning, he called a cardiologist named Peter Pasternack and made an appointment for me.

On October 21, I therefore met with Peter Pasternack and he refused to make light of my angina either. He set up an appointment for a stress test for me. I began to use nitroglycerine patches for relief, but they didn't help much. On October 22, Marty Greenberg and I walked from my apartment to the hotel where the Bouchercon (a mystery convention) was being held. It was only half a mile but I had to stop three times in clear agony. Again I was embarrassed, and also concerned over the fright I was giving Marty.

On October 25, Janet brought a semisweet chocolate female leg (nearly life-sized, but hollow) to the Dutch Treat meeting. It had been given to me by Doubleday as a publication-day present, and Janet was not going to let me eat it all by myself. The club accepted it gladly and had it broken up so that everyone (including me) could get a piece or two for dessert. I expected that Janet, after making the delivery, would be more or less politely ushered out of what was after all a stag meeting, but she wasn't. In gratitude for the gift, she was seated at the head table (while I sat at the usual Jewish table) and they made much of her.

On October 26, I had my stress test and I failed it with flying colors. An isotope picture of my heart was taken and it clearly showed that my coronaries were badly blocked. In my diary for that day I recorded that 1983 was on its way to being far and away my best year as far as income was concerned, but, alas, "I don't expect to long survive it."

Yet life goes on, and even at this crisis I made a trip to Philadelphia to give a talk. On the other hand, I was cautious enough to prepare a new will on November 4.

On November 14, I went to University Hospital for an angiogram. The coronary blockage was pronounced, but still not so bad as to deprive me of what Peter Pasternack called "options." I could have a triple bypass operation or I could choose to live on nitroglycerine tablets and perhaps live out a normal lifetime without an operation, but I'd be more or less a "cardiac cripple."

I said, "What are the chances of dying on the operating table, Peter?"

He said, "About one in a hundred. That counts everyone, however —very old people, people who are suffering emergencies, people who have bad hearts. In your case, the odds would be considerably better."

"And what do you suppose my chances are of dying within a year if I don't have an operation?"

"My guess," said Peter, "is one in six."

"All right," I said, "I'll have the operation."

So Peter made an appointment for me with a surgeon.

(I ought to have started a new novel by now, but I refused to do so until I knew for sure that I would live long enough to finish it. I was *not* going to leave an unfinished novel behind me, as Charles Dickens did, if I could help it. That was why there was a one-year gap before *Robots and Empire* was published. However, I didn't loaf. I was working madly those months on the revision of the *Guide to Science,* hoping to complete a fourth edition before I died.)

On November 29, I went to see Steven Colvin, a young, thin, hyperactive person who was totally dedicated to his work and was, perhaps, the best open-heart surgeon in the world.

Peter had told me this, and, as a testimonial to Colvin's worth, Peter went on to say that his own mother had been operated on by Colvin the year before. I thought about that and then asked a question designed to close an obvious gap in the logic.

"Do you love your mother, Peter?" I asked.

And Peter replied, "Very much!" with such sincerity that I felt I could safely put myself in Colvin's hands.

Colvin, after examining me, asked if I wanted to wait till after Christmas–New Year's for the operation.

Actually, I had a reason to wait, for I wanted to attend the annual banquet of the Baker Street Irregulars on January 6. I was preparing a song to be sung to the tune of "Danny Boy" and I wanted desperately to deliver it.

However, I dared not take a chance. I said, "No, Dr. Colvin, I want the operation at the earliest possible date."

So it was set for December 14, 1983.

I completed the song, sang it into a cassette, and told Janet that she must deliver it to the BSI if I couldn't make it. The prospect of the operation didn't make for a happy tenth wedding anniversary for us when it came the day after my interview with Colvin.

To add to the unhappiness, Sally Greenberg, Marty's dear wife, was also entering the hospital. She had cancer of the kidney and was worse off than I was.

A few days before I was due for the operation, I forgot my condition, and because I was having trouble getting a taxi, I ran for one that finally stopped at a red light. My intention was to get it before someone else did and before it drove away.

The flow of adrenaline kept me going, but after I got into the cab, announced my destination, and settled back, the adrenaline stopped and my heart, unable to get the oxygen it needed, yelled at the top of its voice. I had the worst anginal attack ever, and as I clutched at my chest and gasped for breath, I decided that this was it. I was going to have a second attack and this time it would kill me.

It seemed to me that the driver would reach Doubleday, where I was heading, and find he had a dead man in his cab. Unwilling to go through the red tape of reporting me (so it seemed in my imagination), he would continue his drive, taking me to the East River, tumble me into it, and drive away—leaving Janet to go into a frenzy when I never came home.

I reached for my pad to write my name and address on it in large letters, with directions for calling Janet's number, but as I was about to do so, I felt the pain ebbing and when we got to Doubleday I was normal. —I was badly shaken, of course.

What Stan had told me at the time of my thyroid operation, eleven years earlier, was true. When you are driven by pain, you are not afraid of operations. I could hardly wait for the bypass after this experience.

On Monday, December 12, 1983, I entered the hospital. While there, the anesthesiologist told me the nature of the operation. I asked how a bypass could be made, since obviously a hole would have to be drilled in the aorta and I would bleed to death at once.

"Oh," he said, "we stop the heart."

I turned green. "That gives me five minutes to live."

"No, no. You'll be in a heart-lung machine that will keep the blood circulating and you breathing."

"What if the power shuts off?"

"We've got an emergency generator."

"What if my heart won't start again?"

"It will insist on it. The difficulty is keeping it from starting before we are ready."

I brooded about it and asked to see Paul Esserman. "Paul," I said, "I'm embarrassed to say this to the anesthesiologist because he'll think I'm crazy, but you'll understand. Listen, I must have plenty of oxygen for my brain. I can't afford any shortage that will dim it even slightly. I don't care what happens to my body, within reason, but my brain mustn't be in any way disadvantaged. You'll have to explain to everybody involved in the operation that I have an unusual brain that *must* be protected."

Paul nodded. "I understand, Isaac, and I promise I'll make them understand it too. And I'll test you afterward."

(Years later the New York *Times* ran an article stating that investigation had shown that one in five people subjected to a heart-lung machine suffered some sort of brain damage, not necessarily serious. Paul and Peter both remembered my insistence on plenty of oxygen and both admitted that I had been perfectly right to do so. As it happened, I suffered no brain damage—something I can be sure of because my writing continued undisturbed.)

On the afternoon of the fourteenth, I was wheeled to the elevators and my last words to Janet were: "Remember, if anything happens to me, I have a $75,000 advance for a new novel that you will have to return to Doubleday."

(When it was all over, I told Doubleday this, to impress them with the fact that I had no intention of taking money from them for a book I couldn't do. And they replied, as I might have guessed, with the old refrain: "Don't be silly, Isaac. We wouldn't have accepted the money.")

I had been filled with sedatives and I remember nothing at all after I got into the elevator. I was told afterward, however, that I wouldn't let the operation begin until I had sung a song.

"A song?" I said in surprise. "What song?"

"I don't know," said my informant. "Something about Sherlock Holmes."

Obviously my parody for the BSI was much in my mind. In fact, the evening before my operation, I indulged in an involuntary daydream. I had died on the operating table in my reverie, and Janet, all in black, came to the BSI to deliver the cassette.

"My late husband," she would say, brokenly and in tears, "with the BSI in his last thoughts, asked me to deliver this."

And they would play my parody to the tune of "Danny Boy." The first few lines were:

> Oh, Sherlock Holmes, the Baker Street Irregulars
> Are gathered here to honor you today,
> For in their hearts you glitter like a thousand stars,
> And like the stars, you'll never fade away.

The song would be played and I knew that the audience would be in tears and that when it was done they would stand and applaud and applaud and applaud for twenty minutes. And, in my reverie, I listened to all twenty minutes of the applause, and my eyes filled with tears of happiness.

Then I had the operation and the next thing I knew I was opening my eyes and I realized that I was in the recovery room. I had survived. And my first thought was that now I wouldn't get the kind of applause I would have gotten if I had been dead.

"Oh [expletive deleted]," I said in disappointment.

I have always thought of that moment as the ultimate testimony to the ultimate ham that I was—for I was regretting I had survived because it meant I had lost my applause.

Afterward, Paul told me he had waited after the operation till I opened my eyes and recognized him. I don't remember that, because for a while I kept swimming in and out of consciousness and I remember nothing till consciousness was complete.

I said, in a moment of semi-consciousness, "Hello, Paul."

Paul leaned over, anxious to test the condition of my brain. "Make me up a limerick, Isaac," he said.

I blinked at him, then said slowly:

> There was an old doctor named Paul
> With a penis exceedingly small—

And Paul said austerely, "That's enough, Isaac. You pass."

Once the day dawned, a kindly nurse brought me a New York *Times* and I lay there in the recovery room reading it. Considering that I had had no certain assurance that I would live to see a December 15, 1983, the fact that I was reading a newspaper for that day filled me with elation. I was *alive!*

A doctor passed, stared at me, and said, "What are you doing?"

I looked up in surprise. "Reading the *Times.*"

"In the recovery room?"

"Why not? Reading it won't stop me from recovering."

He walked away, shaking his head. Apparently, patients are not supposed to do anything in the recovery room but lie there in a semi-comatose stupor.

Colvin came to see me. I said to him, "Dr. Colvin, Paul Esserman tells me the operation was a success."

"A success?" said Colvin contemptuously. "It was *perfect.*"

As it turned out, one of my mammary arteries proved to be in excellent shape and it was used for bypassing the largest coronary. A vein from my left leg was used for the other two. The artery can stand much more bashing than a vein can, so the arterial bypass of the main artery was a good thing and left me in that much better shape.

In a way, that was only the beginning, of course. I had to remain in the hospital for two more weeks or so to continue the recovery. It helped to have funds, I can tell you. The harassed nursing staff at the hospital could not begin to give me the kind of care I needed, so Janet simply arranged to have private nurses stay with me on a twenty-four-hour basis, each on an eight-hour shift.

All, I might say, were delightful.

I couldn't have any solid food for days and days, because they were waiting for the excess albumin in my urine to disappear. (The heart-lung machine is hard on the kidneys, and mine have been at less than 100 percent efficiency ever since—though I didn't realize this till long afterward. No one bothered telling me. However, this is not something I can complain about. The kidney condition is not immediately life-threatening and the coronary condition that was cured by the operation was.)

So I lived on soup and Jell-O for days and grew to hate that diet. When the albumin finally receded to a tolerable level, my nurse (a very pretty one who was nursing while waiting for her break in show business) brought me a sandwich of minced chicken on store-bought white bread. In the ordinary way of living, I wouldn't have spit on such a sandwich, but this time I fell on it like a wolf on a lamb chop, chewed it up with the greatest of avidity, then fell back in my bed with a sigh of pleasure and said to the nurse, "Please give my compliments to the chef."

I finally got out of the hospital on December 31, 1983, and could watch the New Year's fireworks in the park from my apartment window. Not only that, but on January 2 I was able to creep to Shun Lee (our local, and excellent, Chinese restaurant) and celebrate my sixty-fourth birthday in the traditional manner with the del Reys, and with Robyn present as an added bonus.

But January 6 was coming, and I plagued Peter Pasternack for permission to attend the Baker Street Irregulars banquet. He finally gave in and said, *"If* the temperature is above freezing and *if* there is no precipitation."

It seemed unlikely, for we had just lived through one of the coldest Decembers on record while I was in the hospital. Lady Fortune smiled at me, however. The evening of January 6, 1984, saw the temperature at 40 degrees and, while cloudy, there was no precipitation. We got into a taxi, told the driver we'd double his tip if he drove slowly (I was in no condition to withstand even a minor collision), and arrived at the banquet during intermission.

Everyone flocked about me to tell me how wonderful I looked (a sure sign that I looked terrible, indeed) and I sang my song rather hoarsely, for I'd had a tube down my throat for six hours while I was on the operating table. I got the applause, but it was only for two minutes, not twenty. There are disadvantages to being alive.

It was important for me to stay home and rest for a while, although, to my relief, it turned out that taking care of my accumulated mail and writing my books was not considered to be strenuous work. (Not physically, anyway.)

That was a great break for me because I had gone into the hospital with the last chapter of the *Guide to Science* not yet revised. I managed to finish it and brought it in personally to Basic Books (now part of the Harper & Row conglomerate) on January 17, 1984, and listened to everyone tell me how great I looked. The fourth edition, *Asimov's New Guide to Science,* was published later that year.

I was left with two physical pieces of disturbance. My voice continued hoarse, and after a while I began to think of cancer of the throat. I said to Janet, "If I've managed to live through a triple bypass and survived just to get cancer of the throat, I shall be seriously annoyed."

We went to my nose and throat man, Noel Cohen, on January 25, and he looked at my vocal cords and said, "It's still slightly inflamed from the tube in the throat. Have you been singing? Shouting? Talking?"

I said, "Yes, yes, and yes."

He said, "For two weeks, whisper."

Those were a hard two weeks—but then the hoarseness was gone.

In addition, the little finger of my left hand was weak and wasn't really under my control. Paul Esserman said there was probably some nerve damage as a result of the manhandling I had received and we just had to wait for it to heal.

"How long?" I asked indignantly.

"It's hard to say," he said, "but we must be patient." (Doctors are *very* patient with their patients' troubles.)

It continued for two and a half months. It may sound like a little thing—what's a little finger—but it interfered with my typing at either the typewriter or the word processor, and there were times when I called out to the Universe in impassioned terms, "Take back the bypass and give me my little finger."

But it did heal, and by mid-March my hands were normal and I could type as well as I ever did—and I had no angina. (My poor father! There were no bypass operations in his day.)

148

Azazel

In the 1980s, I began yet a new series of short stories, one rather unlike any that had gone before. It came about this way—

In early 1980, I began to write the series of mystery stories for *Gallery,* and the first one was a mystery but it did not involve a murder (my mysteries rarely do). Rather, it was a story of a fantastic revenge.

My hero achieved his revenge on an extremely wealthy man by making use of a demon only two centimeters tall who could only do small amounts of magic. What the demon did was to remove certain flecks of paint from extremely valuable paintings that the wealthy man owned. The flecks of paint were those that made up the signatures of Picasso and of others, leaving their paintings worthless.

Gallery printed the story, which I called "Getting Even," in its August 1980 issue. I liked the story so much that I tried to write the second story in the series about the little demon also. At this, however, the editor, Eric Protter, objected. One story about a demon, yes, but no more. So I filed the story away regretfully, because I liked that one too.

Then, after I had allowed it to remain in the drawer, eating its head off for over a year, it suddenly occurred to me that I might sell it elsewhere. I asked Protter and he said yes, provided I made some minor changes so that it would not look as though it was a part of the *Gallery* series.

I promptly invented another situation. There were only two characters, an unnamed narrator (who was transparently I) and a deadbeat named George, who always cadged a meal from me and then told a fantastic story about this small demon he could call up. The demon was named Azazel (a biblical name.)

I submitted the story to *F&SF* and it appeared in the April 1982 issue under the title "One Night of Song."

I proceeded to write others in the series, which became quite stylized. In every story, George tries to help out a friend by means of Azazel's powers, and in every story the help turns out to be a hindrance. The reader is, of course, supposed to guess what will go wrong before I reveal it, and in that sense there is a mystery aspect to it.

In addition, the stories are deliberately overwritten and there is an atmosphere of broad farce about them. The most ridiculous things are said with a straight face, and I get the chance to satirize many of the aspects of society that I think are worth satirizing. And the stories are *funny*—in my estimation, at least.

After I had published two Azazel stories in *F&SF*, Shawna McCarthy, who was by now editor of *IASFM*, objected. She said the stories ought to go into my own magazine.

I said, "But, Shawna, the stories are fantasies. They involve a demon. *F&SF* publishes fantasies, but *IASFM* doesn't."

Shawna said, "So make the demon an extraterrestrial being and give him advanced scientific powers rather than magic."

So I did. My story "To the Victor" appeared in the July 1982 *IASFM* and, thereafter, all my Azazel stories did.

I get occasional letters from readers objecting to the stories on the ground that they are fluff, or frivolous, or insignificant, but I pay no attention to that at all, though I go out of my way to see that some such letters are printed in the magazine. My own attitude is that *IASFM*, under the direction of Shawna McCarthy and then Gardner Dozois, is a very serious magazine, printing stories of a high literary quality that often require considerable concentration if they are to be properly appreciated. An occasional Azazel story, which requires no concentration at all, but moves along merrily, is a welcome change, it seems to me.

Of course, there are people who insist I write them merely because they are so easy to write and that I'm just being lazy. The back of my hand to them if they think that light reading is easy to write. It takes quite a lot of art to be able to write artlessly, and if it were easy to write successfully funny stories, more of them would be written.

By the time I had published seventeen of the Azazel stories, it seemed to me that it was time to put them out in book form and I brought the collection to Doubleday, where Jennifer Brehl had succeeded Kate Medina as my editor. Jennifer objected to Azazel as an extraterrestrial. She wanted him to be a demon. I said that was what he had been at first but my magazine had made me change that. Jennifer said, "Change it back. We want to be able to say this is your first book of fantasies."

I saw the value of that and did as she asked. I also wrote a preliminary story describing how the narrator came to meet George. The book, under the title *Azazel* and with the subtitle *Fantasy Stories,* was published in 1988. I have written eight more Azazel stories since then, and, if I live long enough, I suppose there will eventually be a second collection.

149

Fantastic Voyage II

Apparently, the long-term success of the movie *Fantastic Voyage* (which reappeared on television now and then) and of the novelization I had produced of it inspired some people to think of a sequel. They bought the name of the movie (but not the characters), they planned to get me to write *Fantastic Voyage II,* and then they'd make a movie out of it.

At the William Morris Literary Agency, which was handling the matter, there was a great deal of talk about having a blockbuster bestseller on our hands. I'm not totally immune to the thought of bestsellers, so I was tempted. I was also interested in the suggestion because I had never been satisfied with *Fantastic Voyage* itself, since it had been written from a movie script and was not truly the product of my own imagination. It seemed to me that I could write a much better book on the theme of miniaturized vessels in the human blood-stream if I could go my own way.

I was sent a suggested outline, which was completely unsuitable. It involved *two* vessels in the bloodstream, one American and one Soviet, and what followed was a kind of submicroscopic version of World War III. I wouldn't write anything like that under any circumstances, and I knew they couldn't make me do so. If it came to really writing the book, I would insist on full control of the contents, and if they refused to let me have that, I wouldn't write the book.

After all, as I thought the matter through in cold blood, I began to wonder if they would really make a movie, or if they did, whether I would see a penny of the money it made. (Hollywood is notorious for "creative bookkeeping." They can make many, many millions out of a movie but all of it is skimmed off to actors and direction and what is left, the "net profit," out of which the writers are paid a percentage, usually turns out to be a "net loss.")

So I simply put their suggested outline to one side, told them I would write my own book without reference to any suggestions of theirs, and told them further that I wanted the book published by Doubleday. If there was to be an auction (as they insisted, remarking that they would get a million dollars and more that way), then Doubleday would have to get a fair chance to bid on it. I was, after all, sure that Doubleday would not let it get away and would be the high bidder.

It didn't work out that way. The agent called to tell me that New American Library was the high bidder. I was astonished, so I said, "Well, I'll have to get Doubleday's permission to publish it elsewhere."

The agent said, "Are you contracted to write for them exclusively?"

"Not at all," I said. "Asking their permission is just a matter of honor and ethics." (I didn't expect an agent to make sense out of that statement, but I had no intention of arguing about it.)

What I did not fully appreciate at the time was that Doubleday was going through a period of turmoil because of financial losses. Quite apart from that (which effectively took the minds of the editorial staff off matters of business), my editor, Kate Medina, was having a diffi-cult first pregnancy, comparatively late in life, and was home in bed. Her assistant was out sick as well. There was no one I could speak to about the *Fantastic Voyage II* problem who might be expected to understand the situation. I did manage to reach a reliable editor finally

—Lisa Drew—on September 11. She was holding the fort, and I asked her whether she thought I could do the book for New American Library. Caught by surprise, she said she had better speak to the top brass first.

The next day she called back to say that the top brass objected. (On September 18, however, she left Doubleday, to be followed by loss after loss among the editorial staff, to my great consternation.)

In any case, I was called in to see Sam Vaughan and Henry Reath, both of them at the top of the editorial division.

They told me that Doubleday did not want me to do a science fiction novel for someone else. I said, in confusion, that the agent had said that Doubleday had had a chance to bid on it and had bid low, and they said that, no, Doubleday had never been asked to bid on it.

I was utterly confused by this, and I went back to the agent, who said that he had approached Dell Books for a bid and Dell was a paperback house that was a subsidiary of Doubleday's.

I objected. I said that when I said Doubleday ought to have a chance to bid, I meant *Doubleday,* not Dell. The agent said that from the corporate standpoint that was the same thing, but Sam Vaughan and Henry Reath insisted they had not known of Dell's actions.

The endless telephone conversations on the matter got me more and more confused and I finally decided that I didn't care about the rights and wrongs of the matter; I wasn't going to try to sort out what had been said and done; I was going to stick to fundamentals.

Doubleday was my science fiction publisher. They had worked with me for thirty-four years and some ninety books, including two best-sellers, and I wasn't going to double-cross them. So I told the agent on September 27, 1984, that I wouldn't do *Fantastic Voyage II.*

By October 1, the agent and the movie people he represented were threatening to sue me for breach of contract. I responded with the statement that I had made it perfectly clear, in writing, that my agreement was conditional on Doubleday having a fair chance to bid on the book and that that condition had not been met.

Nevertheless, I felt that I was going to be sued and that, even if I won the case, it would cost a mint in legal fees, in lost time, and in emotional turmoil. So I went to Doubleday again on October 5 (and it was at this time that Henry Reath shook his head and said, "Isaac, you need a keeper," when he found out I had never read the contract with the movie people). I asked what was to be done and Henry said Doubleday would be my keeper, and that their legal staff would take care of everything and bear all the expenses. (Loyalty begets loyalty, in my opinion.)

What Doubleday did, I don't know, but all talk of the lawsuit was dropped and the matter of *Fantastic Voyage II* receded into limbo, to my vast relief.

I went on to finish *Robots and Empire,* which I was working on while the dispute was raging, and it was published in 1985. I then got to work on *Foundation and Earth.* And then, to my total surprise, *Fantastic Voyage II* was reborn. It came about thus—

After I had refused to work on the project, the would-be moviemakers turned to Philip Farmer, an excellent science fiction writer; in fact, a far more skillful writer than I am, if you ask me.

He wrote a novel and sent them the manuscript, but they didn't like it and New American Library didn't like it either. The moviemakers turned to Scott Meredith, perhaps the outstanding literary agent in the world, whom I had known well when I was twenty and he was seventeen. They wanted Scott to get me to reconsider doing the novel. If anyone else had asked me, I would have returned a flat refusal, but an old friend is an old friend, so I temporized and asked to see Phil's manuscript, so I could see what *not* to do.

Scott sent me a copy of the manuscript and I read it. It was not a science fiction novel of the kind that I would want to do, or that I was capable of doing, but it was, in my opinion, terrific. What's more, it stuck tightly to the outline they had once sent me. It dealt with World War III in the bloodstream, and it was full of action and excitement.

I called up the Scott Meredith people and told them that everyone was crazy. They had asked for a particular novel and Farmer had supplied them with the very thing they wanted. There was nothing wrong with it. Why didn't they accept the manuscript, get someone to publish it, and make a movie out of it?

No, no, no, no. They wouldn't hear of it. They wanted me to write the novel. So I carefully made conditions I felt they would reject.

1. They would have to pay Phil Farmer whatever they would have paid him for an accepted novel, for under no circumstances would I undercut a fellow writer.

2. They would have to understand that the novel I wrote would be completely different in plot from what Phil had written (so that he could sell his manuscript elsewhere if he wished) and would in no way match the outline they had once sent me.

3. The hardcover would have to be published by Doubleday.

By that time, Doubleday had changed completely. Betty Prashker, Kate Medina, Sam Vaughan, and Henry Reath had all left, and Dick Malina, whom I had never met, was in Henry Reath's place. On January 27, 1986, Scott Meredith and Dick Malina hammered out the necessary arrangements and New American Library was persuaded to let go of the book.

After that I had to write it, so I began on February 1, 1986. It had similarities to *Fantastic Voyage*, but was longer, more detailed, more scientific, with better characterization—superior in every way, in my opinion. I was very pleased with it, and Doubleday published it in 1987. (By the time the book was published, Dick Malina had left and Nancy Evans replaced him—but none of these repeated changes affected my writing or my relationship with Doubleday as a corporate entity.)

I feel that *Fantastic Voyage II* did not do as well as it might have because I pictured a future in which the Soviet Union and the United States were cautious friends. It dealt not with competing submarines in the bloodstream, but with *one* submarine, with my American hero cooperating (not entirely voluntarily) with four Soviet crew members.

I suppose the story would have been more acceptable if it were a straight matter of Soviet bashing and if the wicked Commies were defeated and slaughtered, but I'm not much good at war stories.

Of course, three years after I wrote it, I grinned wryly as the cold war ended and the United States and the Soviet Union looked as though they were trying to head for greater friendship. Everyone in the United States kept saying, "Who would have thought it?"

Well, *I* had thought it, and *Fantastic Voyage II* turned out to be prescient in that respect. Just the same, it was never made into a movie. The moviemakers should have done as I said, and should have worked with Phil Farmer's novel.

150

Limousines

When I had lived in New York as a poor young man, the subway or the streetcar was my preferred means of transportation. Fares were only a nickel. Taxis, though more convenient, were financially out of reach.

When I returned to New York in a condition of middle-aged affluence, I used taxis as my preferred means of transportation. This was not only a matter of convenience. The subways and buses, having increased their charge from 5 cents to (eventually) $1.15, had naturally increased the dirt and danger in proportion.

The next step upward was the limousine, but I hesitated to make use of them. The trouble was that I am not a limousine person. I feel out of place in one. It is the transportation equivalent of the tuxedo, in which I also feel out of place.

Yet circumstances conspired to make me a limousine person, at least a little bit. As I grew older and more famous and as my reluctance to travel grew ever more pronounced, I was more and more frequently offered limousine transportation as an added inducement. It is hard to turn that down, so Janet and I have become used to getting into a limousine and being driven—sometimes for many miles, once over the distance from New York City to Niagara Falls. (Naturally, we always specify a careful, nonsmoking driver.)

Only once did I have real trouble with a limousine and that was on November 4, 1984. I had been driven about fifty miles upstate to give a talk, which proved very successful. There was a reception afterward and then I was ready to be driven home, but there was no limousine. The person in charge of the talk had to call the limousine people to get one out there for me. There were some hard words from the person about the limousine not having waited for me.

When the limousine came, I got in, while the driver went into the building and (I found out later) exchanged more hard words with the person in charge. I waited patiently in the limousine for about ten minutes before he came out, and when he was driving me home, he was clearly in a bad mood because (I found out later) the person in charge had refused to pay in advance.

Apparently, the driver brooded about that and, when we had gotten halfway home, he stopped the limousine at a roadside phone and, excusing himself, got out to phone his boss. He got back in and began moving the limousine in a way that roused my instant suspicion.

"What are you doing?" I demanded.

"I'm taking you back because I didn't get paid."

"You can't do that. I've got to go home."

"Sorry. My boss says I've got to be paid first."

"How much is it?"

"One hundred fifty dollars."

"I'll pay you. Take me home."

"If I take you home, what if you don't pay me?"

"I'll pay you *now*," I said in exasperation, pulled out the money, and handed it over. So he took me home.

I eventually got the money back from the person who had arranged the talk, but it had been an annoying experience. To be fair, it was the only time when any limousine driver, in my experience, ever failed to do his professional duty in giving the interests of the passenger top billing, so to speak.

151

Humanists

I've never been particularly careful about what label I placed on my beliefs. I believe in the scientific method and the rule of reason as a way of understanding the natural Universe. I don't believe in the existence of entities that cannot be reached by such a method and such a rule and that are therefore "supernatural." I certainly don't believe in the mythologies of our society, in Heaven and Hell, in God and angels, in Satan and demons. I've thought of myself as an "atheist," but that simply described what I *didn't* believe in, not what I did.

Gradually, though, I became aware that there was a movement called "humanism," which used that name because, to put it most simply, Humanists believe that human beings produced the progressive advance of human society and also the ills that plague it. They believe that if the ills are to be alleviated, it is humanity that will have to do the job. They disbelieve in the influence of the supernatural on either the good or the bad of society, on either its ills or the alleviation of those ills.

I received a copy of the "Humanist Manifesto" decades ago when I was still quite young. I read its statement of the principles of humanism, found that I agreed with them, and signed it. When, in the 1970s, an updated statement, "Humanist Manifesto II," was sent me, I agreed with it and signed it as well. That made me an avowed Humanist, something in which Janet, entirely of her own accord (and as a result of principles she had developed before she ever met me), joins me.

As a matter of fact, when we were getting married and were deciding under whose auspices we were to be married, we chose Edward Ericson of the Ethical Culture Society because he too had signed the

Humanist Manifesto both times. And he interrupted his busy schedule to marry us because I had.

My humanism doesn't extend merely to the signing of statements, of course. I have written essays by the dozen that support scientific reasoning and in which I denounce all kinds of pseudoscientific trash. In particular, I have argued vehemently against those religious Fundamentalists who back the Babylonian worldview of the first chapters of the Book of Genesis. These essays have appeared in a number of places, even in the June 14, 1981, issue of *The New York Times Magazine*.

I also wrote an Op-Ed piece in the *Times* in which I disputed strenuously (and with justice, I think) the views of a prominent astronomer who published a book in which he maintained that the Big Bang theory was somehow anticipated by the biblical writers of Genesis and that astronomers were hesitant to accept the Big Bang because they didn't want to support the conventional religious view.

I expanded that Op-Ed piece into a book, *In the Beginning*, in which I went over every verse in the first eleven chapters of Genesis, in as evenhanded and unemotional a method as possible, and compared the literal interpretation of its language with the modern beliefs of science. It was published by Crown in 1981.

Then, of course, there was my earlier two-volume *Asimov's Guide to the Bible*—written from a strictly humanist point of view.

All this resulted in the American Humanist Association selecting me as the "Humanist of the Year" in 1984, and I went to Washington to receive the honor and to speak to the group on April 20, 1984. It was a small group, of course, for we Humanists are few in number. At least, those of us who are willing to identify ourselves as Humanists are few. I suspect that huge numbers of people of Western tradition are Humanists as far as the way they shape their lives is concerned, but that childhood conditioning and social pressures force them to pay lip service to religion and do not allow them even to dream of admitting that it *is* only lip service.

Previous "Humanists of the Year" included Margaret Sanger, Leo Szilard, Linus Pauling, Julian Huxley, Hermann J. Muller, Hudson Hoagland, Erich Fromm, Benjamin Spock, R. Buckminster Fuller, B. F. Skinner, Jonas E. Salk, Andrei Sakharov, Carl Sagan, and a number of others of equal note, so I was in select company.

I gave a humorous talk on the occasion, dealing with the kinds of letters I received from religionists, letters that went to the extreme of praying for my soul, on one hand, to that of consigning me to Hell, on the other. The talk was a huge success; too huge, for it meant that I was eventually asked to become president of the American Humanist Association.

I hesitated, explaining that I didn't travel and that I would be totally unable to attend conventions held anywhere but in New York City, and that, moreover, my schedule was so heavy that I couldn't engage in extended correspondence or involve myself in the political disputes that are inevitable in all organizations.

I was assured that I would not be expected to travel or to do anything I didn't want to do. What they wanted was my name, my writings (which I did anyway), and my signature attached to fund-raising letters.

Even with that settled, I still had to wonder what would happen if I heightened my profile in the Humanist movement to such an extent. My magazine, *IASFM,* was still quite young and one or two people had already canceled their subscriptions "because Isaac Asimov is a Humanist." Would I be killing the magazine altogether if I became president of the AHA?

Then I thought that my editorials in the magazine were completely outspoken—so what worse could my presidency do? Besides, I didn't want to make a decision that was influenced by cowardice. I therefore agreed and I have been president of the American Humanist Association ever since.

The Association has kept its word. I am not expected to travel or to involve myself in organizational procedures. However, I have signed a number of fund-raising letters and I have also continued writing my humanistic essays. The Association is happy about this, because since I have become president, the membership of the Association has increased considerably, and they insist on giving me the credit for that.

152

Senior Citizen

I passed my sixtieth birthday safely, a milestone I had feared I might not reach after my 1977 heart attack. Then I approached my sixty-fifth birthday, another milestone I had feared I might not reach in the nervous month before my triple bypass.

Now here it was. On January 2, 1985, I turned sixty-five, an age that is often considered the official dividing line beyond which a person is a "senior citizen," a phrase I detest with all my heart.

What I was, at sixty-five, was *an old man*.

Sixty-five is, of course, the traditional age for retirement, but that is only true if someone is in a position to fire you and call it retirement. As a free-lance writer, I can be rejected but not fired. Publishers may refuse to put out my books, but they cannot prevent me from writing them.

So I threw a "nonretirement party" for over a hundred people. Janet and I specified "no presents" and "no smoking." A smoke-free party was the best present I could get and it went off magnificently, with all my publishers and friends smiling at me, and my brother, Stan, making a funny speech, and so on.

And my writing career passed right through the sixty-fifth birthday as though there was nothing there.

On February 7, 1985, however, the government caught up to me and I was called in to see some officials who wanted to look at my birth certificate and my tax returns. (I might have mailed them in, but my birth certificate, a fragile piece of old paper from Russia, was not something I cared to trust to the mails—or to the government officials, for that matter.)

I was told that I qualified for Medicare and I accepted that with a certain guilt since I buy ample medical insurance and can afford to pay for my medical care even if I didn't have it. However, I had just gone through a nasty and expensive medical procedure and might have to go through more. I was unwilling to strip myself of a sizable portion of my estate for nothing more than my survival, when I was planning to leave my wife and children as secure as possible after my death. So when the officials told me I *had* to accept Medicare, I acquiesced.

Social security was another thing. I flatly refused to accept that. I said, "I have not retired. I make a good deal of money and will continue to do so. The social security payments are not needed by me and they are needed by others, so keep my payments in the social security fund and pay it out to those others."

The person behind the desk said, "If that's what you want, all right, but only till you're seventy. After you turn seventy, you will have to take your social security payments."

I shrugged that off and forgot about it until January 1990, when a government check arrived that I couldn't account for until I remembered the social security bit. I consulted my accountant, and he said, "You paid for it, Isaac. It's your money."

So it was. And then I thought of the hundreds of thousands of dollars I pay each year in taxes and how much of it finds its way into the pockets of greedy politicians and businessmen—and I hardened my heart and accepted the payment, which, believe me, is not a large one.

153

More About Doubleday

After the *Fantastic Voyage II* imbroglio, conditions at Doubleday continued (to say the least) unsettled. It was clear that Nelson Doubleday, who owned the firm and also the New York Mets baseball team, was interested only in the latter. With the publishing firm losing money, he was looking for a purchaser.

As I mentioned earlier, I lost editor after editor, as all moved on to greener pastures. Nevertheless, I had no thought of doing anything but cling to the firm. I was not of a mind to scuttle off a sinking ship, especially when I wasn't ready to believe it was sinking. I felt Nelson would sell out to some other firm and things would continue well.

Incidentally, each year Nelson would send me an invitation to the Mets' opening game at Shea Stadium, and on April 14, 1986, I actually went to see the game. It was the first time I had seen a baseball game live since I took David to a Red Sox game a quarter century before.

I found that the magic was gone. I no longer enjoyed the surroundings, the compulsive beer drinking, the raucousness, and the fact that I knew that, although I had arrived at Shea Stadium by taxi, I would be going home by subway. (Today, if I had to repeat the matter, I would use a limousine, of course, but it wouldn't be worth it.)

It didn't help the occasion that the Mets lost that opening game and that Dwight Gooden, their star pitcher, whom I had come especially to watch, was knocked out of the box. The Mets then went on to win the next eleven games, which, of course, I didn't watch. After the eleventh victory, I happened to meet Nelson Doubleday at the office elevators.

"Mr. Doubleday," I said, "I saw the Mets lose the opening game at Shea, but since then, when I haven't been in the stands, they have won eleven straight."

"Good," said Doubleday. "In that case, don't go to any more games, Isaac."

"I don't intend to," I said, "but don't you think I ought to be *paid* to stay away?"

In a way, he did pay me, because when the Mets got into the World Series that year, he arranged to let me have four tickets at their face cost (they were being scalped for incredible sums). I, of course, didn't go, but I gave them to Bob Zicklin, my lawyer, at face cost.

In any case, the turmoil at Doubleday left me with a young woman named Jennifer Brehl as my editor. She was only twenty-four years old at the time. She had been working at Doubleday for only two years, had served as Kate Medina's assistant, and inherited me.

As I have explained before, I don't in the least mind having young editors, and I especially didn't mind Jennifer, for it was clear to me that she was enthusiastic, hardworking, completely reliable, and very intelligent. We quickly established a very close working arrangement with which we were both extremely happy. I was a big item for her, her claim to editorial fame, so to speak, so she worked very hard on my behalf and that was exactly what I wanted.

Because I'm not temperamental and agreed readily and happily to anything that was in the least reasonable, Jennifer came to feel a daughterly affection for me, and her concern for my health and welfare seems to run as deeply, almost, as Robyn's does. In fact, in October 1987, when the stock market crashed and lost 500 points, only two people phoned me to find out if I had been, by any chance, wiped out. (Actually, I hadn't been. I remembered the 1929 stock market crash, and my broker, Robert Warnick—a wonderful fellow—had it quite clear in his mind that I would deal only with bonds; no stocks. I was not anxious to make a big killing at the risk of making a big losing. The result was that the stock market crash didn't cost me a penny.)

Robyn was one of the two people who phoned, and I reassured her, but I realized that she had to be concerned about her inheritance, however much she might be far more concerned for my welfare. The second person who phoned was Jennifer, and she had no inheritance to worry about. She was concerned only for me and I was very touched. I reassured her too, of course.

On March 5, 1989, Jennifer told me she had to give up her job at Doubleday in order that she might help her father in his business. The day-to-day work at Doubleday (in connection with me) was then performed by a still younger woman named Jill Roberts, who, like Jennifer, was enthusiastic, hardworking, completely reliable, and very intelligent.

As an example—

In late 1989, a special limited edition of my new novel, *Nemesis,* was prepared. I was supposed to sign every one of the 500 copies to be issued. Each was eventually enclosed in an individual package and these were enclosed, ten at a time, in large boxes. Every book was numbered and put into correspondingly numbered packages, and it was only when all was done and packaged that someone realized that they had never had me sign the books.

I was called in early one morning, and each big box was opened, each small package was opened, each book was signed by me and put back into the small package, and eventually into the big box. I sat there all morning long, signing. It wasn't too difficult, because Jill organized everything so efficiently that the books came streaming out in front of me. All I did was sign while Jill opened boxes, and closed packages, and did all the necessary work so smoothly that not one book ended up in the wrong place. It was a lovely example of efficiency.

Meanwhile, though, I was setting a fine example myself, without knowing it. Generally, an author who is put through some sort of misery entirely through the fault of the publisher gives full vent to his temperament and makes life miserable for everyone in the place, especially if he's an old and venerated author who knows he can get away with it.

But that didn't apply to me. For one thing, I'm not temperamental (at least, not beyond reason). And for another, all I was doing was signing my name, and Jill was doing the hard part, so there was no reason why I couldn't pass the time pleasantly, cracking jokes and singing songs. From all over Doubleday, therefore (so I was told later), people came flocking to the room where I was working in order to peek in and view the anomalous sight of a happy writer.

After it was over, Jill and a couple of others insisted on treating me to lunch, though I assured them it wasn't necessary. It is amazing how the young women flock about me now that I'm old and harmless. Where were they when I could have taken wicked advantage of their affection?

154

Interviews

No writer can escape being interviewed. The appetite for material with which to fill newspapers and magazines is insatiable, and as I grew better known, the number of interviews increased. Even when I was still teaching at the medical school and had only been at the start of my unusual writing career, the Boston *Herald* interviewed me and I ended with an eight-column headline identifying me as a "BU professor."

It was at that time that I was busily fighting to keep my academic title and my foes in the administration at once swooped down upon the headline as an example of my trying to use my position for personal promotion.

It was an easy thing to fight off. The headline was not my doing, and nothing in the interview itself smacked of personal promotion. Besides that, I had granted the interview at the request of the president of the American Chemical Society, which wanted a little publicity push for a meeting of the Society that was about to take place in the city. I had the correspondence to prove this, and I was a little sanctimonious about my duty requiring me to help my professional society when requested to do so. The administration retreated in confusion.

The best interview in print I ever had was the one that appeared in *The New York Times Book Review* on August 3, 1969, the day before my father's death.

I have also been interviewed many times on television. The two most successful interviews (in the sense that I enjoyed them most) were one by Edwin Newman in 1987 and another by Bill Moyers in 1988.

In both those cases, the interview lasted an hour and the interviewer confined himself to asking questions and letting me talk. You would think that this is what an interviewer would be naturally expected to do, but if so, few of them realize it. The usual thing is to have the interviewer compete with you desperately in what seems to be a mad attempt to prove his own erudition. In such cases, since I have no need to prove my own erudition, I would much rather have stayed at home and let the interviewer conduct a monologue.

I once had an interviewer who kept accompanying everything that I said with little sounds of agreement, or perhaps little sounds merely intended to indicate he heard me. I was largely unaware of this when I was recording the interview, but when later I watched the interview on television I was enraged. His constant "ums" and "uh-huhs" drowned me out and made a hash of my appearance.

In the case of both Ed Newman and Bill Moyers, by the way, I did not know beforehand what questions I was going to be asked. There was no rehearsal, no preparation. I simply sat down, was asked questions, and answered. I am too old a hand at public speaking and too clear in my opinions (which I have been working out in innumerable essays) to require preparation, and I speak most easily and eloquently when I *haven't* been chewing the matter over in my mind until most of the taste has been lost.

Then there are telephone interviews. After the advent of television, radio found that most of its entertainment staples had moved over to the new medium. What proliferated, then, was the radio talk show. The hosts of those shows must constantly be interviewing people, and since I won't travel, I accept telephone interviews without objection. It's the only way I'm ever going to be heard by people in Detroit, or Tampa, or San Antonio.

Naturally, such requests for phone interviews come in clusters. Each time a novel of mine appears, or an important nonfiction book, I can count on numerous phone calls asking to set up a time for an interview.

Sometimes, an interview is requested because something has happened that has a scientific or a science fictional angle. When the Viking probes landed on the Martian surface, I had a rash of interviews, the general tenor of which was that since no life was found on Mars, the whole thing was useless and a waste of money, wasn't it, Dr. Asimov?

—And each time I had to explain patiently the enormous value of scientific knowledge concerning Mars even if it did not contain life.

This sort of thing reached its peak after January 28, 1986, when the *Challenger* shuttle blew up shortly after takeoff, killing seven astronauts. The news reached me just as I was walking into the Union Club to preside over a Dutch Treat luncheon. Someone had brought a portable radio so we could all hear the latest bulletins and that was one sad meeting, let me tell you.

But I knew what would come next. My telephone was ringing continually for several days as every radio talk show in the United States wanted my opinion on the matter. What opinion could I have but that it was a desperately deplorable tragedy. And what further opinion could I have but that every great and risk-laden project has its tragedies, yet the projects must continue anyway.

155

Honors

One can't live a normal lifetime and accomplish anything at all above the level of being a drunken bum without getting awards for something. I have been at numerous conventions in the course of my oratorical adventures and there are few of them where awards aren't handed out to various people—sometimes in gratitude (I think) for their consenting to retire.

Even in science fiction, awards keep proliferating. There is the Hugo award (given in ever increasing categories) and the Nebula award. In addition, there are awards in the names of dead superstars of science fiction; awards named for John Campbell, Philip Dick, Ted Sturgeon, and so on. Perhaps in time to come there will be an Isaac Asimov award.

Naturally, I have collected a number of awards (and would collect more if I were willing to travel more than I do). Some are quite trivial, and the most trivial of them, and one I rather like just the same, is a fancy plaque that says on it: "Isaac Asimov, Lovable Lecher." That's something to get an award for, isn't it?

I've also collected diplomas; not only my own legitimate Ph.D., which is framed and up on the wall, but fourteen honorary doctorates as well, stored in a trunk.

I never had an academic robe of my own (I refused to attend my own graduations) and so each school for which I gave a commencement address had to supply me with one, and with a mortarboard and tassel. When I got my honorary doctorate from Columbia, however, they let me keep the academic robe instead of taking it back at the end of the proceedings. What a pleasure! Now I could wear my own.

However, the very first time I wore it at another commencement, it started raining during the address, for the first time it ever had on such an occasion. I had to put up an umbrella while speaking so as to protect my precious robe.

I have never worn it again, because I am getting too old to sit in the sun for two hours and watch hundreds of youngsters get diplomas, just so that I could make a twenty-minute speech.

There were also honors I got for reasons that had nothing to do with my accomplishments, but simply came to me because of where I was born, or the circumstances of my childhood.

Thus, when projects arose for renovating Ellis Island as a kind of museum to honor the achievements of immigrants who had come to the United States during the years when it was the Golden Door to the Promised Land, *Life* magazine decided to find some people who had actually come through Ellis Island. It meant finding old people, for Ellis Island had been shut down decades before.

I was one of the old people they found. On July 28, 1982, I was taken down to the lower tip of Manhattan (in a driving rainstorm, as it happened) and was ferried over to Ellis Island. It was the first time I had set foot on it since that time in 1923 when I arrived and got the measles to celebrate the fact. The buildings were in a state of shabbiest decay and I was photographed sitting rather glumly in the middle of one of them.

The photograph appeared in *Life*, and everyone who saw it asked, "Why are you wearing rubbers?"

And I said, "Because it was raining heavily. Why else?"

A couple of years later, I was awarded some sort of medal or other for having (a) been an immigrant and (b) done something to make the United States not too sorry that I had arrived. I was there in Battery Park with dozens of other well-known immigrants on a gloriously sunny day. Mayor Ed Koch (whom I had introduced on three different occasions as a speaker at Dutch Treat) made a speech, and someone sang "The Star-Spangled Banner," and my name was called out in due course.

Perhaps the most surprising honor I got was to have my name inscribed on a slab of rock on a pathway in the Brooklyn Botanic Gardens. I was not the only one, of course. As one went along that path, there was rock after rock with the names of Brooklyn-born people who had become famous. (Mae West's name was there, for instance.)

When I was told my name was being added, I said I hadn't been born in Brooklyn. They told me that since I had been brought up in Brooklyn from the age of three and had been educated in Brooklyn public schools, that was enough. Janet and I therefore went to the Botanic Gardens on June 8, 1986. When the taxi got us to Grand Army Plaza, we found the whole area blocked off for the party (which was much huger than I had been led to expect) and the taxi would not have been allowed through if one of the policemen hadn't recognized me.

Janet and I followed up the path, read all the names, and met various celebrities who were also being honored. I was asked to say a few words, but the real star present was Danny Kaye, whom I had always admired, and whom I now met for the first and only time. He called me *payess* (Yiddish for "sideburns") and then gave a charming talk.

However, he looked ill and, as a matter of fact, he died on March 3, 1987, only nine months later, at the age of seventy-four.

156

Russian Relatives

I knew, of course, that I had Russian relatives. My father had three brothers and a couple of sisters, and my mother had siblings too. And presumably these had children, and so on. However, there was no contact with them as far as I was concerned, and never had been.

In their early years in the United States, my parents occasionally got letters from Russia, but they did not read them to me or tell me anything about them. (And, to be honest, I wasn't interested.) The result was that I grew up with only my own core family—father, mother, sister, and brother—and was quite contented with that situation. There was my mother's half brother and his wife and son, but they impinged on us only slightly.

After the war, I somehow took it for granted that it was not likely that any of my relatives had survived. Those that joined the army might well have been among the millions who were killed. Those that were trapped by the Nazi invaders might well have been among the millions who were killed by Nazi brutality.

It was only after my earlier autobiographic volumes reached the Soviet Union, however, that I became aware that there were relatives still surviving; or, rather, that they became aware of me.

For years, to be sure, I had been a popular writer of science fiction in the Soviet Union (perhaps helped out by the "-ov" ending of my name), and it was possible that those who bore the same name, or were married to those who had, might have suspected that I was a relative.

Asimov, however, is not an uncommon name in the Uzbek Republic in Central Asia, and it is there spelled (in Cyrillic characters) with an "s." In Byelorussia, where I was born, it was spelled with a "z," but my father had made a spelling mistake when he arrived in the United States. Judging by name only, it was hard for other Byelorussians to tell whether I was a relative or not. In fact, I got word once that there were Uzbekis who claimed relationship.

Once my autobiography came out, however, my birthplace, Petrovichi, became known, as did my grandfather's name, Aaron. That was enough. I began to receive letters, notably from my first cousin, Serafina, the daughter of my father's younger brother, Samuel, who had been an officer in the Soviet army and who had survived the war, but was now dead. (Another younger brother, Ephraim, had died fighting in the Caucasus in 1942.)

My father's youngest brother, Boris, had survived the war and lived in Leningrad, but managed somehow to get out of the Soviet Union in the 1970s and migrated to Israel. My brother, Stan, with a greater sense of family than I had, tracked him down. We thereupon decided what to do (we had to do something, since he was undoubtedly penniless, and he was our father's brother).

I suggested that Marcia carry on a correspondence with Boris in which she would include checks. I would supply the money for those checks, and Stan was to be the decision maker. If Marcia had any questions involving our Uncle Boris, she was to consult Stan, who has the virtual monopoly on common sense in the family.

It didn't work out too well, for Marcia made very heavy weather out of the correspondence, but we managed somehow. Stan even got one of the people at *Newsday,* who happened to be planning a visit to Israel, to promise to look up Boris and see how he was. She did so. He was very old, very feeble, and apparently not quite in his right mind either. He died on August 30, 1986.

This did not put an end to the matter of Russian relatives at all. I had first cousins, second cousins, and people who had married them and had children, and all wrote letters to their famous American relative. Once Mikhail Gorbachev eased conditions in the Soviet Union, a number of them came to the United States and then letters began to come from America.

One letter expressed annoyance that I didn't hasten down to Florida to see my long-lost stranger-relatives. I had to reply politely that I never traveled.

Another group came to the apartment house without warning. When a suspicious concierge called to tell me there were strangers there who claimed they were my relations, I had to go down to see them. When I did, a middle-aged woman threw herself into my arms and wept all over my shoulder at the joy of seeing her beloved something-or-other. I didn't quite find out just exactly how they were related to me, but what they really wanted was for me to find them a place to live. I said that there was a large colony of Russian Jews who had settled in Brighton Beach, but they said they knew that, and wanted a better neighborhood.

Did they expect me to pull an apartment out of my pocket? They eventually left.

Meanwhile, letters still come from various people in the Soviet Union. The family ramifications seem to be incredible.

This is one of those matters that make me wretched. I can't help but feel that most people have extended families, with enormous family feelings, and must live according to a family code whereby any member of the family can call upon any other member of the family for help and be sure of receiving it. I gather that Janet's relatives were like that.

But I have never had an extended family, and I don't feel that sort of togetherness outside Janet, Robyn, and Stan. I don't want to seem cruel and heartless and I'm willing to hand out money to any of them who are down and out, but I can't go beyond that. I just haven't got it in me to greet them with tears of joy and invite them in and make much of them just because they are distant relatives—or say they are.

157

Grand Master

By the time I was sixty-seven years old, it might have seemed I had everything I could possibly want as far as the science fiction world was concerned. I had Hugos, Nebulas, and best-sellers. I was one of the Big Three. I was treated as a monument at science fiction conventions, and young newcomers to the game of science fiction writing viewed me with awe. Thanks to my prominent white sideburns I was routinely recognized in the street and I was sure that, if I traveled, I would find myself recognized all over the world. I was as popular in places like Japan, Spain, and the Soviet Union as I was in the United States, and my books have been translated into over forty languages.

What remained?

One thing! In 1975, the Science Fiction Writers of America instituted a very special Nebula to be called the Grand Master award. This was to go to some science fiction superstar at a Nebula awards banquet for his life's work, rather than for any single production.

The first one went, inevitably, to Robert Heinlein. There was no argument about that. He was the general favorite among science fiction readers and he had pioneered the advance of our kind of science fiction into the slicks and the moving pictures. He was respected outside science fiction as well as inside. Sprague de Camp happened to be at a function along with Heinlein on October 23, 1984, and we took the opportunity to take a photograph in the same pose that had been taken of the three of us back at the NAES exactly thirty years before.

Other Grand Master awards were handed out in later years. Jack Williamson received the second, and Clifford Simak the third. Others went to L. Sprague de Camp, Fritz Leiber, Arthur C. Clarke, and Andre Norton. All were well deserved. All, except Norton, were closely associated with John W. Campbell and the Golden Age.

What's more, all were well stricken in years but had fortunately survived to receive the honor. In fact, I can only think of two people in magazine science fiction who would surely have deserved the honor but who had died before 1975. They were E. E. Smith and John W. Campbell himself.

Naturally, it seemed to me that I was an odds-on favorite to get a Grand Master award someday, but when?

The awards were not given every year. In the eleven years from 1975 to 1986 inclusive, only seven awards had been handed out. All seven Grand Masters were older than I was, and all had begun publishing in the 1930s or 1940s, so I had no quarrel with their getting the awards. Of the writers that remained, two worthy candidates I could think of that were older than I were Lester del Rey and Frederik Pohl, and that might delay my turn anywhere from two to four years.

I was nervous about that. I was having a rash of medical problems that did not fill me with much confidence as to my chance of surviving three or four years, and I certainly didn't want people to go about saying, "We should have given him a Grand Master award before he died." A fat lot of good that would have done me.

It may sound rather greedy of me to hunger for the award, but I'm human too. I wanted it. Besides, I honestly thought I deserved it. However, I kept my hunger entirely within myself. In no way did I campaign for it, and by no word or deed did I ever indicate openly that I was interested.

But the time came at last, and I was still alive. On May 2, 1987, at the Nebula awards banquet, I received my Grand Master award. I was the eighth Grand Master and all of us were still alive, a point I made gleefully in my acceptance speech.

(It was the last opportunity to say that, alas, for in the next year two of the Grand Masters, Robert Heinlein and Clifford Simak, died. What's more, in 1988, the ninth Grand Master was to be Alfred Bester, but he was dying and the award had to be made posthumously. Fortunately, he was told of the award before he died on September 20, 1987, at the age of seventy-four. The tenth award, and the last at this time of writing, went to Ray Bradbury in 1989. I hope that Lester del Rey and Frederik Pohl get one soon. Lester is seventy-five and Fred is seventy, at this time, and they both deserve it in full measure.)

In my acceptance speech, incidentally, I said we all looked for special distinction. Thus, though Bob Heinlein was the first Grand Master, Arthur Clarke was the first British Grand Master, and Andre Norton was the first woman Grand Master. I, although the eighth all told, was the first Jewish Grand Master.

After the banquet, Robert Silverberg (who, next to me, is the most prominent Jewish science fiction writer) said, "Now that you're the first Jewish Grand Master, where does that leave me?"

Unless Bob dies prematurely, he is sure to be a Grand Master someday, and so I said to him, "Bob, you will be the first *handsome* Jewish Grand Master," and he broke into a smile and was pleased.

158

Children's Books

I have written a considerable number of books intended for the teen-age market. In fiction, there were, for instance, the Lucky Starr series, which I did as "Paul French," and the Norby series, which I do with Janet (though she does most of the work by far). In the case of nonfiction, the series of science books I wrote for Abelard-Schuman were aimed at teenagers.

It is not very difficult to write for teenagers if you avoid thinking of them as children. I do *not* simplify my vocabulary for them, though I often add the pronunciations of the technical terms, merely to reduce the terror they inspire visually. I do avoid sentences that are too long and complex and I do not indulge in obscure allusions. What is lacking in a teenager is not intelligence or reasoning ability, but merely experience.

(In fact, and this is a sore point, those portions of my fiction output that are intended for an adult audience are sometimes considered "teenage reading" by the more arrogant critics. This, I presume, arises from the fact that my adult novels eschew violence and graphic sex, and also commit the terrible crime of being clearly written. This means, of course, that intelligent teenagers can read my adult novels with ease and understanding, but that does *not* make them "teenage reading.")

Occasionally, I have also written books for the grade school young-ster—that is, the preteener. That's harder. There you have to be care-ful of your vocabulary. Fiction has to be short, while nonfiction books about science have to be particularly clear.

My first attempt at science fiction for the preteen audience was *The Best New Thing*, which I wrote in early 1962. I intended it for very young children and, since Robyn was about to turn seven at the time, I read it to her and she seemed fascinated. The publisher for whom I wrote it, however, underwent an earthquake of changes and it was not published till 1971 under the World Publishing imprint.

I wrote a number of short stories for *Boys' Life* at a slightly higher age level. My most successful story in this magazine was "Sarah Tops," which was the first of my tales to feature Larry, my junior high school detective. It has been anthologized about a dozen times.

As far as nonfiction is concerned, there was the ill-fated Ginn Science Program, to which I contributed to the text of those volumes intended for the fourth to the eighth grade. I don't want to talk about them.

Much more my own work was a series of four books I did for Walker & Company: *ABC's of Space* (1969), *ABC's of the Ocean* (1970), *ABC's of the Earth* (1971), and *ABC's of Ecology* (1972).

These books sounded good when Beth Walker first suggested them to me. They also sounded easy. As it happened, they turned out to be neither good nor easy.

The point was to pick two words with each letter of the alphabet and define them. Some letters, however, had many possibilities. Thus in the book about space, S could be used for sun, star, Saturn, satellite, space, and so on. Other letters, like Y, had virtually no candidates. The result was that some very important words had to be omitted and some very borderline words had to be admitted. Defining each word clearly and accurately in only three or four lines wasn't easy either.

By the time I did my fourth ABC book, I rebelled and would do no more. The Walkers didn't try to argue with me, for the books didn't do very well either. The *How Did We Find Out About . . . ?* series I have done for Walker for a somewhat older audience was much more satisfactory and did much better financially.

Then, in 1987, a gentleman named Gareth Stevens was establishing a publishing house in Milwaukee, and Marty Greenberg, ever alert to the possibilities of the ground floor, got to know him somehow. The result was a series of children's books on astronomy with me as the author. Marty acted as my agent, and then refused to accept an agent's fee. He is a *very* difficult person to work with, in that respect.

Gareth asked me to do a series of thirty-two books on astronomy. Each of them was to consist of twelve mini-essays on the subject, plus three more on "amazing facts" and yet another three on "puzzling mysteries." In each case, I would get an outline of the subjects to be

covered, as prepared by someone knowledgeable in educational requirements.

The first book in the series, *Did Comets Kill the Dinosaurs?*, was
written on June 19, 1987, and was published before the end of the
year. I believe that one was chosen to initiate the series because it dealt
with dinosaurs and cataclysms, both of which are popular with youngsters. It certainly did the trick, for on the basis of how well that book
was received, Gareth went ahead full speed on the rest.

At the present time of writing, twenty-nine of the series have been
published and two are still in press. The thirty-second and last of the
series came up at a time when my health was such that I couldn't write
it. It was therefore written in-house, but I may be credited with it as
author, for the sake of series uniformity. (If it is, I won't give it a
number.)

These books seem to be successful. They are filled with marvelous
and spectacular artwork, and are popular with schools and libraries.
Gareth, through trips abroad and aggressive promotion, has sold a
large number of foreign editions, all of which (of those I have seen)
keep the size, artwork, and the aura, and translate only my words.

Only one of the topics assigned to the series displeased me. One
book was assigned to UFOs and I objected on the ground that UFOs
were not astronomy, but mythology. However, Gareth said he was
selling the series on the basis of the list of the topics and the one on
UFOs aroused particular interest.

"All right," I said, "but if I do that book, I will make it perfectly
clear that there is no evidence whatever that UFOs are alien spaceships
and I will stress the fact that there is a great deal of hoax and illusion
involved in the subject."

"Go ahead," said Gareth, and that is exactly what I did.

159

Recent Novels

The ending of *Foundation and Earth* had left me in a quandary. It is my custom to try to leave one loose and untied matter at the end of a novel, in the very likely case that I would want to continue the story. At the end of the previous novel of the Foundation series, *Foundation's Edge*, I had even placed at the end the notation: "The End (for now)." Janet had strongly disapproved of that, saying that I would make the readers wait for it when I might not get around to writing a sequel for years.

I did write the sequel quickly, however, but in *Foundation and Earth*, the last paragraph strongly implied that there were complications existing that could only be handled in another book, and I had no idea how those complications could be handled. I still don't know, though five years have passed since I finished the novel.

That may have been one of the reasons I wrote *Fantastic Voyage II*, as one way of putting off the necessary further exploration of the Foundation universe. But when that was done, what was I to do next?

As it happened, I was going up in my apartment elevator one day when a young man said to me that he had read the Foundation series and he always wanted to know what had happened to Hari Seldon when he was young and how he had come to invent psychohistory (the fictional science that underlies the series).

I seized on that, and when the time came to sign contracts for new novels, I suggested that I go back in time and write *Prelude to Foundation*, which would deal with events that took place fifty years before the first book in the series and with Hari Seldon and the establishment of psychohistory.

Jennifer Brehl at once agreed and, sensing my weariness with the

Foundation books, suggested that the novel after that be not part of either the Foundation series or the robot series, but be an entirely independent product, with a completely new background.

I agreed, and began to write *Prelude to Foundation* on February 12, 1987. It was completed nine months later and was published in 1988. It appeared in paperback form in 1989 as the first volume in a new paperback line established by Doubleday/Bantam, that line being called "Foundation" in my honor.

I then began *Nemesis* on February 3, 1988. It was placed closer to our time than was true of either the robot novels or the Foundation novels. It dealt with the colonization of a satellite that circled a Jovian-type planet that, in turn, circled a red-dwarf star. My protagonist was a teenaged girl and I also had two strong adult women characters. I placed considerably more emotion in the novel than was customary for me.

I enjoyed writing it, but it took me thirteen months rather than the ordinary nine, for reasons I will soon explain. The book was published in the fall of 1989 and it was quite successful.

160

Back to Nonfiction

While I was turning out my late novels of the 1980s, I didn't entirely abandon nonfiction. I wrote essays in great numbers and published collections of them. There were *Far as the Human Eye Could See* (Doubleday, 1987) and *The Relativity of Wrong* (Doubleday, 1988), two collections of my *F&SF* essays. There were also several of the *How Did We Find Out About . . . ?* series for Walker and of course the astronomy books for Gareth Stevens.

However, I didn't write any nonfiction books for adults, except for *Beginnings* (Walker, 1987), my account of the evolution of the Universe, of the Earth, and of man, told backward; and my annotation of Gilbert and Sullivan.

I was simply aching to do something, and what I missed most of all were the history books I had written for Houghton Mifflin. The sixteenth and last of these (before Houghton Mifflin decided to end them) was *The Golden Door,* the fourth volume of my history of the United States, which was published in 1977.

Since then, I had not published a single book on history and I had suffered a whole decade of history starvation.

You might wonder why I did not continue the series with another publisher. The thought was indeed in my mind, but somehow the matter had worked itself into something larger. It occurred to me that I ought to do a history of the world from the very beginning, and include all the nations that I could. I would tell it in my way, as a story, with the old-fashioned emphasis on war and politics.

I knew that it was more important to discuss sociology, economics, and cultural events, and I intended to put in as much as possible of that sort of material. Still, the stuff that nowadays is considered the important essence of history is dull, and I wanted the book read for fun. I didn't care what the critics would say; I intended to write the book to please myself and to insert the kind of excitement and drama that makes for fun. That in turn called for war and politics. After all, since I write rather old-fashioned science fiction and rather old-fashioned mysteries, why not write rather old-fashioned histories too?

I got Walker to agree to publish it and they gave me a contract with a $1,000 advance. (I didn't care if they gave me no advance at all; I just wanted it published.) In January 1979, I began writing it, and I kept at it on and off for well over a year, doing nearly half a million words and reaching the year 1850. But then my novels started, and it was clear that the final century and a quarter would take another half a million words at least, so I gave up.

I hated to let all that go for nothing, for I like to boast that I never waste anything and that I publish everything I write, one way or another, but that project defeated me. I didn't consider it a permanent defeat, of course, since I felt, for years, that I would go back to it and finish it someday, but I never did.

(It wasn't even the first large project that failed. During World War II, I wrote notes on everything that was happening, incredible quantities too, because I intended to write a history of the war once it was over. It was never written. I never even began it.)

While I was writing my novels, various publishing houses would advance complex ideas to me. Doubleday itself asked me to do an overview of science in question-and-answer form, and I started it and did quite a bit, but that too died under the pressure of the novels. I handed back Doubleday's fairly sizable advance.

Then, Harper & Row asked me to write a history of science, year by year. I agreed to do it unenthusiastically, for I felt sure that my novel writing would interfere with any large nonfiction project. But then the further suggestion was made that I include in each year something of what was going on in the world outside of science. That filled me with excitement. It would be a kind of *history* book, a general one, and not just one about science.

With my novels going at a hot pace, I couldn't start it, but I kept thinking about it, and dreaming about it. Then, on November 8, 1987, when I was nearly finished with *Prelude to Foundation,* I cast aside caution and began the book I called *Science Timeline.* Eventually, Harper & Row gave it the ungainly, but descriptive name of *Asimov's Chronology of Science and Discovery.*

I have rarely had so much fun in my life. I used my own *Biographical Encyclopedia of Science and Technology* as a mine of names and dates. I got out every other science history in my library. I used my various encyclopedias. I collected data from everywhere and set about telling the story of science, beginning 4 million years ago when the first hominids appeared. In addition, I threw in a great deal of straight history, using my own histories, including even my suspended world history manuscript, and all the history books in my library to supply me with data.

I tried to write it along with *Nemesis* when it came time to do that novel, alternating the two. I used *Nemesis* as a bribe and the *Chronology* as a reward. If I managed to do ten pages of *Nemesis,* I felt free to do twenty of the *Chronology,* and so on.

The advantage was all on the side of the *Chronology.* I knew that *Nemesis* would make ten times as much money as the *Chronology,* but my heart was with nonfiction. The result was that I finished the *Chronology* by the end of 1987, on schedule, but *Nemesis,* which had the same deadline, was still incomplete. Only when Jennifer frowned at me and gave me a final deadline did I get to work and get it in by March 1988.

Both books were published in October 1989. *Asimov's Chronology of Science and Discovery* is a large book, about 700 pages long, with three times the wordage of *Nemesis*, and I was very proud of it indeed, although there were two items about it that bothered me.

One was that preparing the index, though no more difficult than for my other large books, *seemed* more difficult because I was older and because (though I didn't fully realize it at the time) my health was deteriorating, and I was growing tired more rapidly.

The other bothersome item was that I had rather spread myself on the matter of historical events other than science and, on the whole, the nonscientific portion of the book made up a sizable fraction of it. Harper & Row, anxious not to price the book out of the market, and equally anxious not to have to do it in two volumes, cut out much of the straight history, though they cut out not a paragraph of my science history.

I agreed to that without trouble because a new idea had occurred to me.

The recording of historical events in the world, year by year, brought back to mind the failed world history for Walker that I had given up nearly a decade earlier. Why not try it again on a different pattern—one which was closer to that of the *Chronology*? Then I could, perhaps, get Harper & Row to publish it as a companion piece.

I got to work and spent even more time on it than I had on my earlier attempt at such a history. I started 15 billion years ago with the Big Bang creation of the Universe, and it was my intention to come up to the present moment.

I went well past 1850, which had been the cutoff point of the first attempt, partly because I was more systematic in the arrangement of the book and partly because I was being more concise. By the time I reached World War II, however, I realized (once again) that I could not make it up to the present. It would be far too long. It seemed to me that 1945 would be a good point at which to stop and then, sometime in the future, I could write another book dealing with the history of the world since 1945.

Actually, halfway through World War II, I had to stop for reasons I will soon explain, but this time I *know* the stop is only temporary. Barring my death, the book will be finished.

Of course, the one question of ethics in my mind was: What about the contract I had with Walker to do a world history?

I might easily have argued that that didn't matter. Since I had undertaken that first world history, I had published nearly forty books with Walker, so they couldn't complain I was neglecting them.

Nevertheless, there was the $1,000 advance they had paid me for the book. Fortunately, in 1989, Beth Walker became conscious of the approach of the year 2000 and suggested I do a book describing what the earth was like at every millennium as far as human history was concerned. Then, once I got to the present, I would continue with a chapter on what things might be like in the year 3000.

I at once said I would do it if they would let it substitute for the failed world history and would apply the $1,000 advance I had been paid for it toward the new book. They agreed but insisted on paying me an additional thousand. (Publishers rarely let me have my way in the matter of advances. They always shove more money at me than I ask for.)

The book was easy to do and I had it done in a matter of a few months. It will appear under the name of *The Next Millennium*.

161

Robert Silverberg

Robert Silverberg was born in 1936 and his early years may have been much like mine. At least, when he read the first volume of my autobiography, he found a great deal in it, he said, that was reminiscent of his own life.

I can well believe it, for he must undoubtedly have been every bit as bright as I had been, and may have fit into society as poorly as I did. The results were different, though. I was always loud and brash and ready to mix with company, so that those who were unimpressed by me saw in me something of the buffoon. Bob, on the other hand, was serious and grave, and though he had a keen and effective sense of humor, it tended to flash out only periodically—and unexpectedly.

I interpreted this gravity of Bob's as unhappiness and commented on that in the earlier volumes of autobiography. He later told me that he *was* unhappy in his first marriage. But then, so was I, and if we subtract that unhappiness, he was still grave, and I was still brash.

This bothered him a little, I think, for I remember him once saying that he could not indulge in the self-promoting antics of people like Isaac Asimov and Harlan Ellison. I protest, however, that it's not a matter of self-promotion; it's just the way Harlan and I are. If we were not that way by nature, it would be impossible for us to assume the fakery just to promote ourselves. It must come naturally or not at all.

Bob has a lot going for him anyway. In the first place, he is one of the best writers in science fiction, and if he had been born fifteen years earlier, he would have been one of the Big Three, rather than I.

Second, he is extremely prolific. Certainly, he has the capacity to be as prolific as I am, and he has a surprising range too. He has written first-rate nonfiction books, and I remember reading, with enormous pleasure, his books on such subjects as the Mound Builders of pre-Columbian America and on Prester John. In later life, he has also written very good historical novels—I enjoyed one that dealt with Gilgamesh of Sumeria.

The difference between Bob and me, however, rests in this: Bob is more nearly a whole man. He likes to travel and to do a great many other things. That limits his writing. He is also more practical than I am. He deliberately ceased writing nonfiction because it didn't make enough money, whereas I count the fun of writing nonfiction as quite outweighing the financial angle. When he felt that his publishers were allowing most of his books to go out of print, he "retired" from writing for five years. (It would be inconceivable for me to react in that fashion. I would be punishing myself far more than I punished either my publishers or my readers.) Fortunately, Bob returned to writing eventually.

His first published story appeared in 1954, and I met him first at a science fiction convention in Cincinnati toward the end of June in 1957. After I returned to New York in 1970, the del Reys, the Silverbergs, and the Asimovs made a kind of sextet, with the ever-ebullient Judy-Lynn the spark plug. On several occasions, we were all at the Passover seders which Lester insisted on conducting with all the solemnity of a convert. Lester was also an excellent cook, and if I could not work up the necessary religious enthusiasm on these occasions, I at least ate well.

But then Bob decided that New York was not for him and he left for Oakland, California, where he has lived ever since. I was sorry to see him go, of course, and I could not help but think that the migration from New York to California was very much the same thing as the earlier migration from Europe to the United States—a search for greener pastures and a new life. In California, Bob got a divorce and afterward married again, happily (as I had done).

In 1988, Marty Greenberg had an idea. (He has an endless capacity for having ideas.) It occurred to him that aging writers like me had turned out a number of great magazine stories in our youth, stories we had never done anything further with, and didn't plan to do anything further with. Why not get a younger writer to take a classic story and expand it into a novel?

In particular, why not find someone who would take my story "Nightfall," now forty-seven years old, keep the story essentially as written, but add a detailed beginning and a detailed ending to it. I listened to this in some dismay. After all, another writer might ruin the story and write something that wasn't "Asimovian."

Marty said that we could always arrange for me to have full approval of the final novel and even make changes if I felt it necessary. Besides, he thought he would try to get Bob Silverberg to do it, because Bob was so competent.

"Come on," I said disbelievingly, "Bob would never consent to bury his own work in an Asimov story."

"Yes, he will," said Marty, and he was right.

I was still uneasy. After all, I had to do another novel once *Nemesis* was done. It was contracted for, and it had to be another Foundation novel. I still could not manage a sequel for *Foundation and Earth*, so I planned to fill in the gap between *Prelude to Foundation* and *Foundation*.

The new novel, which I called *Forward the Foundation*, was begun on June 4, 1989, but I was really weary of novels. I had written seven of them in the 1980s, for a total of nearly a million words altogether, and I felt ready to take another twenty-year break (if I had only been young enough to do so). In addition, I wanted to complete my world history book, which was approaching its half-million-word mark.

It occurred to me, then, that if Bob wrote a "Nightfall" novel, then that could be the 1990 book of fiction, and I would have a year's respite before having to complete *Forward the Foundation*.

Naturally, there were some little things to argue about. First, what was I to do with my sense of ethics? Would I have the right to place my name on the book if Bob wrote most of it—and to take an equal share of the royalties too? I mentioned this worry to Marty, who promptly pointed out that Bob would have the advantage of a social background ready-made, to say nothing of characters and events that he could work with, and that I would therefore have a full right to my half interest. I let Marty persuade me.

That still left some little things to argue about. I explained to Bob that I didn't want gratuitous sex, unnecessary violence, or vulgar language in the novel, and he agreed to that, indicating that he would be satisfied to let me have the final word on any matters under dispute. When I said "Delete!" it would be deleted, and when I said "Change!" it would be changed.

For his part, Bob wanted to make sure that I wouldn't drown him out by having my name appear more prominently than his (as had happened, not long before, when Arthur Clarke's name completely drowned out that of his collaborator). I told Bob that he little knew me if he thought I would allow such a thing. We would be treated exactly alike (and this time, remembering how poor Karen Frenkel had been treated, I made sure, in advance, that Doubleday understood the necessity of this).

As a matter of fact, it wasn't easy to convince Doubleday of the desirability of the project, for they wanted my new novels rather than an extension of an old story, but when I said I needed the rest, they gave in. As a matter of fact, Doubleday agreed to do three novels. Bob was going to extend not only "Nightfall" but also "The Ugly Little Boy" and "The Positronic Man."

Eventually, I received the extended "Nightfall" manuscript from Bob. Despite everything, I had fearfully anticipated receiving something I couldn't endure and I wondered how I would break the news to Bob and to Marty and to Doubleday.

I need have had no fears. Bob did a wonderful job and I could almost believe I had written the whole thing myself. He remained absolutely faithful to the original story and I had very little to argue with. Bob has already outlined his version of "The Ugly Little Boy." I have seen that outline and approve it heartily.

Bob changed the name of the planet and of one character in "Nightfall" because I had made deliberate use of Sumerian and Egyptian names to lend strangeness without too much strangeness. Bob thought that a mistake and wanted nothing to be too reminiscent of Earth, and he may have been right. In any case, I let him have his way there.

162
Gathering Shadows

In 1972, after I published the first edition of *Asimov's Biographical Encyclopedia of Science and Technology,* I developed the habit of keeping my eye on the New York *Times* obituary page. The reason for that was that I had to know when one of the still-living scientists dealt with in the final pages of the book died. I would then enter the exact day and place of death in a special copy of the book I used for the purpose. This kept me ready for future editions, and I have followed the system ever since.

I began reading the obituaries with a sense of detachment, for death, of course, was something for old people. I was only fifty-two years old when I began my obituary reading and death still seemed far away. However, as I grew older, the obituary page slowly became at once more important to me and more threatening. It has become morbidly obsessive with me now.

I suspect this happens to a great many people. Ogden Nash wrote a line that I have always remembered: "The old men know when an old man dies."

With the years, that line has become ever more poignant to me. After all, an old person to one who has known him for a long time is not an "old person" but is much more likely to be thought of as the younger person who inhabits our memory, vigorous and vibrant. When an old person dies who has been a part of your life, it is part of your youth that dies. And though you survive yourself, you must watch death take away the world of your youth, little by little.

There may be some morbid satisfaction to being a last survivor, but is it so much better than death to be the last leaf on the tree, to find yourself alone in a strange and hostile world where no one remembers you as a boy, and where no one can share with you the memory of that long-gone world that glowed all about you when you were young?

Thoughts like that would beset me, now and then, after I passed my sixty-ninth birthday on January 2, 1989, and knew myself to be within a year of the biblical threescore years and ten.

Mind you, I hadn't turned completely morbid. For the most part, I maintained my cheery and ebullient outlook on the world. I kept up my busy schedule of social get-togethers, speaking engagements, editorial conferences, and endless writing, writing, writing. But in the dead of night sometimes, when sleep wouldn't come, I might think of how few there remained who remembered, with me, how it all was in the beginning.

Science fiction has now become the province of brilliant young men who probably think of me as a living fossil, a remnant of a superannuated clan that has unaccountably survived into modern times, and who think of the great John Campbell—if they think of him at all—as a mythic paleontological personality.

It sometimes seems to me that if I weren't so insistent on speaking of Campbell in my own writings, he would vanish forever from the minds of people—and in that same way, I often think, my own name will vanish too after the first flurry of regret when I die.

I don't expect to live forever, nor do I repine over that, but I am weak enough to want to be remembered forever. —Yet how few of those who have lived, even of those who have accomplished far more than I have, linger on in world memory for even a single century after their death.

This, as you see, verges dangerously on what is to me the most hated of sins—self-pity—and I fight it. There are, however, times when I feel it difficult to bear up under the increasingly rapid drumfire of deaths that come with the passing years.

I have mentioned a number of such deaths in this book so far.

Of my own generation of my family, my sister Marcia's husband, Nicholas, has died, as has Chaucy Bennetts's husband, Leslie, and her older brother, Harold.

Various members of the Trap Door Spiders died, including three who served as models for my characters in the Black Widower stories: Gilbert Cant, Lin Carter, and John D. Clark. So did members of the Dutch Treat Club, including the successive presidents Lowell Thomas and Eric Sloane.

A great many science fiction writers of my own generation died, from Cyril Kornbluth in the 1950s to Alfred Bester in the 1980s. Among the mystery-writing fraternity, there were the deaths of two of my friends, Stanley Ellin and Fred Dannay (Ellery Queen).

Banesh Hoffman, a physicist, who always sat at my left at the Baker Street Irregulars banquets, died in 1986. Robert L. Fish, a mystery writer who always sat at my right, had died even earlier. David Ford, the actor, who had given me the idea for writing the first Black Widower story, died in 1982.

Lloyd Roth, one of my close friends during my early years as a graduate student, and the fellow who had recommended Charles Dawson to me, died in 1986 also, of Alzheimer's disease.

Once on a talk show, where the public could call in, someone phoned and asked me, "Do you remember Al Heikin?"

"Of course," I said. "He was at the NAES with me back in the early 1940s. How is he?"

"He's dead," came the indifferent answer, and I was forced to lose my cool right there on the radio. He had died in November 1986.

Arthur W. Thomas, the professor who befriended me when I was seeking permission to do my Ph.D. research died in 1982 at the age of ninety-two. Louis P. Hammett, who had taught me physical chemistry in 1939—the last time in my life that I did well academically—died in 1987, also at the age of ninety-two.

Richard Wilson, one of the old Futurians, died in 1987 at sixty-six. Bea Mahaffey, for whom I had written my story "Everest" in 1952 while visiting her office in Chicago, died in 1987 at sixty. Bernard Fonoroff, an old pal from Boston days, died in 1987 at sixty-seven.

William C. Boyd, who had first brought me to the medical school, died in 1983 and his first wife, Lyle (also a friend), had died earlier. Matthew Derow, another fellow faculty member at the school, died in 1987 at seventy-eight. Lewis Rohrbaugh, who had succeeded Chester Keefer as head of the medical school, and with whom I had been friendly, died in 1989 at eighty-one.

And so it went. I held more and more passionately to the dwindling group of old friends who survived: Sprague de Camp, Lester del Rey, and Fred Pohl among the science fiction fraternity; Fred Whipple in Boston; and so on.

Unquestionably, twilight was drawing on and the shadows were gathering—and deepening.

163
Threescore Years and Ten

These gloomy ruminations of mine; these sad thoughts of death and dissolution and of an approaching end; were not entirely the result of philosophic thought and of the bitter experience that came to me with the years. There was something more concrete than that. My physical health was deteriorating.

I would not be a good "denier" if I had admitted that deterioration and you can be sure I didn't admit it. Through the summer and fall of 1989, I stubbornly continued my accustomed course, pretending that I did not feel my years.

Janet and I went south to Williamsburg, Virginia, for the fourth time to give a talk. On October 19, 1989, I had the ineffable pleasure of dining at two different places, eating rabbit at one and venison at the other, and finding both absolutely heavenly in their perfection. When I told this to someone, expressing my delight, the disapproving response was: "Do you mean to say that you ate Bambi and Thumper on the same day?"

In Boston, on March 15, 1989, I helped celebrate the sesquicentennial of Boston University. I also gave my makeup talk at Johns Hopkins on June 28, 1989.

Of course, I kept up my writing, completing *Nemesis* and *The Next Millennium* and a couple of *How Did We Find Out About . . . ?* books. I also started *Forward the Foundation,* and helped with the novelization of "Nightfall." In addition I worked endlessly on my huge history book.

Yet all through that summer and autumn, I felt an unaccountable and increasing tendency to weariness. I walked slowly and with an effort. People commented on my loss of ebullience now and then, and, in embarrassment, I tried to be more lively, but only with an ever-increasing effort.

Indeed, I caught myself thinking, now and then, that it would be so pleasant simply to lie down and drift quietly off to sleep and not waken again. Such a thought was so alien to me that, whenever it occurred to me, I shoved it away in horror. I did so with a kind of double horror, in fact, for I could not help but think how Janet and Robyn would react, for one thing, and for another I realized, with complete consternation, that I would be leaving behind unfinished work.

But the thought kept returning.

Yet not a word of this gathering weariness managed to find its way into my diary. I refused to admit openly that it existed. Just the same, there was something wrong that I could not deny because it was a physical manifestation and not something that might be only world-weariness.

As early as March 15, 1984, Paul Esserman had noted that my ankles were a little puffy. I was experiencing fluid retention, and he suggested that I take an occasional diuretic to encourage urination and the elimination of fluid.

Fluid retention is not an uncommon accompaniment of increasing age and Paul was not worried. I was outraged, of course, as I hated any suggestion that the bodily mechanism wasn't working perfectly. What's more, I resisted the necessity of taking diuretics, as I did not wish to suffer the indignity of urinary urgency and the consequent race to the bathroom.

This was only three months after my bypass operation, and what I didn't know (and perhaps what Paul didn't know either at that time) was that my kidneys had been somewhat damaged by the heart-lung machine experience of the bypass and that they were no longer working perfectly.

Janet saw to it that I took an occasional diuretic (she was always on the side of the doctors and would never understand that loyalty should make her side with me against them). That seemed to take care of the water retention, for a while anyway.

Then, at Rensselaerville in 1987, things suddenly got worse. I was cast into the shadows when I found that Izzie Adler had been diagnosed as having a cancerous prostate and I fought depression by eating unwisely, which, in my case, always means—too well.

Furthermore, it was no concern of mine that the food was salty. In fact, I preferred salt. I liked the taste of salt. I loved anchovies, and smoked salmon, and herring, and bacon, and anything else that was nice and salty. If it was nice but not salty, I added salt—and with a liberal hand.

Janet would protest. High blood pressure ran in her family and she had to stay away from salt because it raised blood pressure. I, on the other hand, although I had had my blood pressure taken every time any doctor got within sphygmomanometer range of me, had never—not once—displayed any tendency toward the condition.

So when Janet remonstrated with me over the question of salt, I would answer loftily that high blood pressure was not a problem of mine, and that I did not intend to give up salt. What I did not know, and what I found out quickly after my 1987 stay at Rensselaerville, was that salt powerfully encouraged fluid retention.

I arrived home with a gain of eight pounds, and feet that were visibly swollen. Nor could I deny the seriousness of this, for at Rensselaerville, I had had the greatest difficulty in walking up the slope from the dining room to the dormitory, something that had never given me any trouble before.

Paul Esserman put me on a stronger dose of diuretics and laid down the law. A salt-free diet for me for the rest of my life.

The bitterness of it was overwhelming and the iron entered into my soul. Janet threw herself into the task of preparing salt-free meals enthusiastically—after all, she had to do it for herself anyway—and she monitored my eating habits at restaurants more closely than ever. I submitted to this, but not with any glad cries of joy, you can be sure.

By now, water retention and certain indications in my blood chemistry (a high creatinine value, for instance) made it clear that my kidneys were lying down on the job, so that I came to meet still another physician. This was Jerome Lowenstein, a urologist (or "kidney man" in English), on August 24, 1987. He was a very pleasant, thin-faced, silver-haired gentleman and I was quite taken with him, except that he reinforced the "no salt" order.

I was able to correct the fluid retention I had incurred at Rensselaerville by the lavish use of diuretics, but the problem did not go away. Things were, in fact, hastening to a climax in 1989.

I began to have an occasional day in which I experienced what I referred to in my diary as a "wipeout." There was one such on November 17, 1989, for instance, in which I stayed in bed most of the day. I blamed it on a succession of largely sleepless nights. Of course, that might have had something to do with it. The trouble lay not in my simply having a lazy day, but in not feeling guilty over it. In a wipeout, I felt no anger at staying in bed; rather, I liked it and actively did not want to get up.

Nevertheless, I forced myself to struggle on. I went out to Long Island to help Stan and Ruth celebrate Thanksgiving. (Of course, it snowed, the only snow of significance in all the winter.) On December 4, Janet and I dined at the Peacock Alley with Fred Pohl. Fred was writing a book on the environment and wanted me to cooperate on it. I said, gladly, that I would do so, but that was to be the last normal day I would have for half a year.

On December 6, I was slated to give a three-hour combination of talk, question-and-answer, and book signing, and I got through it only with a great deal of difficulty. It was the first time in many years that I did not enjoy my talk. When it ended, I dashed for home, bone-weary, with Janet sizzling with anger over my having committed myself to a three-hour session. And I was thinking myself that I had bitten off more than I was now able to chew.

The next day, I experienced a wipeout and, thereafter, over a period of days, it was all I could do to drag myself about. My weariness, against which I had been struggling for months, had finally become so overpowering that I was forced to mention its existence in my diary. On December 13, I wrote, "I have no energy. That is the problem."

Actually, that was the symptom. The problem was not something I would have been ready to admit even if I had known it.

For December 14, my diary entry consisted of one word only: "Sick!"

Paul actually made two house calls to check on me and I was rather touched by that. Doctors simply don't make house calls anymore and I took it as a powerful piece of evidence that Paul considered himself my friend as well as my doctor. (As a matter of fact, Paul is utterly dedicated to his profession, as is Peter Pasternack. I am a very fortunate man to have two such physicians taking care of me, although I am careful not to let them know I feel this way, since I prefer to yell at them a lot.)

I spent three weeks in bed, neglecting my work. Of course, the neglect was not total. I managed to keep abreast of my mail, by answering only those letters it was absolutely essential to answer. I also wrote my weekly syndicated column for the Los Angeles *Times*. However, work on my history book stopped. Nor could I add the final touches to *The Next Millennium* or to the two *How Did We Find Out About . . . ?* books I had been working on. I wasn't able to do the thirty-second and last item of the Gareth Stevens astronomy series at all. In fact, the dates of December 17, 18, and 19 in my diary are completely blank.

I managed to struggle to my feet now and then for special occasions. On December 20, Janet and I were taken by limousine to a midtown restaurant to have dinner with Lou Aronica of Bantam Books and a few other Doubleday people. The conversation dealt with plans by Doubleday and Bantam to put out a uniformly bound collection of *all* my fiction—both novels and short stories, both science fiction and mystery.

It was a wonderful idea and I was pleased and flattered—but I also had a niggling little sensation (which I didn't express) that it was the sort of thing usually done for a writer posthumously. Were they—in the fashion of good businessmen—just looking ahead?

If they were, I couldn't blame them, for they would have been doing no more than I was. All through that unhappy December I kept thinking, "I'm so close, so close, but I won't make it to seventy."

It became almost an obsession with me that month. I was dying, I thought, and, in anger, I complained bitterly to Janet at the fate that would not let me reach the magic age of seventy.

What is so magic about seventy? The trouble is that Psalm 90:10 reads: "The years of our life are threescore and ten."

This has been taken, on biblical authority, to be the normal span of human life. Actually, it's not so. The average life span of human beings did not reach seventy over a large section of the population till well into the twentieth century. It took modern medicine and science to see to it that seventy is really the years of our life. But the Bible says seventy, and that figure became magic.

Comparatively early in life, I managed to have it ground into my brain that there was no disgrace in dying after seventy, but that dying before seventy was "premature" and was a reflection on a person's intelligence and character.

It was unreasonable, of course; quite irrational.

Still, I had reached sixty when, after my heart attack, I thought I might not. Then I reached sixty-five when, before my triple bypass, I thought I might not. And now seventy was within reach and I thought, "I won't make it." (It reminded me of the days in 1945 when I was racing to reach twenty-six before I could be drafted—and failed.)

Janet, in despair, tried to reassure me. She said, "You've often told me that January 2 was an artificial birth date assigned to you when you left Russia, and that you were possibly born as long as two or three months earlier. So actually, you are already over seventy."

But I would have none of that. "My official birth date is January 2," I said fiercely. "If I die before then, the New York *Times* obituary will read 'Isaac Asimov, 69' and that's unacceptable. I want 'Isaac Asimov, 70' at the very least."

Yet I hung on. On Christmas Day, Janet, Robyn, and I all went to Leslie Bennetts's to celebrate the day, and to marvel over her nearly ten-month-old baby. And the next day, I went out alone for the first time in three weeks and visited Doubleday.

Nevertheless, I was dragging about and my legs were monstrously edematous. I had what was, in the old days, called "dropsy" and my legs looked like tree trunks. I could not get my shoes on and I had to walk about in slippers, and not too comfortably at that.

Robyn, on hearing all this, grew very excited and demanded that I make an appointment with a cardiologist. Working at a hospital, she was becoming medically oriented, so that now I had two of them, Robyn and Janet, constantly yapping at my heels.

But I did as Robyn asked and saw Peter Pasternack on December 27 at his University Hospital office. He listened to my heart, and said, "You have a murmur."

"I know," I said. "It's probably congenital." I told him that when I was examined for the army in 1945, forty-five years earlier, I had been told by my examining doctors that I had a murmur, but that it wasn't sufficient to keep me out of the army.

Pasternack shook his head. "We can't dismiss it that easily," he said. "In view of your edema, we have to find out exactly how bad the murmur is, for that may be the root of your trouble."

Of course, that meant the beginning of a series of tests.

January 2, 1990, finally dawned and I was seventy years old after all —officially. Janet, Robyn, and I had a celebration dinner at our Chinese restaurant and we had Peking duck. Or, at least, they had it. I ate a small quantity only, for it had salt in it, so it was not exactly a happy birthday even though I was greatly relieved at having reached it. Nor did it make it better that I was beginning to receive cards from all over the world, uniformly wishing me "a happy and a healthy seventieth birthday."

I was having neither, for despite a daily dose of diuretics, I was still badly edematous and Peter was intent on having me continue taking tests.

164
Hospital

Months before, I had agreed to go to Mohonk on the first weekend of January to give a talk to the guests. I didn't want to go, but a promise is a promise. We asked Peter and he said I might risk it, so we talked Mohonk into sending a limousine for us and we were driven up.

I spoke at Mohonk on the evening of January 5, 1990, and, to my intense pleasure, it went well, and I enjoyed it. It seemed a definite indication that though I might be ill, I wasn't dead. We were home on the seventh and I got right into bed—worn out.

On January 9, I made my publishers rounds and also chaired the Dutch Treat meeting for the first time in a month. However, I was so visibly ill, so clearly exhausted, that I badly frightened Jill at Doubleday and Sheila at the magazine. My Dutch Treat comrades were clearly concerned too.

But I refused to take any more medical tests and I had come to a momentous decision.

On January 11, 1990, I went to see Paul Esserman at my own request. There, almost in tears, I made a rather long and eloquent speech, the tenor of which was that I didn't want to take tests, I didn't want hospitalization, I didn't want anything. I just wanted to be allowed to die in peace, and not be made a football to be bounced from doctor to doctor to doctor while all of them experimented with me and began to employ more and more heroic measures to keep me alive.

I had reached seventy, I said, and it was no longer a disgrace to die. I had squirreled away a sizable estate for which I had no personal use, but which was intended to support my wife and children after I was gone, and I didn't want to waste any of it merely for the privilege of maintaining a maimed existence. I ended by saying that I depended on Paul to see that all this was done.

Paul listened to me very carefully and without comment. When I was done, he called University Hospital and got me a private room in the Co-op Care section of the hospital, and by dinnertime that was where I was.

I asked him, in later days, how he had come to do that when I had just spent an arduous half hour telling him *not* to do it. And he said, "Well, *you* might have been ready to die, but I wasn't ready to let you."

The first task at the hospital (where Janet and Robyn took turns staying with me) was to get rid of the edema, and that meant the intravenous injection of a diuretic. I was fitted with something called a "heplock," which opened a passage into a vein in my arm so that material could be injected into my bloodstream at will.

I was pessimistic. It would do no good, I muttered. I was condemned to death and they were merely prolonging my misery.

But I was wrong. The intravenous diuretic did the job beautifully. During my hospital stay, I lost seventeen pounds of fluid and my legs returned to normal. I had been staring at tree trunks so long that I found it unbelievable that they now looked like sticks. I almost thought they wouldn't be strong enough to support my weight.

While there, my left leg (from which a vein had been taken on the occasion of my bypass operation, and which was more susceptible to infection as a result) developed cellulitis, a bacterial inflammation of the skin, which was more likely to happen when that skin was stretched by edema. I had to keep my left leg elevated as much as possible, while I took antibiotics to fight the infection. That was defeated too.

My big problem came on January 16, which was the sixth day of my hospital stay. For months, Doubleday had been planning a party on that day to celebrate both my seventieth birthday and the fortieth anniversary of my first book, *Pebble in the Sky*. It was to be held at Tavern on the Green and it was, to my horror, to be black tie. I insisted that everyone be told that black tie was optional but, of course, *I* would have to get into my tuxedo.

Yet when the day came, there I was in the hospital. I simply couldn't disappoint hundreds of people, however, so I got Paul to conspire with me. He agreed not to tell anyone about the matter and to attend the party so he could keep an eye on me. Janet then "borrowed" a wheelchair and wheeled me out of the hospital at 3 P.M. when no one was looking. Doubleday had sent a limousine, which took us to the apartment. I struggled into my tuxedo and the limousine then drove us around the block to Tavern on the Green, where all my buddies from various publishing houses, all my pals from the Dutch Treat Club and the Trap Door Spiders, all my friends and neighbors, near and far, were waiting.

There was a reception. I greeted everyone happily, from my wheelchair, with my left leg on a stool in front of me. I refused all the dainties everyone was eating (too salty) and made do with orange juice. Nancy Evans, then president of Doubleday, gave me an absolute sweetheart of an introduction and I launched into my talk.

I discussed my earlier near-scrapes with death, going into full detail about my fantasy involving the Baker Street Irregulars at the time of my bypass and what a flash of disappointment I experienced on realizing that I had survived and would not get the applause a dead man would have gotten.

There was wild laughter and applause from everyone, of course, and the only negative comment I got was from Robyn, who was dripping tears, and who came up to complain bitterly to me over my speech.

I said, "But, Robbie, it was *funny*. Everyone laughed."

She said, "I didn't. You may think it's funny to talk about dying, because you're crazy, but *I* don't think it is."

Well, everyone else laughed!

By 9 P.M., I was back in my room, feeling I had handled everything perfectly and no one in the hospital would know.

However, the New York *Times* knew about the party. It appeared in the paper the next day and everyone in the hospital apparently read it, so that I was lectured by the nurses. Lester del Rey (whose own condition wouldn't allow him to attend) called up and raved at me for doing it and endangering my life. All I could say was "Lester! I didn't know you cared!" and that didn't seem to soothe him.

What bothered me most, though, was a matter involving my syndicated column. It was time to do it and the only way I could manage it was to choose a topic that required no reference material, write it out longhand, and then call the Los Angeles *Times* and read it into their recording machine.

I did exactly that, but when I called I got a young woman at the paper who said to me, as soon as I announced my name, "Oh, you bad boy! Why did you sneak out of the hospital?"

It just about broke my heart. I couldn't even carry out an innocent little deception without the whole world knowing.

It meant I couldn't do it twice. A few days later, *Analog* celebrated its sixtieth anniversary, since the magazine, originally called *Astounding Stories of Superscience,* had first come out in early 1930. I had agreed to attend and to give the major talk—and I could not do it. I spent a rather sad lunch hour on the day of the celebration and railed at fate.

Meanwhile I had finally been diagnosed. I was catheterized and CAT-scanned and ultrasounded virtually to death, and it turned out that the murmur, which was probably due to a congenital weakness of the mitral valve in the heart, had gotten worse in 1989. The valve had given way and sprung a leak. As a result, the blood didn't travel efficiently from the right auricle to the right ventricle, but regurgitated somewhat. This cut down the efficiency of the circulation to the lungs, so that I easily got out of breath. What's more, the heart could not work at sufficient efficiency to help my imperfect kidneys expel fluids from my body.

There was, furthermore, a possibility that the mitral valve was infected and that that was what accounted for its failure. In that case, it would have to be replaced. That would mean that I would have to have my chest opened again, precisely as at the bypass, and be subjected to the heart-lung machine. It was a simple operation, they assured me. (Bob Zicklin, my lawyer and good friend, had had a valve replacement operation *three* times, the first time under fairly primitive conditions, and had survived all three handily.)

I was finally released from the hospital on January 26, 1990, fifteen days after I had entered. They told me, however, that I would have to undergo tests to determine whether mitral valve infection really existed. On February 2, I got a call from Peter. Even though the tests for bacterial infection were all negative, they weren't going to take any chances. I would have to return to the hospital the next day and undergo a series of intravenous antibiotic treatments.

On February 3, then, I was back in the hospital, this time in the hospital proper in a private room, and I spent four weeks there. In other words, the entire winter of 1989–90 was spent either in the hospital or in bed at home or creeping about my business feeling very ill.

It was one miserable winter. They had to continue the intravenous drip for four weeks. Twice each day, material was dribbled through a heplock into my veins for an hour or two at a time.

Then, on February 15, the doctors came to me with further news. In view of the fact that no infection could be found, they did not think it wise to subject me to the operation and take a chance on further kidney damage with the heart-lung machine. Therefore, I would not have the operation to replace the leaking mitral valve. They said I could live with mitral regurgitation, that there was no chance that it would suddenly give way and kill me. At the most it would weaken further, my symptoms would get worse, and they would bring me in again for surgery.

On March 3, then, I was back at home and ready to renew my life— with a leaking valve and faulty kidneys. The doctors warned me against involvement in anything beyond my strength, but they agreed that writing (even to the extent that I wrote) was not physically strenuous and that I could continue.

165

New

Autobiography

My winter of illness had produced many unwanted complications in my life. My mail was a disaster. Janet brought in important letters daily while I was in the hospital and I dealt with a few items there.

Most things had to await my return, when my entire two-room section of the apartment seemed crammed with envelopes and packages. Little by little, I took care of everything.

I even rewrote an article on automobiles of the future. A small revision had been plaintively asked for, but it was something I could not do in the hospital.

Fortunately, I routinely kept so far ahead of deadlines in the case of the *F&SF* essays and of the editorials in my magazine that even three months of inaction did not create problems. I was still comfortably ahead when the devastating winter was over and I soon brought myself back to my earlier position of being far in advance.

The syndicated column was another matter. That had to be tied in to some news item, so I could never be more than a week ahead of deadline. I was forced to write a letter explaining that until I could get out of the hospital, I would not be able to do my column, and I hoped that after three years of never having missed a deadline, they could give me some sick leave.

"Of course," they said, and proceeded to fill the space of the four columns that I eventually missed by reprinting ones I had written earlier in the game. That was very kind of them, for it meant that the regular readers of the column would not forget my existence. I promptly wrote another letter saying that I did not expect to be paid for rerun articles, since I had done no work in that connection.

But they must have consulted Doubleday, for back came the answer at once: "Don't be silly, Isaac." They paid me in full.

I had to cancel three talks altogether and—a particular embarrassment—I was late in putting together the data on my income tax for the first time in my life. My accountants had to ask for extensions, but I felt I had a reasonable excuse.

I might say that Janet was a ministering angel throughout, by the way, coming in every day, spending most of the nights with me, bringing in the mail and anything else I needed, always bright and cheerful. She endured my bouts of bad temper and soothed my spirits.

Robyn came in periodically to spell Janet and let her go home for a peaceful nap. I also received visits from Jennifer. I did my best to discourage visits because I felt it was a shame to disrupt people's schedules simply so that they might visit an old slugabed. However, Stan and Ruth visited, as did Don Laventhall, my lawyer, and Robert Warnick, my broker, and other friends as well. Marty Greenberg visited me twice and called me every evening.

And, of course, I had doctors coming in at all hours—Paul Esserman, Peter Pasternack, Jerry Lowenstein, and a raft of others. Nurses came in to take my blood pressure and feed me pills and set up the antibiotic drip. Service people came in to swab the floors and bring the meals and change the water. The place was a madhouse of activity, none of which I particularly welcomed (except the food).

There was nothing I could do while I was being dripped with antibiotics but watch television. I was forced to watch programs that, in my right mind, I wouldn't have allowed in the same house with me, or in the same city, if I could manage that. Yet I watched them with avidity, for it made the dripping time pass that would otherwise have lingered unbearably.

But it wasn't all loss, for January 26, 1990, was the day in the hospital when Janet told me I'd better start the third volume of my autobiography.

I had to smile. She followed a line of wild optimism all through my illness, trying to convince me that I would live forever if I only put my mind to it. That remark, however, made it seem that she felt I had to race the last bit of my life to write the book. I didn't say anything about that; I knew it would upset her, but I did say:

"It's only twelve years since the end of my previous autobiography and since then my life has grown even duller if that is possible. The only thing I would have to say would be that I wrote this, and then I wrote that; that I gave a talk here, and then a talk there. About the only breaks would be my triple bypass and my current illness, and that would make depressing reading."

She said, "Don't give a day-by-day account. Be subjective. Give your thoughts."

I said, "It's still only twelve years."

She said, "Start from the beginning. Cover your whole life in a retrospective, but don't go into unending details. Give the general sweeps and your reactions to it. After all, many people never read the first two volumes, and even if they did, if you tell it all in a different way, they'll be interested."

I didn't really believe any of this. I am not a deep philosopher and I can't make myself believe people are dying to hear my thoughts. However, I know that I have a pleasant writing style and can keep people reading, whatever I write. And I also had the sensation that I *was* racing death. And, as ever and always, I wanted to please Janet.

So I started the book immediately and within a matter of a few pages it had grabbed me. (I am my own favorite subject, as everyone who reads me knows.) I had 105 pages done when I was called back into the hospital for the second siege, and I abandoned the book regretfully and wondered if I would ever finish it.

When I went to the hospital, I took with me, as a matter of course, a bunch of writing pads and several pens just in case time hung heavy on my hands. And of course it did—instantly.

So I began scribbling on the pads. In a few days, I had finished a new Black Widower story, "The Haunted Cabin," and was deeply into an Azazel story. ("The Haunted Cabin" contains an incident that did indeed take place during my first hospitalization. I have since sold it to *EQMM.*)

On February 9, Janet found me scribbling when she came in and asked what I was writing. I told her.

Janet said, "Why are you doing that? Why aren't you writing your autobiography?"

I said, "I need the first two volumes and my diaries to get everything into the right chronological order."

She said, "I told you that you don't need strict chronological order. Just write about incidents as they come into your mind under various headings, and when it is time to prepare final copy, you can always rearrange them to suit yourself."

She was, of course, quite right. I was writing topic by topic, and not day by day, and I could shuffle the topics any way I wished. I worked happily all day, except when I was being dripped or when I had to attend to visitors—whether doctors, nurses, servers, family, or friends. When Janet didn't spend the night with me, I woke up at 5 A.M. (my usual arousal time), turned on the light, and began to write rapidly. There would be three hours before breakfast and that was the best part of the day, with the only interruptions being to have my blood pressure taken, my blood drawn, and my pills handed me (plus Paul's visit).

By the time I was ready to leave the hospital I had written over 250 long pages in reasonably small printing. Not only did this keep me from going mad but it actually put me into a jovial and good-natured mood.

About the only thing I found irritating was that everyone who caught me writing would ask me what I was doing, and when I explained, they would invariably try to sell me on the notion of a laptop computer. I would tell them (and by the tenth person I was getting peevish about it) that I *liked* scribbling by hand, but I don't know that anyone could bring himself or herself to believe me.

Once I got out of the hospital, I continued to work hard on the autobiography. If it is a race with death, then it seems I am winning, for I expect to finish the book today, May 28, 1990, just four months after starting it. I'll have to go over it for some finishing touches, but I hope to have it in to Doubleday in a week or two.

It's a little longer than Doubleday asked for (well, 50 percent longer), but it will all fit into one volume and I shall do my best to keep it from being cut more than cosmetically.

166
New Life

It's not really a new life I have returned to, for I am doing my best to make it as much like my old life as possible. But it's new in that it is considerably modified, and for the worse, I suppose. I am a septuagenarian now, with a leaky heart valve and imperfect kidneys.

I still can't walk very far or very briskly without having to stop to catch my breath, and I do get tired more easily than I like. Nevertheless, it *is* life and I'm getting along.

In addition to this book, I've kept up with my various columns. I've gone over the manuscripts I left hanging when I grew ill. I've returned to making my weekly rounds to the publishers, and the Dutch Treat Club gave me a strong round of applause when I walked in on March 6, 1990, to take over my emcee chores once again. (Every Tuesday that I was in the hospital was sunny. On March 6, of course, it snowed.)

Later in the month, I put together a new collection of *F&SF* essays to be called *The Secret of the Universe.*

Janet and I have been going to the theater more often than before, if anything, and I particularly enjoyed revivals of Sheridan's *The Rivals* and Gay's *The Beggar's Opera*.

On April 6, 1990, I gave my first talk out of town since before my illness. It was at William Patterson College in Wayne, New Jersey, and it went very well. On May 2, I was responded to even more enthusiastically by a standing-room-only crowd at Lehigh University in Bethlehem, Pennsylvania.

I attended a meeting of the Gilbert and Sullivan Society on April 20, and I wrote a new science fiction story, "Kid Brother," and sold it to *IASFM*.

On May 7, I presided over the annual banquet of the Dutch Treat Club, with Victor Borge as the honoree. It was the best I had ever been at and the members were delighted. The next day I attended the eleventh annual Hugh Downs dinner.

On May 15, I gave a talk on Gilbert and Sullivan at the Players Club, introducing five numbers, and on May 18, I finally went to a Trap Door Spiders meeting for the first time in half a year.

Yes, I am carrying on in this new life exactly as I had in the old. I am as busy as ever and I do all the things I always did (except eat freely), but I don't fool myself into thinking this is permanent. The shades of night are still there on the near horizon.

On May 10, 1990, Red Dembner, who published my quiz books, and whom I had made a member of the Dutch Treat Club, phoned me to inquire after my health. His publishing duties kept him away from the club except at infrequent intervals, and he had not seen me in some time.

I assured him I was doing reasonably well, and he said, "I'm so glad. I have a warm spot in my heart for you, Isaac. Let's have lunch together."

I said, "Absolutely, but I know you have a tight schedule. Pick a day that is convenient to you, Red, then call me back and we'll have lunch."

The day never came. On May 14, Red died of a heart attack. It came without warning, and without premonitory symptoms as far as I know. He was sixty-nine years old.

My turn will come too, eventually, but I have had a good life and I have accomplished all I wanted to, and more than I had a right to expect I would.

So I am ready.

But not *too* ready. On May 26, 1990, I introduced Corliss Lamont, the grand old man of humanism, at a luncheon. He is eighty-eight and physically frail, but he stood on his feet for forty-five minutes and delivered an excellent impromptu speech. Clearly, he was in full mental vigor.

So I shall hope.

EPILOGUE
Janet Asimov

One of the deepest desires of a human being is to be known and understood. Hamlet instructs Horatio to tell his story. A child asks to be told a story and is most thrilled when the one he hears has a character like himself in it.

Isaac says in this autobiography that I told him to write it, but the fact remains that he wanted to do so, to share his life with his readers in a way that he did not in the first two autobiographies, which are more detailed, more exactly chronological, and not introspective.

In May 1990, Isaac ended this autobiography with hope, although he knew that he didn't have long to live. He hoped for several more years, but his heart and kidney failure worsened and he died on April 6, 1992.

Isaac wanted this autobiography published right away, so that he could see the book before he died, but this was not done. He also told me that he wanted the book arranged the way it is, in "scenes" written down as they came up in his memory.

After Isaac's death, I took on the job of editing the completed manuscript. The publisher wanted it severely shortened but I think the book should be left much the way Isaac wanted it.

The manuscript ends in May 1990 and reads as if Isaac believed the reader would soon be reading it. I have written this epilogue to give Isaac's readers a brief account of what happened afterward.

Isaac's 1990 diary records May 30 as the day he finished typing the final copy of the autobiography. He writes, "It is now all ready to hand in, 125 days after I started it. Not many can write 235,000 words in that time, while doing other things as well."

The next day we went to Washington, D.C., for a luncheon at the Soviet Embassy. The trip made Isaac feel, for a while, that he was back from illness and part of life again. He was particularly happy about meeting Gorbachev because the ending of the cold war gave hope to the world. Isaac strongly believed all peoples should work together for the common good of humanity.

In the rest of 1990: Isaac gave a talk on Gilbert and Sullivan for Mohonk's music week. In addition to his keynote speech at his last Rensselaerville Institute "Asimov Seminar," he sang and explained all the verses of "The Star-Spangled Banner." There were other meetings, conventions, and speeches, and he even signed books at the outdoor book fair on Fifth Avenue.

In spite of increasing weakness, he wrote every day. He was pleased to discover at the end of 1990 that it had been his best year financially.

He worried about various medical problems—his own and those of his daughter and his brother. For the first time he mentioned his depression and worsening health in his diary, with considerable bitterness. Outwardly, he tried not to depress anyone else, making jokes and being his usual lovable self.

On January 2, 1991, he wrote in his diary, "I made it. I'm 71 today . . . I got a birthday greeting in the 'Garfield' cartoon . . . which probably gave me more exposure than I've ever had before!" Then: "Robyn came and we went to Shun Lee for Peking duck and venison. It was great."

Also in January 1991, he began work on *Asimov Laughs Again,* which lifted his spirits. On April 5, almost exactly a year before he died, he finished the book with a concluding page in which he said that he and I have stayed deeply in love for thirty-two years.

The page ends with: "I'm afraid that my life has just about run its course and I don't really expect to live much longer. However, our love remains and I have no complaints.

"In my life, I have had Janet and I have had my daughter, Robyn, and my son, David; I have had a large number of good friends; I have had my writing and the fame and fortune it has brought me; and no matter what happens to me now, it's been a good life, and I am satisfied with it.

"So please don't worry about me, or feel bad. Instead I only hope that this book has brought you a few laughs."

After he finished and turned in *Asimov Laughs Again* to HarperCollins, he became more withdrawn. The handwriting in his diary deteriorates, and there are fewer, shorter entries. But he went on working as much as possible.

When typing was difficult, he dictated to me, especially his last piece for *The Magazine of Fantasy and Science Fiction*. It was a poignant "Farewell—Farewell" to all his "Gentle Readers." In it he said, "It has always been my ambition to die in harness with my head face down on a keyboard and my nose caught between two of the keys, but that's not the way it worked out."

There continued to be some happy times, and he still enjoyed being president of Dutch Treat, introducing speakers like Mayor Dinkins. We even went to Mohonk once more. Almost the last diary entry is on August 3, 1991, when he said, "I started an editorial for *Asimov's*. It will be a double length on Foundation."

I will not go into any details about Isaac's last months, which were filled with hospitalizations and physical deterioration. Nor will I describe details of his deathbed, except to say that he did not suffer pain —terminal kidney failure brings about a kind of apathy, and eventually peace.

Robyn and I were there when he died, holding his hands and telling him we loved him. His last complete sentence was: "I love you too."

I want to retell something I told Harlan Ellison about an incident from Isaac's last week at home. Isaac couldn't talk much, and was asleep most of the time, but once he woke up looking terribly anxious.

He said to me, "I want . . . I want . . ."

"What is it, Isaac?" I asked.

"I want . . . I want . . ."

"What do you want, darling?"

It seemed to burst out of him. "I want—Isaac Asimov!"

"Yes," I said. "That's you."

Then he said wonderingly, and with triumph, "I AM Isaac Asimov!"

I said, "And Isaac Asimov can rest now."

Isaac smiled happily, said "Okay," and fell asleep again.

Even near the end, his sense of humor was still there. As I said in the memorial service, Robyn, Stan, his wife Ruth, and I were all in Isaac's hospital room the day before he died. I said to him, "Isaac, you're the best there is."

Isaac smiled and shrugged. Then, with a mischievous lift of his eyebrows, he nodded yes, and we all laughed.

Isaac was genuinely proud and happy about his accomplishments. After he died, I came across a piece of paper upon which he'd written in ink (perhaps after he first got sick):

> Over a space of 40 years, I sold
>   an item every ten days on the average.
> Over the space of the second 20 years, I sold
>   an item every six days on the average.
> Over a space of 40 years, I published an average
>   of 1,000 words a day.
> Over the space of the second 20 years, I published
>   an average of 1,700 words a day.

Writing what he wanted to write was an act of joy for him, during which he relaxed and forgot his troubles. He grumbled about having to write so many novels in the last few years, but even those helped. *Forward the Foundation* was hard on him, because in killing Hari Seldon he was also killing himself, yet he transcended the anguish.

He told me what the end of *Forward the Foundation* was going to be—that as Hari Seldon dies, the equations of the future swirl around him and he knows he is looking into the future that he himself has discovered and helped to bring about.

Isaac said, "I don't feel self-pity because I won't be around to see any of the possible futures. Like Hari Seldon, I can look at my work all around me and I'm comforted. I know that I've studied about, imagined, and written down many possible futures—it's as if I've been there."

Once when Isaac and I talked about old age, illness, and death, he said it wasn't so terrible to get sick and old and to die if you've been part of life completing itself as a pattern. Even if you don't make it to old age, it's still worthwhile, there's still pleasure in that vision of being part of the pattern of life—especially a pattern expressed in creativity and shared in love.

Catalogue of Books
Isaac Asimov

PART I—FICTION

Science Fiction Novels

Pebble in the Sky Doubleday, 1950
The Stars, Like Dust— Doubleday, 1951
Foundation Gnome (Doubleday), 1951
David Starr: Space Ranger Doubleday, 1952
Foundation and Empire Gnome (Doubleday), 1952
The Currents of Space Doubleday, 1952
Second Foundation Gnome (Doubleday), 1953
Lucky Starr and the Pirates of the Asteroids Doubleday, 1953
The Caves of Steel Doubleday, 1954
Lucky Starr and the Oceans of Venus Doubleday, 1954
The End of Eternity Doubleday, 1955
Lucky Starr and the Big Sun of Mercury Doubleday, 1956
The Naked Sun Doubleday, 1957
Lucky Starr and the Moons of Jupiter Doubleday, 1957
Lucky Starr and the Rings of Saturn Doubleday, 1958
Fantastic Voyage Houghton Mifflin, 1966
The Gods Themselves Doubleday, 1972
Foundation's Edge Doubleday, 1982
Norby, the Mixed-up Robot (with Janet Asimov) Walker, 1983
The Robots of Dawn Doubleday, 1983
Norby's Other Secret (with Janet Asimov) Walker, 1984
Norby and the Lost Princess (with Janet Asimov) Walker, 1985
Robots and Empire Doubleday, 1985
Norby and the Invaders (with Janet Asimov) Walker, 1985
Foundation and Earth Doubleday, 1986
Norby and the Queen's Necklace (with Janet Asimov) Walker, 1986
Norby Finds a Villain (with Janet Asimov) Walker, 1987
Fantastic Voyage II: Destination Brain Doubleday, 1987
Prelude to Foundation Doubleday, 1988
Norby Down to Earth (with Janet Asimov) Walker, 1988
Nemesis Doubleday, 1989
Norby and Yobo's Great Adventure (with Janet Asimov) Walker, 1989
Norby and the Oldest Dragon (with Janet Asimov) Walker, 1990
Nightfall Doubleday, 1990
The Ugly Little Boy Doubleday, 1992

Norby and the Court Jester (with Janet Asimov) Walker, 1993
Forward the Foundation Doubleday, 1993
The Positronic Man Doubleday, 1993

Mystery Novels

The Death Dealers Avon, 1958
Murder at the ABA Doubleday, 1976

Science Fiction Short Stories and Short Story Collections

I, Robert Gnome (Doubleday), 1950
The Martian Way and Other Stories Doubleday, 1955
Earth Is Room Enough Doubleday, 1957
Nine Tomorrows Doubleday, 1959
The Rest of the Robots Doubleday, 1964
Through a Glass, Clearly New English Library, 1967
Asimov's Mysteries Doubleday, 1968
Nightfall and Other Stories Doubleday, 1969
The Best New Thing World Publishing, 1971
The Early Asimov Doubleday, 1972
The Best of Isaac Asimov Sphere, 1973
Have You Seen These? NESRAA, 1974
Buy Jupiter and Other Stories Doubleday, 1975
The Heavenly Host Walker, 1975
"The Dream," "Benjamin's Dream," and *"Benjamin's Bicentennial Blast"* Private print. 1976
Good Taste Apocalypse, 1976
The Bicentennial Man and Other Stories Doubleday, 1976
Three by Asimov Tart, 1981
The Complete Robot Doubleday, 1982
The Winds of Change and Other Stories Doubleday, 1983
The Edge of Tomorrow Tor, 1985
It's Such a Beautiful Day Creative Education, 1985
The Alternate Asimovs Doubleday, 1986
Science Fiction by Asimov Davis, 1986
The Best Science Fiction of Isaac Asimov Doubleday, 1986
Robot Dreams Byron Preiss, 1986
Other Worlds of Isaac Asimov Avenel, 1987
All the Troubles of the World Creative Education, 1989
Franchise Creative Education, 1989
Robbie Creative Education, 1989
Sally Creative Education, 1989
The Asimov Chronicles Dark Harvest, 1989
Robot Visions Byron Preiss, 1990

Fantasy Short Story Collection

Azazel Doubleday, 1988

Mystery Short Story Collections

Tales of the Black Widowers Doubleday, 1974
More Tales of the Black Widowers Doubleday, 1976
The Key Word and Other Mysteries Walker, 1977
Casebook of the Black Widowers Doubleday, 1980
The Union Club Mysteries Doubleday, 1983
Banquets of the Black Widowers Doubleday, 1984
The Disappearing Man and Other Stories Walker, 1985
The Best Mysteries of Isaac Asimov Doubleday, 1986
Puzzles of the Black Widowers Doubleday, 1990

Anthologies *(Edited by Isaac Asimov)*

The Hugo Winners Doubleday, 1962
Fifty Short Science-fiction Tales (with Groff Conklin) Collier, 1963
Tomorrow's Children Doubleday, 1966
Where Do We Go from Here? Doubleday, 1971
The Hugo Winners, Volume II Doubleday, 1971
Nebula Award Stories Eight Harper, 1973
Before the Golden Age Doubleday, 1974
The Hugo Winners, Volume III Doubleday, 1977
One Hundred Great Science-fiction Short-short Stories (with Martin H. Greenberg and Joseph
    D. Olander) Doubleday, 1978
Isaac Asimov Presents the Great SF Stories, 1: 1939 (with Martin H. Greenberg) DAW Books,
    1979
Isaac Asimov Presents the Great SF Stories, 2: 1940 (with Martin H. Greenberg) DAW Books,
    1979
The Science Fictional Solar System (with Martin H. Greenberg and Charles G. Waugh) Harper
    & Row, 1979
The Thirteen Crimes of Science Fiction (with Martin H. Greenberg and Charles G. Waugh)
    Doubleday, 1979
The Future in Question (with Martin H. Greenberg and Joseph D. Olander) Fawcett, 1980
Microcosmic Tales (with Martin H. Greenberg and Joseph D. Olander) Taplinger, 1980
Isaac Asimov Presents the Great SF Stories, 3: 1941 (with Martin H. Greenberg) DAW Books,
    1980
Who Dun It? (with Alice Laurance) Houghton Mifflin, 1980
Space Mail (with Martin H. Greenberg and Joseph D. Olander) Fawcett, 1980
Microcosmic Tales (with Martin H. Greenberg and Joseph D. Olander) Taplinger, 1980
Isaac Asimov Presents the Great SF Stories, 4: 1942 (with Martin H. Greenberg) DAW Books,
    1980
The Seven Deadly Sins of Science Fiction (with Charles G. Waugh and Martin H. Greenberg)
    Fawcett, 1980
The Future I (with Martin H. Greenberg and Joseph D. Olander) Fawcett, 1980
Isaac Asimov Presents the Great SF Stories, 5: 1943 (with Martin H. Greenberg) DAW Books,
    1981
Catastrophes (with Martin H. Greenberg and Charles G. Waugh) Fawcett, 1981
Isaac Asimov Presents the Best SF of the 19th Century (with Charles G. Waugh and Martin H.
    Greenberg) Beaufort, 1981
The Seven Cardinal Virtues of Science Fiction (with Charles G. Waugh and Martin H.
    Greenberg) Fawcett, 1981
Fantastic Creatures (with Martin H. Greenberg and Charles G. Waugh) Franklin Watts, 1981
Raintree Reading Series I (with Martin H. Greenberg and Charles G. Waugh) Raintree, 1981
Miniature Mysteries (with Martin H. Greenberg and Joseph D. Olander) Taplinger, 1981
The Twelve Crimes of Christmas (with Carol-Lynn Rössel Waugh and Martin H. Greenberg)
    Avon, 1981
Isaac Asimov Presents the Great SF Stories, 6: 1944 (with Martin H. Greenberg) DAW Books,
    1981
Space Mail II (with Martin H. Greenberg and Charles G. Waugh) Fawcett, 1981
Tantalizing Locked Room Mysteries (with Charles G. Waugh and Martin H. Greenberg) Walker,
    1982
TV: 2000 (with Charles G. Waugh and Martin H. Greenberg) Fawcett, 1982
Laughing Space (with J. O. Jeppson) Houghton Mifflin, 1982
Speculations (with Alice Laurance) Houghton Mifflin, 1982
Flying Saucers (with Martin H. Greenberg and Charles G. Waugh) Fawcett, 1982
Raintree Reading Series II (with Martin H. Greenberg and Charles G. Waugh) Raintree, 1982
Dragon Tales (with Martin H. Greenberg and Charles G. Waugh) Fawcett, 1982
Big Apple Mysteries (with Carol-Lynn Rössel Waugh and Martin H. Greenberg) Avon, 1982
Isaac Asimov Presents the Great SF Stories, 7: 1945 (with Martin H. Greenberg) DAW Books,
    1982
The Last Man on Earth (with Martin H. Greenberg and Charles G. Waugh) Fawcett, 1982

Science Fiction A to Z (with Martin H. Greenberg and Charles G. Waugh) Houghton Mifflin, 1982

Isaac Asimov Presents the Best Fantasy of the 19th Century (with Charles G. Waugh and Martin H. Greenberg) Beaufort, 1982

Isaac Asimov Presents the Great SF Stories, 8: 1946 (with Martin H. Greenberg) DAW Books, 1982

Isaac Asimov Presents the Great SF Stories, 9: 1947 (with Martin H. Greenberg) DAW Books, 1983

Show Business Is Murder (with Carol-Lynn Rössel Waugh and Martin H. Greenberg) Avon, 1983

Hallucination Orbit (with Charles G. Waugh and Martin H. Greenberg) Farrar, Straus & Giroux, 1983

Caught in the Organ Draft (with Martin H. Greenberg and Charles G. Waugh) Farrar, Straus & Giroux, 1983

The Science Fiction Weight-Loss Book (with George R. R. Martin and Martin H. Greenberg) Crown, 1983

Isaac Asimov Presents the Best Horror and Supernatural Stories of the 19th Century (with Charles G. Waugh and Martin H. Greenberg) Beaufort, 1983

Starships (with Martin H. Greenberg and Charles G. Waugh) Fawcett, 1983

Isaac Asimov Presents the Great SF Stories, 10: 1948 (with Martin H. Greenberg) DAW Books, 1983

The Thirteen Horrors of Halloween (with Carol-Lynn Rössel Waugh and Martin H. Greenberg) Avon, 1983

Creations (with George Zebrowski and Martin H. Greenberg) Crown, 1983

Wizards (with Martin H. Greenberg and Charles G. Waugh) NAL, 1983

Those Amazing Electronic Machines (with Martin H. Greenberg and Charles G. Waugh) Franklin Watts, 1983

Computer Crimes and Capers (with Martin H. Greenberg and Charles G. Waugh) Academy Chicago, 1983

Intergalactic Empires (with Martin H. Greenberg and Charles G. Waugh) NAL, 1983

Machines That Think (with Patricia S. Warrick and Martin H. Greenberg) Holt, Rinehart and Winston, 1983

100 Great Fantasy Short Stories (with Terry Carr and Martin H. Greenberg) Doubleday, 1984

Raintree Reading Series III (with Martin H. Greenberg and Charles G. Waugh) Raintree, 1984

Isaac Asimov Presents the Great SF Stories, 11: 1949 (with Martin H. Greenberg) DAW Books, 1984

Witches (with Martin H. Greenberg and Charles G. Waugh) NAL, 1984

Murder on the Menu (with Carol-Lynn Rössel Waugh and Martin H. Greenberg) Avon, 1984

Young Mutants (with Martin H. Greenberg and Charles G. Waugh) Harper & Row, 1984

Isaac Asimov Presents the Best Science Fiction Firsts (with Charles G. Waugh and Martin H. Greenberg) Beaufort, 1984

The Science Fictional Olympics (with Martin H. Greenberg and Charles G. Waugh) NAL, 1984

Fantastic Reading (with Martin H. Greenberg and David C. Yeager) Scott, Foresman, 1984

Election Day: 2084 (with Martin H. Greenberg) Prometheus, 1984

Isaac Asimov Presents the Great SF Stories, 12: 1950 (with Martin H. Greenberg) DAW Books, 1984

Young Extraterrestrials (with Martin H. Greenberg and Charles G. Waugh) Harper & Row, 1984

Sherlock Holmes Through Time and Space (with Martin H. Greenberg and Charles G. Waugh) Blue Jay, 1984

Supermen (with Martin H. Greenberg and Charles G. Waugh) NAL, 1984

Thirteen Short Fantasy Novels (with Martin H. Greenberg and Charles G. Waugh) Crown, 1984

Cosmic Knights (with Martin H. Greenberg and Charles G. Waugh) NAL, 1984

The Hugo Winners, Volume IV Doubleday, 1985

Young Monsters (with Martin H. Greenberg and Charles G. Waugh) Harper & Row, 1985

Spells (with Martin H. Greenberg and Charles G. Waugh) NAL, 1985

Great Science Fiction Stories by the World's Great Scientists (with Martin H. Greenberg and Charles G. Waugh) Donald Fine, 1985

Isaac Asimov Presents the Great SF Stories, 13: 1951 (with Martin H. Greenberg) DAW Books, 1985

Amazing Stories Anthology (with Martin H. Greenberg) TSR, Inc., 1985

Young Ghosts (with Martin H. Greenberg and Charles G. Waugh) Harper & Row, 1985
Thirteen Short Science Fiction Novels (with Martin H. Greenberg and Charles G. Waugh) Crown, 1985
Giants (with Martin H. Greenberg and Charles G. Waugh) NAL, 1985
Isaac Asimov Presents the Great SF Stories, 14: 1952 (with Martin H. Greenberg) DAW Books, 1986
Comets (with Martin H. Greenberg and Charles G. Waugh) NAL, 1986
Young Star Travellers (with Martin H. Greenberg and Charles G. Waugh) Harper & Row, 1986
The Hugo Winners, Volume V Doubleday, 1986
Mythical Beasties (with Martin H. Greenberg and Charles G. Waugh) NAL, 1986
Tin Stars (with Martin H. Greenberg and Charles G. Waugh) NAL, 1986
Magical Wishes (with Martin H. Greenberg and Charles G. Waugh) NAL, 1986
Isaac Asimov Presents the Great SF Stories, 15: 1953 (with Martin H. Greenberg) DAW Books, 1986
The Twelve Frights of Christmas (with Charles G. Waugh and Martin H. Greenberg) Avon, 1986
Isaac Asimov Presents the Great SF Stories, 16: 1954 (with Martin H. Greenberg) DAW Books, 1987
Young Witches and Warlocks (with Martin H. Greenberg and Charles G. Waugh) Harper & Row, 1987
Devils (with Martin H. Greenberg and Charles G. Waugh) NAL, 1987
Hound Dunnit (with Martin H. Greenberg and Carol-Lynn Rössel Waugh) Carroll & Graf, 1987
Space Shuttles (with Martin H. Greenberg and Charles G. Waugh) NAL, 1987
Atlantis (with Martin H. Greenberg and Charles G. Waugh) NAL, 1988
Isaac Asimov Presents the Great SF Stories, 17: 1955 (with Martin H. Greenberg) DAW Books, 1988
Encounters (with Martin H. Greenberg and Charles G. Waugh) Headline, 1988
Isaac Asimov Presents the Best Crime Stories of the 19th Century Dembner, 1988
The Mammoth Book of Classic Science Fiction (with Charles G. Waugh and Martin H. Greenberg) Carroll & Graf, 1988
Monsters (with Martin H. Greenberg and Charles G. Waugh) NAL, 1988
Isaac Asimov Presents the Great SF Stories, 18: 1956 (with Martin H. Greenberg) DAW Books, 1988
Ghosts (with Martin H. Greenberg and Charles G. Waugh) NAL, 1988
The Sport of Crime (with Carol-Lynn Rössel Waugh and Martin H. Greenberg) Lynx, 1988
Isaac Asimov Presents the Great SF Stories, 19: 1957 (with Martin H. Greenberg) DAW Books, 1989
Tales of the Occult (with Martin H. Greenberg and Charles G. Waugh) Prometheus, 1989
Purr-fect Crime (with Carol-Lynn Rössel Waugh and Martin H. Greenberg) Lynx, 1989
Robots (with Martin H. Greenberg and Charles G. Waugh) NAL, 1989
Visions of Fantasy (with Martin H. Greenberg) Doubleday, 1989
Curses (with Martin H. Greenberg and Charles G. Waugh) NAL, 1989
The New Hugo Winners: Volume VI (with Martin H. Greenberg) Wynwood, 1989
Senior Sleuths (with Martin H. Greenberg and Carol-Lynn Rössel Waugh) G. K. Hall, 1989
Cosmic Critiques (with Martin H. Greenberg) Writers Digest, 1990
Isaac Asimov Presents the Great SF Stories, 20: 1958 (with Martin H. Greenberg) DAW Books, 1990

PART II—NONFICTION

General Science

Words of Science Houghton Mifflin, 1959
Breakthroughs in Science Houghton Mifflin, 1960
The Intelligent Man's Guide to Science Basic Books, 1960
Asimov's Biographical Encyclopedia of Science and Technology Doubleday, 1964
The New Intelligent Man's Guide to Science Basic Books, 1965
Twentieth Century Discovery Doubleday, 1969
Great Ideas of Science Houghton Mifflin, 1969

Asimov's Biographical Encyclopedia of Science and Technology (Revised Edition) Doubleday, 1972
Asimov's Guide to Science Basic Books, 1972
More Words of Science Houghton Mifflin, 1972
Ginn Science Program—Intermediate Level A Ginn, 1972
Ginn Science Program—Intermediate Level C Ginn, 1972
Ginn Science Program—Intermediate Level B Ginn, 1972
Ginn Science Program—Advanced Level A Ginn, 1973
Ginn Science Program—Advanced Level B Ginn, 1973
Please Explain Houghton Mifflin, 1973
A Choice of Catastrophes Simon & Schuster, 1979
Exploring the Earth and the Cosmos Crown, 1982
Asimov's Biographical Encyclopedia of Science and Technology (2nd Revised Edition) Doubleday, 1982
The Measure of the Universe Harper & Row, 1983
Asimov's New Guide to Science Basic Books, 1984
Beginnings Walker, 1987
Asimov's Chronology of Science and Discovery Harper & Row, 1989
Our Angry Earth (with Frederick Pohl) TOR, 1991

Mathematics

Realm of Numbers Houghton Mifflin, 1959
Realm of Measure Houghton Mifflin, 1960
Realm of Algebra Houghton Mifflin, 1961
Quick and Easy Math Houghton Mifflin, 1964
An Easy Introduction to the Slide Rule Houghton Mifflin, 1965
How Did We Find Out About Numbers? Walker, 1973
The History of Mathematics (a chart) Carolina Biological Supplies, 1989

Astronomy

The Clock We Live On Abelard-Schuman, 1959
The Kingdom of the Sun Abelard-Schuman, 1960
Satellites in Outer Space Random House, 1960
The Double Planet Abelard-Schuman, 1960
Planets for Man Random House, 1964
The Universe Walker, 1966
The Moon Follett, 1967
Environments Out There Scholastic/Abelard-Schuman, 1967
To the Ends of the Universe Walker, 1967
Mars Follett, 1967
Stars Follett, 1968
Galaxies Follett, 1968
ABC's of Space Walker, 1969
What Makes the Sun Shine? Little, Brown, 1971
Comets and Meteors Follett, 1973
The Sun Follett, 1973
Jupiter, the Largest Planet Lothrop, Lee & Shepard, 1973
Our World in Space New York Graphic, 1974
The Solar System Follett, 1975
How Did We Find Out About Comets? Walker, 1975
Eyes on the Universe Houghton Mifflin, 1975
Alpha Centauri, the Nearest Star Lothrop, Lee & Shepard, 1976
The Collapsing Universe Walker, 1977
How Did We Find Out About Outer Space? Walker, 1977
Mars, the Red Planet Lothrop, Lee & Shepard, 1977
How Did We Find Out About Black Holes? Walker, 1978
Saturn and Beyond Lothrop, Lee & Shepard, 1979
Extraterrestrial Civilizations Crown, 1979
Venus: Near Neighbor of the Sun Lothrop, Lee & Shepard, 1981
Visions of the Universe Cosmos Store, 1981

How Did We Find Out About the Universe? Walker, 1982
Asimov's Guide to Halley's Comet Walker, 1985
The Exploding Suns Dutton, 1985
How Did We Find Out About Sunshine? Walker, 1987
Did Comets Kill the Dinosaurs? Gareth Stevens, 1987
Asteroids Gareth Stevens, 1988
Earth's Moon Gareth Stevens, 1988
Mars: Our Mysterious Neighbor Gareth Stevens, 1988
Our Milky Way and Other Galaxies Gareth Stevens, 1988
Quasars, Pulsars, and Black Holes Gareth Stevens, 1988
Rockets, Probes, and Satellites Gareth Stevens, 1988
Our Solar System Gareth Stevens, 1988
The Sun Gareth Stevens, 1988
Uranus: The Sideways Planet Gareth Stevens, 1988
Saturn: The Ringed Beauty Gareth Stevens, 1988
How Was the Universe Born? Gareth Stevens, 1988
Earth: Our Home Base Gareth Stevens, 1988
Ancient Astronomy Gareth Stevens, 1988
Unidentified Flying Objects Gareth Stevens, 1988
The Space Spotter's Guide Gareth Stevens, 1988
Is There Life on Other Planets? Gareth Stevens, 1989
Science Fiction, Science Fact Gareth Stevens, 1989
Mercury: The Quick Planet Gareth Stevens, 1989
Space Garbage Gareth Stevens, 1989
Jupiter: The Spotted Giant Gareth Stevens, 1989
The Birth and Death of Stars Gareth Stevens, 1989
Think About Space (with Frank White) Walker, 1989
Mythology and the Universe Gareth Stevens, 1989
Colonizing the Planets and Stars Gareth Stevens, 1989
Astronomy Today Gareth Stevens, 1989
Pluto: A Double Planet Gareth Stevens, 1989
Piloted Space Flights Gareth Stevens, 1989
Comets and Meteors Gareth Stevens, 1989
Neptune: The Farthest Giant Gareth Stevens, 1990
Venus: A Shrouded Mystery Gareth Stevens, 1990
The World's Space Programs Gareth Stevens, 1990
How Did We Find Out About Neptune? Walker, 1990
How Did We Find Out About Pluto? Walker, 1991

Earth Sciences

Words on the Map Houghton Mifflin, 1962
ABC's of the Ocean Walker, 1970
ABC's of the Earth Walker, 1971
How Did We Find Out the Earth Is Round? Walker, 1973
The Ends of the Earth Weybright & Talley, 1975
How Did We Find Out About Earthquakes? Walker, 1978
How Did We Find Out About Antarctica? Walker, 1979
How Did We Find Out About Oil? Walker, 1980
How Did We Find Out About Coal? Walker, 1980
How Did We Find Out About Volcanoes? Walker, 1981
How Did We Find Out About Atmosphere? Walker, 1985

Chemistry and Biochemistry

Biochemistry and Human Metabolism Williams & Wilkins, 1952
The Chemicals of Life Abelard-Schuman, 1954
Chemistry and Human Health McGraw-Hill, 1956
Building Blocks of the Universe Abelard-Schuman, 1957
The World of Carbon Abelard-Schuman, 1958
The World of Nitrogen Abelard-Schuman, 1958

Life and Energy Doubleday, 1962
The Search for the Elements Basic Books, 1962
The Genetic Code Orion Press, 1963
A Short History of Chemistry Doubleday, 1965
The Noble Gases Basic Books, 1966
The Genetic Effects of Radiation (with Theodosius Dobzhansky) AEC, 1966
Photosynthesis Basic Books, 1969
How Did We Find Out About Vitamins? Walker, 1974
Hos Did We Find Out About DNA? Walker, 1985
How Did We Find Out About Photosynthesis? Walker, 1988

Physics

Inside the Atom Abelard-Schuman, 1956
Inside the Atom (Revised Edition) Abelard-Schuman, 1966
The Neutrino Doubleday, 1966
Understanding Physics, Volume I Walker, 1966
Understanding Physics, Volume II Walker, 1966
Understanding Physics, Volume III Walker, 1966
Light Follett, 1970
Electricity and Man AEC, 1972
Worlds Within Worlds AEC, 1972
How Did We Find Out About Electricity? Walker, 1973
How Did We Find Out About Energy? Walker, 1975
How Did We Find Out About Atoms? Walker, 1976
How Did We Find Out About Nuclear Power? Walker, 1976
How Did We Find Out About Solar Power? Walker, 1981
How Did We Find Out About Computers? Walker, 1984
How Did We Find Out About Robots? Walker, 1984
Robots (with Karen Frenkel) Harmony House, 1985
How Did We Find Out About the Speed of Light? Walker, 1986
How Did We Find Out About Superconductivity? Walker, 1988
How Did We Find Out About Microwaves? Walker, 1989
How Did We Find Out About Lasers? Walker, 1990
Atom Dutton, 1991

Biology

Races and People (with William C. Boyd) Abelard-Schuman, 1955
The Living River Abelard-Schuman, 1960
The Wellsprings of Life Abelard-Schuman, 1960
The Human Body Houghton Mifflin, 1963
The Human Brain Houghton Mifflin, 1964
A Short History of Biology Doubleday, 1964
ABC's of Ecology Walker, 1972
How Did We Find Out About Dinosaurs? Walker, 1973
How Did We Find Out About Germs? Walker, 1974
How Did We Find Out About Our Human Roots? Walker, 1979
How Did We Find Out About Life in the Deep Sea? Walker, 1982
How Did We Find Out About the Beginning of Life? Walker, 1982
How Did We Find Out About Genes? Walker, 1983
How Did We Find Out About Blood? Walker, 1987
How Did We Find Out About the Brain? Walker, 1987
The History of Biology (a chart) Carolina Biological Supplies, 1988
Little Library of Dinosaurs Outlet, 1988

Science Essay Collections

Only a Trillion Abelard-Schuman, 1957
Fact and Fancy Doubleday, 1962
View from a Height Doubleday, 1963

Adding a Dimension Doubleday, 1964
Of Time and Space and Other Things Doubleday, 1965
From Earth to Heaven Doubleday, 1966
Is Anyone There? Doubleday, 1967
Science, Numbers, and I Doubleday, 1968
The Solar System and Back Doubleday, 1970
The Stars in Their Courses Doubleday, 1971
The Left Hand of the Electron Doubleday, 1972
Today and Tomorrow and— Doubleday, 1973
The Tragedy of the Moon Doubleday, 1973
Asimov on Astronomy Doubleday, 1974
Asimov on Chemistry Doubleday, 1974
Of Matters Great and Small Doubleday, 1975
Science Past—Science Future Doubleday, 1975
Asimov on Physics Doubleday, 1976
The Planet That Wasn't Doubleday, 1976
Asimov on Numbers Doubleday, 1977
The Beginning and the End Doubleday, 1977
Quasar, Quasar, Burning Bright Doubleday, 1978
Life and Time Doubleday, 1978
The Road to Infinity Doubleday, 1979
The Sun Shines Bright Doubleday, 1981
Change! Houghton Mifflin, 1981
Counting the Eons Doubleday, 1983
The Roving Mind Prometheus, 1983
X Stands for Unknown Doubleday, 1984
The Subatomic Monster Doubleday, 1985
The Dangers of Intelligence Houghton Mifflin, 1986
Far as the Human Eye Could See Doubleday, 1987
Past, Present and Future Prometheus, 1987
The Relativity of Wrong Doubleday, 1988
The Tyrannosaurus Prescription Prometheus, 1989
Asimov on Science Doubleday, 1989
Frontiers Dutton, 1990
Out of the Everywhere Doubleday, 1990
The Secret of the Universe Doubleday, 1990
Frontiers II Dutton, 1993

Science Fiction Essay Collections

Asimov on Science Fiction Doubleday, 1981
Asimov's Galaxy Doubleday, 1989

History

The Kite That Won the Revolution Houghton Mifflin, 1963
The Greeks Houghton Mifflin, 1965
The Roman Republic Houghton Mifflin, 1966
The Roman Empire Houghton Mifflin, 1967
The Egyptians Houghton Mifflin, 1967
The Near East Houghton Mifflin, 1968
The Dark Ages Houghton Mifflin, 1968
Words from History Houghton Mifflin, 1968
The Shaping of England Houghton Mifflin, 1969
Constantinople Houghton Mifflin, 1970
The Land of Canaan Houghton Mifflin, 1971
The Shaping of France Houghton Mifflin, 1972
The Shaping of North America Houghton Mifflin, 1973
The Birth of the United States Houghton Mifflin, 1974
Earth: Our Crowded Spaceship John Day, 1974
Our Federal Union Houghton Mifflin, 1975

The Golden Door Houghton Mifflin, 1977
The March of the Millennia (with Frank White) Walker, 1991
Asimov's Chronology of the World HarperCollins, 1991

The Bible

Words in Genesis Houghton Mifflin, 1962
Words from the Exodus Houghton Mifflin, 1963
Asimov's Guide to the Bible, Volume I Doubleday, 1968
Asimov's Guide to the Bible, Volume II Doubleday, 1969
The Story of Ruth Doubleday, 1972
Animals in the Bible Doubleday, 1978
In the Beginning Crown, 1981

Literature

Words from the Myths Houghton Mifflin, 1961
Asimov's Guide to Shakespeare, Volume I Doubleday, 1970
Asimov's Guide to Shakespeare, Volume II Doubleday, 1970
Asimov's Annotated Don Juan Doubleday, 1972
Asimov's Annotated Paradise Lost Doubleday, 1974
Familiar Poems, Annotated Doubleday, 1977
Asimov's Sherlockian Limericks Mysterious Press, 1977
The Annotated Gulliver's Travels Clarkson Potter, 1980
How to Enjoy Writing (with Janet Asimov) Walker, 1987
Asimov's Annotated Gilbert & Sullivan Doubleday, 1988

Humor and Satire

Thee Sensuous Dirty Old Man Walker, 1971
Isaac Asimov's Treasury of Humor, Houghton Mifflin, 1971
Lecherous Limericks Walker, 1975
More Lecherous Limericks Walker, 1976
Still More Lecherous Limericks Walker, 1977
Limericks: Too Gross (with John Ciardi) Norton, 1978
A Grossary of Limericks (with John Ciardi) Norton, 1981
Limericks for Children Caedmon, 1984
Asimov Laughs Again HarperCollins, 1992

Autobiography

In Memory Yet Green Doubleday, 1979
In Joy Still Felt Doubleday, 1980
I, Asimov Doubleday, 1994

Miscellaneous

Opus 100 Houghton Mifflin, 1969
Opus 200 Houghton Mifflin, 1979
Isaac Asimov's Book of Facts Grosset & Dunlap, 1979
Isaac Asimov Presents Superquiz (by Ken Fisher) Dembner, 1982
Isaac Asimov Presents Superquiz II (by Ken Fisher) Dembner, 1983
Opus 300 Houghton Mifflin, 1984
Living in the Future (edited) Harmony House, 1985
Future Days Henry Holt, 1986
Isaac Asimov Presents Superquiz III (by Ken Fisher) Dembner, 1987
Isaac Asimov Presents: From Harding to Hiroshima (by Barrington Boardman) Dembner, 1988
Isaac Asimov's Book of Science and Nature Quotations (with Jason A. Shulman) Blue Cliff, 1988
Isaac Asimov's Science Fiction and Fantasy Story-a-Month 1989 Calendar (with Martin H. Greenberg) Pomegranate, 1988
Isaac Asimov Presents Superquiz IV (by Ken Fisher) Dembner, 1989
The Complete Science Fair Handbooks (with Anthony D. Fredericks) Scott, Foresman, 1989